Literature and Culture at the *Fin ∂e Siècle*

Literature and Culture at the *Fin de Siècle*

Talia Schaffer

*Queens College and Graduate Center
of the City University of New York*

Susan J. Wolfson

Associate Editor
Princeton University

PEARSON
Longman

New York   Boston   San Francisco
London   Toronto   Sydney   Tokyo   Singapore   Madrid
Mexico City   Munich   Paris   Cape Town   Hong Kong   Montreal

Editor-in-Chief: *Joseph Terry*
Development Editor: *Christine Halsey*
Marketing Manager: *Ann Stypuloski*
Production Coordinator: *Scarlett Lindsay*
Senior Supplements Editor: *Donna Campion*
Project Coordination, Text Design, and Page Makeup: *Grapevine Publishing Services, Inc.*
Cover Designer/Manager: *John Callahan*
Manufacturing Buyer: *Alfred C. Dorsey*
Printer and Binder: *R.R. Donnelley and Sons Company / Harrisonburg*
Cover Printer: *R.R. Donnelley and Sons Company / Harrisonburg*

Cover Image: John Singer Sargent, American, 1856–1925. Detail of *Dr. Pozzi at Home*, 1881, oil on canvas. The Armand Hammer Collection, gift of the Armand Hammer Foundation. Hammer Museum, Los Angeles, CA.

For permission to use copyrighted material, grateful acknowledgment is made to the copyright holders on pages 595–601, which is hereby made part of this copyright page.

Library of Congress Cataloging-in-Publication Data

Literature and culture at the fin de siècle / [edited by] Talia Schaffer.—1st ed.
    p. cm.
  ISBN 0-321-13217-3
    1. English literature—19th century. 2. English literature—20th century. I. Schaffer, Talia,
1968.

PR1145.L58 2006
820.8'008—dc22

2006018819

Please visit us at www.ablongman.com

ISBN: 0-321-13217-3

1 2 3 4 5 6 7 8 9 0—DOH—09 08 07 06

To my students, who teach me more than I teach them.

Contents

Part III: Mind and Body

Part IV: England and Its Others

Contents:
Alphabetical by Authors and Titles

Table of Dates

1880 George Eliot dies, symbolizing the end of the era of great Victorian realist novels.

1881 W. S. Gilbert and Arthur Sullivan's comic opera *Patience* skewers aesthetes. Henry James, *The Portrait of a Lady*. First Boer War begins.

1882 Married Women's Property Act, allowing wives to retain some of their own property and conduct business in their own names. The Society for Psychical Research founded.

1883 Olive Schreiner, *The Story of an African Farm*; Robert Louis Stevenson, *Treasure Island*.

1884 Amendment to give women the vote defeated by the Prime Minister, William E. Gladstone. "Ouida" (Mary Louise de la Ramée), *Princess Napraxine*.

1885 W. T. Stead's explosive exposé, "The Maiden Tribute of Modern Babylon"; H. Rider Haggard's *King Solomon's Mines*. Leopold II takes over the Congo, initiating a regime of spectacular brutality. Invention of the "safety bicycle," with both wheels the same size, gives women independence and encourages "rational dress." The Indian National Congress forms.

1886 Two novels about the cost of repression: Stevenson, *Dr. Jekyll and Mr. Hyde*, and James, *The Bostonians*. Gladstone introduces the Irish Home Rule bill; it is defeated.

1887 Queen Victoria's Golden Jubilee, celebrating 50 years of her reign. Arthur Conan Doyle's first Sherlock Holmes story, *A Study in Scarlet*.

1888 George Eastman invents the box camera. Rudyard Kipling, *Plain Tales from the Hills*. Jack the Ripper's gruesome murders of prostitutes.

1889 Charles Stewart Parnell, charismatic leader of the Irish independence movement, is destroyed by the revelation of his affair with a married woman, Kitty O'Shea. George Bernard Shaw and Beatrice and Sydney Webb, *Fabian Essays in Socialism*. Deaths of poet Robert Browning, poet Gerard Manley Hopkins, and novelist Wilkie Collins.

1890 W. B. Yeats founds the Rhymers' Club, a group of poets including Ernest Rhys, Ernest Dowson, Lionel Johnson, John Davidson, Richard Le Gallienne, and Arthur Symons. The London Underground (subway) opens. Two scandalously sexual novels: Lucas Malet, *The Wages of Sin*, and Oscar Wilde, *The Picture of Dorian Gray* (serial version; book version in 1891).

1891 George Gissing, *New Grub Street*, and Thomas Hardy, *Tess of the d'Urbervilles*, both cited by conservative critics as evidence of the decline of decency.

1892 Alfred, Lord Tennyson dies, and a deservedly obscure poet named Alfred Austin succeeds him as the Poet Laureate. Wilde, *Lady Windermere's Fan*. Irish Home Rule bill is defeated again.

1893 Henry Ford's first automobile. Two significant plays: Wilde, *A Woman of No Importance*, and Arthur Wing Pinero, *The Second Mrs. Tanqueray*. The most popular New Women novel: Sarah Grand, *The Heavenly Twins*. Another defeat for the Irish Home Rule bill.

1894 The term "New Women" popularized when Grand and Ouida write dueling articles in the *North American Review*. Several controversial New Women novels: Mona Caird, *Daughters of Danaus*, and Iota, *The Yellow Aster*. Debut of the aesthetic journal, *The Yellow Book*, instantly famous for its provocative cover illustrations by Aubrey Beardsley. Kipling, *The Jungle Book*; Shaw, *Arms and the Man*. Stevenson dies.

1895 Two scandalous novels depicting cohabiting couples: Hardy, *Jude the Obscure* (dubbed "Jude the Obscene" by one hostile reviewer), and Grant Allen, *The Woman Who Did*. H. G. Wells publishes *The Time Machine*. Wilde, *The Importance of Being Earnest*, his wittiest play. Max Nordau's *Degeneration* appears (in English translation), accusing Wilde of egoism bordering on madness. In May Wilde is convicted of "gross indecency" and sentenced to two years' hard labor.

1896 John Addington Symonds collaborates with Havelock Ellis on *Sexual Inversion*, suppressed, altered, rejected, and prosecuted in England. A. E. Housman, *A Shropshire Lad*. The Klondike Gold Rush. Kitchener's campaign to reconquer the Sudan.

1897 Queen Victoria's Diamond Jubilee celebrates 60 years on the throne, the longest reign in British history. Two major works of fantasy: Wells, *The Invisible Man*, and Bram Stoker, *Dracula*.

1898 James, *The Turn of the Screw*. Beardsley dies of tuberculosis at 25, begging his friends to destroy his "bawdy drawings" (they didn't). Wilde, "Ballad of Reading Gaol," published with his prison identification C.3.3. as the author's name. Gladstone dies.

1899 Second Boer War begins, pitting the British against the Boers (farmers of Dutch descent) for control of northern South Africa. Kipling, "The White Man's Burden."

1900 Wilde dies in a squalid Paris hotel. Max Planck develops quantum theory. Sigmund Freud, *The Interpretation of Dreams*. Joseph Conrad, *Lord Jim*. Australian Commonwealth forms. Antonio Gaudi designs Parc Guell in Barcelona.

1901 Queen Victoria dies, succeeded by Edward VII. Guglielmo Marconi's wireless transatlantic radio transmission. Bestselling novels: Malet, *The History of Sir Richard Calmady*, and Kipling, *Kim*.

1902 Conrad, *Heart of Darkness*, a landmark study of imperialism's ravages in Africa. The Boers surrender, ending their guerilla campaign. James, *The Wings of the Dove*.

1903 Samuel Butler, *The Way of All Flesh*. The Wright brothers' first successful flight.

1904 Conrad, *Nostromo*; James, *The Golden Bowl*; G. K. Chesterton's *The Napoleon of Notting Hill*; J. M. Synge's *Riders to the Sea*; Shaw, *Man and Superman*; J. M. Barrie, *Peter Pan*. Yeats and his associates found the Abbey Theatre in Dublin to perform Irish plays.

1905 Henri Matisse exhibits his Fauve paintings. Shaw, *Major Barbara*. Sinn Fein, agitating for Irish self-governance, founded.

1906 John Galsworthy, *The Man of Property*. Paul Cézanne dies. The Dreyfus Affair, in which Captain Alfred Dreyfus was framed as a traitor because he was Jewish, ends with Dreyfus formally cleared of all charges.

1907 The Labour bill to give women the vote is defeated. Conrad, *The Secret Agent*. Kipling wins the Nobel Prize. Lord Baden-Powell founds the Boy Scouts.

1908 Kenneth Grahame, *The Wind in the Willows*; Arnold Bennett, *The Old Wives' Tale*; E. M. Forster, *A Room with a View*. Riots in Dublin over Synge's *The Playboy of the Western World*. Henry Ford produces the Model T.

1909 Wells, *Tono-Bungay*. Imprisoned suffragettes go on hunger strike and are force-fed.

1910 Forster, *Howard's End*. Edward VII dies, succeeded by George V. Art historian Roger Fry's Post-Impressionist exhibition, about which Virginia Woolf later reminisces, "on or about December, 1910, human character changed."

Preface

Literature and Culture at the Fin de Siècle is the first reader to make the fascinating texts of the period from 1880 to 1910 available for classroom use. With famous poems, controversial journalism, and moving short stories, *Literature and Culture* gives a wide range of readings suitable for undergraduates and graduate students, designed for easy adaptation to many different types of courses. This book presents texts by major authors like Oscar Wilde, Henry James, Rudyard Kipling, and W. B. Yeats, juxtaposing canonical masterpieces with neglected but significant literary texts. It reveals the period's new theories and new styles of writing, ranging from aestheticism to naturalism, from psychoanalysis to degeneration, from imperialism to the New Women movement. The *fin de siècle's* political and sexual upheavals fascinate students and scholars today, and *Literature and Culture* offers the full range of the era's writing in a way that has never before been possible.

I have organized this volume into four main sections, designed to demonstrate the period's richly complex cultural formations. For instance, "Aestheticism" not only includes the key manifestos of the aesthetic movement by Whistler, Wilde, Beerbohm, and Symons, but also juxtaposes them with Vernon Lee's fascinating dialogues of aesthetic philosophy and Alice Meynell's haunting meditation on the meaning of color. The light comedy of the most famous aesthetic prose finds a darker shadow in Una Ashworth Taylor's sexually charged parables. Similarly, "New Women" reproduces the central documents of this embattled feminist cause, including the pivotal exchange between Sarah Grand and Ouida that popularized the term and the much-discussed George Egerton short story "A Cross Line." But I have also included a range of poetry—not normally perceived to be part of the New Women corpus—that offers voices both militant and jubilant, comical and wistful. Just after Egerton's celebratory tale of female sexual choice I have placed Ella D'Arcy's unforgettable depiction of male cruelty towards precisely this sort of sexually adventurous women. You will find the period's anxieties about social and physical degeneration, urban decay, sexual perversity, and philanthropic and socialist programs represented in "Mind and Body," with urgent prose by George Bernard Shaw, Havelock Ellis, and Charles Booth, not to mention W. T. Stead's infamous exposé of child prostitution. You will also find A. E. Housman's poetry in this section, pointing out the contrast between Housman's willed pastoralism and contemporary urban blight. Another unusual connection emerges in "England and Its Others," when representative works from the Celtic Revival share space with British fantasies about India and Africa, suggesting how the tale of a timeless Irish prehistory might have served English interests as well as nascent Irish nationalism. I have also made a point of contrasting the canonical works of imperialist discourse with other, often less well known, work that writes back against them. Thus Kipling's "Without Benefit of Clergy" meets Alice Perrin's "In the Next Room," which imagines fear, not love, as the keynote of interracial relations, and indeed Kipling's poems and stories find counterparts in work by Laurence Hope and Toru Dutt, women who wrote from (and identified themselves with) India.

By mixing famous works with more unusual texts, I hope to jolt readers into reconsidering, arguing, rethinking what we thought we knew about the late nineteenth century. This book works hard to avoid the usual approach of depicting the period's literary output as composed of the individual iterations of Great Writers who emerged at well-spaced intervals. I have chosen not to reproduce novels that are already widely available in print, some in Longman Cultural Editions: *The Picture of Dorian Gray, Heart of Darkness, Dracula, Jude the Obscure, Tess of the d'Urbervilles, Kim, Trilby, Strange Case of Dr. Jekyll and Mr. Hyde, The War of the Worlds, The Turn of the Screw.* Instead I have selected texts that are just as fascinating but much harder to find. My selections have also been constrained by national and chronological limits: This volume is restricted to the British experience of the *fin de siècle*, across roughly 30 years (1880s–1910s). A wider historical and international range of readings in many of these issues may be found in *The Longman Anthology of British Literature*, vol. 2 (Romantics/Victorians/Twentieth Century) and *The Longman Anthology of World Literature.*

Although the *fin de siècle* was only a few decades long, it boasts an exceptionally rich range of fascinating literature—some newly rediscovered—and I hope you find this anthology an enjoyable way into the period. *Literature and Culture* presents the unquestioned classics of the era, illuminated by the contemporary culture of the periodical press, political cartoons, parodies, and memoirs. From the cheerful nonsense of Gilbert and Sullivan's "If You're Anxious for to Shine" to Stead's despairing "The Maiden Tribute of Modern Babylon," from the optimistic forecast of Grand's "The New Aspect of the Woman Question" to the futile dismay of Synge's *Riders to the Sea*, we can read many different *fin de siècles* in *Literature and Culture*, a collection that tries to communicate and celebrate, not resolve, some of the vast complicated vitality of its chosen era.

Such a project could not have been done alone, and in the past five years of working on this volume I have become acutely aware of how much I have learned and how grateful I am to the scholars from whom I have learned it. I am deeply indebted to the excellent notes in *The Longman Anthology of British Literature*, vol. 2, by William Sharpe and Heather Henderson, and I have tried to emulate their freshness, wit, and range of knowledge. I have learned much from Elleke Boehmer's scrupulously edited and impressively comprehensive collection *Empire Writing: An Anthology of Colonial Literature 1870–1918*. My notes on "The Decay of Lying" benefited from Linda Dowling's admirably thorough scholarship in *Oscar Wilde: The Soul of Man Under Socialism and Selected Critical Prose*. Karl Beckson's *Aesthetes and Decadents of the 1890s* is the pioneering work in this field, and *The Fin de Siècle*, edited by Sally Ledger and Roger Luckhurst, is one of its newest and most useful contributions. These texts have helped me think about how to select and annotate readings; they have taught me what a good anthology should look like.

Almost every page of this volume has notes and facts that other scholars have generously helped me find. Specialists in the *fin de siècle* and Victorianist scholars have generously supported this project; there are too many to name, but I particularly want to thank the members of the VICTORIA listserve who took time to help me track down obscure queries. Specialists in philosophy, astronomy, French, fashion, and other fields equally beyond my range patiently explained various references. My colleagues gave me advice, steered me to resources, and cheered me up. Particular thanks to Joseph Bristow, Nancy Comley, Nicole Cooley, Saros Cowasjee, Elizabeth Ezra, Elaine Freedgood, Carrie Hintz, Linda K. Hughes, Anne Humpherys, Gerhard Joseph, Shuchi Kapila, Richard Kaye, Norman Kelvin, Paula Krebs, Steven Kruger, Mark Samuels Lasner, Diana Maltz, Andrew McCann, Sally Mitchell, George Musser, Anna Neill, Kathy Psomiades, David Richter, Solveig Robinson, Meri-Jane Rochelson, Fred Roden, Caroline Rupprecht, Jonathan Schaffer, Cathy Shuman, Jonah Siegel, Margaret Stetz, Beth Sutton-Ramspeck, Katie Sweeting, Pam Thurschwell, Stan Walker, John Weir, and Nancy Yousef. My students cheerfully endured being guinea pigs for these readings and asked wonderful questions that helped me realize what footnotes we needed. I am so grateful for their good humor and interest in this period.

Many people worked to turn this from just a "good idea" into a real book. David Damrosch encouraged me to send the proposal to Longman, and Jennifer Wicke helped me shape the contents. My research assistants, Kristen Case at the Graduate Center and Marilyn Howard at Queens College, procured many hard-to-find texts. A PSC-CUNY grant sent me to the British Library to find others. Christine Halsey, Dianne Hall, and Chrysta Meadowbrooke patiently answered questions, tabulated pages, and organized manuscript sections. Joseph Terry's and Michele Cronin's support kept the project on track. Above all I am grateful to Susan Wolfson, the most energetic, supportive, and ingenious of editors, who encouraged me to find new ways of thinking about the volume at every level. Susan's wholehearted involvement in the volume almost qualifies her to be listed as a coauthor. She has done more for this book than any "editor" title can reveal.

Finally, I must thank the people who lived through this long process with me. I'm grateful for the love and support and advice, the days out, the barbecues, the long phone calls, and the babysitting from my family: Ann Schaffer, Ben Schaffer, Jonathan Schaffer, Olga Gershenson, Judy Musser, Eva Szekely, George Musser Sr., Bret Musser, Eileen Musser, not to mention Aidan, Katherine, and Kieran Musser. George Musser's unwavering belief in me, and unmatched editorial skill, made all the difference. His strength gave me the confidence to do a book of this magnitude, and his conversation reminded me why it was worth doing. Eliana Musser grew along with this book, and her laughter, curiosity, love, and freshness have made my joy.

TALIA SCHAFFER
Queens College and Graduate Center
of the City University of New York

INTRODUCTION

The *Fin de Siècle*

Everyone who lived through it agreed that the period between the 1870s and 1910s was complex, vital, tumultuous, confusing, and exciting. Writers like Oscar Wilde, Henry James, Joseph Conrad, Thomas Hardy, Lucas Malet, Sarah Grand, Bram Stoker, Sir Arthur Conan Doyle, Olive Schreiner, H. G. Wells, Robert Louis Stevenson, and W. B. Yeats created stylish new ways of writing: aestheticism, naturalism, horror fiction, detective stories, psychological studies, degenerative fables, imperialist allegories, feminist manifestos. A rebellious younger generation of artists, writers, and activists worked to transform British society, instructing their startled elders to change the way they decorated, viewed art, cared for the poor, and displayed the body. Yet the period from the 1870s to the 1910s also has a unique problem: It has no widely accepted name. What can we call this era? "The turn of the century"? "The 1890s"? "Late Victorianism"? "Early modernism"? "The *fin de siècle*" (French for end of the century)? Our nameless era swings up onto the back of the Victorian carriage or clambers onto the running boards of the modernist automobile, tolerated as an extra passenger without being admitted to the full comforts of the vehicle. Its namelessness is not just an inconvenience; it signals something fundamental about the period. The ferment of new ideas—new sciences (psychology, degeneration, sexology), new political movements (Fabian socialism, imperialism), and new cultural forms (New Women, aestheticism, tabloid journalism)—makes the period too complicated to sum up in one succinct label. The fact that the century was ending created psychological stress too. The Victorians' longstanding anxiety about the pace of modernity was exacerbated by this strong presumption that an era was ending. From our perspective, too, the twentieth century's landing right in the middle of our period was highly inconvenient, as it gives us an awkward set of dates that is harder than ever to name.

So which moniker best suits the period? "The turn of the century" focuses on the years between, say, 1895 and 1905: the Jubilee and death of Queen Victoria, Oscar Wilde's imprisonment and death, the Boer War, the imperialist writing of Rudyard Kipling and others, the prosperity of the early Edwardian era. "The 1890s," the term initially preferred by literary historians, focuses on an earlier decade, with Wilde's trial as its climax. If we seek a more chronologically capacious term, we could use "late Victorianism." This designates a long slow twilight of grand Victorian ideas, highlighting writers like Thomas Hardy, A. E. Housman, and Mary Ward. Yet if we like "early modernism," we privilege the literary and cultural experimentation of George Egerton, Arthur Symons, and George Bernard Shaw. Finally, "*fin de siècle*" suggests a longer period than the 1890s, focusing on cultural concerns like degeneration, socialism, New Women, homosexuality, aestheticism, and jingoism. Its star is Oscar Wilde, a key figure in virtually every major cultural movement of the period. In other words, what we call this era suggests whether we prioritize cultural, political, or economic changes; which decades seem most important; and which writers and styles of writing appear most representative.

In this book I have chosen to use "*fin de siècle*" because it presents the period as an entity in itself and offers some flexibility about dates. Moreover, although it is a cumbersome term (especially with that annoying accent), it best embodies the cultural movements of the period. *Fin de siècle* was what writers of the period named their own sense of malaise and uneasiness. "However silly a term *fin de siècle* may be," wrote the German doctor and journalist Max Nordau, "the mental constitution which it indicates is actually present in influential circles." He explained:

> The disposition of the times is curiously confused, a compound of feverish restlessness and blunted discouragement, of fearful presage and hang-dog renunciation. The prevalent feeling is that of imminent perdition and extinction. *Fin de siècle* is at once a confession and a complaint. The old Northern faith contained the fearsome doctrine of the Dusk of the Gods. In our days there have arisen in more highly developed minds vague qualms of a Dusk of the Nations, in which all suns and all stars are gradually waning, and mankind with all its institutions and creations is perishing in the midst of a dying world. (2)

Nordau expresses the dismay of social conservatives, but the insouciant Oscar Wilde also used the term in *The Picture of Dorian Gray*. When Lady Narborough comments, "nowadays all the married men live like bachelors and all the bachelors like married men," Lord Henry replies simply: "Fin de siècle," as if the term explained it all (Wilde, 179). Although Wilde and Nordau despised each other, they shared a sense that the old rules were disappearing and expressed it by the same phrase. Looking back at his youth in the 1890s, historian Holbrook Jackson identified "fin de siècle [as] a pose as well as a fact"; "anything strange or uncanny, anything which savoured of freak and perversity, was swiftly labelled fin de siècle and given a certain topical prominence. The term became a fashion, and writers vied one with another as to which should apply it most aptly" (19, 20).

These "writers" of the *fin de siècle* included Osbert Burdett, W. G. Blaikie Murdoch, and Amy Cruse. Most were born in the 1870s or 1880s, enjoyed the *fin de siècle* in their young adulthood, and wrote their histories in the 1920s and 1930s, surrounded by a hostile new generation of writers who despised the supposedly hidebound, unfashionable Victorian past. No wonder these historians tend to look back nostalgically—and somewhat defensively—at what increasingly seemed like a golden, youthful, prewar paradise of brilliant talents and charismatic personalities. To Burdett it was "the Beardsley Period." The artist Aubrey Beardsley, he proposed, was "a leader," who "bears in himself, in a higher degree of intensity than any of his colleagues, the centre or point of conjunction of the spiritual forces that coalesce among them" (98). In trying to show that the period was vital, brash, and embattled—qualities valued in the modernist period during which they were publishing—these historians were working to save their own memories from what E. P. Thompson has called "the enormous condescension of posterity" (12). Women writers who enjoyed the New Women movement made a special point of describing how invigorated they felt by its fresh ideas about gender and sexuality. Poet Richard Le Gallienne, writing in 1926, celebrated the *fin de siècle* not as the end but as the birth of modernism:

> As one looks back, it is plain that here was not so much the ending of a century as the beginning of a new one. Those last ten years of the nineteenth century properly belong to the twentieth century, and, far from being "decadent," except in certain limited manifestations, they were years of an immense and multifarious renaissance. All our present conditions, socially and artistically, our vaunted new "freedoms" of every kind—including "free verse"—not only began then, but found a more vital and authoritative expression than they have found since. . . . Such achievements as the twentieth century can boast are merely extensions of what the men and women of the '90s began. (78)

Jackson agreed that "the last decade of the last century was, in spite of its many extravagances, a renascent period," (18) indeed "an era of hope and action. People thought anything might happen; and, for the young, any happening sufficiently new was good. . . . [T]he rising generation felt as though it were stepping out of the cages of convention and custom into a freedom full of tremendous possibilities" (30–31). Novelist Netta Syrett captured this feeling in a novel set in the 1890s, *Rose Cottingham, or The Victorians*, when a young woman newly introduced to the heady wonders of the aesthetic movement feels "as though she had exchanged flat beer in pewter mugs, for champagne served in sparkling, slender glasses" (365). "There is no question that people . . . were much more awake in the Nineties," agreed the writer Elizabeth Robins Pennell. Artists, she commented, were

> much more keen about everything, even a fight, or above all a fight, if they thought a fight would clear the air. Those clever young men, self-appointed historians of a period they know only by hearsay, may deplore or envy its decadence. But because a small clique wrote anaemic verse . . . that does not mean decadence. A period of revolt against decadence, of insurrection, of vigorous warfare it seemed to me who lived and worked through it. (118)

Many of the "clever young men" Pennell mentions preferred to cast the period as defunct, contrasting it with their own heroic novelty. They often described a mood of decay or "decadence." W. B. Yeats famously dubbed it the "tragic generation." In 1911 W. G. Blaikie Murdoch described the period as "the twilight of the gods," stressing the fact that the "bright young spirits" Henry Harland, John Davidson, Hubert Crackanthorpe, Ernest Dowson, Frances William Lauderdale Adams, Charles Conder, and H. D. Lowry all died before 1910 (72–75). Max Beerbohm satirizes this prototypical doomed poet in "Enoch Soames," the tale of an inept gloomy writer who sells his soul to the devil. In the 1890s writers were drawn to the notion of "decadence." In 1893 Arthur Symons described decadence as a major new literary movement characterized by "intense self-consciousness, a restless curiosity in research, an over-subtilizing refinement upon refinement, a spiritual and moral perversity" (858–59). Indeed, Symons continued, "its very disease of form" denoted social dissipation, "a civilization grown over-luxurious, over-inquiring, too languid for the relief of action, too uncertain for any emphasis in opinions or in conduct" (859). Symons's stress on "moral perversity" also indicates how decadence accommodated same-sex and other unconventional desires, which could now be coded as a fashionably world-weary amorality. Decadence offered a useful alternative discourse to the punitive late-Victorian medical and juridical codes to which sexuality was increasingly relegated. It was a decadence of the Victorian world: The century was ending, the queen was aging, major figures were dying, and social orders were eroding. Male writers with traditional cultural allegiances (to classically influenced verse, for instance) felt left behind by the brash, bestselling new writings of the New Women, socialists, and imperialists. They recorded their misery as a narrative of decline, as if the relative marginalizing of their particular masculine high-art culture meant the end of civilization itself. As Nordau summed it up, *fin de siècle* "is the impotent despair of a sick man, who feels himself dying by inches in the midst of an eternally living nature blooming insolently for ever," the misery of mortified and exhausted men (3).

Tragic generation or renaissance? Dusk of the nations or modernist birth? Era of a great leader or crowds of fighting youth? The *fin de siècle* meant all these stories, and in the following pages you will find them all.

Works Cited

Burdett, Osbert. *The Beardsley Period: An Essay in Perspective*. 1925; New York: Cooper Square Publishers Inc., 1969.

Cruse, Amy. *After the Victorians*. London: George Allen & Unwin Ltd., 1938.

Jackson, Holbrook. *The Eighteen Nineties*. New York: Alfred A. Knopf, 1922.

Le Gallienne, Richard. *The Romantic '90s*. 1926; London: Robin Clark Ltd., 1993.

Murdoch, W. G. Blaikie. *The Renaissance of the Nineties*. 1911; [Folcroft, PA]: The Folcroft Press, 1970.

Nordau, Max. *Degeneration*. 1895; Lincoln: University of Nebraska Press, 1993.

Pennell, Elizabeth Robins. *Nights: Rome and Venice in the Aesthetic Eighties, London and Paris in the Fighting Nineties*. Philadelphia and London: J.B. Lippincott Company, 1916.

Symons, Arthur. "The Decadent Movement in Literature." *Harper's New Monthly Magazine* November 1893, 858–67.

Syrett, Netta. *Rose Cottingham, or The Victorians*. 1915; Chicago: Academy Press Ltd., 1978.

Thompson, E. P. *The Making of the English Working Class*. New York: Vintage, 1966.

Wilde, Oscar. *The Picture of Dorian Gray*. 1891; Oxford: Oxford University Press, 1981.

Yeats, W. B. "The Tragic Generation," *The Trembling of the Veil*, reprinted in *Autobiographies*. 1922; London: Macmillan, 1955, 300–304.

PART I

Aestheticism

The Art of Living: Introduction to Aestheticism

"One should either be a work of art, or wear a work of art," proclaimed the charismatic Oscar Wilde. At the *fin de siècle*, the aesthetes tried both. Aestheticism, the movement Wilde made famous, was perhaps the most influential and wide-ranging of the period's new ideas. It was both a literary philosophy and a guide for everyday life. Art was a new religion of beauty and a flagrant departure from the Victorian ethos of moral instruction. The aesthetes argued instead that beauty was an end in itself and redesigned every aspect of late-Victorian life: architecture, dress, food, periodicals, book bindings, furniture, church services, tenement housing, museums. No class, no occupation, no object was exempt from the aesthetes' reformist fervor.

Aestheticism (at its height between the 1870s and 1890s) was fundamentally shaped by the Pre-Raphaelite movement of the 1850s. The Pre-Raphaelites (including Dante Gabriel Rossetti, Christina Rossetti, Edward Burne-Jones, and William Morris) produced allegorical, stylized, richly colored, sensuous paintings and poems that evoked medieval styles. Poet Algernon Charles Swinburne flouted conventional morality and celebrated the forbidden in the most addictively lilting of cadences. These earlier artists showed that beauty could be appreciated no matter what it taught. John Ruskin and William Morris explained that the observer needed to look at the object's historical style and honest construction; good art revealed its own truth. Walter Pater celebrated the "hard gemlike flame" of the intense apprehension of beauty as the climax of life. Inspired by these teachers, the aesthetes of the *fin de siècle* devoted themselves to beautifying their surroundings, and their code of connoisseurship became the new mode of critical authority.

The most famous and controversial aesthetes of the 1890s were the febrilely talented Aubrey Beardsley and the brilliantly witty Oscar Wilde. Beardsley's pen-and-ink drawings brought sinuous lines, Japanese simplicity, and perverse uncertainties about gender and sexuality into British art. His spectacular illustrations for *The Yellow Book* caused a scandal. Oscar Wilde, as he pointed out himself in "De Profundis," "was a man who stood in symbolic relations to the art and culture of my age. . . . I summed up all systems in a phrase and all existence in an epigram." Wilde elucidated a vision of art distinct from morality, instead spelling out art's relation to history, imagination, and social class. In *The Picture of Dorian Gray*, short stories, fairy tales, and poems, Wilde explored aesthetic paradox, and his extraordinarily popular plays satirized upper-class assumptions. When he was convicted for "gross indecency," the catastrophe ended his career and ultimately his life. Under the shadow of this scandal, the aesthetic movement collapsed, although its stress on the moral autonomy of art shaped modernism.

This part of the book presents the lively, urgent, and delightful range of *fin-de-siècle* aestheticism. Wilde, Vernon Lee, Max Beerbohm, Arthur Symons, and Alice Meynell rebeled against the notion that art should be measured by its fidelity to real life or socially acceptable morality. Amy Levy, Olive Custance, and the two women writing as "Michael Field" developed a lyric language for lesbian passion, while other female poets questioned standard notions of women's experience. Poets like Wilde, Ernest Dowson, Beerbohm, and Symons delighted in the night side of London—prostitutes, drugs, pollution, artifices, and music halls—with dark consequences. Members of the Rhymers' Club—Dowson, Symons, and Lionel Johnson—died young, poor, and dissipated, exemplifying the love of decay and destruction called "decadence."

Aesthetes shared a fanatical devotion to style, reveling in wit and artfully archaic language, crafting sentences that were little gems in themselves. When Beerbohm writes of "a damosel, prying in her mirror," or Yeats describes "the jewelled crowns that kings have hurled / In shadowy pools, when armies fled," they want us to share their pleasure in their richly evocative language. Aesthetic style could also mean an elegantly simplified, epigrammatic style, as in the famous opening of Meynell's "The Colour of Life": "Red is the colour of violence, or of life broken open, edited, and published."

Fin-de-siècle critics often parodied aestheticism as ridiculously pretentious, but those parodies—like Gilbert and Sullivan's songs in *Patience*—attest to the serious ambitions of the movement. The aesthetic movement provided a coherent philosophy for social reform, decorative and fine art; it transformed the way the British thought about the aim of literature; it provided a discourse for alternative forms of desire; and it produced experimental work that marked a decisive break from high-Victorian realism.

Arguing for Art: Aesthetic Prose

Walter Pater
1839–1894

If Walter Pater had done nothing but coin the phrase "art for art's sake," that alone would have made him a leader of the aesthetic movement. An Oxford don, a dandy, and a lover of religious ritual, Pater also conducted discreet romances with young men. His *Studies in the History of the Renaissance* (1873) presented a new mode of art criticism, a lyrical, impressionistic discourse testifying to the powerful feelings art evokes. His description of Leonardo da Vinci's

Mona Lisa was so evocative that W. B. Yeats declared it the first modern poem, placing it at the beginning of the *Oxford Book of Modern Verse*. Pater's "Conclusion" to *The Renaissance* was controversial because it seemed to advocate intensifying one's experiences through boundless sexual and personal freedom, regardless of morality. Pater urged readers to "grasp at any exquisite passion, or any contribution to knowledge that seems by a lifted horizon to set the spirit free for a moment, or any stirring of the senses." It was embraced as a manifesto by aesthetic youth, including Pater's student Oscar Wilde, and Pater later suppressed it. His later novel, *Marius the Epicurean* (1885), offered dense descriptions and a contemplative tone in lieu of a conventional plot, deeply influencing aesthetic fiction.

from Studies in the History of the Renaissance

from *Leonardo da Vinci* [LA GIOCONDA][1]

La Gioconda is, in the truest sense, Leonardo's masterpiece, the revealing instance of his mode of thought and work. In suggestiveness, only the *Melancholia* of Dürer[2] is comparable to it; and no crude symbolism disturbs the effect of its subdued and graceful mystery. We all know the face and hands of the figure, set in its marble chair, in that circle of fantastic rocks, as in some faint light under sea. Perhaps of all ancient pictures time has chilled it least. As often happens with works in which invention seems to reach its limit, there is an element in it given to, not invented by, the master. In that inestimable folio of drawings, once in the possession of Vasari, were certain designs by Verrocchio,[3] faces of such impressive beauty that Leonardo in his boyhood copied them many times. It is hard not to connect with these designs of the elder, by-past master, as with its germinal principle, the unfathomable smile, always with a touch of something sinister in it, which plays over all Leonardo's work. Besides, the picture is a portrait. From childhood we see this image defining itself on the fabric of his dreams; and but for express historical testimony, we might fancy that this was but his ideal lady, embodied and beheld at last. What was the relationship of a living Florentine to this creature of his thought? By what strange affinities had the dream and the person grown up thus apart, and yet so closely together? Present from the first incorporeally in Leonardo's brain, dimly traced in the designs of Verrocchio, she is found present at last in *Il Giocondo's* house. That there is much of mere portraiture in the picture is attested by the legend that by artificial means, the presence of mimes and flute-players, that subtle expression was protracted on the face. Again, was it in four years and by renewed labour never really completed, or in four months and as by stroke of magic, that the image was projected?

The presence that rose thus so strangely beside the waters, is expressive of what in the ways of a thousand years men had come to desire. Hers is the head upon which all "the ends of the world are come,"[4] and the eyelids are a little weary. It is a beauty wrought out from within upon the flesh, the deposit, little cell by cell, of strange thoughts and fantastic reveries and exquisite passions. Set it for a moment beside one

---

1. Mona Lisa, the wife of Francesco del Giocondo.
2. *Melancholia* (1514) is one of Albrecht Dürer's most celebrated engravings.
3. Giorgio Vasari (1511–74), painter and architect, wrote *Lives of the Artists*. Andrea del Verrocchio (c. 1435–88) was an Italian painter, sculptor, and goldsmith.
4. 1 Corinthians 10.11: "Now all these things happened unto them [idolators] for examples: and they are written for our admonition, upon whom the ends of the world are come."

of those white Greek goddesses or beautiful women of antiquity, and how would they be troubled by this beauty, into which the soul with all its maladies has passed! All the thoughts and experience of the world have etched and moulded there, in that which they have of power to refine and make expressive the outward form, the animalism of Greece, the lust of Rome, the mysticism of the middle age with its spiritual ambition and imaginative loves, the return of the Pagan world, the sins of the Borgias.[5] She is older than the rocks among which she sits; like the vampire, she has been dead many times, and learned the secrets of the grave; and has been a diver in deep seas, and keeps their fallen day about her; and trafficked for strange webs with Eastern merchants and, as Leda, was the mother of Helen of Troy, and, as Saint Anne, the mother of Mary;[6] and all this has been to her but as the sound of lyres and flutes, and lives only in the delicacy with which it has moulded the changing lineaments, and tinged the eyelids and the hands. The fancy of a perpetual life, sweeping together ten thousand experiences, is an old one; and modern philosophy has conceived the idea of humanity as wrought upon by, and summing up in itself, all modes of thought and life. Certainly Lady Lisa might stand as the embodiment of the old fancy, the symbol of the modern idea.

—1871

Conclusion[1]

Λέγει που Ἡράκλειτος ὅτι πάντα χωρεῖ καὶ οὐδὲν μένει[2]

To regard all things and principles of things as inconstant modes or fashions has more and more become the tendency of modern thought. Let us begin with that which is without—our physical life. Fix upon it in one of its more exquisite intervals, the moment, for instance, of delicious recoil from the flood of water in summer heat. What is the whole physical life in that moment but a combination of natural elements to which science gives their names? But those elements, phosphorus and lime and delicate fibres, are present not in the human body alone: we detect them in places most remote from it. Our physical life is a perpetual motion of them—the passage of the blood, the waste and repairing of the lenses of the eye, the modification of the tissues of the brain under every ray of light and sound—processes which science reduces to simpler and more elementary forces. Like the elements of which we are composed, the action of these forces extends beyond us: it rusts iron and ripens corn. Far out on every side of us those elements are broadcast, driven in many currents; and birth and gesture and death and the springing of violets from the grave are but a few out of ten thousand resultant combinations. That clear, perpetual outline of face and limb is but an image of ours, under which we group them—a design in a web, the actual threads of which

---

5. A powerful Italian family of the Renaissance, infamous for its violence.
6. Leda, raped by Zeus in the guise of a swan, gave birth to Helen of Troy. St. Anne was the mother of the Virgin Mary.

---

1. "This brief 'Conclusion' was omitted in the second edition of this book, as I conceived it might possibly mislead some of those young men into whose hands it might fall. On the whole, I have thought it best to reprint it here, with some slight changes which bring it closer to my original meaning. I have dealt more fully in *Marius the Epicurean* with the thoughts suggested by it" [Pater's note to the third edition, 1888].
2. "Heraclitus says, 'All things give way; nothing remaineth'" [Pater's translation, from Plato's "Cratylus"].

pass out beyond it. This at least of flamelike our life has, that it is but the concurrence, renewed from moment to moment, of forces parting sooner or later on their ways.

Or if we begin with the inward world of thought and feeling, the whirlpool is still more rapid, the flame more eager and devouring. There it is no longer the gradual darkening of the eye, the gradual fading of colour from the wall—movements of the shore-side, where the water flows down indeed, though in apparent rest—but the race of the mid-stream, a drift of momentary acts of sight and passion and thought. At first sight experience seems to bury us under a flood of external objects, pressing upon us with a sharp and importunate reality, calling us out of ourselves in a thousand forms of action. But when reflexion begins to play upon those objects they are dissipated under its influence; the cohesive force seems suspended like some trick of magic; each object is loosed into a group of impressions—colour, odour, texture—in the mind of the observer. And if we continue to dwell in thought on this world, not of objects in the solidity with which language invests them, but of impressions, unstable, flickering, inconsistent, which burn and are extinguished with our consciousness of them, it contracts still further: the whole scope of observation is dwarfed into the narrow chamber of the individual mind. Experience, already reduced to a group of impressions, is ringed round for each one of us by that thick wall of personality through which no real voice has ever pierced on its way to us, or from us to that which we can only conjecture to be without. Every one of those impressions is the impression of the individual in his isolation, each mind keeping as a solitary prisoner its own dream of a world. Analysis goes a step farther still, and assures us that those impressions of the individual mind to which, for each one of us, experience dwindles down, are in perpetual flight; that each of them is limited by time, and that as time is infinitely divisible, each of them is infinitely divisible also; all that is actual in it being a single moment, gone while we try to apprehend it, of which it may ever be more truly said that it has ceased to be than that it is. To such a tremulous wisp constantly re-forming itself on the stream, to a single sharp impression, with a sense in it, a relic more or less fleeting, of such moments gone by, what is real in our life fines itself down. It is with this movement, with the passage and dissolution of impressions, images, sensations, that analysis leaves off—that continual vanishing away, that strange, perpetual weaving and unweaving of ourselves.

Philosophiren, says Novalis, *ist dephlegmatisiren vivificiren.*[3] The service of philosophy, of speculative culture, towards the human spirit, is to rouse, to startle it to a life of constant and eager observation. Every moment some form grows perfect in hand or face; some tone on the hills or the sea is choicer than the rest; some mood of passion or insight or intellectual excitement is irresistibly real and attractive to us,—for that moment only. Not the fruit of experience, but experience itself, is the end. A counted number of pulses only is given to us of a variegated, dramatic life. How may we see in them all that is to be seen in them by the finest senses? How shall we pass most swiftly from point to point, and be present always at the focus where the greatest number of vital forces unite in their purest energy?

To burn always with this hard, gemlike flame, to maintain this ecstasy, is success in life. In a sense it might even be said that our failure is to form habits: for, after all, habit is relative to a stereotyped world, and meantime it is only the roughness of the

---

3. *To philosophize is to awaken.* Novalis (Friedrich von Hardenberg) was a German Romantic writer.

eye that makes any two persons, things, situations, seem alike. While all melts under our feet, we may well grasp at any exquisite passion, or any contribution to knowledge that seems by a lifted horizon to set the spirit free for a moment, or any stirring of the senses, strange dyes, strange colours, and curious odours, or work of the artist's hands, or the face of one's friend. Not to discriminate every moment some passionate attitude in those about us, and in the very brilliancy of their gifts some tragic dividing of forces on their ways, is, on this short day of frost and sun, to sleep before evening. With this sense of the splendour of our experience and of its awful brevity, gathering all we are into one desperate effort to see and touch, we shall hardly have time to make theories about the things we see and touch. What we have to do is to be for ever curiously testing new opinions and courting new impressions, never acquiescing in a facile orthodoxy of Comte, or of Hegel,[4] or of our own. Philosophical theories or ideas, as points of view, instruments of criticism, may help us to gather up what might otherwise pass unregarded by us. "Philosophy is the microscope of thought."[5] The theory or idea or system which requires of us the sacrifice of any part of this experience, in consideration of some interest into which we cannot enter, or some abstract theory we have not identified with ourselves, or of what is only conventional, has no real claim upon us.

One of the most beautiful passages of Rousseau is that in the sixth book of the *Confessions*,[6] where he describes the awakening in him of the literary sense. An undefinable taint of death had clung always about him, and now in early manhood he believed himself smitten by mortal disease. He asked himself how he might make as much as possible of the interval that remained; and he was not biassed by anything in his previous life when he decided that it must be by intellectual excitement, which he found just then in the clear, fresh writings of Voltaire.[7] Well! we are all *condamnés*, as Victor Hugo says: we are all under sentence of death but with a sort of indefinite reprieve—*les hommes sont tous condamnés à mort avec des sursis indéfinis*:[8] we have an interval, and then our place knows us no more. Some spend this interval in listlessness, some in high passions, the wisest, at least among "the children of this world,"[9] in art and song. For our one chance lies in expanding that interval, in getting as many pulsations as possible into the given time. Great passions may give us this quickened sense of life, ecstasy and sorrow of love, the various forms of enthusiastic activity, disinterested or otherwise, which come naturally to many of us. Only be sure it is passion— that it does yield you this fruit of a quickened, multiplied consciousness. Of such wisdom, the poetic passion, the desire of beauty, the love of art for its own sake, has most. For art comes to you proposing frankly to give nothing but the highest quality to your moments as they pass, and simply for those moments' sake.

—1873

---

4. 19th-c. French philosopher Auguste Comte (1798–1857) and German philosopher G. W. F. Hegel (1770–1831) both created overarching secular systems to explain the structure of thought.

5. From Victor Hugo (1802–85), *Les Miserables*, Part 5, Bk. 2, Ch. 2. This prolific French Romantic novelist is best known for *Les Miserables* and *Notre Dame de Paris*.

6. French political philosopher Jean-Jacques Rousseau (1712–78) published *Confessions*, a scandalously honest account of his life.

7. Pen name of François-Marie Arouet (1694–1778), the leading skeptic and author of the satirical *Candide*.

8. Hugo, from *Le dernier jour d'un condamné* (1832), translated just prior.

9. From Luke 16.8, Jesus's parable of the "unjust steward" who acts according to the dictates of worldly wisdom rather than divine justice.

James McNeill Whistler
1834–1903

In caricatures of the aesthetic movement, the dandy with the white stripe in his black hair, the glinting monocle, and the bitterly twisted mouth is always James McNeill Whistler. One of the major artists of the *fin de siècle*, the American-born Whistler was celebrated for cutting wit, sartorial elegance, and caustic temperament. He was a rival to Oscar Wilde, whom he accused of poaching his *bon mots*. (Once, when Whistler made a joke, Wilde generously remarked, "I wish I had said that." Whistler riposted: "You will, Oscar, you will.") Strongly influenced by Japanese art, Whistler painted impressionistic portraits and delineated landscapes with simple brushstrokes as pure arrangements of color and line (especially his nearly abstract depictions of the reflected lights in the Thames at night). To enforce this philosophy, he titled his paintings according to their dominant colors, not their subjects. He was also famous for his magnificently gilded Peacock Room, finished in sumptuous style without the owner Frederick R. Leyland's permission. In 1878, in one of the most symbolic moments of the *fin de siècle*'s artistic convulsions, he sued John Ruskin for slandering his mode of art. While he won the case, it ruined him financially. "Mr. Whistler's 'Ten O'Clock'" was delivered on February 20, 1885, to an invited audience of London society figures and art-world experts, at 10 P.M. to accommodate the fashionable audience's dinnertime. It was published in pamphlet form a few years later and reprinted in *The Gentle Art of Making Enemies* (1890), a collection of essays, lectures, and pamphlets completely designed by Whistler, including a series of over 100 different butterflies (his signature). Whistler's interest in the decorative art of book production is as aesthetic as his innovative painting or his stark pronouncements about art.

from Mr. Whistler's "Ten O'Clock"

LADIES AND GENTLEMEN:

It is with great hesitation and much misgiving that I appear before you, in the character of The Preacher.

If timidity be at all allied to the virtue modesty, and can find favour in your eyes, I pray you, for the sake of that virtue, accord me your utmost indulgence.

I would plead for my want of habit, did it not seem preposterous, judging from precedent, that aught save the most efficient effrontery could be ever expected in connection with my subject—for I will not conceal from you that I mean to talk about Art. Yes, Art—that has of late become, as far as much discussion and writing can make it, a sort of common topic for the tea-table.

Art is upon the Town![1]—to be chucked under the chin by the passing gallant—to be enticed within the gates of the householder—to be coaxed into company, as a proof of culture and refinement.

If familiarity can breed contempt, certainly Art—or what is currently taken for it—has been brought to its lowest stage of intimacy.

---

1. For sale on the streets, like a prostitute.

James McNeill Whistler, *Nocturne in Black and Gold: The Falling Rocket* (1875).

The people have been harassed with Art in every guise, and vexed with many methods as to its endurance. They have been told how they shall love Art, and live with it. Their homes have been invaded, their walls covered with paper, their very dress taken to task—until, roused at last, bewildered and filled with the doubts and discomforts of senseless suggestion, they resent such intrusion, and cast forth the false prophets, who have brought the very name of the beautiful into disrepute, and derision upon themselves.[2]

Alas! ladies and gentlemen, Art has been maligned. She has naught in common with such practices. She is a goddess of dainty thought—reticent of habit, abjuring all obtrusiveness, purposing in no way to better others.

She is, withal, selfishly occupied with her own perfection only—having no desire to teach—seeking and finding the beautiful in all conditions and in all times, as did her high priest Rembrandt,[3] when he saw picturesque grandeur and noble dignity in the Jews' quarter of Amsterdam, and lamented not that its inhabitants were not Greeks.

As did Tintoret and Paul Veronese,[4] among the Venetians, while not halting to change the brocaded silks for the classic draperies of Athens.

As did, at the Court of Philip, Velasquez,[5] whose Infantas, clad in inaesthetic hoops, are, as works of Art, of the same quality as the Elgin marbles.[6]

No reformers were these great men—no improvers of the way of others! Their productions alone were their occupation, and, filled with the poetry of their science, they required not to alter their surroundings—for, as the laws of their Art were revealed to them they saw, in the development of their work, that real beauty which, to them, was as much a matter of certainty and triumph as is to the astronomer the verification of the result, foreseen with the light given to him alone. In all this, their world was completely severed from that of their fellow-creatures with whom sentiment is mistaken for poetry; and for whom there is no perfect work that shall not be explained by the benefit conferred upon themselves.

Humanity takes the place of Art, and God's creations are excused by their usefulness. Beauty is confounded with virtue, and, before a work of Art, it is asked: "What good shall it do?"

Hence it is that nobility of action, in this life, is hopelessly linked with the merit of the work that portrays it; and thus the people have acquired the habit of looking, as who should say, not *at* a picture, but *through* it, at some human fact, that shall, or shall not, from a social point of view, better their mental or moral state. So we have come to hear of the painting that elevates, and of the duty of the painter—of the picture that is full of thought, and of the panel that merely decorates.

A favourite faith, dear to those who teach, is that certain periods were especially artistic, and that nations, readily named, were notably lovers of Art.

So we are told that the Greeks were, as a people, worshippers of the beautiful, and that in the fifteenth century Art was engrained in the multitude.

---

2. Art reformers began targeting the British home in the 1850s, when Sir Henry Cole organized the "House of Horrors," a small museum showcasing decorative atrocities. This collection became the core of the South Kensington Museum.

3. Rembrandt van Rijn (1606–69) painted dignified contemporary subjects (many from the Jewish ghetto) in modern dress.

4. Tintoretto (1518–94) was famous for the intensity and energy of his art; Paolo Veronese (1528–88) was admired for the delicacy of his palette.

5. At age 24 Diego Velasquez (1599–1660) was appointed court painter to Philip IV.

6. Sculptural friezes from the Athenian Acropolis, controversially brought to Britain in the early 19th c. by the Earl of Elgin. Their rough-hewn grandeur was prized over neoclassical finish.

That the great masters lived in common understanding with their patrons—that the early Italians were artists—all—and that the demand for the lovely thing produced it.

That we, of to-day, in gross contrast to this Arcadian[7] purity, call for the ungainly, and obtain the ugly.

That, could we but change our habits and climate—were we willing to wander in groves—could we be roasted out of broadcloth[8]—were we to do without haste, and journey without speed, we should again *require* the spoon of Queen Anne, and pick at our peas with the fork of two prongs. And so, for the flock, little hamlets grow near Hammersmith, and the steam horse is scorned.[9]

Useless! quite hopeless and false is the effort!—built upon fable, and all because "a wise man has uttered a vain thing and filled his belly with the East wind."[10]

Listen! There never was an artistic period.

There never was an Art-loving nation.

In the beginning, man went forth each day—some to do battle, some to the chase; others, again, to dig and to delve in the field—all that they might gain and live, or lose and die. Until there was found among them one, differing from the rest, whose pursuits attracted him not, and so he stayed by the tents with the women, and traced strange devices with a burnt stick upon a gourd.

This man, who took no joy in the ways of his brethren—who cared not for conquest, and fretted in the field—this designer of quaint patterns—this deviser of the beautiful—who perceived in Nature about him curious curvings, as faces are seen in the fire—this dreamer apart, was the first artist.

And when, from the field and from afar, there came back the people, they took the gourd—and drank from out of it.

And presently there came to this man another—and, in time, others—of like nature, chosen by the Gods—and so they worked together; and soon they fashioned, from the moistened earth, forms resembling the gourd. And with the power of creation, the heirloom of the artist, presently they went beyond the slovenly suggestion of Nature, and the first vase was born, in beautiful proportion.

And the toilers tilled, and were athirst; and the heroes returned from fresh victories, to rejoice and to feast; and all drank alike from the artists' goblets, fashioned cunningly, taking no note the while of the craftsman's pride, and understanding not his glory in his work; drinking at the cup, not from choice, not from a consciousness that it was beautiful, but because, forsooth, there was none other!

And time, with more state, brought more capacity for luxury, and it became well that men should dwell in large houses, and rest upon couches, and eat at tables; whereupon the artist, with his artificers, built palaces, and filled them with furniture, beautiful in proportion and lovely to look upon.

And the people lived in marvels of art—and ate and drank out of masterpieces—for there was nothing else to eat and to drink out of, and no bad building to live in;

---

7. Rustic, pastoral.
8. Rough cloth used for men's suits.
9. The "flock" means the aesthetes who built model cottages at Hammersmith (associated with William Morris) and eschewed the modern railroad.
10. Job 15.2, condemning worldly men.

no article of daily life, of luxury, or of necessity, that had not been handed down from the design of the master, and made by his workmen.

And the people questioned not, *and had nothing to say in the matter*.

So Greece was in its splendour, and Art reigned supreme—by force of fact, not by election—and there was no meddling from the outsider. The mighty warrior would no more have ventured to offer a design for the temple of Pallas Athene than would the sacred poet have proffered a plan for constructing the catapult.

And the Amateur was unknown—and the Dilettante undreamed of!

And history wrote on, and conquest accompanied civilisation, and Art spread, or rather its products were carried by the victors among the vanquished from one country to another. And the customs of cultivation covered the face of the earth, so that all peoples continued to use what *the artist alone produced*.

And centuries passed in this using, and the world was flooded with all that was beautiful, until there arose a new class, who discovered the cheap, and foresaw fortune in the facture of the sham.

Then sprang into existence the tawdry, the common, the gewgaw.

The taste of the tradesman supplanted the science of the artist, and what was born of the million went back to them, and charmed them, for it was after their own heart; and the great and the small, the statesman and the slave, took to themselves the abomination that was tendered, and preferred it—and have lived with it ever since!

And the artist's occupation was gone, and the manufacturer and the <u>huckster</u> took his place.

And now the heroes filled from the jugs and drank from the bowls—with understanding—noting the glare of their new bravery, and taking pride in its worth.

And the people—this time—had much to say in the matter—and all were satisfied. And Birmingham and Manchester arose in their might[11]—and Art was relegated to the curiosity shop.

Nature contains the elements, in colour and form, of all pictures, as the keyboard contains the notes of all music.

But the artist is born to pick, and choose, and group with science, these elements, that the result may be beautiful—as the musician gathers his notes, and forms his chords, until he bring forth from chaos glorious harmony.

To say to the painter, that Nature is to be taken as she is, is to say to the player, that he may sit on the piano.

That Nature is always right, is an assertion, artistically, as untrue, as it is one whose truth is universally taken for granted. Nature is very rarely right, to such an extent even, that it might almost be said that Nature is usually wrong: that is to say, the condition of things that shall bring about the perfection of harmony worthy a picture is rare, and not common at all.

This would seem, to even the most intelligent, a doctrine almost blasphemous. So incorporated with our education has the supposed aphorism become, that its belief is held to be part of our moral being, and the words themselves have, in our ear, the ring of religion. Still, seldom does Nature succeed in producing a picture.

---

11. Midland industrial cities that produced cheap imitations of quality goods.

The sun blares, the wind blows from the east, the sky is bereft of cloud, and without, all is of iron. The windows of the Crystal Palace[12] are seen from all points of London. The holiday-maker rejoices in the glorious day, and the painter turns aside to shut his eyes.

How little this is understood, and how dutifully the casual in Nature is accepted as sublime, may be gathered from the unlimited admiration daily produced by a very foolish sunset.

The dignity of the snow-capped mountain is lost in distinctness, but the joy of the tourist is to recognise the traveller on the top. The desire to see, for the sake of seeing, is, with the mass, alone the one to be gratified, hence the delight in detail.

And when the evening mist clothes the riverside with poetry, as with a veil, and the poor buildings lose themselves in the dim sky, and the tall chimneys become campanili,[13] and the warehouses are palaces in the night, and the whole city hangs in the heavens, and fairy-land is before us—then the wayfarer hastens home; the working man and the cultured one, the wise man and the one of pleasure, cease to understand, as they have ceased to see, and Nature, who, for once, has sung in tune, sings her exquisite song to the artist alone, her son and her master—her son in that he loves her, her master in that he knows her.

To him her secrets are unfolded, to him her lessons have become gradually clear. He looks at her flower, not with the enlarging lens, that he may gather facts for the botanist, but with the light of the one who sees in her choice selection of brilliant tones and delicate tints, suggestions of future harmonies.

He does not confine himself to purposeless copying, without thought, each blade of grass, as commended by the inconsequent, but, in the long curve of the narrow leaf, corrected by the straight tall stem, he learns how grace is wedded to dignity, how strength enhances sweetness, that elegance shall be the result.

In the citron wing of the pale butterfly, with its dainty spots of orange, he sees before him the stately halls of fair gold, with their slender saffron pillars, and is taught how the delicate drawing high upon the walls shall be traced in tender tones of orpiment,[14] and repeated by the base in notes of graver hue.

In all that is dainty and lovable he finds hints for his own combinations, and *thus* is Nature ever his resource and always at his service, and to him is naught refused.

Through his brain, as through the last alembic,[15] is distilled the refined essence of that thought which began with the Gods, and which they left him to carry out.

Set apart by them to complete their works, he produces that wondrous thing called the masterpiece, which surpasses in perfection all that they have contrived in what is called Nature; and the Gods stand by and marvel, and perceive how far away more beautiful is the Venus of Melos[16] than was their own Eve.

—1888

---

12. The celebrated building housing the Great Exhibition of 1851. Constructed entirely of metal and glass, it was a spectacle of space, light, and air.
13. Bell towers.
14. Bright yellow.
15. A distilling apparatus used in alchemy, an occult science that tried to transmute base metals to gold.
16. The Venus de Milo, the classical sculpture Victorians held as the exemplar of beauty in both art and women.

Oscar Wilde
1854–1900

Oscar Wilde embodies the spirit of the *fin de siècle*. Poet, dramatist, novelist, wit, philosopher, dandy, lover, he led or invented virtually every significant cultural trend of the 1890s. Born in Ireland, the son of Irish patriots, Wilde was famous before he had left college for *bon mots* such as, "I find it harder and harder every day to live up to my blue china." Gilbert and Sullivan lampooned him as a limp and flighty aesthetic poet in *Patience*. Instead of resenting this caricature, Wilde cleverly parlayed it into a lecture tour to enormous crowds in America. He also edited *The Women's World*, reshaping the magazine into a site of women's intellectual culture. In *The Picture of Dorian Gray*, he imagined what it would be like to live as a work of art. His scintillating aesthetic dialogues asserted that art was independent from morality, meant solely to enrich everyday life. His enormously successful plays offered sparkling epigrammatic satires of upper-class English society. Yet in a very different register, Wilde's fairy tales offered simple and poignant allegories.

Although Wilde was married with two children, in the 1890s he led an increasingly open, and increasingly dangerous, homosexual life, with passionate affairs with younger men, particularly Lord Alfred Douglas. Wilde's literary triumphs were shattered in 1895 when he was forced into a courtroom battle by Douglas's father, Lord Queensberry. He was convicted of "gross indecency" and imprisoned for two years with hard labor. Prison destroyed Wilde's health and nearly his sanity. He emerged as a broken man who lived only a few more years. "De Profundis," the agonized letter he wrote Douglas in prison, and "The Ballad of Reading Gaol" are the only two works he was able to produce after his conviction.

Wilde's personal suffering, no less than his literary achievements, have made him an icon today. Gay martyr, Irish outsider, and artist destroyed for challenging his society, Wilde's symbolic importance can hardly be overstated. "The Decay of Lying" and the "Preface" to *Dorian Gray* offer delightfully paradoxical theories of art in perfectly honed witticisms. They challenge the Victorian stricture that art ought to teach morality, instead insisting that art should give only—and entirely—imaginative pleasure. For more information about Wilde, see pp. 83, 148, and 355.

The Decay of Lying[1]

An Observation

A dialogue. Persons: Cyril and Vivian.[2]

SCENE: *The library of a country house in Nottinghamshire.*

CYRIL (*coming in through the open window from the terrace*): My dear Vivian, don't coop yourself up all day in the library. It is a perfectly lovely afternoon. The air is exquisite. There is a mist upon the woods, like the purple bloom upon a plum. Let us go and lie on the grass, and smoke cigarettes, and enjoy Nature.

---

1. Although Wilde pokes fun at the "decadent" movement (aesthetes who found beauty in the disintegration of language and culture), he also evokes it in the word "decay."
2. Named after Wilde's sons, Vyvyan and Cyril.

VIVIAN: Enjoy Nature! I am glad to say that I have entirely lost that faculty. People tell us that Art makes us love Nature more than we loved her before; that it reveals her secrets to us; and that after a careful study of Corot and Constable[3] we see things in her that had escaped our observation. My own experience is that the more we study Art, the less we care for Nature. What Art really reveals to us is Nature's lack of design, her curious crudities, her extraordinary monotony, her absolutely unfinished condition. Nature has good intentions, of course, but, as Aristotle once said, she cannot carry them out. When I look at a landscape I cannot help seeing all its defects. It is fortunate for us, however, that Nature is so imperfect, as otherwise we should have had no art at all. Art is our spirited protest, our gallant attempt to teach Nature her proper place. As for the infinite variety of Nature, that is a pure myth. It is not to be found in Nature herself. It resides in the imagination, or fancy, or cultivated blindness of the man who looks at her.

CYRIL: Well, you need not look at the landscape. You can lie on the grass and smoke and talk.

VIVIAN: But Nature is so uncomfortable. Grass is hard and lumpy and damp, and full of dreadful black insects. Why, even Morris' poorest workman could make you a more comfortable seat than the whole of Nature can. Nature pales before the furniture of "the street which from Oxford has borrowed its name," as the poet you love so much once vilely phrased it.[4] I don't complain. If Nature had been comfortable, mankind would never have invented architecture, and I prefer houses to the open air. In a house we all feel of the proper proportions. Everything is subordinated to us, fashioned for our use and our pleasure. Egotism itself, which is so necessary to a proper sense of human dignity, is entirely the result of indoor life. Out of doors one becomes abstract and impersonal. One's individuality absolutely leaves one. And then Nature is so indifferent, so unappreciative. Whenever I am walking in the park here, I always feel that I am no more to her than the cattle that browse on the slope, or the burdock that blooms in the ditch. Nothing is more evident than that Nature hates Mind. Thinking is the most unhealthy thing in the world, and people die of it just as they die of any other disease. Fortunately, in England at any rate, thought is not catching. Our splendid physique as a people is entirely due to our national stupidity. I only hope we shall be able to keep this great historic bulwark of our happiness for many years to come; but I am afraid that we are beginning to be over-educated; at least everybody who is incapable of learning has taken to teaching—that is really what our enthusiasm for education has come to. In the meantime, you had better go back to your wearisome uncomfortable Nature, and leave me to correct my proofs.

CYRIL: Writing an article! That is not very consistent after what you have just said.

VIVIAN: Who wants to be consistent? The dullard and the doctrinaire, the tedious people who carry out their principles to the bitter end of action, to the *reductio ad absurdum*[5] of practice. Not I. Like Emerson,[6] I write over the door of my library the word "Whim." Besides, my article is really a most salutary and valuable warning. If it is attended to, there may be a new Renaissance of Art.

---

3. Prominent 19th-c. landscape painters.
4. Refers to a line in William Wordsworth, "The Power of Music."
5. An argument carried to an absurd extreme.
6. Ralph Waldo Emerson (1803–82), leading American transcendentalist, essayist, and poet.

CYRIL: What is the subject?

VIVIAN: I intend to call it "The Decay of Lying: A Protest."

CYRIL: Lying! I should have thought that our politicians kept up that habit.

VIVIAN: I assure you that they do not. They never rise beyond the level of misrepresentation, and actually condescend to prove, to discuss, to argue. How different from the temper of the true liar, with his frank, fearless statements, his superb irresponsibility, his healthy, natural disdain of proof of any kind! After all, what is a fine lie? Simply that which is its own evidence. If a man is sufficiently unimaginative to produce evidence in support of a lie, he might just as well speak the truth at once. No, the politicians won't do. Something may, perhaps, be urged on behalf of the Bar. The mantle of the Sophist[7] has fallen on its members. Their feigned ardours and unreal rhetoric are delightful. They can make the worse appear the better cause, as though they were fresh from Leontine schools,[8] and have been known to wrest from reluctant juries triumphant verdicts of acquittal for their clients, even when those clients, as often happens, were clearly and unmistakeably innocent. But they are briefed by the prosaic, and are not ashamed to appeal to precedent. In spite of their endeavours, the truth will out. Newspapers, even, have degenerated. They may now be absolutely relied upon. One feels it as one wades through their columns. It is always the unreadable that occurs. I am afraid that there is not much to be said in favour of either the lawyer or the journalist. Besides, what I am pleading for is Lying in art. Shall I read you what I have written? It might do you a great deal of good.

CYRIL: Certainly, if you give me a cigarette. Thanks. By the way, what magazine do you intend it for?

VIVIAN: For the *Retrospective Review*. I think I told you that the elect had revived it.

CYRIL: Whom do you mean by "the elect"?

VIVIAN: Oh, The Tired Hedonists of course. It is a club to which I belong. We are supposed to wear faded roses in our button-holes when we meet, and to have a sort of cult for Domitian.[9] I am afraid you are not eligible. You are too fond of simple pleasures.

CYRIL: I should be black-balled on the ground of animal spirits, I suppose?

VIVIAN: Probably. Besides, you are a little too old. We don't admit anybody who is of the usual age.

CYRIL: Well, I should fancy you are all a good deal bored with each other.

VIVIAN: We are. That is one of the objects of the club. Now, if you promise not to interrupt too often, I will read you my article.

CYRIL: You will find me all attention.

VIVIAN (*reading in a very clear, musical voice*): "THE DECAY OF LYING: A PROTEST.— One of the chief causes that can be assigned for the curiously commonplace character of most of the literature of our age is undoubtedly the decay of Lying as an art, a science, and a social pleasure. The ancient historians gave us delightful fiction in the form of fact; the modern novelist presents us with dull facts under the guise

---

7. A specious reasoner.
8. Greek colony famous for its schools of rhetoric, led by the sophist Gorgias.
9. Roman emperor Domitian was famous for his vices.

of fiction. The Blue-Book[10] is rapidly becoming his ideal both for method and manner. He has his tedious '*document humain,*' his miserable little '*coin de la création,*'[11] into which he peers with his microscope. He is to be found at the Librairie Nationale, or at the British Museum, shamelessly reading up his subject. He has not even the courage of other people's ideas, but insists on going directly to life for everything, and ultimately, between encyclopaedias and personal experience, he comes to the ground, having drawn his types from the family circle or from the weekly washerwoman, and having acquired an amount of useful information from which never, even in his most meditative moments, can he thoroughly free himself.

"The loss that results to literature in general from this false ideal of our time can hardly be overestimated. People have a careless way of talking about a 'born liar,' just as they talk about a 'born poet.' But in both cases they are wrong. Lying and poetry are arts—arts, as Plato saw, not unconnected with each other—and they require the most careful study, the most disinterested devotion. Indeed, they have their technique, just as the more material arts of painting and sculpture have their subtle secrets of form and colour, their craft-mysteries, their deliberate artistic methods. As one knows the poet by his fine music, so one can recognize the liar by his rich rhythmic utterance, and in neither case will the casual inspiration of the moment suffice. Here, as elsewhere, practice must precede perfection. But in modern days while the fashion of writing poetry has become far too common, and should, if possible, be discouraged, the fashion of lying has almost fallen into disrepute. Many a young man starts in life with a natural gift for exaggeration which, if nurtured in congenial and sympathetic surroundings, or by the imitation of the best models, might grow into something really great and wonderful. But, as a rule, he comes to nothing. He either falls into careless habits of accuracy—"

CYRIL: My dear fellow!

VIVIAN: Please don't interrupt in the middle of a sentence. "He either falls into careless habits of accuracy, or takes to frequenting the society of the aged and the well-informed. Both things are equally fatal to his imagination, as indeed they would be fatal to the imagination of anybody, and in a short time he develops a morbid and unhealthy faculty of truth-telling, begins to verify all statements made in his presence, has no hesitation in contradicting people who are much younger than himself, and often ends by writing novels which are so like life that no one can possibly believe in their probability. This is no isolated instance that we are giving. It is simply one example out of many; and if something cannot be done to check, or at least to modify, our monstrous worship of facts, Art will become sterile, and Beauty will pass away from the land."

"Even Mr. Robert Louis Stevenson,[12] that delightful master of delicate and fanciful prose, is tainted with this modern vice, for we know positively no other

---

10. A government document.

11. Human document; corner of the universe. The phrases come from an essay by Emile Zola. Wilde despised Zola's belief that fiction must scientifically document reality.

12. Stevenson published *Strange Case of Dr. Jekyll and Mr. Hyde* in 1886; the *Lancet* was the period's premier medical journal. Other recent novels to which Wilde may be alluding in this paragraph include H. Rider Haggard's *She* (1887) and *King Solomon's Mines* (1885); Henry James's *Portrait of a Lady* (1881); Hall Caine's *The Deemster* (1887); James Payn's *Lost Sir Massingberd* (1891); William Black's *Daughter of Heth* (1871); Margaret Oliphant's *Chronicles of Carlingford* series (1863–76); F. Marion Crawford's *Mr. Isaacs* (1882); and Mary Ward's *Robert Elsmere* (1888).

name for it. There is such a thing as robbing a story of its reality by trying to make it too true, and *The Black Arrow* is so inartistic as not to contain a single anachronism to boast of, while the transformation of Dr. Jekyll reads danger-ously like an experiment out of the *Lancet*. As for Mr. Rider Haggard, who really has, or had once, the makings of a perfectly magnificent liar, he is now so afraid of being suspected of genius that when he does tell us anything marvel-lous, he feels bound to invent a personal reminiscence, and to put it into a foot-note as a kind of cowardly corroboration. Nor are our other novelists much better. Mr. Henry James writes fiction as if it were a painful duty, and wastes upon mean motives and imperceptible 'points of view' his neat literary style, his felicitous phrases, his swift and caustic satire. Mr. Hall Caine, it is true, aims at the grandiose, but then he writes at the top of his voice. He is so loud that one cannot hear what he says. Mr. James Payn is an adept in the art of concealing what is not worth finding. He hunts down the obvious with the enthusiasm of a short-sighted detective. As one turns over the pages, the suspense of the author becomes almost unbearable. The horses of Mr. William Black's phaeton do not soar towards the sun. They merely frighten the sky at evening into vio-lent chromolithographic[13] effects. On seeing them approach, the peasants take refuge in dialect. Mrs. Oliphant prattles pleasantly about curates, lawn-tennis parties, domesticity, and other wearisome things. Mr. Marion Crawford has immolated himself upon the altar of local colour. He is like the lady in the French comedy who keeps talking about *le beau ciel d'Italie*:[14] Besides, he has fallen into the bad habit of uttering moral platitudes. He is always telling us that to be good is to be good, and that to be bad is to be wicked. At times he is almost edifying. *Robert Elsmere* is of course a masterpiece—a masterpiece of the *genre ennuyeux*,[15] the one form of literature that the English people seems thor-oughly to enjoy. A thoughtful young friend of ours once told us that it reminded him of the sort of conversation that goes on at a meat tea in the house of a seri-ous Nonconformist family, and we can quite believe it. Indeed, it is only in England that such a book could be produced. England is the home of lost ideas. As for that great and daily increasing school of novelists for whom the sun always rises in the East-End,[16] the only thing that can be said about them is that they find life crude, and leave it raw.

"In France, though nothing so deliberately tedious as *Robert Elsmere* had been produced, things are not much better. M. Guy de Maupassant,[17] with his keen mordant irony and his hard vivid style, strips life of the few poor rags that still cover her, and shows us foul sore and festering wound. He writes lurid little tragedies in which everybody is ridiculous; bitter comedies at which one cannot laugh for very tears. M. Zola, true to the lofty principle that he lays down in one of his pronunciamientos on literature, *L'homme de génie n'a jamais d'esprit*, is

---

13. Chromolithography was a method of printing pictures involving bright areas of separate color.
14. French: the beautiful sky of Italy.
15. French: the boring genre.
16. The impoverished "East End" of London; the school includes George Gissing and Arthur Morrison (see Part IV).
17. French authors mentioned in this paragraph include short-story writer Guy de Maupassant (1850–93); natu-ralists Emile Zola (1840–1902) and Alphonse Daudet (1840–97); and the psychological decadent Paul Bourget (1852–1935).

determined to show that, if he has not got genius, he can at least be dull.[18] And how well he succeeds! He is not without power. Indeed at times, as in *Germinal*, there is something almost epic in his work. But his work is entirely wrong from beginning to end, and wrong not on the ground of morals, but on the ground of art. From any ethical standpoint it is just what it should be. The author is perfectly truthful, and describes things exactly as they happen. What more can any moralist desire? We have no sympathy at all with the moral indignation of our time against M. Zola. It is simply the indignation of Tartuffe on being exposed. But from the standpoint of art, what can be said in favour of the author of *L'Assommoir*, *Nana* and *Pot-Bouille*? Nothing. Mr. Ruskin once described the characters in George Eliot's novels as being like the sweepings of a Pentonville omnibus,[19] but M. Zola's characters are much worse. They have their dreary vices, and their drearier virtues. The record of their lives is absolutely without interest. Who cares what happens to them? In literature we require distinction, charm, beauty and imaginative power. We don't want to be harrowed and disgusted with an account of the doings of the lower orders. M. Daudet is better. He has wit, a light touch and an amusing style. But he has lately committed literary suicide. Nobody can possibly care for Delobelle with his *Il faut lutter pour l'art*, or for Valmajour with his eternal refrain about the nightingale, or for the poet in *Jack* with his *mots cruels*, now that we have learned from *Vingt Ans de ma Vie littéraire*[20] that these characters were taken directly from life. To us they seem to have suddenly lost all their vitality, all the few qualities they ever possessed. The only real people are the people who never existed, and if a novelist is base enough to go to life for his personages he should at least pretend that they are creations, and not boast of them as copies. The justification of a character in a novel is not that other persons are what they are, but that the author is what he is. Otherwise the novel is not a work of art. As for M. Paul Bourget, the master of the *roman psychologique*,[21] he commits the error of imagining that the men and women of modern life are capable of being infinitely analysed for an innumerable series of chapters. In point of fact what is interesting about people in good society—and M. Bourget rarely moves out of the Faubourg St. Germain,[22] except to come to London—is the mask that each one of them wears, not the reality that lies behind the mask. It is a humiliating confession, but we are all of us made out of the same stuff. In Falstaff there is something of Hamlet, in Hamlet there is not a little of Falstaff. The fat knight has his moods of melancholy, and the young prince his moments of coarse humour. Where we differ from each other is purely in accidentals: in dress, manner, tone of voice, religious opinions, personal appearance, tricks of habit and the like. The more one analyses people, the more all reasons for analysis disappear. Sooner or later one comes to that dreadful universal thing called human nature. Indeed, as any one who has

---

18. French: The man of genius never has any wit. Zola means that geniuses are too serious to be witty, but Wilde deliberately misreads it as an admission of dullness.
19. In *Fiction Fair and Foul* (1880–81), about *The Mill on the Floss*.
20. French: It is necessary to struggle for art; cruel words; *Twenty years of my literary life*. Daudet's memoirs (1888) were actually entitled *Souvenirs d'un homme de lettres* (Memories of a man of letters) and *Trente ans de Paris* (Thirty years of Paris).
21. French: the psychological novel, referring to Paul Bourget's *Le Disciple* (1889).
22. Fashionable quarter of Paris.

ever worked among the poor knows only too well, the brotherhood of man is no mere poet's dream, it is a most depressing and humiliating reality; and if a writer insists upon analysing the upper classes, he might just as well write of match-girls and costermongers[23] at once." However, my dear Cyril, I will not detain you any further just here. I quite admit that modern novels have many good points. All I insist on is that, as a class, they are quite unreadable.

CYRIL: That is certainly a very grave qualification, but I must say that I think you are rather unfair in some of your strictures. I like *The Deemster*, and *The Daughter of Heth*, and *Le Disciple*, and *Mr. Isaacs*, and as for *Robert Elsmere*, I am quite devoted to it. Not that I can look upon it as a serious work. As a statement of the problems that confront the earnest Christian it is ridiculous and antiquated. It is simply Arnold's *Literature and Dogma*[24] with the literature left out. It is as much behind the age as Paley's *Evidences*, or Colenso's method of Biblical exegesis. Nor could anything be less impressive than the unfortunate hero gravely heralding a dawn that rose long ago, and so completely missing its true significance that he proposes to carry on the business of the old firm under the new name. On the other hand, it contains several clever caricatures, and a heap of delightful quotations, and Green's philosophy very pleasantly sugars the somewhat bitter pill of the author's fiction.[25] I also cannot help expressing my surprise that you have said nothing about the two novelists whom you are always reading, Balzac and George Meredith.[26] Surely they are realists, both of them?

VIVIAN: Ah! Meredith! Who can define him? His style is chaos illumined by flashes of lightning. As a writer he has mastered everything except language: as a novelist he can do everything, except tell a story: as an artist he is everything except articulate. Somebody in Shakespeare—Touchstone, I think—talks about a man who is always breaking his shins over his own wit,[27] and it seems to me that this might serve as the basis for a criticism of Meredith's method. But whatever he is, he is not a realist. Or rather I would say that he is a child of realism who is not on speaking terms with his father. By deliberate choice he has made himself a romanticist. He has refused to bow the knee to Baal, and after all, even if the man's fine spirit did not revolt against the noisy assertions of realism, his style would be quite sufficient of itself to keep life at a respectful distance. By its means he has planted round his garden a hedge full of thorns, and red with wonderful roses. As for Balzac, he was a most remarkable combination of the artistic temperament with the scientific spirit. The latter he bequeathed to his disciples. The former was entirely his own. The difference between such a book as M. Zola's *L'Assommoir* and Balzac's *Illusions Perdues* is the difference between unimaginative realism and imaginative reality. "All Balzac's characters," said Baudelaire, "are gifted with the

---

23. Street vendors of fruit and vegetables.
24. In *Literature and Dogma* (1873), Matthew Arnold argued that spiritual feeling, not literal belief, answered skeptical German biblical scholarship and evolutionary scientific thought. The other references include William Paley's *View of the Evidences of Christianity* (1794) and John William Colenso's *The Pentateuch and Book of Joshua Critically Examined* (1862–63).
25. Mary Ward's *Robert Elsmere* reflects the liberal social reform philosophy of T. H. Green (1836–82), an Oxford professor on whom one of the characters is based.
26. Honoré de Balzac (1799–1850) wrote the vast *Comédie Humaine*, a series of novels about human frailty. Novelist George Meredith (1828–1909) experimented with idiomatic, oblique diction.
27. See *As You Like It* 2.4.

same ardour of life that animated himself. All his fictions are as deeply coloured as dreams. Each mind is a weapon loaded to the muzzle with will. The very scullions have genius." A steady course of Balzac reduces our living friends to shadows, and our acquaintances to the shadows of shades. His characters have a kind of fervent fiery-coloured existence. They dominate us, and defy scepticism. One of the greatest tragedies of my life is the death of Lucien de Rubempré. It is a grief from which I have never been able to completely rid myself. It haunts me in my moments of pleasure. I remember it when I laugh. But Balzac is no more a realist than Holbein was. He created life, he did not copy it. I admit, however, that he set far too high a value on modernity of form, and that, consequently, there is no book of his that, as an artistic masterpiece, can rank with *Salammbo* or *Esmond*, or *The Cloister and the Hearth*, or the *Vicomte de Bragelonne*.[28]

CYRIL: Do you object to modernity of form, then?

VIVIAN: Yes. It is a huge price to pay for a very poor result. Pure modernity of form is always somewhat vulgarising. It cannot help being so. The public imagine that, because they are interested in their immediate surroundings, Art should be interested in them also, and should take them as her subject-matter. But the mere fact that they are interested in these things makes them unsuitable subjects for Art. The only beautiful things, as somebody once said, are the things that do not concern us. As long as a thing is useful or necessary to us, or affects us in any way, either for pain or for pleasure, or appeals strongly to our sympathies, or is a vital part of the environment in which we live, it is outside the proper sphere of art. To art's subject-matter we should be more or less indifferent. We should, at any rate have no preferences, no prejudices, no partisan feeling of any kind. It is exactly because Hecuba is nothing to us that her sorrows are such an admirable motive for a tragedy.[29] I do not know anything in the whole history of literature sadder than the artistic career of Charles Reade. He wrote one beautiful book, *The Cloister and the Hearth*, a book as much above *Romola* as *Romola* is above *Daniel Deronda*,[30] and wasted the rest of his life in a foolish attempt to be modern, to draw public attention to the state of our convict prisons, and the management of our private lunatic asylums. Charles Dickens was depressing enough in all conscience when he tried to arouse our sympathy for the victims of the poor-law administration; but Charles Reade, an artist, a scholar, a man with a true sense of beauty, raging and roaring over the abuses of contemporary life like a common pamphleteer or a sensational journalist, is really a sight for the angels to weep over. Believe me, my dear Cyril, modernity of form and modernity of subject-matter are entirely and absolutely wrong. We have mistaken the common livery of the age for the vesture of the Muses, and spend our days in the sordid streets and hideous suburbs of our vile cities when we should be out on the hillside with Apollo. Certainly we are a degraded race, and have sold our birthright for a mess of facts.

---

28. Historical novels: *Salammbo*, by Gustave Flaubert; *Henry Esmond*, by William Makepeace Thackeray; *The Cloister and the Hearth*, by Charles Reade; *Vicomte de Bragelonne*, by Alexandre Dumas père.

29. Hamlet marvels when an actor weeps real tears: "what's Hecuba to him or he to Hecuba / That he should weep for her?" (2.2).

30. Reade's *The Cloister and the Hearth* and George Eliot's *Romola* have medieval and Renaissance settings respectively; Vivian prefers them to Eliot's modern novel *Daniel Deronda*.

CYRIL: There is something in what you say, and there is no doubt that whatever amusement we may find in reading a purely modern novel, we have rarely any artistic pleasure in re-reading it. And this is perhaps the best rough test of what is literature and what is not. If one cannot enjoy reading a book over and over again, there is no use reading it at all. But what do you say about the return to Life and Nature? This is the panacea that is always being recommended to us.

VIVIAN: I will read you what I say on that subject. The passage comes later on in the article, but I may as well give it to you now:—

"The popular cry of our time is 'Let us return to Life and Nature; they will recreate Art for us, and send the red blood coursing through her veins; they will shoe her feet with swiftness and make her hand strong.' But, alas! we are mistaken in our amiable and well-meaning efforts. Nature is always behind the age. And as for Life, she is the solvent that breaks up Art, the enemy that lays waste her house."

CYRIL: What do you mean by saying that Nature is always behind the age?

VIVIAN: Well, perhaps that is rather cryptic. What I mean is this. If we take Nature to mean natural simple instinct as opposed to self-conscious culture, the work produced under this influence is always old-fashioned, antiquated, and out of date. One touch of Nature may make the whole world kin, but two touches of Nature will destroy any work of Art. If, on the other hand, we regard Nature as the collection of phenomena external to man, people only discover in her what they bring to her. She has no suggestions of her own. Wordsworth went to the lakes, but he was never a lake poet. He found in stones the sermons he had already hidden there. He went moralizing about the district, but his good work was produced when he returned, not to Nature but to poetry. Poetry gave him "Laodamia," and the fine sonnets, and the great Ode, such as it is. Nature gave him "Martha Ray" and "Peter Bell," and the address to Mr. Wilkinson's spade.[31]

CYRIL: I think that view might be questioned. I am rather inclined to believe in the "impulse from a vernal wood," though of course the artistic value of such an impulse depends entirely on the kind of temperament that receives it, so that the return to Nature would come to mean simply the advance to a great personality. You would agree with that, I fancy. However, proceed with your article.

VIVIAN (reading): "Art begins with abstract decoration, with purely imaginative and pleasurable work dealing with what is unreal and nonexistent. This is the first stage. Then Life becomes fascinated with this new wonder, and asks to be admitted into the charmed circle. Art takes life as part of her rough material, recreates it, and refashions it in fresh forms, is absolutely indifferent to fact, invents, imagines, dreams, and keeps between herself and reality the impenetrable barrier of beautiful style, of decorative or ideal treatment. The third stage is when Life gets the upper hand, and drives Art out into the wilderness. This is the true decadence, and it is from this that we are now suffering.

---

31. Romantic poet William Wordsworth (1770–1850) lived in England's Lake District in England and was derided in the reviews as a "Lake poet." In As You Like It 2.1.15–17, the Duke moralizes about finding sermons in stones. The "great Ode" is Wordsworth's Intimations of Immortality, which Vivian prefers to Wordsworth's more rustic poems.

"Take the case of the English drama. At first in the hands of the monks Dramatic Art was abstract, decorative, and mythological. Then she enlisted Life in her service, and using some of life's external forms, she created an entirely new race of beings, whose sorrows were more terrible than any sorrow man has ever felt, whose joys were keener than lover's joys, who had the rage of the Titans and the calm of the gods, who had monstrous and marvellous sins, monstrous and marvellous virtues. To them she gave a language different from that of actual use, a language full of resonant music and sweet rhythm, made stately by solemn cadence, or made delicate by fanciful rhyme, jewelled with wonderful words, and enriched with lofty diction. She clothed her children in strange raiment and gave them masks, and at her bidding the antique world rose from its marble tomb. A new Cæsar stalked through the streets of risen Rome, and with purple sail and flute-led oars another Cleopatra passed up the river to Antioch.[32] Old myth and legend and dream took shape and substance. History was entirely re-written, and there was hardly one of the dramatists who did not recognize that the object of Art is not simple truth but complex beauty. In this they were perfectly right. Art itself is really a form of exaggeration; and selection, which is the very spirit of art, is nothing more than an intensified mode of over-emphasis.

"But Life soon shattered the perfection of the form. Even in Shakespeare we can see the beginning of the end. It shows itself by the gradual breaking up of the blank-verse in the later plays, by the predominance given to prose, and by the over-importance assigned to characterization. The passages in Shakespeare—and they are many—where the language is uncouth, vulgar, exaggerated, fantastic, obscene even, are entirely due to Life calling for an echo of her own voice, and rejecting the intervention of beautiful style, through which alone should Life be suffered to find expression. Shakespeare is not by any means a flawless artist. He is too fond of going directly to life, and borrowing life's natural utterance. He forgets that when Art surrenders her imaginative medium she surrenders everything. Goethe says, somewhere—

In der Beschränkung zeigt sich erst der Meister,[33]

"'It is in working within limits that the master reveals himself,' and the limitation, the very condition of any art is style. However, we need not linger any longer over Shakespeare's realism. *The Tempest* is the most perfect of palinodes.[34] All that we desired to point out was, that the magnificent work of the Elizabethan and Jacobean artists[35] contained within itself the seeds of its own dissolution, and that, if it drew some of its strength from using life as rough material, it drew all its weakness from using life as an artistic method. As the inevitable result of this substitution of an imitative for a creative medium, this surrender of an imaginative form, we have the modern English melodrama. The characters in these plays talk on the

---

32. Scenes in Shakespeare's *Julius Caesar* and *Antony and Cleopatra*.
33. From *Nature and Art* by Johann Wolfgang von Goethe (1749–1832), German Romantic poet, novelist, and playwright.
34. Recantation. Vivian prefers Shakespeare's play about a magician, *The Tempest*, to his more realistic dramas.
35. Eras named for 16th- and 17th-c. monarchs Elizabeth I and James I.

stage exactly as they would talk off it; they have neither aspirations nor aspirates; they are taken directly from life and reproduce its vulgarity down to the smallest detail; they present the gait, manner, costume, and accent of real people; they would pass unnoticed in a third-class railway carriage. And yet how wearisome the plays are! They do not succeed in producing even that impression of reality at which they aim, and which is their only reason for existing. As a method, realism is a complete failure.

"What is true about the drama and the novel is no less true about those arts that we call the decorative arts. The whole history of these arts in Europe is the record of the struggle between Orientalism, with its frank rejection of imitation, its love of artistic convention, its dislike to the actual representation of any object in Nature, and our own imitative spirit. Wherever the former has been paramount, as in Byzantium, Sicily, and Spain, by actual contact, or in the rest of Europe by the influence of the Crusades, we have had beautiful and imaginative work in which the visible things of life are transmuted into artistic conventions, and the things that Life has not are invented and fashioned for her delight. But wherever we have returned to Life and Nature, our work has always become vulgar, common, and uninteresting. Modern tapestry, with its aërial effects, its elaborate perspective, its broad expanses of waste sky, its faithful and laborious realism, has no beauty whatsoever. The pictorial glass of Germany is absolutely detestable. We are beginning to weave possible carpets in England, but only because we have returned to the method and spirit of the East. Our rugs and carpets of twenty years ago, with their solemn depressing truths, their inane worship of Nature, their sordid reproductions of visible objects, have become, even to the Philistine, a source of laughter. A cultured Mahomedan once remarked to us, 'You Christians are so occupied in misinterpreting the fourth commandment that you have never thought of making an artistic application of the second.'[36] He was perfectly right, and the whole truth of the matter is this: The proper school to learn art in is not Life but Art."

And now let me read you a passage which seems to me to settle the question very completely.

"It was not always thus. We need not say anything about the poets, for they, with the unfortunate exception of Mr. Wordsworth, have been really faithful to their high mission, and are universally recognized as being absolutely unreliable. But in the works of Herodotus, who, in spite of the shallow and ungenerous attempts of modern sciolists to verify his history, may justly be called the 'Father of Lies'; in the published speeches of Cicero and the biographies of Suetonius; in Tacitus at his best; in Pliny's *Natural History*; in Hanno's *Periplus*; in all the early chronicles; in the Lives of the Saints; in Froissart and Sir Thomas Mallory; in the travels of Marco Polo; in Olaus Magnus, and Aldrovandus, and Conrad Lycosthenes, with his magnificent *Prodigiorum et Ostentorum Chronicon*; in the autobiography of Benvenuto Cellini; in the memoirs of Casanova; in Defoe's *History of the Plague*; in Boswell's *Life of Johnson*; in Napoleon's despatches, and in the works of our own Carlyle, whose *French Revolution* is one of the most fascinating historical

---

36. The fourth commandment is to keep the Sabbath holy; the second is to make no "graven image."

novels ever written,[37] facts are either kept in their proper subordinate position, or else entirely excluded on the general ground of dullness. Now, everything is changed. Facts are not merely finding a footing-place in history, but they are usurping the domain of Fancy, and have invaded the kingdom of Romance. Their chilling touch is over everything. They are vulgarizing mankind. The crude commercialism of America, its materializing spirit, its indifference to the poetical side of things, and its lack of imagination and of high unattainable ideals, are entirely due to that country having adopted for its national hero a man, who according to his own confession, was incapable of telling a lie, and it is not too much to say that the story of George Washington and the cherry-tree has done more harm, and in a shorter space of time, than any other moral tale in the whole of literature."

CYRIL: My dear boy!

VIVIAN: I assure you it is the case, and the amusing part of the whole thing is that the story of the cherry-tree is an absolute myth. However, you must not think that I am too despondent about the artistic future either of America or of our own country. Listen to this:—

"That some change will take place before this century has drawn to its close we have no doubt whatsoever. Bored by the tedious and improving conversation of those who have neither the wit to exaggerate nor the genius to romance, tired of the intelligent person whose reminiscences are always based upon memory, whose statements are invariably limited by probability, and who is at any time liable to be corroborated by the merest Philistine who happens to be present, Society sooner or later must return to its lost leader, the cultured and fascinating liar. Who he was who first, without ever having gone out to the rude chase, told the wondering cavemen at sunset how he had dragged the Megatherium from the purple darkness of its jasper cave, or slain the Mammoth in single combat and brought back its gilded tusks, we cannot tell, and not one of our modern anthropologists, for all their much-boasted science, has had the ordinary courage to tell us. Whatever was his name or race, he certainly was the true founder of social intercourse. For the aim of the liar is simply to charm, to delight, to give pleasure. He is the very basis of civilized society, and without him a dinner party, even at the mansions of the great, is as dull as a lecture at the Royal Society, or a debate at the Incorporated Authors, or one of Mr. Burnand's farcical comedies.[38]

"Nor will he be welcomed by society alone. Art, breaking from the prison-house of realism, will run to greet him, and will kiss his false, beautiful lips, knowing that he alone is in possession of the great secret of all her manifestations, the secret that Truth is entirely and absolutely a matter of style; while Life—poor,

---

37. Historians, naturalists, and travel writers famous for florid imaginations and vivid narrative style rather than strict accuracy. Herodotus, Cicero, Suetonius, Tacitus, Pliny the Elder, and Hanno are classical historians. His medieval examples include Jean Froissart, Sir Thomas Malory, Marco Polo, Olaus Magnus, Ulisse Aldrovandi, Conrad Lycosthenes, and Benvenuto Cellini. Modern writers are Giacomo Casanova de Seingalt, Daniel Defoe, James Boswell, and Thomas Carlyle. Napoleon Bonaparte strategically downplayed defeats in his dispatches during the Napoleonic Wars.

38. The Royal Society was the most prestigious scientific organization in Britain, while the fictional Incorporated Authors spoofs the Society of Authors founded by Walter Besant in 1884 to represent the interests of authors against publishers. F. C. Burnand edited the humor magazine *Punch* and wrote the anti-aesthetic satirical play *The Colonel* (1881).

probable, uninteresting human life—tired of repeating herself for the benefit of Mr. Herbert Spencer,[39] scientific historians, and the compilers of statistics in general, will follow meekly after him, and try to reproduce, in her own simple and untutored way, some of the marvels of which he talks.

"No doubt there will always be critics who, like a certain writer in the *Saturday Review*, will gravely censure the teller of fairy tales for his defective knowledge of natural history,[40] who will measure imaginative work by their own lack of any imaginative faculty, and will hold up their inkstained hands in horror if some honest gentleman, who has never been farther than the yew-trees of his own garden, pens a fascinating book of travels like Sir John Mandeville, or, like great Raleigh, writes a whole history of the world,[41] without knowing anything whatsoever about the past. To excuse themselves they will try and shelter under the shield of him who made Prospero the magician, and gave him Caliban and Ariel as his servants, who heard the Tritons blowing their horns round the coral reefs of the Enchanted Isle, and the fairies singing to each other in a wood near Athens, who led the phantom kings in dim procession across the misty Scottish heath, and hid Hecate in a cave with the weird sisters. They will call upon Shakespeare—they always do—and will quote that hackneyed passage about Art holding the mirror up to Nature, forgetting that this unfortunate aphorism is deliberately said by Hamlet in order to convince the bystanders of his absolute insanity in all art-matters."[42]

CYRIL: Ahem! Another cigarette, please.

VIVIAN: My dear fellow, whatever you may say, it is merely a dramatic utterance, and no more represents Shakespeare's real views upon art than the speeches of Iago represent his real views upon morals. But let me get to the end of the passage:

"Art finds her own perfection within, and not outside of, herself. She is not to be judged by any external standard of resemblance. She is a veil, rather than a mirror. She has flowers that no forests know of, birds that no woodland possesses. She makes and unmakes many worlds, and can draw the moon from heaven with a scarlet thread. Hers are the 'forms more real than living man,'[43] and hers the great archetypes of which things that have existence are but unfinished copies. Nature has, in her eyes, no laws, no uniformity. She can work miracles at her will, and when she calls monsters from the deep they come. She can bid the almond tree blossom in winter, and send the snow upon the ripe cornfield. At her word the frost lays its silver finger on the burning mouth of June, and the winged lions creep out from the hollows of the Lydian hills.[44] The dryads peer from the thicket as she passes by, and the brown fauns smile strangely at her when she comes near them. She has hawk-faced gods that worship her, and the centaurs gallop at her side."

CYRIL: I like that. I can see it. Is that the end?

---

39. Herbert Spencer (1820–1903), was a major mid-Victorian political theorist, economist, and philosopher.
40. Alluding to the *Saturday Review*'s recent review of Wilde's fairy stories, *The Happy Prince and Other Tales*.
41. Referring to *The Travels of Sir John Mandeville*, a 14th-c. collection of largely imaginary travel stories, and Sir Walter Raleigh's *History of the World* (1614).
42. Referring to characters and events in *The Tempest*, *A Midsummer Night's Dream*, and *Macbeth*. Vivian reinterprets Hamlet's instructions for strict verisimilitude in acting (3.2).
43. Percy Shelley, *Prometheus Unbound*, 1.748.
44. An ancient kingdom, now in modern Turkey.

VIVIAN: No. There is one more passage, but it is purely practical. It simply suggests some methods by which we could revive this lost art of Lying.

CYRIL: Well, before you read it to me, I should like to ask you a question. What do you mean by saying that life, "poor, probable, uninteresting human life," will try to reproduce the marvels of art? I can quite understand your objection to art being treated as a mirror. You think it would reduce genius to the position of a cracked looking-glass. But you don't mean to say that you seriously believe that Life imitates Art, that Life in fact is the mirror, and Art the reality?

VIVIAN: Certainly I do. Paradox though it may seem—and paradoxes are always dangerous things—it is none the less true that Life imitates art far more than Art imitates life. We have all seen in our own day in England how a certain curious and fascinating type of beauty, invented and emphasized by two imaginative painters, has so influenced Life that whenever one goes to a private view or to an artistic salon one sees, here the mystic eyes of Rossetti's dream, the long ivory throat, the strange square-cut jaw, the loosened shadowy hair that he so ardently loved, there the sweet maidenhood of "The Golden Stair," the blossom-like mouth and weary loveliness of the "Laus Amoris," the passion-pale face of Andromeda, the thin hands and lithe beauty of the Vivien in "Merlin's Dream."[45] And it has always been so. A great artist invents a type, and Life tries to copy it, to reproduce it in a popular form, like an enterprising publisher. Neither Holbein nor Vandyck found in England what they have given us.[46] They brought their types with them, and Life with her keen imitative faculty set herself to supply the master with models. The Greeks, with their quick artistic instinct, understood this, and set in the bride's chamber the statue of Hermes or of Apollo, that she might bear children as lovely as the works of art that she looked at in her rapture or her pain. They knew that Life gains from Art not merely spirituality, depth of thought and feeling, soul-turmoil or soul-peace, but that she can form herself on the very lines and colours of art, and can reproduce the dignity of Pheidias as well as the grace of Praxiteles.[47] Hence came their objection to realism. They disliked it on purely social grounds. They felt that it inevitably makes people ugly, and they were perfectly right. We try to improve the conditions of the race by means of good air, free sunlight, wholesome water, and hideous bare buildings for the better housing of the lower orders. But these things merely produce health, they do not produce beauty. For this, Art is required, and the true disciples of the great artist are not his studio-imitators, but those who become like his works of art, be they plastic as in Greek days, or pictorial as in modern times; in a word, Life is Art's best, Art's only pupil.

As it is with the visible arts, so it is with literature. The most obvious and the vulgarest form in which this is shown is in the case of the silly boys who, after reading the adventures of Jack Sheppard or Dick Turpin,[48] pillage the stalls of unfortunate apple-women, break into sweet-shops at night, and alarm old gentlemen who are returning home from the city by leaping out on them in suburban lanes,

---

45. All images from Pre-Raphaelite painters Dante Gabriel Rossetti and Edward Burne-Jones.

46. The German Hans Holbein became the court painter to Henry VIII in the 16th c.; in the 17th c. Sir Anthony Van Dyck was court painter to Charles I.

47. Ancient Greek sculptor Praxiteles was renowned for his delicate marble statuary, and Phidias created the Parthenon frieze.

48. 18th-c. bandit heroes in popular ballads and tales.

with black masks and unloaded revolvers. This interesting phenomenon, which always occurs after the appearance of a new edition of either of the books I have alluded to, is usually attributed to the influence of literature on the imagination. But this is a mistake. The imagination is essentially creative, and always seeks for a new form. The boy-burglar is simply the inevitable result of life's imitative instinct. He is Fact, occupied as Fact usually is, with trying to reproduce Fiction, and what we see in him is repeated on an extended scale throughout the whole of life. Schopenhauer[49] has analysed the pessimism that characterises modern thought, but Hamlet invented it. The world has become sad because a puppet was once melancholy. The Nihilist, that strange martyr who has no faith, who goes to the stake without enthusiasm, and dies for what he does not believe in, is a purely literary product. He was invented by Tourguenieff, and completed by Dostoevski.[50] Robespierre came out of the pages of Rousseau as surely as the People's Palace rose out of the *débris* of a novel.[51] Literature always anticipates life. It does not copy it, but moulds it to its purpose. The nineteenth century, as we know it, is largely an invention of Balzac. Our Luciens de Rubempré, our Rastignacs, and De Marsays made their first appearance on the stage of the *Comédie Humaine*. We are merely carrying out, with footnotes and unnecessary additions, the whim or fancy or creative vision of a great novelist. I once asked a lady, who knew Thackeray intimately, whether he had had any model for Becky Sharp.[52] She told me that Becky was an invention, but that the idea of the character had been partly suggested by a governess who lived in the neighbourhood of Kensington Square, and was the companion of a very selfish and rich old woman. I inquired what became of the governess, and she replied that, oddly enough, some years after the appearance of *Vanity Fair*, she ran away with the nephew of the lady with whom she was living, and for a short time made a great splash in society, quite in Mrs. Rawdon Crawley's style, and entirely by Mrs. Rawdon Crawley's methods. Ultimately she came to grief, disappeared to the Continent, and used to be occasionally seen at Monte Carlo and other gambling places. The noble gentleman from whom the same great sentimentalist drew Colonel Newcome died, a few months after *The Newcomes* had reached a fourth edition, with the word "Adsum" on his lips.[53] Shortly after Mr. Stevenson published his curious psychological story of transformation, a friend of mine, called Mr. Hyde, was in the north of London, and being anxious to get to a railway station, took what he thought would be a short cut, lost his way, and found himself in a network of mean, evil-looking streets. Feeling rather nervous he began to walk extremely fast, when suddenly out

---

49. German philosopher Arthur Schopenhauer (1788–1860) argued that we cannot know reality, only representations.

50. Mid-19th-c. Russian nihilism challenged the validity of all beliefs and institutions, especially in the powerful novels of Ivan Turgenev and Fyodor Dostoevsky.

51. The philosophical thought of Jean-Jacques Rousseau laid the foundation for the French Revolution, which in turn produced Robespierre's Reign of Terror in 1793. Walter Besant's novel *All Sorts and Conditions of Men* (1882) so compellingly described a "People's Palace" (for the entertainment and education of the poor) that the Palace was actually built in 1887.

52. This sexual adventurer, who marries Rawdon Crawley, appears in William Makepeace Thackeray's *Vanity Fair* (1847–48).

53. In Thackeray's *The Newcomes* (1853–55), the loveable Colonel Newcome dies saying "Adsum" (Latin for "here," the answer to roll-call at boarding school).

of an archway ran a child right between his legs. It fell on the pavement, he tripped over it, and trampled upon it. Being, of course, very much frightened and a little hurt, it began to scream, and in a few seconds the whole street was full of rough people who came pouring out of the houses like ants. They surrounded him, and asked him his name. He was just about to give it when he suddenly remembered the opening incident in Mr. Stevenson's story. He was so filled with horror at having realised in his own person that terrible and well-written scene, and at having done acccidentally, though in fact, what the Mr. Hyde of fiction had done with deliberate intent, that he ran away as hard as he could go. He was, however, very closely followed, and finally he took refuge in a surgery, the door of which happened to be open, where he explained to a young assistant, who happened to be there, exactly what had occurred. The humanitarian crowd was induced to go away on his giving them a small sum of money, and as soon as the coast was clear he left. As he passed out, the name on the brass door-plate of the surgery caught his eye. It was "Jekyll." At least it should have been.

Here the imitation, as far as it went, was of course accidental. In the following case the imitation was self-conscious. In the year 1879, just after I had left Oxford, I met at a reception at the house of one of the Foreign Ministers a woman of very curious exotic beauty. We became great friends, and were constantly together. And yet what interested me most in her was not her beauty, but her character, her entire vagueness of character. She seemed to have no personality at all, but simply the possibility of many types. Sometimes she would give herself up entirely to art, turn her drawing-room into a studio, and spend two or three days a week at picture galleries or museums. Then she would take to attending race-meetings, wear the most horsey clothes, and talk about nothing but betting. She abandoned religion for mesmerism, mesmerism for politics, and politics for the melodramatic excitements of philanthropy. In fact, she was a kind of Proteus, and as much a failure in all her transformations as was that wondrous sea-god when Odysseus laid hold of him. One day a serial began in one of the French magazines. At that time I used to read serial stories, and I well remember the shock of surprise I felt when I came to the description of the heroine. She was so like my friend that I brought her the magazine, and she recognised herself in it immediately, and seemed fascinated by the resemblance. I should tell you, by the way, that the story was translated from some dead Russian writer, so that the author had not taken his type from my friend. Well, to put the matter briefly, some months afterwards I was in Venice, and finding the magazine in the reading-room of the hotel, I took it up casually to see what had become of the heroine. It was a most piteous tale, as the girl had ended by running away with a man absolutely inferior to her, not merely in social station, but in character and intellect also. I wrote to my friend that evening about my views on John Bellini, and the admirable ices at Florian's,[54] and the artistic value of gondolas, but added a postscript to the effect that her double in the story had behaved in a very silly manner. I don't know why I added that, but I remember I had a sort of dread over me that she might do the same thing. Before my letter had reached her, she had run away with a man who deserted her

---

54. 15th-c. Venetian painter Giovanni Bellini. Florian's cafe was a fashionable resort on the Piazza San Marco.

in six months. I saw her in 1884 in Paris, where she was living with her mother, and I asked her whether the story had had anything to do with her action. She told me that she had felt an absolutely irresistible impulse to follow the heroine step by step in her strange and fatal progress, and that it was with a feeling of real terror that she had looked forward to the last few chapters of the story. When they appeared, it seemed to her that she was compelled to reproduce them in life, and she did so. It was a most clear example of this imitative instinct of which I was speaking, and an extremely tragic one.

However, I do not wish to dwell any further upon individual instances. Personal experience is a most vicious and limited circle. All that I desire to point out is the general principle that Life imitates Art far more than Art imitates Life, and I feel sure that if you think seriously about it you will find that it is true. Life holds the mirror up to Art, and either reproduces some strange type imagined by painter or sculptor, or realizes in fact what has been dreamed in fiction. Scientifically speaking, the basis of life—the energy of life, as Aristotle would call it—is simply the desire for expression, and Art is always presenting various forms through which this expression can be attained. Life seizes on them and uses them, even if they be to her own hurt. Young men have committed suicide because Rolla did so, have died by their own hand because by his own hand Werther died.[55] Think of what we owe to the imitation of Christ, of what we owe to the imitation of Cæsar.

CYRIL: The theory is certainly a very curious one, but to make it complete you must show that Nature, no less than Life, is an imitation of Art. Are you prepared to prove that?

VIVIAN: My dear fellow, I am prepared to prove anything.

CYRIL: Nature follows the landscape painter then, and takes her effects from him?

VIVIAN: Certainly. Where, if not from the Impressionists,[56] do we get those wonderful brown fogs that come creeping down our streets, blurring the gas-lamps and changing the houses into monstrous shadows? To whom, if not to them and their master, do we owe the lovely silver mists that brood over our river, and turn to faint forms of fading grace curved bridge and swaying barge? The extraordinary change that has taken place in the climate of London during the last ten years is entirely due to this particular school of Art. You smile. Consider the matter from a scientific or a metaphysical point of view, and you will find that I am right. For what is Nature? Nature is no great mother who has borne us. She is our creation. It is in our brain that she quickens to life. Things are because we see them, and what we see, and how we see it, depends on the Arts that have influenced us. To look at a thing is very different from seeing a thing. One does not see anything until one sees its beauty. Then, and then only, does it come into existence. At present, people see fogs, not because there are fogs, but because poets and painters have taught them the mysterious loveliness of such effects. There may have been fogs for centuries in London. I dare say there were. But no one saw them, and so we do not know anything about them. They did not exist till Art had invented them. Now, it must be admitted, fogs are carried to excess. They have become the

---

55. The heroes of Alfred de Musset's *Rolla* (1833) and Goethe's *The Sorrows of Young Werther* (1774) inspired a rash of suicides among despairing young men.

56. A new school of painting, originating in France. Whistler is the "master" of urban "nocturnes."

mere mannerism of a clique, and the exaggerated realism of their method gives dull people bronchitis. Where the cultured catch an effect, the uncultured catch cold. And so, let us be humane, and invite Art to turn her wonderful eyes elsewhere. She has done so already, indeed. That white quivering sunlight that one sees now in France, with its strange blotches of mauve, and its restless violet shadows, is her latest fancy, and, on the whole, Nature reproduces it quite admirably. Where she used to give us Corots and Daubignys, she gives us now exquisite Monets and entrancing Pisaros.[57] Indeed there are moments, rare, it is true, but still to be observed from time to time, when Nature becomes absolutely modern. Of course she is not always to be relied upon. The fact is that she is in this unfortunate position. Art creates an incomparable and unique effect, and, having done so, passes on to other things. Nature, upon the other hand, forgetting that imitation can be made the sincerest form of insult, keeps on repeating this effect until we all become absolutely wearied of it. Nobody of any real culture, for instance, ever talks nowadays about the beauty of a sunset. Sunsets are quite old-fashioned. They belong to the time when Turner was the last note in art.[58] To admire them is a distinct sign of provincialism of temperament. Upon the other hand they go on. Yesterday evening Mrs. Arundel insisted on my going to the window, and looking at the glorious sky, as she called it. Of course I had to look at it. She is one of those absurdly pretty Philistines, to whom one can deny nothing. And what was it? It was simply a very second-rate Turner, a Turner of a bad period, with all the painter's worst faults exaggerated and over-emphasized. Of course, I am quite ready to admit that Life very often commits the same error. She produces her false Renés and her sham Vautrins, just as Nature gives us, on one day a doubtful Cuyp, and on another a more than questionable Rousseau.[59] Still, Nature irritates one more when she does things of that kind. It seems so stupid, so obvious, so unnecessary. A false Vautrin might be delightful. A doubtful Cuyp is unbearable. However, I don't want to be too hard on Nature. I wish the Channel, especially at Hastings, did not look quite so often like a Henry Moore,[60] grey pearl with yellow lights, but then, when Art is more varied, Nature will, no doubt, be more varied also. That she imitates Art, I don't think even her worst enemy would deny now. It is the one thing that keeps her in touch with civilized man. But have I proved my theory to your satisfaction?

CYRIL: You have proved it to my dissatisfaction, which is better. But even admitting this strange imitative instinct in Life and Nature, surely you would acknowledge that Art expresses the temper of its age, the spirit of its time, the moral and social conditions that surround it, and under whose influence it is produced.

VIVIAN: Certainly not! Art never expresses anything but itself. This is the principle of my new aesthetics; and it is this, more than that vital connection between form

---

57. Jean-Baptiste-Camille Corot and Charles-François Daubigny were influential landscape painters; Claude Monet and Camille Pissarro were prominent French Impressionists.

58. The play of light in the paintings of J. W. M. Turner (1775–1851), much admired by John Ruskin.

59. The hero of Chateaubriand's *René* (1805) is a melancholy, erotically obsessed young man; Balzac's Vautrin is a memorable villain. Aelbert Cuyp (1620–91) was a Dutch landscape painter; Henri Rousseau (1844–1910) produced stark, powerful landscapes in a folk-art style.

60. English painter of seascapes (1831–95).

and substance, on which Mr. Pater dwells, that makes music the type of all the arts.[61] Of course, nations and individuals, with that healthy natural vanity which is the secret of existence, are always under the impression that it is of them that the Muses are talking, always trying to find in the calm dignity of imaginative art some mirror of their own turbid passions, always forgetting that the singer of life is not Apollo, but Marsyas.[62] Remote from reality, and with her eyes turned away from the shadows of the cave, Art reveals her own perfection, and the wondering crowd that watches the opening of the marvellous, many-petalled rose fancies that it is its own history that is being told to it, its own spirit that is finding expression in a new form. But it is not so. The highest art rejects the burden of the human spirit, and gains more from a new medium or a fresh material than she does from any enthusiasm for art, or from any lofty passion, or from any great awakening of the human consciousness. She develops purely on her own lines. She is not symbolic of any age. It is the ages that are her symbols.

Even those who hold that Art is representative of time and place and people, cannot help admitting that the more imitative an art is, the less it represents to us the spirit of its age. The evil faces of the Roman emperors look out at us from the foul porphyry and spotted jasper in which the realistic artists of the day delighted to work, and we fancy that in those cruel lips and heavy sensual jaws we can find the secret of the ruin of the Empire. But it was not so. The vices of Tiberius could not destroy that supreme civilization, any more than the virtues of the Antonines[63] could save it. It fell for other, for less interesting reasons. The sibyls and prophets of the Sistine may indeed serve to interpret for some that new birth of the emancipated spirit that we call the Renaissance; but what do the drunken boors and brawling peasants of Dutch art tell us about the great soul of Holland? The more abstract, the more ideal an art is, the more it reveals to us the temper of its age. If we wish to understand a nation by means of its art, let us look at its architecture or its music.

CYRIL: I quite agree with you there. The spirit of an age may be best expressed in the abstract ideal arts, for the spirit itself is abstract and ideal. Upon the other hand, for the visible aspect of an age, for its look, as the phrase goes, we must of course go to the arts of imitation.

VIVIAN: I don't think so. After all, what the imitative arts really give us are merely the various styles of particular artists, or of certain schools of artists. Surely you don't imagine that the people of the Middle Ages bore any resemblance at all to the figures on mediaeval stained glass, or in mediaeval stone and wood carving, or on mediaeval metal-work, or tapestries, or illuminated MSS. They were probably very ordinary-looking people, with nothing grotesque, or remarkable, or fantastic in their appearance. The Middle Ages, as we know them in art, are simply a definite form of style, and there is no reason at all why an artist with this style should not be produced in the nineteenth century. No great artist ever sees things as they

---

61. In "The School of Giorgione," added to the 1877 edition of *Studies in the History of the Renaissance*, Pater advanced his famous theory that "all art constantly aspires to the condition of music."
62. In Greek myth, the mortal Marsyas boasted he could play the flute better than the god Apollo. Apollo accepted his challenge, defeated him, and flayed him alive.
63. Ancient Roman emperor Tiberius was renowned for cruelty; Antoninus Pius and Marcus Aurelius, the Antonines, were much more moderate.

really are. If he did, he would cease to be an artist. Take an example from our own day. I know that you are fond of Japanese things. Now, do you really imagine that the Japanese people, as they are presented to us in art, have any existence? If you do, you have never understood Japanese art at all. The Japanese people are the deliberate self-conscious creation of certain individual artists. If you set a picture by Hokusai, or Hokkei, or any of the great native painters, beside a real Japanese gentleman or lady, you will see that there is not the slightest resemblance between them. The actual people who live in Japan are not unlike the general run of English people; that is to say, they are extremely commonplace, and have nothing curious or extraordinary about them. In fact the whole of Japan is a pure invention. There is no such country, there are no such people. One of our most charming painters went recently to the Land of the Chrysanthemum in the foolish hope of seeing the Japanese. All he saw, all he had the chance of painting, were a few lanterns and some fans. He was quite unable to discover the inhabitants, as his delightful exhibition at Messrs Dowdeswell's Gallery showed only too well.[64] He did not know that the Japanese people are, as I have said, simply a mode of style, an exquisite fancy of art. And so, if you desire to see a Japanese effect, you will not behave like a tourist and go to Tokio. On the contrary, you will stay at home, and steep yourself in the work of certain Japanese artists, and then, when you have absorbed the spirit of their style, and caught their imaginative manner of vision, you will go some afternoon and sit in the Park or stroll down Piccadilly, and if you cannot see an absolutely Japanese effect there, you will not see it anywhere. Or, to return again to the past, take as another instance the ancient Greeks. Do you think that Greek art ever tells us what the Greek people were like? Do you believe that the Athenian women were like the stately dignified figures of the Parthenon frieze, or like those marvellous goddesses who sat in the triangular pediments of the same building? If you judge from the art, they certainly were so. But read an authority, like Aristophanes for instance. You will find that the Athenian ladies laced tightly, wore high-heeled shoes, dyed their hair yellow, painted and rouged their faces, and were exactly like any silly fashionable or fallen creature of our own day. The fact is that we look back on the ages entirely through the medium of Art, and Art, very fortunately, has never once told us the truth.

CYRIL: But modern portraits by English painters, what of them? Surely they are like the people they pretend to represent?

VIVIAN: Quite so. They are so like them that a hundred years from now no one will believe in them. The only portraits in which one believes are portraits where there is very little of the sitter, and a very great deal of the artist. Holbein's drawings of the men and women of his time impress us with a sense of their absolute reality. But this is simply because Holbein compelled life to accept his conditions, to restrain itself within his limitations, to reproduce his type, and to appear as he wished it to appear. It is style that makes us believe in a thing—nothing but style. Most of our modern portrait painters are doomed to absolute oblivion. They never paint what they see. They paint what the public sees, and the public never sees anything.

---

64. Aesthetic artist Mortimer Menpes (1855–1939) gave a Japanese exhibition in 1888.

CYRIL: Well, after that I think I should like to hear the end of your article.

VIVIAN: With pleasure. Whether it will do any good I really cannot say. Ours is certainly the dullest and most prosaic century possible. Why, even Sleep has played us false, and has closed up the gates of ivory, and opened the gates of horn. The dreams of the great middle classes of this country, as recorded in Mr. Myers's two bulky volumes on the subject,[65] and in the Transactions of the Psychical Society, are the most depressing things I have ever read. There is not even a fine nightmare among them. They are commonplace, sordid and tedious. As for the Church, I cannot conceive anything better for the culture of a country than the presence in it of a body of men whose duty it is to believe in the supernatural, to perform daily miracles, and to keep alive that mythopœic faculty which is so essential for the imagination. But in the English Church a man succeeds, not through his capacity for belief, but through his capacity for disbelief. Ours is the only Church where the sceptic stands at the altar, and where St. Thomas[66] is regarded as the ideal apostle. Many a worthy clergyman, who passes his life in admirable works of kindly charity, lives and dies unnoticed and unknown; but it is sufficient for some shallow uneducated passman out of either University to get up in his pulpit and express his doubts about Noah's ark, or Balaam's ass, or Jonah and the whale, for half of London to flock to hear him, and to sit open-mouthed in rapt admiration at his superb intellect. The growth of common sense in the English Church is a thing very much to be regretted. It is really a degrading concession to a low form of realism. It is silly, too. It springs from an entire ignorance of psychology. Man can believe the impossible, but man can never believe the improbable. However, I must read the end of my article:—

"What we have to do, what at any rate it is our duty to do, is to revive this old art of Lying. Much of course may be done, in the way of educating the public, by amateurs in the domestic circle, at literary lunches, and at afternoon teas. But this is merely the light and graceful side of lying, such as was probably heard at Cretan dinner parties. There are many other forms. Lying for the sake of gaining some immediate personal advantage, for instance—lying with a moral purpose, as it is usually called—though of late it has been rather looked down upon, was extremely popular with the antique world. Athena laughs when Odysseus tells her 'his words of sly devising,' as Mr. William Morris phrases it, and the glory of mendacity illumines the pale brow of the stainless hero of Euripidean tragedy, and sets among the noble women of the past the young bride of one of Horace's most exquisite odes. Later on, what at first had been merely a natural instinct was elevated into a self-conscious science. Elaborate rules were laid down for the guidance of mankind, and an important school of literature grew up round the subject. Indeed, when one remembers the excellent philosophical treatise of Sanchez[67] on the whole question, one cannot help regretting that no one has ever thought of publishing a cheap and condensed edition of the works

---

65. Frederic W. H. Myers (1843–1901) cofounded the Society for Psychical Research (see p. 440).
66. The apostle Thomas doubted that Jesus had risen from the dead (John 20.25).
67. The "liar paradox" in philosophy was first propounded by Epimenides, a Cretan, who asked whether he was telling the truth when he said "the Cretans are always liars." Morris translated *The Odyssey* in 1887. The hero of Euripides' *Ion* lies about his origins. In Horace's ode, Hypermnestra saves her husband by lying to her murderous father. Fernando Sanchez wrote *A Treatise on the Noble and High Science of Nescience* (ignorance) in 1581.

of that great casuist. A short primer, 'When to Lie and How,' if brought out in an attractive and not too expensive a form, would no doubt command a large sale, and would prove of real practical service to many earnest and deep-thinking people. Lying for the sake of the improvement of the young, which is the basis of home education, still lingers amongst us, and its advantages are so admirably set forth in the early books of Plato's Republic[68] that it is unnecessary to dwell upon them here. It is a mode of lying for which all good mothers have peculiar capabilities, but it is capable of still further development, and has been sadly overlooked by the School Board. Lying for the sake of a monthly salary is of course well known in Fleet Street,[69] and the profession of a political leader-writer is not without its advantages. But it is said to be a somewhat dull occupation, and it certainly does not lead to much beyond a kind of ostentatious obscurity. The only form of lying that is absolutely beyond reproach is Lying for its own sake, and the highest development of this is, as we have already pointed out, Lying in Art. Just as those who do not love Plato more than Truth cannot pass beyond the threshold of the Academe,[70] so those who do not love Beauty more than Truth never know the inmost shrine of Art. The solid stolid British intellect lies in the desert sands like the Sphinx in Flaubert's marvellous tale, and fantasy, La Chimère, dances round it, and calls to it with her false, flute-toned voice. It may not hear her now, but surely some day, when we are all bored to death with the commonplace character of modern fiction, it will hearken to her and try to borrow her wings.

"And when that day dawns, or sunset reddens, how joyous we shall all be! Facts will be regarded as discreditable, Truth will be found mourning over her fetters, and Romance, with her temper of wonder, will return to the land. The very aspect of the world will change to our startled eyes. Out of the sea will rise Behemoth and Leviathan, and sail round the high-pooped galleys, as they do on the delightful maps of those ages when books on geography were actually readable. Dragons will wander about the waste places, and the phoenix will soar from her nest of fire into the air. We shall lay our hands upon the basilisk, and see the jewel in the toad's head. Champing his gilded oats, the Hippogriff will stand in our stalls,[71] and over our heads will float the Blue Bird singing of beautiful and impossible things, of things that are lovely and that never happen, of things that are not and that should be. But before this comes to pass we must cultivate the lost art of Lying."

CYRIL: Then we must certainly cultivate it at once. But in order to avoid making any error I want you to tell me briefly the doctrines of the new aesthetics.

VIVIAN: Briefly, then, they are these. Art never expresses anything but itself. It has an independent life, just as Thought has, and develops purely on its own lines. It

---

68. Plato banishes artists from his Republic, his utopian vision of a perfect state, because they are liars.
69. The center of the newspaper industry in London.
70. Plato's school in Athens. Wilde reverses Aristotle's statement, "Plato is dear to me, but dearer still is truth," to joke that one must deemphasize truth to enter Plato's school.
71. The "marvellous tale" is The Temptation of Saint Anthony. The beasts are all from fable. The Behemoth is mentioned in the Book of Job; the Leviathan is a sea monster; the basilisk is a reptile that can supposedly kill with a glance; Elizabethan writers believed there was a "jewel in the toad's head," or toadstone; the hippogriff was a Greek monster, part horse.

is not necessarily realistic in an age of realism, nor spiritual in an age of faith. So far from being the creation of its time, it is usually in direct opposition to it, and the only history that it preserves for us is the history of its own progress. Sometimes it returns upon its footsteps, and revives some antique form, as happened in the archaistic movement of late Greek Art, and in the pre-Raphaelite movement of our own day. At other times it entirely anticipates its age, and produces in one century work that it takes another century to understand, to appreciate, and to enjoy. In no case does it reproduce its age. To pass from the art of a time to the time itself is the great mistake that all historians commit.

The second doctrine is this. All bad art comes from returning to Life and Nature, and elevating them into ideals. Life and Nature may sometimes be used as part of Art's rough material, but before they are of any real service to art they must be translated into artistic conventions. The moment Art surrenders its imaginative medium it surrenders everything. As a method Realism is a complete failure, and the two things that every artist should avoid are modernity of form and modernity of subject-matter. To us, who live in the nineteenth century, any century is a suitable subject for art except our own. The only beautiful things are the things that do not concern us. It is, to have the pleasure of quoting myself, exactly because Hecuba is nothing to us that her sorrows are so suitable a motive for a tragedy. Besides, it is only the modern that ever becomes old-fashioned. M. Zola sits down to give us a picture of the Second Empire. Who cares for the Second Empire now? It is out of date. Life goes faster than Realism, but Romanticism is always in front of Life.

The third doctrine is that Life imitates Art far more than Art imitates Life. This results not merely from Life's imitative instinct, but from the fact that the self-conscious aim of Life is to find expression, and that Art offers it certain beautiful forms through which it may realize that energy. It is a theory that has never been put forward before, but it is extremely fruitful, and throws an entirely new light upon the history of Art.

It follows, as a corollary from this, that external Nature also imitates Art. The only effects that she can show us are effects that we have already seen through poetry, or in paintings. This is the secret of Nature's charm, as well as the explanation of Nature's weakness.

The final revelation is that Lying, the telling of beautiful untrue things, is the proper aim of Art. But of this I think I have spoken at sufficient length. And now let us go out on the terrace, where "droops the milk-white peacock like a ghost," while the evening star "washes the dusk with silver."[72] At twilight nature becomes a wonderfully suggestive effect, and is not without loveliness, though perhaps its chief use is to illustrate quotations from the poets. Come! We have talked long enough.

—1888

---

72. From Alfred, Lord Tennyson's *The Princess* and William Blake's "To the Evening Star," respectively.

Preface to *The Picture of Dorian Gray*[1]

—The artist is the creator of beautiful things.
[To reveal art and conceal the artist is art's aim.] —— T.S. Eliot
    The critic is he who can translate into another manner or a new material his impression of beautiful things.
    The highest as the lowest form of criticism is a mode of autobiography.
    Those who find ugly meanings in beautiful things are corrupt without being charming. This is a fault.
    Those who find beautiful meanings in beautiful things are the cultivated. For these there is hope.
    They are the elect to whom beautiful things mean only Beauty.
    There is no such thing as a moral or an immoral book. Books are well written, or badly written. That is all.
    The nineteenth century dislike of Realism is the rage of Caliban[2] seeing his own face in a glass.
    The nineteenth century dislike of Romanticism is the rage of Caliban not seeing his own face in a glass.
    The moral life of man forms part of the subject-matter of the artist, but the morality of art consists in the perfect use of an imperfect medium.
    No artist desires to prove anything. Even things that are true can be proved.
    No artist has ethical sympathies. An ethical sympathy in an artist is an unpardonable mannerism of style.
    No artist is ever morbid. The artist can express everything.
    Thought and language are to the artist instruments of an art.
    Vice and virtue are to the artist materials for an art.
    From the point of view of form, the type of all the arts is the art of the musician.
    From the point of view of feeling, the actor's craft is the type.
    All art is at once surface and symbol.
    Those who go beneath the surface do so at their peril.
    Those who read the symbol do so at their peril.
    It is the spectator, and not life, that art really mirrors.
    Diversity of opinion about a work of art shows that the work is new, complex, and vital.
    When critics disagree the artist is in accord with himself.
    We can forgive a man for making a useful thing as long as he does not admire it. The only excuse for making a useless thing is that one admires it intensely.
    All art is quite useless.

—1891

---

1. *The Picture of Dorian Gray*, first published in *Lippincott's Monthly Magazine* in July 1890, scandalized critics because it seemed to endorse a life of self-gratification. Wilde responded by publishing this "Preface" in *The Fortnightly Review* in March 1891.
2. Caliban is the uncouth barbarian in *The Tempest*.

Vernon Lee
1856–1935

Brilliant, eccentric "Vernon Lee" (Violet Paget) was a novelist, a historian of the eighteenth century, an art critic, a travel writer, an aesthetic philosopher, and a writer specializing in supernatural tales, but in all these genres she focused on the question of what art is and how it appeals to the viewer. She structured her innovative art criticism as dialogues and impressionistic reminiscences that foreground the self's development through encounters with art. In her novel *Miss Brown*, she critiqued aestheticism for objectifying women, and later she developed a theory of "psychological aesthetics," arguing that art registers directly on the body. Lee's love affairs with women ended badly, including a long relationship with poet A. Mary F. Robinson and an intellectual and personal partnership with Kit Anstruther-Thomson. The waning popularity of Lee's work in the twentieth century obscures her high *fin-de-siècle* reputation, when her aesthetic theories, combining scholarly expertise with a Paterian style of personal engagement, won wide admiration. In *Baldwin* and *Althea*, Lee updates Socratic dialogue by infusing it with the psychological realism of nineteenth-century fiction, creating a stylish new form that may have influenced Oscar Wilde's dialogues. In this excerpt, the philosophical guide Baldwin conducts a discussion about the nature of fiction between a typical French author, Marcel, and a typical English one, Mrs. Blake, occasionally joined by friends Dorothy and Carlo.

from Baldwin

Mrs. Blake looked shrewdly at the young man. "It seems to me that they were men also, those of the past," she answered. "They laughed; but they also suffered, and hoped, and hoped, and the laugh seemed to fit in with the rest. Your modern French literature seems to me no longer French: it all somehow comes out of Rousseau. Balzac, Flaubert, Zola, Baudelaire, all that comes out of those 'Confessions' which you choose to place by the side of the 'Vita Nuova.'[1] And as Rousseau, who certainly was not a true Frenchman, has never seemed to be a genuine man either, but a sickly, morbid piece of half-developed precocity; so I cannot admit that the present phase of French literature represents manhood as opposed to the French literature of the past. Had there remained in France more of the old power of laughter, we should not have had your Zolas and Baudelaires, or rather the genius of your Zolas and Baudelaires would have been healthy and useful. Don't wish to lose that laugh of yours, Monsieur Marcel; our moral health here, in England, where evil is brutish, depends upon seriousness; yours, in France, where evil immediately becomes intellectual, depends upon laughter. I am an old woman, so you must not be offended with me."

"There is a deal of truth in what you say," said Baldwin. "The time will come, I am sure, when Frenchmen will look back upon the literature of the last twenty-five years, not as a product of maturity, but rather as a symptom of a particular sort of humourless morbidity which is one of the unbeautiful phases of growth."

---

1. Mrs. Blake prefers Dante's idealized love for Beatrice in his *Vita Nuova* to the sexual honesty of Rousseau's *Confessions* (1782).

Marcel shook his head. "You are merely falling foul of a new form of art because it does not answer to the critical standards which you have deduced from an old one. The art which deals with human emotions real and really appreciated is a growth of our century, and mainly a growth of my country; and you are criticizing it from the standpoint of a quite different art, which made use of only an approximation to psychological reality, for the sake of a tragic or comic effect; it is as if you criticized a landscape by Corot, where beauty is extracted out of the quality of the light, of the soil, and the dampness or dryness of the air, without a thought of the human figure, because it is not like the little bits of conventional landscape which Titian used to complete the scheme of his groups of Saints or Nymphs.[2] Shakespeare and Cervantes are legitimate; but we moderns are legitimate also: they sought for artistic effects new in their day; we seek for artistic effects new in ours."

Baldwin was twisting a long brown rush between his fingers meditatively, looking straight before him upon the endless, grey and purple, thundercloud-coloured undulations of heather.

"I think," he said, "that you imagine you are seeking new artistic effects; but I think, also, that you are mistaken, simply because I feel daily more persuaded that artistic aims are only partially compatible with psychological aims, and that the more the novel becomes psychological the less also will it become artistic. The aim of art, of painting, sculpture, music, and architecture, is, if we put aside the mere display of technical skill, which, as a rule, appeals only to the technically initiated—the aim of art is the production of something which shall give us the particular kind of pleasure associated with the word *beautiful*, pleasure given to our aesthetic faculties, which have a mode of action and necessities as special and as impossible to translate into the mode of action and necessities of our logical and animal faculties as it is impossible to translate the impressions of sight into the impressions of hearing. All art addresses itself, however unconsciously and however much hampered by extraneous necessities, to a desire belonging to these aesthetic faculties, to a desire for the beautiful. What I may call the freely inventive arts, music and architecture, do this most obviously. We are apt to think that painting does so less, because painting is at present seeking for beauty in a region—the region of effects of mere atmosphere, light and colour independent of linear form—where it was not sought in the past, and where we are therefore not prepared to acknowledge it at present, like a certain eminent painter of the old school, who complained to me that Corot had no sense of beauty, because Corot painted grey drizzly skies instead of the blue ones in which beauty used exclusively to reside in former days. But painting, even in the branch which happens to address a non-artistic desire, even in portraiture, is intensely preoccupied with arrangements, the sole aim of which is that specific quality which we call beauty. If a painter select this or that arrangement of light wherein to place what in itself may be ugly; if he say 'such a dress, such an attitude, is better;' if he rack his brains to make his sitter the centre of a scheme of colour; he does this, however, unconsciously, under the impulse of the artistic desire for beauty. We outsiders are apt to overlook, when we see a painter painting some very simple scene or person, neither of which comes up to our idea of beauty, the special sort of beauty which he pur-

---

2. Jean-Baptiste-Camille Corot (1796–1875) was a French landscape painter. Renaissance painter Titian (Tiziano Vecellio) (c. 1485–1576) was a master of portraiture and religious painting.

sues when, for instance, he changes the tint of the sky in order to give a greater value to the tint of the rocks or so forth. We do not perceive the thought and labour expended, for instance, in arranging the hands of several figures, or the fingers of the hands of a single one; still less do we reflect that if the painter were aiming at mere psychological character or truthfulness to nature, he would have placed those hands or those fingers no matter how. Hence, I say, all real art addresses itself mainly, however unconsciously, to a desire for beauty. Now, to postulate such a predominant desire for the beautiful in a literary work dealing exclusively with human emotion and action seems to me utterly absurd. First, because mere beauty, the thing which gives us the specific aesthetic impression, exists, I believe, in its absolute reality only in the domain of the senses and of the sensuous impressions recalled and reconstructed by the intellect; and because I believe that it is merely by analogy, and because we perceive that such a pleasure is neither unreasoning and animal nor intellectual and utilitarian, that we apply to pleasing moral impressions the adjective beautiful. The beautiful, therefore, according to my view, can exist in literature only inasmuch as literature reproduces and reconstructs certain sensuous impressions which we name beautiful; or as it deals with such moral effects as give us an unmixed, direct unutilitarian pleasure analogous to that produced by these sensuous impressions of beauty. Now, human character, emotion, and action not merely present us with a host of impressions which, applying an aesthetical word to moral phenomena, are more or less ugly; but, by the very fatality of things, nearly always require for the production of what we call moral beauty a certain proportion of moral ugliness to make it visible. It is not so in art. A dark background, necessary to throw a figure into full light, is as much part of the beautiful whole as the figure in the light; whereas moral beauty—namely, virtue—can scarcely be conceived as existing, except in a passive and almost invisible condition, unless it be brought out by struggle with vice; so that we can't get rid of ugliness in this department. On the other hand, while the desire for beauty can never be paramount in a work dealing with human character and emotion, at least in anything like the sense in which it is paramount in a work dealing with lines, colours, or sounds; there are connected with this work, dealing with human character and emotion, desires special to itself, independent of, and usually hostile to, the desire of beauty—such desires as those for psychological truth and for dramatic excitement. You may say that these are themselves, inasmuch as they are desires without any proximate practical object, artistic; and that, in this sense, every work that caters for them is subject to artistic necessities. So far you may call them artistic, if you like; but then we must call artistic also every other non-practical desire of our nature: the desire which is gratified by a piece of scientific information, divested of all practical value, will also be artistic, and the man who presents an abstract logical argument in the best order, so that the unimportant be always subordinate to the important, will have to be called an artist. The satisfaction we have in following the workings of a character, when these workings do not awaken sympathy or aversion, is as purely scientific as the satisfaction in following a mathematical demonstration or a physiological experiment; and when these workings of character do awaken sympathy or aversion, this sympathy or aversion is a moral emotion, to which we can apply the aesthetical terms 'beautiful' and 'ugly' only by a metaphor, only in the same way that we apply adjectives of temperature to character, or adjectives belonging to music to qualities of painting. The beautiful, as such, has a far smaller share in the poem, novel, or the drama than in painting, sculpture, or music; and, what is more, the ugly has an immeasurably larger one, both in the actual sense of physical ugliness and in the metaphorical sense of moral deformity. I wonder how much of the desire which makes a painter seek for a peculiar scheme of colour, or a peculiar arrangement of hands, enters into the production of such characters as Regan and Goneril and Cousine Bette and Emma Bovary; into the production of the Pension Vauquer dining-room and the Dissenting chapel in Browning's 'Christmas Eve and Easter Day'?[3] To compare a man who works with such materials, who, every now and then at least, carefully elaborates descriptions of hideous places and odious people, with an artist like Corot, seeking for absolute loveliness in those less showy effects which previous painters have neglected, is simply an absurdity. The arts which deal with man and his passions, and especially the novel, which does so far more exclusively and completely than poetry or the drama, are, compared with painting, or sculpture, or architecture, or music, only half-arts. They can scarcely attain unmixed, absolute beauty; and they are perpetually obliged to deal with unmixed, absolute ugliness."

There was a moment's silence.

"I can't make out our friend Baldwin," said Mrs. Blake; "he is too strangely compounded of a scientific thinker, a moralist, and an aesthete; and each of the three component parts is always starting up when you expect one of the others. Yesterday he was descanting on the sublime superiority of literature over art; now he suddenly tells us that, compared with art, literature is an ugly hybrid."

Dorothy Orme had been listening attentively, and her face wore an expression of vague pain and perplexity.

"I can't understand," she said. "What you say seems dreadfully true; it is what I have often vaguely felt, and what has made me wretched. Human nature does not seem to give one that complete, perfect satisfaction which we get from physical beauty; it is always mixed up, or in conflict with, something that gives pain. And yet one feels, one knows, that it is something much higher and nobler than mere combinations of lines, or sounds, or colours. Oh, why should art that deals with these things be the only real, the only thoroughly perfect art? Why should art that deals with human beings be a mistake? Don't you feel that there is something very wrong and very humiliating in such an admission?—in the admission that an artist is less well employed in showing us real men and women than in showing us a certain amount of heather and cloud and rock like that?"

And Dorothy pointed to the moor which spread, with immediately beneath them a sudden dip, a deep pool of rough, spray-like, blackish-purple heather round half-buried fragments of black rock, for what might be yards or miles or scores of miles; not a house, not a tree, not a track, nothing but the tufts of black and lilac heather and wind-bent rushes being there by which to measure the chain of moors: a sort of second sky, folds and folds and rolls and rolls of grey and purple and black-splashed cloud, swelling out and going in, beneath the folds and folds and rolls and rolls of the real sky, black-splashed, purple and grey, into which the moorland melted, with scarcely a line of division, on the low horizon.

---

3. Referring to King Lear's wicked daughters; the erring heroines of Balzac's novel *Cousine Bette* and Flaubert's *Madame Bovary*; a locale in Balzac's *Old Goriot*. Browning's poem (1850) struggles with issues of faith and Christianity. Dissenters are members of Protestant sects that do not belong to the Church of England.

"I make no such admission, my dear Dorothy," answered Baldwin. "Nay, I think that the artist who shows us real men and women in their emotion and action is a far more important person than the artist who shows us trees and skies, and clouds and rocks; although the one may always give us beauty, and the other may often give us ugliness. I was saying just now that the art dealing with human character and emotion is only half an art, that it cannot fulfil the complete aesthetic purpose of the other arts, and cannot be judged entirely by their standard; but while fiction—let us say at once, the novel—falls short of absolute achievement on one side, it is able to achieve much more, something quite unknown to the rest of the arts, on the other; and while it evades some of the laws of the merely aesthetical, it becomes liable to another set of necessities, the necessities of ethics. The novel has less value in art, but more importance in life. Let me explain my idea. We have seen that there enter into the novel a proportion of interests which are not artistic, interests which are emotional and scientific; desire for the excitement of sympathy and aversion, and desire for the comprehension of psychological problems. Now one of the main differences between these emotional and scientific interests and the merely aesthetic ones is, I think, that the experience accumulated, the sensitiveness increased, by aesthetic stimulation serves merely (except we go hunting for most remote consequences) to fit us for the reception of more aesthetic experiences, for the putting out of more aesthetic sensitiveness; familiarity with beauty training us only for further familiarity with beauty. Whereas, on the contrary, our emotional and scientific experiences obtained from art, however distant all practical object may have been while obtaining them, mingle with other emotional and scientific experiences obtained, with no desire of pleasure, in the course of events; and thus become part of our *viaticum*[4] for life. Emotional and scientific art, or rather emotional and scientific play (for I don't see why the word art should always be used when we do a thing merely to gratify our higher faculties without practical purposes), trains us to feel and comprehend—that is to say, to live. It trains us well or ill; and, the thing done as mere play becoming thus connected with practical matters, it is evident that it must submit to the exigencies of practical matters. From this passive acquiescence in the interests of our lives to an active influence therein is but one step; for the mere play desires receive a strange additional strength from the half-conscious sense that the play has practical results: it is the difference, in point of excitement, between gambling with markers and gambling with money. There is a kind of literature, both in verse and in prose, in which the human figure is but a mere accessory—a doll on which to arrange beautiful brocades and ornaments. But wherever the human figure becomes the central interest, there literature begins to diverge from art; other interests, foreign to those of art, conflicting with the desire for beauty, arise; and these interests, psychological and sympathetic, in mankind, create new powers and necessities. Hence, I say, that although the novel, for instance, is not as artistically valuable as painting, or sculpture, or music, it is practically more important and more noble."

"It is extraordinary," mused Marcel, "how aesthetical questions invariably end in ethical ones when treated by English people; and yet in practice you have given the world as great an artistic literature as any other nation, perhaps even greater."

---

4. Latin: provisions for traveling.

* * * [Baldwin: "]Now what has developed in us such a number and variety of moral notes which did not exist in the gamut of our fathers? What has enabled us to follow consonances and dissonances for which their moral ear was still too coarse? Development? Doubtless; just as development has enabled us to execute, nay, to hear, music which would have escaped the comprehension of the men of former days. But what is development? A mere word, a mere shibboleth, unless we attach to it the conception of a succession of acts which have constituted or produced the change. Now, what, in a case such as this, is that succession of acts? We have little by little become conscious of new harmonies and dissonances, have felt new feelings. But whence came those new harmonies and dissonances, those new feelings? Out of their predecessors: the power of to-day's perception arising out of the fact of yesterday's. But what are such perceptions; and would mere real life suffice to give them? I doubt it. In real life there would be mere dumb, inarticulate, unconscious feeling, at least for the immense majority of humanity, if certain specially gifted individuals did not pick out, isolate, those feelings of real life, show them to us in an ideal condition where they have a merely intellectual value, where we could assimilate them into our conscious ideas. This is done by the moralist, by the preacher, by the poet, by the dramatist; people who have taught mankind to see the broad channels along which its feelings move, who have dug those channels. But in all those things, those finer details of feeling which separate us from the people of the time of Elizabeth, nay, from the people of the time of Fielding,[5] who have been those that have discovered, made familiar, placed within the reach of the immense majority, subtleties of feeling barely known to the minority some hundred years before? The novelists, I think. They have, by playing upon our emotions, immensely increased the sensitiveness, the richness, of this living keyboard; even as a singing-master, by playing on his pupil's throat, increases the number of the musical intervals which he can intone."

"I ask you," went on Baldwin, after a minute, "do you think that our great-grandfathers and great-grandmothers would have been able to understand such situations as those of Dorothea and Casaubon, of the husband and wife in Howells' 'Modern Instance,' as that of the young widow in a novel which I think we must all have read a couple of years ago—Lucas Malet's 'Mrs. Lorimer'?[6] Such situations may have existed, but their very heroes and heroines must have been unconscious of them. I ask you again, Mrs. Blake—for you know the book—could you conceive a modern girl of eighteen, pure and charming and loving, as Fielding represents his Sophia Western, learning the connection between her lover and a creature like Molly Seagrim, without becoming quite morally ill at the discovery?[7] But in the eighteenth century a nice girl had not the feelings, the ideal of repugnances, of a nice girl of our day. In the face of such things it is absurd to pretend, as some people do, that the feelings of mankind and womankind are always the same. Well, to return to my argument. Believing, as I do, in the power of directing human feeling into certain channels rather than into certain others; believing, especially, in the power of reiteration of emotion in consti-

---

5. Elizabeth I ruled in the 15th c.; novelist Henry Fielding wrote in the 18th c.
6. Victorian novels sympathetically depicting women struggling with unhappy marriages. Dorothea and Casaubon are in George Eliot's *Middlemarch* (1871–72); Howells' novel was published in 1881 and Malet's in 1884.
7. In Henry Fielding's novel *Tom Jones* (1749), Sophia Western is horrified to discover that Tom has been sleeping with the gamekeeper's daughter, Molly Seagrim.

tuting our emotional selves, in digging by a constant drop, drop, such moral channels as have already been traced; I must necessarily also believe that the modern human being has been largely fashioned, in all his more delicate peculiarities, by those who have written about him; and most of all, therefore, by the novelist. I believe that were the majority of us, educated and sensitive men and women, able to analyze what we consider our almost inborn, nay, automatic views of life, character, and feeling; able to scientifically assign its origin to each and trace its modifications—I believe that, were this possible, we should find that a good third of what we take to be instinctive knowledge, or knowledge vaguely acquired from personal experience, is really obtained from the novels which we or our friends have read."

* * * [Marcel: "]But I cannot understand how you, Baldwin, who are above the Pharisaism[8] of your nation, and who lay so much—so far too great (I think)—weight upon the ethical importance of the novel, can say that 'Une Vie'[9] is a book that should not have been written. We have, I admit, a class of novel which panders to the worst instincts of the public; and we have also, and I think legitimately, a class of novel which, leaving all practical and moral questions aside, treats life as merely so much artistic material. But 'Une Vie' belongs to neither of these classes. There is, in this novel, a distinct moral purpose; the author feels a duty——"

"I deny it," cried Mrs. Blake, hotly; "the sense of duty in handling indecent things can never lead to their being handled like this; the surgeon washes his hands; and this Guy de Maupassant, nay, rather this French nation, goes through no similar ablution. The man thinks he is obeying his conscience; in reality he is merely obeying his appetite for nastiness and his desire to outdo some other man who has raised the curtain where people have hitherto drawn it."

"Pardon me," answered Marcel, "you seem to me guilty of inconsistency; Baldwin to his theories of the ethical importance of novels: you, Mrs. Blake, to the notions which all English people have about the enlightenment of unmarried women on subjects from which we French most rigorously exclude them. Looking at the question from your own standpoint, you ought to see that such a sickening and degrading revelation as that to which Maupassant's heroine is subjected, is due to that very ignorance of all the realities of married life in which our girls are brought up, and which you consider so immoral. This being the case, what right have you to object to a book which removes the sort of ignorance that turns a woman into a victim, and often into a morally degraded victim?"

"My dear Monsieur Marcel," said Mrs. Blake, "I quite see your argument. I do consider the system of education of your French girls as abominably immoral, since they are brought up in an ignorance which would never be tolerated in entering upon the most trifling contract, and which is downright sinful in entering upon the most terribly binding contract of all. But I say that a woman should get rid of such ignorance gradually, insensibly; in such a manner that she should possess the knowledge without, if I may say so, its ever possessing her, coming upon her in a rush, filling her imagination and emotion, dragging her down by its weight; she ought certainly not to learn it from a book like this, where the sudden, complete, loathsome revelation

---

8. Hypocritical squeamishness.
9. Guy de Maupassant's first novel (1883), about a convent-bred girl whose romantic ideals are crushed by the daily miseries of married life.

would be more degrading than the actual degradation in the reality, because addressed merely to the mind. Hence such a book is more than useless, it is absolutely harmful: a blow, a draught of filthy poison, to the ignorant woman who requires enlightenment; and as to the woman who is not ignorant, who understands such things from experience or from the vicarious experience gleaned throughout years from others and from books, she cannot profit by being presented, in a concentrated, imaginative, emotional form, these facts which she has already learned without any such disgusting concentration of effect. Believe me, respectable, Pharisaic mankind knows what it is about when it taboos such subjects from novels; it may not intellectually understand, but it instinctively guesses, the enervating effect of doubling by the imagination things which exist but too plentifully in reality."

"I perfectly agree with Mrs. Blake," said Baldwin. "We English are inclined to listen to no such pleas as might be presented for 'Une Vie,' and to kick the man who writes a book like this downstairs without more ado; but I regret that, while the instinct which should impel such summary treatment would be perfectly correct, it should with most of my country-people be a mere vague, confused instinct, so that they would be quite unable to answer (except by another kick) the arguments which moral men who write immoral books might urge in defence."

"But why should you wish to kick a man because he does not conceal the truth?" argued Marcel. "Why should that be a sin in an artist which is a virtue in a man of science? Why should you fall foul of a book on account of the baseness of the world which it truthfully reflects? Is not life largely compounded of filthiness and injustice? is it not hopelessly confused and aimless? Does life present us with a lesson, a moral tendency, a moral mood? And if life does not, why should fiction?"

"Because," answered Baldwin, "fiction *is* fiction. Because fiction can manipulate things as they are not manipulated by reality; because fiction addresses faculties which expect, require, a final summing up, a moral, a lesson, a something which will be treasured up, however unconsciously, as a generalization. Life does not appeal to us in the same way, at the same moment, in the same moods, as does literature; less so even than science appeals to us in the same way as art (and yet we should be shocked to hear from a poet what would not shock us from a doctor). We are conscious of life in the very act of living—that is to say, conscious of it in the somewhat confused way in which we are conscious of things going on outside us while other things are going on inside us; conscious by fits and starts, with mind and feelings, not tense, but slack; with attention constantly diverted elsewhere; conscious, as it were, on a full stomach. The things which are washed on to our consciousness, floating on the stream, by the one wave, are washed off again by another wave. It is quite otherwise with literature. We receive its impressions on what, in the intellectual order, corresponds to an empty stomach. We are thinking and feeling about nothing else; we are tense, prepared for receiving and retaining impressions; the faculties concerned therein, and which are continually going off to sleep in reality, are broad awake, on the alert. We are, however unconsciously, prepared to learn a lesson, to be put into a mood, and that lesson learnt will become, remember, a portion of the principles by which we steer our life, that induced mood will become a mood more easily induced among those in which we shall really have to act. Hence we have no right to present to the intellect, which by its nature expects essences, types, lessons, generalizations— we have no right to present to the intellect expecting things which it graves into itself, a casual bit of unarranged, unstudied reality, which is not any of these things; which is only reality, and which ought to have reality's destructibility and fleetingness; a thing which the intellect, the imagination, the imaginative emotions, accept, as they must accept all things belonging to their domain, as the essential, the selected, the thing to be preserved and revived. Hence, also, the immorality, to me, of presenting a piece of mere beastly reality as so much fiction, without demonstrating the proposition which it goes to prove or suggesting the reprobation which it ought to provoke. Still greater, therefore, is the immorality of giving this special value, this durability, this property of haunting the imagination, of determining the judgment, this essentially intellectual (whether imaginative or emotional) weight to things which, in reality, take place below the sphere of the intellect and the intellectual emotions, as, for instance, a man like Rabelais[10] gives an intellectual value, which means obscenity, to acts which in the reality do not tarnish the mind, simply because they don't come in contact with it. In fact, my views may be summed up in one sentence, which is this: Commit to the intellect, which is that which registers, re-arranges, and develops, only such things as we may profit by having registered, re-arranged, and developed." ***

Carlo mused for a moment.

"I don't think you are right," he said; "there still remains, for all that you have been saying, a something in art which does not exist in nature. Do you remember Goethe says somewhere that art is that which gives form? Now, if it gives form, it must evidently give form to something—there must be a contents, a thought contained within this form."

"Art certainly gives form. And do you know to what it gives form?—to its constituent elements, line, colour, light and shade, or sound. The mistake is to suppose, by a false analogy, that this form necessarily encloses something; a mistake due to a metaphor which has quite passed into the language of aesthetics, where we are always talking of contents, of that blessed German invention, Inhalt.[11] Now it so happens that the non-artistic matter of art is in no respect a contents. That is a false metaphorical expression originating probably in the time when art was looked upon as symbolic, its forms being a mere shorthand writing; and when consequently art, like the symbols of ordinary writing, like a letter or a book, got spoken of as having a contents. The form does not contain anything—remember that. It may have attached to it the more or less arbitrary thing called a subject, or it may—I mean the form—be constituted of elements fraught with emotional or imaginative suggestion; but in neither of these two cases does the form contain the subject in the same way as the body was supposed to contain the soul. The elements of the non-imitative arts are fraught with emotional and imaginative suggestion. In the case of music it is the direct nervous power of tone and movement, and the blurred and confused associations of feeling with it; a suggestion due to the fact that tone, rhythm, and so forth, are recognized dimly and unconsciously as having been modes or concomitants of expression. In the case of the imitative arts it is the power of evoking past and distant images and trains of thought owing to the fact of the things used by the artist having been seen before in reality, and suggesting therefore the significance which they had therein. But this emotional and imaginative suggestiveness engrained in the elements

---

10. François Rabelais's 16th-c. novel *Gargantua and Pantagruel* is replete with ribald obscenities.
11. Inherence, or substance.

used by the artist exist equally outside the art, and they may either be deliberately used or deliberately neutralized or merely overlooked by the artist; and whether he deliberately employ or merely neglect these suggestive elements, is a question outside the jurisdiction of his special art, although within that kingdom of emotion and imagination which surrounds it. Some of the art which is most absolutely art is wholly without intellectual contents; you must have remarked this yourself."

"It is true as to pattern art, and colour art, generally," answered Carlo, hesitating. "I suppose there is really no intellectual contents, no *Inhalt*, in a Persian carpet, a Moorish lustre plate, or in the things which come nearest to that—the pattern mosaics of San Vitale and Galla Placidia at Ravenna. And I suppose there are certain Venetian pictures which are pretty well in the same case. Do you remember the little picture of the death of Sophonisba, by Paul Veronese,[12] of which I am so fond? The pale girl in the shot iris and opal dress being stabbed by a red-capped negro, the indifferent young man in scarlet, the indifferent old man in shot purple and yellow— all these are as simply and entirely so many notes of colour as are the pale sky and the opalescent clouds. The absolute negation of interest on the part of actors and artist in what is going on makes it perfectly impossible to feel the slightest interest or emotion connected with this picture. I suppose you would say, Baldwin, that such a picture as this appeals to us in the same way as a sunset or an evening sky?"

"Not only this picture, but every picture, in so far as it is a picture. Some of the noblest works of linear art (for you have been speaking of colour), not merely arabesques of carving or stalactite of architectural decoration, but actual human figures, appeal to us, and can appeal to us, only as form: the draped fragments from the Parthenon, the Belvedere Mercury, the naked men of Signorelli, the draped virgins of Andrea[13]—all these appeal to us as exclusively by their form as does a pattern in lace. It is useless to object that they represent something, namely, men and women; we perceive that only as part of the fact of their being form, and form only. In none of these things, if we enjoy them, do we seek for an *Inhalt*."

"Don't you think you are turning artistic enjoyment into something rather soulless, Baldwin?"

"My dear Carlo, I am merely arguing that we enjoy art in the same way that we enjoy nature; and I have never heard it called soulless to enjoy nature. Ask yourself where is the difference? Don't the marvellous peacock harmonies, the branching, spreading, and interlacing sea blue, and sea green, and russet gold of those Ravenna mosaics, appeal to the same faculties as the even more marvellous colour harmonies of the peacock's tail and breast; don't the sun-permeated flesh and shot draperies of Veronese's pictures affect us exactly as would the sun-permeated flesh, the shot draperies of some living woman; and don't the throat and neck and head of the youths in Signorelli's frescoes arrest our attention as would the similar throat and neck and head of a beautiful real youth? We do not seek for an explanation of the how and why, for an expression of the artist's nature, in natural things; nor for an intellectual contents of their beauty; and, as a matter of fact, we do not look for any

---

12. Venetian painter of the Renaissance.
13. The Belvedere "Mercury" may be the renowned Greek sculpture the Apollo Belvedere; Luca Signorelli was an Italian Renaissance painter; another Renaissance painter, Andrea del Sarto, achieved renewed fame in the Victorian era as the speaker of Robert Browning's dramatic monologue "Andrea del Sarto" (1855).

of these things at the moment that we are really enjoying art. And therefore I say that art merely adds to the stock of beauty which nature has given us: it completes and multiplies it when deficient." * * *

"I don't believe the least in innate ideas," answered Baldwin, amused at the young man's look of horror; "but I don't believe either that our minds and feelings are merely whitewashed walls, on which the external world projects its magic-lantern figures. Every real impression that we receive decomposes and leaves behind it a greater or lesser amount of fragments of itself: broken-down impressions, sometimes a mere minute dust, which live on within us. And the aggregate, constantly shifting, of all this living dust of broken impressions, lives and has its necessities of life, its sympathies and desires. In speaking of the aesthetic or imaginative sides of our life," went on Baldwin, "we are apt to think of them as composed of distinct impressions, voluntary and well-defined, the seeing of a picture or piece of architecture, the reading of a poem, the hearing of a song or symphony. Nothing could be further from the fact. Our aesthetic life goes on within us, or if not constantly in fact, constantly at all events potentially; and in this the new sights or sounds play no more part—nay, I think, play less—than do new facts in our intellectual life. As this latter is an almost permanent process—a process of constant weighing and comparing and classifying of our ideas—so likewise is our aesthetic life an almost permanent process, infinitely vaguer and more delicate, and, to a great extent, unconscious, a kaleidoscopic shifting and rearranging of all pleasant impressions of colour, sound, form, or emotion. The fact is, that we live much more in the past of our aesthetic impressions than in their present: our aesthetic life consists really in the fluctuations, the movements, of these, if I may call them so, living molecules of aesthetic feeling; it consists of the action and reaction produced within us by any new impression that we receive. It is for this reason that the value of art must not be measured, as I said, by conformity to a reality which is outside us, but by conformity to these feelings within us. Remember, what you realists forget, that there is not merely the real constitution of external nature to be taken into account; there is, what is much more important, the real nature of our soul."

For a moment Carlo did not answer.

"Then, according to you," he said, as they walked along a narrow lane between the ridges of corn and hemp, where goats and sheep nibbled at the fern and honeysuckle; "according to you, art is there, so to speak, for the express purpose of gratifying the fantastic requirements of this fantastic living mass of heterogeneous broken-down impressions within us—art is not there to register our knowledge of reality?"

"Only incidentally, so far as reality is, after all, the storehouse whence the majority of our impressions come. Art registers our knowledge of reality when reality happens to coalesce with that which constitutes, as I have said, our aesthetic life; when, in short, reality is what we term beautiful."

"But art is continually doing the very opposite, registering reality pure and simple, merely because it is reality, Baldwin."

"Art does it, and does it especially at present; but to do so is, whenever it happens, a new, a false start, due to the mixing up of scientific interests, or to the usurpations of technical knowledge or skill, the usurpations of the *power of doing*. But you will find that while left to itself, while in possession of unexhausted means, and while absolutely spontaneous, all art tends, as Pater has said, to the condition of music. I don't know what Pater exactly meant by that remark."

"I think he was probably merely repeating Hegel's old theories about music being the romantic art, and all other arts tending towards the romantic condition," interrupted Carlo.

"I dare say he did. But the saying to me expresses a far more important truth: all art tends to the condition of music, that is to say, to the condition of producing freely, with reference not to a pre-existing reality, but to the desires of our soul."

"At that rate," answered Carlo, incredulously, "a perfect piece of artificiality, a monstrosity, like the opera, is the typical form of art."

Baldwin was not at all put out by this remark.

"Exactly so," he said; "and so, from the Greek tragedy to the great ceremonial altar-pieces of the Venetians, where madonnas and saints and real people sit and stand among clouds and lamps and garlands, none taking heed of his companions, all the greatest and most spontaneous art has been. And this is exactly what I want to prove to you, and what I shall prove to you in five minutes, I hope—I mean that realistic art is an after-thought, an artificial growth; and idealistic, unreal art, a direct, spontaneous one. * * * "

—1886

Alice Meynell
1847–1922

"A saint and a sibyl smoking a cigarette," one admirer aptly described Alice Meynell. A devout Catholic, Meynell often addressed themes of divine love and martyrdom, yet also explored changes in women's roles (she was a strong supporter of suffrage) and expressed surprising ambivalence about motherhood (she had seven children). Her journalism and poetry were widely admired for an intellectual playfulness at once meticulous and reticent. The writing is extremely complex and offers startlingly original pronouncements challenging Victorians' assumptions about women's feelings. "The Colour of Life," probably Meynell's most famous prose piece, appeared in the "Wares of Autoloycus" column, a notable venue for women's writing in *The Pall Mall Gazette* in 1895. She revised it substantially for *The Colour of Life* (1896). Because Meynell skillfully uses an elaborate aesthetic rhetoric about colors, she manages to discuss such unsaintly topics as murdered women and the naked bodies of homeless boys. For more information about Meynell, see pp. 117 and 236.

The Colour of Life

Red has been praised for its nobility as the colour of life. But the true colour of life is not red. Red is the colour of violence, or of life broken open, edited, and published. Or if red is indeed the colour of life, it is so only on condition that it is not seen. Once fully visible, red is the colour of life violated, and in the act of betrayal and of waste. Red is the secret of life, and not the manifestation thereof. It is one of the things the value of which is secrecy, one of the talents that are to be hidden in a napkin. The true colour of life is the colour of the body, the colour of the covered red, the implicit and not explicit red of the living heart and the pulses. It is the modest colour of the unpublished blood.

So bright, so light, so soft, so mingled, the gentle colour of life is outdone by all the colours of the world. Its very beauty is that it is white, but less white than milk; brown, but less brown than earth; red, but less red than sunset or dawn. It is lucid, but less lucid than the colour of lilies. It has the hint of gold that is in all fine colour; but in our latitudes the hint is almost elusive. Under Sicilian skies, indeed, it is deeper than old ivory; but under the misty blue of the English zenith, and the warm gray of the London horizon, it is as delicately flushed as the paler wild roses, out to their utmost, flat as stars, in the hedges of the end of June.

For months together London does not see the colour of life in any mass. The human face does not give much of it, what with features, and beards, and the shadow of the top-hat and *chapeau melon*[1] of man, and of the veils of woman. Besides, the colour of the face is subject to a thousand injuries and accidents. The popular face of the Londoner has soon lost its gold, its white, and the delicacy of its red and brown. We miss little beauty by the fact that it is never seen freely in great numbers out-of-doors. You get it in some quantity when all the heads of a great indoor meeting are turned at once upon a speaker; but it is only in the open air, needless to say, that the colour of life is in perfection, in the open air, "clothed with the sun,"[2] whether the sunshine be golden and direct, or dazzlingly diffused in gray.

The little figure of the London boy it is that has restored to the landscape the human colour of life. He is allowed to come out of all his ignominies, and to take the late colour of the midsummer north-west evening, on the borders of the Serpentine.[3] At the stroke of eight he sheds the slough of nameless colours—all allied to the hues of dust, soot, and fog, which are the colours the world has chosen for the clothing of its boys—and he makes, in his hundreds, a bright and delicate flush between the gray-blue water and the gray-blue sky. Clothed now with the sun, he is crowned by-and-by with twelve stars as he goes to bathe, and the reflection of an early moon is under his feet.[4]

So little stands between a gamin and all the dignities of Nature. They are so quickly restored. There seems to be nothing to do, but only a little thing to undo. It is like the art of Eleonora Duse.[5] The last and most finished action of her intellect, passion, and knowledge was, as it were, the flicking away of some insignificant thing mistaken for art by other actors, some little obstacle to the way and liberty of Nature.

All the squalor is gone in a moment, kicked off with the second boot, and the child goes shouting to complete the landscape with the lacking colour of life. You are inclined to wonder that, even undressed, he still shouts with a Cockney accent.[6] You half expect pure vowels and elastic syllables from his restoration, his spring, his slen-

---

1. Bowler hat.
2. "And there appeared a great wonder in heaven; a woman clothed with the sun, and the moon under her feet, and upon her head a crown of twelve stars" (Revelations 12.1).
3. Artificial lake in Hyde Park.
4. See n. 2.
5. Italian actress famed for her natural style of acting.
6. Working-class London accent.

derness, his brightness, and his glow. Old ivory and wild rose in the deepening mid-summer sun, he gives his colours to his world again.

It is easy to replace man, and it will take no great time, when Nature has lapsed, to replace Nature. It is always to do, by the happily easy way of doing nothing. The grass is always ready to grow in the streets—and no streets could ask for a more charming finish than your green grass. The gasometer[7] even must fall to pieces unless it is renewed; but the grass renews itself. There is nothing so remediable as the work of modern man—"a thought which is also," as Mr. Pecksniff said, "very soothing."[8] And by remediable I mean, of course, destructible. As the bathing child shuffles off his garments—they are few, and one brace suffices him—so the land might always, in reasonable time, shuffle off its yellow brick and purple slate, and all the things that collect about railway stations. A single night almost clears the air of London.

But if the colour of life looks so well in the rather sham scenery of Hyde Park, it looks brilliant and grave indeed on a real sea-coast. To have once seen it there should be enough to make a colourist. O memorable little picture! The sun was gaining colour as it neared setting, and it set not over the sea, but over the land. The sea had the dark and rather stern, but not cold, blue of that aspect—the dark and not the opal tints. The sky was also deep. Everything was very definite, without mystery, and exceedingly simple. The most luminous thing was the shining white of an edge of foam, which did not cease to be white because it was a little golden and a little rosy in the sunshine. It was still the whitest thing imaginable. And the next most luminous thing was the little unclad child, also invested with the sun and the colour of life.

In the case of women, it is of the living and unpublished blood that the violent world has professed to be delicate and ashamed. See the curious history of the political rights of woman under the Revolution. On the scaffold she enjoyed an ungrudged share in the fortunes of party. Political life might be denied her, but that seems a trifle when you consider how generously she was permitted political death. She was to spin and cook for her citizen in the obscurity of her living hours; but to the hour of her death was granted a part in the largest interests, social, national, international. The blood wherewith she should, according to Robespierre,[9] have blushed to be seen or heard in the tribune, was exposed in the public sight unsheltered by her veins.

Against this there was no modesty. Of all privacies, the last and the innermost—the privacy of death—was never allowed to put obstacles in the way of public action for a public cause. Women might be, and were, duly silenced when, by the mouth of Olympe de Gouges,[10] they claimed a "right to concur in the choice of representatives for the formation of the laws"; but in her person, too, they were liberally allowed to bear political responsibility to the Republic. Olympe de Gouges was guillotined. Robespierre thus made her public and complete amends.

—1896

---

7. Huge industrial metal structures used to store gas for lighting and heating towns.
8. A hypocritical character in Charles Dickens' *Martin Chuzzlewit* (1843–44).
9. The architect of the Reign of Terror in 1793.
10. This author of the "Declaration of the Rights of Woman" agitated for equal rights for French women in the new Republic and was sent to the guillotine in 1793.

Max Beerbohm
1872–1956

Max Beerbohm, paradoxically, prided himself on his modesty. Yet this most dapper of *fin-de-siècle* dandies produced caricatures (in art and words) that are among the most memorable summations of the period. His cartoons skewer writers and politicians; his stories, essays, and novel (*Zuleika Dobson*) perfectly parody the period's literary culture. As an Oxford undergraduate, Beerbohm published in *The Yellow Book* and befriended virtually every member of the aesthetic movement. George Bernard Shaw summed him up: "the younger generation is knocking on the door; and as I open it, there steps spritely in the incomparable Max." Beerbohm succeeded Shaw as *The Saturday Review*'s drama critic, a post he held for twelve years (his brother, Herbert Beerbohm Tree, was one of the period's most renowned actors) until he retired to Rapallo, Italy, with his first wife, where he continued to produce occasional, finely honed, devastating short pieces. When "A Defence of Cosmetics" was published in the first number of *The Yellow Book* (1894), it outraged Victorian readers who associated cosmetics with prostitutes. To assuage the outcry, Beerbohm wrote the "Letter to the Editor," protesting that he was merely joking. His gleefully exuberant language, reveling in frivolity and artificiality, however, suggests that he enjoyed aesthetic style at least as much as he satirized it. For more information about Beerbohm, see p. 128.

A Defence of Cosmetics

Nay, but it is useless to protest. Artifice must queen it once more in the town, and so, if there be any whose hearts chafe at her return, let them not say, "We have come into evil times," and be all for resistance, reformation or angry cavilling. For did the king's sceptre send the sea retrograde, or the wand of the sorcerer avail to turn the sun from its old course? And what man or what number of men ever stayed that reiterated process by which the cities of this world grow, are very strong, fail and grow again? Indeed, indeed, there is charm in every period, and only fools and flutter-pates do not seek reverently for what is charming in their own day. No martyrdom, however fine, nor satire, however splendidly bitter, has changed by a little tittle the known tendency of things. It is the times that can perfect us, not we the times, and so let all of us wisely acquiesce. Like the little wired marionettes, let us acquiesce in the dance.

For behold! The Victorian era comes to its end and the day of sancta simplicitas[1] is quite ended. The old signs are here and the portents to warn the seer of life that we are ripe for a new epoch of artifice. Are not men rattling the dice-box and ladies dipping their fingers in the rouge-pots? At Rome, in the keenest time of her *dégringolade*,[2] when there was gambling even in the holy temples, great ladies (does not Lucian[3] tell us?) did not scruple to squander all they had upon unguents from Arabia. Nero's mistress and unhappy wife, Poppæa, of shameful memory, had in her travelling retinue fifteen—or, as some say, fifty—she-asses, for the sake of their milk,

---

1. Latin: blessed simplicity.
2. French: decadence.
3. 2nd-c. Greek writer.

Aubrey Beardsley, *Cover Design for the Yellow Book, Vol. III* (1894).

that was thought an incomparable guard against cosmetics with poison in them. Last century, too, when life was lived by candle-light, and ethics was but etiquette, and even art a question of punctilio, women, we know, gave the best hours of the day to the crafty larding of their faces and the towering of their coiffures. And men, throwing passion into the wine-bowl to sink or swim, turned out thought to browse upon the green cloth. Cannot we even now in our fancy see them, those silent exquisites round the long table at Brooks', masked, all of them, "lest the countenance should betray feeling," in quinze masks, through whose eyelets they sat peeping, peeping, while macao brought them riches or ruin? We can see them, those silent rascals, sitting there with their cards and their rouleaux and their wooden money-bowls, long after the dawn had crept up St. James' and pressed its haggard face against the window of the little club. Yes, we can raise their ghosts—and, more, we can see manywhere a devotion to hazard fully as meek as theirs. In England there has been a wonderful revival of cards. Roulette may rival dead faro in the tale of her devotees. Her wheel is spinning busily in every house and ere long it may be that tender parents will be waiting to complain of the compulsory baccarat in our public schools.[4]

In fact, we are all gamblers once more, but our gambling is on a finer scale than ever it was. We fly from the card-room to the heath, and from the heath to the City, and from the City to the coast of the Mediterranean. And just as no one seriously encourages the clergy in its frantic efforts to lay the spirit of chance, that has thus resurged among us, so no longer are many faces set against that other great sign of a more complicated life, the love for cosmetics. No longer is a lady of fashion blamed if, to escape the outrageous persecution of time, she fly for sanctuary to the toilet-table; and if a damosel, prying in her mirror, be sure that with brush and pigment she can trick herself into more charm, we are not angry. Indeed, why should we ever have been? Surely it is laudable, this wish to make fair the ugly and overtop fairness, and no wonder that within the last five years the trade of the makers of cosmetics has increased immoderately—twenty-fold, so one of these makers has said to me. We need but walk down any modish street and peer into the little broughams[5] that flit past, or (in Thackeray's phrase) under the bonnet of any woman we meet,[6] to see over how wide a kingdom rouge reigns. We men, who, from Juvenal[7] down to that discourteous painter of whom Lord Chesterfield[8] tells us, have especially shown a dislike of cosmetics, are quite yielding; and there are, I fancy, many such husbands as he who, suddenly realising that his wife was painted, bade her sternly, "Go up and take it all off," and, on her reappearance, bade her with increasing sternness, "Go up and put it all on again."

But now that the use of pigments is becoming general, and most women are not so young as they are painted, it may be asked curiously how the prejudice ever came into being. Indeed, it is hard to trace folly, for that it is inconsequent, to its start; and perhaps it savours too much of reason to suggest that the prejudice was due to

---

4. Accoutrements of fashionable life in the 18th and early 19th c. Brooks' was a men's club; St. James's Park had aristocratic associations; a quinze mask was worn by gamblers playing a French card game; 18th-c. gambling games included quinze, macao, hazard, faro, baccarat; rouleaux are rolls of money.
5. Closed carriages.
6. General Tufto examines women this way in Ch. 28 of Thackeray's *Vanity Fair* (1847–48).
7. 2nd-c. Roman satirist.
8. An 18th-c. wit and worldly politician.

the tristful[9] confusion man has made of soul and surface. Through trusting so keenly to the detection of the one by keeping watch upon the other, and by force of the thousand errors following, he has come to think of surface even as the reverse of soul. He supposes that every clown beneath his paint and lip-salve is moribund and knows it, (though in verity, I am told, clowns are as cheerful a class of men as any other), that the fairer the fruit's rind and the more delectable its bloom, the closer are packed the ashes within it. The very jargon of the hunting-field connects cunning with a mask. And so perhaps came man's anger at the embellishment of women—that lovely mask of enamel with its shadows of pink and tiny pencilled veins, what must lurk behind it? Of what treacherous mysteries may it not be the screen? Does not the heathen lacquer her dark face, and the harlot paint her cheeks, because sorrow has made them pale?

After all, the old prejudice is a-dying. We need not pry into the secret of its birth. Rather is this a time of jolliness and glad indulgence. For the era of rouge is upon us, and as only in an elaborate era can man by the tangled accrescency of his own pleasures and emotions reach that refinement which is his highest excellence, and by making himself, so to say, independent of Nature, come nearest to God, so only in an elaborate era is woman perfect. Artifice is the strength of the world, and in that same mask of paint and powder, shadowed with vermeil tinct[10] and most trimly pencilled, is woman's strength.

For see! We need not look so far back to see woman under the direct influence of Nature. Early in this century, our grandmothers, sickening of the odour of faded exotics and spilt wine, came out into the daylight once more and let the breezes blow around their faces and enter, sharp and welcome, into their lungs. Artifice they drove forth, and they set Martin Tupper[11] upon a throne of mahogany to rule over them. A very reign of terror set in. All things were sacrificed to the fetish Nature. Old ladies may still be heard to tell how, when they were girls, affectation was not; and, if we verify their assertion in the light of such literary authorities as Dickens, we find that it is absolutely true. Women appear to have been in those days utterly natural in their conduct—flighty, gushing, blushing, fainting, giggling and shaking their curls. They knew no reserve in the first days of the Victorian era. No thought was held too trivial, no emotion too silly, to express. To Nature everything was sacrificed. Great heavens! And in those barren days what influence was exerted by women? By men they seem not to have been feared nor loved, but regarded rather as "dear little creatures" or "wonderful little beings," and in their relation to life as foolish and ineffectual as the landscapes they did in water-colour. Yet, if the women of those years were of no great account, they had a certain charm and they at least had not begun to trespass upon men's ground; if they touched not thought, which is theirs by right, at any rate they refrained from action, which is ours. Far more serious was it when, in the natural trend of time, they became enamoured of rinking and archery and galloping along the Brighton Parade.[12] Swiftly they have sped on since then from horror to horror. The invasion of the tennis-courts and of the golf-links, the seizure of the tricycle and

---

9. Sad, regrettable.
10. Bright red hue.
11. Moralistic Victorian poet.
12. Seafront resort, south of London.

of the type-writer, were but steps preliminary in that campaign which is to end with the final victorious occupation of St. Stephen's.[13] But stay! The horrific pioneers of womanhood who gad hither and thither and, confounding wisdom with the device on her shield, shriek for the unbecoming, are doomed. Though they spin their tricycle-treadles so amazingly fast, they are too late. Though they scream victory, none follow them. Artifice, that fair exile, has returned.

Yes, though the pioneers know it not, they are doomed already. For of the curiosities of history not the least strange is the manner in which two social movements may be seen to overlap, long after the second has, in truth, given its death-blow to the first. And, in like manner as one has seen the limbs of a murdered thing in lively movement, so we need not doubt that, though the voices of those who cry out for reform be very terribly shrill, they will soon be hushed. Dear Artifice is with us. It needed but that we should wait.

Surely, without any of my pleading, women will welcome their great and amiable protectrix, as by instinct. For (have I not said?) it is upon her that all their strength, their life almost, depends. Artifice's first command to them is that they should repose. With bodily activity their powder will fly, their enamel crack. They are butterflies who must not flit, if they love their bloom. Now, setting aside the point of view of passion, from which very many obvious things might be said, (and probably have been by the minor poets), it is, from the intellectual point of view, quite necessary that a woman should repose. Hers is the resupinate[14] sex. On her couch she is a goddess, but so soon as ever she put her foot to the ground—lo, she is the veriest little sillypop and quite done for. She cannot rival us in action, but she is our mistress in the things of the mind. Let her not by second-rate athletics, nor indeed by any exercise soever of the limbs, spoil the pretty procedure of her reason. Let her be content to remain the guide, the subtle suggester of what *we* must do, the strategist whose soldiers we are, the little architect whose workmen.

"After all," as a pretty girl once said to me, "women are a sex by themselves, so to speak," and the sharper the line between their worldly functions and ours, the better. This greater swiftness and less erring subtlety of mind, their forte and privilege, justifies the painted mask that Artifice bids them wear. Behind it their minds can play without let. They gain the strength of reserve. They become important, as in the days of the Roman Empire were the Emperor's mistresses, as was the Pompadour at Versailles,[15] as was our Elizabeth. Yet do not their faces become lined with thought; beautiful and without meaning are their faces.

And, truly, of all the good things that will happen with the full renascence of cosmetics, one of the best is that surface will finally be severed from soul. That damnable confusion will be solved by the extinguishing of a prejudice which, as I suggest, itself created. Too long has the face been degraded from its rank as a thing of beauty to a mere vulgar index of character or emotion. We had come to troubling ourselves, not with its charm of colour and line, but with such questions as whether the lips were sensuous, the eyes full of sadness, the nose indicative of determination. I have no quarrel with physiognomy. For my own part, I believe in it. But it has tended to

13. The House of Commons in Parliament.
14. Bent or angled backward.
15. The mistress of Louis XV; Versailles was the royal palace.

degrade the face æsthetically, in such wise as the study of cheirosophy[16] has tended
to degrade the hand. And the use of cosmetics, the masking of the face, will change
this. We shall gaze at a woman merely because she is beautiful, not stare into her face
anxiously, as into the face of a barometer.

How fatal it has been, in how many ways, this confusion of soul and surface!
Wise were the Greeks in making plain masks for their mummers to play in, and
dunces we not to have done the same! Only the other day, an actress was saying that
what she was most proud of in her art—next, of course, to having appeared in some
provincial pantomime at the age of three—was the deftness with which she contrived, in parts demanding a rapid succession of emotions, to dab her cheeks quite
quickly with rouge from the palm of her right hand, or powder from the palm of her
left. Gracious goodness! why do not we have masks upon the stage? Drama is the presentment of the soul in action. The mirror of the soul is the voice. Let the young critics, who seek a cheap reputation for austerity, by cavilling at "incidental music," set
their faces rather against the attempt to justify inferior dramatic art by the subven-
tion of a quite alien art like painting, of any art, indeed, whose sphere is only surface.
Let those, again, who sneer, so rightly, at the "painted anecdotes of the Academy,"
censure equally the writers who trespass on painter's ground.[17] It is a proclaimed sin
that a painter should concern himself with a good little girl's affection for a Scotch
greyhound, or the keen enjoyment of their port by elderly gentlemen of the early 'forties. Yet, for a painter to prod the soul with his paint-brush is no worse than for a novelist to refuse to dip under the surface, and the fashion of avoiding a psychological
study of grief by stating that the owner's hair turned white in a single night, or of
shame by mentioning a sudden rush of scarlet to the cheeks, is as lamentable as may
be. But! But with the universal use of cosmetics and the consequent secernment[18] of
soul and surface, which, at the risk of irritating a reader, I must again insist upon, all
those old properties that went to bolster up the ordinary novel—the trembling lips,
the flashing eyes, the determined curve of the chin, the nervous trick of biting the
moustache—aye and the hectic spot of red on either cheek—will be made spiflicate,
as the puppets were spiflicated by Don Quixote.[19] Yes, even now Demos[20] begins to
discern. The same spirit that has revived rouge, smote his mouth as it grinned at the
wondrous painter of mist and river, and now sends him sprawling for the pearls that
Meredith[21] dived for in the deep waters of romance.

Indeed the revival of cosmetics must needs be so splendid an influence, conjur-
ing boons innumerable, that one inclines almost to mutter against the inexorable law
by which Artifice must perish from time to time. That such branches of painting as
the staining of glass or the illuminating of manuscripts should fall into disuse seems,
in comparison, so likely; these were esoteric arts; they died with the monastic spirit.
But personal appearance is art's very basis. The painting of the face is the first kind of
painting man can have known. To make beautiful things—is it not an impulse laid

---

16. The study of the hand.
17. The Royal Academy, which displayed officially approved art.
18. Separation.
19. Defunct. The hero of Miguel de Cervantes's 17th-c. *Don Quixote* is so engaged by a puppet show depicting the
Moors fighting the Spanish that he draws his sword and hacks the puppets to pieces.
20. Greek: the people.
21. Novelist George Meredith (1828–1909) experimented with idiomatic, oblique diction.

upon few? But to make oneself beautiful is an universal instinct. Strange that the resultant art could never perish! So fascinating an art too! So various in its materials from stimmis, psimythium and fuligo to bismuth and arsenic,[22] so simple in that its ground and its subject-matter are one, so marvellous in that its very subject-matter becomes lovely when an artist has selected it! For surely this is no idle nor fantastic saying. To deny that "make-up" is an art, on the pretext that the finished work of its exponents depends for beauty and excellence upon the ground chosen for the work, is absurd. At the touch of a true artist, the plainest face turns comely. As subject-matter the face is no more than suggestive, as ground, merely a loom round which the *beatus artifex*[23] may spin the threads of any gold fabric:

> *Quae nunc nomen habent operosi signa Maronis*
> *Pondus iners quondam duraque massa fuit.*
> *Multa viros nescire decet, pars maxima rerum*
> *Offendat, si non interiora tegas,*[24]

and, as Ovid[25] would seem to suggest, by pigments any tone may be set aglow on a woman's cheek, from enamel the features take any form. Insomuch that surely the advocates of soup-kitchens and free-libraries and other devices for giving people what providence did not mean them to receive, should send out pamphlets in the praise of self-embellishment. For it will place Beauty within easy reach of many who could not otherwise hope to attain it.

But of course Artifice is rather exacting. In return for the repose she forces— so wisely!—upon her followers when the sun is high or the moon is blown across heaven, she demands that they should pay her long homage at the sun's rising. The initiate may not enter lightly upon her mysteries. For, if a bad complexion be inexcusable, to be ill-painted is unforgiveable; and when the toilet is laden once more with the fullness of its elaboration, we shall hear no more of the proper occupation for women. And think, how sweet an energy, to sit at the mirror of coquetry! See the dear merits of the toilet as shown on old vases, or upon the walls of Roman dwellings, or, rather still, read Böttinger's alluring, scholarly description of "Morgenscenen in Puttzimmer Einer Reichen Römerin."[26] Read of Sabina's face as she comes through the curtain of her bed-chamber to the chamber of her toilet. The slave-girls have long been chafing their white feet upon the marble floor. They stand, those timid Greek girls, marshalled in little battalions. Each has her appointed task, and all kneel in welcome as Sabina stalks, ugly and frowning, to the toilet chair. Scaphion steps forth from among them, and, dipping a tiny sponge in a bowl of hot milk, passes it lightly, ever so lightly, over her mistress' face. The Poppæan pastes melt beneath it like snow. A cooling lotion is poured over her

---

22. Chemicals used in cosmetics; fuligo was a rouge, arsenic was a whitener.
23. Latin: happy artist.
24. Latin (Karl Beckson's translation): That which is now called the statue of laborious Maro was once an inert mass and a hard rock. It is proper that men should remain ignorant of many things; most things would cause offence if one did not hide their interior.
25. Witty Roman poet who wrote *The Art of Love.*
26. Böttinger's work was translated as *Sabine ou Matinée d'une Dame Romaine à sa Toilette* (French trans., 1813), describing the daily rituals of a lady's grooming.

brow and is fanned with feathers. Phiale comes after, a clever girl, captured in some sea-skirmish in the Aegean. In her left hand she holds the ivory box wherein are the phucus and that white powder, psimythium; in her right a sheaf of slim brushes. With how sure a touch does she mingle the colours, and in what sweet proportion blushes and blanches her lady's upturned face. Phiale is the cleverest of all the slaves. Now Calamis dips her quill in a certain powder that floats, liquid and sable, in the hollow of her palm. Standing upon tip-toe and with lips parted, she traces the arch of the eyebrows. The slaves whisper loudly of their lady's beauty, and two of them hold up a mirror to her. Yes, the eyebrows are rightly arched. But why does Psecas abase herself? She is craving leave to powder Sabina's hair with a fine new powder. It is made of the grated rind of the cedar-tree, and a Gallic perfumer, whose stall is near the Circus, gave it to her for a kiss. No lady in Rome knows of it. And so, when four special slaves have piled up the headdress, out of a perforated box this glistening powder is showered. Into every little brown ringlet it enters, till Sabina's hair seems like a pile of gold coins. Lest the breezes send it flying, the girls lay the powder with sprinkled attar. Soon Sabina will start for the Temple of Cybele.

Ah! Such are the lures of the toilet that none will for long hold aloof from them. Cosmetics are not going to be a mere prosaic remedy for age or plainness, but all ladies and all young girls will come to love them. Does not a certain blithe Marquise, whose *lettres intimes* from the Court of Louis Seize are less read than their wit would merit, tell us how she was scandalised to see *"même les toutes jeunes demoiselles émaillées comme ma tabatière?"*[27] So it shall be with us. Surely the common prejudice against painting the lily can be based on mere ground of economy. That which is already fair is complete, it may be urged—urged implausibly, for there are not so many lovely things in this world that we can afford not to know each one of them by heart. There is only one white lily, and who that has ever seen—as I have—a lily really well painted could grudge the artist so fair a ground for his skill? Scarcely do you believe through how many nice metamorphoses a lily may be passed by him. In like manner, we all know the young girl, with her simpleness, her goodness, her wayward ignorance. And a very charming ideal for England must she have been, and a very natural one, when a young girl sat even on the throne. But no nation can keep its ideal for ever and it needed none of Mr. Gilbert's delicate satire in "Utopia"[28] to remind us that she had passed out of her ken with the rest of the early Victorian era. What writer of plays, as lately asked some pressman, who had been told off to attend many first nights and knew what he was talking about, ever dreams of making the young girl the centre of his theme? Rather he seeks inspiration from the tried and tired woman of the world, in all her intricate maturity, whilst, by way of comic relief, he sends the young girl flitting in and out with a tennis-racket, the poor εἴδωλον ἀμαυρόν[29] of her former self. The season of the unsophisticated is gone by, and the young girl's final extinction beneath the rising tides of cosmetics will leave no gap in life and will rob art of nothing.

---

27. French: even the very young girls enameled like my tobacco case.
28. "Utopia, Limited" (1893) describes a South Sea Island whose British-educated Princess Zara inspires inhabitants to emulate British customs and laws.
29. Greek (Beckson's translation): wasted image.

"Tush," I can hear some damned flutterpate exclaim, "girlishness and innocence are as strong and as permanent as womanhood itself! Why, a few months past, the whole town went mad over Miss Cissie Loftus! Was not hers a success of girlish innocence and the absence of rouge? If such things as these be outmoded, why was she so wildly popular?" Indeed, the triumph of that clever girl, whose début made London nice even in August, is but another witness to the truth of my contention. In a very sophisticated time, simplicity has a new dulcedo. Hers was a success of contrast. Accustomed to clever malaperts like Miss Lloyd or Miss Reeve,[30] whose experienced pouts and smiles under the sun-bonnet are a standing burlesque of innocence and girlishness, Demos was really delighted, for once and away, to see the real presentment of these things upon his stage. Coming after all those sly serios, coming so young and mere with her pink frock and straightly combed hair, Miss Cissie Loftus had the charm which things of another period often do possess. Besides, just as we adored her for the abrupt nod with which she was wont at first to acknowledge the applause, so we were glad for her to come upon the stage with nothing to tinge the ivory of her cheeks. It seemed so strange, that neglect of convention. To be behind footlights and not rouged! Yes, hers was a success of contrast. She was like a daisy in the window at Solomons'. She was delightful. And yet, such is the force of convention, that when last I saw her, playing in some burlesque at the Gaiety, her fringe was curled and her pretty face rouged with the best of them. And, if further need be to show the absurdity of having called her performance "a triumph of naturalness over the jaded spirit of modernity," let us reflect that the little mimic was not a real old-fashioned girl after all. She had none of that restless naturalness that would seem to have characterised the girl of the early Victorian days. She had no pretty ways—no smiles nor blushes nor tremors. Posssibly Demos could not have stood a presentment of girlishness unrestrained.

But with her grave insouciance, Miss Cissie Loftus had much of the reserve that is one of the factors of feminine perfection, and to most comes only, as I have said, with artifice. Her features played very, very slightly. And in truth, this may have been one of the reasons of her great success. For expression is but too often the ruin of a face; and, since we cannot as yet so order the circumstances of life that women shall never be betrayed into "an unbecoming emotion," when the brunette shall never have cause to blush, and the lady who looks well with parted lips be kept in a permanent state of surprise, the safest way by far is to create, by brush and pigments, artificial expressions for every face.

And this—say you?—will make monotony? You are mistaken, toto cœlo[31] mistaken. When your mistress has wearied you with one expression, then it will need but a few touches of that pencil, a backward sweep of that brush, and lo, you will be revelling in another. For though, of course, the painting of the face is, in manner, most like the painting of canvas, in outcome it is rather akin to the art of music—lasting, like music's echo, not for very long. So that, no doubt, of the many little appurtenances of the Reformed Toilet Table, not the least vital will be a list of the emotions that become its owner, with recipes for simulating them. According to the colour she wills her hair to be for the time—black or yellow or, peradventure, burnished red—

30. Music-hall stars during the *fin de siècle*.
31. Latin: wholly.

she will blush for you, sneer for you, laugh or languish for you. The good combinations of line and colour are nearly numberless, and by their means poor restless woman will be able to realise her moods in all their shades and lights and dappledoms, to live many lives and masquerade through many moments of joy. No monotony will be. And for us men matrimony will have lost its sting.

But be it remembered! Though we men will garner these oblique boons, it is into the hands of women that Artifice gives her pigments. I know, I know that many men in a certain sect of society have shown a marked tendency to the use of cosmetics. I speak not of the countless gentlemen who walk about town in the time of its desertion from August to October, artificially bronzed, as though they were fresh from the moors or from the Solent.[32] This, I conceive, is done for purely social reasons and need not concern me here. Rather do I speak of those who make themselves up, seemingly with an aesthetic purpose. Doubtless—I wish to be quite just—there are many who look the better for such embellishment; but, at the hazard of being thought old-fashioned and prejudiced, I cannot speak of the custom with anything but strong disapproval. If men are to lie among the rouge-pots, inevitably it will tend to promote that amalgamation of the sexes which is one of the chief planks in the decadent platform and to obtund[33] that piquant contrast between him and her, which is one of the redeeming features of creation. Besides, really, men have not the excuse of facial monotony, that holds in the case of women. Have we not hair upon our chins and upper lips? And can we not, by diverting the trend of our moustache or by growing our beard in this way or that, avoid the boredom of looking the same for long? Let us beware. For if, in violation of unwritten sexual law, men take to trifling with the paints and brushes that are feminine heritage, it may be that our great ladies will don false imperials, and the little doner deck her pretty chin with a Newgate fringe![34] After all, I think we need not fear that many men will thus trespass. Most of them are in the City nowadays, and the great wear and tear of that place would put their use of rouge—that demands bodily repose from its dependents—quite outside the range of practical æsthetics.

But that in the world of women they will not neglect this art, so ripping in itself, in its result so wonderfully beneficent, I am sure indeed. Much, I have said, is already done for its full renascence. The spirit of the age has made straight the path of its professors. Fashion has made Jezebel[35] surrender her monopoly of the rouge-pot. As yet, the great art of self-embellishment is for us but in its infancy. But if Englishwomen can bring it to the flower of an excellence so supreme as never yet has it known, then, though Old England may lose her martial and commercial supremacy, we patriots will have the satisfaction of knowing that she has been advanced at one bound to a place in the councils of æsthetic Europe. And, in sooth, is this hoping too high of my countrywomen? True that, as the art seems always to have appealed to the ladies of Athens, and it was not until the waning time of the Republic that Roman ladies learned to love the practice of it, so Paris, Athenian in this as in all other things, has been noted hitherto as a far more vivid centre of the art than London. But it was in

32. The western part of the English Channel.
33. Dull, blunt.
34. A beard that grew from below the jawline.
35. The infamous painted woman of the biblical story, wife of King Ahab.

Rome, under the Emperors, that unguentaria[36] reached its zenith, and shall it not be in London, soon, that unguentaria shall outstrip its Roman perfection? Surely there must be among us artists as cunning in the use of brush and puff as any who lived at Versailles. Surely the splendid, impalpable advance of good taste, as shown in dress and in the decoration of houses, may justify my hope of the preëminence of Englishwomen in the cosmetic art. By their innate delicacy of touch they will accomplish much, and much, of course, by their swift feminine perception. Yet it were well that they should know something also of the theoretical side of the craft. Modern authorities upon the mysteries of the toilet are, it is true, rather few; but among the ancients many a writer would seem to have been fascinated by them. Archigenes, a man of science at the Court of Cleopatra, and Criton at the Court of the Emperor Trajan, both wrote treatises upon cosmetics—doubtless most scholarly treatises that would have given many a precious hint. It is a pity they are not extant. From Lucian, or from Juvenal, with his bitter picture of a Roman *levée*,[37] much may be learnt; from the staid pages of Xenophon and Aristophanes' dear farces. But best of all is that fine book of the *Ars Amatoria*[38] that Ovid has set aside for the consideration of dyes, perfumes and pomades. Written by an artist who knew the allurements of the toilet and understood its philosophy, it remains without rival as a treatise upon Artifice. It is more than a poem, it is a manual; and if there be left in England any lady who cannot read Latin in the original, she will do well to procure a discreet translation. In the Bodleian Library[39] there is treasured the only known copy of a very poignant and delightful rendering of this one book of Ovid's masterpiece. It was made by a certain Wye Waltonstall, who lived in the days of Elizabeth,[40] and, seeing that he dedicated it to "the Vertuous Laydes and Gentlewomen of Great Britain," I am sure that the gallant writer, could he know of our great renascence of cosmetics, would wish his little work to be placed once more within their reach. "Inasmuch as to you, ladyes and gentlewomen," so he writes in his queer little dedication, "my booke of pigments doth first addresse itself, that it may kisse your hands and afterward have the lines thereof in reading sweetened by the odour of your breath, while the dead letters formed into words by your divided lips may receive new life by your passionate expression, and the words marryed in that Ruby coloured temple may thus happily united, multiply your contentment." It is rather sad to think that, at this crisis in the history of pigments, the Vertuous Ladyes and Gentlewomen cannot read the *libellus*[41] of Wye Waltonstall, who did so dearly love pigments.

But since the days when these great critics wrote their treatises, with what gifts innumerable has Artifice been loaded by Science! Many little partitions must be added to the *narthecium*[42] before it can comprehend all the new cosmetics that have been quietly devised since classical days, and will make the modern toilet chalks away more splendid in its possibilities. A pity that no one has devoted himself to the compiling of a new list; but doubtless all the newest devices are known to the admirable

---

36. Scented salve.
37. Originally a nobleman's morning rituals; later, the morning reception held by royalty.
38. Latin: *The Art of Love.*
39. At Oxford University.
40. 16th c.
41. Latin: little book.
42. Ointment box.

unguentarians of Bond Street, who will impart them to their clients. Our thanks, too, should be given to Science for ridding us of the old danger that was latent in the use of cosmetics. Nowadays they cannot, being purged of any poisonous element, do harm to the skin that they make beautiful. There need be no more sowing the seeds of destruction in the furrows of time, no martyrs to the cause like Georgina Gunning, that fair dame but infelix,[43] who died, so they relate, from the effect of a poisonous rouge upon her lips. No, we need have no fears now. Artifice will claim not another victim from among her worshippers.

Loveliness shall sit at the toilet, watching her oval face in the oval mirror. Her smooth fingers shall flit among the paints and powder, to tip and mingle them, catch up a pencil, clasp a phial, and what not and what *not*, until the mask of vermeil tinct has been laid aptly, the enamel quite hardened. And, heavens, how she will charm us and ensorcel[44] our eyes! Positively rouge will rob us for a time of all our reason; we shall go mad over masks. Was it not at Capua that they had a whole street where nothing was sold but dyes and unguents? We must have such a street, and, to fill our new Seplasia,[45] our Arcade of the Unguents, all herbs and minerals and live creatures shall give of their substance. The white cliffs of Albion[46] shall be ground to powder for loveliness, and perfumed by the ghost of many a little violet. The fluffy eider-ducks, that are swimming round the pond, shall lose their feathers, that the powder-puff may be moon-like as it passes over loveliness's lovely face. Even the camels shall become ministers of delight, giving their hair in many tufts to be stained by the paints in her colour-box, and across her cheek the swift hare's foot shall fly as of old. The sea shall offer her the phucus, its scarlet weed. We shall spill the blood of mulberries at her bidding. And, as in another period of great ecstasy, a dancing wanton, la belle Aubrey, was crowned upon a church's lighted altar, to Arsenic, that "green-tress'd goddess," ashamed at length of skulking between the soup of the unpopular and the test-tubes of the Queen's analyst, shall be exalted to a place of highest honour upon loveliness's toilet-table.

All these things shall come to pass. Times of jolliness and glad indulgence! For Artifice, whom we drove forth, has returned among us, and, though her eyes are red with crying, she is smiling forgiveness. She is kind. Let us dance and be glad, and trip the cockawhoop! Artifice, sweetest exile, is come into her kingdom. Let us dance her a welcome!

—1894

A Letter to the Editor

Dear Sir,—

When The Yellow Book appeared I was in Oxford. So literary a little town is Oxford that its undergraduates see a newspaper nearly as seldom as the Venetians see a horse, and until yesterday, when coming to London, I found in the album of a friend certain newspaper cuttings, I had not known how great was the wrath of the pressmen.

---

43. Unfortunate.
44. Enchant, as a sorceress.
45. Major street in the Roman town of Capua.
46. "Albion" (white) is a poetic term for England, referring to the white cliffs of Dover.

What in the whole volume seems to have provoked the most ungovernable fury is, I am sorry to say, an essay about Cosmetics that I myself wrote. Of this it was impossible for any one to speak calmly. The mob lost its head, and, so far as any one in literature can be lynched, I was. In speaking of me, one paper dropped the usual prefix of "Mr." as though I were a well-known criminal, and referred to me shortly as "Beerbohm"; a second allowed me the "Mr." but urged that "a short Act of Parliament should be passed to make this kind of thing illegal"; a third suggested, rather tamely, that I should read one of Mr. William Watson's[1] sonnets. More than one comic paper had a very serious poem about me, and a known adherent to the humour which, forest-like, is called new, declared my essay to be "the rankest and most nauseous thing in all literature." It was a bomb thrown by a cowardly decadent, another outrage by one of that desperate and dangerous band of madmen who must be mercilessly stamped out by a comity of editors. May I, Sir, in justice to myself and to you, who were gravely censured for harbouring me, step forward, and assure the affrighted mob that it is the victim of a hoax? May I also assure it that I had no notion that it would be taken in? Indeed, it seems incredible to me that any one on the face of the earth could fail to see that my essay, so grotesque in subject, in opinion so flippant in style so wildly affected, was meant for a burlesque upon the "precious" school of writers. If I had only signed myself D. Cadent or Parrar Docks, or appended a note to say that the MS. had been picked up not a hundred miles from Tite Street,[2] all the pressmen would have said that I had given them a very delicate bit of satire. But I did not. And *hinc*, as they themselves love to say, *illæ lacrimæ*.[3]

After all, I think it is a sound rule that a writer should not kick his critics. I simply wish to make them a friendly philosophical suggestion. It seems to be thought that criticism holds in the artistic world much the same place as, in the moral world, is held by punishment—"the vengeance taken by the majority upon such as exceed the limits of conduct imposed by that majority." As in the case of punishment, then, we must consider the effect produced by criticism upon its object, how far is it reformatory? Personally I cannot conceive how any artist can be hurt by remarks dropped from a garret into a gutter. Yet it is incontestable that many an illustrious artist has so been hurt. And these very remarks, so far from making him change or temper his method, have rather made that method intenser, have driven him to retire further within his own soul, by shewing him how little he may hope for from the world but insult and ingratitude.

In fact, the police-constable mode of criticism is a failure. True that, here and there, much beautiful work of the kind has been done. In the old, old Quarterlies is many a slashing review, that, however absurd it be as criticism, we can hardly wish unwritten.[4] In the *National Observer*,[5] before its reformation, were countless fine examples of the cavilling method. The paper was rowdy, venomous and insincere. There was libel in every line of it. It roared with the lambs and bleated with the lions.

---

1. A late-Victorian poet.
2. Wilde lived at 16 Tite Street, in Chelsea, with Dante Gabriel Rossetti nearby.
3. Latin: hence . . . those tears.
4. Reviews in these 19th-c. journals were known for both style and viciousness. *The Quarterly Review*'s treatments of John Keats and Charlotte Brontë were infamous.
5. When W. E. Henley took over the *Scots Observer* he renamed it the *National Observer* but kept its pugnacious tone, gleefully attacking *The Picture of Dorian Gray*.

It was a disgrace to journalism and a glory to literature. I think of it often with tears and desiderium.[6] But the men who wrote these things stand upon a very different plane to the men employed as critics by the press of Great Britain. These must be judged, not by their workmanship, which is naught, but by the spirit that animates them and the consequence of their efforts. If only they could learn that it is for the critic to seek after beauty and to try to interpret it to others, if only they would give over their eternal fault-finding and not presume to interfere with the artist at his work, then with an equally small amount of ability our pressmen might do nearly as much good as they have hitherto done harm. Why should they regard writers with such enmity? The average pressman, reviewing a book of stories or of poems by an unknown writer, seems not to think "where are the beauties of this work that I may praise them, and by my praise quicken the sense of beauty in others?" He steadily applies himself to the ignoble task of plucking out and gloating over its defects. It is a pity that critics should show so little sympathy with writers, and curious when we consider that most of them tried to be writers themselves, once. Every new school that has come into the world, every new writer who has brought with him a new mode, they have rudely persecuted. The dullness of Ibsen, the obscurity of Meredith, the horrors of Zola—all these are household words. It is not until the pack has yelled itself hoarse that the level voice of justice is heard in praise. To pretend that no generation is capable of gauging the greatness of its own artists is the merest bauble-tit.[7] Were it not for the accursed abuse of their function by the great body of critics, no poet need "live uncrown'd, apart." Many and irreparable are the wrongs that our critics have done. At length let them repent with ashes upon their heads. Where they see not beauty, let them be silent, reverently feeling that it may yet be there, and train their dull senses in quest of it.

Now is a good time for such penance. There are signs that our English literature has reached that point, when, like the literatures of all the nations that have been, it must fall at length into the hands of the decadents. The qualities that I tried in my essay to travesty—paradox and marivaudage,[8] lassitude, a love of horror and all unusual things, a love of argot and archaism and the mysteries of style—are not all these displayed, some by one, some by another of *les jeunes écrivains*?[9] Who knows but that Artifice is in truth at our gates and that soon she may pass through our streets? Already the windows of Grub Street[10] are crowded with watchful, evil faces. They are ready, the men of Grub Street, to pelt her, as they have pelted all that came before her. Let them come down while there is still time, and hang their houses with colours, and strew the road with flowers. Will they not, for once, do homage to a new queen? By the time this letter appears, it *may* be too late!

Meanwhile, Sir, I am, your obedient servant,

MAX BEERBOHM

Oxford, May '94

—1894

---

6. Deep longing.
7. Nonsensical flummery.
8. Affected, exaggeratedly sentimental style, like the writer Marivaux's.
9. French: the young writers.
10. The locale associated with impecunious journalists, especially after George Gissing's novel, *New Grub Street* (1891).

Arthur Symons
1865–1945

Daring, rebellious, and drawn to the dark side of London, Arthur Symons was among the most "decadent" of the aesthetes. The son of a Wesleyan Methodist minister, Symons edited the journal *The Savoy* for a year and had a nervous breakdown in 1908. "The Decadent Movement in Literature" became a manifesto for an art that celebrated decline and death. Heavily influenced by French poets Stephane Mallarmé and Paul Verlaine, Symons became an expert on contemporary, experimental French literature. His criticism was no less important than his poetry, and *The Symbolist Movement in Literature* (1899) helped shape the modernist poetic sensibility. For more information about Symons, see pp. 75 and 401.

from The Decadent Movement in Literature

The latest movement in European literature has been called by many names, none of them quite exact or comprehensive—Decadence, Symbolism, Impressionism, for instance. It is easy to dispute over words, and we shall find that Verlaine objects to being called a Decadent, Maeterlinck to being called a Symbolist, Huysmans to being called an Impressionist.[1] These terms, as it happens, have been adopted as the badge of little separate cliques, noisy, brainsick young people who haunt the brasseries of the Boulevard Saint-Michel,[2] and exhaust their ingenuities in theorizing over the works they cannot write. But, taken frankly as epithets which express their own meaning, both Impressionism and Symbolism convey some notion of that new kind of literature which is perhaps more broadly characterized by the word Decadence. The most representative literature of the day—the writing which appeals to, which has done so much to form, the younger generation—is certainly not classic, nor has it any relation with that old antithesis of the Classic, the Romantic. After a fashion it is no doubt a decadence; it has all the qualities that mark the end of great periods, the qualities that we find in the Greek, the Latin, decadence: an intense self-consciousness, a restless curiosity in research, an over-subtilizing refinement upon refinement, a spiritual and moral perversity. If what we call the classic is indeed the supreme art— those qualities of perfect simplicity, perfect sanity, perfect proportion, the supreme qualities—then this representative literature of to-day, interesting, beautiful, novel as it is, is really a new and beautiful and interesting disease.

Healthy we cannot call it, and healthy it does not wish to be considered. The Goncourts, in their prefaces, in their *Journal*, are always insisting on their own pet malady, *la névrose*.[3] It is in their work, too, that Huysmans notes with delight "le style

---

1. Paul Verlaine (1844–96), leading French symbolist poet; Maurice Maeterlinck (1862–1949), Belgian playwright, poet, and novelist; Joris-Karl Huysmans (1848–1907), French decadent novelist famous for *À Rebours* (Against Nature) (1884), which depicted a debilitated aristocrat searching for new sensations.
2. Cafés in the left-bank artists' quarter of Paris.
3. Brothers Edmond and Jules de Goncourt, French brothers whose *Journal* carefully recorded their psychological states. La névrose: affected sensitivity.

tacheté et faisandé"—high-flavored and spotted with corruption—which he himself possesses in the highest degree. "Having desire without light, curiosity without wisdom, seeking God by strange ways, by ways traced by the hands of men; offering rash incense upon the high places to an unknown God, who is the God of darkness"— that is how Ernest Hello,[4] in one of his apocalyptic moments, characterizes the nineteenth century. And this unreason of the soul—of which Hello himself is so curious a victim—this unstable equilibrium, which has overbalanced so many brilliant intelligences into one form or another of spiritual confusion, is but another form of the *maladie fin de siècle*.[5] For its very disease of form, this literature is certainly typical of a civilization grown over-luxurious, over-inquiring, too languid for the relief of action, too uncertain for any emphasis in opinion or in conduct. It reflects all the moods, all the manners, of a sophisticated society; its very artificiality is a way of being true to nature: simplicity, sanity, proportion—the classic qualities—how much do we possess them in our life, our surroundings, that we should look to find them in our literature—so evidently the literature of a decadence?

Taking the word Decadence, then, as most precisely expressing the general sense of the newest movement in literature, we find that the terms Impressionism and Symbolism define correctly enough the two main branches of that movement. Now Impressionist and Symbolist have more in common than either supposes; both are really working on the same hypothesis, applied in different directions. What both seek is not general truth merely, but *la vérité vraie*, the very essence of truth—the truth of appearances to the senses, of the visible world to the eyes that see it; and the truth of spiritual things to the spiritual vision. The Impressionist, in literature as in painting, would flash upon you in a new, sudden way so exact an image of what you have just seen, just as you have seen it, that you may say, as a young American sculptor, a pupil of Rodin,[6] said to me on seeing for the first time a picture of Whistler's, "Whistler seems to think his picture upon canvas—and there it is!" Or you may find, with Sainte-Beuve,[7] writing of Goncourt, the "soul of the landscape"—the soul of whatever corner of the visible world has to be realized. The Symbolist, in this new, sudden way, would flash upon you the "soul" of that which can be apprehended only by the soul—the finer sense of things unseen, the deeper meaning of things evident. And naturally, necessarily, this endeavor after a perfect truth to one's impression, to one's intuition—perhaps an impossible endeavor—has brought with it, in its revolt from ready-made impressions and conclusions, a revolt from the ready-made of language, from the bondage of traditional form, of a form become rigid. In France, where this movement began and has mainly flourished, it is Goncourt who was the first to invent a style in prose really new, impressionistic, a style which was itself almost sensation. It is Verlaine who has invented such another new style in verse.

—1893

---

4. French philosopher and essayist (1828–85), an ardent Catholic.
5. French: illness of the end of the century.
6. Auguste Rodin (1840–1917), French sculptor.
7. Eminent French literary critic Charles Augustin Sainte-Beuve (1804–69).

Incantatory Art: Aesthetic Poems

Ernest Dowson
1867–1900

Tubercular, alcoholic, and hopelessly smitten by a teenage Polish girl who worked in her father's eating-house, Ernest Dowson emblematizes what W. B. Yeats called the "tragic generation" of the *fin de siècle*. A member of the Rhymers' Club along with Yeats, Lionel Johnson, and Arthur Symons, Dowson was deeply steeped in French verse, experimented with meters, and adopted French symbolist theories for English poetry. His most famous poem, nicknamed "Cynara," sums up Dowson's iconically decadent short life of weary dissipation. His melancholic phrases have become cultural touchstones: "gone with the wind" ("Cynara"); "the days of wine and roses" ("They Are Not Long").

Non Sum Qualis Eram Bonae Sub Regno Cynarae[1]

Last night, ah, yesternight, betwixt her lips and mine
There fell thy shadow, Cynara! thy breath was shed
Upon my soul between the kisses and the wine;
And I was desolate and sick of an old passion,
   Yea, I was desolate and bowed my head: 5
I have been faithful to thee, Cynara! in my fashion.

All night upon mine heart I felt her warm heart beat,
Night-long within mine arms in love and sleep she lay;
Surely the kisses of her bought red mouth were sweet;
But I was desolate and sick of an old passion,   10
   When I awoke and found the dawn was gray:
I have been faithful to thee, Cynara! in my fashion.

I have forgot much, Cynara! gone with the wind,
Flung roses, roses riotously with the throng,
Dancing, to put thy pale, lost lilies out of mind;   15
But I was desolate and sick of an old passion,
   Yea, all the time, because the dance was long:
I have been faithful to thee, Cynara! in my fashion.

I cried for madder music and for stronger wine,
But when the feast is finished and the lamps expire,   20

---

1. "I am not what I was under the reign of good Cynara." Horace's ode 4.1 pleads with Venus to free him from desire, since he is too old to love.

Then falls thy shadow, Cynara! the night is thine;
And I am desolate and sick of an old passion,
    Yea hungry for the lips of my desire:
I have been faithful to thee, Cynara! in my fashion.

—1891

Lionel Johnson
1867–1902

Lionel Johnson, perhaps the most learned of the aesthetes, wrote highly disciplined Latinate poetry and was a member of the Rhymers' Club. Johnson led a spartan, scholarly, celibate life but died at thirty-five from ill health partly caused by alcoholism. Like many of the aesthetes, he was drawn to Roman Catholicism and converted in 1891. Like the rest of the "tragic generation," he was a promising young man destroyed by intense drives; he was, for instance, highly ambivalent about decadence's celebration of sensuality. His poems enact this struggle of pent-up passions against extremely disciplined form.

The Destroyer of a Soul

To—.[1]

I hate you with a necessary hate.
First, I sought patience: passionate was she:
My patience turned in very scorn of me,
That I should dare forgive a sin so great,
As this, through which I sit disconsolate;   5
Mourning for that live soul, I used to see;
Soul of a saint, whose friend I used to be:
Till you came by! a cold, corrupting, fate.

Why come you now? You, whom I cannot cease
With pure and perfect hate to hate? Go, ring   10
The death-bell with a deep, triumphant toll!
Say you, my friend sits by me still? Ah, peace!
Call you this thing my friend? this nameless thing?
This living body, hiding its dead soul?

—1892

---

1. Probably addressed to Wilde. In 1891 Johnson introduced Wilde to the man who became his lover, Lord Alfred Douglas. This expression of hatred is structured as a Petrarchan sonnet, ironically, a form usually identified with love poetry.

A Decadent's Lyric

Sometimes, in very joy of shame,
Our flesh becomes one living flame:
And she and I
Are no more separate, but the same.

Ardour and agony unite;   5
Desire, delirium, delight:
And I and she
Faint in the fierce and fevered night.

Her body music is: and ah,
The accords of lute and viola!   10
When she and I
Play on live limbs love's opera!

—1897

Arthur Symons
1865–1945

Arthur Symons's poetry celebrates artifice, sensation, and sensuality. As he explained in "The Decadent Movement in Literature," a "spiritual and moral perversity" was the aim of the new art, and its favorite site was the London underworld of garish street life, music halls, brothels, and alcoholism. For more information about Symons, see pp. 71 and 401.

Renée

Rain, and the night, and the old familiar door,
And the archway dim, and the roadway desolate;
Faces that pass, and faces, and more, yet more:
Renée! come, for I wait.

Pallid out of the darkness, adorably white,   5
Pale as the spirit of rain, with the night in her hair,
Renée undulates, shadow-like, under the light,
Into the outer air.

Mournful, beautiful, calm with that vague unrest,
Sad with that sensitive, vaguely ironical mouth;   10
Eyes a-flame with the loveliest, deadliest
Fire of passionate youth;

Mournful, beautiful, sister of night and rain,
Elemental, fashioned of tears and fire,
Ever desiring, ever desired in vain,   15
Mother of vain desire;

Renée comes to me, she the sorceress, Fate,
Subtly insensible, softly invincible, she,
Renée, who waits for another, for whom I wait,
To linger a moment with me.   20

—1895

White Heliotrope

The feverish room and that white bed,
   The tumbled skirts upon a chair,
   The novel flung half-open, where
Hat, hair-pins, puffs, and paints, are spread;

The mirror that has sucked your face   5
   Into its secret deep of deeps,
   And there mysteriously keeps
Forgotten memories of grace;

And you, half dressed and half awake,
   Your slant eyes strangely watching me,   10
   And I, who watch you drowsily,
With eyes that, having slept not, ache;

This (need one dread? nay, dare one hope?)
   Will rise, a ghost of memory, if
   Ever again my handkerchief   15
Is scented with White Heliotrope.

—1895

Morbidezza[1]

White girl, your flesh is lilies
Grown 'neath a frozen moon,
So still is
The rapture of your swoon
Of whiteness, snow or lilies.   5

---

1. Delicate, soft representation of flesh.

The virginal revealment,
Your bosom's wavering slope,
Concealment,
'Neath fainting heliotrope,
Of whitest white's revealment,   10

Is like a bed of lilies,
A jealous-guarded row,
Whose will is
Simply chaste dreams:——but oh,
The alluring scent of lilies!   15

—1892

Maquillage[1]

The charm of rouge on fragile cheeks,
Pearl-powder, and, about the eyes,
The dark and lustrous Eastern dyes;
The floating odour that bespeaks
A scented boudoir and the doubtful night   5
Of alcoves curtained close against the light.

Gracile and creamy white and rose,
Complexioned like the flower of dawn,
Her fleeting colours are as those
That, from an April sky withdrawn,   10
Fade in a fragrant mist of tears away
When weeping noon leads on the altered day.

—1892

Lord Alfred Douglas
1870–1945

"It is a marvel that those red rose-leaf lips of yours should have been made no less for music of song than for madness of kisses," wrote an entranced Oscar Wilde to his lover, the young poet Lord Alfred Douglas. Douglas is famous as the golden lad Wilde was imprisoned for adoring. His life was marked by extreme swings; having been Wilde's lover, he turned against Wilde when he read Wilde's bitter prison letter, *De Profundis*; having been a leading aesthete, he later sued his former friends; having led an uninhibitedly open homosexual life, he suddenly mar-

---

1. Cosmetics.

ried the poet Olive Custance; having advocated daring literature in his youth, he became a traditional Catholic and then a Nazi sympathizer. "Two Loves," a poem Douglas wrote as an undergraduate, became famous when it was read at Wilde's trial, spurring Wilde to a sudden eloquent defense of male love. "The love that dare not speak its name" is both the legal term for male homosexuality, "inter Christianos non nomindum" ("the crime not to be named among Christians," from Sir William Blackstone's *Commentaries on the Laws of England* [1765–69]), and, more generally, a way of mourning the difficulty of expressing same-sex desire in a hostile culture.

Two Loves

    I dreamed I stood upon a little hill,
And at my feet there lay a ground that seemed
    Like a waste garden, flowering at its will
With buds and blossoms. There were pools that dreamed
    Black and unruffled; there were white lilies   5
A few, and crocuses, and violets,
    Purple or pale, snake-like fritillaries[1]
Scarce seen for the rank grass, and through green nets
    Blue eyes of shy pervenche[2] winked in the sun.
And there were curious flowers, before unknown,   10
Flowers that were stained with moonlight, or with shades
    Of Nature's wilful moods; and here a one
    That had drunk in the transitory tone
Of one brief moment in a sunset; blades
    Of grass that in an hundred springs had been   15
    Slowly but exquisitely nurtured by the stars,
And watered with the scented dew long cupped
    In lilies, that for rays of sun had seen
    Only God's glory, for never a sunrise mars
The luminous air of Heaven. Beyond, abrupt,   20
    A grey stone wall, o'ergrown with velvet moss,
    Uprose; and gazing I stood long, all mazed
To see a place so strange, so sweet, so fair.
    And as I stood and marvelled, lo! across
    The garden came a youth; one hand he raised   25
To shield him from the sun, his wind-tossed hair
    Was twined with flowers, and in his hand he bore
A purple bunch of bursting grapes, his eyes
Were clear as crystal, naked all was he,
    White as the snow on pathless mountains frore,[3]   30
    Red were his lips as red wine-spilth that dyes

---

1. Flowers.
2. Periwinkles, blue flowers.
3. Frozen.

A marble floor, his brow chalcedony.[4]
    And he came near me, with his lips uncurled
And kind, and caught my hand and kissed my mouth,
And gave me grapes to eat, and said, "Sweet friend,   35
    Come, I will show thee shadows of the world
And images of life. See from the South
Comes the pale pageant that hath never an end."
    And lo! within the garden of my dream
I saw two walking on a shining plain   40
    Of golden light. The one did joyous seem
And fair and blooming, and a sweet refrain
    Came from his lips; he sang of pretty maids
And joyous love of comely girl and boy;
    His eyes were bright, and 'mid the dancing blades   45
Of golden grass his feet did trip for joy;
    And in his hands he held an ivory lute
With strings of gold that were as maidens' hair,
    And sang with voice as tuneful as a flute,
And round his neck three chains of roses were.   50
    But he that was his comrade walked aside;
He was full sad and sweet, and his large eyes
    Were strange with wondrous brightness, staring wide
With gazing; and he sighed with many sighs
    That moved me, and his cheeks were wan and white   55
Like pallid lilies, and his lips were red
    Like poppies, and his hands he clenchèd tight
And yet again unclenchèd, and his head
    Was wreathed with moon-flowers pale as lips of death.
A purple robe he wore, o'erwrought in gold   60
    With the device of a great snake, whose breath
Was like curved flame: which when I did behold
    I fell a-weeping, and I cried, "Sweet youth,
Tell me why, sad and sighing, thou dost rove
    These pleasant realms? I pray thee, speak me sooth,   65
What is thy name?" He said, "My name is Love."
    Then straight the first did turn himself to me
And cried: "He lieth, for his name is Shame,
    But I am Love, and I was wont to be
Alone in this fair garden, till he came   70
    Unasked by night; I am true Love, I fill
The hearts of boy and girl with mutual flame."
    Then sighing, said the other: "Have thy will,
I am the love that dare not speak its name."

        —1894

---

4. Translucent quartz.

W. B. Yeats
1865–1939

William Butler Yeats's early poetry—the material in this volume—celebrated Ireland's richly symbolic, mythic, occult legacy, although in his mature poetry Yeats forged a newly concise style that helped shape the modernist poetic sensibility. Yeats spent virtually all of his adult life hopelessly in love with fellow Irish nationalist Maud Gonne, who refused to marry him. Eventually Yeats managed a happy marriage to his friend Georgiana Hyde-Lees and spent much of his later life involved in nationalist work and spiritualist experiments. In 1891, Yeats organized the Rhymers' Club, which included Ernest Dowson, Lionel Johnson, and Arthur Symons. Yeats's early poems have the allegorical intensity, densely visual descriptiveness, archaic language, and intricate patterning of the Pre-Raphaelite movement, yet Yeats's deep ties to the Irish landscape allowed him to place these formal elements in the service of Irish legend and Irish national pride. Unlike his fellow members of the Rhymers' Club, Yeats shows little interest in the seamy underworld of London, with its alcohol and prostitutes and music halls. Instead, Yeats's aestheticism focuses on densely packed symbols, allegorical tales, and richly beautiful historical and folkloric survivals. For more information about Yeats, see p. 576.

When You are Old

When you are old and grey and full of sleep,
And nodding by the fire, take down this book,
And slowly read, and dream of the soft look
Your eyes had once, and of their shadows deep;

How many loved your moments of glad grace,   5
And loved your beauty with love false or true,
But one man loved the pilgrim soul in you,
And loved the sorrows of your changing face;

And bending down beside the glowing bars,
Murmur, a little sadly, how Love fled   10
And paced upon the mountains overhead
And hid his face amid a crowd of stars.

—1893

The Lover Tells of the Rose in His Heart

All things uncomely and broken, all things worn out and old,
The cry of a child by the roadway, the creak of a lumbering cart,
The heavy steps of the ploughman, splashing the wintry mould,
Are wronging your image that blossoms a rose in the deeps of my heart.

The wrong of unshapely things is a wrong too great to be told;   5
I hunger to build them anew and sit on a green knoll apart,
With the earth and the sky and the water, re-made, like a casket of gold
For my dreams of your image that blossoms a rose in the deeps of my heart.

—1899

He Remembers Forgotten Beauty

When my arms wrap you round I press
My heart upon the loveliness
That has long faded from the world;
The jewelled crowns that kings have hurled
In shadowy pools, when armies fled;   5
The love-tales wrought with silken thread
By dreaming ladies upon cloth
That has made fat the murderous moth;
The roses that of old time were
Woven by ladies in their hair,   10
The dew-cold lilies ladies bore
Through many a sacred corridor
Where such grey clouds of incense rose
That only God's eyes did not close:
For that pale breast and lingering hand   15
Come from a more dream-heavy land,
A more dream-heavy hour than this;
And when you sigh from kiss to kiss
I hear white Beauty sighing, too,
For hours when all must fade like dew,   20
But flame on flame, and deep on deep,
Throne over throne where in half sleep,
Their swords upon their iron knees,
Brood her high lonely mysteries.

—1899

The Secret Rose

Far-off, most secret, and inviolate Rose,
Enfold me in my hour of hours; where those
Who sought thee in the Holy Sepulchre,
Or in the wine-vat, dwell beyond the stir
And tumult of defeated dreams; and deep   5
Among pale eyelids, heavy with the sleep
Men have named beauty. Thy great leaves enfold
The ancient beards, the helms of ruby and gold

Of the crowned Magi;[1] and the king[2] whose eyes
Saw the Pierced Hands and Rood[3] of elder rise   10
In Druid vapour and make the torches dim;
Till vain frenzy awoke and he died; and him
Who met Fand walking among flaming dew
By a grey shore where the wind never blew,
And lost the world and Emer for a kiss;[4]   15
And him who drove the gods out of their liss,[5]
And till a hundred morns had flowered red
Feasted, and wept the barrows of his dead;
And the proud dreaming king who flung the crown
And sorrow away, and calling bard and clown   20
Dwelt among wine-stained wanderers in deep woods;
And him who sold tillage, and house, and goods,[6]
And sought through lands and islands numberless years,
Until he found, with laughter and with tears,
A woman of so shining loveliness   25
That men threshed corn at midnight by a tress,
A little stolen tress. I, too, await
The hour of thy great wind of love and hate.
When shall the stars be blown about the sky,
Like the sparks blown out of a smithy, and die?   30
Surely thine hour has come, thy great wind blows,
Far-off, most secret, and inviolate Rose?

—1899

He Wishes for the Cloths of Heaven

Had I the heavens' embroidered cloths,
Enwrought with golden and silver light,
The blue and the dim and the dark cloths
Of night and light and the half-light,
I would spread the cloths under your feet: 5
But I, being poor, have only my dreams;
I have spread my dreams under your feet;
Tread softly because you tread on my dreams.

—1899

---

1. The three kings who visited Jesus in the manger.
2. Conchubar at the Crucifixion. When his Druid told him what the uproar meant, Conchubar died, becoming the first Christian martyr.
3. The Rood is the Cross.
4. Cuchulain was married to Emer but had an affair with Fand, wife of the sea-god.
5. Legendary king Eochaid Airim ploughed up the "lios," underground shelter, of his supernatural rival in love.
6. A character from *West Irish Folk Tales and Romances* (1893), peasant tales collected and translated by William Larminie.

Oscar Wilde
1854–1900

Today most people know Oscar Wilde for his wit, but in his own lifetime he was famous as a poet. "The Sphinx" demonstrates his elaborate early style. It is written in an exceptionally complex form, with end-rhyme hooking a word in the middle of the next line, and it bursts with the most exuberantly esoteric vocabulary Wilde could find. "The Harlot's House" and "Impression du Matin" are typical aesthetic poems from his middle period, using strong visual imagery and unconventional subjects. By contrast, "The Ballad of Reading Gaol" uses stringently simple Anglo-Saxon words in the service of a plain ballad form, relying on the starkness of the message. It was written after Wilde's prison sentence, commemorating an execution, and he insisted on publishing it under his prison code, C.3.3. For more information about Wilde, see pp. 19, 148, and 355.

from The Sphinx[1]

In a dim corner of my room for longer than my fancy thinks
A beautiful and silent Sphinx has watched me through the shifting gloom.

Inviolate and immobile she does not rise she does not stir
For silver moons are naught to her and naught to her the suns that reel.

Red follows grey across the air the waves of moonlight ebb and flow　　　　5
But with the Dawn she does not go and in the night-time she is there.

Dawn follows dawn and Nights grow old and all the while this curious cat
Lies crouching on the Chinese mat with eyes of satin rimmed with gold.

Upon the mat she lies and leers and on the tawny throat of her
Flutters the soft and silky fur or ripples to her pointed ears.　　　　　10

Come forth, my lovely seneschal! so somnolent, so statuesque!
Come forth you exquisite grotesque! half woman and half animal!

Come forth my lovely languorous Sphinx! and put your head upon my knee!
And let me stroke your throat and see your body spotted like the Lynx!

And let me touch those curving claws of yellow ivory and grasp　　　　15
The tail that like a monstrous Asp coils round your heavy velvet paws!

A thousand weary centuries are thine while I have hardly seen
Some twenty summers cast their green for Autumn's gaudy liveries.

---

1. The Sphinx, with woman's breast and lion's body, posed a riddle to Oedipus about the nature of man.

But you can read the Hieroglyphs on the great sandstone obelisks,
And you have talked with Basilisks, and you have looked on Hippogriffs.[2]   20

O tell me, were you standing by when Isis to Osiris knelt?
And did you watch the Egyptian melt her union for Antony

And drink the jewel-drunken wine and bend her head in mimic awe
To see the huge proconsul draw the salted tunny from the brine?

And did you mark the Cyprian kiss white Adon on his catafalque?[3]   25
And did you follow Amenalk, the God of Heliopolis?[4]

And did you talk with Thoth,[5] and did you hear the moon-horned Io weep?
And know the painted kings who sleep beneath the wedge-shaped Pyramid?

Lift up your large black satin eyes which are like cushions where one sinks!
Fawn at my feet, fantastic Sphinx! and sing me all your memories!   30

Sing to me of the Jewish maid who wandered with the Holy Child,
And how you led them through the wild, and how they slept beneath your shade.

Sing to me of that odorous green eve when couching by the marge
You heard from Adrian's gilded barge the laughter of Antinous[6]

And lapped the stream and fed your drouth and watched with hot and
     hungry stare   35
The ivory body of that rare young slave with his pomegranate mouth!

Sing to me of the Labyrinth in which the twiformed bull was stalled![7]
Sing to me of the night you crawled across the temple's granite plinth

When through the purple corridors the screaming scarlet Ibis flew
In terror, and a horrid dew dripped from the moaning Mandragores,[8]   40

And the great torpid crocodile within the tank shed slimy tears,
And tare the jewels from his ears and staggered back into the Nile,

And the priests cursed you with shrill psalms as in your claws you seized their snake
And crept away with it to slake your passion by the shuddering palms.

---

2. Greek mythological monsters: The basilisk's gaze turned people to stone; hippogriffs combined the bodies of horses and griffons.
3. Aphrodite (the Cyprian) kissed Adonis as he died, and his blood drops sprang up into flowers. A catafalque is a hearse.
4. Egyptian god Ammon/Amun, seen as the source of all creation. Heliopolis was a major religious center.
5. Bird-headed god of ancient Egypt, patron of scribes; in Greek myth, Io was pursued by Zeus and transformed into a heifer.
6. Beautiful youth and favorite of the Emperor (H)adrian.
7. The prison held the Minotaur, a monstrous bull.
8. Ibis: an Egyptian bird. Mandragore: the mandrake, a narcotic plant that supposedly shrieked when plucked.

Who were your lovers? who were they who wrestled for you in the dust?   45
Which was the vessel of your Lust? What Leman[9] had you, every day?

Did giant Lizards come and crouch before you on the reedy banks?
Did Gryphons[10] with great metal flanks leap on you in your trampled couch?

Did monstrous hippopotami come sidling toward you in the mist?
Did gilt-scaled dragons writhe and twist with passion as you passed them by?   50

And from the brick-built Lycian bomb what horrible Chimera[11] came
With fearful heads and fearful flame to breed new wonders from your womb?

* * *

Or did huge Apis from his car leap down and lay before your feet
Big blossoms of the honey-sweet and honey-coloured nenuphar?[12]

How subtle-secret is your smile! Did you love none then? Nay, I know
Great Ammon was your bedfellow! He lay with you beside the Nile!

The river-horses in the slime trumpeted when they saw him come   75
Odorous with Syrian galbanum and smeared with spikenard[13] and with thyme.

He came along the river bank like some tall galley argent-sailed,
He strode across the waters, mailed in beauty, and the waters sank.

He strode across the desert sand: he reached the valley where you lay:
He waited till the dawn of day: then touched your black breasts with his hand.   80

You kissed his mouth with mouths of flame: you made the hornèd god your own:
You stood behind him on his throne: you called him by his secret name.

You whispered monstrous oracles into the caverns of his ears:
With blood of goats and blood of steers you taught him monstrous miracles.

White Ammon was your bedfellow! Your chamber was the steaming Nile!   85
And with your curved archaic smile you watched his passion come and go.

With Syrian oils his brows were bright: and wide-spread as a tent at noon
His marble limbs made pale the moon and lent the day a larger light.

His long hair was nine cubits' span and coloured like that yellow gem
Which hidden in their garment's hem the merchants bring from Kurdistan.   90

His face was as the must that lies upon a vat of new-made wine:
The seas could not insapphirine the perfect azure of his eyes.

---

9. Lover.
10. Monsters with a lion's body and eagle's head and wings, associated with Zeus.
11. Monster combining lion, serpent, and goat.
12. Apis: bull-headed god. Nenuphar: water lily.
13. Galbanum: gum resin. Spikenard: aromatic oil.

His thick soft throat was white as milk and threaded with the veins of blue:
And curious pearls like frozen dew were broidered on his flowing silk.

On pearl and porphyry pedestalled he was too bright to look upon: 95
For on his ivory breast there shone the wondrous' ocean-emerald,

That mystic moonlit jewel which some diver of the Colchian caves
Had found beneath the blackening waves and carried to the Colchian witch.[14]

Before his gilded galiot ran naked vine-wreathed corybants,[15]
And lines of swaying elephants knelt down to draw his chariot,   100

And lines of swarthy Nubians bare up his litter as he rode
Down the great granite-paven road between the nodding peacock-fans.

The merchants brought him steatite from Sidon in their painted ships:
The meanest cup that touched his lips was fashioned from a chrysolite.

The merchants brought him cedar chests of rich apparel bound with cords: 105
His train was borne by Memphian lords: young kings were glad to be his guests.

Ten hundred shaven priests did bow to Ammon's altar day and night,
Ten hundred lamps did wave their light through Ammon's carven House—and now

Foul snake and speckled adder with their young ones crawl from stone to stone
For ruined is the house and prone the great rose-marble monolith!   110

Wild ass or trotting jackal comes and couches in the mouldering gates:
Wild satyrs call unto their mates across the fallen fluted drums.

And on the summit of the pile the blue-faced ape of Horus sits
And gibbers while the fig-tree splits the pillars of the peristyle.[16]

* * *

Why are you tarrying? Get hence! I weary of your sullen ways,
I weary of your steadfast gaze, your somnolent magnificence.   150

Your horrible and heavy breath makes the light flicker in the lamp,
And on my brow I feel the damp and dreadful dews of night and death.

Your eyes are like fantastic moons that shiver in some stagnant lake,
Your tongue is like a scarlet snake that dances to fantastic tunes,

Your pulse makes poisonous melodies, and your black throat is like the hole   155
Left by some torch or burning coal on Saracenic tapestries.

Away! The sulphur-coloured stars are hurrying through the Western gate!
Away! Or it may be too late to climb their silent silver cars!

---

14. Medea fell in love with Jason when he sought the Golden Fleece in Colchis.
15. Galiot: small boat. Corybant: worshipper of Cybele, the mother goddess.
16. A circular enclosure of columns.

Max Beerbohm, *Oscar Wilde* (c. 1894).

See, the dawn shivers round the grey gilt-dialled towers, and the rain
Streams down each diamonded pane and blurs with tears the wannish day.   160

What snake-tressed fury fresh from Hell, with uncouth gestures and unclean,
Stole from the poppy-drowsy queen and led you to a student's cell?

What songless tongueless ghost of sin crept through the curtain of the night,
And saw my taper burning bright, and knocked, and bade you enter in?

Are there not others more accursed, whiter with leprosies than I?   165
Are Abana and Pharphar[17] dry that you come here to slake your thirst?

Get hence, you loathsome mystery! Hideous animal, get hence!
You wake in me each bestial sense, you make me what I would not be.

You make my creed a barren sham, you wake foul dreams of sensual life,
And Atys with his blood-stained knife[18] were better than the thing I am.   170

False Sphinx! False Sphinx! By reedy Styx old Charon, leaning on his oar,
Waits for my coin.[19] Go thou before, and leave me to my crucifix,

Whose pallid burden, sick with pain, watches the world with wearied eyes,
And weeps for every soul that dies, and weeps for every soul in vain.

—1894

The Harlot's House

We caught the tread of dancing feet,
We loitered down the moonlit street,
And stopped beneath the harlot's house.

Inside, above the din and fray,
We heard the loud musicians play   5
The "Treues Liebes Herz" of Strauss.[1]

Like strange mechanical grotesques,
Making fantastic arabesques,
The shadows raced across the blind.

We watched the ghostly dancers spin   10
To sound of horn and violin,
Like black leaves wheeling in the wind.

---

17. Rivers in Damascus (Kings 2.5).
18. Cybele's beloved, a Phrygian shepherd who castrated himself and died.
19. Charon ferried the souls of the dead across the River Styx into the underworld.

---

1. "True loving heart," by an Austrian composer of famous waltzes.

Like wire-pulled automatons,
Slim silhouetted skeletons
Went sidling through the slow quadrille.   15

They took each other by the hand,
And danced a stately saraband;[2]
Their laughter echoed thin and shrill.

Sometimes a clockwork puppet pressed
A phantom lover to her breast,   20
Sometimes they seemed to try to sing.

Sometimes a horrible marionette
Came out, and smoked its cigarette
Upon the steps like a live thing.

Then, turning to my love, I said,   25
"The dead are dancing with the dead,
The dust is whirling with the dust."

But she—she heard the violin,
And left my side, and entered in:
Love passed into the house of lust.   30

Then suddenly the tune went false,
The dancers wearied of the waltz,
The shadows ceased to wheel and whirl.

And down the long and silent street,
The dawn, with silver-sandalled feet,   35
Crept like a frightened girl.

—1885, 1908

Impression du Matin

The Thames nocturne of blue and gold
    Changed to a harmony in gray:[1]
    A barge with ochre-coloured hay
Dropt from the wharf: and chill and cold

The yellow fog came creeping down   5
    The bridges, till the houses' walls

2. A slow Spanish dance.

1. Allusions to Whistler's nocturnes (night scenes) and harmonies (day scenes). Matin is morning.

Seemed changed to shadows and St. Paul's[2]
Loomed like a bubble o'er the town.

Then suddenly arose the clang
   Of waking life; the streets were stirred   10
   With country wagons: and a bird
Flew to the glistening roofs and sang.

But one pale woman all alone,
   The daylight kissing her wan hair,
   Loitered beneath the gas lamps' flare,   15
With lips of flame and heart of stone.

—1877, 1881

The Ballad[1] of Reading Gaol

IN MEMORIAM
C. T. W.[2]
Sometime Trooper of The Royal Horse Guards
Obiit H.M. Prison, Reading, Berkshire
July 7th, 1896

I

He did not wear his scarlet coat,
   For blood and wine are red,
And blood and wine were on his hands
   When they found him with the dead,
The poor dead woman whom he loved,   5
   And murdered in her bed.

He walked amongst the Trial Men
   In a suit of shabby grey;
A cricket cap was on his head,
   And his step seemed light and gay;   10
But I never saw a man who looked
   So wistfully at the day.

I never saw a man who looked
   With such a wistful eye

---

2. Sir Christopher Wren's famous cathedral.

---

1. A folk narrative transmitted through oral tradition. Ballad meter uses four feet in the first and third lines, three in the second and fourth lines.
2. Charles Thomas Wooldridge, aged 30, hanged on July 7, 1896, for murdering his wife.

Upon that little tent of blue   15
   Which prisoners call the sky,
And at every drifting cloud that went
   With sails of silver by.

I walked, with other souls in pain,
   Within another ring,   20
And was wondering if the man had done
   A great or little thing,
When a voice behind me whispered low,
   "That fellow's got to swing."

Dear Christ! the very prison walls   25
   Suddenly seemed to reel,
And the sky above my head became
   Like a casque of scorching steel;
And, though I was a soul in pain,
   My pain I could not feel.   30

I only knew what hunted thought
   Quickened his step, and why
He looked upon the garish day
   With such a wistful eye;
The man had killed the thing he loved,   35
   And so he had to die.

Yet each man kills the thing he loves,
   By each let this be heard,
Some do it with a bitter look,
   Some with a flattering word,   40
The coward does it with a kiss,
   The brave man with a sword!

Some kill their love when they are young,
   And some when they are old;
Some strangle with the hands of Lust,   45
   Some with the hands of Gold;
The kindest use a knife, because
   The dead so soon grow cold.

Some love too little, some too long
   Some sell, and others buy;   50
Some do the deed with many tears,
   And some without a sigh:
For each man kills the thing he loves,
   Yet each man does not die.

He does not die a death of shame   55
   On a day of dark disgrace,
Nor have a noose about his neck,
   Nor a cloth upon his face,
Nor drop feet foremost through the floor
   Into an empty space.   60

He does not sit with silent men
   Who watch him night and day;
Who watch him when he tries to weep,
   And when he tries to pray;
Who watch him lest himself should rob   65
   The prison of its prey.

He does not wake at dawn to see
   Dread figures throng his room,
 The shivering Chaplain robed in white,
   The Sheriff stern with gloom,   70
And the Governor all in shiny black,
   With the yellow face of Doom.

He does not rise in piteous haste
   To put on convict-clothes,
While some coarse-mouthed Doctor gloats, and notes   75
   Each new and nerve-twitched pose,
Fingering a watch whose little ticks
   Are like horrible hammer-blows.

He does not know that sickening thirst
   That sands one's throat, before   80
The hangman with his gardener's gloves
   Slips through the padded door,
And binds one with three leathern thongs,
   That the throat may thirst no more.

He does not bend his head to hear   85
   The Burial Office read,
Nor, while the terror of his soul
   Tells him he is not dead,
Cross his own coffin, as he moves
   Into the hideous shed.   90

He does not stare upon the air
   Through a little roof of glass:
He does not pray with lips of clay
   For his agony to pass;

Nor feel upon his shuddering cheek   95
　　The kiss of Caiaphas.[3]

II

Six weeks our guardsman walked the yard,
　　In the suit of shabby grey:
His cricket cap was on his head,
　　And his step seemed light and gay,   100
But I never saw a man who looked
　　So wistfully at the day.

I never saw a man who looked
　　With such a wistful eye
Upon that little tent of blue   105
　　Which prisoners call the sky,
And at every wandering cloud that trailed
　　Its ravelled fleeces by.

He did not wring his hands, as do
　　Those witless men who dare
To try to rear the changeling Hope   110
　　In the cave of black Despair:
He only looked upon the sun,
　　And drank the morning air.

He did not wring his hands nor weep,   115
　　Nor did he peek or pine,
But he drank the air as though it held
　　Some healthful anodyne;
With open mouth he drank the sun
　　As though it had been wine!   120

And I and all the souls in pain,
　　Who tramped the other ring,
Forgot if we ourselves had done
　　A great or little thing,
And watched with gaze of dull amaze   125
　　The man who had to swing.

And strange it was to see him pass
　　With a step so light and gay,
And strange it was to see him look
　　So wistfully at the day,   130

---

3. Governor of Jerusalem who ordered Jesus's execution.

And strange it was to think that he
  Had such a debt to pay.

For oak and elm have pleasant leaves
  That in the spring-time shoot:
But grim to see is the gallows-tree,   135
  With its adder-bitten root,
And, green or dry, a man must die
  Before it bears its fruit!

The loftiest place is that seat of grace
  For which all worldlings try: 140
But who would stand in hempen band
  Upon a scaffold high,
And through a murderer's collar take
  His last look at the sky?

It is sweet to dance to violins   145
  When Love and Life are fair:
To dance to flutes, to dance to lutes
  Is delicate and rare:
But it is not sweet with nimble feet
  To dance upon the air!   150

So with curious eyes and sick surmise
  We watched him day by day,
And wondered if each one of us
  Would end the self-same way,
For none can tell to what red Hell   155
  His sightless soul may stray.

At last the dead man walked no more
  Amongst the Trial Men,
And I knew that he was standing up
  In the black dock's dreadful pen,   160
And that never would I see his face
  In God's sweet world again.

Like two doomed ships that pass in storm
  We had crossed each other's way:
But we made no sign, we said no word,   165
  We had no word to say:
For we did not meet in the holy night,
  But in the shameful day.

A prison wall was round us both,
  Two outcast men we were: 170

The world had thrust us from its heart,
    And God from out His care:
And the iron gin that waits for Sin
    Had caught us in its snare.

III

In Debtors' Yard the stones are hard,   175
    And the dripping wall is high,
So it was there he took the air
    Beneath the leaden sky,
And by each side a Warder walked,
    For fear the man might die.   180

Or else he sat with those who watched
    His anguish night and day;
Who watched him when he rose to weep,
    And when he crouched to pray;
Who watched him lest himself should rob   185
    Their scaffold of its prey.

The Governor was strong upon
    The Regulations Act:
The Doctor said that Death was but
    A scientific fact: 190
And twice a day the Chaplain called,
    And left a little tract.

And twice a day he smoked his pipe,
    And drank his quart of beer:
His soul was resolute, and held   195
    No hiding-place for fear:
He often said that he was glad
    The hangman's hands were near.

But why he said so strange a thing
    No Warder dared to ask: 200
For he to whom a watcher's doom
    Is given as his task
Must set a lock upon his lips,
    And make his face a mask.

Or else he might be moved, and try   205
    To comfort or console:
And what should Human Pity do
    Pent up in Murderers' Hole?
What word of grace in such a place
    Could help a brother's soul?   210

With slouch and swing around the ring
    We trod the Fools' Parade!
We did not care: we knew we were
    The Devil's Own Brigade:
And shaven head and feet of lead   215
    Make a merry masquerade.

We tore the tarry rope to shreds
    With blunt and bleading nails;
We rubbed the doors, and scrubbed the floors,
    And cleaned the shining rails: 220
And, rank by rank, we soaped the plank,
    And clattered with the pails.

We sewed the sacks, we broke the stones,
    We turned the dusty drill:
We banged the tins, and bawled the hymns,   225
    And sweated on the mill:
But in the heart of every man
    Terror was lying still.

So still it lay that every day
    Crawled like a weed-clogged wave: 230
And we forgot the bitter lot
    That waits for fool and knave,
Till once, as we tramped in from work,
    We passed an open grave.

With yawning mouth the yellow hole   235
    Gaped for a living thing;
The very mud cried out for blood
    To the thirsty asphalte ring:
And we knew that ere one dawn grew fair
    Some prisoner had to swing.   240

Right in we went, with soul intent
    On Death and Dread and Doom:
The hangman, with his little bag,
    Went shuffling through the gloom:
And each man trembled as he crept   245
    Into his numbered tomb.

That night the empty corridors
    Were full of forms of Fear,
And up and down the iron town
    Stole feet we could not hear,   250
And through the bars that hide the stars
    White faces seemed to peer.

He lay as one who lies and dreams
   In a pleasant meadow-land,
The watchers watched him as he slept,   255
   And could not understand
How one could sleep so sweet a sleep
   With a hangman close at hand.

But there is no sleep when men must weep
   Who never yet have wept: 260
So we—the fool, the fraud, the knave—
   That endless vigil kept,
And through each brain on hands of pain
   Another's terror crept.

Alas! it is a fearful thing   265
   To feel another's guilt!
For, right within, the sword of Sin
   Pierced to its poisoned hilt,
And as molten lead were the tears we shed
   For the blood we had not spilt.   270

The Warders with their shoes of felt
   Crept by each padlocked door,
And peeped and saw, with eyes of awe,
   Grey figures on the floor,
And wondered why men knelt to pray   275
   Who never prayed before.

All through the night we knelt and prayed,
   Mad mourners of a corse!
The troubled plumes of midnight were
   The plumes upon a hearse: 280
And bitter wine upon a sponge
   Was the savour of Remorse.

The grey cock crew, the red cock crew,
   But never came the day:
And crooked shapes of Terror crouched,   285
   In the corners where we lay:
And each evil sprite that walks by night
   Before us seemed to play.

They glided past, they glided fast,
   Like travellers through a mist: 290
They mocked the moon in a rigadoon
   Of delicate turn and twist,
And with formal pace and loathsome grace
   The phantoms kept their tryst,

With mop and mow, we saw them go,   295
    Slim shadows hand in hand:
About, about, in ghostly rout
    They trod a saraband:
And the damned grotesques made arabesques,
    Like the wind upon the sand!   300

With the pirouettes of marionettes,
    They tripped on pointed tread:
But with flutes of Fear they filled the ear,
    As their grisly masque they led,
And loud they sang, and long they sang,   305
    For they sang to wake the dead.

'Oho!' they cried, 'the world is wide,
    But fettered limbs go lame!
And once, or twice, to throw the dice
    Is a gentlemanly game,   310
But he does not win who plays with Sin
    In the secret House of Shame.'

No things of air these antics were,
    That frolicked with such glee:
To men whose lives were held in gyves   315
    And whose feet might not go free,
Ah! wounds of Christ! they were living things,
    Most terrible to see.

Around, around, they waltzed and wound;
    Some wheeled in smirking pairs;   320
With the mincing step of a demirep
    Some sidled up the stairs:
And with subtle sneer, and fawning leer,
    Each helped us at our prayers.

The morning wind began to moan,   325
    But still the night went on:
Through its giant loom the web of gloom
    Crept till each thread was spun:
And, as we prayed, we grew afraid
    Of the Justice of the Sun.   330

The moaning wind went wandering round
    The weeping prison-wall:
Till like a wheel of turning steel
    We felt the minutes crawl:
O moaning wind! what had we done   335
    To have such a seneschal?

At last I saw the shadowed bars,
   Like a lattice wrought in lead,
Move right across the whitewashed wall
   That faced my three-planked bed,   340
And I knew that somewhere in the world
   God's dreadful dawn was red.

At six o'clock we cleaned our cells,
   At seven all was still,
But the sough and swing of a mighty wing   345
   The prison seemed to fill,
For the Lord of Death with icy breath
   Had entered in to kill.

He did not pass in purple pomp,
   Nor ride a moon-white steed.   350
Three yards of cord and a sliding board
   Are all the gallows' need:
So with rope of shame the Herald came
   To do the secret deed.

We were as men who through a fen   355
   Of filthy darkness grope:
We did not dare to breathe a prayer,
   Or to give our anguish scope:
Something was dead in each of us,
   And what was dead was Hope.   360

For man's grim Justice goes its way,
   And will not swerve aside:
It slays the weak, it slays the strong,
   It has a deadly stride:
With iron heel it slays the strong,   365
   The monstrous parricide!

We waited for the stroke of eight:
   Each tongue was thick with thirst:
For the stroke of eight is the stroke of Fate
   That makes a man accursed,   370
And Fate will use a running noose
   For the best man and the worst.

We had no other thing to do,
   Save to wait for the sign to come:
So, like things of stone in a valley lone,   375
   Quiet we sat and dumb:
But each man's heart beat thick and quick,
   Like a madman on a drum!

With sudden shock the prison-clock
  Smote on the shivering air,   380
And from all the gaol rose up a wail
  Of impotent despair,
Like the sound that frightened marshes hear
  From some leper in his lair.

And as one sees most fearful things   385
  In the crystal of a dream,
We saw the greasy hempen rope
  Hooked to the blackened beam,
And heard the prayer the hangman's snare
  Strangled into a scream.   390

And all the woe that moved him so
  That he gave that bitter cry,
And the wild regrets, and the bloody sweats,
  None knew so well as I:
For he who lives more lives than one   395
  More deaths than one must die.

IV

There is no chapel on the day
  On which they hang a man:
The Chaplain's heart is far too sick,
  Or his face is far too wan,   400
Or there is that written in his eyes
  Which none should look upon.

So they kept us close till nigh on noon,
  And then they rang the bell,
And the Warders with their jingling keys   405
  Opened each listening cell,
And down the iron stair we tramped,
  Each from his separate Hell.

Out into God's sweet air we went,
  But not in wonted way,   410
For this man's face was white with fear,
  And that man's face was grey,
And I never saw sad men who looked
  So wistfully at the day.

I never saw sad men who looked   415
  With such a wistful eye
Upon that little tent of blue
  We prisoners called the sky,

And at every careless cloud that passed
  In happy freedom by.   420

But there were those amongst us all
  Who walked with downcast head,
And knew that, had each got his due,
  They should have died instead:
He had but killed a thing that lived,   425
  Whilst they had killed the dead.

For he who sins a second time
  Wakes a dead soul to pain,
And draws it from its spotted shroud,
  And makes it bleed again,   430
And makes it bleed great gouts of blood,
  And makes it bleed in vain!

Like ape or clown, in monstrous garb
  With crooked arrows starred,
Silently we went round and round   435
  The slippery asphalte yard;
Silently we went round and round,
  And no man spoke a word.

Silently we went round and round,
  And through each hollow mind   440
The Memory of dreadful things
  Rushed like a dreadful wind,
And Horror stalked before each man,
  And Terror crept behind.

The Warders strutted up and down,   445
  And kept their herd of brutes,
Their uniforms were spick and span,
  And they wore their Sunday suits,
But we knew the work they had been at,
  By the quicklime on their boots.   450

For where a grave had opened wide,
  There was no grave at all:
Only a stretch of mud and sand
  By the hideous prison-wall,
And a little heap of burning lime,   455
  That the man should have his pall.

For he has a pall, this wretched man,
  Such as few men can claim:

Deep down below a prison-yard,
   Naked for greater shame,   460
He lies, with fetters on each foot,
   Wrapt in a sheet of flame!

And all the while the burning lime
   Eats flesh and bone away,
It eats the brittle bone by night,   465
   And the soft flesh by day,
It eats the flesh and bone by turns,
   But it eats the heart alway.

For three long years they will not sow
   Or root or seedling there: 470
For three long years the unblessed spot
   Will sterile be and bare,
And look upon the wondering sky
   With unreproachful stare.

They think a murderer's heart would taint   475
   Each simple seed they sow.
It is not true! God's kindly earth
   Is kindlier than men know,
And the red rose would but blow more red,
   The white rose whiter blow.   480

Out of his mouth a red, red rose!
   Out of his heart a white!
For who can say by what strange way,
   Christ brings His will to light,
Since the barren staff the pilgrim bore   485
   Bloomed in the great Pope's sight?

But neither milk-white rose nor red
   May bloom in prison-air;
The shard, the pebble, and the flint,
   Are what they give us there: 490
For flowers have been known to heal
   A common man's despair.

So never will wine-red rose or white,
   Petal by petal, fall
On that stretch of mud and sand that lies   495
   By the hideous prison-wall,
To tell the men who tramp the yard
   That God's Son died for all.

Yet though the hideous prison-wall
  Still hems him round and round,
And a spirit may not walk by night
  That is with fetters bound,
And a spirit may but weep that lies
  In such unholy ground,

                  500

He is at peace—this wretched man—
  At Peace, or will be soon:
There is no thing to make him mad,
  Nor does Terror walk at noon,
For the lampless Earth in which he lies
  Has neither Sun nor Moon.

                  505

                  510

They hanged him as a beast is hanged:
  They did not even toll
A requiem that might have brought
  Rest to his startled soul,
But hurriedly they took him out,
  And hid him in a hole.

                  515

They stripped him of his canvas clothes,
  And gave him to the flies:
They mocked the swollen purple throat,
  And the stark and staring eyes:
And with laughter loud they heaped the shroud
  In which their convict lies.

                  520

The Chaplain would not kneel to pray
  By his dishonoured grave:
Nor mark it with that blessed Cross
  That Christ for sinners gave,
Because the man was one of those
  Whom Christ came down to save.

                  525

Yet all is well; he has but passed
  To Life's appointed bourne:
And alien tears will fill for him
  Pity's long-broken urn,
For his mourners will be outcast men,
  And outcasts always mourn.

                  530

V

I know not whether Laws be right,
  Or whether Laws be wrong;
All that we know who lie in gaol
  Is that the wall is strong;

                  535

And that each day is like a year,
   A year whose days are long.   540

But this I know, that every Law
   That men have made for Man,
Since first Man took his brother's life,
   And the sad world began,
But straws the wheat and saves the chaff   545
   With a most evil fan.

This too I know—and wise it were
   If each could know the same—
That every prison that men build
   Is built with bricks of shame,   550
And bound with bars lest Christ should see
   How men their brothers maim.

With bars they blur the gracious moon,
   And blind the goodly sun:
And they do well to hide their Hell,   555
   For in it things are done
That Son of God nor son of Man
   Ever should look upon!

The vilest deeds, like poison weeds,
   Bloom well in prison-air;   560
It is only what is good in Man
   That wastes and withers there:
Pale Anguish keeps the heavy gate,
   And the Warder is Despair.

For they starve the little frightened child,   565
   Till it weeps both night and day:
And they scourge the weak, and flog the fool,
   And gibe the old and grey,
And some grow mad, and all grow bad,
   And none a word may say.   570

Each narrow cell in which we dwell
   Is a foul and dark latrine,
And the fetid breath of living Death
   Chokes up each grated screen,
And all, but Lust, is turned to dust   575
   In Humanity's machine.

The brackish water that we drink
   Creeps with a loathsome slime,

And the bitter bread they weigh in scales
   Is full of chalk and lime,
And Sleep will not lie down, but walks
   Wild-eyed, and cries to Time.   580

But though lean Hunger and green Thirst
   Like asp with adder fight,
We have little care of prison fare,
   For what chills and kills outright   585
Is that every stone one lifts by day
   Becomes one's heart by night.

With midnight always in one's heart,
   And twilight in one's cell,
We turn the crank, or tear the rope,   590
   Each in his separate Hell,
And the silence is more awful far
   Than the sound of a brazen bell.

And never a human voice comes near   595
   To speak a gentle word:
And the eye that watches through the door
   Is pitiless and hard:
And by all forgot, we rot and rot,
   With soul and body marred.   600

And thus we rust Life's iron chain
   Degraded and alone:
And some men curse, and some men weep,
   And some men make no moan:
But God's eternal Laws are kind   605
   And break the heart of stone.

And every human heart that breaks,
   In prison-cell or yard,
Is as that broken box that gave
   Its treasure to the Lord,   610
And filled the unclean leper's house
   With the scent of costliest nard.

Ah! happy they whose hearts can break
   And peace of pardon win!
How else may man make straight his plan   615
   And cleanse his soul from Sin:
How else but through a broken heart
   May Lord Christ enter in?

And he of the swollen purple throat,
   And the stark and staring eyes,   620
Waits for the holy hands that took
   The Thief to Paradise;
And a broken and a contrite heart
   The Lord will not despise.

The man in red who reads the Law   625
   Gave him three weeks of life,
Three little weeks in which to heal
   His soul of his soul's strife,
And cleanse from every blot of blood
   The hand that held the knife.   630

And with tears of blood he cleansed the hand,
   The hand that held the steel:
For only blood can wipe out blood,
   And only tears can heal:
And the crimson stain that was of Cain   635
   Became Christ's snow-white seal.

VI

In Reading gaol by Reading town
   There is a pit of shame,
And in it lies a wretched man
   Eaten by teeth of flame,   640
In a burning winding-sheet he lies,
   And his grave has got no name.

And there, till Christ call forth the dead,
   In silence let him lie:
No need to waste the foolish tear,   645
   Or heave the windy sigh:
The man had killed the thing he loved,
   And so he had to die.

And all men kill the thing they love,
   By all let this be heard,   650
Some do it with a bitter look,
   Some with a flattering word,
The coward does it with a kiss,
   The brave man with a sword!

—1898

Michael Field

(Katharine Bradley) (Edith Cooper)
1846–1914   1862–1913

It is hard to pick a pronoun for "Michael Field": he? she? they? This was the pen name of Katharine Bradley and Edith Cooper, lovers, cowriters, and aunt and niece. They collaborated on twenty-seven poetic dramas and eight volumes of poetry, including *Long Ago* (1889), translating and completing Sappho's fragments; *Sight and Song* (1892), offering poetic analogues for paintings; and *Whym Chow: Flames of Love* (1906), celebrating animal drives. Their work is remarkable for its celebration of female sexuality, all the more unusual as cowritten love poems addressed to each other. "Come, Gorgo, put the rug in place" (*Long Ago*) daringly retains Sappho's female subject to emphasize the poem's lesbian erotic charge. "La Gioconda" and "A Pen-Drawing of Leda" were published in *Sight and Song*, aiming to "translate into verse what the lines and colours of certain chosen pictures sing in themselves."

Come, Gorgo, put the rug in place

'Αλλὰ, μὴ μεγαλύνεο δακτυλίω πέρι[1]

Come, Gorgo, put the rug in place,
  And passionate recline;
I love to see thee in thy grace,
  Dark, virulent, divine.

But wherefore thus thy proud eyes fix   5
  Upon a jewelled band?
Art thou so glad the sardonyx[2]
  Becomes thy shapely hand?

Bethink thee! 'Tis for such as thou
  Zeus leaves his lofty seat;   10
'Tis at thy beauty's bidding how
  Man's mortal life shall fleet;
Those fairest hands—dost thou forget
  Their power to thrill and cling?
O foolish woman, dost thou set   15
  Thy pride upon a ring?

—1889

---

1. Foolish woman, do not pride yourself on a ring.
2. A gemstone.

I Love You With My Life

I love you with my life—'tis so I love you;
    I give you as a ring
The cycle of my days till death:
    I worship with the breath
That keeps me in the world with you and spring: 5
And God may dwell behind, but not above you.

Mine, in the dark, before the world's beginning:
    The claim of every sense,
    Secret and source of every need;
    The goal to which I speed,   10
And at my heart a vigour more immense
Than will itself to urge me to its winning.

—1892

The Mummy Invokes his Soul

Down to me quickly, down! I am such dust,
Baked, pressed together; let my flesh be fanned
With thy fresh breath; come from thy reedy land
Voiceful with birds; divert me, for I lust
To break, to crumble—prick with pores this crust!—   5
And fall apart, delicious, loosening sand.
Oh, joy, I feel thy breath, I feel thy hand
That searches for my heart, and trembles just
Where once it beat. How light thy touch, thy frame!
Surely thou perchest on the summer trees . . .   10
And the garden that we loved? Soul, take thine ease,
I am content, so thou enjoy the same
Sweet terraces and founts, content, for thee,
To burn in this immense torpidity.

—1892

Unbosoming

The love that breeds
    In my heart for thee!
As the iris is full, brimful of seeds,
And all that it flowered for among the reeds
Is packed in a thousand vermilion-beads   5
That push, and riot, and squeeze, and clip,
Till they burst the sides of the silver scrip,
And at last we see

What the bloom, with its tremulous, bowery fold
Of zephyr-petal at heart did hold: 10
So my breast is rent
With the burthen and strain of its great content;
For the summer of fragrance and sighs is dead,
The harvest-secret is burning red,
And I would give thee, after my kind,   15
The final issues of heart and mind.

—1892

La Gioconda[1]

Leonardo Da Vinci

THE LOUVRE

Historic, side-long, implicating eyes;
A smile of velvet's lustre on the cheek;
Calm lips the smile leads upward; hand that lies
Glowing and soft, the patience in its rest
Of cruelty that waits and doth not seek   5
For prey; a dusky forehead and a breast
Where twilight touches ripeness amorously:
Behind her, crystal rocks, a sea and skies
Of evanescent blue on cloud and creek;
Landscape that shines suppressive of its zest   10
For those vicissitudes by which men die.

—1892

A Pen-Drawing of Leda[1]

Sodoma[2]

THE GRAND DUKE'S PALACE AT WEIMAR[3]

'Tis Leda lovely, wild and free,
Drawing her gracious Swan down through the grass to see
        Certain round eggs without a speck:
One hand plunged in the reeds and one dinting the downy neck,
        Although his hectoring bill   5
        Gapes toward her tresses,
She draws the fondled creature to her will.

---

1. Compare to Pater's famous meditation on the Mona Lisa ("La Gioconda"; see p. 9).

---

1. In the form of a swan, Zeus raped Leda, who then gave birth to Clytemnestra and Helen of Troy.
2. Nickname of Italian Renaissance painter Giovanni Antonio Bazzi.
3. Site of this painting.

She joys to bend in the live light
Her glistening body toward her love, how much more bright!
    Though on her breast the sunshine lies   10
And spreads its affluence on the wide curves of her waist and thighs,
    To her meek, smitten gaze
    Where her hand presses
The Swan's white neck sink Heaven's concentred rays.

—1892

Amy Levy
1861–1889

The short, tumultuous, passionate, tragic life of Amy Levy almost overshadows her writing. As a Jewish lesbian, she felt doubly marginalized, a sense of isolation that only deepened as she lost her hearing. Her novel *Reuben Sachs* (1888) shows her profound ambivalence about London's Jewish community, while her journalism and poetry reveal passionately conflicted feelings, particularly about love. Levy killed herself at the age of 27. Her poetry articulates unusual subjects: sexual desire for women, the beauty of London, the pleasure of female independence, and anger at women's suppression. "To Vernon Lee" is a love poem addressed to the prominent writer who never reciprocated Levy's affection. "Xantippe," one of Levy's earliest poems, uses a dramatic monologue to present Socrates's wife as a feminist heroine. For more information about Levy, see p. 248.

To Vernon Lee

On Bellosguardo,[1] when the year was young,
We wandered, seeking for the daffodil
And dark anemone, whose purples fill
The peasant's plot, between the corn-shoots sprung.

Over the grey, low wall the olive flung   5
Her deeper greyness; far off, hill on hill
Sloped to the sky, which, pearly-pale and still,
Above the large and luminous landscape hung.

A snowy blackthorn flowered beyond my reach;
You broke a branch and gave it to me there;   10
I found for you a scarlet blossom rare.

---

1. A hill above Florence, where Vernon Lee lived.

Thereby ran on of Art and Life our speech;
And of the gifts the gods had given to each—
Hope unto you, and unto me Despair.

—1889

Xantippe

(*A Fragment*)

What, have I waked again? I never thought
To see the rosy dawn, or ev'n this grey,
Dull, solemn stillness, ere the dawn has come.
The lamp burns low; low burns the lamp of life:
The still morn stays expectant, and my soul,   5
All weighted with a passive wonderment,
Waiteth and watcheth, waiteth for the dawn.
Come hither, maids; too soundly have ye slept
That should have watched me; nay, I would not chide—
Oft have I chidden, yet I would not chide   10
In this last hour;—now all should be at peace,
I have been dreaming in a troubled sleep
Of weary days I thought not to recall;
Of stormy days, whose storms are hushed long since;
Of gladsome days, of sunny days; alas   15
In dreaming, all their sunshine seem'd so sad,
As though the current of the dark To-Be
Had flow'd, prophetic, through the happy hours.
And yet, full well, I know it was not thus;
I mind me sweetly of the summer days,   20
When, leaning from the lattice, I have caught
The fair, far glimpses of a shining sea;
And, nearer, of tall ships which thronged the bay,
And stood out blackly from a tender sky
All flecked with sulphur, azure, and bright gold;   25
And in the still, clear air have heard the hum
Of distant voices; and me thinks there rose
No darker fount to mar or stain the joy
Which sprang ecstatic in my maiden breast
Than just those vague desires, those hopes and fears,   30
Those eager longings, strong, though undefined,
Whose very sadness makes them seem so sweet.
What cared I for the merry mockeries
Of other maidens sitting at the loom?
Or for sharp voices, bidding me return   35
To maiden labour? Were we not apart—
I and my high thoughts, and my golden dreams,

My soul which yearned for knowledge, for a tongue
That should proclaim the stately mysteries
Of this fair world, and of the holy gods?   40
Then followed days of sadness, as I grew
To learn my woman-mind had gone astray,
And I was sinning in those very thoughts—
For maidens, mark, such are not woman's thoughts—
(And yet, 'tis strange, the gods who fashion us   45
Have given us such promptings). . . .
                              Fled the years,
Till seventeen had found me tall and strong,
And fairer, runs it, than Athenian maids
Are wont to seem; I had not learnt it well—
My lesson of dumb patience—and I stood   50
At Life's great threshold with a beating heart,
And soul resolved to conquer and attain. . . .
Once, walking 'thwart the crowded market-place,
With other maidens, bearing in the twigs
White doves for Aphrodite's sacrifice,   55
I saw him, all ungainly and uncouth,
Yet many gathered round to hear his words,
Tall youths and stranger-maidens—Sokrates—
I saw his face and marked it, half with awe,
Half with a quick repulsion at the shape. . . .   60
The richest gem lies hidden furthest down,
And is the dearer for the weary search;
We grasp the shining shells which strew the shore,
Yet swift we fling them from us; but the gem
We keep for aye and cherish. So a soul,   65
Found after weary searching in the flesh
Which half repelled our senses, is more dear,
For that same seeking, than the sunny mind
Which lavish Nature marks with thousand hints
Upon a brow of beauty. We are prone   70
To overweigh such subtle hints, then deem,
In after disappointment, we are fooled. . . .
And when, at length, my father told me all,
That I should wed me with great Sokrates,
I, foolish, wept to see at once cast down   75
The maiden image of a future love,
Where perfect body matched the perfect soul.
But slowly, softly did I cease to weep;
Slowly I 'gan to mark the magic flash
Leap to the eyes, to watch the sudden smile   80
Break round the mouth, and linger in the eyes;
To listen for the voice's lightest tone—
Great voice, whose cunning modulations seemed

Like to the notes of some sweet instrument.
So did I reach and strain, until at last   85
I caught the soul athwart the grosser flesh.
Again of thee, sweet Hope, my spirit dreamed!
I, guided by his wisdom and his love,
Led by his words, and counselled by his care,
Should lift the shrouding veil from things which be,   90
And at the flowing fountain of his soul
Refresh my thirsting spirit. . . .
                                   And indeed,
In those long days which followed that strange day
When rites and song, and sacrifice and flow'rs,
Proclaimed that we were wedded, did I learn,   95
In sooth, a-many lessons; bitter ones
Which sorrow taught me, and not love inspired,
Which deeper knowledge of my kind impressed
With dark insistence on reluctant brain;—
But that great wisdom, deeper, which dispels   100
Narrowed conclusions of a half-grown mind,
And sees athwart the littleness of life
Nature's divineness and her harmony,
Was never poor Xantippe's. . . .
                                   I would pause
And would recall no more, no more of life,   105
Than just the incomplete, imperfect dream
Of early summers, with their light and shade,
Their blossom-hopes, whose fruit was never ripe;
But something strong within me, some sad chord
Which loudly echoes to the later life,   110
Me to unfold the after-misery
Urges, with plaintive wailing in my heart.
Yet, maidens, mark; I would not that ye thought
I blame my lord departed, for he meant
No evil, so I take it, to his wife.   115
'Twas only that the high philosopher,
Pregnant with noble theories and great thoughts,
Deigned not to stoop to touch so slight a thing
As the fine fabric of a woman's brain—
So subtle as a passionate woman's soul.   120
I think, if he had stooped a little, and cared,
I might have risen nearer to his height,
And not lain shattered, neither fit for use
As goodly household vessel, nor for that
Far finer thing which I had hoped to be. . . .   125
Death, holding high his retrospective lamp,
Shows me those first, far years of wedded life,
Ere I had learnt to grasp the barren shape

Of what the Fates had destined for my life
Then, as all youthful spirits are, was I   130
Wholly incredulous that Nature meant
So little, who had promised me so much.
At first I fought my fate with gentle words,
With high endeavours after greater things;
Striving to win the soul of Sokrates,   135
Like some slight bird, who sings her burning love
To human master, till at length she finds
Her tender language wholly misconceived,
And that same hand whose kind caress she sought,
With fingers flippant flings the careless corn. . . .   140
I do remember how, one summer's eve,
He, seated in an arbour's leafy shade,
Had bade me bring fresh wine-skins. . . .
                                        As I stood
Ling'ring upon the threshold, half concealed
By tender foliage, and my spirit light   145
With draughts of sunny weather, did I mark
An instant the gay group before mine eyes.
Deepest in shade, and facing where I stood,
Sat Plato, with his calm face and low brows
Which met above the narrow Grecian eyes,   150
The pale, thin lips just parted to the smile,
Which dimpled that smooth olive of his cheek.
His head a little bent, sat Sokrates,
With one swart finger raised admonishing,
And on the air were borne his changing tones.   155
Low lounging at his feet, one fair arm thrown
Around his knee (the other, high in air
Brandish'd a brazen amphor, which yet rained
Bright drops of ruby on the golden locks
And temples with their fillets of the vine),   160
Lay Alkibiades the beautiful.[1]
And thus, with solemn tone, spake Sokrates:
'This fair Aspasia, which our Perikles[2]
Hath brought from realms afar, and set on high
In our Athenian city, hath a mind,   165
I doubt not, of a strength beyond her race;
And makes employ of it, beyond the way
Of women nobly gifted: woman's frail—
Her body rarely stands the test of soul;
She grows intoxicate with knowledge; throws   170
The laws of custom, order, 'neath her feet,

---

1. A favorite pupil of Socrates and a ward of Pericles.
2. An Athenian leader; his mistress Aspasia was a philosophically astute woman whom Socrates admired.

Feasting at life's great banquet with wide throat.'
Then sudden, stepping from my leafy screen,
Holding the swelling wine-skin o'er my head,
With breast that heaved, and eyes and cheeks aflame,   175
Lit by a fury and a thought, I spake:
'By all great powers around us! can it be
That we poor women are empirical?
That gods who fashioned us did strive to make
Beings too fine, too subtly delicate,   180
With sense that thrilled response to ev'ry touch
Of nature's, and their task is not complete?
That they have sent their half-completed work
To bleed and quiver here upon the earth?
To bleed and quiver, and to weep and weep,   185
To beat its soul against the marble walls
Of men's cold hearts, and then at last to sin!'
I ceased, the first hot passion stayed and stemmed
And frighted by the silence: I could see,
Framed by the arbour foliage, which the sun   190
In setting softly gilded with rich gold,
Those upturned faces, and those placid limbs;
Saw Plato's narrow eyes and niggard mouth,
Which half did smile and half did criticise,
One hand held up, the shapely fingers framed   195
To gesture of entreaty—'Hush, I pray,
Do not disturb her; let us hear the rest;
Follow her mood, for here's another phase
Of your black-browed Xantippe. . . .'
                              Then I saw
Young Alkibiades, with laughing lips   200
And half-shut eyes, contemptuous shrugging up
Soft, snowy shoulders, till he brought the gold
Of flowing ringlets round about his breasts.
But Sokrates, all slow and solemnly,
Raised, calm, his face to mine, and sudden spake: 205
'I thank thee for the wisdom which thy lips
Have thus let fall among us: prythee tell
From what high source, from what philosophies
Didst cull the sapient notion of thy words?'
Then stood I straight and silent for a breath,   210
Dumb, crushed with all that weight of cold contempt;
But swiftly in my bosom there uprose
A sudden flame, a merciful fury sent
To save me; with both angry hands I flung
The skin upon the marble, where it lay   215
Spouting red rills and fountains on the white;
Then, all unheeding faces, voices, eyes,

I fled across the threshold, hair unbound—
White garment stained to redness—beating heart
Flooded with all the flowing tide of hopes   220
Which once had gushed out golden, now sent back
Swift to their sources, never more to rise. . . .
I think I could have borne the weary life,
The narrow life within the narrow walls,
If he had loved me; but he kept his love   225
For this Athenian city and her sons;
And, haply, for some stranger-woman, bold
With freedom, thought, and glib philosophy. . . .
Ah me! the long, long weeping through the nights,
The weary watching for the pale-eyed dawn   230
Which only brought fresh grieving: then I grew
Fiercer, and cursed from out my inmost heart
The Fates which marked me an Athenian maid.
Then faded that vain fury; hope died out;
A huge despair was stealing on my soul,   235
A sort of fierce acceptance of my fate,—
He wished a household vessel—well 'twas good,
For he should have it! He should have no more
The yearning treasure of a woman's love,
But just the baser treasure which he sought.   240
I called my maidens, ordered out the loom,
And spun unceasing from the morn till eve;
Watching all keenly over warp and woof,
Weighing the white wool with a jealous hand.
I spun until, methinks, I spun away   245
The soul from out my body, the high thoughts
From out my spirit; till at last I grew
As ye have known me,—eye exact to mark
The texture of the spinning; ear all keen
For aimless talking when the moon is up,   250
And ye should be a-sleeping; tongue to cut
With quick incision, 'thwart the merry words
Of idle maidens. . . .
                         Only yesterday
My hands did cease from spinning; I have wrought
My dreary duties, patient till the last.   255
The gods reward me! Nay, I will not tell
The after years of sorrow; wretched strife
With grimmest foes—sad Want and Poverty;—
Nor yet the time of horror, when they bore
My husband from the threshold; nay, nor when   260
The subtle weed had wrought its deadly work.
Alas! alas! I was not there to soothe
The last great moment; never any thought

Of her that loved him—save at least the charge,
All earthly, that her body should not starve. . . .   265
You weep, you weep; I would not that ye wept;
Such tears are idle; with the young, such grief
Soon grows to gratulation, as, 'her love
Was withered by misfortune; mine shall grow
All nurtured by the loving,' or, 'her life   270
Was wrecked and shattered—mine shall smoothly sail.'
Enough, enough. In vain, in vain, in vain!
The gods forgive me! Sorely have I sinned
In all my life. A fairer fate befall
You all that stand there. . . .
                Ha! the dawn has come;   275
I see a rosy glimmer—nay! it grows dark;
Why stand ye so in silence? throw it wide,
The casement, quick; why tarry?—give me air—
O fling it wide, I say, and give me light!

—1881

Alice Meynell
1847–1922

Alice Meynell's poetry is as disciplined and complex as her prose. As her admirer Vita Sackville-West wrote, "her Thought was stone: O frugal poet, hard / Cut the spare chisel on each separate gem— / Jaspar and onyx, emerald and sard: / Craft and integrity have fashioned them." The selections here demonstrate Meynell's interest in paradox; renouncement is love ("Renouncement") and refusal is honor ("Why Wilt Thou Chide?"). Other poems show how Meynell challenged conventional pieties about women. "Cradle-Song at Twilight" is no lullaby, while "Maternity" expresses maternal love only in the chilling context of loss. "Easter Night" shows another side of Meynell, her ardent Catholicism. For more information about Meynell, see pp. 54 and 236.

Renouncement[1]

I must not think of thee; and, tired yet strong,
    I shun the thought that lurks in all delight—
  The thought of thee—and in the blue Heaven's height,
And in the sweetest passage of a song.

---

1. This Petrarchan sonnet (a form associated with love poems) is supposedly addressed to Father Dignam, a priest with whom Meynell had fallen in love.

O just beyond the fairest thoughts that throng   5
   This breast, the thought of thee waits, hidden yet bright;
   But it must never, never come in sight;
I must stop short of thee the whole day long.

But when sleep comes to close each difficult day,
   When night gives pause to the long watch I keep,   10
     And all my bonds I needs must loose apart,

Must doff my will as raiment laid away,—
   With the first dream that comes with the first sleep
     I run, I run, I am gathered to thy heart.

—1882

Cradle-Song at Twilight

The child not yet is lulled to rest.
   Too young a nurse, the slender Night
So laxly holds him to her breast
   That throbs with flight.

He plays with her, and will not sleep.   5
   For other playfellows she sighs;
An unmaternal fondness keep
   Her alien eyes.

—1895

Why Wilt Thou Chide?

Why wilt thou chide,
   Who hast attained to be denied?[1]
O learn, above
All price is my refusal, Love.
   My sacred Nay   5
Was never cheapened by the way.
Thy single sorrow crowns thee lord
Of an unpurchasable word.

   O strong, O pure:
As Yea makes happier loves secure,   10
   I vow thee this
Unique rejection of a kiss.

---

1. Probably addressed to one of the eminent writers who adored her: Coventry Patmore, George Meredith, Francis Thompson.

I guard for thee
This jealous sad monopoly.
I seal this honour thine; none dare   15
Hope for a part in thy despair.

—1896

Maternity

One wept whose only child was dead,
    New-born, ten years ago.
'Weep not; he is in bliss,' they said.
    She answered, 'Even so,

'Ten years ago was born in pain   5
    A child, not now forlorn.
But oh, ten years ago, in vain,
    A mother, a mother was born.'

—1913

Easter Night

All night had shout of men and cry
        Of woeful women filled His way;
Until that noon of sombre sky
        On Friday, clamour and display
Smote Him; no solitude had He,   5
No silence, since Gethsemane.[1]

Public was Death; but Power, but Might,
        But Life again, but Victory,
Were hushed within the dead of night,
        The shutter'd dark, the secrecy.   10
And all alone, alone, alone
He rose again behind the stone.

—1915

---

1. The garden where Jesus suffered through the night before Judas betrayed him.

Graham R. Tomson
1860–1911

The life of poet "Graham R. Tomson" (Rosamund Marriott Watson) was so romantically adventurous it nearly derailed her literary reputation. First married to George Armytage, she left him to marry Arthur Graham Tomson, then left Tomson for H. B. Marriott Watson, a sequence of divorces and cohabitations that scandalized her contemporaries (and produced frequent name changes that confounded her readers). Her ballads adapt traditional, folk-tale elements to tell terrifying stories of dangerous love, grief, and loss; in her journalism, she wittily elaborates aesthetic theories about dress, home decoration, and gardening into complexly layered reviews. Her love life demanded courage but produced the pervasive sadness we can see in her poems, for in the nineteenth century an adulterous wife could not have custody of her children. Thus when the poet left Armytage she had to abandon her two daughters, and when she left Tomson she lost her son. "Aubade" is a celebration of dawning love, while "Ballad of the Bird-Bride" imagines a lost, eerie, domestic idyll. For more about Tomson, see p. 249

Aubade[1]

The lights are out in the street, and a cool wind swings
Loose poplar plumes on the sky;
Deep in the gloom of the garden the first bird sings:
Curt, hurried steps go by
Loud in the hush of the dawn past the linden screen,   5
Lost in a jar and a rattle of wheels unseen
Beyond on the wide highway:—
Night lingers dusky and dim in the pear-tree boughs,
Hangs in the hollows of leaves, though the thrushes rouse,
And the glimmering lawn grows grey.   10
Yours, my heart knoweth, yours only, the jewelled gloom,
Splendours of opal and amber, the scent, the bloom,
Yours all, and your own demesne[2]—
Scent of the dark, of the dawning, of leaves and dew;
Nothing that was but hath changed—'tis a world made new—   15
A lost world risen again.

The lamps are out in the street, and the air grows bright—
Come—lest the miracle fade in the broad, bare light,
The new world wither away:
Clear is your voice in my heart, and you call me—whence?   20
Come—for I listen, I wait,—bid me rise, go hence,
Or ever the dawn turn day.

—1891

---

1. A poem saluting the dawn, often after a night of love.
2. Domain.

Ballad of the Bird-Bride

(Eskimo)

They never come back, though I loved them well;
   I watch the South in vain;
The snow-bound skies are blear and grey,
Waste and wide is the wild gull's way,
   And she comes never again.   5

Years agone, on the flat white strand,
   I won my sweet sea-girl:
Wrapped in my coat of the snow-white fur,
I watched the wild birds settle and stir,
   The grey gulls gather and whirl.   10

One, the greatest of all the flock,
   Perched on an ice-floe bare,
Called and cried as her heart were broke,
And straight they were changed, that fleet bird-folk,
   To women young and fair.   15

Swift I sprang from my hiding-place
   And held the fairest fast;
I held her fast, the sweet, strange thing:
Her comrades skirled, but they all took wing,
   And smote me as they passed.   20

I bore her safe to my warm snow house;
   Full sweetly there she smiled;
And yet, whenever the shrill winds blew,
She would beat her long white arms anew,
   And her eyes glanced quick and wild.   25

But I took her to wife, and clothed her warm
   With skins of the gleaming seal;
Her wandering glances sank to rest
When she held a babe to her fair, warm breast,
   And she loved me dear and leal.   30

Together we tracked the fox and the seal,
   And at her behest I swore
That bird and beast my bow might slay
For meat and for raiment, day by day,
   But never a grey gull more.   35

A weariful watch I keep for aye
   'Mid the snow and the changeless frost:

Woe is me for my broken word!
Woe, woe's me for my bonny bird,
   My bird and the love-time lost!   40

Have ye forgotten the old keen life?
   The hut with the skin-strewn floor?
O winged white wife, and children three,
Is there no room left in your hearts for me,
   Or our home on the low sea-shore?   45

Once the quarry was scarce and shy,
   Sharp hunger gnawed us sore,
My spoken oath was clean forgot,
My bow twanged thrice with a swift, straight shot,
   And slew me sea-gulls four.   50

The sun hung red on the sky's dull breast,
   The snow was wet and red;
Her voice shrilled out in a woeful cry,
She beat her long white arms on high,
   'The hour is here,' she said.   55

She beat her arms, and she cried full fain
   As she swayed and wavered there.
'Fetch me the feathers, my children three,
Feathers and plumes for you and me,
   Bonny grey wings to wear!'   60

They ran to her side, our children three,
   With the plumage black and grey;
Then she bent her down and drew them near,
She laid the plumes on our children dear,
   'Mid the snow and the salt sea-spray.   65

'Babes of mine, of the wild wind's kin,
   Feather ye quick, nor stay.
Oh, oho! the wild winds blow!
Babes of mine, it is time to go:
   Up, dear hearts, and away!'   70

And lo! the grey plumes covered them all,
   Shoulder and breast and brow.
I felt the wind of their whirling flight:
Was it sea or sky? was it day or night?
   It is always night-time now.   75

Dear, will you never relent, come back?
   I loved you long and true.
O winged white wife, and our children three,

Of the wild wind's kin though ye surely be,
   Are ye not of my kin too?   80

Ay, ye once were mine, and, till I forget,
   Ye are mine forever and aye,
Mine, wherever your wild wings go,
While shrill winds whistle across the snow
   And the skies are blear and grey.   85

                                              —1889

Olive Custance
1874–1944

It is hard to imagine a more aesthetic poet than Olive Custance, who wrote intensely descriptive, highly mannered, and sexually charged verse, some published in *The Yellow Book*. Her first book was *Opals* (1897), expressing a typically aesthetic love of gems (and the sort of title Max Beerbohm parodied with "Fungoids" ["Enoch Soames," 128]). She befriended Aubrey Beardsley, and in 1902 she married Oscar Wilde's former lover Lord Alfred Douglas. She had also fallen in love with decadent poet John Gray, the author of the famously precious *Silverpoints*, and Natalie Clifford Barney, the leader of a prominent lesbian coterie in Paris and the probable subject of "Doubts" and "The White Witch."

Doubts

A web of gold is the western sky!
   Golden strands of the sun's bright hair
   Caught in the grey clouds everywhere!
Or the tangled skeins of day's broidery?

. . . And now it is that the twilight sings;   5
   Twilight . . . whose voice is full of tears,
   Trailing athwart our hopes and fears
The drooping bows of her dusky wings!

In the fading light we dream of death
   And closer cling in a long embrace.   10
   O! pure pale girl with the passionate face
Life strips us naked . . . but leaves us breath.

But when our bodies lie strange and still
   They will bury us swiftly out of sight,
   Shut us away from the warm sunlight . . .   15
How dark the darkness will be and chill!

But ah! I forgot, we shall not feel
    Folded safe in our last deep sleep
    Never again to kiss and weep—
While our lips' rose colour the roses steal.   20

Dear, never again to know regret,
    With its iron hand laid on the leaping heart
    Its fingers thrust where the wide wounds smart,
The wounds of memory bleeding yet. . . .

Ah! but the kisses—the tears—the fleet   25
    Delights—slow sorrows, are *life*—in vain
    To praise white peace when the wine of pain,
Fate's purple wine, is so fiery sweet!

Think you we should be glad to die
    Now . . . when the stars are coming soon   30
    And the daylight pales, and the primrose moon
Is a stemless flower in a silver sky. . . .

              —1897

The White Witch

Her body is a dancing joy, a delicate delight,
Her hair a silver glamour in a net of golden light.

Her face is like the faces that a dreamer sometimes meets,
A face that Leonardo[1] would have followed through the streets.

Her eyelids are like clouds that spread white wings across blue skies,   5
Like shadows in still water are the sorrows in her eyes.

How flower-like are the smiling lips so many have desired,
Curled lips that love's long kisses have left a little tired.

              —1902

---

1. Leonardo da Vinci (1452–1519), Renaissance painter famous for depicting mystical and delicate female expressions.

The Art of Conversation: Aesthetic Fiction and Drama

W. S. Gilbert
1836–1911

The irascible, bombastic, brilliant lyricist William Schwenk Gilbert found a perfect match in the composer Arthur Sullivan. Together, they wrote fourteen comic operas between 1871 and 1896, performed at the Savoy Theatre by their own company, overseen by Richard D'Oyly Carte. These immensely popular pieces parody British institutions (the navy, the law) and skewer supposedly sacred emotions (sentimental motherhood, British patriotism). In *The Pirates of Penzance*, *H.M.S. Pinafore*, *The Mikado*, and *The Gondoliers*, characters eagerly endorse official emotions or identities to absurd extremes while a respectful chorus echoes their key words. *Patience* (1881) mocked the aesthetic movement, with excessively affected poets Bunthorne and Grosvenor (based on Oscar Wilde and James McNeill Whistler). In "If You're Anxious for to Shine," Bunthorne confesses he is pretending to be aesthetic to attract women. This suspicion also animates George du Maurier's anti-aesthetic *Punch* cartoons and shows that before Wilde's trial, the male aesthetes' effeminate luxury was read as an aggressive heterosexual ploy rather than a sign of same-sex desire.

If You're Anxious for to Shine

Am I alone,
   And unobserved? I am!
Then let me own
   I'm an aesthetic sham!
This air severe   5
   Is but a mere
         Veneer!
This cynic smile
   Is but a wile
         Of guile!   10
This costume chaste
   Is but good taste
         Misplaced!
Let me confess!
A languid love for lilies does *not* blight me!   15
Lank limbs and haggard cheeks do *not* delight me!
I do *not* care for dirty greens
   By any means.
I do *not* long for all one sees

That's Japanese.[1]   20
I am *not* fond of uttering platitudes
    In stained-glass attitudes.
In short, my mediaevalism's[2] affectation,
Born of a morbid love of admiration!

Song

If you're anxious for to shine in the high aesthetic line as a man of culture rare,   25
You must get up all the germs of the transcendental[3] terms, and plant them
    everywhere.
You must lie upon the daisies and discourse in novel phrases of your complicated
    state of mind,
The meaning doesn't matter if it's only idle chatter of a transcendental kind.
            And every one will say,
            As you walk your mystic way,   30
"If this young man expresses himself in terms too deep for *me*,
Why, what a very singularly deep young man this deep young man must be!"

Be eloquent in praise of the very dull old days which have long since passed away,
And convince 'em, if you can, that the reign of good Queen Anne[4] was Culture's
    palmiest day.
Of course you will pooh-pooh whatever's fresh and new, and declare it's crude
    and mean,   35
For Art stopped short in the cultivated court of the Empress Josephine.[5]
            And every one will say,
            As you walk your mystic way,
"If that's not good enough for him which is good enough for *me*,
Why, what a very cultivated kind of youth this kind of youth must be!"   40

Then a sentimental passion of a vegetable fashion must excite your languid spleen,
An attachment *à la* Plato for a bashful young potato, or a not-too-French French
    bean![6]
Though the Philistines[7] may jostle, you will rank as an apostle in the high aesthetic
    band,

---

1. Aesthetic mania for Japanese art, associated with Whistler.
2. Many aesthetes yearned for a medieval model of artistic and social community.
3. Transcendentalism was an American philosophical movement, a philosophy of material nature infused with spiritual life. *The Germ* (meaning "seed") was the Pre-Raphaelite journal that aimed to start a new growth of spiritual art in England.
4. The aesthetes adored the "Queen Anne style" (derived from the early-18th-c. monarch's reign) for its quaint ornamentation and quirky architecture.
5. Wife of Napoleon Bonaparte, known for her love of highly ornamented artifacts.
6. Jokes about purity. Wilde called lilies and sunflowers the most perfect models of art, but Gilbert extends this "vegetable passion" to less romantic plants. Bunthorne has a Platonic (i.e., nonsexual) relationship with a potato, or admiration of a bean that is "not-too-French" (i.e., not too sexually liberated).
7. Middle-class vulgarians.

THE SIX-MARK TEA-POT.

Æsthetic Bridegroom. "It is quite consummate, is it not?"
Intense Bride. "It is, indeed! Oh, Algernon, let us live up to it!"

George du Maurier, *The Six-Mark Teapot* (1880).
"*Aesthetic Bridegroom:* 'It is quite consummate, is it not?'
Intense Bride: 'It is, indeed! Oh, Algernon, let us live up to it!'"

If you walk down Piccadilly[8] with a poppy or a lily in your mediaeval hand.
And every one will say,   45
As you walk your flowery way,
"If he's content with a vegetable love which would certainly not suit *me*,
Why, what a most particularly pure young man this pure young man must be!"

—1881

Max Beerbohm
1872–1956

In "Enoch Soames," Max Beerbohm himself figures as a character, a naïve young observer recording the oddities of his elders. This playful story captures the ultra-aesthetic milieu of the 1890s perfectly, for every character mentioned in the story really existed except (presumably) Enoch Soames. For more information about Beerbohm, see p. 57.

Enoch Soames

When a book about the literature of the eighteen-nineties was given by Mr. Holbrook Jackson[1] to the world, I looked eagerly in the index for SOAMES, ENOCH. I had feared he would not be there. He was not there. But everybody else was. Many writers whom I had quite forgotten, or remembered but faintly, lived again for me, they and their work, in Mr. Holbrook Jackson's pages. The book was as thorough as it was brilliantly written. And thus the omission found by me was an all the deadlier record of poor Soames' failure to impress himself on his decade.

I daresay I am the only person who noticed the omission. Soames had failed so piteously as all that! Nor is there a counterpoise in the thought that if he had had some measure of success he might have passed, like those others, out of my mind, to return only at the historian's beck. It is true that had his gifts, such as they were, been acknowledged in his life-time, he would never have made the bargain I saw him make—that strange bargain whose results have kept him always in the foreground of my memory. But it is from those very results that the full piteousness of him glares out.

Not my compassion, however, impels me to write of him. For his sake, poor fellow, I should be inclined to keep my pen out of the ink. It is ill to deride the dead. And how can I write about Enoch Soames without making him ridiculous? Or rather, how am I to hush up the horrid fact that he *was* ridiculous? I shall not be able to do

---

8. Fashionable, bustling street in London. When asked how he could have walked down Piccadilly carrying a flower, Wilde responded, "to have done it was nothing, but to make people think one had done it was a triumph."

---

1. Critic and historian of the 1890s (1874–1948).

that. Yet, sooner or later, write about him I must. You will see, in due course, that I have no option. And I may as well get the thing done now.

In the Summer Term of '93 a bolt from the blue flashed down on Oxford. It drove deep, it hurtlingly embedded itself in the soil. Dons and undergraduates stood around, rather pale, discussing nothing but it. Whence came it, this meteorite? From Paris. Its name? Will Rothenstein.[2] Its aim? To do a series of twenty-four portraits in lithograph. These were to be published from the Bodley Head, London.[3] The matter was urgent. Already the Warden of A, and the Master of B, and the Regius Professor of C, had meekly "sat."[4] Dignified and doddering old men, who had never consented to sit to any one, could not withstand this dynamic little stranger. He did not sue: he invited; he did not invite: he commanded. He was twenty-one years old. He wore spectacles that flashed more than any other pair ever seen. He was a wit. He was brimful of ideas. He knew Whistler. He knew Edmond de Goncourt.[5] He knew every one in Paris. He knew them all by heart. He was Paris in Oxford. It was whispered that, so soon as he had polished off his selection of dons, he was going to include a few undergraduates. It was a proud day for me when I—I—was included. I liked Rothenstein not less than I feared him; and there arose between us a friendship that has grown ever warmer, and been more and more valued by me, with every passing year.

At the end of Term he settled in—or rather, meteoritically into—London. It was to him I owed my first knowledge of that forever enchanting little world-in-itself, Chelsea, and my first acquaintance with Walter Sickert[6] and other august elders who dwelt there. It was Rothenstein that took me to see, in Cambridge Street, Pimlico, a young man whose drawings were already famous among the few—Aubrey Beardsley, by name.[7] With Rothenstein I paid my first visit to the Bodley Head. By him I was inducted into another haunt of intellect and daring, the domino room of the Café Royal.

There, on that October evening—there, in that exuberant vista of gilding and crimson velvet set amidst all those opposing mirrors and upholding caryatids, with fumes of tobacco ever rising to the painted and pagan ceiling, and with the hum of presumably cynical conversation broken into so sharply now and again by the clatter of dominoes shuffled on marble tables, I drew a deep breath, and "This indeed," said I to myself, "is life!"

It was the hour before dinner. We drank vermouth. Those who knew Rothenstein were pointing him out to those who knew him only by name. Men were constantly coming in through the swing-doors and wandering slowly up and down in search of vacant tables, or of tables occupied by friends. One of these rovers interested me because I was sure he wanted to catch Rothenstein's eye. He had twice

---

2. Will Rothenstein (1872–1945) really did make dashing sketches of Oxford luminaries.
3. The major publisher of the aesthetic movement, the Bodley Head Press, issued work by Oscar Wilde and George Egerton and also published *The Yellow Book.*
4. Posed for portraits.
5. French writer (1822–96), whose journal (co-written with his brother Jules) focused on their psychological states.
6. British painter (1860–1942) who specialized in scenes of urban realism.
7. Aubrey Beardsley's perverse, undulating, superb line drawings scandalized and titillated the British public. One of the most controversial of aesthetes, in his short life (1872–98) Beardsley also produced some of the most extraordinarily skillful images of the period, creating what some observers dubbed "the Beardsley Period." See p. 58.

passed our table, with a hesitating look; but Rothenstein, in the thick of a disquisition on Puvis de Chavannes,[8] had not seen him. He was a stooping, shambling person, rather tall, very pale, with longish and brownish hair. He had a thin vague beard—or rather, he had a chin on which a large number of hairs weakly curled and clustered to cover its retreat. He was an odd-looking person; but in the 'nineties odd apparitions were more frequent, I think, than they are now. The young writers of that era—and I was sure this man was a writer—strove earnestly to be distinct in aspect. This man had striven unsuccessfully. He wore a soft black hat of clerical kind but of Bohemian intention, and a grey waterproof cape which, perhaps because it was waterproof, failed to be romantic. I decided that "dim" was the *mot juste*[9] for him. I had already essayed to write, and was immensely keen on the *mot juste*, that Holy Grail of the period.

The dim man was now again approaching our table, and this time he made up his mind to pause in front of it. "You don't remember me," he said in a toneless voice.

Rothenstein brightly focussed him. "Yes, I do," he replied after a moment, with pride rather than effusion—pride in a retentive memory. "Edwin Soames."

"Enoch Soames," said Enoch.

"Enoch Soames," repeated Rothenstein in a tone implying that it was enough to have hit on the surname. "We met in Paris two or three times when you were living there. We met at the Café Groche."

"And I came to your studio once."

"Oh yes; I was sorry I was out."

"But you were in. You showed me some of your paintings, you know. . . . I hear you're in Chelsea[10] now."

"Yes."

I almost wondered that Mr. Soames did not, after this monosyllable, pass along. He stood patiently there, rather like a dumb animal, rather like a donkey looking over a gate. A sad figure, his. It occurred to me that "hungry" was perhaps the *mot juste* for him; but—hungry for what? He looked as if he had little appetite for anything. I was sorry for him; and Rothenstein, though he had not invited him to Chelsea, did ask him to sit down and have something to drink.

Seated, he was more self-assertive. He flung back the wings of his cape with a gesture which—had not those wings been waterproof—might have seemed to hurl defiance at things in general. And he ordered an absinthe. "*Je me tiens toujours fidèle,*" he told Rothenstein, "*à la sorcière glauque.*"[11]

"It is bad for you," said Rothenstein dryly.

"Nothing is bad for one," answered Soames. "*Dans ce monde il n'y a ni de bien ni de mal.*"[12]

"Nothing good and nothing bad? How do you mean?"

"I explained it all in the preface to 'Negations.'"

"'Negations'?"

---

8. 19th-c. French muralist (1824–98) specializing in classical and allegorical figures.
9. French: the perfect word.
10. A bohemian quarter of London, where Dante Gabriel Rossetti and Wilde lived.
11. French: "I am always faithful to the glaucous sorcerer," i.e., absinthe, the reputedly poisonous intoxicant favored by the aesthetes.
12. French: "In this world there is nothing good and nothing bad."

"Yes; I gave you a copy of it."

"Oh yes, of course. But did you explain—for instance—that there was no such thing as bad or good grammar?"

"N–no," said Soames. "Of course in Art there is the good and the evil. But in Life—no." He was rolling a cigarette. He had weak white hands, not well washed, and with finger-tips much stained by nicotine. "In Life there are illusions of good and evil, but"—his voice trailed away to a murmur in which the words "vieux jeu" and "rococo" were faintly audible. I think he felt he was not doing himself justice, and feared that Rothenstein was going to point out fallacies. Anyhow, he cleared his throat and said *"Parlons d'autre chose."*[13]

It occurs to you that he was a fool? It didn't to me. I was young, and had not the clarity of judgment that Rothenstein already had. Soames was quite five or six years older than either of us. Also, he had written a book.

It was wonderful to have written a book.

If Rothenstein had not been there, I should have revered Soames. Even as it was, I respected him. And I was very near indeed to reverence when he said he had another book coming out soon. I asked if I might ask what kind of book it was to be.

"My poems," he answered. Rothenstein asked if this was to be the title of the book. The poet meditated on this suggestion, but said he rather thought of giving the book no title at all. "If a book is good in itself—" he murmured, waving his cigarette.

Rothenstein objected that absence of title might be bad for the sale of a book. "If," he urged, "I went into a bookseller's and said simply 'Have you got?' or 'Have you a copy of?' how would they know what I wanted?"

"Oh, of course I should have my name on the cover," Soames answered earnestly. "And I rather want," he added, looking hard at Rothenstein, "to have a drawing of myself as frontispiece." Rothenstein admitted that this was a capital idea, and mentioned that he was going into the country and would be there for some time. He then looked at his watch, exclaimed at the hour, paid the waiter, and went away with me to dinner. Soames remained at his post of fidelity to the glaucous witch.

"Why were you so determined not to draw him?" I asked.

"Draw him? Him? How can one draw a man who doesn't exist?"

"He is dim," I admitted. But my *mot juste* fell flat. Rothenstein repeated that Soames was non-existent.

Still, Soames had written a book. I asked if Rothenstein had read "Negations." He said he had looked into it, "but," he added crisply, "I don't profess to know anything about writing." A reservation very characteristic of the period! Painters would not then allow that any one outside their own order had a right to any opinion about painting. This law (graven on the tablets brought down by Whistler from the summit of Fujiyama)[14] imposed certain limitations. If other arts than painting were not utterly unintelligible to all but the men who practised them, the law tottered—the Monroe Doctrine,[15] as it were, did not hold good. Therefore no painter would

---

13. French: "Let's speak of something else."

14. Beerbohm satirizes Whistler's Japanese-inspired rules about the proper form of art by comparing them to the Ten Commandments.

15. The American declaration of 1823 divided the world into American-dominated and European-dominated hemispheres.

offer an opinion of a book without warning you at any rate that his opinion was worthless. No one is a better judge of literature than Rothenstein; but it wouldn't have done to tell him so in those days; and I knew that I must form an unaided judgment on "Negations."

Not to buy a book of which I had met the author face to face would have been for me in those days an impossible act of self-denial. When I returned to Oxford for the Christmas Term I had duly secured "Negations." I used to keep it lying carelessly on the table in my room, and whenever a friend took it up and asked what it was about I would say "Oh, it's rather a remarkable book. It's by a man whom I know." Just "what it was about" I never was able to say. Head or tail was just what I hadn't made of that slim green volume. I found in the preface no clue to the exiguous labyrinth of contents, and in that labyrinth nothing to explain the preface.

> Lean near to life. Lean very near—nearer.
> Life is web, and therein nor warp nor woof is, but web only.
> It is for this I am Catholick in church and in thought, yet do let swift Mood weave there what the shuttle of Mood wills.

These were the opening phrases of the preface, but those which followed were less easy to understand. Then came "Stark: A Conte," about a midinette who, so far as I could gather, murdered, or was about to murder, a mannequin. It was rather like a story by Catulle Mendès[16] in which the translator had either skipped or cut out every alternate sentence. Next, a dialogue between Pan and St. Ursula—lacking, I felt, in "snap." Next, some aphorisms (entitled ἀφορίσματα). Throughout, in fact, there was a great variety of form; and the forms had evidently been wrought with much care. It was rather the substance that eluded me. Was there, I wondered, any substance at all? It did now occur to me: suppose Enoch Soames was a fool! Up cropped a rival hypothesis: suppose I was! I inclined to give Soames the benefit of the doubt. I had read "L'Après-midi d'un Faune"[17] without extracting a glimmer of meaning. Yet Mallarmé—of course—was a Master. How was I to know that Soames wasn't another? There was a sort of music in his prose, not indeed arresting, but perhaps, I thought, haunting, and laden perhaps with meanings as deep as Mallarmé's own. I awaited his poems with an open mind.

And I looked forward to them with positive impatience after I had had a second meeting with him. This was on an evening in January. Going into the aforesaid domino room, I passed a table at which sat a pale man with an open book before him. He looked from his book to me, and I looked back over my shoulder with a vague sense that I ought to have recognised him. I returned to pay my respects. After exchanging a few words, I said with a glance to the open book, "I see I am interrupting you," and was about to pass on, but "I prefer," Soames replied in his toneless voice, "to be interrupted," and I obeyed his gesture that I should sit down.

I asked him if he often read here. "Yes; things of this kind I read here," he answered, indicating the title of his book—The Poems of Shelley.

---

16. Poet of the French Parnassian school (1841–1909).
17. "The Afternoon of a Faun," French poet Stéphane Mallarmé's famously obscure poem c. 1865.

"Anything that you really"—and I was going to say "admire?" But I cautiously left my sentence unfinished, and was glad that I had done so, for he said, with unwonted emphasis, "Anything second-rate."

I had read little of Shelley, but "Of course," I murmured, "he's very uneven."

"I should have thought evenness was just what was wrong with him. A deadly evenness. That's why I read him here. The noise of this place breaks the rhythm. He's tolerable here." Soames took up the book and glanced through the pages. He laughed. Soames' laugh was a short, single and mirthless sound from the throat, unaccompanied by any movement of the face or brightening of the eyes. "What a period!" he uttered, laying the book down. And "What a country!" he added.

I asked rather nervously if he didn't think Keats had more or less held his own against the drawbacks of time and place. He admitted that there were "passages in Keats," but did not specify them. Of "the older men," as he called them, he seemed to like only Milton.[18] "Milton," he said, "wasn't sentimental." Also, "Milton had a dark insight." And again, "I can always read Milton in the reading-room."

"The reading-room?"

"Of the British Museum. I go there every day."

"You do? I've only been there once. I'm afraid I found it rather a depressing place. It—it seemed to sap one's vitality."

"It does. That's why I go there. The lower one's vitality, the more sensitive one is to great art. I live near the Museum. I have rooms in Dyott Street."

"And you go round to the reading-room to read Milton?"

"Usually Milton." He looked at me. "It was Milton," he certificatively added, "who converted me to Diabolism."[19]

"Diabolism? Oh yes? Really?" said I, with that vague discomfort and that intense desire to be polite which one feels when a man speaks of his own religion. "You—worship the Devil?"

Soames shook his head. "It's not exactly worship," he qualified, sipping his absinthe. "It's more a matter of trusting and encouraging."

"Ah, yes. . . . But I had rather gathered from the preface to 'Negations' that you were a—a Catholic."

"Je l'étais à cette époque.[20] Perhaps I still am. Yes, I'm a Catholic diabolist."

This profession he made in an almost cursory tone. I could see that what was upmost in his mind was the fact that I had read "Negations." His pale eyes had for the first time gleamed. I felt as one who is about to be examined, viva voce,[21] on the very subject in which he is shakiest. I hastily asked him how soon his poems were to be published. "Next week," he told me.

"And are they to be published without a title?"

"No. I found a title, at last. But I shan't tell you what it is," as though I had been so impertinent as to inquire. "I am not sure that it wholly satisfies me. But it is the

---

18. The Romantic poet John Keats was famous for his lush poetry and early death; 17th-c. poet John Milton's *Paradise Lost* describes the fall of Satan.
19. A joke about Romantic Satanism, the practice of reading Satan as the noble tragic hero of *Paradise Lost*.
20. French: "I was at that time."
21. Latin: oral examination.

best I can find. It suggests something of the quality of the poems. . . . Strange growths, natural and wild, yet exquisite," he added, "and many-hued, and full of poisons."

I asked him what he thought of Baudelaire. He uttered the snort that was his laugh, and "Baudelaire," he said, "was a *bourgeois malgré lui*." France had had only one poet: Villon; "and two-thirds of Villon were sheer journalism." Verlaine was "an *épicier malgré lui*." Altogether, rather to my surprise, he rated French literature lower than English. There were "passages" in Villiers de l'Isle-Adam.[22] But "I," he summed up, "owe nothing to France." He nodded at me. "You'll see," he predicted.

I did not, when the time came, quite see that. I thought the author of *Fungoids* did—unconsciously, of course—owe something to the young Parisian décadents, or to the young English ones who owed something to *them*. I still think so. The little book—bought by me in Oxford—lies before me as I write. Its pale grey buckram cover and silver lettering have not worn well. Nor have its contents. Through these, with a melancholy interest, I have again been looking. They are not much. But at the time of their publication I had a vague suspicion that they *might* be. I suppose it is my capacity for faith, not poor Soames' work, that is weaker than it once was. . . .

To a Young Woman

Thou art, who hast not been!
    Pale tunes irresolute
    And traceries of old sounds
    Blown from a rotted flute
Mingle with noise of cymbals rouged with rust,
Nor not strange forms and epicene
    Lie bleeding in the dust,
      Being wounded with wounds.
    For this it is
That in thy counterpart
    Of age-long mockeries
Thou hast not been nor art!

There seemed to me a certain inconsistency as between the first and last lines of this. I tried, with bent brows, to resolve the discord. But I did not take my failure as wholly incompatible with a meaning in Soames' mind. Might it not rather indicate the depth of his meaning? As for the craftsmanship, "rouged with rust" seemed to me a fine stroke, and "nor not" instead of "and" had a curious felicity. I wondered who the Young Woman was, and what she had made of it all. I sadly suspect that Soames could not have made more of it than she. Yet, even now, if one doesn't try to make any sense at all of the poem, and reads it just for the sound, there is a certain grace of cadence. Soames was an artist—in so far as he was anything, poor fellow!

---

22. French: "bourgeois in spite of himself," and "a grocer in spite of himself" (alluding to Molière's *Le Médecin Malgré Lui* [The Doctor in Spite of Himself]). All these French writers influenced the aesthetes. Charles Baudelaire (1821–67) wrote *Les Fleurs du Mal* (Flowers of Evil), a poetic celebration of sin; François Villon was a 15th-c. poet translated by both Rossetti and Swinburne; Verlaine was famous for his dissolute life, including an episode where he shot his lover the poet Arthur Rimbaud; Villiers de l'Isle-Adam wrote *L'Eve Future*, a novel about the building of a perfect female automaton.

It seemed to me, when first I read "Fungoids," that, oddly enough, the Diabolistic side of him was the best. Diabolism seemed to be a cheerful, even a wholesome, influence in his life.

Nocturne

Round and round the shutter'd Square
I stroll'd with the Devil's arm in mine.
No sound but the scrape of his hoofs was there
And the ring of his laughter and mine.
   We had drunk black wine.

I scream'd, "I will race you, Master!"
"What matter," he shriek'd, "to-night
Which of us runs the faster?
There is nothing to fear to-night
   In the foul moon's light!"

Then I look'd him in the eyes,
And I laugh'd full shrill at the lie he told
And the gnawing fear he would fain disguise.
It was true, what I'd time and again been told:
   He was old—old.

There was, I felt, quite a swing about that first stanza—a joyous and rollicking note of comradeship. The second was slightly hysterical perhaps. But I liked the third: it was so bracingly unorthodox, even according to the tenets of Soames' peculiar sect in the faith. Not much "trusting and encouraging" here! Soames triumphantly exposing the Devil as a liar, and laughing "full shrill," cut a quite heartening figure, I thought—then! Now, in the light of what befell, none of his poems depresses me so much as "Nocturne."

I looked out for what the metropolitan reviewers would have to say. They seemed to fall into two classes: those who had little to say and those who had nothing. The second class was the larger, and the words of the first were cold; insomuch that

Strikes a note of modernity throughout. . . . These tripping numbers.—*Preston Telegraph*

was the only lure offered in advertisements by Soames' publisher. I had hopes that when next I met the poet I could congratulate him on having made a stir; for I fancied he was not so sure of his intrinsic greatness as he seemed. I was but able to say, rather coarsely, when next I did see him, that I hoped "Fungoids" was "selling splendidly." He looked at me across his glass of absinthe and asked if I had bought a copy. His publisher had told him that three had been sold. I laughed, as at a jest.

"You don't suppose I *care*, do you?" he said, with something like a snarl. I disclaimed the notion. He added that he was not a tradesman. I said mildly that I wasn't, either, and murmured that an artist who gave truly new and great things to the world had always to wait long for recognition. He said he cared not a sou for recognition. I agreed that the act of creation was its own reward.

His moroseness might have alienated me if I had regarded myself as a nobody. But ah! hadn't both John Lane and Aubrey Beardsley suggested that I should write an essay for the great new venture that was afoot—"The Yellow Book"? And hadn't Henry Harland, as editor, accepted my essay?[23] And wasn't it to be in the very first number? At Oxford I was still *in statu pupillari*.[24] In London I regarded myself as very much indeed a graduate now—one whom no Soames could ruffle. Partly to show off, partly in sheer good-will, I told Soames he ought to contribute to "The Yellow Book." He uttered from the throat a sound of scorn for that publication.

Nevertheless, I did, a day or two later, tentatively ask Harland if he knew anything of the work of a man called Enoch Soames. Harland paused in the midst of his characteristic stride around the room, threw up his hands towards the ceiling, and groaned aloud: he had often met "that absurd creature" in Paris, and this very morning had received some poems in manuscript from him.

"Has he *no* talent?" I asked.

"He has an income. He's all right." Harland was the most joyous of men and most generous of critics, and he hated to talk of anything about which he couldn't be enthusiastic. So I dropped the subject of Soames. The news that Soames had an income did take the edge off solicitude. I learned afterwards that he was the son of an unsuccessful and deceased bookseller in Preston, but had inherited an annuity of £300 from a married aunt, and had no surviving relatives of any kind. Materially, then, he was "all right." But there was still a spiritual pathos about him, sharpened for me now by the possibility that even the praises of *The Preston Telegraph* might not have been forthcoming had he not been the son of a Preston man. He had a sort of weak doggedness which I could not but admire. Neither he nor his work received the slightest encouragement; but he persisted in behaving as a personage: always he kept his dingy little flag flying. Wherever congregated the *jeunes féroces*[25] of the arts, in whatever Soho restaurant they had just discovered, in whatever music-hall they were most frequenting, there was Soames in the midst of them, or rather on the fringe of them, a dim but inevitable figure. He never sought to propitiate his fellow-writers, never bated a jot of his arrogance about his own work or of his contempt for theirs. To the painters he was respectful, even humble; but for the poets and prosaists of "The Yellow Book," and later of "The Savoy,"[26] he had never a word but of scorn. He wasn't resented. It didn't occur to anybody that he or his Catholic Diabolism mattered. When, in the autumn of '96, he brought out (at his own expense, this time) a third book, his last book, nobody said a word for or against it. I meant, but forgot, to buy it. I never saw it, and am ashamed to say I don't even remember what it was called. But I did, at the time of its publication, say to Rothenstein that I thought poor old Soames was really a rather tragic figure, and that I believed he would literally die for want of recognition. Rothenstein scoffed. He said I was trying to get credit for a kind heart which I didn't possess; and perhaps this was so. But at the private view of the New English Art Club, a few weeks later, I beheld a pastel portrait of "Enoch Soames, Esq." It was very like him, and very like Rothenstein to have done it. Soames was standing near it, in his soft hat and his waterproof cape, all through the afternoon. Anybody who knew him

---

23. Beerbohm's "Defence of Cosmetics" (p. 57) did indeed appear in the first number of *The Yellow Book*.
24. Latin: had the status of a pupil.
25. French: young rebels.
26. *The Savoy* was a short-lived successor to *The Yellow Book*.

would have recognised the portrait at a glance, but nobody who didn't know him would have recognised the portrait from its bystander: it "existed" so much more than he; it was bound to. Also, it had not that expression of faint happiness which on this day was discernible, yes, in Soames' countenance. Fame had breathed on him. Twice again in the course of the month I went to the New English, and on both occasions Soames himself was on view there. Looking back, I regard the close of that exhibition as having been virtually the close of his career. He had felt the breath of Fame against his cheek—so late, for such a little while; and at its withdrawal he gave in, gave up, gave out. He, who had never looked strong or well, looked ghastly now—a shadow of the shade he had once been. He still frequented the domino room, but, having lost all wish to excite curiosity, he no longer read books there. "You read only at the Museum now?" asked I, with attempted cheerfulness. He said he never went there now. "No absinthe there," he muttered. It was the sort of thing that in the old days he would have said for effect; but it carried conviction now. Absinthe, erst but a point in the "personality" he had striven so hard to build up, was solace and necessity now. He no longer called it "la sorcière glauque." He had shed away all his French phrases. He had become a plain, unvarnished, Preston man.

Failure, if it be a plain, unvarnished, complete failure, and even though it be a squalid failure, has always a certain dignity. I avoided Soames because he made me feel rather vulgar. John Lane had published, by this time, two little books of mine, and they had had a pleasant little success of esteem. I was a—slight but definite—"personality." Frank Harris had engaged me to kick up my heels in *The Saturday Review*,[27] Alfred Harmsworth was letting me do likewise in *The Daily Mail*.[28] I was just what Soames wasn't. And he shamed my gloss. Had I known that he really and firmly believed in the greatness of what he as an artist had achieved, I might not have shunned him. No man who hasn't lost his vanity can be held to have altogether failed. Soames' dignity was an illusion of mine. One day in the first week of June, 1897, that illusion went. But on the evening of that day Soames went too.

I had been out most of the morning, and, as it was too late to reach home in time for luncheon, I sought "the Vingtième." This little place—Restaurant du Vingtième Siècle,[29] to give it its full title—had been discovered in '96 by the poets and prosaists, but had now been more or less abandoned in favour of some later find. I don't think it lived long enough to justify its name; but at that time there it still was, in Greek Street, a few doors from Soho Square, and almost opposite to that house where, in the first years of the century, a little girl, and with her a boy named De Quincey, made nightly encampment in darkness and hunger among dust and rats and old legal parchments.[30] The Vingtième was but a small whitewashed room, leading out into the street at one end and into a kitchen at the other. The proprietor and cook was a Frenchman, known to us as Monsieur Vingtième; the waiters were his two daughters, Rose and Berthe; and the food, according to faith, was good. The tables were so

27. Harris, a boisterous and untrustworthy literary man, edited the *Saturday Review* and hired Beerbohm as the paper's drama critic when George Bernard Shaw left.
28. Harmsworth, later Lord Northcliffe, was a newspaper magnate.
29. French: Restaurant of the Twentieth Century.
30. An episode in De Quincey's *Confessions of an Opium Eater* (1821).

narrow, and were set so close together, that there was space for twelve of them, six jutting from either wall.

Only the two nearest to the door, as I went in, were occupied. On one side sat a tall, flashy, rather Mephistophelian[31] man whom I had seen from time to time in the domino room and elsewhere. On the other side sat Soames. They made a queer contrast in that sunlit room—Soames sitting haggard in that hat and cape which nowhere at any season had I seen him doff, and this other, this keenly vital man, at sight of whom I more than ever wondered whether he were a diamond merchant, a conjurer, or the head of a private detective agency. I was sure Soames didn't want my company; but I asked, as it would have seemed brutal not to, whether I might join him, and took the chair opposite to his. He was smoking a cigarette, with an untasted salmi[32] of something on his plate and a half-empty bottle of Sauterne before him; and he was quite silent. I said that the preparations for the Jubilee[33] made London impossible. (I rather liked them, really.) I professed a wish to go right away till the whole thing was over. In vain did I attune myself to his gloom. He seemed not to hear me nor even to see me. I felt that his behaviour made me ridiculous in the eyes of the other man. The gangway between the two rows of tables at the Vingtième was hardly more than two feet wide (Rose and Berthe, in their ministrations, had always to edge past each other, quarrelling in whispers as they did so), and any one at the table abreast of yours was practically at yours. I thought our neighbour was amused at my failure to interest Soames, and so, as I could not explain to him that my insistence was merely charitable, I became silent. Without turning my head, I had him well within my range of vision. I hoped I looked less vulgar than he in contrast with Soames. I was sure he was not an Englishman, but what *was* his nationality? Though his jet-black hair was *en brosse*,[34] I did not think he was French. To Berthe, who waited on him, he spoke French fluently, but with a hardly native idiom and accent. I gathered that this was his first visit to the Vingtième; but Berthe was off-hand in her manner to him: he had not made a good impression. His eyes were handsome, but—like the Vingtième's tables—too narrow and set too close together. His nose was predatory, and the points of his moustache, waxed up beyond his nostrils, gave a fixity to his smile. Decidedly, he was sinister. And my sense of discomfort in his presence was intensified by the scarlet waistcoat which tightly, and so unseasonably in June, sheathed his ample chest. This waistcoat wasn't wrong merely because of the heat, either. It was somehow all wrong in itself. It wouldn't have done on Christmas morning. It would have struck a jarring note at the first night of *Hernani*.[35] I was trying to account for its wrongness when Soames suddenly and strangely broke silence. "A hundred years hence!" he murmured, as in a trance.

"We shall not be here!" I briskly but fatuously added.

"We shall not be here. No," he droned, "but the Museum will still be just where it is. And the reading-room, just where it is. And people will be able to go and read there." He inhaled sharply, and a spasm as of actual pain contorted his features.

---

31. Demonic.
32. Stew.
33. The 1887 celebration of Queen Victoria's fifty years on the throne.
34. French: brushed, a crewcut.
35. At the opening night of Verdi's opera *Hernani*, Théophile Gautier famously donned a bright pink vest.

I wondered what train of thought poor Soames had been following. He did not enlighten me when he said, after a long pause, "You think I haven't minded."

"Minded what, Soames?"

"Neglect. Failure."

"*Failure?*" I said heartily. "Failure?" I repeated vaguely. "Neglect—yes, perhaps; but that's quite another matter. Of course you haven't been—appreciated. But what then? Any artist who—who gives—" What I wanted to say was, "Any artist who gives truly new and great things to the world has always to wait long for recognition"; but the flattery would not out: in the face of his misery, a misery so genuine and so unmasked, my lips would not say the words.

And then—he said them for me. I flushed. "That's what you were going to say, isn't it?" he asked.

"How did you know?"

"It's what you said to me three years ago, when 'Fungoids' was published." I flushed the more. I need not have done so at all, for "It's the only important thing I ever heard you say," he continued. "And I've never forgotten it. It's a true thing. It's a horrible truth. But—d'you remember what I answered? I said 'I don't care a sou for recognition.' And you believed me. You've gone on believing I'm above that sort of thing. You're shallow. What should *you* know of the feelings of a man like me? You imagine that a great artist's faith in himself and in the verdict of posterity is enough to keep him happy. . . . You've never guessed at the bitterness and loneliness, the"—his voice broke; but presently he resumed, speaking with a force that I had never known in him. "Posterity! What use is it to *me*? A dead man doesn't know that people are visiting his grave—visiting his birthplace—putting up tablets to him—unveiling statues of him. A dead man can't read the books that are written about him. A hundred years hence! Think of it! If I could come back to life *then*—just for a few hours—and go to the reading-room, and *read*! Or better still: if I could be projected, now, at this moment, into that future, into that reading-room, just for this one afternoon! I'd sell myself body and soul to the devil, for that! Think of the pages and pages in the catalogue: 'SOAMES, ENOCH' endlessly—endless editions, commentaries, prolegomena, biographies"—but here he was interrupted by a sudden loud creak of the chair at the next table. Our neighbour had half risen from his place. He was leaning towards us, apologetically intrusive.

"Excuse—permit me," he said softly. "I have been unable not to hear. Might I take a liberty? In this little restaurant-sans-façon"—he spread wide his hands—"might I, as the phrase is, 'cut in'?"

I could but signify our acquiescence. Berthe had appeared at the kitchen door, thinking the stranger wanted his bill. He waved her away with his cigar, and in another moment had seated himself beside me, commanding a full view of Soames.

"Though not an Englishman," he explained, "I know my London well, Mr. Soames. Your name and fame—Mr. Beerbohm's too—very known to me. Your point is: who am *I*?" He glanced quickly over his shoulder, and in a lowered voice said, "I am the Devil."

I couldn't help it: I laughed. I tried not to, I knew there was nothing to laugh at, my rudeness shamed me, but—I laughed with increasing volume. The Devil's quiet dignity, the surprise and disgust of his raised eyebrows, did but the more dissolve me. I rocked to and fro, I lay back aching. I behaved deplorably.

"I am a gentleman, and," he said with intense emphasis, "I thought I was in the company of *gentlemen*."

"Don't!" I gasped faintly. "Oh, don't!"

"Curious, *nicht wahr?*"[36] I heard him say to Soames. "There is a type of person to whom the very mention of my name is—oh-so-awfully-funny! In your theatres the dullest *comédien* needs only to say 'The Devil!' and right away they give him 'the loud laugh that speaks the vacant mind.' Is it not so?"

I had now just breath enough to offer my apologies. He accepted them, but coldly, and re-addressed himself to Soames.

"I am a man of business," he said, "and always I would put things through 'right now,' as they say in the States. You are a poet. *Les affaires*[37]—you detest them. So be it. But with me you will deal, eh? What you have said just now gives me furiously to hope."

Soames had not moved, except to light a fresh cigarette. He sat crouched forward, with his elbows squared on the table, and his head just above the level of his hands, staring up at the Devil. "Go on," he nodded. I had no remnant of laughter in me now.

"It will be the more pleasant, our little deal," the Devil went on, "because you are—I mistake not?—a Diabolist."

"A Catholic Diabolist," said Soames.

The Devil accepted the reservation genially. "You wish," he resumed, "to visit now—this afternoon as-ever-is—the reading-room of the British Museum, yes? but of a hundred years hence, yes? *Parfaitement.*[38] Time—an illusion. Past and future—they are as ever-present as the present, or at any rate only what you call 'just-round-the-corner.' I switch you on to any date. I project you—pouf! You wish to be in the reading-room just as it will be on the afternoon of June 3, 1997? You wish to find yourself standing in that room, just past the swing-doors, this very minute, yes? and to stay there till closing time? Am I right?"

Soames nodded.

The Devil looked at his watch. "Ten past two," he said. "Closing time in summer same then as now: seven o'clock. That will give you almost five hours. At seven o'clock—pouf!—you find yourself again here, sitting at this table. I am dining tonight *dans le monde—dans le higlif.*[39] That concludes my present visit to your great city. I come and fetch you here, Mr. Soames, on my way home."

"Home?" I echoed.

"Be it never so humble!" said the Devil lightly.

"All right," said Soames.

"Soames!" I entreated. But my friend moved not a muscle.

The Devil had made as though to stretch forth his hand across the table and touch Soames' forearm; but he paused in his gesture.

"A hundred years hence, as now," he smiled, "no smoking allowed in the reading-room. You would better therefore——"

---

36. German: "isn't it?"
37. French: business affairs.
38. French: Perfectly.
39. French: in society—in the high life.

Soames removed the cigarette from his mouth and dropped it into his glass of Sauterne.

"Soames!" again I cried. "Can't you"—but the Devil had now stretched forth his hand across the table. He brought it slowly down on—the table-cloth. Soames' chair was empty. His cigarette floated sodden in his wine-glass. There was no other trace of him.

For a few moments the Devil let his hand rest where it lay, gazing at me out of the corners of his eyes, vulgarly triumphant.

A shudder shook me. With an effort I controlled myself and rose from my chair. "Very clever," I said condescendingly. "But—*The Time Machine*[40] is a delightful book, don't you think? So entirely original!"

"You are pleased to sneer," said the Devil, who had also risen, "but it is one thing to write about an impossible machine; it is a quite other thing to be a Supernatural Power." All the same, I had scored.

Berthe had come forth at the sound of our rising. I explained to her that Mr. Soames had been called away, and that both he and I would be dining here. It was not until I was out in the open air that I began to feel giddy. I have but the haziest recollection of what I did, where I wandered, in the glaring sunshine of that endless afternoon. I remember the sound of carpenters' hammers all along Piccadilly, and the bare chaotic look of the half-erected "stands." Was it in the Green Park, or in Kensington Gardens, or *where* was it that I sat on a chair beneath a tree, trying to read an evening paper? There was a phrase in the leading article that went on repeating itself in my fagged mind—"Little is hidden from this august Lady full of the garnered wisdom of sixty years of Sovereignty." I remember wildly conceiving a letter (to reach Windsor by express messenger told to await answer):

> MADAM,—Well knowing that your Majesty is full of the garnered wisdom of sixty years of Sovereignty, I venture to ask your advice in the following delicate matter. Mr. Enoch Soames, whose poems you may or may not know, . . .

Was there *no* way of helping him—saving him? A bargain was a bargain, and I was the last man to aid or abet any one in wriggling out of a reasonable obligation. I wouldn't have lifted a little finger to save Faust.[41] But poor Soames!—doomed to pay without respite an eternal price for nothing but a fruitless search and a bitter disillusioning. . . .

Odd and uncanny it seemed to me that he, Soames, in the flesh, in the waterproof cape, was at this moment living in the last decade of the next century, poring over books not yet written, and seeing and seen by men not yet born. Uncannier and odder still, that to-night and evermore he would be in Hell. Assuredly, truth was stranger than fiction.

Endless that afternoon was. Almost I wished I had gone with Soames—not indeed to stay in the reading-room, but to sally forth for a brisk sight-seeing walk around a new London. I wandered restlessly out of the Park I had sat in. Vainly I tried to imagine myself an ardent tourist from the eighteenth century. Intolerable

---

40. H. G. Wells's famous time-travel science-fiction novel (1895).
41. The legendary German scholar who sells his soul to the Devil, dramatized by Christopher Marlowe in the 16th c. and Johann Wolfgang von Goethe in the 19th c.

was the strain of the slow-passing and empty minutes. Long before seven o'clock I was back at the Vingtième.

I sat there just where I had sat for luncheon. Air came in listlessly through the open door behind me. Now and again Rose or Berthe appeared for a moment. I had told them I would not order any dinner till Mr. Soames came. A hurdy-gurdy began to play, abruptly drowning the noise of a quarrel between some Frenchmen further up the street. Whenever the tune was changed I heard the quarrel still raging. I had bought another evening paper on my way. I unfolded it. My eyes gazed ever away from it to the clock over the kitchen door. . . .

Five minutes, now, to the hour! I remembered that clocks in restaurants are kept five minutes fast. I concentrated my eyes on the paper. I vowed I would not look away from it again. I held it upright, at its full width, close to my face, so that I had no view of anything but it. . . . Rather a tremulous sheet? Only because of the draught, I told myself.

My arms gradually became stiff; they ached; but I could not drop them—now. I had a suspicion, I had a certainty. Well, what then? . . . What else had I come for? Yet I held tight that barrier of newspaper. Only the sound of Berthe's brisk footstep from the kitchen enabled me, forced me, to drop it, and to utter:

"What shall we have to eat, Soames?"

"*Il est souffrant, ce pauvre Monsieur Soames?*"[42] asked Berthe.

"He's only—tired." I asked her to get some wine—Burgundy—and whatever food might be ready. Soames sat crouched forward against the table, exactly as when last I had seen him. It was as though he had never moved—he who had moved so unimaginably far. Once or twice in the afternoon it had for an instant occurred to me that perhaps his journey was not to be fruitless—that perhaps we had all been wrong in our estimate of the works of Enoch Soames. That we had been horribly right was horribly clear from the look of him. But "Don't be discouraged," I falteringly said. "Perhaps it's only that you—didn't leave enough time. Two, three centuries hence, perhaps—"

"Yes," his voice came. "I've thought of that."

"And now—now for the more immediate future! Where are you going to hide? How would it be if you caught the Paris express from Charing Cross? Almost an hour to spare. Don't go on to Paris. Stop at Calais.[43] Live in Calais. He'd never think of looking for you in Calais."

"It's like my luck," he said, "to spend my last hours on earth with an ass." But I was not offended. "And a treacherous ass," he strangely added, tossing across to me a crumpled bit of paper which he had been holding in his hand. I glanced at the writing on it—some sort of gibberish, apparently. I laid it impatiently aside.

"Come, Soames! pull yourself together! This isn't a mere matter of life and death. It's a question of eternal torment, mind you! You don't mean to say you're going to wait limply here till the Devil comes to fetch you?"

"I can't do anything else. I've no choice."

"Come! This is 'trusting and encouraging' with a vengeance! This is Diabolism run mad!" I filled his glass with wine. "Surely, now that you've *seen* the brute——"

---

42. French: "Is he sick, poor Mr. Soames?"
43. A tawdry, unfashionable French port city where English passengers disembarked.

"It's no good abusing him."

"You must admit there's nothing Miltonic about him, Soames."

"I don't say he's not rather different from what I expected."

"He's a vulgarian, he's a swell-mobsman, he's the sort of man who hangs about the corridors of trains going to the Riviera and steals ladies' jewel-cases. Imagine eternal torment presided over by *him*!"

"You don't suppose I look forward to it, do you?"

"Then why not slip quietly out of the way?"

Again and again I filled his glass, and always, mechanically, he emptied it; but the wine kindled no spark of enterprise in him. He did not eat, and I myself ate hardly at all. I did not in my heart believe that any dash for freedom could save him. The chase would be swift, the capture certain. But better anything than this passive, meek, miserable waiting. I told Soames that for the honour of the human race he ought to make some show of resistance. He asked what the human race had ever done for him. "Besides," he said, "can't you understand that I'm in his power? You saw him touch me, didn't you? There's an end of it. I've no will. I'm sealed."

I made a gesture of despair. He went on repeating the word "sealed." I began to realise that the wine had clouded his brain. No wonder! Foodless he had gone into futurity, foodless he still was. I urged him to eat at any rate some bread. It was maddening to think that he, who had so much to tell, might tell nothing. "How was it all," I asked, "yonder? Come! Tell me your adventures."

"They'd make first-rate 'copy,' wouldn't they?"

"I'm awfully sorry for you, Soames, and I make all possible allowances; but what earthly right have you to insinuate that I should make 'copy,' as you call it, out of you?"

The poor fellow pressed his hands to his forehead. "I don't know," he said. "I had some reason, I know . . . I'll try to remember."

"That's right. Try to remember everything. Eat a little more bread. What did the reading-room look like?"

"Much as usual," he at length muttered.

"Many people there?"

"Usual sort of number."

"What did they look like?"

Soames tried to visualise them. "They all," he presently remembered, "looked very like one another."

My mind took a fearsome leap. "All dressed in Jaeger?"[44]

"Yes. I think so. Greyish-yellowish stuff."

"A sort of uniform?" He nodded. "With a number on it, perhaps?—a number on a large disc of metal sewn on to the left sleeve? DKF 78,910—that sort of thing?" It was even so. "And all of them—men and women alike—looking very well-cared-for? very Utopian? and smelling rather strongly of carbolic? and all of them quite hairless?" I was right every time. Soames was only not sure whether the men and women were hairless or shorn. "I hadn't time to look at them very closely," he explained.

"No, of course not. But——"

---

44. Supposedly health-promoting woolen clothing favored by George Bernard Shaw.

"They stared at *me*, I can tell you. I attracted a great deal of attention." At last he had done that! "I think I rather scared them. They moved away whenever I came near. They followed me about at a distance, wherever I went. The men at the round desk in the middle seemed to have a sort of panic whenever I went to make inquiries."

"What did you do when you arrived?"

Well, he had gone straight to the catalogue, of course—to the S volumes, and had stood long before SN-SOF, unable to take this volume out of the shelf, because his heart was beating so. . . . At first, he said, he wasn't disappointed—he only thought there was some new arrangement. He went to the middle desk and asked where the catalogue of *twentieth*-century books was kept. He gathered that there was still only one catalogue. Again he looked up his name, stared at the three little pasted slips he had known so well. Then he went and sat down for a long time. . . .

"And then," he droned, "I looked up the *Dictionary of National Biography* and some encyclopaedias. . . . I went back to the middle desk and asked what was the best modern book on late nineteenth-century literature. They told me Mr. T. K. Nupton's book was considered the best. I looked it up in the catalogue and filled in a form for it. It was brought to me. My name wasn't in the index, but—Yes!" he said with a sudden change of tone. "That's what I'd forgotten. Where's that bit of paper? Give it me back."

I, too, had forgotten that cryptic screed. I found it fallen on the floor, and handed it to him.

He smoothed it out, nodding and smiling at me disagreeably. "I found myself glancing through Nupton's book," he resumed. "Not very easy reading. Some sort of phonetic spelling. . . . All the modern books I saw were phonetic."

"Then I don't want to hear any more, Soames, please."

"The proper names seemed all to be spelt in the old way. But for that, I mightn't have noticed my own name."

"Your own name? Really? Soames, I'm *very* glad."

"And yours."

"No!"

"I thought I should find you waiting here to-night. So I took the trouble to copy out the passage. Read it."

I snatched the paper. Soames' handwriting was characteristically dim. It, and the noisome spelling, and my excitement, made me all the slower to grasp what T. K. Nupton was driving at.

The document lies before me at this moment. Strange that the words I here copy out for you were copied out for me by poor Soames just seventy-eight years hence. . . .

From p. 234 of "Inglish Littracher 1890–1900" bi T. K. Nupton, publishd bi th Stait, 1992:

> Fr egzarmpl, a riter ov th time, naimd Max Beerbohm, hoo woz stil alive in th twentieth senchri, rote a stauri in wich e pautraid an immajnari karrakter kauld 'Enoch Soames'—a thurd-rait poit hoo beleevz imself a grate jeneus an maix a bargin with th Devvl in auder ter no wot posterriti thinx ov im! It iz a sumwot labud sattire but not without vallu az showing hou seriusli the yung men ov th aiteen-ninetiz took themselvz. Nou that the littreri profeshn haz bin auganized az a departmnt of publik servis, our riters hav found their

levvl an hav lernt ter doo their duti without thort ov th morro. 'Th laibrer iz werthi ov hiz hire,' an that iz aul. Thank hevvn we hav no Enoch Soameses amung us to-dai!

I found that by murmuring the words aloud (a device which I commend to my reader) I was able to master them, little by little. The clearer they became, the greater was my bewilderment, my distress and horror. The whole thing was a nightmare. Afar, the great grisly background of what was in store for the poor dear art of letters; here, at the table, fixing on me a gaze that made me hot all over, the poor fellow whom—whom evidently . . . but no: whatever down-grade my character might take in coming years, I should never be such a brute as to—

Again I examined the screed. "Immajnari"—but here Soames was, no more imaginary, alas! than I. And "labud"—what on earth was that? (To this day, I have never made out that word.) "It's all very—baffling," I at length stammered.

Soames said nothing, but cruelly did not cease to look at me.

"Are you sure," I temporised, "quite sure you copied the thing out correctly?"

"Quite."

"Well, then it's this wretched Nupton who must have made—must be going to make—some idiotic mistake. . . . Look here, Soames! you know me better than to suppose that I . . . After all, the name 'Max Beerbohm' is not at all an uncommon one, and there must be several Enoch Soameses running around—or rather, 'Enoch Soames' is a name that might occur to any one writing a story. And I don't write stories: I'm an essayist, an observer, a recorder. . . . I admit that it's an extraordinary co-incidence. But you must see——"

"I see the whole thing," said Soames quietly. And he added, with a touch of his old manner, but with more dignity than I had ever known in him, "*Parlons d'autre chose.*"

I accepted that suggestion very promptly. I returned straight to the more immediate future. I spent most of the long evening in renewed appeals to Soames to slip away and seek refuge somewhere. I remember saying at last that if indeed I was destined to write about him, the supposed "stauri" had better have at least a happy ending. Soames repeated those last three words in a tone of intense scorn. "In Life and in Art," he said, "all that matters is an *inevitable* ending."

"But," I urged, more hopefully than I felt, "an ending that can be avoided *isn't* inevitable."

"You aren't an artist," he rasped. "And you're so hopelessly not an artist that, so far from being able to imagine a thing and make it seem true, you're going to make even a true thing seem as if you'd made it up. You're a miserable bungler. And it's like my luck."

I protested that the miserable bungler was not I—was not going to be I—but T. K. Nupton; and we had a rather heated argument, in the thick of which it suddenly seemed to me that Soames saw he was in the wrong: he had quite physically cowered. But I wondered why—and now I guessed with a cold throb just why—he stared so, past me. The bringer of that "inevitable ending" filled the doorway.

I managed to turn in my chair and to say, not without a semblance of lightness, "Aha, come in!" Dread was indeed rather blunted in me by his looking so absurdly like a villain in a melodrama. The sheen of his tilted hat and of his shirt-front, the repeated twists he was giving to his moustache, and most of all the magnificence of his sneer, gave token that he was there only to be foiled.

He was at our table in a stride. "I am sorry," he sneered witheringly, "to break up your pleasant party, but—"

"You don't: you complete it," I assured him. "Mr. Soames and I want to have a little talk with you. Won't you sit? Mr. Soames got nothing—frankly nothing—by his journey this afternoon. We don't wish to say that the whole thing was a swindle—a common swindle. On the contrary, we believe you meant well. But of course the bargain, such as it was, is off."

The Devil gave no verbal answer. He merely looked at Soames and pointed with rigid forefinger to the door. Soames was wretchedly rising from his chair when, with a desperate quick gesture, I swept together two dinner-knives that were on the table, and laid their blades across each other. The Devil stepped sharp back against the table behind him, averting his face and shuddering.

"You are not superstitious!" he hissed.

"Not at all," I smiled.

"Soames!" he said as to an underling, but without turning his face, "put those knives straight!"

With an inhibitive gesture to my friend, "Mr. Soames," I said emphatically to the Devil, "is a *Catholic* Diabolist"; but my poor friend did the Devil's bidding, not mine; and now, with his master's eyes again fixed on him, he arose, he shuffled past me. I tried to speak. It was he that spoke. "Try," was the prayer he threw back at me as the Devil pushed him roughly out through the door, "*try* to make them know that I did exist!"

In another instant I too was through that door. I stood staring all ways—up the street, across it, down it. There was moonlight and lamplight, but there was not Soames nor that other.

Dazed, I stood there. Dazed, I turned back, at length, into the little room; and I suppose I paid Berthe or Rose for my dinner and luncheon, and for Soames': I hope so, for I never went to the Vingtième again. Ever since that night I have avoided Greek Street altogether. And for years I did not set foot even in Soho Square, because on that same night it was there that I paced and loitered, long and long, with some such dull sense of hope as a man has in not straying far from the place where he has lost something. . . . "Round and round the shutter'd Square"—that line came back to me on my lonely beat, and with it the whole stanza, ringing in my brain and bearing in on me how tragically different from the happy scene imagined by him was the poet's actual experience of that prince in whom of all princes we should put not our trust.

But—strange how the mind of an essayist, be it never so stricken, roves and ranges!—I remember pausing before a wide doorstep and wondering if perchance it was on this very one that the young De Quincey lay ill and faint while poor Ann flew as fast as her feet would carry her to Oxford Street, the "stony-hearted step-mother" of them both, and came back bearing that "glass of port wine and spices" but for which he might, so he thought, actually have died. Was this the very doorstep that the old De Quincey used to revisit in homage?[45] I pondered Ann's fate, the cause of

---

45. Another episode from De Quincey's *Confessions*. He befriended this young prostitute but was never able to find her subsequently.

her sudden vanishing from the ken of her boyfriend; and presently I blamed myself for letting the past override the present. Poor vanished Soames!

And for myself, too, I began to be troubled. What had I better do? Would there be a hue and cry—Mysterious Disappearance of an Author, and all that? He had last been seen lunching and dining in my company. Hadn't I better get a hansom and drive straight to Scotland Yard?[46] . . . They would think I was a lunatic. After all, I reassured myself, London was a very large place, and one very dim figure might easily drop out of it unobserved—now especially, in the blinding glare of the near Jubilee. Better say nothing at all, I thought.

And I was right. Soames' disappearance made no stir at all. He was utterly forgotten before any one, so far as I am aware, noticed that he was no longer hanging around. Now and again some poet or prosaist may have said to another, "What has become of that man Soames?" but I never heard any such question asked. The solicitor through whom he was paid his annuity may be presumed to have made inquiries, but no echo of these resounded. There was something rather ghastly to me in the general unconsciousness that Soames had existed, and more than once I caught myself wondering whether Nupton, that babe unborn, were going to be right in thinking him a figment of my brain.

In that extract from Nupton's repulsive book there is one point which perhaps puzzles you. How is it that the author, though I have here mentioned him by name and have quoted the exact words he is going to write, is not going to grasp the obvious corollary that I have invented nothing? The answer can be only this: Nupton will not have read the later passages of this memoir. Such lack of thoroughness is a serious fault in any one who undertakes to do scholar's work. And I hope these words will meet the eye of some contemporary rival to Nupton and be the undoing of Nupton.

I like to think that some time between 1992 and 1997 somebody will have looked up this memoir, and will have forced on the world his inevitable and startling conclusions. And I have reasons for believing that this will be so. You realise that the reading-room into which Soames was projected by the Devil was in all respects precisely as it will be on the afternoon of June 3, 1997. You realise, therefore, that on that afternoon, when it comes round, there the self-same crowd will be, and there Soames too will be, punctually, he and they doing precisely what they did before. Recall now Soames' account of the sensation he made. You may say that the mere difference of his costume was enough to make him sensational in that uniformed crowd. You wouldn't say so if you had ever seen him. I assure you that in no period could Soames be anything but dim. The fact that people are going to stare at him, and follow him around, and seem afraid of him, can be explained only on the hypothesis that they will somehow have been prepared for his ghostly visitation. They will have been awfully waiting to see whether he really would come. And when he does come the effect will of course be—awful.

An authentic, guaranteed, proven ghost, but—only a ghost, alas! Only that. In his first visit, Soames was a creature of flesh and blood, whereas the creatures into whose midst he was projected were but ghosts, I take it—solid, palpable, vocal, but unconscious and automatic ghosts, in a building that was itself an illusion. Next

---

46. The British police headquarters.

time, that building and those creatures will be real. It is of Soames that there will be but the semblance. I wish I could think him destined to revisit the world actually, physically, consciously. I wish he had this one brief escape, this one small treat, to look forward to. I never forget him for long. He is where he is, and forever. The more rigid moralists among you may say he has only himself to blame. For my part, I think he has been very hardly used. It is well that vanity should be chastened; and Enoch Soames' vanity was, I admit, above the average, and called for special treatment. But there was no need for vindictiveness. You say he contracted to pay the price he is paying; yes; but I maintain that he was induced to do so by fraud. Well-informed in all things, the Devil must have known that my friend would gain nothing by his visit to futurity. The whole thing was a very shabby trick. The more I think of it, the more detestable the Devil seems to me.

Of him I have caught sight several times, here and there, since that day at the Vingtième. Only once, however, have I seen him at close quarters. This was in Paris. I was walking, one afternoon, along the Rue d'Antin, when I saw him advancing from the opposite direction—over-dressed as ever, and swinging an ebony cane, and altogether behaving as though the whole pavement belonged to him. At thought of Enoch Soames and the myriads of other sufferers eternally in this brute's dominion, a great cold wrath filled me, and I drew myself up to my full height. But—well, one is so used to nodding and smiling in the street to anybody whom one knows that the action becomes almost independent of oneself: to prevent it requires a very sharp effort and great presence of mind. I was miserably aware, as I passed the Devil, that I nodded and smiled to him. And my shame was the deeper and hotter because he, if you please, stared straight at me with the utmost haughtiness.

To be cut[47]—deliberately cut—by *him*! I was, I still am, furious at having had that happen to me.

—1914

Oscar Wilde
1854–1900

In the play presented here, it is better to be named Ernest than to be earnest, to have the style rather than the substance. This delightfully subversive substitution is characteristic of Oscar Wilde's last and greatest play, *The Importance of Being Earnest*, with its perfectly absurdly balanced plot, its sparkling epigrammatic dialogue, and its dizzyingly comic reversals. The play opened on Valentine's Day in 1895, but when Wilde was tried for "gross indecency" in April his name was removed from the theater marquee, and the play closed shortly thereafter. In *Earnest*, Wilde praised the delights of a secret life of pleasure ("Bunburying," with its suggestively homoerotic sound), rather than dutiful male earnestness. Wilde's marvelous fantasy world makes truth into a game too. Diaries are not private glimpses of true feeling, but "some-

---

47. Snubbed socially.

thing sensational to read in the train," or records of imaginary relationships "intended for publication," while novels and babies are exchangeable equivalents. At the end of the play it seems that traditional relationships have been restored, with each man pinned down to a bride, a proper name, and a place in the patriarchal family, but when Jack comments, "it is a terrible thing for a man to find out suddenly that all his life he has been speaking nothing but the truth," Gwendolen reassures him, "I feel that you are sure to change." Truth and earnestness get restored accidentally, but Wilde promises us that the true values of the play, wit, laughter, language, and pleasure, will return. For more information about Wilde, see pp. 19, 83, and 355.

The Importance of Being Earnest

A Trivial Comedy for Serious People

FIRST ACT

SCENE: *Morning-room in Algernon's flat in Half Moon Street.*[1] *The room is luxuriously and artistically furnished. The sound of a piano is heard in the adjoining room.*

> [*Lane is arranging afternoon tea on the table, and after the music has ceased, Algernon enters.*]

ALGERNON: Did you hear what I was playing, Lane?

LANE: I didn't think it polite to listen, sir.

ALGERNON: I'm sorry for that, for your sake. I don't play accurately—anyone can play accurately—but I play with wonderful expression. As far as the piano is concerned, sentiment is my forte. I keep science for Life.

LANE: Yes, sir.

ALGERNON: And, speaking of the science of Life, have you got the cucumber sandwiches cut for Lady Bracknell?

LANE: Yes, sir. [*Hands them on a salver.*]

ALGERNON [*inspects them, takes two, and sits down on the sofa*]: Oh! . . . by the way, Lane, I see from your book that on Thursday night, when Lord Shoreham and Mr. Worthing were dining with me, eight bottles of champagne are entered as having been consumed.

LANE: Yes, sir; eight bottles and a pint.

ALGERNON: Why is it that at a bachelor's establishment the servants invariably drink the champagne? I ask merely for information.

LANE: I attribute it to the superior quality of the wine, sir. I have often observed that in married households the champagne is rarely of a first-rate brand.

ALGERNON: Good Heavens! Is marriage so demoralizing as that?

LANE: I believe it *is* a very pleasant state, sir. I have had very little experience of it myself up to the present. I have only been married once. That was in consequence of a misunderstanding between myself and a young person.

ALGERNON [*languidly*]: I don't know that I am much interested in your family life, Lane.

LANE: No, sir; it is not a very interesting subject. I never think of it myself.

---

1. A fashionable and wealthy area in London.

ALGERNON: Very natural, I am sure. That will do, Lane, thank you.

LANE: Thank you, sir. [*Lane goes out.*]

ALGERNON: Lane's views on marriage seem somewhat lax. Really, if the lower orders don't set us a good example, what on earth is the use of them? They seem, as a class, to have absolutely no sense of moral responsibility.

 [*Enter Lane.*]

LANE: Mr. Ernest Worthing.

 [*Enter Jack. Lane goes out.*]

ALGERNON: How are you, my dear Ernest? What brings you up to town?

JACK: Oh, pleasure, pleasure! What else should bring one anywhere? Eating as usual, I see, Algy!

ALGERNON [*stiffly*]: I believe it is customary in good society to take some slight refreshment at five o'clock. Where have you been since last Thursday?

JACK [*sitting down on the sofa*]: In the country.

ALGERNON: What on earth do you do there?

JACK [*pulling off his gloves*]: When one is in town one amuses oneself. When one is in the country one amuses other people. It is excessively boring.

ALGERNON: And who are the people you amuse?

JACK [*airily*]: Oh, neighbours, neighbours.

ALGERNON: Got nice neighbours in your part of Shropshire?[2]

JACK: Perfectly horrid! Never speak to one of them.

ALGERNON: How immensely you must amuse them! [*Goes over and takes sandwich.*] By the way, Shropshire is your county, is it not?

JACK: Eh? Shropshire? Yes, of course. Hallo! Why all these cups? Why cucumber sandwiches? Why such reckless extravagance in one so young? Who is coming to tea?

ALGERNON: Oh! merely Aunt Augusta and Gwendolen.

JACK: How perfectly delightful!

ALGERNON: Yes, that is all very well; but I am afraid Aunt Augusta won't quite approve of your being here.

JACK: May I ask why?

ALGERNON: My dear fellow, the way you flirt with Gwendolen is perfectly disgraceful. It is almost as bad as the way Gwendolen flirts with you.

JACK: I am in love with Gwendolen. I have come up to town expressly to propose to her.

ALGERNON: I thought you had come up for pleasure? . . . I call that business.

JACK: How utterly unromantic you are!

ALGERNON: I really don't see anything romantic in proposing. It is very romantic to be in love. But there is nothing romantic about a definite proposal. Why, one may be accepted. One usually is, I believe. Then the excitement is all over. The very essence of romance is uncertainty. If I ever get married, I'll certainly try to forget the fact.

JACK: I have no doubt about that, dear Algy. The Divorce Court was specially invented for people whose memories are so curiously constituted.

---

2. Jack's estate is actually in Hertfordshire (near London), quite far from Shropshire on the northwest border of England.

ALGERNON: Oh! there is no use speculating on that subject. Divorces are made in Heaven—[*Jack puts out his hand to take a sandwich. Algernon at once interferes.*] Please don't touch the cucumber sandwiches. They are ordered specially for Aunt Augusta. [*Takes one and eats it.*]

JACK: Well, you have been eating them all the time.

ALGERNON: That is quite a different matter. She is my aunt. [*Takes plate from below.*] Have some bread and butter. The bread and butter is for Gwendolen. Gwendolen is devoted to bread and butter.

JACK [*advancing to table and helping himself*]: And very good bread and butter it is too.

ALGERNON: Well, my dear fellow, you need not eat as if you were going to eat it all. You behave as if you were married to her already. You are not married to her already, and I don't think you ever will be.

JACK: Why on earth do you say that?

ALGERNON: Well, in the first place girls never marry the men they flirt with. Girls don't think it right.

JACK: Oh, that is nonsense!

ALGERNON: It isn't. It is a great truth. It accounts for the extraordinary number of bachelors that one sees all over the place. In the second place, I don't give my consent.

JACK: Your consent!

ALGERNON: My dear fellow, Gwendolen is my first cousin. And before I allow you to marry her, you will have to clear up the whole question of Cecily. [*Rings bell.*]

JACK: Cecily! What on earth do you mean? What do you mean, Algy, by Cecily? I don't know anyone of the name of Cecily.
    [*Enter Lane.*]

ALGERNON: Bring me that cigarette case Mr. Worthing left in the smoking-room the last time he dined here.

LANE: Yes, sir. [*Lane goes out.*]

JACK: Do you mean to say you have had my cigarette case all this time? I wish to goodness you had let me know. I have been writing frantic letters to Scotland Yard[3] about it. I was very nearly offering a large reward.

ALGERNON: Well, I wish you would offer one. I happen to be more than usually hard up.

JACK: There is no good offering a large reward now that the thing is found.
    [*Enter Lane with the cigarette case on a salver. Algernon takes it at once. Lane goes out.*]

ALGERNON: I think that is rather mean of you, Ernest, I must say. [*Opens case and examines it.*] However, it makes no matter, for, now that I look at the inscription inside, I find that the thing isn't yours after all.

JACK: Of course it's mine. [*Moving to him.*] You have seen me with it a hundred times, and you have no right whatsoever to read what is written inside. It is a very ungentlemanly thing to read a private cigarette case.

ALGERNON: Oh! it is absurd to have a hard-and-fast rule about what one should read and what one shouldn't. More than half of modern culture depends on what one shouldn't read.

---

3. Police headquarters.

JACK: I am quite aware of the fact, and I don't propose to discuss modern culture. It isn't the sort of thing one should talk of in private. I simply want my cigarette case back.

ALGERNON: Yes; but this isn't your cigarette case. This cigarette case is a present from someone of the name of Cecily, and you said you didn't know anyone of that name.

JACK: Well, if you want to know, Cecily happens to be my aunt.

ALGERNON: Your aunt!

JACK: Yes. Charming old lady she is, too. Lives at Tunbridge Wells.[4] Just give it back to me, Algy.

ALGERNON [retreating to back of sofa]: But why does she call herself little Cecily if she is your aunt and lives at Tunbridge Wells? [Reading.] "From little Cecily with her fondest love."

JACK [moving to sofa and kneeling upon it]: My dear fellow, what on earth is there in that? Some aunts are tall, some aunts are not tall. That is a matter that surely an aunt may be allowed to decide for herself. You seem to think that every aunt should be exactly like your aunt! That is absurd! For Heaven's sake give me back my cigarette case. [Follows Algernon round the room.]

ALGERNON: Yes. But why does your aunt call you her uncle? "From little Cecily, with her fondest love to her dear Uncle Jack." There is no objection, I admit, to an aunt being a small aunt, but why an aunt, no matter what her size may be, should call her own nephew her uncle, I can't quite make out. Besides, your name isn't Jack at all; it is Ernest.

JACK: It isn't Ernest; it's Jack.

ALGERNON: You have always told me it was Ernest. I have introduced you to everyone as Ernest. You answer to the name of Ernest. You look as if your name was Ernest. You are the most earnest looking person I ever saw in my life. It is perfectly absurd your saying that your name isn't Ernest. It's on your cards. Here is one of them. [Taking it from case.] "Mr. Ernest Worthing, B. 4, The Albany." I'll keep this as a proof that your name is Ernest if ever you attempt to deny it to me, or to Gwendolen, or to anyone else. [Puts the card in his pocket.]

JACK: Well, my name is Ernest in town and Jack in the country, and the cigarette case was given to me in the country.

ALGERNON: Yes, but that does not account for the fact that your small Aunt Cecily, who lives at Tunbridge Wells, calls you her dear uncle. Come, old boy, you had much better have the thing out at once.

JACK: My dear Algy, you talk exactly as if you were a dentist. It is very vulgar to talk like a dentist when one isn't a dentist. It produces a false impression.

ALGERNON: Well, that is exactly what dentists always do. Now, go on! Tell me the whole thing. I may mention that I have always suspected you of being a confirmed and secret Bunburyist, and I am quite sure of it now.

JACK: Bunburyist? What on earth do you mean by a Bunburyist?

ALGERNON: I'll reveal to you the meaning of that incomparable expression as soon as you are kind enough to inform me why you are Ernest in town and Jack in the country.

---

4. A rather dreary resort town.

JACK: Well, produce my cigarette case first.

ALGERNON: Here it is. [*Hands cigarette case.*] Now produce your explanation, and pray make it improbable. [*Sits on sofa.*]

JACK: My dear fellow, there is nothing improbable about my explanation at all. In fact it's perfectly ordinary. Old Mr. Thomas Cardew, who adopted me when I was a little boy, made me in his will guardian to his granddaughter, Miss Cecily Cardew. Cecily who addresses me as her uncle from motives of respect that you could not possibly appreciate, lives at my place in the country under the charge of her admirable governess, Miss Prism.

ALGERNON: Where is that place in the country, by the way?

JACK: That is nothing to you, dear boy. You are not going to be invited. . . . I may tell you candidly that the place is not in Shropshire.

ALGERNON: I suspected that, my dear fellow! I have Bunburyed all over Shropshire on two separate occasions. Now, go on. Why are you Ernest in town and Jack in the country?

JACK: My dear Algy, I don't know whether you will be able to understand my real motives. You are hardly serious enough. When one is placed in the position of guardian, one has to adopt a very high moral tone on all subjects. It's one's duty to do so. And as a high moral tone can hardly be said to conduce very much to either one's health or one's happiness, in order to get up to town I have always pretended to have a younger brother of the name of Ernest, who lives in the Albany, and gets into the most dreadful scrapes. That, my dear Algy, is the whole truth pure and simple.

ALGERNON: The truth is rarely pure and never simple. Modern life would be very tedious if it were either, and modern literature a complete impossibility!

JACK: That wouldn't be at all a bad thing.

ALGERNON: Literary criticism is not your forte, my dear fellow. Don't try it. You should leave that to people who haven't been at a University. They do it so well in the daily papers. What you really are is a Bunburyist. I was quite right in saying you were a Bunburyist. You are one of the most advanced Bunburyists I know.

JACK: What on earth do you mean?

ALGERNON: You have invented a very useful younger brother called Ernest, in order that you may be able to come up to town as often as you like. I have invented an invaluable permanent invalid called Bunbury, in order that I may be able to go down into the country whenever I choose. Bunbury is perfectly invaluable. If it wasn't for Bunbury's extraordinary bad health, for instance, I wouldn't be able to dine with you at Willis's[5] tonight, for I have been really engaged[6] to Aunt Augusta for more than a week.

JACK: I haven't asked you to dine with me anywhere tonight.

ALGERNON: I know. You are absurdly careless about sending out invitations. It is very foolish of you. Nothing annoys people so much as not receiving invitations.

JACK: You had much better dine with your Aunt Augusta.

ALGERNON: I haven't the smallest intention of doing anything of the kind. To begin with, I dined there on Monday, and once a week is quite enough to dine with

---

5. A fashionable London restaurant.
6. Promised to attend her dinner.

one's own relations. In the second place, whenever I do dine there I am always treated as a member of the family, and sent down[7] with either no woman at all, or two. In the third place, I know perfectly well whom she will place me next to, tonight. She will place me next Mary Farquhar, who always flirts with her own husband across the dinner-table. That is not very pleasant. Indeed, it is not even decent . . . and that sort of thing is enormously on the increase. The amount of women in London who flirt with their own husbands is perfectly scandalous. It looks so bad. It is simply washing one's clean linen in public. Besides, now that I know you to be a confirmed Bunburyist I naturally want to talk to you about Bunburying. I want to tell you the rules.

JACK: I'm not a Bunburyist at all. If Gwendolen accepts me, I am going to kill my brother, indeed I think I'll kill him in any case. Cecily is a little too much interested in him. It is rather a bore. So I am going to get rid of Ernest. And I strongly advise you to do the same with Mr. . . . with your invalid friend who has the absurd name.

ALGERNON: Nothing will induce me to part with Bunbury, and if you ever get married, which seems to me extremely problematic, you will be very glad to know Bunbury. A man who marries without knowing Bunbury has a very tedious time of it.

JACK: That is nonsense. If I marry a charming girl like Gwendolen, and she is the only girl I ever saw in my life that I would marry, I certainly won't want to know Bunbury.

ALGERNON: Then your wife will. You don't seem to realize, that in married life three is company and two is none.

JACK [sententiously]: That, my dear young friend, is the theory that the corrupt French Drama[8] has been propounding for the last fifty years.

ALGERNON: Yes; and that the happy English home has proved in half the time.

JACK: For heaven's sake, don't try to be cynical. It's perfectly easy to be cynical.

ALGERNON: My dear fellow, it isn't easy to be anything nowadays. There's such a lot of beastly competition about. [The sound of an electric bell is heard.] Ah! that must be Aunt Augusta. Only relatives, or creditors, ever ring in that Wagnerian[9] manner. Now, if I get her out of the way for ten minutes, so that you can have an opportunity for proposing to Gwendolen, may I dine with you tonight at Willis's?

JACK: I suppose so, if you want to.

ALGERNON: Yes, but you must be serious about it. I hate people who are not serious about meals. It is so shallow of them.

   [Enter Lane.]

LANE: Lady Bracknell and Miss Fairfax.

   [Algernon goes forward to meet them. Enter Lady Bracknell and Gwendolen.]

LADY BRACKNELL: Good afternoon, dear Algernon, I hope you are behaving very well.

ALGERNON: I'm feeling very well, Aunt Augusta.

LADY BRACKNELL: That's not quite the same thing. In fact the two things rarely go together. [Sees Jack and bows to him with icy coldness.]

ALGERNON [to Gwendolen]: Dear me, you are smart!

---

7. Matched with a woman whom he would escort to the dining room and sit by.
8. French fiction and drama frequently showed extramarital liaisons.
9. Grand, crashing chords characteristic of operas by German composer Richard Wagner.

GWENDOLEN: I am always smart! Aren't I, Mr. Worthing?

JACK: You're quite perfect, Miss Fairfax.

GWENDOLEN: Oh! I hope I am not that. It would leave no room for developments, and I intend to develop in many directions. [*Gwendolen and Jack sit down together in the corner.*]

LADY BRACKNELL: I'm sorry if we are a little late, Algernon, but I was obliged to call on dear Lady Harbury. I hadn't been there since her poor husband's death. I never saw a woman so altered; she looks quite twenty years younger. And now I'll have a cup of tea, and one of those nice cucumber sandwiches you promised me.

ALGERNON: Certainly, Aunt Augusta. [*Goes over to tea-table.*]

LADY BRACKNELL: Won't you come and sit here, Gwendolen?

GWENDOLEN: Thanks, mamma, I'm quite comfortable where I am.

ALGERNON [*picking up empty plate in horror*]: Good heavens! Lane! Why are there no cucumber sandwiches? I ordered them specially.

LANE [*gravely*]: There were no cucumbers in the market this morning, sir. I went down twice.

ALGERNON: No cucumbers!

LANE: No, sir. Not even for ready money.

ALGERNON: That will do, Lane, thank you.

LANE: Thank you, sir. [*Goes out.*]

ALGERNON: I am greatly distressed, Aunt Augusta, about there being no cucumbers, not even for ready money.

LADY BRACKNELL: It really makes no matter, Algernon. I had some crumpets with Lady Harbury, who seems to me to be living entirely for pleasure now.

ALGERNON: I hear her hair has turned quite gold from grief.

LADY BRACKNELL: It certainly has changed its colour. From what cause I, of course, cannot say. [*Algernon crosses and hands tea.*] Thank you. I've quite a treat for you tonight, Algernon. I am going to send you down with Mary Farquhar. She is such a nice woman, and so attentive to her husband. It's delightful to watch them.

ALGERNON: I am afraid, Aunt Augusta, I shall have to give up the pleasure of dining with you tonight after all.

LADY BRACKNELL [*frowning*]: I hope not, Algernon. It would put my table completely out. Your uncle would have to dine upstairs. Fortunately he is accustomed to that.

ALGERNON: It is a great bore, and, I need hardly say, a terrible disappointment to me, but the fact is I have just had a telegram to say that my poor friend Bunbury is very ill again. [*Exchanges glances with Jack.*] They seem to think I should be with him.

LADY BRACKNELL: It is very strange. This Mr. Bunbury seems to suffer from curiously bad health.

ALGERNON: Yes; poor Bunbury is a dreadful invalid.

LADY BRACKNELL: Well, I must say, Algernon, that I think it is high time that Mr. Bunbury made up his mind whether he was going to live or to die. This shilly-shallying with the question is absurd. Nor do I in any way approve of the modern sympathy with invalids. I consider it morbid. Illness of any kind is hardly a thing to be encouraged in others. Health is the primary duty of life. I am always telling that to your poor uncle, but he never seems to take much notice . . . as far as any improvement in his ailments goes. I should be much obliged if you would ask Mr. Bunbury, from me, to be kind enough not to have a relapse on Saturday, for I rely on you to arrange my music for me. It is my last reception, and one wants something that will encourage conversation, particularly at the end of the season[10] when everyone has practically said whatever they had to say, which, in most cases, was probably not much.

ALGERNON: I'll speak to Bunbury, Aunt Augusta, if he is still conscious, and I think I can promise you he'll be all right by Saturday. Of course the music is a great difficulty. You see, if one plays good music, people don't listen, and if one plays bad music people don't talk. But I'll run over the programme I've drawn out, if you will kindly come into the next room for a moment.

LADY BRACKNELL: Thank you, Algernon. It is very thoughtful of you. [*Rising, and following Algernon.*] I'm sure the programme will be delightful, after a few expurgations. French songs I cannot possibly allow. People always seem to think that they are improper, and either look shocked, which is vulgar, or laugh, which is worse. But German sounds a thoroughly respectable language, and indeed, I believe is so. Gwendolen, you will accompany me.

GWENDOLEN: Certainly, mamma.

[*Lady Bracknell and Algernon go into the music-room, Gwendolen remains behind.*]

JACK: Charming day it has been, Miss Fairfax.

GWENDOLEN: Pray don't talk to me about the weather, Mr. Worthing. Whenever people talk to me about the weather, I always feel quite certain that they mean something else. And that makes me so nervous.

JACK: I do mean something else.

GWENDOLEN: I thought so. In fact, I am never wrong.

JACK: And I would like to be allowed to take advantage of Lady Bracknell's temporary absence . . .

GWENDOLEN: I would certainly advise you to do so. Mamma has a way of coming back suddenly into a room that I have often had to speak to her about.

JACK [*nervously*]: Miss Fairfax, ever since I met you I have admired you more than any girl . . . I have ever met since . . . I met you.

GWENDOLEN: Yes, I am quite aware of the fact. And I often wish that in public, at any rate, you had been more demonstrative. For me you have always had an irresistible fascination. Even before I met you I was far from indifferent to you. [*Jack looks at her in amazement.*] We live, as I hope you know, Mr. Worthing, in an age of ideals. The fact is constantly mentioned in the more expensive monthly magazines, and has reached the provincial pulpits I am told: and my ideal has always been to love some one of the name of Ernest. There is something in that name that inspires absolute confidence. The moment Algernon first mentioned to me that he had a friend called Ernest, I knew I was destined to love you.

JACK: You really love me, Gwendolen?

GWENDOLEN: Passionately!

JACK: Darling! You don't know how happy you've made me.

GWENDOLEN: My own Ernest!

JACK: But you don't really mean to say that you couldn't love me if my name wasn't Ernest?

---

10. The fashionable London social season ran from late spring through July, when people left for their country estates.

GWENDOLEN: But your name is Ernest.

JACK: Yes, I know it is. But supposing it was something else? Do you mean to say you couldn't love me then?

GWENDOLEN [*glibly*]: Ah! that is clearly a metaphysical speculation, and like most metaphysical speculations has very little reference at all to the actual facts of real life, as we know them.

JACK: Personally, darling, to speak quite candidly, I don't much care about the name of Ernest . . . I don't think the name suits me at all.

GWENDOLEN: It suits you perfectly. It is a divine name. It has a music of its own. It produces vibrations.

JACK: Well, really, Gwendolen, I must say that I think there are lots of other much nicer names. I think Jack, for instance, a charming name.

GWENDOLEN: Jack? . . . No, there is very little music in the name Jack, if any at all, indeed. It does not thrill. It produces absolutely no vibrations . . . I have known several Jacks, and they all, without exception, were more than usually plain. Besides, Jack is a notorious domesticity for John! And I pity any woman who is married to a man called John. She would probably never be allowed to know the entrancing pleasure of a single moment's solitude. The only really safe name is Ernest.

JACK: Gwendolen, I must get christened at once—I mean we must get married at once. There is no time to be lost.

GWENDOLEN: Married, Mr. Worthing?

JACK [*astounded*]: Well . . . surely. You know that I love you, and you led me to believe, Miss Fairfax, that you were not absolutely indifferent to me.

GWENDOLEN: I adore you. But you haven't proposed to me yet. Nothing has been said at all about marriage. The subject has not even been touched on.

JACK: Well . . . may I propose to you now?

GWENDOLEN: I think it would be an admirable opportunity. And to spare you any possible disappointment, Mr. Worthing, I think it only fair to tell you quite frankly beforehand that I am fully determined to accept you.

JACK: Gwendolen!

GWENDOLEN: Yes, Mr. Worthing, what have you got to say to me?

JACK: You know what I have got to say to you.

GWENDOLEN: Yes, but you don't say it.

JACK: Gwendolen, will you marry me? [*Goes on his knees.*]

GWENDOLEN: Of course I will, darling. How long you have been about it! I am afraid you have had very little experience in how to propose.

JACK: My own one, I have never loved anyone in the world but you.

GWENDOLEN: Yes, but men often propose for practice. I know my brother Gerald does. All my girl-friends tell me so. What wonderfully blue eyes you have, Ernest! They are quite, quite, blue. I hope you will always look at me just like that, especially when there are other people present.

[*Enter Lady Bracknell.*]

LADY BRACKNELL: Mr. Worthing! Rise, sir, from this semi-recumbent posture. It is most indecorous.

GWENDOLEN: Mamma! [*He tries to rise; she restrains him.*] I must beg you to retire. This is no place for you. Besides, Mr. Worthing has not quite finished yet.

LADY BRACKNELL: Finished what, may I ask?

GWENDOLEN: I am engaged to Mr. Worthing, mamma. [*They rise together.*]

LADY BRACKNELL: Pardon me, you are not engaged to anyone. When you do become engaged to some one, I, or your father, should his health permit him, will inform you of the fact. An engagement should come on a young girl as a surprise, pleasant or unpleasant, as the case may be. It is hardly a matter that she could be allowed to arrange for herself. . . . And now I have a few questions to put to you, Mr. Worthing. While I am making these inquiries, you, Gwendolen, will wait for me below in the carriage.

GWENDOLEN [*reproachfully*]: Mamma!

LADY BRACKNELL: In the carriage, Gwendolen! [*Gwendolen goes to the door. She and Jack blow kisses to each other behind Lady Bracknell's back. Lady Bracknell looks vaguely about as if she could not understand what the noise was. Finally turns round.*] Gwendolen, the carriage!

GWENDOLEN: Yes, mamma. [*Goes out, looking back at Jack.*]

LADY BRACKNELL [*sitting down*]: You can take a seat, Mr. Worthing.
      [*Looking in her pocket for note-book and pencil.*]

JACK: Thank you, Lady Bracknell, I prefer standing.

LADY BRACKNELL [*pencil and note-book in hand*]: I feel bound to tell you that you are not down on my list of eligible young men, although I have the same list as the dear Duchess of Bolton has. We work together, in fact. However, I am quite ready to enter your name, should your answers be what a really affectionate mother requires. Do you smoke?

JACK: Well, yes, I must admit I smoke.

LADY BRACKNELL: I am glad to hear it. A man should always have an occupation of some kind. There are far too many idle men in London as it is. How old are you?

JACK: Twenty-nine.

LADY BRACKNELL: A very good age to be married at. I have always been of opinion that a man who desires to get married should know either everything or nothing. Which do you know?

JACK [*after some hesitation*]: I know nothing, Lady Bracknell.

LADY BRACKNELL: I am pleased to hear it. I do not approve of anything that tampers with natural ignorance. Ignorance is like a delicate exotic fruit; touch it and the bloom is gone. The whole theory of modern education is radically unsound. Fortunately in England, at any rate, education produces no effect whatsoever. If it did, it would prove a serious danger to the upper classes, and probably lead to acts of violence in Grosvenor Square.[11] What is your income?

JACK: Between seven and eight thousand a year.

LADY BRACKNELL [*makes a note in her book*]: In land, or in investments?

JACK: In investments, chiefly.

LADY BRACKNELL: That is satisfactory. What between the duties expected of one during one's lifetime, and the duties exacted from one after one's death,[12] land has ceased to be either a profit or a pleasure. It gives one position, and prevents one from keeping it up. That's all that can be said about land.

---

11. A wealthy enclave.
12. Estate taxes.

JACK: I have a country house with some land, of course, attached to it, about fifteen hundred acres, I believe; but I don't depend on that for my real income. In fact, as far as I can make out, the poachers are the only people who make anything out of it.

LADY BRACKNELL: A country house! How many bedrooms? Well, that point can be cleared up afterwards. You have a town house, I hope? A girl with a simple, unspoiled nature, like Gwendolen, could hardly be expected to reside in the country.

JACK: Well, I own a house in Belgrave Square,[13] but it is let by the year to Lady Bloxham. Of course, I can get it back whenever I like, at six months' notice.

LADY BRACKNELL: Lady Bloxham? I don't know her.

JACK: Oh, she goes about very little. She is a lady considerably advanced in years.

LADY BRACKNELL: Ah, nowadays that is no guarantee of respectability of character. What number in Belgrave Square?

JACK: 149.

LADY BRACKNELL [*shaking her head*]: The unfashionable side. I thought there was something. However, that could easily be altered.

JACK: Do you mean the fashion, or the side?

LADY BRACKNELL [*sternly*]: Both, if necessary, I presume. What are your politics?

JACK: Well, I am afraid I really have none. I am a Liberal Unionist.[14]

LADY BRACKNELL: Oh, they count as Tories. They dine with us. Or come in the evening, at any rate. Now to minor matters. Are your parents living?

JACK: I have lost both my parents.

LADY BRACKNELL: Both? To lose one parent may be regarded as a misfortune—to lose *both* seems like carelessness. Who was your father? He was evidently a man of some wealth. Was he born in what the Radical papers call the purple of commerce, or did he rise from the ranks of the aristocracy?

JACK: I am afraid I really don't know. The fact is, Lady Bracknell, I said I had lost my parents. It would be nearer the truth to say that my parents seem to have lost me . . . I don't actually know who I am by birth. I was . . . well, I was found.

LADY BRACKNELL: Found!

JACK: The late Mr. Thomas Cardew, an old gentleman of a very charitable and kindly disposition, found me, and gave me the name of Worthing, because he happened to have a first-class ticket for Worthing in his pocket at the time. Worthing is a place in Sussex. It is a seaside resort.

LADY BRACKNELL: Where did the charitable gentleman who had a first-class ticket for this seaside resort find you?

JACK [*gravely*]: In a hand-bag.

LADY BRACKNELL: A hand-bag?

JACK [*very seriously*]: Yes, Lady Bracknell. I was in a hand-bag—a somewhat large, black leather hand-bag, with handles to it—an ordinary hand-bag in fact.

LADY BRACKNELL: In what locality did this Mr. James, or Thomas, Cardew come across this ordinary hand-bag?

JACK: In the cloak-room at Victoria Station. It was given to him in mistake for his own.

LADY BRACKNELL: The cloak-room at Victoria Station?

---

13. An area of London associated with the hereditary aristocracy.
14. In 1886, the Liberal Unionists joined the Conservatives (Tories) to vote against Irish Home Rule.

JACK: Yes. The Brighton line.

LADY BRACKNELL: The line is immaterial. Mr. Worthing, I confess I feel somewhat bewildered by what you have just told me. To be born, or at any rate bred, in a hand-bag, whether it had handles or not, seems to me to display a contempt for the ordinary decencies of family life that reminds one of the worst excesses of the French Revolution. And I presume you know what that unfortunate movement led to? As for the particular locality in which the hand-bag was found, a cloak-room at a railway station might serve to conceal a social indiscretion—has probably, indeed, been used for that purpose before now—but it could hardly be regarded as an assured basis for a recognized position in good society.

JACK: May I ask you then what you would advise me to do? I need hardly say I would do anything in the world to ensure Gwendolen's happiness.

LADY BRACKNELL: I would strongly advise you, Mr. Worthing, to try and acquire some relations as soon as possible, and to make a definite effort to produce at any rate one parent, of either sex, before the season is quite over.

JACK: Well, I don't see how I could possibly manage to do that. I can produce the hand-bag at any moment. It is in my dressing-room at home. I really think that should satisfy you, Lady Bracknell.

LADY BRACKNELL: Me, sir! What has it to do with me? You can hardly imagine that I and Lord Bracknell would dream of allowing our only daughter—a girl brought up with the utmost care—to marry into a cloak-room, and form an alliance with a parcel? Good morning, Mr. Worthing!

[*Lady Bracknell sweeps out in majestic indignation.*]

JACK: Good morning! [*Algernon, from the other room, strikes up the Wedding March. Jack looks perfectly furious, and goes to the door.*] For goodness' sake don't play that ghastly tune, Algy! How idiotic you are!

[*The music stops, and Algernon enters cheerily.*]

ALGERNON: Didn't it go off all right, old boy? You don't mean to say Gwendolen refused you? I know it is a way she has. She is always refusing people. I think it is most ill-natured of her.

JACK: Oh, Gwendolen is as right as a trivet. As far as she is concerned, we are engaged. Her mother is perfectly unbearable. Never met such a Gorgon[15] . . . I don't really know what a Gorgon is like, but I am quite sure Lady Bracknell is one. In any case, she is a monster, without being a myth, which is rather unfair . . . I beg your pardon, Algy, I suppose I shouldn't talk about your own aunt in that way before you.

ALGERNON: My dear boy, I love hearing my relations abused. It is the only thing that makes me put up with them at all. Relations are simply a tedious pack of people, who haven't got the remotest knowledge of how to live, nor the smallest instinct about when to die.

JACK: Oh, that is nonsense!

ALGERNON: It isn't!

JACK: Well, I won't argue about the matter. You always want to argue about things.

ALGERNON: That is exactly what things were originally made for.

---

15. Mythological monster who could turn to stone anyone who glanced at her.

JACK: Upon my word, if I thought that, I'd shoot myself . . . [*A pause.*] You don't
think there is any chance of Gwendolen becoming like her mother in about a
hundred and fifty years, do you Algy?

ALGERNON: All women become like their mothers. That is their tragedy. No man
does. That's his.

JACK: Is that clever?

ALGERNON: It is perfectly phrased! and quite as true as any observation in civilized
life should be.

JACK: I am sick to death of cleverness. Everybody is clever nowadays. You can't go
anywhere without meeting clever people. The thing has become an absolute public nuisance. I wish to goodness we had a few fools left.

ALGERNON: We have.

JACK: I should extremely like to meet them. What do they talk about?

ALGERNON: The fools? Oh! about the clever people, of course.

JACK: What fools!

ALGERNON: By the way, did you tell Gwendolen the truth about your being Ernest
in town, and Jack in the country?

JACK [*in a very patronizing manner*]: My dear fellow, the truth isn't quite the sort of
thing one tells to a nice sweet refined girl. What extraordinary ideas you have
about the way to behave to a woman!

ALGERNON: The only way to behave to a woman is to make love to her,[16] if she is
pretty, and to someone else if she is plain.

JACK: Oh, that is nonsense.

ALGERNON: What about your brother? What about the profligate Ernest?

JACK: Oh, before the end of the week I shall have got rid of him. I'll say he died in
Paris of apoplexy. Lots of people die of apoplexy, quite suddenly, don't they?

ALGERNON: Yes, but it's hereditary, my dear fellow. It's a sort of thing that runs in
families. You had much better say a severe chill.

JACK: You are sure a severe chill isn't hereditary, or anything of that kind?

ALGERNON: Of course it isn't!

JACK: Very well, then. My poor brother Ernest is carried off suddenly in Paris, by a
severe chill. That gets rid of him.

ALGERNON: But I thought you said that . . . Miss Cardew was a little too much interested in your poor brother Ernest? Won't she feel his loss a good deal?

JACK: Oh, that is all right. Cecily is not a silly romantic girl, I am glad to say. She has
got a capital appetite, goes for long walks, and pays no attention at all to her lessons.

ALGERNON: I would rather like to see Cecily.

JACK: I will take very good care you never do. She is excessively pretty, and she is
only just eighteen.

ALGERNON: Have you told Gwendolen yet that you have an excessively pretty ward
who is only just eighteen?

JACK: Oh! one doesn't blurt these things out to people. Cecily and Gwendolen are
perfectly certain to be extremely great friends. I'll bet you anything you like that
half an hour after they have met, they will be calling each other sister.

---

16. Flirt with her.

ALGERNON: Women only do that when they have called each other a lot of other things first. Now, my dear boy, if we want to get a good table at Willis's, we really must go and dress. Do you know it is nearly seven?

JACK [irritably]: Oh! it always is nearly seven.

ALGERNON: Well, I'm hungry.

JACK: I never knew you when you weren't. . . .

ALGERNON: What shall we do after dinner? Go to a theatre?

JACK: Oh no! I loathe listening.

ALGERNON: Well, let us go to the Club?

JACK: Oh, no! I hate talking.

ALGERNON: Well, we might trot round to the Empire[17] at ten?

JACK: Oh, no! I can't bear looking at things. It is so silly.

ALGERNON: Well, what shall we do?

JACK: Nothing!

ALGERNON: It is awfully hard work doing nothing. However, I don't mind hard work where there is no definite object of any kind.

[Enter Lane.]

LANE: Miss Fairfax.

[Enter Gwendolen. Lane goes out.]

ALGERNON: Gwendolen, upon my word!

GWENDOLEN: Algy, kindly turn your back. I have something very particular to say to Mr. Worthing.

ALGERNON: Really, Gwendolen, I don't think I can allow this at all.

GWENDOLEN: Algy, you always adopt a strictly immoral attitude towards life. You are not quite old enough to do that.

[Algernon retires to the fireplace.]

JACK: My own darling!

GWENDOLEN: Ernest, we may never be married. From the expression on mamma's face I fear we never shall. Few parents nowadays pay any regard to what their children say to them. The old-fashioned respect for the young is fast dying out. Whatever influence I ever had over mamma, I lost at the age of three. But although she may prevent us from becoming man and wife, and I may marry someone else, and marry often, nothing that she can possibly do can alter my eternal devotion to you.

JACK: Dear Gwendolen!

GWENDOLEN: The story of your romantic origin, as related to me by mamma, with unpleasing comments, has naturally stirred the deeper fibres of my nature. Your Christian name has an irresistible fascination. The simplicity of your character makes you exquisitely incomprehensible to me. Your town address at the Albany I have. What is your address in the country?

JACK: The Manor House, Woolton, Hertfordshire.

[Algernon, who has been carefully listening, smiles to himself, and writes the address on his shirt-cuff. Then picks up the Railway Guide.]

---

17. A music hall.

GWENDOLEN: There is a good postal service, I suppose? It may be necessary to do something desperate. That of course will require serious consideration. I will communicate with you daily.

JACK: My own one!

GWENDOLEN: How long do you remain in town?

JACK: Till Monday.

GWENDOLEN: Good! Algy, you may turn round now.

ALGERNON: Thanks, I've turned round already.

GWENDOLEN: You may also ring the bell.

JACK: You will let me see you to your carriage, my own darling?

GWENDOLEN: Certainly.

JACK [to Lane, who now enters]: I will see Miss Fairfax out.

LANE: Yes, sir. [Jack and Gwendolen go off.]
    [Lane presents several letters on a salver to Algernon. It is to be surmised that they are bills, as Algernon, after looking at the envelopes, tears them up.]

ALGERNON: A glass of sherry, Lane.

LANE: Yes, sir.

ALGERNON: Tomorrow, Lane, I'm going Bunburying.

LANE: Yes, sir.

ALGERNON: I shall probably not be back till Monday. You can put up my dress clothes, my smoking jacket, and all the Bunbury suits . . .

LANE: Yes, sir. [Handing sherry.]

ALGERNON: I hope tomorrow will be a fine day, Lane.

LANE: It never is, sir.

ALGERNON: Lane, you're a perfect pessimist.

LANE: I do my best to give satisfaction, sir.
    [Enter Jack. Lane goes off.]

JACK: There's a sensible, intellectual girl! the only girl I ever cared for in my life.
    [Algernon is laughing immoderately.] What on earth are you so amused at?

ALGERNON: Oh, I'm a little anxious about poor Bunbury, that is all.

JACK: If you don't take care, your friend Bunbury will get you into a serious scrape some day.

ALGERNON: I love scrapes. They are the only things that are never serious.

JACK: Oh, that's nonsense, Algy. You never talk anything but nonsense.

ALGERNON: Nobody ever does.
    [Jack looks indignantly at him, and leaves the room. Algernon lights a cigarette, reads his shirt-cuff, and smiles.]

ACT DROP

SECOND ACT

SCENE: Garden at the Manor House. A flight of gray stone steps leads up to the house. The garden, an old-fashioned one, full of roses. Time of year, July. Basket chairs, and a table covered with books, are set under a large yew tree.

[Miss Prism discovered seated at the table. Cecily is at the back watering flowers.]

MISS PRISM [*calling*]: Cecily, Cecily! Surely such a utilitarian occupation as the watering of flowers is rather Moulton's duty than yours? Especially at a moment when intellectual pleasures await you. Your German grammar is on the table. Pray open it at page fifteen. We will repeat yesterday's lesson.

CECILY [*coming over very slowly*]: But I don't like German. It isn't at all a becoming language. I know perfectly well that I look quite plain after my German lesson.

MISS PRISM: Child, you know how anxious your guardian is that you should improve yourself in every way. He laid particular stress on your German, as he was leaving for town yesterday. Indeed, he always lays stress on your German when he is leaving for town.

CECILY: Dear Uncle Jack is so very serious! Sometimes he is so serious that I think he cannot be quite well.

MISS PRISM [*drawing herself up*]: Your guardian enjoys the best of health, and his gravity of demeanour is especially to be commended in one so comparatively young as he is. I know no one who has a higher sense of duty and responsibility.

CECILY: I suppose that is why he often looks a little bored when we three are together.

MISS PRISM: Cecily! I am surprised at you. Mr. Worthing has many troubles in his life. Idle merriment and triviality would be out of place in his conversation. You must remember his constant anxiety about that unfortunate young man his brother.

CECILY: I wish Uncle Jack would allow that unfortunate young man, his brother, to come down here sometimes. We might have a good influence over him, Miss Prism. I am sure you certainly would. You know German, and geology, and things of that kind influence a man very much. [*Cecily begins to write in her diary.*]

MISS PRISM [*shaking her head*]: I do not think that even I could produce any effect on a character that according to his own brother's admission is irretrievably weak and vacillating. Indeed I am not sure that I would desire to reclaim him. I am not in favour of this modern mania for turning bad people into good people at a moment's notice. As a man sows so let him reap.[18] You must put away your diary, Cecily. I really don't see why you should keep a diary at all.

CECILY: I keep a diary in order to enter the wonderful secrets of my life. If I didn't write them down I should probably forget all about them.

MISS PRISM: Memory, my dear Cecily, is the diary that we all carry about with us.

CECILY: Yes, but it usually chronicles the things that have never happened, and couldn't possibly have happened. I believe that Memory is responsible for nearly all the three-volume novels that Mudie[19] sends us.

MISS PRISM: Do not speak slightly of the three-volume novel, Cecily. I wrote one myself in earlier days.

CECILY: Did you really, Miss Prism? How wonderfully clever you are! I hope it did not end happily? I don't like novels that end happily. They depress me so much.

MISS PRISM: The good ended happily, and the bad unhappily. That is what Fiction means.

---

18. Paraphrase of Galatians 6.7.
19. Mudie's Select Library bought expensive three-volume novels and lent them, a volume at a time, to borrowers who paid a fee. Buying only novels that met his moral approval, Mudie was accused of keeping a stranglehold on British fiction. By the 1890s, cheaper production methods (and more varied lengths for novels) allowed publishers to sell novels directly to customers.

CECILY: I suppose so. But it seems very unfair. And was your novel ever published?

MISS PRISM: Alas! no. The manuscript unfortunately was abandoned. I use the word in the sense of lost or mislaid. To your work, child, these speculations are profit-less.

CECILY [smiling]: But I see dear Dr. Chasuble[20] coming up through the garden.

MISS PRISM [rising and advancing]: Dr. Chasuble! This is indeed a pleasure.

[Enter Canon Chasuble.]

CHASUBLE: And how are we this morning? Miss Prism, you are, I trust, well?

CECILY: Miss Prism has just been complaining of a slight headache. I think it would do her so much good to have a short stroll with you in the Park, Dr. Chasuble.

MISS PRISM: Cecily, I have not mentioned anything about a headache.

CECILY: No, dear Miss Prism, I know that, but I felt instinctively that you had a headache. Indeed I was thinking about that, and not about my German lesson, when the Rector came in.

CHASUBLE: I hope Cecily, you are not inattentive.

CECILY: Oh, I am afraid I am.

CHASUBLE: That is strange. Were I fortunate enough to be Miss Prism's pupil, I would hang upon her lips. [Miss Prism glares.] I spoke metaphorically.—My metaphor was drawn from bees. Ahem! Mr. Worthing I suppose, has not returned from town yet?

MISS PRISM: We do not expect him till Monday afternoon.

CHASUBLE: Ah yes, he usually likes to spend his Sunday in London. He is not one of those whose sole aim is enjoyment, as, by all accounts, that unfortunate young man his brother seems to be. But I must not disturb Egeria[21] and her pupil any longer.

MISS PRISM: Egeria? My name is Laetitia, Doctor.

CHASUBLE [bowing]: A classical allusion merely, drawn from the Pagan authors. I shall see you both no doubt at Evensong?[22]

MISS PRISM: I think, dear Doctor, I will have a stroll with you. I find I have a headache after all, and a walk might do it good.

CHASUBLE: With pleasure, Miss Prism, with pleasure. We might go as far as the schools and back.

MISS PRISM: That would be delightful. Cecily, you will read your Political Economy in my absence. The chapter on the Fall of the Rupee you may omit.[23] It is some-what too sensational. Even these metallic problems have their melodramatic side. [Goes down the garden with Dr. Chasuble.]

CECILY [picks up books and throws them back on table]: Horrid Political Economy! Hor-rid Geography! Horrid, horrid German!

[Enter Merriman with a card on a salver.]

MERRIMAN: Mr. Ernest Worthing has just driven over from the station. He has brought his luggage with him.

---

20. A chasuble is a clergyman's robe, worn in Catholic services. Rev. Chasuble is a High Church Anglican (Episcopalian), closest to Catholicism.

21. A Roman woman of great learning.

22. Evening services, associated with Catholic worship.

23. A rupee is Indian currency.

CECILY [*takes the card and reads it*]: "Mr. Ernest Worthing, B.4 The Albany, W." Uncle Jack's brother! Did you tell him Mr. Worthing was in town?

MERRIMAN: Yes, Miss. He seemed very much disappointed. I mentioned that you and Miss Prism were in the garden. He said he was anxious to speak to you privately for a moment.

CECILY: Ask Mr. Ernest Worthing to come here. I suppose you had better talk to the housekeeper about a room for him.

MERRIMAN: Yes, Miss. [*Merriman goes off.*]

CECILY: I have never met any really wicked person before. I feel rather frightened. I am so afraid he will look just like everyone else.

  [*Enter Algernon, very gay and debonair.*]

  He does!

ALGERNON [*raising his hat*]: You are my little cousin Cecily, I'm sure.

CECILY: You are under some strange mistake. I am not little. In fact, I believe I am more than usually tall for my age. [*Algernon is rather taken aback.*] But I am your cousin Cecily. You, I see from your card, are Uncle Jack's brother, my cousin Ernest, my wicked cousin Ernest.

ALGERNON: Oh! I am not really wicked at all, cousin Cecily. You mustn't think that I am wicked.

CECILY: If you are not, then you have certainly been deceiving us all in a very inexcusable manner. I hope you have not been leading a double life, pretending to be wicked and being really good all the time. That would be hypocrisy.

ALGERNON [*looks at her in amazement*]: Oh! Of course I have been rather reckless.

CECILY: I am glad to hear it.

ALGERNON: In fact, now you mention the subject, I have been very bad in my own small way.

CECILY: I don't think you should be so proud of that, although I am sure it must have been very pleasant.

ALGERNON: It is much pleasanter being here with you.

CECILY: I can't understand how you are here at all. Uncle Jack won't be back till Monday afternoon.

ALGERNON: That is a great disappointment. I am obliged to go up by the first train on Monday morning. I have a business appointment that I am anxious . . . to miss.

CECILY: Couldn't you miss it anywhere but in London?

ALGERNON: No: the appointment is in London.

CECILY: Well, I know, of course, how important it is not to keep a business engagement, if one wants to retain any sense of the beauty of life, but still I think you had better wait till Uncle Jack arrives. I know he wants to speak to you about your emigrating.

ALGERNON: About my what?

CECILY: Your emigrating. He has gone up to buy your outfit.

ALGERNON: I certainly wouldn't let Jack buy my outfit. He has no taste in neckties at all.

CECILY: I don't think you will require neckties. Uncle Jack is sending you to Australia.[24]

---

24. By the 1890s Australia was no longer a penal colony, but it had a reputation as a rough land where unsuccessful men could try to start over.

ALGERNON: Australia! I'd sooner die.

CECILY: Well, he said at dinner on Wednesday night, that you would have to choose between this world, the next world, and Australia.

ALGERNON: Oh, well! The accounts I have received of Australia and the next world are not particularly encouraging. This world is good enough for me, cousin Cecily.

CECILY: Yes, but are you good enough for it?

ALGERNON: I'm afraid I'm not that. That is why I want you to reform me. You might make that your mission, if you don't mind, cousin Cecily.

CECILY: I'm afraid I've no time, this afternoon.

ALGERNON: Well, would you mind my reforming myself this afternoon?

CECILY: It is rather Quixotic of you. But I think you should try.

ALGERNON: I will. I feel better already.

CECILY: You are looking a little worse.

ALGERNON: That is because I am hungry.

CECILY: How thoughtless of me. I should have remembered that when one is going to lead an entirely new life, one requires regular and wholesome meals. Won't you come in?

ALGERNON: Thank you. Might I have a buttonhole[25] first? I never have any appetite unless I have a buttonhole first.

CECILY: A Maréchal Niel?[26] [*Picks up scissors.*]

ALGERNON: No, I'd sooner have a pink rose.

CECILY: Why? [*Cuts a flower.*]

ALGERNON: Because you are like a pink rose, Cousin Cecily.

CECILY: I don't think it can be right for you to talk to me like that. Miss Prism never says such things to me.

ALGERNON: Then Miss Prism is a short-sighted old lady. [*Cecily puts the rose in his buttonhole.*] You are the prettiest girl I ever saw.

CECILY: Miss Prism says that all good looks are a snare.

ALGERNON: They are a snare that every sensible man would like to be caught in.

CECILY: Oh! I don't think I would care to catch a sensible man. I shouldn't know what to talk to him about.

[*They pass into the house. Miss Prism and Dr. Chasuble return.*]

MISS PRISM: You are too much alone, dear Dr. Chasuble. You should get married. A misanthrope I can understand—a womanthrope, never!

CHASUBLE [*with a scholar's shudder*]: Believe me, I do not deserve so neologistic[27] a phrase. The precept as well as the practice of the Primitive Church[28] was distinctly against matrimony.

MISS PRISM [*sententiously*]: That is obviously the reason why the Primitive Church has not lasted up to the present day. And you do not seem to realize, dear Doctor, that by persistently remaining single, a man converts himself into a permanent

---

25. A flower worn in a man's buttonhole.
26. A yellow rose.
27. New-worded (combining English and Greek).
28. The original Catholic Church before its doctrinal splits.

public temptation. Men should be more careful; this very celibacy leads weaker vessels astray.

CHASUBLE: But is a man not equally attractive when married?

MISS PRISM: No married man is ever attractive except to his wife.

CHASUBLE: And often, I've been told, not even to her.

MISS PRISM: That depends on the intellectual sympathies of the woman. Maturity can always be depended on. Ripeness can be trusted. Young women are green. [*Dr. Chasuble starts.*] I spoke horticulturally. My metaphor was drawn from fruits. But where is Cecily?

CHASUBLE: Perhaps she followed us to the schools.

  [*Enter Jack slowly from the back of the garden. He is dressed in the deepest mourning, with crape hat-band and black gloves.*]

MISS PRISM: Mr. Worthing!

CHASUBLE: Mr. Worthing?

MISS PRISM: This is indeed a surprise. We did not look for you till Monday afternoon.

JACK [*shakes Miss Prism's hand in a tragic manner*]: I have returned sooner than I expected. Dr. Chasuble, I hope you are well?

CHASUBLE: Dear Mr. Worthing, I trust this garb of woe does not betoken some terrible calamity?

JACK: My brother.

MISS PRISM: More shameful debts and extravagance?

CHASUBLE: Still leading his life of pleasure?

JACK [*shaking his head*]: Dead!

CHASUBLE: Your brother Ernest dead?

JACK: Quite dead.

MISS PRISM: What a lesson for him! I trust he will profit by it.

CHASUBLE: Mr. Worthing, I offer you my sincere condolence. You have at least the consolation of knowing that you were always the most generous and forgiving of brothers.

JACK: Poor Ernest! He had many faults, but it is a sad, sad blow.

CHASUBLE: Very sad indeed. Were you with him at the end?

JACK: No. He died abroad; in Paris, in fact. I had a telegram last night from the manager of the Grand Hotel.

CHASUBLE: Was the cause of death mentioned?

JACK: A severe chill, it seems.

MISS PRISM: As a man sows, so shall he reap.

CHASUBLE [*raising his hand*]: Charity, dear Miss Prism, charity! None of us are perfect. I myself am peculiarly susceptible to draughts. Will the interment take place here?

JACK: No. He seemed to have expressed a desire to be buried in Paris.

CHASUBLE: In Paris! [*Shakes his head.*] I fear that hardly points to any very serious state of mind at the last. You would no doubt wish me to make some slight allusion to this tragic domestic affliction next Sunday. [*Jack presses his hand convulsively.*] My sermon on the meaning of the manna in the wilderness[29] can be adapted to almost

---

29. Exodus 16.

any occasion, joyful, or, as in the present case, distressing. [*All sigh.*] I have preached it at harvest celebrations, christenings, confirmations, on days of humiliation and festal days. The last time I delivered it was in the Cathedral, as a charity sermon on behalf of the Society for the Prevention of Discontent among the Upper Orders. The Bishop, who was present, was much struck by some of the analogies I drew.

JACK: Ah! that reminds me, you mentioned christenings I think, Dr. Chasuble? I suppose you know how to christen all right? [*Dr. Chasuble looks astounded.*] I mean, of course, you are continually christening, aren't you?

MISS PRISM: It is, I regret to say, one of the Rector's most constant duties in this parish. I have often spoken to the poorer classes on the subject. But they don't seem to know what thrift is.

CHASUBLE: But is there any particular infant in whom you are interested, Mr. Worthing? Your brother was, I believe, unmarried, was he not?

JACK: Oh, yes.

MISS PRISM [*bitterly*]: People who live entirely for pleasure usually are.

JACK: But it is not for any child, dear Doctor. I am very fond of children. No! the fact is, I would like to be christened myself, this afternoon, if you have nothing better to do.

CHASUBLE: But surely, Mr. Worthing, you have been christened already?

JACK: I don't remember anything about it.

CHASUBLE: But have you any grave doubts on the subject?

JACK: I certainly intend to have. Of course I don't know if the thing would bother you in any way, or if you think I am a little too old now.

CHASUBLE: Not at all. The sprinkling, and, indeed, the immersion of adults is a perfectly canonical practice.

JACK: Immersion!

CHASUBLE: You need have no apprehensions. Sprinkling is all that is necessary, or indeed I think advisable. Our weather is so changeable. At what hour would you wish the ceremony performed?

JACK: Oh, I might trot round about five if that would suit you.

CHASUBLE: Perfectly, perfectly! In fact I have two similar ceremonies to perform at that time. A case of twins that occurred recently in one of the outlying cottages on your own estate. Poor Jenkins the carter, a most hard-working man.

JACK: Oh! I don't see much fun in being christened along with other babies. It would be childish. Would half-past five do?

CHASUBLE: Admirably! Admirably! [*Takes out watch.*] And now, dear Mr. Worthing, I will not intrude any longer into a house of sorrow. I would merely beg you not to be too much bowed down by grief. What seem to us bitter trials are often blessings in disguise.

MISS PRISM: This seems to me a blessing of an extremely obvious kind.

[*Enter Cecily from the house.*]

CECILY: Uncle Jack! Oh, I am pleased to see you back. But what horrid clothes you have got on! Do go and change them.

MISS PRISM: Cecily!

CHASUBLE: My child! my child!

[*Cecily goes towards Jack; he kisses her brow in a melancholy manner.*]

CECILY: What is the matter, Uncle Jack? Do look happy! You look as if you had toothache, and I have got such a surprise for you. Who do you think is in the dining-room? Your brother!

JACK: Who?

CECILY: Your brother Ernest. He arrived about half an hour ago.

JACK: What nonsense! I haven't got a brother.

CECILY: Oh, don't say that. However badly he may have behaved to you in the past he is still your brother. You couldn't be so heartless as to disown him. I'll tell him to come out. And you will shake hands with him, won't you, Uncle Jack? [*Runs back into the house.*]

CHASUBLE: These are very joyful tidings.

MISS PRISM: After we had all been resigned to his loss, his sudden return seems to me peculiarly distressing.

JACK: My brother is in the dining-room? I don't know what it all means. I think it is perfectly absurd.

[*Enter Algernon and Cecily hand in hand. They come slowly up to Jack.*]

JACK: Good heavens! [*Motions Algernon away.*]

ALGERNON: Brother John, I have come down from town to tell you that I am very sorry for all the trouble I have given you, and that I intend to lead a better life in the future.

[*Jack glares at him and does not take his hand.*]

CECILY: Uncle Jack, you are not going to refuse your own brother's hand?

JACK: Nothing will induce me to take his hand. I think his coming down here disgraceful. He knows perfectly well why.

CECILY: Uncle Jack, do be nice. There is some good in everyone. Ernest has just been telling me about his poor invalid friend Mr. Bunbury whom he goes to visit so often. And surely there must be much good in one who is kind to an invalid, and leaves the pleasures of London to sit by a bed of pain.

JACK: Oh! he has been talking about Bunbury has he?

CECILY: Yes, he has told me all about poor Mr. Bunbury, and his terrible state of health.

JACK: Bunbury! Well, I won't have him talk to you about Bunbury or about anything else. It is enough to drive one perfectly frantic.

ALGERNON: Of course I admit that the faults were all on my side. But I must say that I think that Brother John's coldness to me is peculiarly painful. I expected a more enthusiastic welcome, especially considering it is the first time I have come here.

CECILY: Uncle Jack, if you don't shake hands with Ernest I will never forgive you.

JACK: Never forgive me?

CECILY: Never, never, never!

JACK: Well, this is the last time I shall ever do it. [*Shakes hands with Algernon and glares.*]

CHASUBLE: It's pleasant, is it not, to see so perfect a reconciliation? I think we might leave the two brothers together.

MISS PRISM: Cecily, you will come with us.

CECILY: Certainly, Miss Prism. My little task of reconciliation is over.

CHASUBLE: You have done a beautiful action today, dear child.

MISS PRISM: We must not be premature in our judgements.

CECILY: I feel very happy. [*They all go off.*]

JACK: You young scoundrel, Algy, you must get out of this place as soon as possible. I don't allow any Bunburying here.

[*Enter Merriman.*]

MERRIMAN: I have put Mr. Ernest's things in the room next to yours, sir. I suppose that is all right?

JACK: What?

MERRIMAN: Mr. Ernest's luggage, sir. I have unpacked it and put it in the room next to your own.

JACK: His luggage?

MERRIMAN: Yes, sir. Three portmanteaus, a dressing-case, two hat-boxes, and a large luncheon-basket.

ALGERNON: I am afraid I can't stay more than a week this time.

JACK: Merriman, order the dog-cart[30] at once. Mr. Ernest has been suddenly called back to town.

MERRIMAN: Yes, sir. [*Goes back into the house.*]

ALGERNON: What a fearful liar you are, Jack. I have not been called back to town at all.

JACK: Yes, you have.

ALGERNON: I haven't heard anyone call me.

JACK: Your duty as a gentleman calls you back.

ALGERNON: My duty as a gentleman has never interfered with my pleasures in the smallest degree.

JACK: I can quite understand that.

ALGERNON: Well, Cecily is a darling.

JACK: You are not to talk of Miss Cardew like that. I don't like it.

ALGERNON: Well, I don't like your clothes. You look perfectly ridiculous in them. Why on earth don't you go up and change? It is perfectly childish to be in deep mourning for a man who is actually staying for a whole week with you in your house as a guest. I call it grotesque.

JACK: You are certainly not staying with me for a whole week as a guest or anything else. You have got to leave . . . by the four-five train.

ALGERNON: I certainly won't leave you so long as you are in mourning. It would be most unfriendly. If I were in mourning you would stay with me, I suppose. I should think it very unkind if you didn't.

JACK: Well, will you go if I change my clothes?

ALGERNON: Yes, if you are not too long. I never saw anybody take so long to dress, and with such little result.

JACK: Well, at any rate, that is better than being always over-dressed as you are.

ALGERNON: If I am occasionally a little over-dressed, I make up for it by being always immensely over-educated.

JACK: Your vanity is ridiculous, your conduct an outrage, and your presence in my garden utterly absurd. However, you have got to catch the four-five, and I hope you will have a pleasant journey back to town. This Bunburying, as you call it, has not been a great success for you. [*Goes into the house.*]

---

30. Open carriage adapted for carrying hounds for hunting.

ALGERNON: I think it has been a great success. I'm in love with Cecily, and that is
    everything.
    [Enter Cecily at the back of the garden. She picks up the can and begins to water the
    flowers.]
    But I must see her before I go, and make arrangements for another Bunbury. Ah,
    there she is.
CECILY: Oh, I merely came back to water the roses. I thought you were with Uncle
    Jack.
ALGERNON: He's gone to order the dog-cart for me.
CECILY: Oh, is he going to take you for a nice drive?
ALGERNON: He's going to send me away.
CECILY: Then have we got to part?
ALGERNON: I am afraid so. It's a painful parting.
CECILY: It is always painful to part from people whom one has known for a very brief
    space of time. The absence of old friends one can endure with equanimity. But
    even a momentary separation from anyone to whom one has just been introduced
    is almost unbearable.
ALGERNON: Thank you.
    [Enter Merriman.]
MERRIMAN: The dog-cart is at the door, sir.
    [Algernon looks appealingly at Cecily.]
CECILY: It can wait, Merriman . . . for . . . five minutes.
MERRIMAN: Yes, Miss. [Exit Merriman.]
ALGERNON: I hope, Cecily, I shall not offend you if I state quite frankly and openly
    that you seem to me to be in every way the visible personification of absolute
    perfection.
CECILY: I think your frankness does you great credit, Ernest. If you will allow me I
    will copy your remarks into my diary. [Goes over to table and begins writing in diary.]
ALGERNON: Do you really keep a diary? I'd give anything to look at it. May I?
CECILY: Oh no. [Puts her hand over it.] You see, it is simply a very young girl's record
    of her own thoughts and impressions, and consequently meant for publication.
    When it appears in volume form I hope you will order a copy. But pray, Ernest,
    don't stop. I delight in taking down from dictation. I have reached "absolute per-
    fection." You can go on. I am quite ready for more.
ALGERNON [somewhat taken aback]: Ahem! Ahem!
CECILY: Oh, don't cough, Ernest. When one is dictating one should speak fluently
    and not cough. Besides, I don't know how to spell a cough. [Writes as Algernon
    speaks.]
ALGERNON [speaking very rapidly]: Cecily, ever since I first looked upon your won-
    derful and incomparable beauty, I have dared to love you wildly, passionately, de-
    votedly, hopelessly.
CECILY: I don't think that you should tell me that you love me wildly, passionately,
    devotedly, hopelessly. Hopelessly doesn't seem to make much sense, does it?
ALGERNON: Cecily!
    [Enter Merriman.]
MERRIMAN: The dog-cart is waiting, sir.
ALGERNON: Tell it to come round next week, at the same hour.

MERRIMAN [*looks at Cecily, who makes no sign*]: Yes, sir. [*Merriman retires.*]

CECILY: Uncle Jack would be very much annoyed if he knew you were staying on till next week, at the same hour.

ALGERNON: Oh, I don't care about Jack. I don't care for anybody in the whole world but you. I love you, Cecily. You will marry me, won't you?

CECILY: You silly boy! Of course. Why, we have been engaged for the last three months.

ALGERNON: For the last three months?

CECILY: Yes, it will be exactly three months on Thursday.

ALGERNON: But how did we become engaged?

CECILY: Well, ever since dear Uncle Jack first confessed to us that he had a younger brother who was very wicked and bad, you of course have formed the chief topic of conversation between myself and Miss Prism. And of course a man who is much talked about is always very attractive. One feels there must be something in him after all. I daresay it was foolish of me, but I fell in love with you, Ernest.

ALGERNON: Darling! And when was the engagement actually settled?

CECILY: On the 14th of February last.[31] Worn out by your entire ignorance of my existence, I determined to end the matter one way or the other, and after a long struggle with myself I accepted you under this dear old tree here. The next day I bought this little ring in your name, and this is the little bangle with the true lovers' knot I promised you always to wear.

ALGERNON: Did I give you this? It's very pretty, isn't it?

CECILY: Yes, you've wonderfully good taste, Ernest. It's the excuse I've always given for your leading such a bad life. And this is the box in which I keep all your dear letters. [*Kneels at table, opens box, and produces letters tied up with blue ribbon.*]

ALGERNON: My letters! But my own sweet Cecily, I have never written you any letters.

CECILY: You need hardly remind me of that, Ernest. I remember only too well that I was forced to write your letters for you. I wrote always three times a week, and sometimes oftener.

ALGERNON: Oh, do let me read them, Cecily?

CECILY: Oh, I couldn't possibly. They would make you far too conceited. [*Replaces box.*] The three you wrote me after I had broken off the engagement are so beautiful, and so badly spelled, that even now I can hardly read them without crying a little.

ALGERNON: But was our engagement ever broken off?

CECILY: Of course it was. On the 22nd of last March. You can see the entry if you like. [*Shows diary.*] "Today I broke off my engagement with Ernest. I feel it is better to do so. The weather still continues charming."

ALGERNON: But why on earth did you break it off? What had I done? I had done nothing at all. Cecily, I am very much hurt indeed to hear you broke it off. Particularly when the weather was so charming.

CECILY: It would hardly have been a really serious engagement if it hadn't been broken off at least once. But I forgave you before the week was out.

---

31. The opening night of *Earnest*.

ALGERNON [*crossing to her, and kneeling*]: What a perfect angel you are, Cecily.

CECILY: You dear romantic boy. [*He kisses her, she puts her fingers through his hair.*] I hope your hair curls naturally, does it?

ALGERNON: Yes, darling, with a little help from others.

CECILY: I am so glad.

ALGERNON: You'll never break off our engagement again, Cecily?

CECILY: I don't think I could break it off now that I have actually met you. Besides, of course, there is the question of your name.

ALGERNON: Yes, of course. [*Nervously.*]

CECILY: You must not laugh at me, darling, but it had always been a girlish dream of mine to love some one whose name was Ernest. [*Algernon rises, Cecily also.*] There is something in that name that seems to inspire absolute confidence. I pity any poor married woman whose husband is not called Ernest.

ALGERNON: But, my dear child, do you mean to say you could not love me if I had some other name?

CECILY: But what name?

ALGERNON: Oh, any name you like—Algernon—for instance . . .

CECILY: But I don't like the name of Algernon.

ALGERNON: Well, my own dear, sweet, loving little darling, I really can't see why you should object to the name of Algernon. It is not at all a bad name. In fact, it is rather an aristocratic name. Half of the chaps who get into the Bankruptcy Court are called Algernon. But seriously, Cecily . . . [*moving to her*] . . . if my name was Algy, couldn't you love me?

CECILY [*rising*]: I might respect you, Ernest, I might admire your character, but I fear that I should not be able to give you my undivided attention.

ALGERNON: Ahem! Cecily! [*Picking up hat.*] Your Rector here is, I suppose, thoroughly experienced in the practice of all the rites and ceremonials of the Church?

CECILY: Oh yes. Dr. Chasuble is a most learned man. He has never written a single book, so you can imagine how much he knows.

ALGERNON: I must see him at once on a most important christening—I mean on most important business.

CECILY: Oh!

ALGERNON: I shan't be away more than half an hour.

CECILY: Considering that we have been engaged since February the 14th, and that I only met you today for the first time, I think it is rather hard that you should leave me for so long a period as half an hour. Couldn't you make it twenty minutes?

ALGERNON: I'll be back in no time. [*Kisses her and rushes down the garden.*]

CECILY: What an impetuous boy he is! I like his hair so much. I must enter his proposal in my diary.
    [*Enter Merriman.*]

MERRIMAN: A Miss Fairfax has just called to see Mr. Worthing. On very important business Miss Fairfax states.

CECILY: Isn't Mr. Worthing in his library?

MERRIMAN: Mr. Worthing went over in the direction of the Rectory some time ago.

CECILY: Pray ask the lady to come out here; Mr. Worthing is sure to be back soon. And you can bring tea.

MERRIMAN: Yes, Miss. [*Goes out.*]

CECILY: Miss Fairfax! I suppose one of the many good elderly women who are associated with Uncle Jack in some of his philanthropic work in London. I don't quite like
women who are interested in philanthropic work. I think it is so forward of them.
[*Enter Merriman.*]

MERRIMAN: Miss Fairfax.

[*Enter Gwendolen. Exit Merriman.*]

CECILY [*advancing to meet her*]: Pray let me introduce myself to you. My name is
Cecily Cardew.

GWENDOLEN: Cecily Cardew? [*Moving to her and shaking hands.*] What a very sweet
name! Something tells me that we are going to be great friends. I like you already
more than I can say. My first impressions of people are never wrong.

CECILY: How nice of you to like me so much after we have known each other such a
comparatively short time. Pray sit down.

GWENDOLEN [*still standing up*]: I may call you Cecily, may I not?

CECILY: With pleasure!

GWENDOLEN: And you will always call me Gwendolen, won't you.

CECILY: If you wish.

GWENDOLEN: Then that is all quite settled, is it not?

CECILY: I hope so.

[*A pause. They both sit down together.*]

GWENDOLEN: Perhaps this might be a favourable opportunity for my mentioning
who I am. My father is Lord Bracknell. You have never heard of papa, I suppose?

CECILY: I don't think so.

GWENDOLEN: Outside the family circle, papa, I am glad to say, is entirely unknown. I
think that is quite as it should be. The home seems to me to be the proper sphere
for the man. And certainly once a man begins to neglect his domestic duties he
becomes painfully effeminate, does he not? And I don't like that. It makes men so
very attractive. Cecily, mamma, whose views on education are remarkably strict,
has brought me up to be extremely short-sighted; it is part of her system; so do you
mind my looking at you through my glasses?

CECILY: Oh! not at all, Gwendolen. I am very fond of being looked at.

GWENDOLEN: [*after examining Cecily carefully through a lorgnette*]: You are here on a
short visit I suppose.

CECILY: Oh no! I live here.

GWENDOLEN [*severely*]: Really? Your mother, no doubt, or some female relative of advanced years, resides here also?

CECILY: Oh no! I have no mother, nor, in fact, any relations.

GWENDOLEN: Indeed?

CECILY: My dear guardian, with the assistance of Miss Prism, has the arduous task of
looking after me.

GWENDOLEN: Your guardian?

CECILY: Yes, I am Mr. Worthing's ward.

GWENDOLEN: Oh! It is strange he never mentioned to me that he had a ward. How
secretive of him! He grows more interesting hourly. I am not sure, however, that
the news inspires me with feelings of unmixed delight. [*Rising and going to her.*] I
am very fond of you, Cecily; I have liked you ever since I met you! But I am bound
to state that now that I know that you are Mr. Worthing's ward, I cannot help

expressing a wish you were—well just a little older than you seem to be—and not quite so very alluring in appearance. In fact, if I may speak candidly—

CECILY: Pray do! I think that whenever one has anything unpleasant to say, one should always be quite candid.

GWENDOLEN: Well, to speak with perfect candour, Cecily, I wish that you were fully forty-two, and more than usually plain for your age. Ernest has a strong upright nature. He is the very soul of truth and honour. Disloyalty would be as impossible to him as deception. But even men of the noblest possible moral character are extremely susceptible to the influence of the physical charms of others. Modern, no less than Ancient History, supplies us with many most painful examples of what I refer to. If it were not so, indeed, History would be quite unreadable.

CECILY: I beg your pardon, Gwendolen, did you say Ernest?

GWENDOLEN: Yes.

CECILY: Oh, but it is not Mr. Ernest Worthing who is my guardian. It is his brother—his elder brother.

GWENDOLEN [*sitting down again*]: Ernest never mentioned to me that he had a brother.

CECILY: I am sorry to say they have not been on good terms for a long time.

GWENDOLEN: Ah! that accounts for it. And now that I think of it I have never heard any man mention his brother. The subject seems distasteful to most men. Cecily, you have lifted a load from my mind. I was growing almost anxious. It would have been terrible if any cloud had come across a friendship like ours, would it not? Of course you are quite, quite sure that it is not Mr. Ernest Worthing who is your guardian?

CECILY: Quite sure. [*A pause.*] In fact, I am going to be his.

GWENDOLEN [*enquiringly*]: I beg your pardon?

CECILY [*rather shy and confidingly*]: Dearest Gwendolen, there is no reason why I should make a secret of it to you. Our little county newspaper is sure to chronicle the fact next week. Mr. Ernest Worthing and I are engaged to be married.

GWENDOLEN [*quite politely, rising*]: My darling Cecily, I think there must be some slight error. Mr. Ernest Worthing is engaged to me. The announcement will appear in the "Morning Post" on Saturday at the latest.

CECILY [*very politely, rising*]: I am afraid you must be under some misconception. Ernest proposed to me exactly ten minutes ago. [*Shows diary.*]

GWENDOLEN [*examines diary through her lorgnette carefully*]: It is certainly very curious, for he asked me to be his wife yesterday afternoon at 5.30. If you would care to verify the incident, pray do so. [*Produces diary of her own.*] I never travel without my diary. One should always have something sensational to read in the train. I am so sorry, dear Cecily, if it is any disappointment to you, but I am afraid I have the prior claim.

CECILY: It would distress me more than I can tell you, dear Gwendolen, if it caused you any mental or physical anguish, but I feel bound to point out that since Ernest proposed to you he clearly has changed his mind.

GWENDOLEN [*meditatively*]: If the poor fellow has been entrapped into any foolish promise I shall consider it my duty to rescue him at once, and with a firm hand.

CECILY [*thoughtfully and sadly*]: Whatever unfortunate entanglement my dear boy may have got into, I will never reproach him with it after we are married.

GWENDOLEN: Do you allude to me, Miss Cardew, as an entanglement? You are presumptuous. On an occasion of this kind it becomes more than a moral duty to speak one's mind. It becomes a pleasure.

CECILY: Do you suggest, Miss Fairfax, that I entrapped Ernest into an engagement? How dare you? This is no time for wearing the shallow mask of manners. When I see a spade I call it a spade.

GWENDOLEN [*satirically*]: I am glad to say that I have never seen a spade. It is obvious that our social spheres have been widely different.

[*Enter Merriman, followed by the footman. He carries a salver, table cloth, and plate stand. Cecily is about to retort. The presence of the servants exercises a restraining influence, under which both girls chafe.*]

MERRIMAN: Shall I lay tea here as usual, Miss?

CECILY [*sternly, in a calm voice*]: Yes, as usual.

[*Merriman begins to clear table and lay cloth. A long pause. Cecily and Gwendolen glare at each other.*]

GWENDOLEN: Are there many interesting walks in the vicinity, Miss Cardew?

CECILY: Oh! yes! a great many. From the top of one of the hills quite close one can see five counties.

GWENDOLEN: Five counties! I don't think I should like that. I hate crowds.

CECILY [*sweetly*]: I suppose that is why you live in town?

[*Gwendolen bites her lip, and beats her foot nervously with her parasol.*]

GWENDOLEN [*looking round*]: Quite a well-kept garden this is, Miss Cardew.

CECILY: So glad you like it, Miss Fairfax.

GWENDOLEN: I had no idea there were any flowers in the country.

CECILY: Oh, flowers are as common here, Miss Fairfax, as people are in London.

GWENDOLEN: Personally, I cannot understand how anybody manages to exist in the country, if anybody who is anybody does. The country always bores me to death.

CECILY: Ah! This is what the newspapers call agricultural depression,[32] is it not? I believe the aristocracy are suffering very much from it just at present. It is almost an epidemic amongst them, I have been told. May I offer you some tea, Miss Fairfax?

GWENDOLEN [*with elaborate politeness*]: Thank you. [*Aside.*] Detestable girl! But I require tea!

CECILY [*sweetly*]: Sugar?

GWENDOLEN [*superciliously*]: No, thank you. Sugar is not fashionable any more.

[*Cecily looks angrily at her, takes up the tongs and puts four lumps of sugar into the cup.*]

CECILY [*severely*]: Cake or bread and butter?

GWENDOLEN [*in a bored manner*]: Bread and butter, please. Cake is rarely seen at the best houses nowadays.

CECILY [*cuts a very large slice of cake, and puts it on the tray*]: Hand that to Miss Fairfax.

[*Merriman does so, and goes out with footman. Gwendolen drinks the tea and makes a grimace. Puts down cup at once, reaches out her hand to the bread and butter, looks at it, and finds it is cake. Rises in indignation.*]

---

32. The economic decline of British farming and the gloom felt by the upper-class landowners whose revenues derived from farmers' rents.

GWENDOLEN: You have filled my tea with lumps of sugar, and though I asked most distinctly for bread and butter, you have given me cake. I am known for the gentleness of my disposition, and the extraordinary sweetness of my nature, but I warn you, Miss Cardew, you may go too far.

CECILY [*rising*]: To save my poor, innocent, trusting boy from the machinations of any other girl there are no lengths to which I would not go.

GWENDOLEN: From the moment I saw you I distrusted you. I felt that you were false and deceitful. I am never deceived in such matters. My first impressions of people are invariably right.

CECILY: It seems to me, Miss Fairfax, that I am trespassing on your valuable time. No doubt you have many other calls of a similar character to make in the neighbourhood.

[*Enter Jack.*]

GWENDOLEN [*catching sight of him*]: Ernest! My own Ernest!

JACK: Gwendolen! Darling! [*Offers to kiss her.*]

GWENDOLEN [*drawing back*]: A moment! May I ask if you are engaged to be married to this young lady? [*Points to Cecily.*]

JACK [*laughing*]: To dear little Cecily! Of course not! What could have put such an idea into your pretty little head?

GWENDOLEN: Thank you. You may! [*Offers her cheek.*]

CECILY [*very sweetly*]: I knew there must be some misunderstanding, Miss Fairfax. The gentleman whose arm is at present round your waist is my dear guardian, Mr. John Worthing.

GWENDOLEN: I beg your pardon?

CECILY: This is Uncle Jack.

GWENDOLEN [*receding*]: Jack! Oh!

[*Enter Algernon.*]

CECILY: Here is Ernest.

ALGERNON [*goes straight over to Cecily without noticing anyone else*]: My own love! [*Offers to kiss her.*]

CECILY [*drawing back*]: A moment, Ernest! May I ask you—are you engaged to be married to this young lady?

ALGERNON [*looking round*]: To what young lady? Good heavens! Gwendolen!

CECILY: Yes, to good heavens, Gwendolen, I mean to Gwendolen.

ALGERNON [*laughing*]: Of course not! What could have put such an idea into your pretty little head?

CECILY: Thank you. [*Presenting her cheek to be kissed.*] You may. [*Algernon kisses her.*]

GWENDOLEN: I felt there was some slight error, Miss Cardew. The gentleman who is now embracing you is my cousin, Mr. Algernon Moncrieff.

CECILY [*breaking away from Algernon*]: Algernon Moncrieff! Oh! [*The two girls move towards each other and put their arms round each other's waists as if for protection.*]

CECILY: Are you called Algernon?

ALGERNON: I cannot deny it.

CECILY: Oh!

GWENDOLEN: Is your name really John?

JACK [*standing rather proudly*]: I could deny it if I liked. I could deny anything if I liked. But my name certainly is John. It has been John for years.

CECILY [*to Gwendolen*]: A gross deception has been practised on both of us.

GWENDOLEN: My poor wounded Cecily!

CECILY: My sweet wronged Gwendolen!

GWENDOLEN [*slowly and seriously*]: You will call me sister, will you not?

[*They embrace. Jack and Algernon groan and walk up and down.*]

CECILY [*rather brightly*]: There is just one question I would like to be allowed to ask my guardian.

GWENDOLEN: An admirable idea! Mr. Worthing, there is just one question I would like to be permitted to put to you. Where is your brother Ernest? We are both engaged to be married to your brother Ernest, so it is a matter of some importance to us to know where your brother Ernest is at present.

JACK [*slowly and hesitatingly*]: Gwendolen—Cecily—It is very painful for me to be forced to speak the truth. It is the first time in my life that I have ever been reduced to such a painful position, and I am really quite inexperienced in doing anything of the kind. However I will tell you quite frankly that I have no brother Ernest. I have no brother at all. I never had a brother in my life, and I certainly have not the smallest intention of ever having one in the future.

CECILY [*surprised*]: No brother at all?

JACK [*cheerily*]: None!

GWENDOLEN [*severely*]: Had you never a brother of any kind?

JACK [*pleasantly*]: Never. Not even of any kind.

GWENDOLEN: I am afraid it is quite clear, Cecily, that neither of us is engaged to be married to anyone.

CECILY: It is not a very pleasant position for a young girl suddenly to find herself in. Is it?

GWENDOLEN: Let us go into the house. They will hardly venture to come after us there.

CECILY: No, men are so cowardly, aren't they?

[*They retire into the house with scornful looks.*]

JACK: This ghastly state of things is what you call Bunburying, I suppose?

ALGERNON: Yes, and a perfectly wonderful Bunbury it is. The most wonderful Bunbury I have ever had in my life.

JACK: Well, you've no right whatsoever to Bunbury here.

ALGERNON: That is absurd. One has a right to Bunbury anywhere one chooses. Every serious Bunburyist knows that.

JACK: Serious Bunburyist! Good heavens!

ALGERNON: Well, one must be serious about something, if one wants to have any amusement in life. I happen to be serious about Bunburying. What on earth you are serious about I haven't got the remotest idea. About everything, I should fancy. You have such an absolutely trivial nature.

JACK: Well, the only small satisfaction I have in the whole of this wretched business is that your friend Bunbury is quite exploded. You won't be able to run down to the country quite so often as you used to do, dear Algy. And a very good thing too.

ALGERNON: Your brother is a little off colour, isn't he, dear Jack? You won't be able to disappear to London quite so frequently as your wicked custom was. And not a bad thing either.

JACK: As for your conduct towards Miss Cardew, I must say that your taking in a sweet, simple, innocent girl like that is quite inexcusable. To say nothing of the fact that she is my ward.

ALGERNON: I can see no possible defence at all for your deceiving a brilliant, clever, thoroughly experienced young lady like Miss Fairfax. To say nothing of the fact that she is my cousin.

JACK: I wanted to be engaged to Gwendolen, that is all. I love her.

ALGERNON: Well, I simply wanted to be engaged to Cecily. I adore her.

JACK: There is certainly no chance of your marrying Miss Cardew.

ALGERNON: I don't think there is much likelihood, Jack, of you and Miss Fairfax being united.

JACK: Well, that is no business of yours.

ALGERNON: If it was my business, I wouldn't talk about it. [Begins to eat muffins.] It is very vulgar to talk about one's business. Only people like stockbrokers do that, and then merely at dinner parties.

JACK: How you can sit there, calmly eating muffins when we are in this horrible trouble, I can't make out. You seem to me to be perfectly heartless.

ALGERNON: Well, I can't eat muffins in an agitated manner. The butter would probably get on my cuffs. One should always eat muffins quite calmly. It is the only way to eat them.

JACK: I say it's perfectly heartless your eating muffins at all, under the circumstances.

ALGERNON: When I am in trouble, eating is the only thing that consoles me. Indeed, when I am in really great trouble, as anyone who knows me intimately will tell you, I refuse everything except food and drink. At the present moment I am eating muffins because I am unhappy. Besides, I am particularly fond of muffins. [Rising.]

JACK [rising]: Well, that is no reason why you should eat them all in that greedy way.

[Takes muffins from Algernon.]

ALGERNON [offering tea-cake]: I wish you would have tea-cake instead. I don't like tea-cake.

JACK: Good heavens! I suppose a man may eat his own muffins in his own garden.

ALGERNON: But you have just said it was perfectly heartless to eat muffins.

JACK: I said it was perfectly heartless of you, under the circumstances. That is a very different thing.

ALGERNON: That may be. But the muffins are the same. [He seizes the muffin-dish from Jack.]

JACK: Algy, I wish to goodness you would go.

ALGERNON: You can't possibly ask me to go without having some dinner. It's absurd. I never go without my dinner. No one ever does, except vegetarians and people like that. Besides I have just made arrangements with Dr. Chasuble to be christened at a quarter to six under the name of Ernest.

JACK: My dear fellow, the sooner you give up that nonsense the better. I made arrangements this morning with Dr. Chasuble to be christened myself at 5.30, and

I naturally will take the name of Ernest. Gwendolen would wish it. We can't both be christened Ernest. It's absurd. Besides, I have a perfect right to be christened if I like. There is no evidence at all that I ever have been christened by anybody. I should think it extremely probable I never was, and so does Dr. Chasuble. It is entirely different in your case. You have been christened already.

ALGERNON: Yes, but I have not been christened for years.

JACK: Yes, but you have been christened. That is the important thing.

ALGERNON: Quite so. So I know my constitution can stand it. If you are not quite sure about your ever having been christened, I must say I think it rather dangerous your venturing on it now. It might make you very unwell. You can hardly have forgotten that someone very closely connected with you was very nearly carried off this week in Paris by a severe chill.

JACK: Yes, but you said yourself that a severe chill was not hereditary.

ALGERNON: It usen't to be, I know—but I daresay it is now. Science is always making wonderful improvements in things.

JACK [picking up the muffin-dish]: Oh, that is nonsense; you are always talking nonsense.

ALGERNON: Jack, you are at the muffins again! I wish you wouldn't. There are only two left. [Takes them.] I told you I was particularly fond of muffins.

JACK: But I hate tea-cake.

ALGERNON: Why on earth then do you allow tea-cake to be served up for your guests? What ideas you have of hospitality!

JACK: Algernon! I have already told you to go. I don't want you here. Why don't you go!

ALGERNON: I haven't quite finished my tea yet, and there is still one muffin left.

[Jack groans, and sinks into a chair. Algernon still continues eating.]   ACT DROP

THIRD ACT

SCENE: Morning-room[33] at the Manor House.

[Gwendolen and Cecily are at the window, looking out into the garden.]

GWENDOLEN: The fact that they did not follow us at once into the house, as anyone else would have done, seems to me to show that they have some sense of shame left.

CECILY: They have been eating muffins. That looks like repentance.

GWENDOLEN [after a pause]: They don't seem to notice us at all. Couldn't you cough?

CECILY: But I haven't got a cough.

GWENDOLEN: They're looking at us. What effrontery!

CECILY: They're approaching. That's very forward of them.

GWENDOLEN: Let us preserve a dignified silence.

CECILY: Certainly. It's the only thing to do now.

[Enter Jack followed by Algernon. They whistle some dreadful popular air from a British Opera.][34]

---

33. An informal room for receiving visitors.
34. A dig at Gilbert and Sullivan, whose parody of aestheticism, Patience (1881), helped make Wilde famous.

GWENDOLEN: This dignified silence seems to produce an unpleasant effect.

CECILY: A most distasteful one.

GWENDOLEN: But we will not be the first to speak.

CECILY: Certainly not.

GWENDOLEN: Mr. Worthing, I have something very particular to ask you. Much depends on your reply.

CECILY: Gwendolen, your common sense is invaluable. Mr. Moncrieff, kindly answer me the following question. Why did you pretend to be my guardian's brother?

ALGERNON: In order that I might have an opportunity of meeting you.

CECILY [to Gwendolen]: That certainly seems a satisfactory explanation, does it not?

GWENDOLEN: Yes, dear, if you can believe him.

CECILY: I don't. But that does not affect the wonderful beauty of his answer.

GWENDOLEN: True. In matters of grave importance, style, not sincerity is the vital thing. Mr. Worthing, what explanation can you offer to me for pretending to have a brother? Was it in order that you might have an opportunity of coming up to town to see me as often as possible?

JACK: Can you doubt it, Miss Fairfax?

GWENDOLEN: I have the gravest doubts upon the subject. But I intend to crush them. This is not the moment for German scepticism.[35] [Moving to Cecily.] Their explanations appear to be quite satisfactory, especially Mr. Worthing's. That seems to me to have the stamp of truth upon it.

CECILY: I am more than content with what Mr. Moncrieff said. His voice alone inspires one with absolute credulity.

GWENDOLEN: Then you think we should forgive them?

CECILY: Yes. I mean no.

GWENDOLEN: True! I had forgotten. There are principles at stake that one cannot surrender. Which of us should tell them? The task is not a pleasant one.

CECILY: Could we not both speak at the same time?

GWENDOLEN: An excellent idea! I nearly always speak at the same time as other people. Will you take the time from me?

CECILY: Certainly.

[Gwendolen beats time with uplifted finger.]

GWENDOLEN AND CECILY [speaking together]: Your Christian names are still an insuperable barrier. That is all!

JACK AND ALGERNON [speaking together]: Our Christian names! Is that all? But we are going to be christened this afternoon.

GWENDOLEN [to Jack]: For my sake you are prepared to do this terrible thing?

JACK: I am.

CECILY [to Algernon]: To please me you are ready to face this fearful ordeal?

ALGERNON: I am!

GWENDOLEN: How absurd to talk of the equality of the sexes! Where questions of self-sacrifice are concerned, men are infinitely beyond us.

JACK: We are. [Clasps hands with Algernon.]

---

35. Famous for treating the Bible as a historical document or source for interpretation rather than revealed truth.

CECILY: They have moments of physical courage of which we women know absolutely nothing.

GWENDOLEN [to Jack]: Darling!

ALGERNON [to Cecily]: Darling! [They fall into each other's arms.]

[Enter Merriman. When he enters he coughs loudly, seeing the situation.]

MERRIMAN: Ahem! Ahem! Lady Bracknell!

JACK: Good heavens!

[Enter Lady Bracknell. The couples separate in alarm.] [Exit Merriman.]

LADY BRACKNELL: Gwendolen! What does this mean?

GWENDOLEN: Merely that I am engaged to be married to Mr. Worthing, mamma.

LADY BRACKNELL: Come here. Sit down. Sit down immediately. Hesitation of any kind is a sign of mental decay in the young, of physical weakness in the old. [Turns to Jack.] Apprised, sir, of my daughter's sudden flight by her trusty maid, whose confidence I purchased by means of a small coin, I followed her at once by a luggage train. Her unhappy father is, I am glad to say, under the impression that she is attending a more than usually lengthy lecture by the University Extension Scheme on the Influence of a Permanent Income on Thought. I do not propose to undeceive him. Indeed I have never undeceived him on any question. I would consider it wrong. But of course, you will clearly understand that all communication between yourself and my daughter must cease immediately from this moment. On this point, as indeed on all points, I am firm.

JACK: I am engaged to be married to Gwendolen, Lady Bracknell!

LADY BRACKNELL: You are nothing of the kind, sir. And now, as regards Algernon! . . . Algernon!

ALGERNON: Yes, Aunt Augusta.

LADY BRACKNELL: May I ask if it is in this house that your invalid friend Mr. Bunbury resides?

ALGERNON [stammering]: Oh! No! Bunbury doesn't live here. Bunbury is somewhere else at present. In fact, Bunbury is dead.

LADY BRACKNELL: Dead! When did Mr. Bunbury die? His death must have been extremely sudden.

ALGERNON [airily]: Oh! I killed Bunbury this afternoon. I mean poor Bunbury died this afternoon.

LADY BRACKNELL: What did he die of?

ALGERNON: Bunbury? Oh, he was quite exploded.

LADY BRACKNELL: Exploded! Was he the victim of a revolutionary outrage? I was not aware that Mr. Bunbury was interested in social legislation. If so, he is well punished for his morbidity.

ALGERNON: My dear Aunt Augusta, I mean he was found out! The doctors found out that Bunbury could not live, that is what I mean—so Bunbury died.

LADY BRACKNELL: He seems to have had great confidence in the opinion of his physicians. I am glad, however, that he made up his mind at the last to some definite course of action, and acted under proper medical advice. And now that we have finally got rid of this Mr. Bunbury, may I ask, Mr. Worthing, who is that young person whose hand my nephew Algernon is now holding in what seems to me a peculiarly unnecessary manner?

JACK: That lady is Miss Cecily Cardew, my ward.

[*Lady Bracknell bows coldly to Cecily.*]

ALGERNON: I am engaged to be married to Cecily, Aunt Augusta.

LADY BRACKNELL: I beg your pardon?

CECILY: Mr. Moncrieff and I are engaged to be married, Lady Bracknell.

LADY BRACKNELL [*with a shiver, crossing to the sofa and sitting down*]: I do not know whether there is anything peculiarly exciting in the air of this particular part of Hertfordshire, but the number of engagements that go on seems to me considerably above the proper average that statistics have laid down for our guidance. I think some preliminary enquiry on my part would not be out of place. Mr. Worthing, is Miss Cardew at all connected with any of the larger railway stations in London? I merely desire information. Until yesterday I had no idea that there were any families or persons whose origin was a Terminus.

[*Jack looks perfectly furious, but restrains himself.*]

JACK [*in a clear, cold voice*]: Miss Cardew is the granddaughter of the late Mr. Thomas Cardew of 149, Belgrave Square, S.W.; Gervase Park, Dorking, Surrey; and the Sporran, Fifeshire, N.B.[36]

LADY BRACKNELL: That sounds not unsatisfactory. Three addresses always inspire confidence, even in tradesmen. But what proof have I of their authenticity?

JACK: I have carefully preserved the Court Guides[37] of the period. They are open to your inspection, Lady Bracknell.

LADY BRACKNELL [*grimly*]: I have known strange errors in that publication.

JACK: Miss Cardew's family solicitors are Messrs Markby, Markby, and Markby.

LADY BRACKNELL: Markby, Markby, and Markby? A firm of the very highest position in their profession. Indeed I am told that one of the Mr. Markbys is occasionally to be seen at dinner parties. So far I am satisfied.

JACK [*very irritably*]: How extremely kind of you, Lady Bracknell! I have also in my possession, you will be pleased to hear, certificates of Miss Cardew's birth, baptism, whooping cough, registration, vaccination, confirmation, and the measles; both the German and the English variety.

LADY BRACKNELL: Ah! A life crowded with incident, I see; though perhaps somewhat too exciting for a young girl. I am not myself in favour of premature experiences. [*Rises, looks at her watch.*] Gwendolen! the time approaches for our departure. We have not a moment to lose. As a matter of form, Mr. Worthing, I had better ask you if Miss Cardew has any little fortune?

JACK: Oh! about a hundred and thirty thousand pounds in the Funds.[38] That is all. Goodbye, Lady Bracknell. So pleased to have seen you.

LADY BRACKNELL [*sitting down again*]: A moment, Mr. Worthing. A hundred and thirty thousand pounds! And in the Funds! Miss Cardew seems to me a most attractive young lady, now that I look at her. Few girls of the present day have any really solid qualities, any of the qualities that last, and improve with time. We live, I regret to say, in an age of surfaces. [*To Cecily.*] Come over here, dear. [*Cecily goes across.*] Pretty child! your dress is sadly simple, and your hair seems almost as Nature might have left it. But we can soon alter all that. A thoroughly experi-

---

36. North Britain, or Scotland.

37. Annual listings of upper-class names and addresses.

38. Government bonds, a safe investment. Cecily's fortune is enormous.

enced French maid produces a really marvellous result in a very brief space of time. I remember recommending one to young Lady Lancing, and after three months her own husband did not know her.

JACK [*aside*]: And after six months nobody knew her.

LADY BRACKNELL [*glares at Jack for a few moments. Then bends, with a practised smile, to Cecily.*]: Kindly turn round, sweet child. [*Cecily turns completely round.*] No, the side view is what I want. [*Cecily presents her profile.*] Yes, quite as I expected. There are distinct social possibilities in your profile. The two weak points in our age are its want of principle and its want of profile. The chin a little higher, dear. Style largely depends on the way the chin is worn. They are worn very high, just at present. Algernon!

ALGERNON: Yes, Aunt Augusta!

LADY BRACKNELL: There are distinct social possibilities in Miss Cardew's profile.

ALGERNON: Cecily is the sweetest, dearest, prettiest girl in the whole world. And I don't care twopence about social possibilities.

LADY BRACKNELL: Never speak disrespectfully of Society, Algernon. Only people who can't get into it do that. [*To Cecily.*] Dear child, of course you know that Algernon has nothing but his debts to depend upon. But I do not approve of mercenary marriages. When I married Lord Bracknell I had no fortune of any kind. But I never dreamed for a moment of allowing that to stand in my way. Well, I suppose I must give my consent.

ALGERNON: Thank you, Aunt Augusta.

LADY BRACKNELL: Cecily, you may kiss me!

CECILY [*kisses her*]: Thank you, Lady Bracknell.

LADY BRACKNELL: You may also address me as Aunt Augusta for the future.

CECILY: Thank you, Aunt Augusta.

LADY BRACKNELL: The marriage, I think, had better take place quite soon.

ALGERNON: Thank you, Aunt Augusta.

CECILY: Thank you, Aunt Augusta.

LADY BRACKNELL: To speak frankly, I am not in favour of long engagements. They give people the opportunity of finding out each other's character before marriage, which I think is never advisable.

JACK: I beg your pardon for interrupting you, Lady Bracknell, but this engagement is quite out of the question. I am Miss Cardew's guardian, and she cannot marry without my consent until she comes of age. That consent I absolutely decline to give.

LADY BRACKNELL: Upon what grounds may I ask? Algernon is an extremely, I may almost say an ostentatiously, eligible young man. He has nothing, but he looks everything. What more can one desire?

JACK: It pains me very much to have to speak frankly to you, Lady Bracknell, about your nephew, but the fact is that I do not approve at all of his moral character. I suspect him of being untruthful.

[*Algernon and Cecily look at him in indignant amazement.*]

LADY BRACKNELL: Untruthful! My nephew Algernon? Impossible! He is an Oxonian.[39]

---

39. From Oxford University.

JACK: I fear there can be no possible doubt about the matter. This afternoon, during my temporary absence in London on an important question of romance, he obtained admission to my house by means of the false pretence of being my brother. Under an assumed name he drank, I've just been informed by my butler, an entire pint bottle of my Perrier-Jouet, Brut, '89; a wine I was specially reserving for myself. Continuing his disgraceful deception, he succeeded in the course of the afternoon in alienating the affections of my only ward. He subsequently stayed to tea, and devoured every single muffin. And what makes his conduct all the more heartless is, that he was perfectly well aware from the first that I have no brother, that I never had a brother, and that I don't intend to have a brother, not even of any kind. I distinctly told him so myself yesterday afternoon.

LADY BRACKNELL: Ahem! Mr. Worthing, after careful consideration I have decided entirely to overlook my nephew's conduct to you.

JACK: That is very generous of you, Lady Bracknell. My own decision, however, is unalterable. I decline to give my consent.

LADY BRACKNELL [to Cecily]: Come here, sweet child. [Cecily goes over.] How old are you, dear?

CECILY: Well, I am really only eighteen, but I always admit to twenty when I go to evening parties.

LADY BRACKNELL: You are perfectly right in making some slight alteration. Indeed, no woman should ever be quite accurate about her age. It looks so calculating. . . . [In a meditative manner.] Eighteen, but admitting to twenty at evening parties. Well, it will not be very long before you are of age and free from the restraints of tutelage. So I don't think your guardian's consent is, after all, a matter of any importance.

JACK: Pray excuse me, Lady Bracknell, for interrupting you again, but it is only fair to tell you that according to the terms of her grandfather's will Miss Cardew does not come legally of age till she is thirty-five.

LADY BRACKNELL: That does not seem to me to be a grave objection. Thirty-five is a very attractive age. London society is full of women of the very highest birth who have, of their own free choice, remained thirty-five for years. Lady Dumbleton is an instance in point. To my own knowledge she has been thirty-five ever since she arrived at the age of forty, which was many years ago now. I see no reason why our dear Cecily should not be even still more attractive at the age you mention than she is at present. There will be a large accumulation of property.

CECILY: Algy, could you wait for me till I was thirty-five?

ALGERNON: Of course I could, Cecily. You know I could.

CECILY: Yes, I felt it instinctively, but I couldn't wait all that time. I hate waiting even five minutes for anybody. It always makes me rather cross. I am not punctual myself, I know, but I do like punctuality in others, and waiting, even to be married, is quite out of the question.

ALGERNON: Then what is to be done, Cecily?

CECILY: I don't know, Mr. Moncrieff.

LADY BRACKNELL: My dear Mr. Worthing, as Miss Cardew states positively that she cannot wait till she is thirty-five—a remark which I am bound to say seems to me to show a somewhat impatient nature—I would beg of you to reconsider your decision.

JACK: But my dear Lady Bracknell, the matter is entirely in your own hands. The moment you consent to my marriage with Gwendolen, I will most gladly allow your nephew to form an alliance with my ward.

LADY BRACKNELL [*rising and drawing herself up*]: You must be quite aware that what you propose is out of the question.

JACK: Then a passionate celibacy is all that any of us can look forward to.

LADY BRACKNELL: That is not the destiny I propose for Gwendolen. Algernon, of course, can choose for himself. [*Pulls out her watch.*] Come, dear; [*Gwendolen rises.*] we have already missed five, if not six, trains. To miss any more might expose us to comment on the platform.

    [*Enter Dr. Chasuble.*]

CHASUBLE: Everything is quite ready for the christenings.

LADY BRACKNELL: The christenings, sir! Is not that somewhat premature?

CHASUBLE [*looking rather puzzled, and pointing to Jack and Algernon*]: Both these gentlemen have expressed a desire for immediate baptism.

LADY BRACKNELL: At their age? The idea is grotesque and irreligious! Algernon, I forbid you to be baptized. I will not hear of such excesses. Lord Bracknell would be highly displeased if he learned that that was the way in which you wasted your time and money.

CHASUBLE: Am I to understand then that there are to be no christenings at all this afternoon?

JACK: I don't think that, as things are now, it would be of much practical value to either of us, Dr. Chasuble.

CHASUBLE: I am grieved to hear such sentiments from you, Mr. Worthing. They savour of the heretical views of the Anabaptists,[40] views that I have completely refuted in four of my unpublished sermons. However, as your present mood seems to be one peculiarly secular, I will return to the church at once. Indeed, I have just been informed by the pew-opener that for the last hour and a half Miss Prism has been waiting for me in the vestry.

LADY BRACKNELL [*starting*]: Miss Prism! Did I hear you mention a Miss Prism?

CHASUBLE: Yes, Lady Bracknell. I am on my way to join her.

LADY BRACKNELL: Pray allow me to detain you for a moment. This matter may prove to be one of vital importance to Lord Bracknell and myself. Is this Miss Prism a female of repellent aspect, remotely connected with education?

CHASUBLE [*somewhat indignantly*]: She is the most cultivated of ladies, and the very picture of respectability.

LADY BRACKNELL: It is obviously the same person. May I ask what position she holds in your household?

CHASUBLE [*severely*]: I am a celibate, madam.

JACK [*interposing*]: Miss Prism, Lady Bracknell, has been for the last three years Miss Cardew's esteemed governess and valued companion.

LADY BRACKNELL: In spite of what I hear of her, I must see her at once. Let her be sent for.

CHASUBLE [*looking off*]: She approaches; she is nigh.

    [*Enter Miss Prism hurriedly.*]

---

40. A 16th-c. Protestant sect that baptized adults.

MISS PRISM: I was told you expected me in the vestry, dear Canon. I have been waiting for you there for an hour and three quarters. [*Catches sight of Lady Bracknell
who has fixed her with a stony glare. Miss Prism grows pale and quails. She looks anxiously round as if desirous to escape.*]

LADY BRACKNELL [*in a severe, judicial voice*]: Prism! [*Miss Prism bows her head in shame.*]
Come here, Prism! [*Miss Prism approaches in a humble manner.*] Prism! Where is that
baby? [*General consternation. The Canon starts back in horror. Algernon and Jack pretend to be anxious to shield Cecily and Gwendolen from hearing the details of a terrible
public scandal.*] Twenty-eight years ago, Prism, you left Lord Bracknell's house,
Number 104, Upper Grosvenor Street, in charge of a perambulator that contained
a baby, of the male sex. You never returned. A few weeks later, through the elaborate investigations of the Metropolitan police, the perambulator was discovered at
midnight, standing by itself in a remote corner of Bayswater.[41] It contained the
manuscript of a three-volume novel of more than usually revolting sentimentality.
[*Miss Prism starts in involuntary indignation.*] But the baby was not there! [*Everyone
looks at Miss Prism.*] Prism! Where is that baby? [*A pause.*]

MISS PRISM: Lady Bracknell, I admit with shame that I do not know. I only wish I
did. The plain facts of the case are these. On the morning of the day you mention,
a day that is for ever branded on my memory, I prepared as usual to take the baby
out in its perambulator. I had also with me a somewhat old, but capacious hand-
bag in which I had intended to place the manuscript of a work of fiction that I had
written during my few unoccupied hours. In a moment of mental abstraction, for
which I never can forgive myself, I deposited the manuscript in the bassinette, and
placed the baby in the hand-bag.

JACK [*who has been listening attentively*]: But where did you deposit the hand-bag?

MISS PRISM: Do not ask me, Mr. Worthing.

JACK: Miss Prism, this is a matter of no small importance to me. I insist on knowing
where you deposited the hand-bag that contained that infant.

MISS PRISM: I left it in the cloak-room of one of the larger railway stations in London.

JACK: What railway station?

MISS PRISM [*quite crushed*]: Victoria. The Brighton line. [*Sinks into a chair.*]

JACK: I must retire to my room for a moment. Gwendolen, wait here for me.

GWENDOLEN: If you are not too long, I will wait here for you all my life.

[*Exit Jack in great excitement.*]

CHASUBLE: What do you think this means, Lady Bracknell?

LADY BRACKNELL: I dare not even suspect, Dr. Chasuble. I need hardly tell you that
in families of high position strange coincidences are not supposed to occur. They
are hardly considered the thing.

[*Noises heard overhead as if someone was throwing trunks about. Everyone looks up.*]

CECILY: Uncle Jack seems strangely agitated.

CHASUBLE: Your guardian has a very emotional nature.

LADY BRACKNELL: This noise is extremely unpleasant. It sounds as if he was having an argument. I dislike arguments of any kind. They are always vulgar, and
often convincing.

---

41. Fashionable area near Kensington Gardens in London.

CHASUBLE [*looking up*]: It has stopped now. [*The noise is redoubled.*]

LADY BRACKNELL: I wish he would arrive at some conclusion.

GWENDOLEN: This suspense is terrible. I hope it will last.

[*Enter Jack with a hand-bag of black leather in his hand.*]

JACK [*rushing over to Miss Prism*]: Is this the hand-bag, Miss Prism? Examine it carefully before you speak. The happiness of more than one life depends on your answer.

MISS PRISM [*calmly*]: It seems to be mine. Yes, here is the injury it received through the upsetting of a Gower Street omnibus in younger and happier days. Here is the stain on the lining caused by the explosion of a temperance beverage, an incident that occurred at Leamington. And here, on the lock, are my initials. I had forgotten that in an extravagant mood I had had them placed there. The bag is undoubtedly mine. I am delighted to have it so unexpectedly restored to me. It has been a great inconvenience being without it all these years.

JACK [*in a pathetic voice*]: Miss Prism, more is restored to you than this hand-bag. I was the baby you placed in it.

MISS PRISM [*amazed*]: You?

JACK [*embracing her*]: Yes . . . mother!

MISS PRISM [*recoiling in indignant astonishment*]: Mr. Worthing! I am unmarried!

JACK: Unmarried! I do not deny that is a serious blow. But after all, who has the right to cast a stone against one who has suffered?[42] Cannot repentance wipe out an act of folly? Why should there be one law for men, and another for women? Mother, I forgive you. [*Tries to embrace her again.*]

MISS PRISM [*still more indignant*]: Mr. Worthing, there is some error. [*Pointing to Lady Bracknell.*] There is the lady who can tell you who you really are.

JACK [*after a pause*]: Lady Bracknell, I hate to seem inquisitive, but would you kindly inform me who I am?

LADY BRACKNELL: I am afraid that the news I have to give you will not altogether please you. You are the son of my poor sister, Mrs. Moncrieff, and consequently Algernon's elder brother.

JACK: Algy's elder brother! Then I have a brother after all. I knew I had a brother! I always said I had a brother! Cecily—how could you have ever doubted that I had a brother. [*Seizes hold of Algernon.*] Dr. Chasuble, my unfortunate brother. Miss Prism, my unfortunate brother. Gwendolen, my unfortunate brother. Algy, you young scoundrel, you will have to treat me with more respect in the future. You have never behaved to me like a brother in all your life.

ALGERNON: Well, not till today, old boy, I admit. I did my best, however, though I was out of practice. [*Shakes hands.*]

GWENDOLEN [*to Jack*]: My own! But what own are you? What is your Christian name, now that you have become someone else?

JACK: Good heavens! . . . I had quite forgotten that point. Your decision on the subject of my name is irrevocable, I suppose?

GWENDOLEN: I never change, except in my affections.

CECILY: What a noble nature you have, Gwendolen!

---

42. Jesus, rescuing a woman about to be stoned for adultery, says, "He that is without sin among you, let him first cast a stone at her" (John 8.7).

JACK: Then the question had better be cleared up at once. Aunt Augusta, a moment. At the time when Miss Prism left me in the hand-bag, had I been christened already?

LADY BRACKNELL: Every luxury that money could buy, including christening, had been lavished on you by your fond and doting parents.

JACK: Then I was christened! That is settled. Now, what name was I given? Let me know the worst.

LADY BRACKNELL: Being the eldest son you were naturally christened after your father.

JACK [*irritably*]: Yes, but what was my father's Christian name?

LADY BRACKNELL [*meditatively*]: I cannot at the present moment recall what the General's Christian name was. But I have no doubt he had one. He was eccentric, I admit. But only in later years. And that was the result of the Indian climate, and marriage, and indigestion, and other things of that kind.

JACK: Algy! Can't you recollect what our father's Christian name was?

ALGERNON: My dear boy, we were never even on speaking terms. He died before I was a year old.

JACK: His name would appear in the Army Lists of the period, I suppose, Aunt Augusta?

LADY BRACKNELL: The General was essentially a man of peace, except in his domestic life. But I have no doubt his name would appear in any military directory.

JACK: The Army Lists of the last forty years are here. These delightful records should have been my constant study. [*Rushes to bookcase and tears the books out.*] M. Generals . . . Mallam, Maxbohm,[43] Magley, what ghastly names they have—Markby, Migsby, Mobbs, Moncrieff! Lieutenant 1840, Captain, Lieutenant-Colonel, Colonel, General 1869, Christian names, Ernest John. [*Puts book very quietly down and speaks quite calmly.*] I always told you, Gwendolen, my name was Ernest, didn't I? Well, it is Ernest after all. I mean it naturally is Ernest.

LADY BRACKNELL: Yes, I remember now that the General was called Ernest. I knew I had some particular reason for disliking the name.

GWENDOLEN: Ernest! My own Ernest! I felt from the first that you could have no other name!

JACK: Gwendolen, it is a terrible thing for a man to find out suddenly that all his life he has been speaking nothing but the truth. Can you forgive me?

GWENDOLEN: I can. For I feel that you are sure to change.

JACK: My own one!

CHASUBLE [*to Miss Prism*]: Laetitia! [*Embraces her.*]

MISS PRISM [*enthusiastically*]: Frederick! At last!

ALGERNON: Cecily! [*Embraces her.*] At last!

JACK: Gwendolen! [*Embraces her.*] At last!

LADY BRACKNELL: My nephew, you seem to be displaying signs of triviality.

JACK: On the contrary, Aunt Augusta, I've now realized for the first time in my life the vital Importance of Being Earnest.

—1894, performed 1895, 1899

---

43. A jocular contraction of Max Beerbohm's name.

Una Ashworth Taylor
1857–1922

Una Ashworth Taylor wrote allegorical stories in aesthetic style. She came from a literary family; her father was the prominent Victorian poet Henry Taylor, and both her sisters, Ida and Eleanor, were successful novelists. Family friends included Alfred Tennyson, Anthony Trollope, and Lewis Carroll. Taylor's novel *The City of Sarras* (1887) and her book of short stories *Nets for the Wind* (1896) set up complex patterns among symbolic characters in carefully archetypal or semi-Arthurian settings. "Seed of the Sun" is a parable about fear of a monstrous pregnancy, while "The Truce of God" triangulates the relationship between artist and artwork, asking where the woman fits in. These unconventional stories may have been too highly wrought for their audience at the time, but they testify to the innovative ways aesthetes used fairy-tale and mythic elements to develop alternatives to realism.

Seed of the Sun

"We sell our score, but she her threescore," the other flower-sellers in the market-place said of the flower-girl whose name was Raël. "Fortune's sun shines on her."

But a day came when for Raël fortune's sun set.

It was spring. Raël loitered on her homeward way through the gay streets of the old city. She watched the fountain; its drops were jewelled with western lights of amber and rose-colour. She lingered by the open gate of a great garden wood, where the narcissus blossoms starred the ground under the myrtle-trees, and then she passed on beneath the shadows of great houses, on towards the streets where the poor people dwelt.

Near by her home was a ruined court, at one side of it was a shrine, where a pale Madonna looked down from her moss-grown niche. In the midst of the court was the statue of a lost god.[1] Raël did not know either his name or his godhead, but the statue she loved. Its face was so grey and mutilated that it seemed to her nothing could be older, yet its open lips were so young that it seemed to her nothing could be younger. All other youth was as age beside it.

Raël entered the court; she climbed upon a broken ledge near by the statue's pedestal, and she put her bluest violets one by one amongst its curls. Then she laughed softly and went singing on her way.

A flight of stone stairs led upwards to the little room which was her home; she could see them from the further end of the straight narrow street. At the foot of the stairway a man clad in rags was sitting. As she came near he rose and met her; she thought he was a beggar, but he did not beg of her. He stretched out his hand to her; in it lay a small seed, the size of a bean seed, brown and shrivelled.

"To him that hath shall be given," he said. "You have youth and innocence and joy and hope—I bring you a gift." He laid the brown seed in her hand. "Plant it and

---

1. Probably Apollo (god of art and light), since the story's title identifies him with the sun and Apollo was often depicted with curly hair.

water it, and let the sun shine upon it, cherish and tend it, and it will germinate and grow, yet its life will not come from the water-drops nor yet from the sunshine. When it is grown it will put forth strange leaves, and the leaves you will see; and one day it will blossom, but the blossom you will not see."

He waited for no answer, but passed swiftly from her sight.

Raël looked at the beggar's gift; she touched it with the finger of her right hand, doubtful and wondering. Then she took it home with her.

Next morning she wakened early; she rose and she looked again at the seed. It was so parched and dead that it seemed a husk and no seed.

She sought the house of an old physician; he knew many things and he had many books, and in his garden many strange and rare and health-giving herbs flourished and blossomed. Daily to him Raël brought her freshest spring flowers.

"Give me, I pray you," now she asked him, "a pot, and earth wherewith to fill it, that in it I may plant the seed to which I would give life."

And she said—

"Of what plant is the seed?"

She unclosed her hand that she might show the seed to him; as it lay in her palm it appeared to her that the brown was less withered.

"I do not know," the old man said.

He searched many books, but though they told of many seeds, of this seed they told nothing.

He gave Raël the pot, and the earth to fill it with, and she planted the seed and set it in her window, and watered it. When that evening she came back from the market-place, it seemed to her that the little white-walled room was no longer empty. That night she dreamt that beneath the earth the seed had broken its husk. Waking, she felt that she was no more solitary—and she was glad.

The days passed. In the city, amongst her companions, Raël was lonely; by night she was no longer alone, the beggar's gift was with her. Once at midnight she started from her sleep, she thought some one had called her by name. Next morning at dawn the crust of the earth which filled the pot was cracked; above its surface was a small red-tipped sheath, the first sheath-leaf of the fertilised seed. Raël leant over it, her breath touched it; the chill of winter was in the grey daybreak and she shivered, then a great faintness stole over her for joy that the plant was born.

That day she counted the hours as she sat in the market-place—each hour seemed a whole day's length—until evening came. Her eyes were like mist with the sun behind it; the malady of her joy had left its mark.

"What has befallen her?" her companions questioned. But Raël was silent.

At sundown she hastened homeward, the little shut sheath was there; she watered it, and then she slept the sleep of troubled happiness. In the morning a seam showed itself in the sheath; the night following, the seam split and the stem raised itself, and afterwards two leaves came, one on either side, and the plant grew, yet it was only in the night that it grew. Raël recalled the beggar's words, "not of the raindrops nor yet of the sunshine should its life spring forth." She pondered them.

The summer heat had stolen the red from her lips; in the market the buyers passed her without buying.

But the plant flourished and grew. One day the old physician stopped her in the street. It was long since she had seen him.

"How fares it with the seed?" he asked.

"It sprouted and is green—the stem bears many leaves," she answered him.

"I will come and see it," he said, "that I may know its name."

He came and he looked upon the plant, yet its name he could not tell. The leaf was not grown in his garden nor engraved in his books.

He looked upon Raël.

"Beware," he said. "There are herbs which are for health-giving—there are also herbs which breathe out strange maladies."

When he was gone Raël stood and watched the veined leaves in the sunshine; they were strong and young, very strong and very young. She touched them with her hands, which were languid and thin, and the leaves were warm with the sun and her hands were chill. A terror grew in her heart, a great grey fear, and her terror and fear were of the plant she had planted.

"I will fly from it," she said.

She fled—fled from the city out into the plains beyond the city, and beyond the plains to the blue sea. Her feet were wet with the dew of grasses, her lips were fanned by the sea-wind, and soft sea-mists were on her hair, but the fever-dream dreamt on at her heart, and the dream was of the plant.

"To-day it will fade," she said the first morning. And the next day she said, "It dies."

And its dying was her anguish.

"Maybe it is already dead," she told herself; "I will return and see."

So she returned. Up the narrow street she went with ever-quickening steps, up the steep stair with panting breath, and at her heart a hope and a despair.

The stem drooped, the green leaves were discoloured. Raël bathed them with her tears, and the stem lifted itself and the leaves revived.

After that Raël left it no more. In the market-place her seat was empty.

"When I am absent it is alone," she cried.

Poverty came to her, she begged for bread in the street.

"She has grown a poison-plant," her companions said, and they shrank from her; she was very pale, her face was like a shadow that fades, but the line of her straight lips was like the colour of a geranium flower.

A day came when bread itself failed. That day a stranger sought the narrow street where she lived. The fame of that strange plant had reached his ears. By the window stood the plant, beside it Raël sat silent; hunger shadowed her eyes, her small feet were bare on the stones and her gown was ragged.

"Sell to me," said the stranger. "For the plant that you have grown I will give much gold—even the price of a king's ransom. Hunger you shall know no more, nor poverty, nor any labour, and the stones of the street shall forget the touch of your feet."

Raël lifted her head and smiled.

"I will not sell one single leaf of its blossoming," she answered.

Nor would she listen to any entreating. And the plant still grew. It bore one bud, a close-furled bud. All day long Raël tended and watched it. Presently a narrow streak of a nameless rose-colour showed through the sheath of the bud.

Autumn had come, hot and breathless and feverish. The old physician climbed the stair. He stood by Raël.

"It feeds upon thy life," he said. "Come from it or cast it forth."

"Go from it I cannot. I went and I returned. Cast it forth I will not," she answered.

"Listen," he spoke once more, "and choose. Its health is your malady, its strength your faintness. Break the stem, let the root wither and parch. It lives of your dying, its blossom will be born of your death."

Then he said—

"It is ill to die in life's April."

He left her.

To die in life's spring!

The old man's words echoed on in her ears through the hours of the long afternoon.

To die—she or it. One must slay the other or be slain.

Day by day, hour by hour, it was stealing the colour from her face, the strength from her hands, the food from her lips, the blood from her veins. It was her enemy, her antagonist. There it was with the fair strong leaves and the straight stalk, and the folded bud with the scarlet thread of the blossom within, waiting, struggling, panting to be free. She looked at it; it seemed to watch her, and soon it would strike her with the death-wound of its first blossoming. The mutiny of life stirred within her; she would live and not die!

In the small still room the two adversaries were alone together—between them was a combat, a silent, unequal combat.

Go from it! She had gone and had returned. Sell it! No: though breast and brow and lips were printed with hunger. Cast it forth—break the stem, let the root wither!

She looked at her wasted hands. If they tore the plant, would it cry? would the leaves wail if she cast them forth?

It must blossom or it must die. Was there no compromise with death, no middle road for her or for it?

The leaves of the plant shone green as emerald in the red sunset. Before the morning came the bud must be broken, or—it must blossom. There was no compromise with death.

She turned from it and lay upon her couch with hidden face. And the tide of the battle ebbed and flowed. Life was fair, and life's desire quickened within her. A bird sang. She heard the beat of flying wings, and remembrance of old days wakened, of days when the seed was not, and the whole earth was very glad to her. And the world was still beautiful, and it was very great. Sky after sky would redden as it reddened now, and April would come and violets would come, and anemones and yellow crocuses. A hundred plants would spring, although that one plant of all plants lay dead in the dry street dust; a hundred blossoms would blossom although that one blossom of all earth's blossomings had never broken its bud.

Were there no other joys, save the joy of its verdure, no other loves with which she could love, was there nothing else in all the world for her save that one plant? Her lips answered her "Yes," but her heart answered her, "Nothing." She raised herself on her arm; the gold dusk of the twilight dazzled her, the plant was dark against it. The combat was keen, and it was a mortal combat. She looked through the yellow haze to trace the outline of each leaf—the leaves that must die!

And after? After the battle, when the strife was over and her antagonist was slain? When the leaf to which her breath had given life, her tears, rain—when the bud which had been born of her nearness—were rent from their stem?

The tints of sunset faded, her heart sickened and failed her. The tide of the contest turned in the balance. How beautiful it was—this child of her cherishing, this life of her life, this sweetness of her upbringing. And was it such a great matter to be slain of its slaying?

A new languor stole over her limb by limb, it weighed softly on her eyelids—in it was something of the imprisoning sweetness of sleep—it seemed to her as though it were the advance guard of death. Fear fell from her. Was this all?

Dusk was gone. In its place night—a translucent night without darkness—was come, and in the night the plant was drawing her to it, drawing and drawing and drawing her to its side. She felt it through the breathless stillness of that grey light—it called her—it wanted her—its need was her compulsion. She rose, as a sleepwalker rises; with slow, pausing feet she crossed the little room.

"I am coming," she said softly. "I come." She saw the small square of the starred sky set in the whiteness of the wall, and the window's ledge, and the earthen pot, and the one bud where the scarlet blossom struggled to break free. It was waiting for her, waiting for the nativity of her kiss. Raël knelt beside it. She lifted her hands to caress the leaves she had tended, she lifted her face to the bud she had cherished, then with shut eyes she kissed the bud with her lips.

And in the dawn the blossom of the plant broke like the flame of the sunrise. But the blossom Raël did not see.

"Bury it with her," the old physician bade them when they made ready to carry her to her grave.

And he laid the scarlet blossom on her breast, and the root he cast forth to die.

—1896

The Truce of God[1]

Hermas stood beside the statue and Mèril stood by him. The statue was the figure of a youth; in the hand of the youth was a sword, and upon his head a crown of laurel leaves; his eyes were closed. Hermas had made the statue, its temples had the wings of sleep.

"The statue is stronger than I," said the sculptor. "It has no needs. Without bread it will not starve, without water it will not thirst. Pain, before which man is powerless, before it is impotent."

Across the sunlight which flooded the great bare room the shadow of a flying swallow passed in a swift curve. Hermas paused to watch the bird's flight through the summer air. Then he went on—

"Men and beasts agonise, plants have their health and their maladies, flower gives birth to flower, and bird mates with bird. But spring-time and harvest-time, winter and summer, stone remains stone, and marble marble. The statue is stronger than I."

---

1. This title alludes to the medieval rule that combat must cease on saints' days. It is probably the idea of an inhuman intercession in personal, human conflict that Taylor wants to convey.

He expected no reply, how should Mèril answer him?

"Of old," he continued, after a brief pause, "we are told men made gods of stone; was it in truth that they in stone discerned a God?"

Mèril laughed softly. She loved Hermas; she had his hands to kiss, his face to look on, his voice to hear; she knew no more. Of what lay beyond Hermas she questioned nothing. She had neither past nor future, for her yesterday and to-morrow were not. What signified to her those eternal interrogations of eternal mysteries? what mattered it to her those vulnerabilities of humanity, or that sterile inviolability of stone? Even while he spoke Hermas had raised his hand once more to the marble, indenting a wound-mark above the heart.

"Nor when I strike does it suffer," he said moodily.

Mèril laughed again, thrusting her scarlet-tinged face between the sculptor and his work; she twined her arms round the statue, and with her feet poised on the stone base she reached the eyelids of the youth with her soft lips.

"Nor, if I cherish it, will it love," she cried gaily. "Its loss is infinite."

Her touch was the touch of a flower, her face in its sensitive uncertainty was like a reflection, vivid in sunlight, pale in shadow.

"Take heed, Mèril." Hermas set her on the ground. "There is a legend that once, playing heedlessly, a youth set his marriage ring upon the open hand of a stone Venus. She shut her fingers on the gift and held him bondsman."

Mèril kissed the hand in which hers lay.

"Ah, Hermas!" she said, "you, like that old lost world, think that because marble is not mortal it is God; that to be less than human is to be half divine."

They were the haphazard words of an intelligence that only mirrored the images of life upon its surface, but they turned the current of his thoughts.

"And to be less than woman," he jested, "is to be—Mèril."

"Am I less than woman?" she asked, a little cloud of trouble overcasting her face.

His speculative eyes rested upon her evasive loveliness; and the speculation died out of them. "You are the soul of a rose—if roses have souls," he answered her caressingly, "where others feel needs you only follow impulses, where they pursue aims you only obey instincts."

"What is the distinction?" she persisted.

"How should you understand!" he said. "Want is the consciousness of a void, it is the pang of hunger and the torture of thirst. Impulse is to the joy of bread without hunger, to the joy of dew without fever's parching."

For a moment a faint gleam of comprehension lay in her eyes, then lifting his hand she laid it on her hair.

"What is it to me, what is anything to me without or within?" she cried. "Love is enough!"

She loved so much. She had a genius for love; it is a genius which demands great things of those to whom it is given. Further, it has the sacrificial quality of all genius, it produces no works even for the merchandise of the heart. Likewise Hermas loved her, but with a difference. Mèril needed her whole self—Hermas had to be only part of himself—to love. Mèril, by reason of her love, could do many things; Hermas had to put aside many things to love.

When Hermas made the statue he was poor, the great house which was their home was beautiful as a palace and bare as a prison. Mèril loved its bareness, it was so white and still. There is a restlessness to some women in the presence even of things inanimate.

But after the winged statue was made, Hermas became famous and he became rich. Men and women came and went in the rooms which once were solitary. The world entered Mèril's paradise. At its hands she demanded nothing, to Hermas it gave all that he demanded. Soon there remained nothing for him to strive for save the unattainable; he suffered the supreme defeat of victory. When a man has won all that is winable, he can hereafter only draw blanks. It is an inevitable penalty of success— Hermas grew hardened to it; as it became a custom it ceased to be a sensation, but the accent of life was lost.

Often he left Mèril. When he left her she lived alone in the great echoing house. She needed no companionship. Hermas was present or Hermas was absent, and when he was absent her life lay between a memory and an expectation. She was not unhappy, for her memories and her expectations were both of joy. Only in the stillness and the solitude she grew like a shadow; waiting, she wasted away with her heart's home-sickness for his arms.

Once he came back to her suddenly. She had not known his return, she had not heard his footsteps. She had fallen asleep in the white room where the winged statue stood upon his pedestal with his closed eyelids and parted lips. There Hermas found her. The sunshine of the late afternoon flooded the room with dusty radiance. The cobweb threads of her hair had caught both the radiance and the dustiness; they shone as if powdered with gold, like the feathers of a gold-moth's wings, but her face was very white, and in the full summer heat she lay as if the chill of winter encompassed her. A dumb terror held Hermas for a moment speechless, then kneeling beside her he wakened her with kisses. He saw the colour spring back to her face, the lagging pulses beat swiftly, and still his kisses touched her lips as never before they had touched them. Under those kisses her eyes shone like mad stars.

"You are my life," she whispered. "Life of my life!" Then with a swift recoil of terror she shrank from him.

"See!" she cried, "the statue bleeds!"

He turned. By some freak of reflected light a sun-ray, dyed red as blood by the ruby crystal of a great cup set on a high shelf above, struck its stain upon the beauty of the statue—and on the breast of the statue, above its heart, was the wound-mark Hermas had cut in the marble.

He saw and laughed.

"It bleeds because of my kisses," he said. "Stone is a jealous god." Then his laughter died away. "Jealous and strong," he added, as if compelled by some after-thought of indefinite distrust.

Again his gaze reverted to Mèril. He saw once more her face as he had seen it in sleep, white and still. Even now it seemed to him as if the crimson flush, new-born with his coming, was fading and giving place to that former pallor. It was like the contagion of marble.

Mèril had risen; she was standing close beside the statue; her eyes were drowsily raised towards it, as if she half expected to see the flow of the wound and the drip of the life-blood from its cleft heart. But the red stain was gone; the sunlight had shifted; the sun sank fast in throbbing colours behind the walls and roofs of the city streets, and as it sank it left behind it a sky of amber and orange, flecked with rose-red clouds. Presently these too faded, and a clear twilight which was like white fire filled the room.

Neither of the two had spoken for many minutes, but Hermas was watching Mèril with a sharpening sense of disquietude. At last he broke the silence.

"Why were you sleeping?" he demanded, with a certain urgency.

Mèril crept back to him; she leant against him, and drew his passive hand softly over her eyelids.

"I wanted it," she said. Then after a short pause, "I want it still," she murmured, with a gesture of profoundest languor. He let her sleep, but the slumber seemed to him like the invasion of an enemy—it had the remoteness of death.

The next day, and the next, something of that shadowy drowsiness clung to her; her life lay beneath it as the muted strings of a violin. Then by slow degrees its muffled stillness was broken; beneath his hands the film which overspread her vitality dispersed; warmth, and colour, and movement revived. In those days his love changed. Before, he had loved her, now he became her lover. She was aware of some change, with a vague, indefinite consciousness. The perception brought with it an unaccustomed burthen; a sense of inadequacy to respond to some new demand oppressed her. Her joy was gone. The unfamiliarities of life's relations are like estrangements to women; a new nearness is like a separation.

"I have a grief, Hermas," she said.

"I see no tears," he answered lightly, yet wondering.

"To you I gave all," she continued, paying no heed to his words, "I gave all, and more than all can no woman give. Now, you who were once content need more."

He made no response. She moved restlessly, striving to disentangle the thread of her thoughts.

"To give more, I must be more," she went on.

"More than Mèril?" he said, smiling. But he could not dispel that troubled sense of incompleteness.

She lifted wistful eyes to his; their wistfulness was like a passion.

"Ah, Hermas!" she cried, "I cannot, cannot understand, it is like lying between a waking and a sleep, between a life and a death—and neither are mine. But the sleep is stronger than the waking and the death than the life."

"Death is not stronger than life," he asserted, stirred to denial by some sense of contest. His own fantastic imaginings had found utterance in her words.

"It is stronger, it is stronger," she reiterated. "Its expression is in impotence, the helplessness of dead lips, the weakness of dead hands, but behind the dead is the death-giver, and he is stronger than all."

Mèril clasped her arms round Hermas.

"Give me life," she said, "give me life, that I may give back to you all you demand."

• • •

It was evening. A gay crowd thronged hall and stairs and corridors. Mèril passed among the guests with the face of a woman to whom a crowd is a solitude.

Once her lips trembled and her colour came and went, as Hermas for a moment lin-gered at her side.

A woman near by laughed.

"You are his bondswoman," she said.

"To be bondswoman of one is to be freed-woman of many," Mèril answered.

The woman who jeered paused. She had fought with the world and won, yet con-fronted by Mèril's eyes with their remote enfranchisement, her triumphs shrank into littleness. What were they but tributes to the world's empire? To conquer a world is to proclaim that the world is worth conquest. She was a thrall to her victories.

Yet—she knew Hermas—once she had loved him. She looked from him to Mèril; from the god who was dust, to the worship which was infinite—looked and was silent, and turned away, lest in place of pity she should envy the emancipation of the bondage she derided.

The hours wore on to midnight. But for Mèril the lassitude of the summer night had no fatigue, and the turmoil of laughter and jests had no unrest. Her heart waited; enclosed in its own quietude, for the hour when no voice, save the voice of Hermas should sound in her ears, when no eyes save her eyes should look upon his face. And yet even as she waited, she was conscious of coming change—the ear of some spiri-tual sense caught as it were the whirr of fortune's wheel which turned. Something was coming—coming that very night. It would come, as day comes after a dream, reality after an image—the same, yet not the same.

She stole from the crowd, away from the voices, away from the lights and the glitter, and the movement—they oppressed her like a narrowed horizon. The grey night was in the summer-garden—its hand lay upon the eyes of the flowers. The air was like the breath of the earth's fever, but it was silent. She was not tired, but she would rest; without weariness she craved for repose in that dumb greyness. In a niche, beneath a high stone wall, was a seat of stone, shadowed from the twilight; she sought it. The soft dark plumes of the cypresses against the sky were motionless; there were star-shadows on the grass, and something was calling her to sleep, and she was sink-ing, sinking into the utmost recess of slumber, where even dreams are forgotten and out of mind.

Within the house the lights burnt lower and lower. Men and women came from it in twos and threes, singly, or in loitering companies. Presently they came no more. All was still—the last footstep had died away, and the windows one by one darkened in the wall.

Hermas waited. Soon Mèril would come to him—come with words or with silence, with the grace of unashamed caresses, or with the half-fear of her heart's sur-rendering worship. He was patient for her coming, with the patience bred of security, the decoy which ensnares men to inaction until joy's hour has passed by beyond recall, uncaptured and unpossessed.

Without Mèril slept. From time to time, in that leaden slumber, she stirred with some fret of restless awakening; once with wide-open eyes she looked upon the night, then again sleep re-entangled her in its meshes, and her weighted lids re-closed.

Within, Hermas passed from room to room. He had waited, and Mèril had not come. He sought her. He would find her somewhere sleeping, as once before in the afternoon sunlight he had found her, and she would waken, as then she had wakened. But he sought in vain. Each room was tenantless and forlorn, as solitude assumes to itself forlorness when once it has been peopled. He called her name. No answer came. Then all the darkness and the vacancy became vitalised with fears—on every threshold a terror stood sentinel—the very silence became a menace.

He relinquished his unavailing search—he fled from the empty house, and unsought he found her. The fire of his kisses was on her lips and her eyelids and her hands, but no least quiver of response, the answer of life to life, came from the quiet figure, wrapped in that inanimate repose. He lifted her in his arms and retraced his steps; he laid her on the low window-seat where before he had found her on the first day of his home-coming. When day came, day would waken her, he told his despair, and his despair answered him. He waited and watched and waited; and the statue, with its winged brows, stood near by in sinister whiteness, with the mark of the bloodless scar, and the muteness of its passive secrecy. Over Hermas the old fantasy regained ascendency. The marble lived, lived with an evasive vitality, which, like the breath of a malignant herb poisoned the air with unknown malady: and the statue was stronger than he, in that strange half-life which eluded his grasp. And he, Hermas, had given to the marble a form, had endowed that passive, dormant life within it, with the fashioning of a man's shape, had set a weapon in its hands, and, under the image of a death-wound, had ascribed to the senseless figure a heart.

He left Mèril and drew near the statue.

· · ·

And Mèril still slept, held in the soft prison of that tenacious slumber.

Without, the early dawn radiated in silver tints across the sky, the steel glimmers of light caught the dew-drenched grass, and penetrating the windows, struck here and there upon a glass cup or a bright metal. Then sudden shafts of opal fires shot across the silver, and flakes of scarlet flame drifted like burning spray upon the wide expanse of the mornings's blueness.

With the shock of a cry Mèril wakened. The cry still rang in her ears—the cry of a dream. For a moment she lay confused, doubting, wondering, until memory's balance readjusted itself, and life the substantial divided itself from life the unsubstantial, and wakefulness, with which all wakefulness she had ever known became as a blurred phantom, swept over her senses with a vividness that pierced and stung.

"Hermas!" she cried, and she repeated, "Hermas!" Against the pedestal, where once the statue had stood, Hermas was leaning. At his feet the statue lay shattered upon the marble floor. The shaft of its weapon was broken, the hilt severed from the hand which had held it, and in the hand of Hermas lay the point of the splintered blade.

"The statue is dead," said Hermas.

Mèril came swiftly towards him; her eyes saw him alone, her heart beat for the captivity of his hand.

"I slept," she said, "but I have wakened."

Her eyes shone; the whole joy of the summer daybreak, its strength and its fullness was in the beating of her pulses, its rose-colour on her lips.

Hermas stirred, he moved as if to meet her—then fell back to the same posture.

"The statue is dead," he repeated. She was beside him, she clasped her arms round his neck—his words had no significance to her ears.

"Life has come to me," she whispered. "It has come that I may give it back to you—give all that you demand. My grief is gone."

Hermas raised himself erect. He held her to him and with blind lips sought hers. When he released her, her eyes fell upon the sword-point. It lay where it had fallen from his hand—the sword-point which he had drawn from his breast.

"Hermas," Mèril cried with sudden terror, "the blade is wet."

—1896

DONNA QUIXOTE.

["A world of disorderly notions *picked out of books*, crowded into his (her) imagination."—*Don Quixote*.

Punch, Donna Quixote (1894). "A world of disorderly notions *picked out of books*, crowded into his (her) imagination." Based on Gustave Doré's "Don Quixote in his Library" (1863).

PART II

New Women

The New Women: Introduction

In 1894, the critic W. F. Barry warned, "The New Woman ought to be aware that her condition is morbid, or, at least, hysterical; that the true name of science falsely so-called may be 'brain-poisoning'; that 'ideas' and love affairs, when mixed in unequal proportions, may explode like dynamite." This dangerous "New Woman" was a middle-class woman agitating for such "dynamite" ideas as the right to walk without a chaperone, to hold a job, to live alone in a flat, to go to college, and to wear sensible clothing. Moreover, she wanted to remake Victorian marriage. New Women asked men to exercise sexual self-discipline, demanded women have access to honest sex education, and tried to popularize alternatives to marriage (ranging from free unions to easier divorces). To modern readers, a movement in which prosperous young women agitated for the right to cut their hair, ride bicycles, and study might not seem terribly radical. Yet as Barry's warning shows, the New Women shocked and confounded *fin-de-siècle* observers and gained notoriety out of all proportion to the number of its actual participants.

The New Women emerged from a century of argument about women's proper role. By the mid-nineteenth century, the Enlightenment model of equal rights propounded by Mary Wollstonecraft's *Vindication of the Rights of Women* (1792) had been replaced by widespread cultural belief that men and women were inherently different. Conservatives argued that since women were naturally domestic they should remain at home; reformers demanded that women be able to use their nurturing skills for the public good by training in caretaking professions. By the late nineteenth century, however, this discourse changed as new data suggested that British women significantly outnumbered men. Even if all women married, some would be "left over" and those "odd women" would have to work in order to support themselves. While traditionalists warned that women who eschewed marriage and motherhood were "unsexing" themselves, with horrendous physical and psychological consequences, activists could use the "odd women" problem to insist on the legitimacy of women's independent lives.

What's more, the New Woman could take advantage of modern life in her desire for independence. Did young women seek jobs? They could be secretaries, using new technologies like typewriters and telephones; they could be clerks in the new department stores; they could teach in the recently established progressive girls' schools; they could do philanthropic nursing work in urban centers. How would they live? They could rent a flat, ride omnibuses or pedal bicycles to work, eat in the new Aerated Bread Company cafeterias (designed to provide a safe nonalcoholic alternative to pubs). The literature of the New Woman described the excitements and frustrations of these young women's lives. Just as aestheticism expanded male roles, making the sensitive, poetic, artistic man into a culturally acceptable persona, so did the New Women movement reform women's roles, popularizing the idea of an energetic, self-sufficient, hard-working woman.

Meanwhile, the media celebrated and condemned this New Woman. Most famously, Sarah Grand and Ouida exchanged a series of tart rebuttals in the *North American Review* in 1894 over the identity and value of the New Woman. Cartoons in *Punch* perpetuated the image of the New Woman as a bespectacled, angular, ridiculous spinster. *The Nineteenth Century* ran a series of ardent debates between mothers and "revolting daughters," initiated by an article by B. A. Crackanthorpe. New Women novels sympathetically depicted women's difficulty carving out satisfactory lives. Probably the most controversial New Woman novels were Sarah Grand's *The Heavenly Twins*, which angrily depicts women's sexual victimhood in marriage, and—from a very different perspective—Grant Allen's *The Woman Who Did*, which idealizes extramarital unions. Mona Caird's *Daughters of Danaus* demonstrates how family duties overwhelm a gifted composer. Similarly, talented young women writers' struggles occupy *Story of a Modern Woman* by Ella Hepworth Dixon and *A Writer of Books* by "George Paston" (Emily Morse Symonds). Among the most critically acclaimed New Women novels are Thomas Hardy's *Jude the Obscure*, George Gissing's *The Odd Women*, and Olive Schreiner's *Story of an African Farm*, which uses innovative nonrealist techniques to depict the tortured life of the independent woman Lyndall. Among writers of short fiction, the most celebrated was "George Egerton" (Mary Chavelita Dunne Clairmonte Bright), whose *Keynotes* and *Discords* reinvent the short story, making it impressionistic, nonlinear, and fragmented, with multiple points of view. Stories by Mabel E. Wotton, Ella D'Arcy, and Charlotte Perkins Gilman portrayed the terrible harm that paternalistic ideologies wreaked on the women they entrapped.

Because New Women writers were often journalists who saw their writing as part of an ongoing campaign, they usually wrote in prose, but they did produce some poetry too. The poems presented here reflect the martial or critical moods characteristic of New Women activism, although the same poets' more contemplative, description-rich verse is recognizably aesthetic.

Fin-de-siècle critics despised what they saw as the sloppy writing and undeserved sales of most New Women novels, but what seem like literary faults may actually be important proto-modernist innovations. With multiple characters' shifting points of view, hallucinatory dream sequences, fragmentary glimpses of alternate modes, refusal of closure, suspension of conventional plot, and an urgent, contemporary, transparent prose style borrowed from journalism, the New Women's writing differed noticeably from the aesthetes' symbolic, allusive, learned prose. Above all, however, the

New Women novels were the first, most recognizable, and bestselling corpus of explicitly feminist literature. They deserve attention as an attempt to articulate women's needs in a tumultuous time.

New Women in the Popular Press

Sarah Grand
1854–1943

The prolific, controversial writer "Sarah Grand" (Frances Elizabeth Bellenden Clarke McFall) seemed to be everywhere at the *fin de siècle*. Her impassioned journalism defined the New Women for the public; her scandalous fiction became a byword for conservative critics. First gaining notoriety with *Ideala* (1888), Grand outdid herself in *The Heavenly Twins* (1893). *The Heavenly Twins* shocked readers with its insistence that women needed sex education to protect themselves from their syphilitic husbands. *The Beth Book* (1897) is an autobiographically based account of a woman's growth. Grand had an alcoholic father and an unhappy marriage to a doctor who treated prostitutes suffering from venereal disease. Her publication of *Ideala* gave her enough money to leave her husband and son and embark on her career as a writer and lecturer on women's issues. A strong supporter of suffrage, she was also "Lady Mayoress" of Bath for six years. Presented here is the first in her famous series of articles in the *North American Review* denouncing men's ethical failure to live up to the New Woman's standards, and it helped establish the term *New Woman*. Although Grand largely accepts women's inherent difference from men, she argues that women must extend their uniquely domestic skills into public work to enhance the nation.

The New Aspect of the Woman Question

It is amusing as well as interesting to note the pause which the new aspect of the woman question has given to the Bawling Brothers[1] who have hitherto tried to howl down every attempt on the part of our sex to make the world a pleasanter place to live in. That woman should ape man and desire to change places with him was conceivable to him as he stood on the hearth-rug in his lord-and-master-monarch-of-all-I-survey attitude, well inflated with his own conceit; but that she should be content to develop the good material which she finds in herself and be only dissatisfied with the poor quality of that which is being offered to her in man, her mate, must appear to him to be a thing as monstrous as it is unaccountable. "If women don't want to be men, what do they want?" asked the Bawling Brotherhood when the first misgiving of the truth flashed upon them; and then,

---

1. Grand's coinage, meant to match Eliza Lynn Linton's earlier misogynist nickname, "the Shrieking Sisters" (1870).

to reassure themselves, they pointed to a certain sort of woman in proof of the contention that we were all unsexing ourselves.

It would be rational for us now to declare that men generally are Bawling Brothers or to adopt the hasty conclusion which makes all men out to be fiends on the one hand and all women fools on the other. We have our Shrieking Sisterhood, as the counterpart of the Bawling Brotherhood. The latter consists of two sorts of men. First of all is he who is satisfied with the cow-kind of woman as being most convenient; it is the threat of any strike among his domestic cattle for more consideration that irritates him into loud and angry protests. The other sort of Bawling Brother is he who is under the influence of the scum of our sex, who knows nothing better than women of that class in and out of society, preys upon them or ruins himself for them, takes his whole tone from them, and judges us all by them. Both the cow-woman and the scum-woman are well within range of the comprehension of the Bawling Brotherhood, but the new woman is a little above him, and he never even thought of looking up to where she has been sitting apart in silent contemplation all these years, thinking and thinking, until at last she solved the problem and proclaimed for herself what was wrong with Home-is-theWoman's-Sphere, and prescribed the remedy.

What she perceived at the outset was the sudden and violent upheaval of the suffering sex in all parts of the world. Women were awaking from their long apathy, and, as they awoke, like healthy hungry children unable to articulate, they began to whimper for they knew not what. They might have been easily satisfied at that time had not society, like an ill-conditioned and ignorant nurse, instead of finding out what they lacked, shaken them and beaten them and stormed at them until what was once a little wail became convulsive shrieks and roused up the whole human household. Then man, disturbed by the uproar, came upstairs all anger and irritation, and, without waiting to learn what was the matter, added his own old theories to the din, but, finding they did not act rapidly, formed new ones, and made an intolerable nuisance of himself with his opinions and advice. He was in the state of one who cannot comprehend because he has no faculty to perceive the thing in question, and that is why he was so positive. The dimmest perception that you may be mistaken will save you from making an ass of yourself.

We must look upon man's mistakes, however, with some leniency, because we are not blameless in the matter ourselves. We have allowed him to arrange the whole social system and manage or mismanage it all these ages without ever seriously examining his work with a view to considering whether his abilities and his motives were sufficiently good to qualify him for the task. We have listened without a smile to his preachments, about our place in life and all we are good for, on the text that "there is no understanding a woman." We have endured most poignant misery for his sins, and screened him when we should have exposed him and had him punished. We have allowed him to exact all things of us, and have been content to accept the little he grudgingly gave us in return. We have meekly bowed our heads when he called us bad names instead of demanding proofs of the superiority which alone would give him a right to do so. We have listened much edified to man's sermons on the subject of virtue, and have acquiesced uncomplainingly in the convenient arrangement by which this quality has come to be altogether practised for him by us vicariously. We have seen him set up Christ as an example for all men to follow, which argues his belief in the possibility of doing so, and have not only allowed his weakness and hypocrisy in the matter to pass without comment, but, until lately, have not even seen the humor of his pretensions when contrasted with his practices nor held him up to that wholesome ridicule which is a stimulating corrective. Man deprived us of all proper education, and then jeered at us because we had no knowledge. He narrowed our outlook on life so that our view of it should be all distorted, and then declared that our mistaken impression of it proved us to be senseless creatures. He cramped our minds so that there was no room for reason in them, and then made merry at our want of logic. Our divine intuition was not to be controlled by him, but he did his best to damage it by sneering at it as an inferior feminine method of arriving at conclusions; and finally, after having had his own way until he lost his head completely, he set himself up as a sort of a god and required us to worship him, and, to our eternal shame be it said, we did so. The truth has all along been in us, but we have cared more for man than for truth, and so the whole human race has suffered. We have failed of our effect by neglecting our duty here, and have deserved much of the obloquy that was cast upon us. All that is over now, however, and while on the one hand man has shrunk to his true proportions in our estimation, we, on the other, have been expanding to our own; and now we come confidently forward to maintain, not that this or that was "intended," but that there are in ourselves, in both sexes, possibilities hitherto suppressed or abused, which, when properly developed, will supply to either what is lacking in the other.

The man of the future will be better, while the woman will be stronger and wiser. To bring this about is the whole aim and object of the present struggle, and with the discovery of the means lies the solution of the Woman Question. Man, having no conception of himself as imperfect from the woman's point of view, will find this difficult to understand, but we know his weakness, and will be patient with him, and help him with his lesson. It is the woman's place and pride and pleasure to teach the child, and man morally is in his infancy. There have been times when there was a doubt as to whether he was to be raised or woman was to be lowered, but we have turned that corner at last; and now woman holds out a strong hand to the child man, and insists, but with infinite tenderness and pity, upon helping him up.

He must be taught consistency. There are ideals for him which it is to be presumed that he tacitly agrees to accept when he keeps up an expensive establishment to teach them: let him live up to them. Man's faculty for shirking his own responsibility has been carried to such an extent in the past that, rather than be blamed himself when it did not answer to accuse woman, he imputed the whole consequence of his own misery-making peculiarities to God.

But with all his assumption man does not make the most of himself. He has had every advantage of training to increase his insight, for instance, but yet we find him, even at this time of day, unable to perceive that woman has a certain amount of self-respect and practical good sense—enough at all events to enable her to use the proverb about the bird in the hand to her own advantage. She does not in the least intend to sacrifice the privileges she enjoys on the chance of obtaining others, especially of the kind which man seems to think she must aspire to as so much more desirable. Woman may be foolish, but her folly has never been greater than man's conceit, and the one is not more disastrous to the understanding than the other. When a man talks about knowing the world and having lived and that sort of thing, he means something objectionable; in seeing life he generally includes doing wrong; and it is in these respects he is apt to accuse us of wishing to ape him. Of old if a woman ventured to be at all unconventional, man was allowed to slander her with the imputation that she must be abandoned, and he really believed it because with him liberty meant license. He has never accused us of trying to emulate him in any noble, manly quality, because the cultivation of noble qualities has not hitherto been a favorite pursuit of his, not to the extent at least of entering into his calculations and making any perceptible impression on public opinion; and he never, therefore, thought of considering whether it might have attractions for us. The cultivation of noble qualities has been individual rather than general, and the person who practised it is held to be one apart, if not actually eccentric. Man acknowledges that the business of life carried on according to his methods corrodes, and the state of corrosion is a state of decay; and yet he is fatuous enough to imagine that our ambition must be to lie like him for our own benefit in every public capacity. Heaven help the child to perceive with what travail and sorrow we submit to the heavy obligation, when it is forced upon us by our sense of right, of showing him how things ought to be done.

We have been reproached by Ruskin for shutting ourselves up behind park palings and garden walls, regardless of the waste world that moans in misery without,[2] and that has been too much our attitude; but the day of our acquiescence is over. There is that in ourselves which forces us out of our apathy; we have no choice in the matter. When we hear the "Help! help! help!" of the desolate and the oppressed, and still more when we see the awful dumb despair of those who have lost even the hope of help, we must respond. This is often inconvenient to man, especially when he has seized upon a defenceless victim whom he would have destroyed had we not come to the rescue; and so, because it is inconvenient to be exposed and thwarted, he snarls about the end of all true womanliness, cants on the subject of the Sphere, and threatens that if we do not sit still at home with cotton-wool in our ears so that we cannot be stirred into having our sympathies aroused by his victims when they shriek, and with shades over our eyes that we may not see him in his degradation, we shall be afflicted with short hair, coarse skins, unsymmetrical figures, loud voices, tastelessness in dress, and an unattractive appearance and character generally, and then he will not love us any more or marry us. And this is one of the most amusing of his threats, because he has said and proved on so many occasions that he cannot live without us whatever we are. O man! man! you are a very funny fellow now we know you! But take care. The standard of your pleasure and convenience has already ceased to be our conscience. On one point, however, you may reassure yourself. True womanliness is not in danger, and the sacred duties of wife and mother will be all the more honorably performed when women have a reasonable hope of becoming wives and mothers of *men*. But there is the difficulty. The trouble is not because women are mannish, but because men grow ever more effeminate. Manliness is at a premium now because there is so little of it, and we are accused of aping men in order to conceal the side from which the contrast should evidently be drawn. Man in his manners becomes more and more wanting until we seem to be near the time when there will be nothing left of him but the old Adam, who said, "It wasn't me."

---

2. In "Of Queens' Gardens" (1864).

Of course it will be retorted that the past has been improved upon in our day; but that is not a fair comparison. We walk by the electric light: our ancestors had only oil-lamps. We can see what we are doing and where we are going, and should be as much better as we know how to be. But where are our men? Where is the chivalry, the truth, and affection, the earnest purpose, the plain living, high thinking, and noble self-sacrifice that make a man? We look in vain among the bulk of our writers even for appreciation of these qualities. With the younger men all that is usually cultivated is that flippant smartness which is synonymous with cheapness. There is such a want of wit amongst them, too, such a lack of variety, such monotony of threadbare subjects worked to death! Their "comic" papers subsist upon repetitions of those three venerable jests, the mother-in-law, somebody drunk, and an edifying deception successfully practised by an unfaithful husband or wife. As they have nothing true so they have nothing new to give us, nothing either to expand the heart or move us to happy mirth. Their ideas of beauty threaten always to be satisfied with the ballet dancer's legs, pretty things enough in their way, but not worth mentioning as an aid to the moral, intellectual, and physical strength that make a man. They are sadly deficient in imagination, too; that old fallacy to which they cling, that because an evil thing has always been, therefore it must always continue, in as much the result of want of imagination as of the man's trick of evading the responsibility of seeing right done in any matter that does not immediately affect his personal comfort. But there is one thing the younger men are especially good at, and that is giving their opinion; this they do to each other's admiration until they verily believe it to be worth something. Yet they do not even know where we are in the history of the world. One of them only lately, doubtless by way of ingratiating himself with the rest of the Bawling Brotherhood, actually proposed to reintroduce the Acts of the Apostles-of-the-Pavements;[3] he was apparently quite unaware of the fact that the mothers of the English race are too strong to allow themselves to be insulted by the reimposition of another most shocking degradation upon their sex. Let him who is responsible for the economic position which forces women down be punished for the consequence. If any are unaware of cause and effect in that matter, let them read The Struggle for Life which the young master wrote in Wreckage.[4] As the workingman says with Christ-like compassion: "They wouldn't be there, poor things, if they were not driven to it."

There are upwards of a hundred thousand women in London doomed to damnation by the written law of man if they dare to die, and to infamy for a livelihood if they must live; yet the man at the head of affairs wonders what it is that we with the power are protesting against in the name of our sex. But is there any wonder we women wail for the dearth of manliness when we find men from end to end of their rotten social system forever doing the most cowardly deed in their own code, striking at the defenceless woman, especially when she is down?

The Bawling Brotherhood have been seeing reflections of themselves lately which did not flatter them, but their conceit survives, and they cling confidently to

---

3. The Contagious Diseases Acts (CDA) of the 1860s gave police the right to examine any woman suspected of prostitution, searching for venereal disease. Although repealed in the1880s, the Acts were proposed for reintroduction throughout the 1880s and 1890s. Grand's involvement in the major feminist cause of fighting the CDA led her to publicize the facts about venereal disease in The Heavenly Twins.
4. Hubert Crackanthorpe (1870–96), writer of highly stylized aesthetic fiction, published Wreckage in 1893.

the delusion that they are truly all that is admirable, and it is the mirror that is in fault. Mirrors may be either a distorting or a flattering medium, but women do not care to see life any longer in a glass darkly. Let there be light. We suffer in the first shock of it. We shriek in horror at what we discover when it is turned on that which was hidden away in dark corners; but the first principle of good housekeeping is to have no dark corners, and as we recover ourselves we go to work with a will to sweep them out. It is for us to set the human household in order, to see to it that all is clean and sweet and comfortable for the men who are fit to help us to make home in it. We are bound to raise the dust while we are at work, but only those who are in it will suffer any inconvenience from it, and the self-sufficing and self-supporting are not afraid. For the rest it will be all benefits. The Woman Question is the Marriage Question, as shall be shown hereafter.

—1894

Ouida
1839–1908

"Her style is a veritable cascade," marveled Max Beerbohm about the dauntingly prolific "Ouida" (Marie Louise de la Ramée), whose novels depict gorgeous aristocratic beauties engaged in epic passions. Ouida lived much of her life in Italy, where she behaved like a true aesthete, spending a fortune on hothouse flowers and priceless china, designing her own gowns, and pursuing romantic adventures with men. Her 46 novels and numerous plays, short stories, and articles helped make her a "Circulating Library Queen," a bestselling popular author. Ouida's fiction often focuses on dandies, uses homoerotic tension, and describes luxurious surroundings in visually rich passages studded with epigrams. However, her journalism could be much more carping than her aesthetic fiction. The article presented here is probably the first to use the capitalized phrase "the New Woman." Because of the nastily exasperated opening paragraphs, this essay is often cited as antifeminist, but in the rest of the article Ouida actually scolds the New Women for insufficient radicalism. She demands that women show a better social conscience toward the working class and do a better job of supporting animal rights (Ouida was a major figure in the anti-vivisectionist movement). The changing politics of this article indicate just how complicated *fin-de-siècle* gender ideas could be.

The New Woman

It can scarcely be disputed, I think, that in the English language there are conspicuous at the present moment two words which designate two unmitigated bores: The Workingman and the Woman. The Workingman and the Woman, the New Woman, be it remembered, meet us at every page of literature written in the English tongue; and each is convinced that on its own especial W hangs the future of the world. Both he and she want to have their values artificially raised and rated, and a status given to them by favor in lieu of desert. In an age in which persistent clamor is generally crowned by success they have both obtained considerable attention; is it offensive to say much more of it than either deserves? Your contributor avers that the Cow-Woman and the Scum-Woman, man understands; but that the New Woman is above him. The elegance of these appellatives is not calculated to recommend them to readers of either sex; and as a specimen of style forces one to hint that the New Woman who, we are told, "has been sitting apart in silent contemplation all these years" might in all these years have studied better models of literary composition. We are farther on told "that the dimmest perception that you may be mistaken, will save you from making an ass of yourself." It appears that even this dimmest perception has never dawned upon the New Woman.

We are farther told that "thinking and thinking" in her solitary sphynx-like contemplation she solved the problem and prescribed the remedy (the remedy to a problem!); but what this remedy was we are not told, nor did the New Woman apparently disclose it to the rest of womankind, since she still hears them in "sudden and violent upheaval" like "children unable to articulate whimpering for they know not what." It is sad to reflect that they might have been "easily satisfied at that time" (at what time?), "but society stormed at them until what was a little wail became convulsive shrieks"; and we are not told why the New Woman who had "the remedy for the problem," did not immediately produce it. We are not told either in what country or at what epoch this startling upheaval of volcanic womanhood took place in which "man merely made himself a nuisance with his opinions and advice," but apparently did quell this wailing and gnashing of teeth since it would seem that he has managed still to remain more masterful than he ought to be.

We are further informed that women "have allowed him to arrange the whole social system and manage or mismanage it all these ages without ever seriously examining his work with a view to considering whether his abilities and his methods were sufficiently good to qualify him for the task."

There is something deliciously comical in the idea, thus suggested, that man has only been allowed to "manage or mismanage" the world because woman has graciously refrained from preventing his doing so. But the comic side of this pompous and solemn assertion does not for a moment offer itself to the New Woman sitting aloof and aloft in her solitary meditation on the superiority of her sex. For the New Woman there is no such thing as a joke. She has listened without a smile to her enemy's "preachments"; she has "endured poignant misery for his sins," she has "meekly bowed her head" when he called her bad names; and she has never asked for "any proof of the superiority" which could alone have given him a right to use such naughty expressions. The truth has all along been in the possession of woman; but strange and sad perversity of taste! she has "cared more for man than for truth, and so the whole human race has suffered!"

"All that is over, however," we are told, and "while on the one hand man has shrunk to his true proportions" she has, all the time of this shrinkage, been herself expanding, and has in a word come to "fancy herself" extremely. So that he has no longer the slightest chance of imposing upon her by his game-cock airs.

Man, "having no conception of himself as imperfect," will find this difficult to understand at first; but the New Woman "knows his weakness," and will "help him with his lesson." "*Man morally is in his infancy.*" There have been times when there was a doubt as to whether he was to be raised to her level, or woman to be lowered to his, but we "have turned that corner at last and now woman holds out a strong hand to the child man and insists upon helping him up." The child-man (Bismarck? Herbert Spencer? Edison? Gladstone? Alexander III.? Lord Dufferin? the Duc d'Aumale?)[1] the child man must have his tottering baby steps guided by the New Woman, and he must be taught to live up to his ideals. To live up to an ideal, whether our own or somebody else's, is a painful process; but man must be made to do it. For, oddly enough, we are assured that despite "all his assumption he does not make the best of himself," which is not wonderful if he be still only in his infancy; and he has the incredible stupidity to be blind to the fact that "woman has self-respect and good sense," and that "she does not in the least intend to sacrifice the privileges she enjoys on the chance of obtaining others."

I have written amongst other *pensées éparses*[2] which will some day see the light, the following reflection:

> L'école nouvelle des femmes libres oubliée qu'on ne puisse pas a la fait combattre l'homme sur son propre terrain et attendre de lui des politesses, des tendresses et des galanteries. Il ne faut pas aux même moment prendre de l'homme son chaise à l'Université et sa place dans l'omnibus; si on lui arrâche son gagnepain, on ne peut pas exiger qu'il offre aussi sa parapluie.[3]

The whole kernel of the question lies in this. Your contributor says that the New Woman will not surrender her present privileges; *i. e.*, she will still expect the man to stand that she may sit; the man to get wet through that she may use his umbrella. But if she retain those privileges she can only do so by an appeal to his chivalry, *i. e.*, by a confession that she is weaker than he. But she does not want to do this: she wants to get the comforts and concessions due to feebleness, at the same time as she demands the lion's share of power due to superior force alone. It is this overweening and unreasonable grasping at both positions which will end in making her odious to man and in her being probably kicked back roughly by him into the seclusion of a harem.

Before me lies an engraving in an illustrated journal of a woman's meeting; whereat a woman is demanding in the name of her sovereign sex the right to vote at political elections. The speaker is middle-aged and plain of feature; she wears an inverted plate on her head tied on with strings under her double-chin; she has balloon-sleeves, a bodice tight to bursting, a waist of ludicrous dimensions in proportion to her portly person; she is gesticulating with one hand, of which all the fingers are stuck out in ungraceful defiance of all artistic laws of gesture.[4] Now, why cannot this

---

1. All outstanding political and scientific leaders of the late-19th c. Otto von Bismarck was the architect of German unification; Herbert Spencer (1820–1903) was a major mid-Victorian political theorist, economist, and philosopher; the American inventor Thomas Alva Edison developed electric light (among other things); William Ewart Gladstone (1809–98) served as British prime minister four times between 1868 and 1894; Alexander III was Czar of Russia from 1881 to 1894; Lord Dufferin was viceroy of India and Governor-General of Canada; the Duc d'Aumale (1822–97), a son of the French king Louis Philippe, was a soldier, politician, historian, and bibliophile who became governor of Algeria.
2. French: scattered thoughts.
3. French: The new school of liberated women has forgotten that one cannot fight man on his proper ground and expect from him politenesses, tendernesses, and gallantries. It is not possible at the same moment to take man's chair at University and his place in the omnibus; if one wants to strip him of his job, one cannot also demand that he offers one his umbrella.
4. Probably based on Linley Sambourne's cartoon, "The Angel in the 'House'; or, the Result of Female Suffrage. (A Troubled Dream of the Future)," *Punch*, 14 June 1884, 279.

orator learn to gesticulate and learn to dress, instead of clamoring for a franchise? She violates in her own person every law, alike of common-sense and artistic fitness, and yet comes forward as a fit and proper person to make laws for others. She is an exact representative of her sex.

Woman, whether new or old, has immense fields of culture untilled, immense areas of influence wholly neglected. She does almost nothing with the resources she possesses, because her whole energy is concentrated on desiring and demanding those she has not. She can write and print anything she chooses; and she scarcely ever takes the pains to acquire correct grammar or elegance of style before wasting ink and paper. She can paint and model any subjects she chooses, but she imprisons herself in men's *ateliers*[5] to endeavor to steal their technique and their methods, and thus loses any originality she might possess. Her influence on children might be so great that through them she would practically rule the future of the world; but she delegates her influence to the vile school boards if she be poor, and if she be rich to governesses and tutors; nor does she in ninety-nine cases out of a hundred ever attempt to educate or control herself into fitness for the personal exercise of such influence. Her precept and example in the treatment of the animal creation might be of infinite use in mitigating the hideous tyranny of humanity over them, but she does little or nothing to this effect; she wears dead birds and the skins of dead creatures; she hunts the hare and shoots the pheasant, she drives and rides with more brutal recklessness than men; she watches with delight the struggles of the dying salmon, of the gralloched[6] deer; she keeps her horses standing in snow and fog for hours with the muscles of their heads and necks tied up in the torture of the bearing rein; when asked to do anything for a stray dog, a lame horse, a poor man's donkey, she is very sorry, but she has so many claims on her already; she never attempts by orders to her household, to her *fournisseurs*,[7] to her dependents, to obtain some degree of mercy in the treatment of sentient creatures and in the methods of their slaughter.

The immense area which lies open to her in private life is almost entirely uncultivated, yet she wants to be admitted into public life. Public life is already overcrowded, verbose, incompetent, fussy, and foolish enough without the addition of her in her sealskin coat with the dead humming bird on her hat. Woman in public life would exaggerate the failings of men, and would not have even their few excellencies. Their legislation would be, as that of men is too often, the offspring of panic or prejudice; and she would not put on the drag of common-sense as man frequently does in public assemblies. There would be little to hope from her humanity, nothing from her liberality; for when she is frightened she is more ferocious than he, and when she has power more merciless.

"Men," says your contributor, "deprived us of all proper education and then jeered at us because we had no knowledge." How far is this based on facts? Could not Lady Jane Grey learn Greek and Latin as she chose? Could not Hypatia lecture? Were George Sand or Mrs. Somerville withheld from study? Could not in every age every woman choose a Corinna or Cordelia as her type? become either Helen or Penelope?

---

5. French: art studios.
6. Disemboweled.
7. French: suppliers.

If the vast majority have not either the mental or physical gifts to become either, that was Nature's fault, not man's. Aspasia and Adelina Patti were born, not made.[8] In all eras and all climes a woman of great genius or of great beauty has done what she chose; and if the majority of women have led obscure lives, so have the majority of men. The chief part of humanity is insignificant, whether it be male or female. In most people there is very little character indeed, and as little mind. Those who have much never fail to make their marks, be they of which sex they may.

The unfortunate idea that there is no good education without a college curriculum is as injurious as it is erroneous. The college education may have excellencies for men in its *frottement*,[9] its preparation for the world, its rough destruction of personal conceit; but for women it can only be hardening and deforming. If study be delightful to a woman, she will find her way to it as the hart to water brooks. The author of *Aurora Leigh* was not only always at home, but she was an invalid;[10] yet she became a fine classic, and found her path to fame. A college curriculum would have done nothing to improve her rich and beautiful mind; it might have done much to debase it.

The perpetual contact of men with other men may be good for them, but the perpetual contact of women with other women is very far from good. The publicity of a college must be odious to a young girl of refined and delicate feeling.

The "Scum-woman" and the "Cow-woman," to quote the elegant phraseology of your contributor, are both of them less of a menace to humankind than the New Woman with her fierce vanity, her undigested knowledge, her over-weening estimate of her own value and her fatal want of all sense of the ridiculous.

When scum comes to the surface it renders a great service to the substance which it leaves behind it; when the cow yields pure nourishment to the young and the suffering, her place is blessed in the realm of nature; but when the New Woman splutters blistering wrath on mankind she is merely odious and baneful.

The error of the New Woman (as of many an old one) lies in speaking of women as the victims of men, and entirely ignoring the frequency with which men are the victims of women. In nine cases out of ten the first to corrupt the youth is the woman. In nine cases out of ten also she becomes corrupt herself because she likes it.

It is all very well to say that prostitutes were at the beginning of their career victims of seduction; but it is not probable and it is not provable. Love of drink and of finery, and a dislike to work, are the more likely motives and origin. It never seems to occur to the accusers of man that women are just as vicious and as lazy as he is in nine cases out of ten, and need no invitation from him to become so.

A worse prostitution than that of the streets, *i. e.*, that of loveless marriages of convenience, are brought about by women, not by men. In such unions the man

---

8. Outstanding women of learning. Lady Jane Grey was very briefly queen; Hypatia was an Egyptian mathematician and leading Neoplatonist philosopher; "George Sand" (Amantine-Aurore-Lucile Dupin) was a famously daring, cross-dressing French writer of scandalous Romantic novels; Mary Somerville was a celebrated Victorian astronomer. Ouida contrasts Corinne, who refuses marriage to pursue poetic genius in Mme. de Staël's *Corinne, or Italy* (1807) with Cordelia (the loving daughter in *King Lear*) and the seductive Helen of Troy with the faithful wife Penelope. Brilliant Aspasia was Pericles's consort in ancient Greece. Adelina Patti was a famous operatic singer.
9. French: rubbing or scraping.
10. Elizabeth Barrett Browning (1806–61), although she wrote her book-length poem, *Aurora Leigh*, after recovering from her invalidism.

always gives much more than he gains, and the woman in almost every instance is persuaded or driven into it by women—her mother, her sisters, her acquaintances. It is rarely that the father interferes to bring about such a marriage.

In even what is called a well-assorted marriage, the man is frequently sacrificed to the woman. As I wrote long ago, Andrea del Sarto's wife has many sisters. Correggio dying of the burden of the family, has many brothers.[11] Men of genius are often dragged to earth by their wives. In our own day a famous statesman is made very ridiculous by his wife; frequently the female influences brought to bear on him render a man of great and original powers and disinterested character, a time-server, a conventionalist, a mere seeker of place. Woman may help man sometimes, but she certainly more often hinders him. Her self-esteem is immense and her self-knowledge very small. I view with dread for the future of the world the power which modern inventions place in the hands of woman. Hitherto her physical weakness has restrained her in a great measure from violent action; but a woman can make a bomb and throw it, can fling vitriol, and fire a repeating revolver as well as any man can. These are precisely the deadly, secret, easily handled modes of warfare and revenge, which will commend themselves to her ferocious feebleness.

Jules Ruchard has written:

"J'ai professé de l'anatomie pendant des longues années, j'ai passé une bonne partie de ma vie dans les amphithéatres, mais je n'en ai pas moins éprouvé un sentiment penible en trouvant dans toutes les maisons d'education des squilettes d'animaux et des mannequins anatomiques entre les mains des fillettes."[12]

I suppose this passage will be considered as an effort "to withhold knowledge from women," but it is one which is full of true wisdom and honorable feeling. When you have taken her into the physiological and chemical laboratories, when you have extinguished pity in her, and given weapons to her dormant cruelty which she can use in secret, you will be hoist with your own petard—your pupil will be your tyrant, and then she will meet with the ultimate fate of all tyrants.

In the pages of this REVIEW a physician has lamented the continually increasing unwillingness of women of the world to bear children, and the consequent increase of ill-health, whilst to avoid child-bearing is being continually preached to the working classes by those who call themselves their friends.

The elegant epithet of Cow-woman implies the contempt with which maternity is viewed by the New Woman who thinks it something fine to vote at vestries, and shout at meetings, and lay bare the spines of living animals, and haul the gasping salmon from the river pool, and hustle male students off the benches of amphitheatres.

Modesty is no doubt a thing of education or prejudice, a conventionality artificially stimulated; but it is an exquisite grace, and womanhood without it loses its most

---

11. 16th-c. painter Andrea del Sarto's supposed suffering under a wifely virago was popularized by Robert Browning's dramatic monologue of 1855; Antonio Correggio, another 16th-c. painter, died young.
12. French: I have lectured on anatomy for many years, I have passed a good part of my life in the amphitheaters, but I have nonetheless felt dismay in finding in all the educational establishments the animal skeletons and anatomical mannequins in the hands of the young girls.

subtle charm. Nothing tends so to destroy modesty as the publicity and promiscuity of schools, of hotels, of railway trains and sea voyages. True modesty shrinks from the curious gaze of other women as from the coarser gaze of man.

Men, moreover, are in all except the very lowest classes more careful of their talk before young girls than women are. It is very rarely that a man does not respect real innocence; but women frequently do not. The jest, the allusion, the story which sullies her mind and awakes her inquisitiveness, will much oftener be spoken by women than men. It is not from her brothers, nor her brother's friends, but from her female companions that she will understand what the grosser laugh of those around her suggests. The biological and pathological curricula complete the loveless disflowering of her maiden soul.

Everything which tends to obliterate the contrast of the sexes, like your mixture of boys and girls in your American common schools, tends also to destroy the charm of intercourse, the savor and sweetness of life. Seclusion lends an infinite seduction to the girl, as the rude and bustling publicity of modern life robs woman of her grace. Packed like herrings in a railway carriage, sleeping in odious vicinity to strangers on a shelf, going days and nights without a bath, exchanging decency and privacy for publicity and observation, the women who travel, save those rich enough to still purchase seclusion, are forced to cast aside all refinement and delicacy.

It is said that travel enlarges the mind. There are many minds which can no more be enlarged, by any means whatever, than a nut or a stone. The fool remains a fool, though you carry him or her about over the whole surface of the globe, and it is certain that the promiscuous contact and incessant publicity of travel, which may not hurt the man, do injure the woman.

Neither men nor women of genius are, I repeat, any criterion for the rest of their sex; nay, they belong, as Plato placed them, to a third sex which is above the laws of the multitude. But even whilst they do so they are always the foremost to recognize that it is the difference, not the likeness, of sex which makes the charm of human life. Barry Cornwall[13] wrote long ago:

> "As the man beholds the woman,
>   As the woman sees the man;
> Curiously they note each other,
>   As each other only can.
>
> "Never can the man divest her
>   Of that mystic charm of sex;
> Ever must she, gazing on him,
>   That same mystic charm annex."

That mystic charm will long endure despite the efforts to destroy it of orators in tight stays and balloon sleeves, who scream from platforms, and the beings so justly abhorred of Mrs. Lynn Lynton, who smoke in public carriages and from the waist upward are indistinguishable from the men they profess to despise.

---

13. A friend of Keats's, a poet whose real name was Bryan Waller Procter (1788–1874).

But every word, whether written or spoken, which urges the woman to antago-
nism against the man, every word which is written or spoken to try and make of her
a hybrid, self-contained, opponent of men, makes a rift in the lute to which the world
looks for its sweetest music.

The New Woman reminds me of an agriculturist who, discarding a fine farm of
his own, and leaving it to nettles, stones, thistles, and wire-worms, should spend his
whole time in demanding neighboring fields which are not his. The New Woman will
not even look at the extent of ground indisputably her own, which she leaves
unweeded and untilled.

Not to speak of the entire guidance of childhood, which is certainly already
chiefly in the hands of woman (and of which her use does not do her much honor),
so long as she goes to see one of her own sex dancing in a lion's den, the lions being
meanwhile terrorized by a male brute; so long as she wears dead birds as millinery and
dead seals as coats; so long as she goes to races, steeplechases, coursing and pigeon
matches; so long as she "walks with the guns"; so long as she goes to see an American
lashing horses to death in idiotic contest with velocipedes; so long as she courtesies
before princes and emperors who reward the winners of distance-rides; so long as she
receives physiologists in her drawing-rooms, and trusts to them in her maladies; so
long as she invades literature without culture and art without talent; so long as she
orders her court-dress in a hurry; so long as she makes no attempt to interest herself
in her servants, in her animals, in the poor slaves of her tradespeople; so long as she
shows herself as she does at present without scruple at every brutal and debasing spectacle which is considered fashionable; so long as she understands nothing of the
beauty of meditation, of solitude, of Nature; so long as she is utterly incapable of
keeping her sons out of the shambles of modern sport, and lifting her daughters above
the pestilent miasma of modern society—so long as she does not, can not, or will not
either do, or cause to do, any of these things, she has no possible title or capacity to
demand the place or the privilege of man.

—1894

B. A. Crackanthorpe
1847–1928

While Sarah Grand and Ouida were famous novelists, Blanche Alethea Crackanthorpe is
more typical of those who thrashed out the New Women issue in the popular press.
Crackanthorpe was a respected participant in *fin-de-siècle* cultural circles but not a leading
writer. She married lawyer and writer Montague Cookson (they changed their surname in
1888 because of a legacy) and moved in artistic and literary circles, with friends including
Henry James and Thomas Hardy. Their son, short-story writer Hubert Crackanthorpe, wrote
highly mannered tales published in *The Yellow Book*. Crackanthorpe published chatty articles
on cultural events and at least one novel, *Milly's Story*, while her husband became a leading
eugenics proponent. Her "Revolt of the Daughters" has the plaintive tone of a progressive
who finds herself outdone by the next generation. Published in the general-interest journal

The Nineteenth Century, this article reveals how conflicted many women felt about the new movement. The article provoked a storm of responses, among which Kathleen Cuffe's witty rejoinder is perhaps the most memorable.

The Revolt of the Daughters

These are the days of strikes. No sooner is one happily closed than another, more serious it may be, and farther reaching in its effects, comes up for next consideration. A big trade strike is just ended; another, of a totally different complexion, is fast approaching. Not every one possesses the power of reading sky signs aright, yet for months past very large and plain specimens have been on view. More than one of the public prints has beguiled this year's autumn dulness by opening its columns to a majority of daughters, who have therein detailed their intimate and personal home grievances. They in their turn have been answered by a minority of mothers champing under the sense of the burning ingratitude, and more, the general unseemliness of their offspring. With a frankness that would be indecent were it not absolutely tragic both sets of combatants have exposed to a gaping audience their naked griefs and unveiled wrongs. As the controversy ended precisely where it began, in mere hot statement, no one was any the better, and not a few were considerably the worse. Neither did the question itself get any "forrader" towards solution. This was a large and vulgar sky "skeleton," but others, more subtle, yet to the full as significant, are not lacking.

When an *habitué* of London Society, himself a keen observer of manners, is heard to remark that this question must be ripe, seeing the very large percentage of households where war, open or concealed, exists between mothers and daughters, it is serious. When a leading London doctor confides to a friend that he is much concerned by a new phenomenon in his practice, to wit, the frequent presence in his waiting-room of mothers broken down in body and perplexed in mind over "difficulties" with their grown-up daughters, and of daughters come to consult him privately whose nerves have "gone wrong" because, as they put their case, they are not "understood" nor "sympathised with" by their mothers, this is significant indeed. The evil cannot be lightly laughed away as a passing trouble, to be speedily cured by marriage in the one case, and in the other—where the mothers' inappropriate youthfulness is a chief disturbing cause—by the certain grip of relentless old age. For our own part we believe the psychological moment has arrived in which to probe, to diagnose, and to prescribe for, the hidden disease.

Let it be granted, for the sake of convenience, that the premises above stated are correct, and that a case is so far proven. With whom does the fault lie? on whose shoulders should rest the main burden of responsibility for the dead-lock, if it exists as stated by these experts? In this latest strike we will call the mothers the employers, and the daughters the operatives. The capital of the employers is here represented by a wide experience, which should carry in its train wisdom, far-reaching vision, and a balance of patient staying power which ought never to be wholly drawn out. The operatives bring as their contribution to the carrying out of the existing social contract, youth, vitality, "go," and the muscle strength that enables them to pick themselves up and go home after a deadly encounter, only a surface bruise or two the worse, whilst their elder and less supple opponent has possibly received wounds which, bleeding inwardly, poison the joy of life at its purest source.

For our own part we are prepared to state frankly at the outset that, whilst admitting to the full the provocative nature, the egoism, the governing unreasonableness, which too often characterise the attitude of the daughters during the struggle for supremacy, everything in fact which goes to form that expressive yet inelegant word *tiresome*, we yet find ourselves ranged on the side of the younger generation. Let their case be first stated. They are young. They are vital. The springs of life, the thirst to taste its joys, run very strong in their veins. They desire ardently to try things on their own account. They long for the "unexpected," not always the "properly introduced," still less the "well accredited" of that sage and prudent ambassador their mother. Far from them is the desire for things that are wrong in themselves. They have no unwholesome hankering for forbidden fruit. Their individuality is at this moment the strongest—and the most inconvenient—thing about them. They pray passionately to be allowed to travel ever so short a way alone. Should an obstructive pebble lie in their path and threaten for a moment to upset their youthful equilibrium, they resent hotly the immediate application of the hand of a guardian to the small of their back. So have we seen a rebellious baby, just able to run, hit out impotently, but with deadly intent, at the over-conscientious nurse who stood by ready to "save" it from that wholesome tumble provided by a wise nature as experience-lesson. Girls want to make their own minor mistakes and not to be strictly limited by unwritten law to producing feeble imitations of their mothers' best copies. And why not, since mistakes have to be made? No one is worth a thought who has not made them, and he, or she, who has lost the capacity for their manufacture, as an occasional indulgence, is far on towards old age. To look upon trivial errors, whether of speech, manner, or action, as *anathema maranatha*[1]—and this is the real bogey of the good mother—is but to make complacent display of her own limited intelligence. Other and graver plaints has the daughter, plaints which perhaps she has never actually formulated, but of the existence of which she is intensely sub-conscious. Does uncongenial atmosphere go for nothing as a shaping influence? What of the suffering of a girl on whom tricksy Nature, or some remote ancestress, has bestowed a romantic, gipsy-minded personality, and who finds herself in a well-ordered and accurately balanced *entourage* where this side of her—a side she can no more help than the colour of her hair or the shape of her nose—is conscientiously repressed, disapproved of, and ignored?

We have of late years elected to educate everybody, our daughters included. Girton and Newnham, the "halls," and all kinds of minor establishments of a like kind fill the land.[2] "Higher Education," "University Extension," are common form, whilst diplomas of proficiency—not, be it observed, of efficiency—are more plentiful than were blackberries last year. The attempt to open wide the doors one side the house, and to hermetically close them the other, is a trifle illogical, and no one but politicians anxious to buy votes and not eager to pay the full price, or women who demand heaven and earth at the same moment, would make such an attempt. Wisely or foolishly—it is yet an open question—we have said that our daughters are to know. They, in their turn, insist that they shall be allowed the free use of the weapon with which we ourselves have furnished them. Are they to be blamed for this?

---

1. Cursed, outcast (1 Corinthians 16.22).
2. The first women's colleges at Cambridge (founded in the 1870s).

It is not so usual now as it was twenty years ago for the head of a middle-class household to cheerfully spend a thousand pounds or more on each boy's training, first at a public school, than at a University, to "fit him for taking his place in the world," whilst his daughters, were they many or few, had to put up with equal shares in the talents of one lady with the indulgence of occasional snap-shots at music and dancing masters. The injustice of his proceeding is, at this time of day, more visible to the naked eye, though we fear the practice is not altogether obsolete. For our own part we have no hesitation in saying that the girl who sees her brothers equipped for any professions they may choose, whilst she herself is confined to the single one of marriage, is a really ill-used person. Marriage *is* the best profession for a woman; we all know and acknowledge it; but, for obvious reasons, all women cannot enter its strait and narrow gate. When the moment comes in which the daughter sees clearly that success for her, if it comes at all, must come on other lines, and that the sense of modest achievement alone gives zest and fire to life, can it be gainsaid that if she then goes to her father and says, "Give me a portion, a fraction of what you have laid out on Dick and Tom, to enable me to make my experiment, to try to do my little bit of world's work," and he refuses her on the score that a woman's place is entirely at home till she is called higher by a husband, she has a very real grievance indeed?

So far, and it is a long way, in their plea for a larger liberty, not license—the liberty that claims the right to be an individual as well as a daughter—we are entirely with the girls in their revolt. Justice, however, now demands that the mirror should be presented to them with a stern command that they do take a long look therein. It will not be a beautiful vision that will meet their gaze. For inner barrenness of spirit, manifesting itself in ugly outside action, few things can match the ruthless young daughter pulling her own way against her mother, and generally getting it too. She is, by reason of her youth, perfectly insensible to, absolutely regardless of, the agony she is causing and the wounds she is inflicting. For the time being she presents to the observer a curious mental compound of which the fundamental basis is egoism. Such imagination as she possesses is so self-centred, its light so turned on the point she desires either to secure or to avoid, that it stands her in no stead at all as an illuminator of her own or other people's conduct. During this state she distinctly becomes that hideous product, a non-human *thing*, governed only by its own innate stubbornness (this a quality, by the way, too often pinnacle-placed by women of all ages, who christen it firmness, and then chant secret psalms in its honour). This is indeed a parlous state, and the animating spirit possessing her for the time being is not to be exorcised save by prayer and fasting. It may be that the true vision of herself is withheld from her for many a long day, but it comes at last, possibly when the little drama is repeated—with this little difference, that she now fills the other rôle. For time always calls to a reckoning. Accounts in that book are never crossed off unpaid, and it is only the fool who says in his heart, "For me there is no judgment-day."

The Attitude of the Mothers

Ce n'est que le premier pas qui coûte[3] is a fiction familiar to most of us. We have often found, to our cost, that bad as was the first step, those that come after were a hun-

---

3. French: It is only the first step that hurts.

dred-fold darker and more slippery. So will it be with the New Strike. "Flags are Flying," Björnson's title,[4] becomes now very apt. The tom-tom is heard at the street-corners calling out the younger levies, who answer in glad haste; whilst far away in upper chambers sit the legitimate rulers of the rebels in deep consultation—anxious, waiting, determined. No wonder they wear a care-lined air. For in their souls they know full well that whatever the results may be—whoever stands or whoever falls—the responsibility of the situation is their own. A little more magnanimity, a larger sense of the rights of the individual, although the individual in question be that sacred product their own daughter, a little more of that most difficult of all forms of altruism, the tucking-in of their own skirts to make room for the new-comers, and the present dead-lock would never have arisen at all. This is their burden, and a pretty heavy one it proves. They would not be the mothers of their own daughters if they were deficient in stubbornness. Watch them as they sit round the table with tightened lips and mouths that have a comic resemblance to the steel-clasped bag of our youth—how viciously it used to snap!—note the angry sparkle in their eyes, and then marvel at the thought that in spite of all the outward show of righteous wrath these women are in their hearts enduring the torture of remorse for neglected opportunities and wasted chances.

Can it be denied that mothers are oftentimes mortally stupid? Their intentions are, indeed, excellent, but only to supply another illustration of the proverb. For stupid it is not to recognise facts and tendencies, which, after all, are but facts in their first stage; still more stupid is it when to ignore them is no longer possible, not to admit their consideration frankly, and to let conduct be guided, nay, altered thereby. Principles make excellent consulting physicians, but it would fare ill with many of us in the affairs of life were we to be deprived of those useful general practitioners, tact and expediency. Let mothers, especially "good" mothers, practise in secret the art of contemplating their daughters as part of a vast "collective" youth, and not as highly specialised young females on whom no wind is to blow roughly, whose ears are to be stuffed with medicated cotton-wool, and whose sight is to be ever safeguarded by good substantial blinkers well tied on by the prudent parent. Let us again protect ourselves by repeating that we are *not* writing of girls in their teens, but of women turned twenty. With sons this course has to be taken, as every mother of sons knows. Often the lesson is bitter and hard, but the wiser and more catholic the woman, the quicker she will be in mastering it. Her best-loved son must have his *wanderjahre*.[5] She cannot hold him back. She can only gaze after his retreating form from the watch-tower of her love; too often he departs with never a backward glance at her. But in her heart a silent witness speaketh, telling her to have patience, for he will return in the end. Why not allow the possibility that nice girls, well-disposed girls, may also desire a mild sort of *wanderjahre* period, during which they, too, want not to break fences, but to get occasional glimpses of the landscape beyond the family domain? Blunders not a few they may make, but not of the kind that need be counted with. The far-seeing mother will consent to sit a quiet and smiling spectator when her daughter ventures on small, or even comparatively big, social experiments. She will not employ her leisure moments in crushing every troublesome symptom of individuality, nor in flat-

---

4. Norwegian writer Bjornstjerne Björnson's (1832–1910) 1889 collection of essays.
5. German: wanderlust.

ironing the surface creases that may from time to time appear. She will be slow to blame and quick to praise. A saving sense of humour, if the gods have smiled at her birth, will help her greatly, for we do not for a moment pretend that this will be the happiest or most careless period of the mother's reign. But if she has made a friend of her girl *in childhood*—and it is vain to think this can be done later on—nothing will really come between them. Yet, after all, in any collision between them, her suffering is a hundred times acuter than that of her daughter, for, unfortunately, women are addicted to feeling more and not less as they grow older, and if, as has been well said, in every contest only one of the combatants is booted and spurred, it must be admitted that more often than not these advantages remain with the daughter.

Once, a mother, Celtic and nervous edged, suffering from friction with her elder daughter, Saxon and stolid, addressed herself in her tribulation to the sage of the household, who happened in this instance to be its youngest member, aged fourteen. "Mother," said the child, after listening sympathetically to the plaint, "do you think you love Mary quite enough? She needs loving." Thus out of the mouth of the babe and suckling dropped the word of truth which furnishes a key to part, though by no means to the whole, of the situation.

So much for the lighter aspects; when we come to the other and graver side, it is, we fear, a serious indictment that many mothers have to meet. We would ask them what have been the methods they have chosen by which to rear and train their difficult young? How much personal time, personal influence, and personal effort have they expended on the task during the critical years which lie between ten and seventeen—the only moulding time in a girl's life? Would thirty hours a week cover it? Would twenty? Would ten? Have they not rather—we write of the majority—selected from the very moment of birth the very best outside help they could obtain, beginning with the certificated wet-nurse and ending with the diplomaed lady who, for a hundred a year, undertakes the herculean task of administering tongues and social wisdom in equal doses to her charges, the mothers themselves falling the while into the sin that most easily besets them—namely, that of overlooking the work instead of bearing a hand in it?

When, if ever, did real friendship between them and their daughters begin? What are the guiding principles of conduct they have been careful to instil—no, to get instilled—into them during the few years when alone the process is easy of accomplishment? And, lastly, in every conflict of opinion that may have arisen since, what has been the true motive at the back which underlies their disapprobation and commands both the quantity and the quality of their frowns?

The moment has come for the secrets of the maternal heart to be disclosed. Is it not true that the marriage "ring" is the governing authority which the mothers acknowledge and obey, although not for a moment will they admit it? The things that make or mar a girl's chances *there* are the mother's realities. We believe that the mother we describe would prefer her daughter to steal spoons (she would carefully return them next morning) to her committing any social misdemeanour, of no moment whatever, which should militate against these chances. To take an example. A girl wants exceedingly to hear Chevalier sing.[6] This innocent desire can only, we

---

6. Music-hall star Albert Chevalier (1861–1923).

will suppose, be gratified by a visit to a music-hall in charge of a brother. Now music-halls are not "nice" places—a nice girl, *i.e.* a promising candidate in the marriage market, must on no account be seen in one. The domestic fiat is pronounced; the girl rages inwardly over the shams that govern her life. There is her sister, only a year or two older, who married but a few months ago—she is free to visit a music-hall with her husband and friends. "Where is truth?" cries the girl.

When it comes to actual marriage—we feel we are here on very delicate ground, but forward we must go—the mother we describe makes but one inquiry, after ways and means are satisfactorily established. Is the man free *now* from entanglements of any kind, and can he be depended upon to remain so? Of the girl's passionate ideals, of her hot burning heart, of the purity she brings as a flame to the altar—for, in spite of the sound of laughter in the air, we maintain that to many a girl marriage is still a sacrament—the mother recks not at all. Her "knowledge of the world" enables her to assure her daughter that "Mr. Jones will make a good and 'dependable' husband." Is it too much to say that many mothers would be exceedingly shocked if their daughter came to them saying she would like to be assured that the man she was about to marry had no "past" to bury? And yet here the girl's instinct is surely a right one, for if the "burying of the past" means the putting aside a woman who has faith-fully filled the place of wife and mother for many years, that girl is not far wrong who feels that, under these conditions, she is after all but the lawful mistress, the other remaining the unlawful wife. Not so very long ago a mother anxious to secure the best *parti*[7] of many seasons achieved at last this signal triumph, and bore him tri-umphantly away for her daughter from a horde of angry rivals. At the close of the interview which took place between her gratified self and the half-indifferent son-in-law-to-be he remarked carelessly, "Well, you had better take ——'s," mentioning the name of a legal expert, "opinion as to whether I am free or not," which the lady did, her daughter lending no unwilling hand. Together they sought the gentleman of the long robe, and being satisfied that the thing was sufficiently "safe," the wed-ding came off. (Admission to the church was by ticket only, lest unwelcome and uninvited guests should present themselves.) It is almost a satisfaction to remember that the last stage of that marriage was even worse than the first. Repulsive as this story is, it is true.

Not a little curious is it that the mothers who so carefully shield their daugh-ters from the faintest breath of adverse criticism before marriage appear to be absolutely indifferent to what is said openly of these same daughters when marriage has set them free. Is this a reality, or is it a monstrous unreality, leading to every kind of social hypocrisy? On all sides we are told that society, both at the top and at the bottom, is rotten to its core. These are the factors that go to produce such rottenness. It has been suggested that nothing but a clean sweep of it can purify the stable, and that a boat should be started, say, every Wednesday morning from Tilbury Dock,[8] bearing one week its load of West-End loungers, and the next a like load of East-End loafers,[9] the cargo to be discharged in mid-ocean. So would the "impossible" elements of our civilisation be happily disposed of, "scum" and "dregs"

---

7. French: eligible bachelor.
8. Dock on the river Thames.
9. The West End was the fashionable side of London; the East End had the slums.

alike, and the way at last left clear for the onward march of the resolute and the purposeful of all classes. Over-population being the problem of the hour, this experiment might be worth the trying.

Salvation comes from within always and everywhere. Since the capitalists have failed them, the operatives must work out their own. Then perhaps shall we have the woman of to-morrow, pure of heart and fearless of speech, who demands of herself and of every one else, not a flimsy and superficial "correctness," but that inward sincerity which enables her both to say and to hear, "I have erred," with equanimity. Of this woman it will truly be said, Blessed are the pure in heart, for God-like possibilities will be plain to her clear vision, not only in the suffering pavement-dweller, but, far harder still, in the lady of high place, set with every outward circumstance of prosperity, who decorates herself with lovers as lightly as with the diamonds in her hair.

We are told that, in view of the threatened "Union of Daughters," "mothers' meetings" will shortly be organised not only in Mayfair and Belgravia,[10] but throughout the provinces. We should like to suggest the following as test questions to be set at each meeting. On their right answering would, to our mind, depend the placing of each individual mother on the alternative "wise" or "foolish" list.

(1) Give an example of a possible difference of opinion between mother and daughter, and state the line of least resistance you would be prepared to adopt.

(2) If your daughter, turned twenty years of age, should desire to pursue an acquaintance which you, from instinctive or sentimental reasons (reasons which might be absolutely just), did not consider a valuable one for her, would you, or would you not, make it difficult for her to try its value for herself?

But all these well-meant efforts may fail, and, as in other strikes, a Board of Conciliation may be the only way of meeting the difficulty. Delegates from both camps will doubtless be eager to attend. But where is the President to come from who will be acceptable to both camps? Would Mr. Gladstone[11] crown the glories of his long life by accomplishing this Union of Hearts as his final public act? Or, failing him, would the Archbishop of Canterbury (in his robes), and carrying Dodo[12] of Lambeth as text-book, undertake the task?

One word more. As during the late coal strike entire districts in the midlands remained wholly unaffected by it, work going forward continuously the while, and the harmonious understanding between masters and men remaining unbroken, so in what we have fancifully called the New Strike, we are thankfully aware that there are whole strata of society in which no difficulty has arisen nor, in all probability, ever will arise. Such a state of things is only to be reached by the mothers recognising betimes that loyal friendship is the only lasting basis for this as for all other human relationships. There lies the root of the matter. Not of the happy households where this truth obtains are these pages written.

—1894

---

10. Not a real union but a spoof of contemporary socialist discussions of trade unions (see Part III). Mayfair and Belgravia were elite regions of London.

11. Prime Minister W. E. Gladstone (1809–98).

12. The comic novel *Dodo* (1893) satirized upper-class women's flirtatious behavior and was written by E. F. Benson, son of the Archbishop of Canterbury Edward White Benson (the archbishop's palace is in Lambeth).

Kathleen Cuffe
1872–1938

"A Reply from the Daughters" presents Kathleen Cuffe as a typical New Woman, but in reality, she was one of the most privileged scions of the British aristocracy. She was Lady Kathleen Mary Alexina Cuffe, the only child of the Earl of Desart, and the year after she wrote "A Reply from the Daughters," she married Sir Thomas Edward Milborne-Swinnerton-Pilkington, twelfth baronet in a family lineage dating back to the thirteenth century. Cuffe settled down to become a model county lady, bearing four children, enjoying her family's hunting and racing activities, organizing the Ladies' Kennel Association Show, overseeing local charities, and founding a hospital for disabled soldiers. She seems never to have published anything else, although the delightfully witty and confident writing style of "A Reply from the Daughters" shows considerable talent. Her contribution is a useful reminder that the New Woman movement was limited to prosperous women, for they were the ones suffocating under the stringent etiquette and surveillance their society required to ensure they remained respectable for the marriage market. While working-class girls could and did move around without chaperones, such independence would have been impossible for the young heiress of the Earl of Desart.

A Reply from the Daughters

As a daughter, but, I trust, not in any sense a "revolting" one, may I take up a brief in defence of the much abused girl of the present day? I have read with attention the interesting and instructive mass of information contributed of late to English periodicals about her, and the equally instructive comments made thereon by critics, wise and otherwise.

Whether we owe most to friend or enemy it is indeed hard to say. According to one view, the modern maiden sits wringing her hands all day at home, exhausting herself in querulous laments over her inability to indulge in *Wanderjahre*,[1] even in one mild *Wanderjahr*, and filling the surrounding air in general, and her unfortunate family's ears in particular, with irritating iterations of the things she would do if she was let.

According to another, her sole occupation consists in reading Ibsen's works, *Dodo*, and *The Heavenly Twins*, and learning by heart quotations from *The Second Mrs. Tanqueray*, arranged in a text-book for morning and evening use.[2]

As to aspirations, our desires to develop our Personality (with a very big P), satisfy the cravings of our souls for something beyond the commonplace (the commonplace of home duties and making the best of our natural surroundings), are inseparable from an equally intense longing to frequent music-halls and possess latchkeys, and a

---

1. German: wanderlust.
2. Controversial *fin-de-siècle* books. Henrik Ibsen's plays offer realistic portrayals of unhappy marriages; E. F. Benson's *Dodo* (1893) has a flirtatious heroine; Sir Arthur Wing Pinero's *The Second Mrs. Tanqueray* is a sympathetic account of a reformed mistress.

vehement appeal to poor, much taxed Providence to remove the lingering prejudice against women smoking in public.

To criticise one's elders may seem to savour somewhat of impertinence; but is it wrong for me as a girl of the period (in the literal, not the Mrs. Lynn Linton,[3] sense of the phrase) to try and disentangle the things we do want from the things we are supposed to want? The latter, thanks to the masterly way many persons have wielded their pens of late, no one can pretend to be totally in ignorance of. But the former are considerably less well known, and I am beginning to be afraid that the likes and dislikes of the *fin-de-siècle* maiden may be destined to share the fate of Mr. Gladstone's intentions,[4] and be only known by the guesswork of their admirers or detractors. Young people's opinions are seldom asked, perhaps because on most subjects they are given without that trifling formality; still, it strikes me as strange that, amid the "all sorts and conditions of men" and women who have taken part in this discussion, not a single girl has come to the front in explanation or defence of her views, real and supposed.

Surely the modern damsel ought to be sufficiently mistress of her pen and her grammar to be able to break a lance in her own cause. It is a cruel fate that has caused us to be painted in glaring colours, and held up to the ridicule of the cynical and the horror of the "unco guid:"[5] so will you allow me to put the subject before you as *we* look upon it?

When I say "we," I do not mean the highly educated, examination-passing Girton[6] girl, with her vast schemes for regenerating mankind, or ousting our lords and masters from the paths where women are at present not allowed to follow. Nor do I mean the happy few whose talents for music, drawing, or any other art open out to them vistas of endless occupation and happiness. I want to speak in the name of the average more or less unemployed, tea-drinking, lawn-tennis playing, ball-going damsel, whose desire for greater emancipation does not run in the same lines as those of the independent shop-girl, or of the young woman with a mission.

I should not like to assert that, were we given the free use of latchkeys and the entrée of music-halls, we should not avail ourselves of, and at the moment enjoy, these prerogatives keenly. But we do not adopt as our highest ideals these very frivolous and evanescent pleasures of the average hobbledehoy; nor do we imagine that by so doing we should be most likely to gain that freedom and emancipation so many of us long for, though we do consider ourselves bound by many senseless prejudices, meaningless restrictions, and annoying trammels.

The most entrancing of possibilities fade into insignificance before the very smallest of realities. Parental prejudices, doubtless born of affection, but still prejudices, have existed, do exist, and will continue to exist; and, so long as they do thus exist, we don't see any chance of the much-talked-of *Wanderjahr* having a place in the education of our young womanhood. But while we are ready to admit that this belongs to the eternal fitness of things, we do not see why we must therefore give up

---

3. Eliza Lynn Linton's famous attack on modern women, "The Girl of the Period," appeared in the *Saturday Review* (1868).
4. Prime Minister W. E. Gladstone's feelings about women's suffrage were unclear; although he claimed to support the cause, he stopped suffrage bills from passing.
5. Scottish: "uncommonly virtuous."
6. Girton was the first women's college at Cambridge.

all our other aspirations, supposed or admitted. How many girls are there not at this moment whose position in life is best described by the old simile of a round peg in a square hole? There is hardly a single large family—or small one either, for the matter of that—which cannot show some member whose tastes, ideas, and ambitions differ radically from those of their enforced surroundings.

If this member be a boy, it matters but little. School and college keep him occupied and interested until the time when he can choose his career, all trades and all careers being, at any rate to a certain extent, open to him; and after that it lies in his own power to determine whether his life be a failure or a success.

But not so the girl.

If only the great mass of parents and guardians who, despite their many assertions to the contrary, do of course guide the destinies of England's coming womanhood, would agree to cast off to a small extent the fear of Mrs. Grundy[7] and the dread of malicious and spiteful gossip, I am sure they would never have cause to regret their decision, and they would gain their daughters' deep and lasting gratitude.

Naturally, I do not wish to deny that there will always be a certain number who will look on the acquisition of the inch of liberty we ask for as the stepping-stone for the ell of complete emancipation and the shaking-off of all conventional rules and regulations whatsoever; and whose greater freedom in pursuit of amusements would only lead to the committal of follies of every description. But no one could ever succeed in doing good to the many if they reflected on the evil they might be doing to the few, and in our case it is just these few who are the obstacles to our attaining the freedom we crave.

Far be it from me to say that it is essential to every young woman's welfare or happiness that she should be pursuing some vague ideal—whether amusing or instructive—at the greatest possible distance from her home. I only think that there are many cases in which a girl might, at the expense merely of a few malicious words, and that only in the first instances, be allowed to do a lot of things which she is not permitted to do now, which would make all the difference in the world to her and could harm no one. At least in my eyes and those of my contemporary friends they do not appear capable of harming anyone, and we do think there is harm in the present system.

For example, it has always struck me that there is an increase in the number of unhappy marriages; and I cannot resist the conclusion that they arise often from girls plunging into matrimony simply and solely to escape from a home life whose restrictions they imagine less endurable than a loveless marriage of convenience. The novelty of the situation for a time makes things go smoothly, but the awakening comes all too surely, and two wrecked lives are the result.

Now we say that if a girl were, whilst at home, of course within reasonable bounds, permitted to follow the natural bent of her mind, she would not be impelled by her boredom and discontent into marrying the first person, whether congenial or not, who appeared on her limited horizon.

Set down in plain black and white, her requirements may appear very trifling; but, as the philosopher said, the world is made up of trifles. And these are trifles that cause an incredible amount of discontent, grumbling and irritation.

---

7. Personification of conventional society, from Thomas Morton's comic play, *Speed the Plough* (1798).

What she wants, first of all, is the abolition of chaperons on all possible occasions. This at once results in a deadlock between the modern mother and her yet more modern daughter: the difference of opinion as to which are possible occasions, and which are not. I will quote a few that appear very possible.

She considers it hard that she cannot walk the length of two or three—even five or six—streets to visit a friend, without having first provided herself with an unhappy maid or attendant of some description, presumably to prevent her from losing her way or getting run over. Or, if the friend she wishes to visit reside at a greater distance, she is not considered capable, without the aforesaid chaperon, of driving quietly in a hansom as far as that abode.

So it is in everything. No early morning stroll in the Park, or afternoon tea-party, may be undertaken without the same faithful domestic walking gloomily by her side, or waiting drearily for her in alien front halls.

A young married woman does not wear her wedding ring in her nose or other prominent spot to assure the passer-by of her social status; and, owing to prevailing fashions, her clothes do little to distinguish her from her unwedded sister. Yet she can walk through the streets alone, and drive in hansoms alone. Why cannot the girl?

Is it that her parents do not trust her for one second when out of their sight to behave in a rational and lady-like manner? Or is it that they do not think she has common sense and presence of mind enough to find her way about the streets, to avoid being run over by omnibuses in their wild career, or to pay her cabby the necessary shilling? If so, there is little to be said and much to be deplored. But is it not rather that the real reason is to be found in the constantly repeated formula, "People would talk so if . . ."

Surely the mothers might enter into a treaty to allow their respective daughters the privilege of walking a mile or so, or driving that distance—alone—in the most civilised capital in Europe. They do not rebel against chaperons from a wanton desire to be aggressively independent, or always to go about alone. But, in the nature of things, there are so many harmless pleasures they enjoy which to their parents and guardians are mere weariness and vexation of spirit. Under existing circumstances, either the latter must endure long periods of boredom or the former give up an equal amount of innocent enjoyment. Why cannot something be arranged to prevent this constant necessity for sacrifices on both sides, sacrifices irritating because they are so small and useless?

Without going to see either Mrs. *Tanqueray* or Ibsen, there are many matinées and concerts which girls might attend but for the ever necessary satellite who cannot be spared to go with them. They even must have one to accompany them to church.

Talking of church reminds me of another thing. If, spurred on to sudden charitable energy by a rousing sermon of a favourite parson, they are seized with an earnest wish to go and "do good" in the East End,[8] their inspirations are nipped in the bud by the usual formula, and the subject, and any good they might possibly do, are alike abandoned. For who has ever heard of anyone "slumming" under the protecting care of a chaperon?

There is another point to mention: the question of friendship between men and girls, as distinguished from flirtation. It does indeed seem a mistaken system

---

8. Poor area of London.

which prevents a man and a girl knowing anything in reality of each other's characters until they are engaged, when, unless they be people unusually indifferent to gossip and kindred annoyances, it is too late to make any alterations or repair mistaken impressions.

Inter-feminine conversation has never been famed for its depth of ideas or intellect: why may not the girls enjoy a little of the superior article from masculine lips without being suspected of ulterior designs on their hearts, if the men be poor, or on their fortunes, if they be rich? They never get a chance of finding out what a man thinks; and the married woman in the ball-room routs them with ignominy, simply because with her the unmarried man can chat at his ease, secure of not being angled for if he be rich, or warned off the premises if he be poor.

The so-called revolting maiden only asks for a small amount of liberty. The average girl, as Mr. Besant[9] might call her, does not want it for any of the weird and wild purposes set forth to the world of late. She does not want to read the books forbidden by her parents, or to see the plays they prefer she should not see. She only wishes to enjoy the minor pleasures and duties of life without the now inevitable bored and wearied chaperon. She does not want anything very startling or very important. And, as things are now, if she wanted to be great, how could she? What heroine of antiquity could have achieved renown on such terms?

Can we picture to ourselves Una, in the days of yore, wandering through the desert with her lion and her lady's-maid?[10] If it be urged that the lion acted as chaperon, I can only say that if properly tamed lions, warranted not to roar or bite, be provided, they would be gladly accepted[11] in lieu of the maids and governesses and duennas of the present time.

The refusal of parents and guardians to grant these desires, or even to sympathise with them, probably arises from the fact that in their young days—those times to modern minds so terribly dull and unenterprising—such sentiments were as unknown as the electric light. But they have admitted the practicability of the latter, and it is to be trusted that they may eventually acknowledge the advisability of the former.

Rome was not built in a day: and girls cannot expect to prove in that space of time their fitness for either liberty or latchkeys. But many littles make a mickle,[12] and perhaps the time may not be very far off when it will occur to the elders that, if the juniors were allowed by degrees a modicum of freedom in everyday life, they would not be so liable, on the unavoidable occasions when they suddenly get a comparatively large amount, to be carried away by the novelty of the situation, and commit such an infinitude of follies.

Perhaps we may even see the day when a chaperon will be as little known as a great auk or other creature of a past era.

—1894

---

9. Prolific author, social reformer, and founder of the Society of Authors (1836–1901).
10. Allegorical heroine of Edmund Spenser's 16th-c. poem *The Faerie Queene*.
11. In the 19th c., "a lion" meant "a celebrity."
12. Scottish: little things add up.

A. G. P. Sykes

Who was "A. G. P. Sykes"? There is no record of him in any nineteenth century documents. "Sykes" was almost certainly a pseudonym, but because so few of the records of *The Westminster Review* in the 1890s have survived, it is impossible to identify the real author with certainty. One possibility, however, is that this piece was written by the influential theater critic Clement Scott (1841–1904). Its style matches Scott's dashing, opinionated writing; its political and theatrical opinions are identical with Scott's; and its familiarity with drama suggests that the author was a theater reviewer. Scott was the theater critic for the *Daily Telegraph* newspaper for almost thirty years, and his prolific, intemperate criticism appeared in many *fin-de-siècle* newspapers. Whether or not Scott is the real Sykes, this article usefully summarizes some of the dominant—and contradictory—cultural fears of the New Women. Sykes worries about female revolt yet claims that women prefer slavish domesticity; he fears women's literary success but insists on the inferiority of women's writing. In spite of the article's confident, authoritative tone, Sykes was clearly worried about the way his world was heading.

The Evolution of the Sex

It is not possible to ride by road or rail, to read a review, a magazine or a newspaper, without being continually reminded of the subject which lady-writers love to call the Woman Question. "The Eternal Feminine," the "Revolt of the Daughters," the Woman's Volunteer Movement, Women's Clubs, are significant expressions and effective landmarks. Woman at the present epoch has persuaded herself that she is the salt of the earth as well as the sweet, that her intelligence, her faculties, her fads, and crazes are greater and of more importance than they ever have been, and, mentally, she adds, greater than anything else in the evolvements of the *fin de siècle*.

A combination of superficial observations and attempts at epigram, of strong language and weak significance, of unconventionality in purpose and in action interpenetrated by the strongest contempt for the weakness and vileness of Man, is regarded by many of both sexes as a modern divinity before whom all of different calibre should lift up their voices in praise.

The Girton and Newnham periods[1] were child's play in comparison. *Punch*[2] and the comments of their more sensible (if less advanced) sisters have convinced students that slovenliness of dress, ugly shoes, dishevelled hair, no corsets, and pince-nez, are not indispensable accessories to the acquirement of knowledge, nor are they to be accepted as infallible outward signs of a clever woman.

This epoch is past. Girton and Newnham are supplemented by so many other homes of learning for the fair sex, and their initiation into the callings which hitherto have been the appropriation of men has become such an accomplished fact, that scarcely any bar of conventionality exists between the two. It has already been stated in more than one "popular novel" that not only is the bar thrown down, but the

---

1. Women's colleges at Cambridge; Girton was founded in 1869 and Newnham in 1871.
2. Influential British humor magazine that satirized New Women.

woman desires it to remain so. Equality, liberty and fraternity is their cry,[3] but, as yet, chastity is still to exist, an intellectual woman being in fact "sexless," although she desires the homage and admiration of men. Since not even Mr. Herbert Spencer[4] has suggested a method of cultivating sexuality out of existence however, the question arises as to where all this "flinging of javelins" is likely to lead?

Man, says the modern authoress,[5] is an inferior animal morally (and frequently physically!). His coarse nature cannot appreciate the delicate sensitiveness, the refinement, the purity of a good woman, and he must be exiled from their society as a leper, an outcast, a pariah. He takes his pleasure with ephemeral content, which is akin to crime in the eyes of woman, who desires constant repetition and eternal assurance of what is frequently quite as firmly rooted in him as in her.

The outcry against man's villainy is not made by the average pretty girl who has still in her heart a strong liking for masculine attributes as portrayed by men, and who can enlarge her knowledge without either losing her womanly delicacy or breaking down her beliefs. It may be assumed that these are still so weak-minded that they are occasionally guilty of the folly of "falling in love" and that this state of ecstatic bliss may even exist after marriage. But the modern feminine conveys the impression that she is above such inanity; whilst the modern masculine is told to efface his most contemptible personality in order that she, for the time being, may absorb attention on all sides, and in artistic, dramatic, or literary *rôles* win victory after victory.

Women's pictures, women's plays, women's books. What is it that makes them temporarily so successful, and eternally so wanting? Daring and unconventionality? If a woman produces something which is constructed on lines of her own, she straightway believes it to be a work of genius, and declares that the mortals who hold to beaten tracks are not worthy to be mentioned in the same breath with her.

A strong tide of emotion, with a dash of piquancy to redeem it from commonplace, a command of detail rarely possessed by men, a fund of loquacious discourse, a love of the unnatural and of depicting ludicrously inhuman characters incapable of natural or lasting affection—in each and all of these phases a woman is in her element. Given any one of them, and she evolves a novel which is treated as a scientific experiment or as mere pastime, intended to bewilder or shock the reader, as who should say: "Do not imagine that this is by any means my best work. You are only a shuttlecock to be tossed whither I please. If I chose to be in down-right earnest—!" And these apologies for literature become "popular novels" despite their illiteracy, tautology, slovenliness, slip-shod vernacular, profanity, and reckless, not to say repulsive, exposure of psychological hypotheses and the errors of humanity, in the knowledge of which the writers are clearly no novices. So long as the world lasts, the history of human failings and peccadilloes will never cease; and a judicious author frequently accomplishes more than a dozen sermons; but when fools rush in to stop a gap the inevitable consequences are that the gap is widened and made worse than before.

And the pity of it. When one thinks of the vast amount of good that women have done within the last thirty years to enlarge their own sphere and give vent to

---

3. The slogan of the French Revolution.
4. A major mid-Victorian political theorist, economist, and philosopher.
5. Alludes to Sarah Grand's "The New Aspect of the Woman Question" (see p. 205).

their individuality, of the added comforts they can give to themselves and to their people, of the pleasure and satisfaction which a pure-minded woman feels when she has an aim in life that can be fulfilled without detriment to her womanly sympathies and that sensitive delicacy which is her greatest claim to any man's chivalry and strength, it seems a pity to have such good work marred by the mischievous, foolish, and ignorant style of fiction which continues to be poured into the market by women, and, since pure imitativeness, always asserts its sway for the time being, by men also.

The representation of a natural, pure-minded woman, who is at the same time no fool, seems to be shirked or tossed aside, both on the stage and in the novel of the circulating library. Whether one argues that the theatre has no business to seek to instruct or not, it is decided that it must amuse, and a certain influence is created which may, or may not, vanish outside of the theatre. Such a play as *The Second Mrs. Tanqueray*,[6] a model of dramatic perfection, could but leave a painful impression on the mind, in whichever light one regarded the unfortunate Paula. *The Transgressor*,[7] however, had a fair run at the same time. The Lady Brandon, in Dr. Todhunter's *Comedy of Sighs*,[8] made a desperate and self-satisfied effort to prolong her senseless, cheap philosophies, but revealed herself as a neurotic bad-tempered being, devoid of the lovable qualities and sensitive generosity which enlisted sympathy—perhaps unwillingly—for Paula Tanqueray. *Mrs. Lessingham*[9] wearied her listeners, and totally failed to arouse their interest. At the present time a wave of unwholesome, unsavoury matter has spread itself over literature generally, the palate is vitiated, for there is nothing so contagious as a thirst for the unique, and few have the mental strength to decide that a thing may be the most mischievous trash, although it has created a furore, possibly by a reason of there being a grain of truth amongst its illiterate chaff.

To achieve success, cry many, a thing must be seasoned with naughtiness, and seasoned so very thoroughly that the most blunted taste can perceive it.

Do the feminine authors of the novels of the last two or three years delude themselves by the hope that they will be remembered and quoted as George Eliot, George Sand, Jane Austen, Charlotte Bronté [*sic*], are still? And will be for many long days yet. It was Porson who said of Southey that his works would be read when Homer and Virgil were forgotten; to which Byron supplemented: "And not till then."[10]

But what can be expected when a writer like Mr. Le Gallienne[11] says: "Man for the present seems to be at a standstill, if not actually retrograde, and the onward movement of the world to be embodied in woman"? whilst Mr. Havelock Ellis, in *Man and Woman*, declares that woman is Nature's favourite: "She bears the special characteristics of humanity in a higher degree than man."

For spontaneity of thought, for following up a clue, for brightly written transcripts of life embracing rapid glances at phases of human character and existence,

---

6. Arthur Wing Pinero's play, with a sympathetic account of reformed mistress Paula Tanqueray.
7. *The Transgressor: A Play in Four Acts*, by Alexander Frederick Frank.
8. Irish poet John Todhunter's 1894 play, advertised by an Aubrey Beardsley poster.
9. 1894 play by "George Fleming" (Constance Fletcher). Prominent actress, manager, and author Elizabeth Robins starred.
10. Early 19th-c. critic Richard Porson, commenting on Romantic poet Robert Southey.
11. Poet and dandy Richard Le Gallienne (1866–1947).

woman novelists are far ahead of the men. For, as has been said by Paul Lafitte,[12] the value of the details in a woman's book is greater than the value of the whole. They can build up elaborate structures by laborious effort, but their architecture is neither inventive nor striking; pure imagination is wanting, and the finished work from the standpoint of idealisation, classic style, and consummate art, is not a success.

It may be that the future will alter this. The emancipation of woman is not at its height, say its votaries, and as universal education is to produce enlightenment, and subdue savagery amongst the masses, possibly the gradual development of woman's sphere will restrain her impulses and sober down her impetuosity. The world is before them. If they are to conquer in the same way that they have endured, conquer they certainly will, and due honour will be paid them.

But there is much to be done yet; and it is a pitiable sign of the present day's taste in literature that mere eccentricity in a heroine should be regarded for any length of time as a mark of merit, and that the work of true talent should be jostled by the outpourings of all the irrepressible writers who succeed in finding a reservoir for their verbosity. Fidelity to human nature is the keynote[13] to success, and if women wish to use their influence in the subduing of present evils, if they desire to raise the moral tone of men's lives, they will work to far greater advantage by employing their more subtle wit and keen perception, by retaining the power of their physical weakness and mental strength, their shrinking from vice, and adroitness in amusing, than by inveterate hectoring and probing and petty tilting in the lists on unequal terms, or still more open warfare.

There is another aspect which demands especial attention. I refer to it briefly, since it is a very vital point in the "Woman Question." Those less fortunate than Mrs. Humphrey [sic] Ward,[14] who has already realised a very comfortable fortune from her three lengthy books, have to face a very difficult and well-nigh insuperable barrier in the pursuit of a career, especially so in the literary world, and most particularly when journalism is their calling.

When men and young and attractive women can work daily together, without danger to the latter, the millennium will have been reached. *Ce n'est que le premier pas qui coute.*[15]

The woman who determines to succeed, will, after the preliminary struggle, face the inevitable. When she has to depend upon herself, when she has thrown off the trammels of home and imbibed a taste for Bohemianism, she will, by-and-by, cease her demands for a higher standard of morality amongst men, because she herself has cast conventionality to the winds. This is not a pleasant prospect: nevertheless, it is the greatest danger of the "Woman Question."

—1895

---

12. Probably turn-of-the-century artist Jean Paul Lafitte.
13. Alludes to the Keynote Series of women's fiction, named after George Egerton's controversial *Keynotes* (1893).
14. Prolific and serious turn-of-the-century novelist (1851–1920).
15. French: It is only the first step that hurts.

Mona Caird
1855–1932

"Does Marriage Hinder a Woman's Self-development?" is immediately recognizable as Alice Mona Caird's work, with its characteristically clever reversal and pithy style. Caird, who was among the most prominent writers of the New Women movement, stirred up outrage for her forthright denunciation of Victorian marriage. Caird's own family life appears to have been happy (she married in 1877 and had one son), but she opposed the institution of marriage because it victimized women. In *The Morality of Marriage* (1897) she argued that marriage often oppressed women, and her most famous novel, *The Daughters of Danaus* (1894), depicts a talented female composer trapped by family duties. In 1899, the magazine *The Ladies' Realm* asked a number of women writers to discuss whether marriage hindered a woman's self-development. Caird's response is presented here.

Does Marriage Hinder a Woman's Self-development?

Perhaps it might throw some light on the question whether marriage interferes with a woman's self-development and career, if we were to ask ourselves honestly how a man would fare in the position, say, of his own wife.

We will take a mild case, so as to avoid all risk of exaggeration.

Our hero's wife is very kind to him. Many of his friends have far sadder tales to tell. Mrs. Brown is fond of her home and family. She pats the children on the head when they come down to dessert, and plies them with chocolate creams, much to the detriment of their health; but it amuses Mrs. Brown. Mr. Brown superintends the bilious attacks, which the lady attributes to other causes. As she never finds fault with the children, and generally remonstrates with their father, in a good-natured way, when *he* does so, they are devoted to the indulgent parent, and are inclined to regard the other as second-rate.

Meal-times are often trying in this household, for Sophia is very particular about her food; sometimes she sends it out with a rude message to the cook. Not that John objects to this. He wishes she would do it oftener, for the cook gets used to Mr. Brown's second-hand version of his wife's language. He simply cannot bring himself to hint at Mrs. Brown's robust objurgations. She *can* express herself when it comes to a question of her creature comforts!

John's faded cheeks, the hollow lines under the eyes, and hair out of curl, speak of the struggle for existence as it penetrates to the fireside. If Sophia but knew what it meant to keep going the multitudinous details and departments of a household! Her idea of adding housemaids and pageboys whenever there is a jolt in the machinery has landed them in expensive disasters, time out of mind. And then, it hopelessly cuts off all margin of income for every other purpose. It is all rather discouraging for the hero of this petty, yet gigantic tussle, for he works, so to speak, in a hostile camp, with no sympathy from his entirely unconscious spouse, whom popular sentiment nevertheless regards as the gallant protector of his manly weakness.

If incessant vigilance, tact, firmness, foresight, initiative, courage and judgment—in short, all the qualities required for governing a kingdom, and more—have made things go smoothly, the wife takes it as a matter of course; if they go wrong, she naturally lays the blame on the husband. In the same way, if the children are a credit to their parents, that is only as it should be. But if they are naughty, and fretful, and stupid, and untidy, is it not clear that there must be some serious flaw in the system which could produce such results in the offspring of Mrs. Brown? What word in the English language is too severe to describe the man who neglects to watch with sufficient vigilance over his children's health and moral training, who fails to see that his little boys' sailor-suits and knickerbockers are in good repair, that their boot-lace ends do not fly out from their ankles at every step, that their hair is not like a hearth-brush, that they do not come down to dinner every day with dirty hands?

To every true man, the cares of fatherhood and home are sacred and all-sufficing. He realises, as he looks around at his little ones, that they are his crown and recompense.

John often finds that *his* crown-and-recompense gives him a racking headache by war-whoops and stampedes of infinite variety, and there are moments when he wonders in dismay if he is really a true man! He has had the privilege of rearing and training five small crowns and recompenses, and he feels that he could face the future if further privilege, of this sort, were denied him. Not but that he is devoted to his family. Nobody who understands the sacrifices he has made for them could doubt that. Only, he feels that those parts of his nature which are said to distinguish the human from the animal kingdom, are getting rather effaced.

He remembers the days before his marriage, when he was so bold, in his ignorant youth, as to cherish a passion for scientific research. He even went so far as to make a chemical laboratory of the family box-room, till attention was drawn to the circumstance by a series of terrific explosions, which shaved off his eyebrows, blackened his scientific countenance, and caused him to be turned out, neck and crop, with his crucibles, and a sermon on the duty that lay nearest him,—which resolved itself into that of paying innumerable afternoon calls with his father and brothers, on acquaintances selected—as he declared in his haste—for their phenomenal stupidity. His father pointed out how selfish it was for a young fellow to indulge his own little fads and fancies, when he might make himself useful in a nice manly way, at home.

When, a year later, the scapegrace Josephine, who had caused infinite trouble and expense to all belonging to her, showed a languid interest in chemistry, a spare room was at once fitted up for her, and an extraordinary wealth of crucibles provided by her delighted parents; and when explosions and smells pervaded the house, her father, with a proud smile, would exclaim: "What genius and enthusiasm that dear girl does display!" Josephine afterwards became a distinguished professor, with an awestruck family, and a husband who made it his chief duty and privilege to save her from all worry and interruption in her valuable work.

John, who knows in his heart of hearts that he could have walked round Josephine, in the old days, now speaks with manly pride of his sister, the Professor. His own bent, however, has always been so painfully strong that he even yet tries to snatch spare moments for his researches; but the strain in so many directions has broken down his health. People always told him that a man's constitution was not fitted for severe brain-work. He supposes it is true.

During those odd moments, he made a discovery that seemed to him of value, and he told Sophia about it, in a mood of scientific enthusiasm. But she burst out laughing, and said he would really be setting the Thames on fire if he didn't take care.

"Perhaps you will excuse my remarking, my dear, that I think you might be more usefully, not to say becomingly employed, in attending to your children and your household duties, than in dealing with explosive substances in the back dining-room."

And Sophia tossed off her glass of port in such an unanswerable manner, that John felt as if a defensive reply would be almost of the nature of a sacrilege. So he remained silent, feeling vaguely guilty. And as Johnny took measles just then, and it ran through the house, there was no chance of completing his work, or of making it of public value.

Curiously enough, a little later, Josephine made the very same discovery—only rather less perfect—and every one said, with acclamation, that science had been revolutionised by a discovery before which that of gravitation paled.

John still hoped, after twenty years of experience, that presently, by some different arrangement, some better management on his part, he would achieve leisure and mental repose to do the work that his heart was in; but that time never came.

No doubt John was not infallible, and made mistakes in dealing with his various problems: do the best of us achieve consummate wisdom? No doubt, if he had followed the advice that we could all have supplied him with, in such large quantities, he might have done rather more than he did. But the question is: Did his marriage interfere with his self-development and career, and would many other Johns, in his circumstances, have succeeded much better?

—1899

Alice Meynell
1847–1922

Although Alice Meynell was most revered for her poetry, her "princely journalism" (as one admirer called it) is equally remarkable. "A Woman in Grey" describes the exhilarating experience of watching a woman ride a bicycle. This recently invented machine enabled women to travel independently for the first time. Moreover, it was too dangerous to wear voluminous skirts and constricting corsets while bicycling, so riders adopted new "rational dress" styles, sometimes including modified trousers. The bicycle swiftly became the emblem of liberation, independence, and modernity. Although Meynell herself adhered to a more traditional feminine model, the essay shows her fascination with her counterparts' experiments. For more information about Meynell, see pp. 54 and 117.

A Woman in Grey

The mothers of Professors were indulged in the practice of jumping at conclusions, and were praised for their impatience of the slow process of reason.

Professors have written of the mental habits of women as though they accumulated generation by generation upon women, and passed over their sons. Professors take it for granted, obviously by some process other than the slow process of reason, that women derive from their mothers and grandmothers, and men from their fathers and grand-fathers. This, for instance, was written lately: "This power [it matters not what][1] would be about equal in the two sexes but for the influence of heredity, which turns the scale in favour of the woman, as for long generations the surroundings and conditions of life of the female sex have developed in her a greater degree of the power in question than circumstances have required from men." "Long generations" of subjection are, strangely enough, held to excuse the timorousness and the shifts of women to-day. But the world, unknowing, tampers with the courage of its sons by such a slovenly indulgence. It tamp-ers with their intelligence by fostering the ignorance of women.

And yet Shakespeare confessed the participation of man and woman in their common heritage. It is Cassius who speaks:

> Have you not love enough to bear with me
> When that rash humour which my mother gave me
> Makes me forgetful?

And Brutus who replies:

> Yes, Cassius, and from henceforth
> When you are over-earnest with your Brutus
> He'll think your mother chides, and leave you so.[2]

Dryden confessed it also in his praises of Anne Killigrew:

> If by traduction[3] came thy mind,
> Our wonder is the less to find
> A soul so charming from a stock so good.
> Thy father was transfused into thy blood.[4]

The winning of Waterloo upon the Eton playgrounds[5] is very well; but there have been some other, and happily minor, fields that were not won—that were more or less lost. Where did this loss take place, if the gains were secured at football? This inquiry is not quite so cheerful as the other. But while the victories were once going forward in the playground, the defeats or disasters were once going forward in some other place, presumably. And this was surely the place that was not a playground, the place where the future wives of the football players were sitting still while their future husbands were playing football.

This is the train of thought that followed the grey figure of a woman on a bicy-cle in Oxford Street.[6] She had an enormous and top-heavy omnibus at her back. All

---

1. Meynell's note.
2. *Julius Caesar* 4.3.
3. Transmission from father to daughter.
4. From Dryden's memorial ode of 1686 for the painter and poet Anne Killigrew, whose father was also a poet.
5. The Duke of Wellington's phrase, meaning that the British public schools fostered values that produced supe-rior fighting forces.
6. Major shopping street in central London.

the things on the near side of the street—the things going her way—were going at different paces, in two streams, overtaking and being overtaken. The tributary streets shot omnibuses and carriages, cabs and carts—some to go her own way, some with an impetus that carried them curving into the other current, and other some making a straight line right across Oxford Street into the street opposite. Besides all the unequal movement, there were the stoppings. It was a delicate tangle to keep from knotting. The nerves of the mouths of horses bore the whole charge and answered it, as they do every day.

The woman in grey, quite alone, was immediately dependent on no nerves but her own, which almost made her machine sensitive. But this alertness was joined to such perfect composure as no flutter of a moment disturbed. There was the steadiness of sleep, and a vigilance more than that of an ordinary waking.

At the same time, the woman was doing what nothing in her youth could well have prepared her for. She must have passed a childhood unlike the ordinary girl's childhood, if her steadiness or her alertness had ever been educated, if she had been rebuked for cowardice, for the egoistic distrust of general rules, or for claims of exceptional chances. Yet here she was, trusting not only herself but a multitude of other people; taking her equal risk; giving a watchful confidence to averages—that last, perhaps, her strangest and greatest success.

No exceptions, were hers, no appeals, and no forewarnings. She evidently had not in her mind a single phrase, familiar to women, made to express no confidence except in accidents, and to proclaim a prudent foresight of the less probable event. No woman could ride a bicycle along Oxford Street with any such baggage as that about her.

The woman in grey had a watchful confidence not only in a multitude of men but in a multitude of things. And it is very hard for any untrained human being to practise confidence in things in motion—things full of force, and, what is worse, of forces. Moreover, there is a supreme difficulty for a mind accustomed to search timorously for some little place of insignificant rest on any accessible point of stable equilibrium; and that is the difficulty of holding itself nimbly secure in an equilibrium that is unstable. Who can deny that women are generally used to look about for the little stationary repose just described? Whether in intellectual or in spiritual things, they do not often live without it.

She, none the less, fled upon unstable equilibrium, escaped upon it, depended upon it, trusted it, was 'ware of it, was on guard against it, as she sped amid her crowd: her own unstable equilibrium, her machine's, that of the judgment, the temper, the skill, the perception, the strength of men and horses.

She had learnt the difficult peace of suspense. She had learnt also the lowly and self-denying faith in common chances. She had learnt to be content with her share—no more—in common security, and to be pleased with her part in common hope. For all this, it may be repeated, she could have had but small preparation. Yet no anxiety was hers, no uneasy distrust and disbelief of that human thing—an average of life and death.

To this courage the woman in grey had attained with a spring, and she had seated herself suddenly upon a place of detachment between earth and air, freed from the principal detentions, weights, and embarrassments of the usual life of fear. She had made herself, as it were, light, so as not to dwell either in security or danger, but to pass between them. She confessed difficulty and peril by her delicate evasions, and consented to rest in neither. She would not owe safety to the mere motionlessness of a seat on the solid earth, but she used gravitation to balance the slight burdens of her wariness and her confidence. She put aside all the pride and vanity of terror, and leapt into an unsure condition of liberty and content.

She leapt, too, into a life of moments. No pause was possible to her as she went, except the vibrating pause of a perpetual change and of an unflagging flight. A woman, long educated to sit still, does not suddenly learn to live a momentary life without strong momentary resolution. She has no light achievement in limiting not only her foresight, which must become brief, but her memory, which must do more; for it must rather cease than become brief. Idle memory wastes times and other things. The moments of the woman in grey as they dropped by must needs disappear, and be simply forgotten, as a child forgets. Idle memory, by the way, shortens life, or shortens the sense of time, by linking the immediate past clingingly to the present. Here may possibly be found one of the reasons for the length of a child's time, and for the brevity of the time that succeeds. The child lets his moments pass by and quickly become remote through a thousand little successive oblivions. He has not yet the languid habit of recall.

"Thou art my warrior," said Volumnia. "I holp to frame thee."[7]

Shall a man inherit his mother's trick of speaking, or her habit and attitude, and not suffer something, against his will, from her bequest of weakness, and something, against his heart, from her bequest of folly? From the legacies of an unlessoned mind, a woman's heirs-male are not cut off in the Common Law of the generations of mankind. Brutus knew that the valour of Portia[8] was settled upon his sons.

—1896

New Women Poetry

May Kendall
1861–1943

Emma Goldworth (May) Kendall wrote delightfully unconventional poetry. She strongly supported women's equality and sympathized passionately with impoverished people. Never married, Kendall worked alongside men and enjoyed using scientific jargon for her comic and incisive verses. Kendall also wrote in several other genres: three novels between 1887 and 1893, short stories about the Armenian massacre in *Turkish Bonds* (1898), and economic treatises in collaboration with Seebohm Rowntree in 1913 and 1918. "Woman's Future" was published in *Dreams to Sell* (1887).

---

7. *Coriolanus* 5.3, a mother speaking to her son.
8. In *Julius Caesar*, Brutus's wife Portia bravely attempts to uncover the plot against Caesar.

Woman's Future

Complacent they tell us, hard hearts and derisive,
    In vain is our ardour: in vain are our sighs:
Our intellects, bound by a limit decisive,
    To the level of Homer's may never arise.
We heed not the falsehood, the base innuendo,   5
    The laws of the universe, these are our friends.
Our talents shall rise in a mighty crescendo,
    We trust Evolution to make us amends!

But ah, when I ask you for food that is mental,
    My sisters, you offer me ices and tea!   10
You cherish the fleeting, the mere accidental,
    At cost of the True, the Intrinsic, the Free.
Your feelings, compressed in Society's mangle,
    Are vapid and frivolous, pallid and mean.
To slander you love; but you don't care to wrangle: 15
    You bow to Decorum, and cherish Routine.

Alas, is it woolwork you take for your mission,
    Or Art that your fingers so gaily attack?[1]
Can patchwork atone for the mind's inanition?
    Can the soul, oh my sisters, be fed on a *plaque?*[2]   20
Is this your vocation? My goal is another,
    And empty and vain is the end you pursue.
In antimacassars[3] the world you may smother;
    But intellect marches o'er them and o'er you.

On Fashion's vagaries your energies strewing,   25
    Devoting your days to a rug or a screen,
Oh, rouse to a lifework—do something worth doing!
    Invent a new planet, a flying-machine.
Mere charms superficial, mere feminine graces,
    That fade or that flourish, no more you may prize;   30
But the knowledge of Newton[4] will beam from your faces,
    The soul of a Spencer[5] will shine in your eyes.

---

1. In the 1850s Berlin-wool work was a popular hobby—stitching bright yarns onto preprinted patterns—but by the 1870s the new craze was for "art" crafts.
2. A patch in patchwork, but also refers to the decorative ceramic plaques made by women in the Arts and Crafts movement.
3. A decorative mat covering the back of a chair to protect it from hair oil.
4. Sir Isaac Newton (1642–1727), astronomer, philosopher, and mathematician who developed the sciences of optics and gravity.
5. See p. 212, n. 1.

Envoy

Though jealous exclusion may tremble to own us,
    Oh, wait for the time when our brains shall expand!
When once we're enthroned, you shall never dethrone us—   35
    The poets, the sages, the seers of the land!

—1887

Conſtance Naden
1858–1889

This remarkably talented poet excelled in science, poetry, languages, art, and philosophy. Influenced by Herbert Spencer's evolutionary philosophy, Constance Naden became an outspoken atheist and came to believe in a radically solipsistic theory that the perceiving self shapes the universe. She wrote rigorously learned essays on philosophical and scientific subjects (published posthumously), produced flower paintings celebrated for their accuracy, traveled in Europe and India, and published two books of poetry before her untimely death at age 31 from an operation to remove ovarian cysts. "The New Orthodoxy" is Part II of a four-part series called "Evolutional Erotics," published in *A Modern Apostle, The Elixir of Life and Other Poems* (1887).

The New Orthodoxy[1]

So, dear Fred, you're not content
Though I quote the books you lent,
And I've kept that spray you sent
    Of the milk-white heather;
For you fear I'm too "advanced"   5
To remember all that chanced
In the old days, when we danced,
    Walked, and rode together.

Trust me, Fred, beneath the curls
Of the most "advanced" of girls,   10
Many a foolish fancy whirls,
    Bidding Fact defiance,
And the simplest village maid
Needs not to be much afraid
Of her sister, sage and staid,   15
    Bachelor of Science.

---

1. Victorian women often rejected men for inadequate religious feeling; Naden creates a comic reversal.

Ah! while yet our hope was new
Guardians thought 'twould never do
That Sir Frederick's heir should woo
   Little Amy Merton: 20
So the budding joy they snatched
From our hearts, so meetly matched—
You to Oxford they despatched,
   Me they sent to Girton.[2]

Were the vows all writ in dust?   25
No—you're one-and-twenty—just
And you write—"We will, we must
   Now, at once, be married!"
Nay, you plan the wedding trip!
Softly, sir! there's many a slip   30
Ere the goblet to the lip
   Finally is carried.

Oh, the wicked tales I hear!
Not that you at Ruskin[3] jeer,
Nor that at Carlyle[4] you sneer,   35
   With his growls dyspeptic:
But that, having read in vain
Huxley, Tyndall, Clifford, Bain,[5]
All the scientific train—
   You're a hardened sceptic!   40

Things with fin, and claw, and hoof
Join to give us perfect proof
That our beings' warp and woof
   We from near and far win;
Yet your flippant doubts you vaunt,   45
And—to please a maiden aunt—
You've been heard to say you can't
   Pin your faith to Darwin!

Then you jest, because Laplace[6]
Said this Earth was nought but gas   50
Till the vast rotating mass
   Denser grew and denser:[7]

---

2. Pioneering women's college at Cambridge, founded in 1869.
3. Influential 19th-c. art critic who expounded socialist ideals.
4. Victorian sage Thomas Carlyle—who was indeed dyspeptic (had bad digestion)—condemned the excesses of industrial capitalism.
5. All important 19th-c. scientists. Thomas Henry Huxley was a biologist, John Tyndall a physicist, W. K. Clifford a mathematician, and Alexander Bain an educational reformer.
6. Pierre Simon, Marquis de Laplace (1749–1827) revolutionized astronomy.
7. The "nebular hypothesis," generally credited to both Immanuel Kant and Laplace.

Something worse they whisper too,
But I'm sure it *can't* be true—
For they tell me, Fred, that you   55
Scoff at Herbert Spencer![8]

Write—or telegraph—or call!
Come yourself and tell me all:
No fond hope shall me enthrall,
   No regret shall sway me: 60
Yet—until the worst is said,
Till I know your faith is dead,
I remain, dear doubting Fred,
Your believing
          AMY.   65

          —1887

Dora Sigerson Shorter
1866–1918

An Irish poet, Dora Sigerson Shorter was central to the social cliques of women poets in the 1890s. A close friend of Katharine Tynan, she knew W. B. Yeats and other Irish poets, but because she married the writer and editor Clement Shorter, her literary circles also included many of the prominent English writers of the period. Shorter was a talented artist (painter and sculptor), a legendarily beautiful woman, and a passionate supporter of Irish independence and Irish nationalism. Indeed, her death may have been hastened by her misery at the failure of the 1916 Easter Uprising, when rebels led by Padraic Pearse declared the Republic of Ireland but, after a week of fighting, were forced to surrender and were executed. Her poems show strong yearnings for Celtic myth and a resolute Irish patriotism, as well as concerns about women's status. In the sly poem "Cecilia's Way," Shorter rewrites Alfred, Lord Tennyson's iconic "The Lady of Shalott." Whereas Tennyson depicts his Lady as silent, imprisoned, and doomed, Shorter gleefully sends hers outside on a fearless walk.

Cecilia's Way

Lighted by the lady moon,
Breezes blow and aspens quiver,[1]
By the stream's enchanted tune
Singing to the distant river,
Walks Cecilia.   5

---

8. Major political theorist, economist, and philosopher (1820–1903).

---

1. Rewrites lines from Tennyson's "The Lady of Shalott."

Such an hour for love and song,
Lover's kiss and maiden's laughter.
Who would wish the night less long
Or fail to weep it back hereafter?
Sighs Cecilia.   10

'Neath the aspen moves a shade,—
Shadow dark! The saints defend her!
Any lass would fly afraid
On the wings that fear would lend her!
Smiles Cecilia.   15

Who would brave the shaping gloom,
Hiding form and hidden face,
Phantom arms that would entomb,
Who dares go to that embrace?—
Why, Cecilia.   20

—1903

E. Nesbit
1858–1924

Although Edith Nesbit became famous as a writer of Edwardian children's stories, in the 1890s she was a political reformer and aesthetic poet, using carefully crafted language to express uneducated speakers' deep but inarticulate emotions. Nesbit and her husband Hubert Bland led a wildly unconventional lifestyle, each taking lovers, and Nesbit reared two of her husband's illegitimate children alongside her own three. As a founding member of the socialist group advocating parliamentary reform, the Fabian Society, Nesbit wrote socialist poems about labor and the slums. "Accession" is a good example of the mixed feelings in many New Woman texts, in which writers project a vision of powerful, independent women only to undermine it at the end. Here Nesbit depicts a woman who triumphantly rules herself, yet also suggests that such independence is tragic.

Accession

Once I loved, and my heart bowed down,
    Subject and slave, for Love was a King;
He sat above with sceptre and crown,
    Turning his eyes from my sorrowing.
The laugh of a god on his lips lay light—   5
    His lips victorious that mocked my pain,
And I mourned in the cold and the outer night,
    And my tears and my prayers were vain.

Now the old spell is over and done,
   Myself I wear the ermine and gold,   10
My brows are crowned, I ascend the throne,
   I have taken the sceptre and orb to hold.
I smile victorious, set far above
   The music of voices that moan and pray,
My feet are wet with the tears of love,   15
   And I turn my eyes away.

—1905

Dollie Radford
1858–1920

Dollie (Caroline) Radford wrote ambitious poems, children's books, and witty verses that were often published in the periodical press, including some work in *The Yellow Book*. Like Dora Sigerson Shorter, Radford was a central participant in the social networks of the 1890s; a committed socialist and radical thinker, her friends included reformist writers like H. G. Wells, George Bernard Shaw, D. H. Lawrence, W. B. Yeats, William Morris, and Olive Schreiner. Radford's husband Ernest Radford was also a poet and belonged to the Rhymers' Club, but his poetry was generally conceded to be inferior to his wife's. Like many Victorian women writers, Radford often found her work dismissed as "charming"—agreeable without being serious—but "From Our Emancipated Aunt in Town" is clearly a serious account of changing feminist goals. The poem sensitively depicts relations between two generations, the older aesthetically oriented women who regard their younger, more politically active New Women "nieces" with wry and somewhat envious pride.

From Our Emancipated Aunt in Town

All has befallen as I say,
The old régime has passed away,
     And quite a new one

Is being fashioned in a fire,
The fervours of whose burning tire   5
     And quite undo one.

The fairy prince has passed from sight,
Away into the ewigkeit,[1]
     With best intention

---

1. German: eternity.

I served him, as you know my dears,   10
Unfalteringly through more years
          Than ladies mention.

And though the fairy prince has gone,
With all the props I leaned upon,
          And I am stranded,   15

With old ideals blown away,
And all opinions, in the fray,
          Long since disbanded.

And though he's only left to me,
Of course quite inadvertently,   20
          The faintest glimmer

Of humour, to illume my way,
I'm thankful he has had his day,
          His shine and shimmer.

Le roi est mort[2]—but what's to come?—   25
Surcharged the air is with the hum
          Of startling changes,

And our great "question" is per force[3]
The vital one, o'er what a course
          It boldly ranges!   30

Strange gentlemen to me express
At quiet "at homes" their willingness,
          To ease our fetters

And ladies, in a fleeting car,
Will tell me that the moderns are   35
          My moral betters.

My knees I know are much too weak
To mount the high and shaky peak
          Of latest ethics,

---

2. French: The king is dead.
3. The "Woman Question," what rights and duties women should have.

I'm tabulated, and I stand   40
By evolution, in a band
    Of poor pathetics

Who cannot go alone, who cling
To many a worn out tottering thing
    Of a convention;   45

To many a prejudice and hope,
And to the old proverbial rope
    Of long dimension.

It is to you to whom I look
To beautify our history book,   50
    For coming readers,

To you my nieces, who must face
Our right and wrong, and take your place
    As future leaders.

And I, meanwhile, shall still pursue   55
All that is weird and wild and new,
    In song and ballet,

In lecture, drama, verse and prose,
With every cult that comes and goes
    Your aunt will dally.   60

A microscopic analyst
Of female hearts, she will subsist
    On queerest notions,

And subtlest views of maid and wife
Ever engaged in deadly strife   65
    With the emotions.

But while you walk, and smile at her,
In quiet lanes, which you prefer
    To public meetings,

Remember she prepares your way,   70
With many another Aunt to-day,
    And send her greetings.

        —1895

Amy Levy
1861–1889

Amy Levy, a brilliant and miserable writer of the *fin de siècle*, had a lot to contend with. When not fighting her bad health, including encroaching deafness, she was trying to come to terms with her love of women and her Judaism, traits that made her feel marginalized from mainstream British society. Levy's bitter, witty, concise poetry expresses these tensions but also celebrates the identity with which Levy found most comfort: the New Woman. Living alone in a London flat, traveling independently on omnibuses, Levy found her freedom exhilarating. She even named one of her books of poetry *A London Plane-Tree* (1889), defiantly identifying with the hardy shrub that grows out of the stony pavements of the city, rather than more conventionally pastoral or mythological greenery. For more information about Levy, see p. 110.

Captivity

The lion remembers the forest,
   The lion in chains;
To the bird that is captive a vision
   Of woodland remains.

One strains with his strength at the fetter,   5
   In impotent rage;
One flutters in flights of a moment,
   And beats at the cage.

If the lion were loosed from the fetter,
   To wander again;   10
He would seek the wide silence and shadow
   Of his jungle in vain.

He would rage in his fury, destroying;
   Let him rage, let him roam!
Shall he traverse the pitiless mountain,   15
   Or swim through the foam?

If they opened the cage and the casement,
   And the bird flew away;
He would come back at evening, heartbroken,
   A captive for aye.   20

Would come if his kindred had spared him,
   Free birds from afar—
There was wrought what is stronger than iron
   In fetter and bar.

I cannot remember my country,   25
    The land whence I came;
Whence they brought me and chained me and made me
    Nor wild thing nor tame.

This only I know of my country,
    This only repeat:—   30
It was free as the forest, and sweeter
    Than woodland retreat.

When the chain shall at last be broken,
    The window set wide;
And I step in the largeness and freedom   35
    Of sunlight outside;

Shall I wander in vain for my country?
    Shall I seek and not find?
Shall I cry for the bars that encage me
    The fetters that bind?   40

—1889

Graham R. Tomson
1860–1911

At the *fin de siècle*, "Graham R. Tomson" (Rosamund Marriott Watson) was famous for her ethereal beauty, her adventurous love life, her beautifully descriptive prose, and her evocative, haunting poetry. She wrote prose work about gardens, interior design, and fashions, but her poetry tended to deal with more mythic elements, simple natural scenes transformed by visitations from the dead, people enchanted into animals, or legendary figures. "On the Road" uses Tomson's typically stark, simple metrical form. It was published in *The Bird-Bride*, whose title itself indicates some of her fascination with mythic change. For more information about Tomson, see p. 120.

On the Road

The snow is white, the way is stern and sore,
Wide, blinding wastes behind us and before,
And though we soon shall see a stiller shore,
        The road is long.

The gaunt grey wolves are famished for their prey,   5
But we are bound, and hungrier than they;
The fruit will fall when we ourselves are clay—
        The road is long.

We leave strong hands to cleanse away the stain,
Though we plod on along the shuddering plain   10
To marching music of the creaking chain—
      The road is long.

The sands of Tyranny are slow to run.
Alas! that this and many a morrow's sun
Must see the goal ungained, the work undone!   15
      The road is long.

Our lives were ladder-rungs: the Cause moves on;
The light shines fair as ever it has shone;
'Twill blaze full bright ere many years be gone—
      The road is long.   20

We are but bubbles breaking in the sea,
The strong slow tide that one day will be free;
We shall not know it—yea, but it will be:
      The road is long.

—1889

Mathilde Blind
1841–1896

It is no exaggeration to call Mathilde Blind heroic. Blind, who also wrote under the name of "Claude Lake," was a poet, translator, literary critic, and novelist with strong views about the women's movement. An ardent supporter of women's education, she wrote about radicals she admired (including Mary Wollstonecraft and Percy Bysshe Shelley), dedicated poems to Giuseppe Mazzini and the cause of the Italian republic, translated *The Journal of Marie Bashkirtseff* (1890), and wrote long poems about atheism, the suffering of crofters in the Scottish Highlands, and evolution. Blind's poetry is passionate and imaginative. Unmarried, Blind formed strong friendships with women, traveled widely, and bequeathed her estate to Newnham College, Cambridge, to found a scholarship for women. Throughout her life, she wrote and worked for the causes in which she believed, and her epic book-length set of poems, *The Ascent of Man* (1889), is no exception. *The Ascent of Man*, from which this Prelude is taken, rethinks Darwin's *The Descent of Man* (1871) by reading human history as a triumphant progression toward revolutionary society and poetic creativity.

Prelude. Wings.

Ascend, oh my Soul, with the wings of the lark ascend!
   Soaring away and away far into the blue.
Or with the shrill seagull to the breakers bend,

Or with the bee, where the grasses and field-flowers blend,
    Drink out of golden cups of the honey-dew.   5

Ascend, oh my Soul, on the wings of the wind as it blows,
    Striking wild organ-blasts from the forest trees,
Or on the zephyr bear love of the rose to the rose,
Or with the hurricane sower cast seed as he goes
    Limitless ploughing the leagues of the sibilant seas.   10

Ascend, oh my Soul, on the wings of the choral strain,
    Invisible tier above tier upbuilding sublime;
Note as it scales after note in a rhythmical chain
Reaching from chaos and welter of struggle and pain,
    Far into vistas empyreal receding from time.   15

Ascend! take wing on the thoughts of the Dead, my Soul,
    Breathing in colour and stone, flashing through epic and song:
Thoughts that like avalanche snows gather force as they roll,
Mighty to fashion and knead the phenomenal throng
    Of generations of men as they thunder along.   20

—1889

New Women Fiction

George Egerton
1859–1945

In the 1890s, the short stories "George Egerton" (Mary Chavelita Dunne) wrote made her infamous. Published as *Keynotes* and *Discords*, these stories depicted women as independent, sexually assertive beings not bound to matrimony. Egerton depicted her characters' lives in mere glimpses, dreams, and hints, and she frequently left their problems unresolved. *Keynotes* was such a sensation that the publisher, John Lane, began a Keynote Series featuring books by women writers, with covers by Aubrey Beardsley. Egerton married and had a child, but she divorced her husband and later remarried; in the twentieth century she turned to novels and dramatic writing. "A Cross Line" emphasizes bodily experience—including sexual desire—as the key to emotions, and its depiction of its female character's fantasies was considered scandalous. This erotic material, however, serves a eugenic and evolutionary purpose, as the woman sizes up her husband's body for its mating potential and ultimately decides on her romantic partner based on reproductive considerations.

A Cross Line[1]

The rather flat notes of a man's voice float out into the clear air, singing the refrain of a popular music-hall ditty. There is something incongruous between the melody and the surroundings. It seems profane, indelicate, to bring this slangy, vulgar tune, and with it the mental picture of footlight flare and fantastic dance, into the lovely freshness of this perfect spring day.

A woman sitting on a felled tree turns her head to meet its coming, and an expression flits across her face in which disgust and humorous appreciation are subtly blended. Her mind is nothing if not picturesque; her busy brain, with all its capabilities choked by a thousand vagrant fancies, is always producing pictures and finding associations between the most unlikely objects. She has been reading a little sketch written in the daintiest language of a fountain scene in Tanagra,[2] and her vivid imagination has made it real to her. The slim, graceful maids grouped around it filling their exquisitely-formed earthen jars, the dainty poise of their classic heads, and the flowing folds of their draperies have been actually present with her; and now,—why, it is like the entrance of a half-tipsy vagabond player bedizened in tawdry finery: the picture is blurred. She rests her head against the trunk of a pine-tree behind her, and awaits the singer. She is sitting on an incline in the midst of a wilderness of trees; some have blown down, some have been cut down, and the lopped branches lie about; moss and bracken and trailing bramble bushes, fir-cones, wild rose-bushes, and speckled red "fairy hats" fight for life in wild confusion. A disused quarry to the left is an ideal haunt of pike, and to the right a little river rushes along in haste to join a greater sister that is fighting a troubled way to the sea. A row of stepping-stones cross it, and if you were to stand on one you would see shoals of restless stone-loach "beardies"[3] darting from side to side. The tails of several ducks can be seen above the water, and the paddle of their balancing feet and the gurgling suction of their bills as they search for larvae can be heard distinctly between the hum of insect, twitter of bird, and rustle of stream and leaf. The singer has changed his lay to a whistle, and presently he comes down the path a cool, neat, gray-clad figure, with a fishing creel slung across his back, and a trout rod held on his shoulder. The air ceases abruptly, and his cold, gray eyes scan the seated figure with its gypsy ease of attitude, a scarlet shawl that has fallen from her shoulders forming an accentuative background to the slim roundness of her waist.

Persistent study, coupled with a varied experience of the female animal, has given the owner of the said gray eyes some facility in classing her, although it has not supplied him with any definite data as to what any one of the species may do in a given circumstance. To put it in his own words, in answer to a friend who chaffed him on his untiring pursuit of women as an interesting problem,—

"If a fellow has had much experience of his fellow-man he may divide him into types, and given a certain number of men and a certain number of circumstances, he is pretty safe on hitting on the line of action each type will strike. 'Taint so with

---

1. Cross-line fishing means putting multiple hooks on one line stretching across a river, generally considered unfair entrapment.
2. Greek town famous for terra-cotta statuettes.
3. Small freshwater fish with barbels, resembling whiskers, around the mouth.

woman. You may always look out for the unexpected; she generally upsets a fellow's calculations, and you are never safe in laying odds on her. Tell you what, old chappie, we may talk about superior intellect; but if a woman wasn't handicapped by her affection or need of it, the cleverest chap in Christendom would be just a bit of putty in her hands. I find them more fascinating as problems than anything going. Never let an opportunity slip to get new data—never!"

He did not now. He met the frank, unembarrassed gaze of eyes that would have looked with just the same bright inquiry at the advent of a hare or a toad, or any other object that might cross her path, and raised his hat with respectful courtesy, saying, in the drawling tone habitual with him,—

"I hope I am not trespassing?"

"I can't say; you may be; so may I, but no one has ever told me so!"

A pause. His quick glance has noted the thick wedding-ring on her slim brown hand and the flash of a diamond in its keeper. A lady decidedly. Fast?—perhaps. Original?—undoubtedly. Worth knowing?—rather.

"I am looking for a trout stream, but the directions I got were rather vague; might I—"

"It's straight ahead; but you won't catch anything now, at least not here,—sun's too glaring and water too low; a mile up you may in an hour's time."

"Oh, thanks awfully for the tip. You fish then?"

"Yes, sometimes."

"Trout run big here?" (What odd eyes the woman has! kind of magnetic.)

"No, seldom over a pound; but they are very game."

"Rare good sport, isn't it, whipping a stream? There is so much besides the mere catching of fish; the river and the trees and the quiet sets a fellow thinking; kind of sermon; makes a chap feel good, don't it?"

She smiles assentingly, and yet what the devil is she amused at, he queries mentally. An inspiration! he acts upon it, and says eagerly,—

"I wonder—I don't half like to ask, but fishing puts people on a common footing, don't it? You knowing the stream, you know, would you tell me what are the best flies to use?"

"I tie my own, but—"

"Do you? How clever of you! Wish I could;" and sitting down on the other end of the tree, he takes out his fly-book. "But I interrupted you, you were going to say—"

"Only,"—stretching out her hand, of a perfect shape but decidedly brown, for the book,—"that you might give the local fly-tyer a trial; he'll tell you. Later on, end of next month, or perhaps later, you might try the oak-fly,—the natural fly, you know. A horn is the best thing to hold them in, they get out of anything else; and put two on at a time."

"By Jove, I must try that dodge!"

He watches her as she handles his book and examines the contents critically, turning aside some with a glance, fingering others almost tenderly, holding them daintily, and noting the cock of wings and the hint of tinsel, with her head on one side,—a trick of hers, he thinks.

"Which do you like most, wet or dry fly?" She is looking at some dry flies.

"Oh," with that rare smile, "at the time I swear by whichever happens to catch most fish,—perhaps really dry fly. I fancy most of these flies are better for Scotland or

England. Up to this, March-brown has been the most killing thing. But you might try an 'orange-grouse,'—that's always good here,—with perhaps a 'hare's ear' for a change, and put on a 'coachman' for the evenings. My husband [he steals a side look at her] brought home some beauties yesterday evening."

"Lucky fellow!"

She returns the book. There is a tone in his voice as he says this that jars on her, sensitive as she is to every inflection of a voice, with an intuition that is almost second sight. She gathers up her shawl,—she has a cream-colored woollen gown on, and her skin looks duskily foreign by contrast. She is on her feet before he can regain his, and says, with a cool little bend of her head: "Good afternoon, I wish you a full basket!"

Before he can raise his cap she is down the slope, gliding with easy steps that have a strange grace, and then springing lightly from stone to stone across the stream. He feels small, snubbed someway; and he sits down on the spot where she sat, and lighting his pipe says, "Check!"

. . .

She is walking slowly up the garden path; a man in his shirt-sleeves is stooping among the tender young peas; a bundle of stakes lies next him, and he whistles softly and all out of tune as he twines the little tendrils round each new support. She looks at his broad shoulders and narrow flanks; his back is too long for great strength she thinks. He hears her step, and smiles up at her from under the shadow of his broad-leafed hat.

"How do you feel now, old woman?"

"Beastly! I've got that horrid qualmish feeling again. I can't get rid of it."

He has spread his coat on the side of the path, and pats it for her to sit down.

"What is it?" anxiously. "If you were a mare I'd know what to do for you. Have a nip of whiskey?"

He strides off without waiting for her reply, and comes back with it and a biscuit, kneels down and holds the glass to her lips. "Poor little woman, buck up! You'll see that'll fix you. Then you go, by-and-by, and have a shy at the fish."

She is about to say something, when a fresh qualm attacks her and she does not. He goes back to his tying.

"By Jove!" he says suddenly, "I forgot; got something to show you!"

After a few minutes he returns, carrying a basket covered with a piece of sacking; a dishevelled-looking hen, with spread wings trailing and her breast bare from sitting on her eggs, screeches after him. He puts it carefully down and uncovers it, disclosing seven little balls of yellow fluff splashed with olive-green; they look up sideways with bright round eyes, and their little spoon-bills disproportionately large.

"Aren't they beauties?" enthusiastically. "This one is just out," taking up an egg; "mustn't let it get chilled; there is a chip out of it and a piece of hanging skin. Isn't it funny?" he asks, showing her how it is curled in the shell, with its paddles flattened and its bill breaking through the chip, and the slimy feathers sticking to its violet skin.

She suppresses an exclamation of disgust, and looks at his fresh-tinted skin instead. He is covering basket, hen, and all.

"How you love young things!" she says.

"Some! I had a filly once; she turned out a lovely mare! I cried when I had to sell her; I wouldn't have let any one in God's world mount her."

"Yes, you would!"

"Who?" with a quick look of resentment.

"Me!"

"I wouldn't!"

"What! you wouldn't?"

"I wouldn't!"

"I think you would if I wanted to!" with a flash out of the tail of her eye.

"No, I wouldn't!"

"Then you would care more for her than for me. I would give you your choice," passionately, "her or me!"

"What nonsense!"

"Maybe," concentrated; "but it's lucky she isn't here to make deadly sense of it." A humble-bee buzzes close to her ear, and she is roused to a sense of facts, and laughs to think how nearly they have quarrelled over a mare that was sold before she knew him.

Some evenings later she is stretched motionless in a chair; and yet she conveys an impression of restlessness,—a sensitively nervous person would feel it. She is gazing at her husband; her brows are drawn together, and make three little lines. He is reading, reading quietly, without moving his eyes quickly from side to side of the page as she does when she reads, and he pulls away at a big pipe with steady enjoyment. Her eyes turn from him to the window, and follow the course of two clouds; then they close for a few seconds, then open to watch him again. He looks up and smiles.

"Finished your book?"

There is a singular, soft monotony in his voice; the organ with which she replies is capable of more varied expression.

"Yes, it is a book makes one think. It would be a greater book if he were not an Englishman; he's afraid of shocking the big middle class. You wouldn't care about it."

"Finished your smoke?"

"No, it went out; too much fag[4] to light up again! No," protestingly, "never you mind, old boy, why do you?"

He has drawn his long length out of his chair, and kneeling down beside her guards a lighted match from the incoming evening air. She draws in the smoke contentedly, and her eyes smile back with a general vague tenderness.

"Thank you, dear old man!"

"Going out again?" Negative head-shake.

"Back aching?" Affirmative nod, accompanied by a steadily aimed puff of smoke, that she has been carefully inhaling, into his eyes.

"Scamp! Have your booties off?"

"Oh, don't you bother! Lizzie will do it."

He has seized a foot from under the rocker, and sitting on his heels holds it on his knee, while he unlaces the boot; then he loosens the stocking under her toes, and strokes her foot gently. "Now the other!" Then he drops both boots outside the door,

---

4. Trouble.

and fetching a little pair of slippers, past their first smartness, from the bedroom, puts one on. He examines the left foot: it is a little swollen round the ankle, and he presses his broad fingers gently round it as one sees a man do to a horse with windgalls. Then he pulls the rocker nearer to his chair, and rests the slipperless foot on his thigh. He relights his pipe, takes up his book, and rubs softly from ankle to toes as he reads.

She smokes, and watches him, diverting herself by imagining him in the hats of different periods. His is a delicate skinned face, with regular features; the eyes are fine in color and shape, with the luminous clearness of a child's; his pointed beard is soft and curly. She looks at his hand,—a broad, strong hand with capable fingers; the hand of a craftsman, a contradiction to the face with its distinguished delicacy. She holds her own up, with a cigarette poised between the first and second fingers, idly pleased with its beauty of form and delicate, nervous slightness. One speculation chases the other in her quick brain: odd questions as to race arise; she dives into theories as to the why and wherefore of their distinctive natures, and holds a mental debate in which she takes both sides of the question impartially. He has finished his pipe, laid down his book, and is gazing dreamily into space, with his eyes darkened by their long lashes and a look of tender melancholy in their clear depths.

"What are you thinking of?" There is a look of expectation in her quivering nervous little face.

He turns to her, chafing her ankle again. "I was wondering if lob-worms would do for—"

He stops: a strange look of disappointment flits across her face and is lost in an hysterical peal of laughter.

"You are the best emotional check I ever knew," she gasps.

He stares at her in utter bewilderment, and then a slow smile creeps to his eyes and curves the thin lips under his mustache,—a smile at her. "You seem amused, Gypsy!"

She springs out of her chair, and takes book and pipe; he follows the latter anxiously with his eyes until he sees it laid safely on the table. Then she perches herself, resting her knees against one of his legs, while she hooks her feet back under the other.

"Now I am all up, don't I look small?"

He smiles his slow smile. "Yes, I believe you are made of gutta percha."[5]

She is stroking out all the lines in his face with the tip of her finger; then she runs it through his hair. He twists his head half impatiently; she desists.

"I divide all the people in the world," she says, "into those who like their hair played with, and those who don't. Having my hair brushed gives me more pleasure than anything else; it's delicious. I'd *purr* if I knew how. I notice," meditatively, "I am never in sympathy with those who don't like it. I am with those who do; I always get on with them."

"You are a queer little devil!"

"Am I? I shouldn't have thought you would have found out I was the latter at all. I wish I were a man! I believe if I were a man, I'd be a disgrace to my family."

"Why?"

"I'd go on a jolly old spree!"

---

5. Dense elastic material resembling rubber.

He laughs: "Poor little woman! is it so dull?"

There is a gleam of deviltry in her eyes, and she whispers solemnly,—

"Begin with a D," and she traces imaginary letters across his forehead, and end-ing with a flick over his ear, says, "and that is the tail of the y!" After a short silence she queries: "Are you fond of me?" She is rubbing her chin up and down his face.

"Of course I am, don't you know it?"

"Yes, perhaps I do," impatiently; "but I want to be told it. A woman doesn't care a fig for a love as deep as the death-sea and as silent; she wants something that tells her it in little waves all the time. It isn't the *love*, you know, it's the *being loved*; it isn't really the *man*, it's his *loving*!"

"By Jove, you're a rum un!"

"I wish I wasn't, then. I wish I was as commonplace as—You don't tell me any-thing about myself," a fierce little kiss; "you might, even if it were lies. Other men who cared for me told me things about my eyes, my hands, anything. I don't believe you notice."

"Yes I *do*, little one, only I think it."

"Yes, but I don't care a bit for your thinking; if I can't see what's in your head, what good is it to me?"

"I wish I could understand you, dear!"

"I wish to God you could! Perhaps if you were badder and I were gooder we'd meet half-way. *You* are an awfully good old chap; it's just men like you send women like me to the devil!"

"But you are good," kissing her,—"a real good chum! You understand a fellow's weak points; you don't blow him up if he gets on a bit. Why," enthusiastically, "being married to you is like chumming with a chap! Why," admiringly, "do you remember before we were married, when I let that card fall out of my pocket? Why, I couldn't have told another girl about her! she wouldn't have believed that I *was* straight; she'd have thrown me over, and you sent her a quid[6] because she was sick. You are a great little woman!"

"Don't see it!" she is biting his ear. "Perhaps I was a man last time, and some hereditary memories are cropping up in this incarnation!"

He looks so utterly at sea that she must laugh again, and, kneeling up, shuts his eyes with kisses, and bites his chin and shakes it like a terrier in her strong little teeth.

"You imp! was there ever such a woman!"

Catching her wrists, he parts his knees and drops her on to the rug; then perhaps the subtle magnetism that is in her affects him, for he stoops and snatches her up and carries her up and down, and then over to the window, and lets the fading light with its glimmer of moonshine play on her odd face with its tantalizing changes, and his eyes dilate and his color deepens as he crushes her soft little body to him and carries her off to her room.

• • •

Summer is waning, and the harvest is ripe for ingathering, and the voice of the reaping machine is loud in the land. She is stretched on her back on the short, heather-mixed moss at the side of a bog stream. Rod and creel are flung aside, and the

---

6. Slang: a pound.

wanton breeze with the breath of coolness it has gathered in its passage over the murky dykes of black bog-water is playing with the tail-fly, tossing it to and fro with a half threat to fasten it to a prickly spine of golden gorse. Bunches of bog-wool nod their fluffy heads, and through the myriad indefinite sounds comes the regular scrape of a strickle on the scythe of a reaper in a neighboring meadow. Overhead a flotilla of clouds is steering from the south in a northeasterly direction. Her eyes follow them,—old-time galleons, she thinks, with their wealth of snowy sail spread, riding breast to breast up a wide, blue fjord after victory. The sails of the last are rose-flushed, with a silver edge. Someway she thinks of Cleopatra sailing down to meet Antony,[7] and a great longing fills her soul to sail off somewhere too,—away from the daily need of dinner-getting and the recurring Monday with its washing, life with its tame duties and virtuous monotony. She fancies herself in Arabia on the back of a swift steed; flashing eyes set in dark faces surround her, and she can see the clouds of sand swirl, and feel the swing under her of his rushing stride; and her thoughts shape themselves into a wild song,—a song to her steed of flowing mane and satin skin, an uncouth rhythmical jingle with a feverish beat; a song to the untamed spirit that dwells in her. Then she fancies she is on the stage of an ancient theatre, out in the open air, with hundreds of faces upturned toward her. She is gauze-clad in a cobweb garment of wondrous tissue; her arms are clasped by jewelled snakes, and one with quivering diamond fangs coils round her hips; her hair floats loosely, and her feet are sandal-clad, and the delicate breath of vines and the salt freshness of an incoming sea seem to fill her nostrils. She bounds forward and dances, bends her lissome waist, and curves her slender arms, and gives to the soul of each man what he craves, be it good or evil. And she can feel now, lying here in the shade of Irish hills, with her head resting on her scarlet shawl and her eyes closed, the grand, intoxicating power of swaying all these human souls to wonder and applause. She can see herself with parted lips and panting, rounded breasts, and a dancing devil in each glowing eye, sway voluptuously to the wild music that rises, now slow, now fast, now deliriously wild, seductive, intoxicating, with a human note of passion in its strain. She can feel the answering shiver of emotion that quivers up to her from the dense audience, spellbound by the motion of her glancing feet; and she flies swifter and swifter, and lighter and lighter, till the very serpents seem alive with jewelled scintillations. One quivering, gleaming, daring bound, and she stands with outstretched arms and passion-filled eyes, poised on one slender foot, asking a supreme note to finish her dream of motion; and the men rise to a man and answer her, and cheer, cheer till the echoes shout from the surrounding hills and tumble wildly down the crags.

The clouds have sailed away, leaving long feathery streaks in their wake. Her eyes have an inseeing look, and she is tremulous with excitement; she can hear yet that last grand shout, and the strain of that old-time music that she has never heard in this life of hers, save as an inner accompaniment to the memory of hidden things, born with her, not of this time.

And her thoughts go to other women she has known, women good and bad, school friends, casual acquaintances, women workers,—joyless machines for grinding daily corn, unwilling maids grown old in the endeavor to get settled, patient wives

---

7. In Shakespeare's *Antony and Cleopatra*, Cleopatra sails down the Nile on a gilded barge.

who bear little ones to indifferent husbands until they wear out,—a long array. She busies herself with questioning. Have they, too, this thirst for excitement, for change, this restless craving for sun and love and motion? Stray words, half confidences, glimpses through soul-chinks of suppressed fires, actual outbreaks, domestic catastrophes,—how the ghosts dance in the cells of her memory! And she laughs, laughs softly to herself, because the denseness of man, his chivalrous, conservative devotion to the female idea he has created, blinds him, perhaps happily, to the problems of her complex nature. "Ay," she mutters musingly, "the wisest of them can only say we are enigmas; each one of them sets about solving the riddle of the *ewig weibliche*,[8]—and well it is that the workings of our hearts are closed to them, that we are cunning enough or *great* enough to seem to be what they would have us, rather than be what we are. But few of them have had the insight to find out the key to our seeming contradictions,—the why a refined, physically fragile woman will mate with a brute, a mere male animal with primitive passions, and love him; the why strength and beauty appeal more often than the more subtly fine qualities of mind or heart; the why women (and not the innocent ones) will condone sins that men find hard to forgive in their fellows. They have all overlooked the eternal wildness, the untamed primitive savage temperament that lurks in the mildest, best woman. Deep in through ages of convention this primeval trait burns,—an untamable quantity that may be concealed but is never eradicated by culture, the keynote of woman's witchcraft and woman's strength. But it is there, sure enough, and each woman is conscious of it in her truth-telling hours of quiet self-scrutiny; and each woman in God's wide world will deny it, and each woman will help another to conceal it,—for the woman who tells the truth and is not a liar about these things is untrue to her sex and abhorrent to man, for he has fashioned a model on imaginary lines, and he has said, 'So I would have you!' and every woman is an unconscious liar, for so man loves her. And when a Strindberg or a Nietzsche[9] arises and peers into the recesses of her nature and dissects her ruthlessly, the men shriek out louder than the women, because the truth is at all times unpalatable, and the gods they have set up are dear to them—"

"Dreaming, or speering into futurity? You have the look of a seer. I believe you are half a witch!" And he drops his gray-clad figure on the turf; he has dropped his drawl long ago in midsummer.

"Is not every woman that? Let us hope I'm for my friends a white one."

"A-ah! Have you many friends?"

"That is a query! If you mean many correspondents, many persons who send me Christmas cards, or remember my birthday, or figure in my address book,—no."

"Well, grant I don't mean that!"

"Well, perhaps, yes. Scattered over the world, if my death were belled out, many women would give me a tear, and some a prayer; and many men would turn back a page in their memory and give me a kind thought, perhaps a regret, and go back to their work with a feeling of having lost something that they never possessed. I am a creature of moments. Women have told me that I came into their lives just when they needed me; men had no need to tell me, I felt it. People have needed me more

---

8. German: the eternal feminine.
9. August Strindberg, 19th-c. Swedish playwright who wrote stark, psychologically driven dramas; Friedrich Nietzsche, 19th-c. German philosopher famous for his theories of power and tragedy.

than I them. I have given freely whatever they craved from me in the way of understanding or love; I have touched sore places they showed me, and healed them,—but they never got at me. I have been for myself, and helped myself, and borne the burden of my own mistakes. Some have chafed at my self-sufficiency, and have called me fickle,—not understanding that they gave me nothing, and that when I had served them their moment was ended, and I was to pass on. I read people easily, I am written in black letter to most—"

"To your husband?"

"He," quickly,—"we will not speak of him; it is not loyal."

"Do not I understand you a little?"

"You do not misunderstand me."

"That is something."

"It is much!"

"Is it?" searching her face. "It is not one grain of sand in the desert that stretches between you and me, and you are as impenetrable as a sphinx at the end of it. This," passionately, "is my moment, and what have you given me?"

"Perhaps less than other men I have known; but you want less. You are a little like me,—you can stand alone; and yet," her voice is shaking, "have I given you nothing?"

He laughs, and she winces; and they sit silent, and they both feel as if the earth between them is laid with infinitesimal electric threads vibrating with a common pain. Her eyes are filled with tears that burn but don't fall; and she can see his some way through her closed lids, see their cool grayness troubled by sudden fire, and she rolls her handkerchief into a moist cambric ball between her cold palms.

"You have given me something, something to carry away with me,—an infernal want. You ought to be satisfied: I am infernally miserable. You," nearer, "have the most tantalizing mouth in the world when your lips tremble like that. I—What! can you cry? You?"

"Yes, even I can cry!"

"You dear woman!" pause; "and I can't help you?"

"You can't help me; no man can. Don't think it is because you are you I cry, but because you probe a little nearer into the real me that I feel so."

"Was it necessary to say that?" reproachfully; "do you think I don't know it? I can't for the life of me think how you, with that free gypsy nature of yours, could bind yourself to a monotonous country life, with no excitement, no change. I wish I could offer you my yacht; do you like the sea?"

"I love it; it answers one's moods."

"Well, let us play pretending, as the children say. Grant that I could, I would hang your cabin with your own colors, fill it with books (all those I have heard you say you care for), make it a nest as rare as the bird it would shelter. You would reign supreme. When your highness would deign to honor her servant, I would come and humor your every whim. If you were glad, you could clap your hands and order music, and we would dance on the white deck, and we would skim through the sunshine of Southern seas on a spice-scented breeze. You make me poetical. And if you were angry, you could vent your feelings on me, and I would give in and bow my head to your mood. And we would drop anchor, and stroll through strange cities,—go far inland and glean folklore out of the beaten track of everyday tourists; and at night, when the harbor slept, we would sail out through the moonlight over silver seas. You are smiling,—you look so different when you smile; do you like my picture?"

"Some of it!"

"What not?"

"You!"

"Thank you."

"You asked me. Can't you understand where the spell lies? It is the freedom, the freshness, the vague danger, the unknown that has a witchery for me,—ay, for every woman!"

"Are you incapable of affection, then?"

"Of course not. I share," bitterly, "that crowning disability of my sex; but not willingly,—I chafe under it. My God! if it were not for that, we women would master the world! I tell you, men would be no match for us! At heart we care nothing for laws, nothing for systems; all your elaborately reasoned codes for controlling morals or man do not weigh a jot with us against an impulse, an instinct. We learn those things from you,—you tamed, amenable animals; they are not natural to us. It is a wise disposition of Providence that this untamableness of ours is corrected by our affections. We forge our own chains in a moment of softness, and then," bitterly, "we may as well wear them with a good grace. Perhaps many of our seeming contradictions are only the outward evidences of inward chafing. Bah! the qualities that go to make a Napoleon—superstition, want of honor, disregard of opinion, and the eternal I—are oftener to be found in a woman than a man. Lucky for the world, perhaps, that all these attributes weigh as nothing in the balance with the need to love, if she be a good woman; to be loved, if she is of a coarser fibre."

"I never met any one like you; you are a strange woman!"

"No, I am merely a truthful one. Women talk to me—why? I can't say; but always they come, strip their hearts and souls naked, and let me see the hidden folds of their natures. The greatest tragedies I have ever read are child's play to those I have seen acted in the inner life of outwardly commonplace women. A woman must beware of speaking the truth to a man; he loves her the less for it. It is the elusive spirit in her, that he divines but cannot seize, that fascinates and keeps him."

There is a long silence; the sun is waning and the scythes are silent, and overhead the crows are circling,—a croaking, irregular army, homeward bound from a long day's pillage.

She has made no sign, yet so subtilely is the air charged with her that he feels but a few moments remain to him. He goes over and kneels beside her, and fixes his eyes on her odd, dark face. They both tremble, yet neither speaks. His breath is coming quickly, and the bistre[10] stains about her eyes seem to have deepened, perhaps by contrast, as she has paled.

"Look at me!"

She turns her head right round and gazes straight into his face; a few drops of sweat glisten on his forehead.

"You witch woman! what am I to do with myself? Is my moment ended?"

"I think so."

---

10. Brown pigment used in watercolors.

"Lord, what a mouth!"

"Don't! oh, don't!"

"No, I won't. But do you mean it? Am I, who understand your every mood, your restless spirit, to vanish out of your life? You can't mean it! Listen!—are you listening to me? I can't see your face; take down your hands. Go back over every chance meeting you and I have had together since I met you first by the river, and judge them fairly. To-day is Monday: Wednesday afternoon I shall pass your gate, and if—if my moment is ended, and you mean to send me away, to let me go with this weary aching—"

"A-ah!" she stretches out one brown hand appealingly, but he does not touch it. *"Hang something white on the lilac bush!"*

She gathers up creel and rod, and he takes her shawl, and wrapping it round her holds her a moment in it, and looks searchingly into her eyes, then stands back and raises his hat, and she glides away through the reedy grass.

. . .

Wednesday morning she lies watching the clouds sail by. A late rose-spray nods into the open window, and the petals fall every time. A big bee buzzes in and fills the room with his bass note, and then dances out again. She can hear his footstep on the gravel. Presently he looks in over the half window,—

"Get up and come out,—'t will do you good; have a brisk walk!"

She shakes her head languidly, and he throws a great soft, dewy rose with sure aim on her breast.

"Shall I go in and lift you out and put you, 'nighty' and all, into your tub?"

"No!" impatiently. "I'll get up just now."

The head disappears, and she rises wearily and gets through her dressing slowly, stopped every moment by a feeling of faintness. He finds her presently rocking slowly to and fro with closed eyes, and drops a leaf with three plums in it on to her lap.

"I have been watching four for the last week, but a bird, greedy beggar, got one this morning early: try them. Don't you mind, old girl, I'll pour out my own tea!"

She bites into one and tries to finish it, but cannot. "You are a good old man!" she says, and the tears come unbidden to her eyes, and trickle down her cheeks, dropping on to the plums, streaking their delicate bloom.

He looks uneasily at her, but doesn't know what to do; and when he has finished his breakfast he stoops over her chair and strokes her hair, saying, as he leaves a kiss on the top of her head, "Come out into the air, little woman; do you a world of good!"

And presently she hears the sharp thrust of his spade above the bee's hum, leaf rustle, and the myriad late summer sounds that thrill through the air. It irritates her almost to screaming point; there is a practical non-sympathy about it; she can distinguish the regular one, two, three, the thrust, interval, then pat, pat, on the upturned sod. To-day she wants some one, and her thoughts wander to, and she wonders what, the gray-eyed man who never misunderstands her, would say to her. Oh, she wants some one so badly to soothe her; and she yearns for the little mother who is twenty years under the daisies,—the little mother who is a faint memory strengthened by a daguerreotype in which she sits with silk-mittened hands primly crossed on the lap of her moiré gown, a diamond brooch fastening the black-velvet ribbon crossed so stiffly over her lace collar, the shining tender eyes looking steadily out, and her hair in the fashion of fifty-six. How that spade dominates over every sound! and what a sickening pain she has, an odd pain; she never felt it before. Supposing she were to die, she tries to fancy how she would look; they would be sure to plaster her curls down. He might be digging her grave—no, it is the patch where the early peas grew, the peas that were eaten with the twelve weeks' ducklings: she remembers them, little fluffy golden balls with waxen bills, and such dainty paddles,—remembers holding an egg to her ear and listening to it cheep inside before even there was a chip in the shell. Strange how things come to life! What! she sits bolt upright and holds tightly to the chair, and a questioning, awesome look comes over her face; and then the quick blood creeps up through her olive skin right up to her temples, and she buries her face in her hands and sits so a long time.

The maid comes in and watches her curiously, and moves softly about. The look in her eyes is the look of a faithful dog, and she loves her with the same rare fidelity. She hesitates, then goes into the bedroom and stands thoughtfully, with her hands clasped over her breast. She is a tall, thin, flat-waisted woman, with misty blue eyes and a receding chin. Her hair is pretty. She turns as her mistress comes in, with an expectant look on her face. She has taken up a nightgown, but holds it idly.

"Lizzie, had you ever a child?"

The girl's long left hand is ringless; yet she asks it with a quiet insistence, as if she knew what the answer would be, and her odd eyes read her face with an almost cruel steadiness. The girl flushes painfully, and then whitens; her very eyes seem to pale, and her under lip twitches as she jerks out huskily,—

"Yes!"

"What happened to it?"

"It died, M'am."

"Poor thing! Poor old Liz!"

She pats the girl's hand softly, and the latter stands dumbly and looks down at both hands, as if fearful to break the wonder of a caress. She whispers hesitatingly,—

"Have you—have you any little things left?"

And she laughs such a soft, cooing little laugh, like the chirring of a ring-dove, and nods shyly back in reply to the tall maid's questioning look. The latter goes out, and comes back with a flat, red-painted deal box, and unlocks it. It does not hold very much, and the tiny garments are not of costly material; but the two women pore over them as a gem collector over a rare stone. She has a glimpse of thick-crested paper[11] as the girl unties a packet of letters, and looks away until she says tenderly,—

"Look, M'am!"

A little bit of hair inside a paper heart. It is almost white, so silky and so fine that it is more like a thread of bog-wool than a baby's hair; and the mistress, who is a wife, puts her arms round the tall maid, who has never had more than a moral claim to the name, and kisses her in her quick way.

The afternoon is drawing on; she is kneeling before an open trunk, with flushed cheeks and sparkling eyes. A heap of unused, dainty lace-trimmed ribbon-decked cambric garments are scattered around her. She holds the soft, scented web to her cheek and smiles musingly; and then she rouses herself and sets to work, sorting out

---

11. Denoting an aristocratic crest, or motto and coat of arms.

the finest, with the narrowest lace and tiniest ribbon, and puckers her swarthy brows, and measures lengths along her middle finger, and then gets slowly up, as if careful of herself as a precious thing, and half afraid.

"Lizzie!"

"Yes, M'am!"

"Wasn't it lucky they were too fine for every day? They will be so pretty. Look at this one with the tiny valenciennes edging. Why, one nightgown will make a dozen little shirts,—such elfin-shirts as they are too; and Lizzie!"

"Yes, M'am!"

"Just hang it out on the lilac-bush,—mind, the lilac-bush!"

"Yes, M'am!"

"Or, Lizzie, wait: I'll do it myself!"

—1893

Ella D'Arcy
1856?–1939

Ella D'Arcy wrote comparatively little (her exasperated editors sometimes called her "lazy"), but what she did write was influential and widely admired. Originally trained as an artist at the Slade School, D'Arcy turned to literature when her eyesight began to fail. She became the assistant literary editor of *The Yellow Book*, where she published several stories. In spite of this aesthetic affiliation, D'Arcy's stories often have a hard-edged, caustic tone more characteristic of New Women writing. She participated in the many coteries of aesthetic women writers in the 1890s and subsequently moved to Paris, remaining unmarried. "The Pleasure-Pilgrim," originally published in *The Yellow Book* in 1895, shows that the New Woman was devastatingly indecipherable for a traditional Englishman.

The Pleasure-Pilgrim

I

Campbell was on his way to Schloss Altenau,[1] for a second quiet season with his work. He had spent three profitable months there a year ago, and he was hoping now for a repetition of that good fortune. His thoughts outran the train; and long before his arrival at the Hamelin railway station, he was enjoying his welcome by the Ritterhausens, was revelling in the ease and comfort of the old castle, and was contrasting the pleasures of his home-coming—for he looked upon Schloss Altenau as a sort of temporary home—with his recent cheerless experiences of lodging-houses in London, hotels in Berlin, and strange indifferent faces everywhere. He thought with especial satisfaction of the Maynes, and of the good talks Mayne and he would have

---

1. German: Old Castle.

together, late at night, before the great fire in the hall, after the rest of the household had gone to bed. He blessed the adverse circumstances which had turned Schloss Altenau into a boarding-house, and had reduced the Freiherr Ritterhausen to eke out his shrunken revenues by the reception, as paying guests, of English and American pleasure-pilgrims.

He rubbed the blurred window-pane with the fringed end of the strap hanging from it, and, in the snow-covered landscape reeling towards him, began to recognize objects that were familiar. Hamelin could not be far off. . . . In another ten minutes the train came to a standstill.

He stepped down with a sense of relief from the overheated atmosphere of his compartment into the cold bright February afternoon, and saw through the open station doors one of the Ritterhausen carriages awaiting him, with Gottlieb in his second-best livery on the box. Gottlieb showed every reasonable consideration for the Baron's boarders, but had various methods of marking his sense of the immense abyss separating them from the family. The use of his second-best livery was one of these methods. Nevertheless, he turned a friendly German eye up to Campbell, and in response to his cordial "Guten Tag, Gottlich. Wie geht's? Und die Herrschaften?"[2] expressed his pleasure at seeing the young man back again.

While Campbell stood at the top of the steps that led down to the carriage and the Platz, looking after the collection of his luggage and its bestowal by Gottlieb's side, he became aware of two persons, ladies, advancing towards him from the direction of the Wartsaal.[3] It was surprising to see any one at any time in Hamelin station. It was still more surprising when one of these ladies addressed him by name.

"You are Mr. Campbell, are you not?" she said. "We have been waiting for you to go back in the carriage together. When we found this morning that there was only half an hour between your train and ours, I told the Baroness it would be perfectly absurd to send to the station twice. I hope you won't mind our company?"

The first impression Campbell received was of the magnificent apparel of the lady before him; it would have been noticeable in Paris or Vienna—it was extravagant here. Next, he perceived that the face beneath the upstanding feathers and the curving hat-brim was that of so very young a girl as to make the furs and velvets seem more incongruous still. But the sense of incongruity vanished with the intonation of her first phrase, which told him she was an American. He had no standards for American conduct. It was clear that the speaker and her companion were inmates of the Schloss.

He bowed, and murmured the pleasure he did not feel. A true Briton, he was intolerably shy; and his heart sank at the prospect of a three-mile drive with two strangers who evidently had the advantage of knowing all about him, while he was in ignorance of their very names. As he took his place opposite to them in the carriage, he unconsciously assumed a cold, blank stare, pulling nervously at his moustache, as was his habit in moments of discomposure. Had his companions been British also, the ordeal of the drive must have been a terrible one; but these young American ladies showed no sense of embarrassment whatever.

---

2. German: "Good day, Gottlieb. How are you? And the master and mistress?"
3. German: waiting-room.

"We've just come back from Hanover," said the girl who had already spoken to him. "I go over once a week for a singing lesson, and my little sister comes along to take care of me."

She turned a narrow, smiling glance from Campbell to her little sister, and then back to Campbell again. She had red hair, freckles on her nose, and the most singular eyes he had ever seen; slit-like eyes, set obliquely in her head, Chinese fashion.

"Yes, Lulie requires a great deal of taking care of," assented the little sister sedately, though the way in which she said this seemed to imply something less simple than the words themselves. The speaker bore no resemblance to Lulie. She was smaller, thinner, paler. Her features were straight, a trifle peaked; her skin sallow; her hair of a nondescript brown. She was much less gorgeously dressed. There was even a suggestion of shabbiness in her attire, though sundry isolated details of it were handsome too. She was also much less young; or so, at any rate, Campbell began by pronouncing her. Yet presently he wavered. She had a face that defied you to fix her age. Campbell never fixed it to his own satisfaction, but veered in the course of that drive (as he was destined to do during the next few weeks) from point to point up and down the scale from eighteen to thirty-five. She wore a spotted veil, and beneath it a pince nez, the lenses of which did something to temper the immense amount of humorous meaning which lurked in her gaze. When her pale prominent eyes met Campbell's, it seemed to the young man that they were full of eagerness to add something at his expense to the stores of information they had already garnered up. They chilled him with misgivings; there was more comfort to be found in her sister's shifting, red-brown glances.

"Hanover is a long way to go for lessons," he observed, forcing himself to be conversational. "I used to go there myself about once a week, when I first came to Schloss Altenau, for tobacco, or note-paper, or to get my hair cut. But later on I did without, or contented myself with what Hamelin, or even the village, could offer me."

"Nannie and I," said the young girl, "meant to stay only a week at Altenau, on our way to Hanover, where we were going to pass the winter; but the Castle is just too lovely for anything." She raised her eyelids the least little bit as she looked at him, and such a warm and friendly gaze shot out, that Campbell was suddenly thrilled. Was she pretty, after all? He glanced at Nannie; she, at least, was indubitably plain. "It's the very first time we've ever stayed in a castle," Lulie went on; "and we're going to remain right along now, until we go home in the spring. Just imagine living in a house with a real moat, and a drawbridge, and a Rittersaal,[4] and suits of armor that have been actually worn in battle! And oh, that delightful iron collar and chain! You remember it, Mr. Campbell? It hangs right close to the gateway on the courtyard side. And you know, in old days the Ritterhausens used it for the punishment of their serfs. There are horrible stories connected with it. Mr. Mayne can tell you them. But just think of being chained up there like a dog! So wonderfully picturesque."

"For the spectator perhaps," said Campbell, smiling. "I doubt if the victim appreciated the picturesque aspect of the case."

With this Lulie disagreed. "Oh, I think he must have been interested," she said. "It must have made him feel so absolutely part and parcel of the Middle Ages. I persuaded Mr. Mayne to fix the collar round my neck the other day; and though it was

---

4. German: knights' hall.

very uncomfortable, and I had to stand on tiptoe, it seemed to me that all at once the courtyard was filled with knights in armor, and crusaders, and palmers, and things; and there were flags flying and trumpets sounding; and all the dead and gone Ritterhausens had come down from their picture-frames, and were walking about in brocaded gowns and lace ruffles."

"It seemed to require a good deal of persuasion to get Mr. Mayne to unfix the collar again," said the little sister. "How at last did you manage it?"

But Lulie replied irrelevantly: "And the Ritterhausens are such perfectly lovely people, aren't they, Mr. Campbell? The old Baron is a perfect dear. He has such a grand manner. When he kisses my hand I feel nothing less than a princess. And the Baroness is such a funny, busy, delicious little round ball of a thing. And she's always playing bagatelle, isn't she? Or else cutting up skeins of wool for carpet-making." She meditated a moment. "Some people always *are* cutting things up in order to join them together again," she announced, in her fresh drawling young voice.

"And some people cut things up, and leave other people to do the reparation," commented the little sister, enigmatically.

And meantime the carriage had been rattling over the cobble-paved streets of the quaint mediæval town, where the houses stand so near together that you may shake hands with your opposite neighbor; where allegorical figures, strange birds and beasts, are carved and painted over the windows and doors; and where to every distant sound you lean your ear to catch the fairy music of the Pied Piper, and at every street corner you look to see his tatterdemalion form with the frolicking children at his heels.

Then the Weser bridge was crossed, beneath which the ice-floes jostled and ground themselves together, as they forced their way down the river; and the carriage was rolling smoothly along country roads, between vacant snow-decked fields.

Campbell's embarrassment began to wear off. Now that he was getting accustomed to the girls, he found neither of them awe-inspiring. The red-haired one had a simple childlike manner that was charming. Her strange little face, with its piquant irregularity of line, its warmth of color, began to please him. What though her hair was red, the uncurled wisp which strayed across her white forehead was soft and alluring; he could see soft masses of it tucked up beneath her hat-brim as she turned her head. When she suddenly lifted her red-brown lashes, those queer eyes of hers had a velvety softness too. Decidedly, she struck him as being pretty—in a peculiar way. He felt an immense accession of interest in her. It seemed to him that he was the discoverer of her possibilities. He did not doubt that the rest of the world called her plain, or at least odd-looking. He, at first, had only seen the freckles on her nose, her oblique-set eyes. He wondered now what she thought of herself, how she appeared to Nannie. Probably as a very ordinary little girl; sisters stand too close to see each other's qualities. She was too young to have had much opportunity of hearing flattering truths from strangers; and, besides, the average stranger would see nothing in her to call for flattering truths. Her charm was something subtle, out-of-the-common, in defiance of all known rules of beauty. Campbell saw superiority in himself for recognizing it, for formulating it; and he was not displeased to be aware that it would always remain caviare to the multitude.

The carriage had driven through the squalid village of Dürrendorf, had passed the great Ritterhausen barns and farm-buildings, on the tie-beams of which are carved Bible texts in old German; had turned in at the wide-open gates of Schloss Altenau, where Gottlieb always whipped up his horses to a fast trot. Full of feeling both for the pocket and the dignity of the Ritterhausens, he would not use up his beasts in unnecessary fast driving. But it was to the credit of the family that he should reach the Castle in fine style. And so he thundered across the drawbridge, and through the great archway pierced in the north wing, and over the stones of the cobbled courtyard, to pull up before the door of the hall, with much clattering of hoofs and a final elaborate whip-flourish.

II

"I'm jolly glad to have you back," Mayne said, that same evening, when, the rest of the boarders having retired to their rooms, he and Campbell were lingering over the hall-fire for a talk and smoke. "I've missed you awfully, old chap, and the good times we used to have here. I've often meant to write to you, but you know how one shoves off letter-writing day after day, till at last one is too ashamed of one's indolence to write at all. But tell me—you had a pleasant drive from Hamelin? What do you think of our young ladies?"

"Those American girls? But they're charming," said Campbell, with enthusiasm. "The red-haired one is particularly charming."

At this Mayne laughed so strangely that Campbell questioned him in surprise. "Isn't she charming?"

"My dear chap," Mayne told him, "the red-haired one, as you call her, is the most remarkably charming young person I've ever met or read of. We've had a good many American girls here before now—you remember the good old Choate family, of course—they were here in your time, I think?—but we've never had anything like this Miss Lulie Thayer. She is something altogether unique."

Campbell was struck with the name. "Lulie—Lulie Thayer," he repeated. "How pretty it is!" And, full of his great discovery, he felt he must confide it to Mayne, at least. "Do you know," he went on, "*she* is really very pretty too? I didn't think so at first, but after a bit I discovered that she is positively quite pretty—in an odd sort of way."

Mayne laughed again. "Pretty, pretty!" he echoed in derision. "Why, *lieber Gott im Himmel*,[5] where are your eyes? Pretty! The girl is beautiful, gorgeously beautiful; every trait, every tint, is in complete, in absolute harmony with the whole. But the truth is, of course, we've all grown accustomed to the obvious, the commonplace; to violent contrasts; blue eyes, black eyebrows, yellow hair; the things that shout for recognition. You speak of Miss Thayer's hair as red. What other color would you have, with that warm, creamy skin? And then, what a red it is! It looks as though it had been steeped in red wine."

"Ah, what a good description!" said Campbell, appreciatively. "That's just it— steeped in red wine."

"Though it's not so much her beauty," Mayne continued. "After all, one has met beautiful women before now. It's her wonderful generosity, her complaisance. She doesn't keep her good things to herself. She doesn't condemn you to admire from a distance."

---

5. German: "dear God in Heaven."

"How do you mean?" Campbell asked, surprised again.

"Why, she's the most egregious little flirt I've ever met. And yet, she's not exactly a flirt, either. I mean she doesn't flirt in the ordinary way. She doesn't talk much, or laugh, or apparently make the least claims on masculine attention. And so all the women like her. I don't believe there's one, except my wife, who has an inkling as to her true character. The Baroness, as you know, never observes anything. *Seigneur Dieu!*[6] if she knew the things I could tell her about Miss Lulie! For I've had opportunities of studying her. You see, I'm a married man, and not in my first youth, and the looker-on generally gets the best view of the game. But you, who are young and charming and already famous—we've had your book here, by the by, and there's good stuff in it—you're going to have no end of pleasant experiences. I can see she means to add you to her ninety-and-nine other spoils; I saw it from the way she looked at you at dinner. She always begins with those velvety red-brown glances. She began that way with March and Prendergast and Willie Anson, and all the men we've had here since her arrival. The next thing she'll do will be to press your hand under the tablecloth."

"Oh, come, Mayne, you're joking," cried Campbell, a little brusquely. He thought such jokes in bad taste. He had a high ideal of Woman, an immense respect for her; he could not endure to hear her belittled, even in jest. "Miss Thayer is refined and charming. No girl of her class would do such things."

"But what is her class? Who knows anything about her? All we know is that she and her uncanny little friend—her little sister, as she calls her, though they're no more sisters than you and I are—they're not even related—all we know is, that she and Miss Dodge (that's the little sister's name)—arrived here one memorable day last October from the Kronprinz Hotel at Waldeck-Pyrmont. By the by, it was the Choates, I believe, who told her of the Castle—hotel acquaintances—you know how travelling Americans always cotton to each other. And we've picked up a few little auto and biographical notes from her and Miss Dodge since. *Zum Beispiel,*[7] she's got a rich father somewhere away back in Michigan, who supplies her with all the money she wants. And she's been travelling about since last May: Paris, Vienna, the Rhine, Düsseldorf, and so on here. She must have had some rich experiences, by Jove, for she's done everything. Cycled in Paris: you should see her in her cycling costume,[8] she wears it when the Baron takes her out shooting—she's an admirable shot by the way, an accomplishment learned, I suppose, from some American cow-boy; then in Berlin she did a month's hospital nursing; and now she's studying the higher branches of the Terpsichorean art. You know she was in Hanover to-day. Did she tell you what she went for?"

"To take a singing lesson," said Campbell, remembering the reason she had given.

"A singing lesson! Do you sing with your legs? A dancing lesson, *mein lieber.*[9] A dancing lesson from the ballet-master of the Hof Theater. She could deposit a kiss on your forehead with her foot, I don't doubt. I must ask her if she can do the *grand écart*[10] yet." And when Campbell, in astonishment, wondered why on earth

---

6. French: "Lord God!"
7. German: "For example."
8. Cycling was associated with rebellious, experimental young women.
9. German: "my dear."
10. French: "great leap."

she should wish to learn such things, "Oh, to extend her opportunities," Mayne explained, "and to acquire fresh sensations. She's an adventuress. Yes, an adventuress, but an end-of-the-century one. She doesn't travel for profit, but for pleasure. She has no desire to swindle her neighbor, but to amuse herself. And she's clever; she's read a good deal; she knows how to apply her reading to practical life. Thus, she's learned from Herrick not to be coy; and from Shakespeare that sweet-and-twenty is the time for kissing and being kissed.[11] She honors her masters in the observance. She was not in the least abashed when, one day, I suddenly came upon her teaching that damned idiot, young Anson, two new ways of kissing."

Campbell's impressions of the girl were readjusting themselves completely, but for the moment he was unconscious of the change. He only knew that he was partly angry, partly incredulous, and inclined to believe that Mayne was chaffing him.

"But Miss Dodge," he objected, "the little sister, she is older; old enough to look after her friend. Surely she could not allow a young girl placed in her charge to behave in such a way—"

"Oh, that little Dodge girl," said Mayne contemptuously. "Miss Thayer pays the whole shot, I understand, and Miss Dodge plays gooseberry, sheep-dog, jackal, what you will. She finds her reward in the other's cast-off finery. The silk blouse she was wearing tonight, I've good reason for remembering, belonged to Miss Lulie. For, during a brief season, I must tell you, my young lady had the caprice to show attentions to your humble servant. I suppose my being a married man lent me a factitious fascination. But I didn't see it. That kind of girl doesn't appeal to me. So she employed Miss Dodge to do a little active canvassing. It was really too funny; I was coming in one day after a walk in the woods; my wife was trimming bonnets, or had neuralgia, or something. Anyhow, I was alone, and Miss Dodge contrived to waylay me in the middle of the courtyard. 'Don't you find it vurry dull walking all by yourself?' she asked me; and then, blinking up in her strange little short-sighted way—she's really the weirdest little creature—'Why don't you make love[12] to Lulie?' she said; 'you'd find her vurry charming.' It took me a minute or two to recover presence of mind enough to ask her whether Miss Thayer had commissioned her to tell me so. She looked at me with that cryptic smile of hers; 'She'd like you to do so, I'm sure,' she finally remarked, and pirouetted away. Though it didn't come off, owing to my bashfulness, it was then that Miss Dodge appropriated the silk 'waist;' and Providence, taking pity on Miss Thayer's forced inactivity, sent along March, a young fellow reading for the army, with whom she had great doings. She fooled him to the top of his bent; sat on his knee; gave him a lock of her hair, which, having no scissors handy, she burned off with a cigarette taken from his mouth; and got him to offer her marriage. Then she turned round and laughed in his face, and took up with a Dr. Weber, a cousin of the Baron's, under the other man's very eyes. You never saw anything like the unblushing coolness with which she would permit March to catch her in Weber's arms."

"Come," Campbell protested again, "aren't you drawing it rather strong?"

"On the contrary, I'm drawing it mild, as you'll discover presently for yourself; and then you'll thank me for forewarning you. For she makes love—desperate love,

---

11. 17th-c. Cavalier poet Robert Herrick urged "gather ye rosebuds while ye may" in "To the Virgins to Make Much of Time." Shakespeare wrote "then come and kiss me, sweet and twenty / Youth's a stuff will not endure," in *Twelfth Night* 2.2.
12. Flirt.

mind you—to every man she meets. And goodness knows how many she hasn't met in the course of her career, which began presumably at the age of ten, in some 'Amur'can' hotel or watering-place. Look at this." Mayne fetched an alpenstock[13] from a corner of the hall; it was decorated with a long succession of names, which, ribbon-like, were twisted round and round it, carved in the wood. "Read them," insisted Mayne, putting the stick in Campbell's hands. "You'll see they're not the names of the peaks she has climbed, or the towns she has passed through; they're the names of the men she has fooled. And there's room for more; there's still a good deal of space, as you see. There's room for yours."

Campbell glanced down the alpenstock—reading here a name, there an initial, or just a date—and jerked it impatiently from him on to a couch. He wished with all his heart that Mayne would stop, would talk of something else, would let him get away. The young girl had interested him so much; he had felt himself so drawn towards her; he had thought her so fresh, so innocent. But Mayne, on the contrary, was warming to his subject, was enchanted to have some one to listen to his stories, to discuss his theories, to share his cynical amusement.

"I don't think, mind you," he said, "that she is a bit interested herself in the men she flirts with. I don't think she gets any of the usual sensations from it, you know. My theory is, she does it for mere devilry, for a laugh. Or, and this is another theory, she is actuated by some idea of retribution. Perhaps some woman she was fond of— her mother even—who knows?—was badly treated at the hands of a man. Perhaps this girl has constituted herself the Nemesis for her sex, and goes about seeing how many masculine hearts she can break, by way of revenge. Or can it be that she is simply the newest development of the New Woman—she who in England preaches and bores you, and in America practises and pleases? Yes, I believe she's the American edition, and so new that she hasn't yet found her way into fiction. She's the pioneer of the army coming out of the West, that's going to destroy the existing scheme of things and rebuild it nearer to the heart's desire."

"Oh, damn it all, Mayne," cried Campbell, rising abruptly, "why not say at once that she's a wanton, and have done with it? Who wants to hear your rotten theories?" And he lighted his candle without another word, and went off to bed.

III

It was four o'clock, and the Baron's boarders were drinking their afternoon coffee, drawn up in a semicircle round the hall fire. All but Campbell, who had carried his cup away to a side-table, and, with a book open beside him, appeared to be reading assiduously. In reality he could not follow a line of what he read; he could not keep his thoughts from Miss Thayer. What Mayne had told him was germinating in his mind. Knowing his friend as he did, he could not on reflection doubt his word. In spite of much superficial cynicism, Mayne was incapable of speaking lightly of any young girl without good cause. It now seemed to Campbell that, instead of exaggerating the case, Mayne had probably understated it. He asked himself with horror, what had this girl not already known, seen, permitted? When now and again his eyes travelled over perforce to where she sat, her red head leaning against Miss Dodge's

---

13. A stout stick for walking.

knee, and seeming to attract to, and concentrate upon itself all the glow of the fire, his forehead set itself in frowns, and he returned to his book with an increased sense of irritation.

"I'm just sizzling up, Nannie," Miss Thayer presently complained, in her child-like, drawling little way; "this fire is too hot for anything." She rose and shook straight her loose tea-gown, a marvellous plush and lace garment created in Paris, which would have accused a duchess of wilful extravagance. She stood smiling round a moment, pulling on and off with her right hand a big diamond ring which decorated the left. At the sound of her voice Campbell had looked up, and his cold, unfriendly eyes encountered hers. He glanced rapidly past her, then back to his book. But she, undeterred, with a charming sinuous movement and a frou-frou of trailing silks, crossed over towards him. She slipped into an empty chair next his.

"I'm going to do you the honor of sitting beside you, Mr. Campbell," she said sweetly.

"It's an honor I've done nothing whatever to merit," he answered, without looking at her, and turned a page.

"The right retort," she approved; "but you might have said it a little more cordially."

"I don't feel cordial."

"But why not? What has happened? Yesterday you were so nice."

"Ah, a good deal of water has run under the bridge since yesterday."

"But still the river remains as full," she told him smiling, "and still the sky is as blue. The thermometer has even risen six degrees."

"What did you go into Hanover for yesterday?" Campbell suddenly asked her.

She flashed him a comprehending glance from half-shut eyes. "I think men gossip a great deal more than women," she observed, "and they don't understand things either. They try to make all life suit their own pre-conceived theories. And why, after all, should I not wish to learn dancing thoroughly? There's no harm in that."

"Only, why call it singing?" Campbell inquired.

Miss Thayer smiled. "Truth is so uninteresting!" she said, and paused. "Except in books. One likes it there. And I wanted to tell you, I think your books perfectly lovely. I know them, most all. I've read them away home. They're very much thought of in America. Only last night I was saying to Nannie how glad I am to have met you, for I think we're going to be great friends, aren't we, Mr. Campbell? At least, I hope so, for you can do me so much good, if you will. Your books always make me feel real good; but you yourself can help me much more."

She looked up at him with one of her warm, narrow red-brown glances, which yesterday would have thrilled his blood, and to-day merely stirred it to anger.

"You overestimate my abilities," he said coldly; "and, on the whole, I fear you will find writers a very disappointing race. You see, they put their best into their books. So not to disillusion you too rapidly"—he rose—"will you excuse me? I have some work to do." And he left her sitting there alone.

But he did no work when he got to his room. Whether Lulie Thayer was actually present or not, it seemed that her influence was equally disturbing to him. His mind was full of her: of her singular eyes, her quaint intonation, her sweet, seductive praise. Twenty-four hours ago such praise would have been delightful to him: what young author is proof against appreciation of his books? Now Campbell simply told himself that she laid the butter on too thick; that it was in some analogous manner she had flattered up March, Anson, and all the rest of the men that Mayne had spoken of. He supposed it was the first step in the process by which he was to be fooled, twisted round her finger, added to the list of victims who strewed her conquering path. He had a special fear of being fooled. For beneath a somewhat supercilious exterior, the dominant note of his character was timidity, distrust of his own merits; and he knew he was single-minded—one-idea'd almost—if he were to let himself go, to get to care very much for a woman, for such a girl as this girl, for instance, he would lose himself completely, be at her mercy absolutely. Fortunately, Mayne had let him know her character. He could feel nothing but dislike for her,—disgust, even. And yet he was conscious how pleasant it would be to believe in her innocence, in her candor. For she was so adorably pretty; her flower-like beauty grew upon him; her head, drooping a little on one side when she looked up, was so like a flower bent by its own weight. The texture of her cheeks, her lips, was delicious as the petals of a flower. He found he could recall with perfect accuracy every detail of her appearance; the manner in which the red hair grew round her temples; the way in which it was loosely and gracefully fastened up behind with just a single tortoise-shell pin. He recollected the suspicion of a dimple that shadowed itself in her cheek when she spoke, and deepened into a delicious reality every time she smiled. He remembered her throat: her hands, of a beautiful whiteness, with pink palms and pointed fingers. It was impossible to write. He speculated long on the ring she wore on her engaged finger. He mentioned this ring to Mayne the next time he saw him.

"Engaged? very much so, I should say. Has got a *fiancé* in every capital of Europe probably. But the ring-man is the *fiancé en titre*.[14] He writes to her by every mail, and is tremendously in love with her. She shows me his letters. When she's had her fling, I suppose, she'll go back and marry him. That's what these little American girls do, I'm told; sow their wild oats here with us, and settle down into *bonnes ménagères*[15] over yonder. Meanwhile, are you having any fun with her? Aha, she presses your hand? The 'gesegnete Mahlzeit'[16] business after dinner is an excellent institution, isn't it? She'll tell you how much she loves you soon; that's the next move in the game."

But so far she had done neither of these things, for Campbell gave her no opportunities. He was guarded in the extreme, ungenial; avoiding her even at the cost of civility. Sometimes he was downright rude. That especially occurred when he felt himself inclined to yield to her advances. For she made him all sorts of silent advances, speaking with her eyes, her sad little mouth, her beseeching attitude. And then one evening she went further still. It occurred after dinner in the little green drawing-room. The rest of the company were gathered together in the big drawing-room beyond. The small room has deep embrasures to the windows. Each embrasure holds two old faded green velvet sofas in black oaken frames, and an oaken oblong table stands between them. Campbell had flung himself down on one of these sofas in the corner nearest the window. Miss Thayer, passing through the room, saw him, and sat down opposite. She leaned her elbows on the table, the laces of her sleeves falling away from her round white arms, and clasped her hands.

14. French: "titular or official fiancé."
15. French: "good household managers."
16. German: "good appetite," a traditional mealtime greeting.

"Mr. Campbell, tell me what have I done? How have I vexed you? You have hardly spoken two words to me all day. You always try to avoid me." And when he began to utter evasive banalities, she stopped him with an imploring "Ah, don't! I love you. You know I love you. I love you so much I can't bear you to put me off with mere phrases."

Campbell admired the well-simulated passion in her voice, remembered Mayne's prediction, and laughed aloud.

"Oh, you may laugh," she said, "but I am serious. I love you, I love you with my whole soul." She slipped round the end of the table, and came close beside him. His first impulse was to rise; then he resigned himself to stay. But it was not so much resignation that was required as self-mastery, cool-headedness. Her close proximity, her fragrance, those wonderful eyes raised so beseechingly to his, made his heart beat.

"Why are you so cold?" she said. "I love you so; can't you love me a little too?"

"My dear young lady," said Campbell, gently repelling her, "what do you take me for? A foolish boy like your friends Anson and March? What you are saying is monstrous, preposterous. Ten days ago you'd never even seen me."

"What has length of time to do with it?" she said. "I loved you at first sight."

"I wonder," he observed judicially, and again gently removed her hand from his, "to how many men you have not already said the same thing."

"I've never meant it before," she said quite earnestly, and nestled closer to him, and kissed the breast of his coat, and held her mouth up towards his. But he kept his chin resolutely high, and looked over her head.

"How many men have you not already kissed ever since you've been here?"

"But there've not been many here to kiss!" she exclaimed naïvely.

"Well, there was March; you kissed him?"

"No, I'm quite sure I didn't."

"And young Anson; what about him? Ah, you don't answer! And then the other fellow—what's his name—Prendergast—you've kissed him?"

"But, after all, what is there in a kiss?" she cried ingenuously. "It means nothing, absolutely nothing. Why, one has to kiss all sorts of people one doesn't care about."

Campbell remembered how Mayne had said she had probably known strange kisses since the age of ten; and a wave of anger with her, of righteous indignation, rose within him.

"To me," said he, "to all right-thinking people, a young girl's kisses are something pure, something sacred, not to be offered indiscriminately to every fellow she meets. Ah, you don't know what you have lost! You have seen a fruit that has been handled, that has lost its bloom? You have seen primroses, spring flowers, gathered and thrown away in the dust? And who enjoys the one, or picks up the others? And this is what you remind me of,—only you have deliberately, of your own perverse will, tarnished your beauty, and thrown away all the modesty, the reticence, the delicacy, which make a young girl so infinitely dear. You revolt me, you disgust me. I want nothing from you but to be let alone. Kindly take your hands away, and let me go."

He shook her roughly off and got up, then felt a moment's curiosity to see how she would take the repulse.

Miss Thayer never blushed; had never, he imagined, in her life done so. No faintest trace of color now stained the warm pallor of her rose-leaf skin; but her eyes filled up with tears. Two drops gathered on the under lashes, grew large, trembled an instant, and then rolled unchecked down her cheeks. Those tears somehow put him in the wrong, and he felt he had behaved brutally to her for the rest of the night.

He began to seek excuses for her: after all, she meant no harm; it was her upbringing, her *genre*; it was a *genre* he loathed; but perhaps he need not have spoken so harshly. He thought he would find a more friendly word for her next morning; and he loitered about the Mahlsaal,[17] where the boarders come in to breakfast, as in an hotel, just when it suits them, till past eleven; but she did not come. Then, when he was almost tired of waiting, Miss Dodge put in an appearance, in a flannel wrapper, and her front hair twisted up in steel pins.

Campbell judged Miss Dodge with even more severity than he did Miss Thayer; there was nothing in this weird little creature's appearance to temper justice with mercy. It was with difficulty that he brought himself to inquire after her friend.

"Lulie is sick this morning," she told him. "I've come down to order her some broth. She couldn't sleep any last night, because of your unkindness to her. She's vurry, vurry unhappy about it."

"Yes, I'm sorry for what I said. I had no right to speak so strongly, I suppose. But I spoke strongly because I feel strongly. However, there's no reason why my bad manners should make her unhappy."

"Oh, yes, there's vurry good reason," said Miss Dodge. "She's vurry much in love with you."

Campbell looked at the speaker long and earnestly to try and read her mind; but the prominent blinking eyes, the cryptic physiognomy, told him nothing.

"Look here," he said brusquely, "what's your object in trying to fool me like this? I know all about your friend. Mayne has told me. She has cried 'Wolf' too often before to expect to be believed now."

"But, after all," argued Miss Dodge, blinking more than ever behind her glasses, "the wolf did really come at last, you know; didn't he? Lulie is really in love this time. We've all made mistakes in our lives, haven't we? But that's no reason for not being right at last. And Lulie has cried herself sick."

Campbell was a little shaken. He went and repeated the conversation to Mayne, who laughed derisively.

"Capital, capital!" he cried; "excellently contrived. It quite supports my latest theory about our young friend. She's an actress, a born comédienne. She acts always, and to every one: to you, to me, to the Ritterhausens, to the Dodge girl—even to herself when she is quite alone. And she has a great respect for her art; she'll carry out her rôle, *coûte que coûte*,[18] to the bitter end. She chooses to pose as in love with you; you don't respond; the part now requires that she should sicken and pine. Consequently she takes to her bed, and sends her confidante to tell you so. Oh, it's colossal, it's *famos*."

IV

"If you can't really love me," said Lulie Thayer,—"and I know I've been a bad girl and don't deserve that you should,—at least, will you allow me to go on loving you?"

---

17. German: banqueting hall.
18. French: "cost what it may."

She walked by Campbell's side, through the solitary uncared-for park of Schloss Altenau. It was three weeks later in the year, and the spring feeling in the air stirred the blood. All round were signs and tokens of spring: in the busy gayety of bird and insect life; in the purple flower-tufts which thickened the boughs of the ash-trees; in the young green things pushing up pointed heads from amidst last season's dead leaves and grasses. The snow-wreaths, that had for so long decorated the distant hills, were shrinking perceptibly away beneath the strong March sunshine.

There was every invitation to spend one's time out of doors, and Campbell passed long mornings in the park, or wandering through the woods and the surrounding villages. Miss Thayer often accompanied him. He never invited her to do so, but when she offered him her company, he could not, or at least did not, refuse it.

"May I love you? Say," she entreated.

"'Wenn ich Dich liche, was geht's Dich an?'"[19] he quoted lightly. "Oh, no, it's nothing to me, of course. Only don't expect me to believe you,—that's all."

This disbelief of his was the recurring decimal of their conversation. No matter on what subject they began, they always ended thus. And the more sceptical he showed himself, the more eager she became. She exhausted herself in endeavors to convince him.

They had reached the corner in the park where the road to the Castle turns off at right angles from the road to Dürrendorf. The ground rises gently on the park-side to within three feet of the top of the boundary wall, although on the other side there is a drop of at least twenty feet. The broad wall-top makes a convenient seat. Campbell and the girl sat down on it; at his last words she wrung her hands together in her lap.

"But how can you disbelieve me?" she cried, "when I tell you I love you, I adore you? When I swear it to you? And can't you see for yourself? Why, every one at the Castle sees it."

"Yes, you afford the Castle a good deal of unnecessary amusement. And that shows you don't understand what love really is. Real love is full of delicacy, of reticences, and would feel itself profaned if it became the jest of the servants' hall."

"It's not so much my love for you, as your rejection of it, which has made me talked about."

"Isn't it rather on account of the favors you've lavished on all my predecessors?"

She sprang to her feet, and walked up and down in agitation.

"But after all, surely, mistakes of that sort are not to be counted against us? I did really think I was in love with Mr. March. Willie Anson doesn't count. He's an American too, and he understands things. Besides, he is only a boy. And how could I know I should love you before I had met you? And how can I help loving you now I have? You're so different from other men. You're good, you're honorable, you treat women with respect. Oh, I do love you so, I do love you! Ask Nannie if I don't."

The way in which Campbell shrugged his shoulders clearly expressed the amount of reliance he would place on any testimony from Miss Dodge. He could not forget her "Why don't you make love to Lulie?" addressed to a married man. Such a want of principle argued an equal want of truth.

---

19. German: "If I love you, what business is that of yours?" from Johann Wolfgang von Goethe's *Wilhelm Meister's Apprenticeship* (1795–96).

Lulie seemed on the brink of weeping.

"I wish I were dead," she struggled to say; "life's impossible if you won't believe me. I don't ask you any longer to love me. I know I've been a bad girl, and I don't deserve that you should; but if you won't believe that I love you I don't want to live any longer."

Campbell confessed to himself that she acted admirably, but that the damnable iteration of the one idea became monotonous. He sought a change of subject. "Look there," he said, "close by the wall, what's that jolly little blue flower? It's the first I've seen this year."

He showed her where, at the base of the wall, a solitary blossom rose above a creeping stem and glossy dark green leaves.

Lulie, all smiles again, picked it with childlike pleasure. "Oh, if that's the first you've seen." she cried, "you can take a wish. Only you mustn't speak until some one asks you a question."

She began to fasten it in his coat. "It's just as blue as your eyes," she said. "You have such blue and boyish eyes, you know. Stop, stop, that's not a question," and, seeing that he was about to speak, she laid her finger across his mouth. "You'll spoil the charm."

She stepped back, folded her arms, and seemed to dedicate herself to eternal silence; then relenting suddenly,—

"Do you believe me?" she entreated.

"What's become of your ring?" Campbell answered beside the mark. He had noticed its absence from her finger while she had been fixing in the flower.

"Oh, my engagement's broken."

Campbell asked how the *fiancé* would like that.

"Oh, he won't mind. He knows I only got engaged because he worried so. And it was always understood between us that I was to be free if I ever met any one I liked better."

Campbell asked her what sort of fellow this accommodating *fiancé* was.

"Oh, he's all right. And he's very good too. But he's not a bit clever, and don't let us talk about him. He makes me tired."

"But you're wrong," Campbell told her, "to throw away a good, a sincere affection. If you really want to reform and turn over a new leaf, as you are always telling me you do, I should advise you to go home and marry him."

"What, when I'm in love with you?" she cried reproachfully. "Would that be right?"

"It's going to rain," said Campbell. "Didn't you feel a drop just then? And it's getting near lunch-time. Shall we go in?"

Their shortest way led through the little cemetery in which the departed Ritterhausens lay at peace in the shadow of their sometime home.

"When I die the Baron has promised I shall be buried here," said Lulie pensively; "just here, next to his first wife. Don't you think it would be lovely to be buried in a beautiful, peaceful baronial graveyard, instead of in some horrid crowded city cemetery?"

Mayne met them as they entered the hall. He noticed the flower in his friend's coat. "Ah, my dear chap, been treading the—periwinkle path of dalliance, I see? How many desirable young men have I not witnessed led down the same broad way by the same seductive lady! Always the same thing; nothing changes but the flower according to the season."

When Campbell reached his room he took the poor periwinkle out of his coat, and threw it away into the stove.

And yet, had it not been for Mayne, Miss Thayer might have triumphed after all; might have convinced Campbell of her passion, or have added another victim to her long list. But Mayne had set himself as determinedly to spoil her game as she was bent on winning it. He had always the cynical word, the apt reminiscence ready, whenever he saw signs on Campbell's part of surrender. He was very fond of Campbell. He did not wish him to fall a prey to the wiles of this little American siren. He had watched her conduct in the past with a dozen different men; he genuinely believed she was only acting in the present.

Campbell, for his part, began to experience an ever-increasing exasperation in the girl's presence. Yet he did not avoid it; he could not well avoid it, she followed him about so persistently; but his speech would overflow with bitterness towards her. He would say the cruellest things; then, remembering them when alone, be ashamed of his brutalities. But nothing he said ever altered her sweetness of temper or weakened the tenacity of her purpose. His rebuffs made her beautiful eyes run over with tears, but the harshest of them never elicited the least sign of resentment. There would have been something touching as well as comic in this dog-like humility, which accepted everything as welcome at his hands, had he not been imbued with Mayne's conviction that it was all an admirable piece of acting. Or when for a moment he forgot the histrionic theory, then invariably there would come a chance word in her conversation which would fill him with cold rage. They would be talking of books, travels, sport, what not, and she would drop a reference to this man or to that. So-and-so had taken her to Bullier's, she had learned skating with this other; Duroy, the *prix de Rome*[20] man, had painted her as Hebe; Franz Weber had tried to teach her German by means of Heine's poems.[21] And he got glimpses of long vistas of amourettes played in every State in America, in every country of Europe, since the very beginning, when, as a mere child, elderly men, friends of her father's, had held her on their knee and fed her on sweetmeats and kisses. It was sickening to think of, it was pitiable. So much youth and beauty tarnished; the possibility for so much good thrown away. For if one could only blot out her record, forget it, accept her for what she chose to appear, a more endearing companion no man could desire.

V

It was a wet afternoon, the rain had set in at midday with a gray determination which gave no hopes of clearing. Nevertheless, Mayne had accompanied his wife and the Baroness into Hamelin. "To take up a servant's character, and expostulate with a recalcitrant dressmaker," he explained to Campbell, and wondered what women would do to fill up their days were it not for the perennial crimes of dressmakers and domestic servants. He himself was going to look in at the English Club; wouldn't Campbell come too? There was a fourth seat in the carriage. But Campbell was in no social mood; he felt his temper going all to pieces; a quarter of an hour of Mrs. Mayne's society would have brought on an explosion. He thought he must be alone;

---

20. A prize given to the best painting every year at the Paris Conservatory.
21. German Romantic poet Heinrich Heine (1797–1856).

and yet when he had read for half an hour in his room he wondered vaguely what Lulie was doing; he had not seen her since luncheon. She always gave him her society when he could very well dispense with it, but on a wet day like this, when a little conversation would be tolerable, of course she stayed away. Then there came down the long Rittersaal the tapping of high heels, and a well-known knock at his door. He went over and opened it; Miss Thayer, in the plush and lace tea-gown, fronted him serenely.

"Am I disturbing you?" she asked; and his mood was so capricious that, now she was standing there on his threshold, he thought he was annoyed at it. "It's so dull," she said, persuasively. "Nannie's got a sick headache, and I daren't go downstairs, or the Baron will annex me to play Halma. He always wants to play Halma on wet days."

"And what do you want to do?" said Campbell, leaning against the doorpost, and letting his eyes rest on the strange piquant face in its setting of red hair.

"To be with you, of course."

"Well," said he, coming out and closing the door, "I'm at your service. What next?"

They strolled together through the room, and listened to the falling rain. The Rittersaal occupies all the space on the first floor that the hall and four drawing-rooms do below. Wooden pillars support the ceiling, dividing the apartment lengthwise into a nave and two aisles. Down the middle are long tables used for ceremonial banquets. Six windows look into the courtyard, and six out over the open country. The centre pane of each window is emblazoned with a Ritterhausen shield. Between the windows hang family portraits, and the sills are broad and low, and cushioned in faded velvet.

"How it rains!" said Lulie, stopping before one of the south windows; "why, you can't see anything for the rain, and there's no sound at all but the rain either. I like it. It makes me feel as though we had the whole world to ourselves."

Then, "Say, what would you like to do?" she asked him. "Shall I fetch over my pistols, and we'll practise with them? You've no notion how well I can shoot. We couldn't hurt anything here, could we?"

Campbell thought they might practise there without inconvenience, and Lulie, bundling up the duchess tea-gown over one arm, danced off in very unduchess-like fashion to fetch the case.

It was a charming little box of cedar-wood and mother-o'-pearl, lined with violet velvet; and two tiny revolvers lay inside, hardly more than six inches long, with silver engraved handles.

"I won them in a bet," she observed complacently, "with the Hon. Billie Thornton. He's an Englishman, you know, the son of Lord Thornton. I knew him in Washington two years ago last fall. He bet I couldn't hit a three-cent piece at twenty yards, and I did. Aren't they perfectly sweet? Now, can't you contrive a target?"

Campbell went back to his room, drew out a rough diagram, and pasted it down on to a piece of cardboard. Then this was fixed up by means of a penknife driven into the wood of one of the pillars, and Campbell, with his walking-stick laid down six successive times, measured off the distance required, and set a chalk mark across the floor. Lulie took the first shot. She held the little weapon up at arm's length above her head, the first finger stretched out along the barrel; then, dropping her hand sharply so that the finger pointed straight at the butt, she pulled the trigger with the third. There was a sharp report, the tiny smoke film; and when Campbell went up to examine results, he found she had only missed the very centre by a quarter of an inch.

Lulie was exultant. "I don't seem to have got out of practice any," she remarked. "I'm so glad, for I used to be a very good shot. It was Hiram P. Ladd who taught me. He's the crack shot of Montana. What! you don't know Hiram P.? Why, I should have supposed every one must have heard of him. He had the next ranche to my Uncle Samuel's, where I used to go summers, and he made me do an hour's pistol practice every morning after bathing. It was he who taught me swimming too—in the river."

"Damnation," said Campbell under his breath, then shot in his turn, and shot wide. Lulie made another bull's-eye, and after that a white. She urged Campbell to continue, which he sullenly did, and again missed.

"You see I don't come up to your Hiram P. Ladd," he remarked savagely, and put the pistol down, and walked over to the window. He stood with one foot on the cushioned seat, staring out at the rain, and pulling moodily at his moustache.

Lulie followed him, nestled up to him, lifted the hand that hung passive by his side, put it round her waist and held it there. Campbell, lost in thought, let it remain so for a second; then remembered how she had doubtless done this very same thing with other men in this very room. All her apparently spontaneous movements, he told himself, were but the oft-used pieces in the game she played so skilfully.

"Let go," he said, and flung himself down on the window-seat, looking up at her with darkening eyes.

She, sitting meekly in the other corner, folded her offending hands in her lap.

"Do you know your eyes are not a bit nice when you're cross?" she said; "they seem to become quite black."

He maintained a discouraging silence.

She looked over at him meditatively.

"I never cared a bit for Hiram P., if that's what you mean," she remarked presently.

"Do you suppose I care a button if you did?"

"Then why did you leave off shooting, and why won't you talk to me?"

He vouchsafed no reply.

Lulie spent some moments immersed in thought. Then she sighed deeply, and recommenced on a note of pensive regret:—

"Ah, if I'd only met you sooner in life, I should be a very different girl."

The freshness which her quaint, drawling enunciation lent to this time-dishonored formula made Campbell smile, till, remembering all its implications, his forehead set in frowns again.

Lulie continued her discourse. "You see," said she, "I never had any one to teach me what was right. My mother died when I was quite a child, and my father has always let me do exactly as I pleased, so long as I didn't bother him. Then I've never had a home, but have always lived around in hotels and places: all winter in New York or Washington, and summers out at Longbranch or Saratoga. It's true we own a house in Detroit, on Lafayette Avenue, that we reckon as home, but we don't ever go there. It's a bad sort of life for a girl, isn't it?" she pleaded.

"Horrible," he said mechanically. His mind was at work. The loose threads of his angers, his irritations, his desires, were knitting themselves together, weaving themselves into something overmastering and definite.

The young girl meanwhile was moving up towards him along the seat, for the effect which his sharpest rebuke produced on her never lasted more than four minutes. She now again possessed herself of his hand, and, holding it between her own, began to caress it in childlike fashion, pulling the fingers apart and closing them again, spreading it palm downwards on her lap, and laying her own little hand over it, to exemplify the differences between them. He let her be; he seemed unconscious of her proceedings.

"And then," she continued, "I've always known a lot of young fellows who've liked to take me round; and no one ever objected to my going with them, and so I went. And I enjoyed it, and there wasn't any harm in it, just kissing, and making believe, and nonsense. But I never really cared for one of them. I can see that now, when I compare them with you,—when I compare what I felt for them with what I feel for you. Oh, I do love you so much," she murmured; "don't you believe me?" She lifted his hand to her lips and covered it with kisses.

He pulled it roughly from her. "I wish you'd give over such fool's play," he told her, got up, walked to the table, came back again, stood looking at her with sombre eyes and dilating pupils.

"But I do love you," she repeated, rising and advancing towards him.

"For God's sake, drop that damned rot," he cried out with sudden fury. "It wearies me, do you hear? it sickens me. Love, love, my God, what do you know about? Why, if you really loved me, really loved any man,—if you had any conception of what the passion of love is, how beautiful, how fine, how sacred,—the mere idea that you could not come to your lover fresh, pure, untouched, as a young girl should, that you had been handled, fondled, and God knows what besides, by this man and the other,—would fill you with such horror for yourself, with such supreme disgust, you would feel yourself so unworthy, so polluted . . . that . . . that . . . by God! you would take up that pistol there, and blow your brains out!"

Lulie seemed to find the idea quite entertaining. She picked the pistol up from where it lay in the window, examined it critically, with her pretty head drooping on one side, and then sent one of her long, red-brown caressing glances up towards him.

"And suppose I were to," she asked lightly, "would you believe me then?"

"Oh, . . . well . . . then, perhaps! If you showed sufficient decency to kill yourself, perhaps I might," said he, with ironical laughter. His ebullition had relieved him; his nerves were calmed again. "But nothing short of that would ever make me."

With her little tragic air, which seemed to him so like a smile disguised, she raised the weapon to the bosom of her gown. There came a sudden, sharp crack, a tiny smoke-film. She stood an instant swaying slightly, smiling certainly, distinctly outlined against the background of rain-washed window, of gray falling rain, the top of her head cutting in two the Ritterhausen escutcheon. Then all at once there was nothing at all between him and the window; he saw the coat-of-arms entire; but a motionless, inert heap of plush and lace, and fallen wine-red hair, lay at his feet upon the floor.

"Child, child, what have you done?" he cried with anguish, and, kneeling beside her, lifted her up, and looked into her face.

When from a distance of time and place Campbell was at last able to look back with some degree of calmness on the catastrophe, the element in it which stung him most keenly was this: he could never convince himself that Lulie had really loved him after all. And the only two persons who had known them both and the circumstances of the case sufficiently well to have resolved his doubts one way or the other, held diametrically opposite views.

"Well, listen, then, and I'll tell you how it was," Miss Nannie Dodge had said to him impressively, the day before he left Schloss Altenau forever. "Lulie was tremendously, terribly in love with you. And when she found that you wouldn't care about her, she didn't want to live any more. As to the way in which it happened, you don't need to reproach yourself for that. She'd have done it, anyhow; if not then, why, later. But it's all the rest of your conduct to her that was so mean, your cold, cruel, complacent British unresponsiveness. I guess you'll never find another woman to love you as Lulie did. She was just the darlingest, the sweetest, the most loving girl in the world."

Mayne, on the other hand, summed it up in this way: "Of course, old chap, it's horrible to think of; horrible, horrible, horrible! I can't tell you how badly I feel about it. For she was a gorgeously beautiful creature. That red hair of hers—Good Lord! You won't come across such hair as that again in a lifetime. But, believe me, she was only fooling with you. Once she had you in her hunting-noose, once her buccaneering instincts satisfied, and she'd have chucked you as she did all the rest. As to her death, I've got three theories,—no, two,—for the first being that she compassed it in a moment of genuine emotion, we may dismiss, I think, as quite untenable. The second is, that it arose from pure misadventure. You had both been shooting, hadn't you? Well, she took up the pistol and pulled the trigger from mere mischief, to frighten you, and quite forgetting one barrel was still loaded. And the third is, it was just her histrionic sense of the fitness of things. The rôle she had played so long and so well now demanded a sensational finale in the centre of the stage. And it's the third theory I give the preference to. She was the most consummate little actress I ever met."

—1895

Mabel E. Wotton
1863–1927

This short-story writer was best known for *Day-Books* (1896), published by John Lane in the Keynote Series devoted to promising women writers. She wrote one novel, *A Girl Diplomatist* (1892), which was roundly panned. Its failure left her embittered about authorship and publishing. "The Fifth Edition" (from *Day-Books*) shows a typical New Woman awareness of literature as a business, with its marketing ploys, multiple editions, and obsession with sales. Although this new professionalism assisted many New Women who were able to get paid work at the new magazines, "The Fifth Edition" shows how women writers could be victimized due to their ignorance of business matters and ladylike reluctance to ask for money. Nor is the story entirely fictional; although Wotton has imagined these particular characters, arrangements in which obscure women ghost-wrote fiction for more famous male authors did indeed occur in the 1890s.

The Fifth Edition

His afternoon had not been a success. Miss Elliott, whom he particularly wanted to see, had not been "at home",[1] which was the more vexing as she knew he intended to call; and an overzealous friend had posted him a paper containing a paragraph which had greatly annoyed him, and which otherwise he might not have seen. So when he bethought himself that he was near Maxwell's rooms, he instantly resolved to look him up, and see if the young actor could not give him a stall somewhere or other for that night. He had an intense hatred of even a passing discomfort, and he wanted something fresh to think about.

Maxwell's rooms were in Museum Street, and Leyden had been in them so often, that when he found the street door ajar, he unceremoniously pushed it open, and walked up to the second floor. Probably the small maid-of-all-work had gone to post a letter, or to a near shop, and it was useless ringing a bell which would not be answered.

Once in the room the first thing that struck him was that Maxwell must have been tidying-up,—the next, that the transformation was too complete to be so interpreted. The numberless photographs which, grimed with dust, were wont to adorn the mantelpiece and the top of the hanging book-shelf which was always guiltless of books, were now conspicuous by their absence. The stacks of newspapers, which Leyden used to complain made locomotion difficult, had wholly vanished, together with the pipe-racks and the tobacco jars. The familiar furniture seemed set at more convenient angles, a few good engravings had been hung on the walls, and a work-basket yawned on the windowsill. On the table was a pot of daffodils, and a book. It was evident that Maxwell had at last fulfilled his weekly threat, and had betaken himself and his chattels elsewhere. It was equally evident that the room was now the property of a woman.

The intruder looked about him with approving eyes. It was all very quiet and restful, he thought, and the place had acquired a certain self-respecting atmosphere which results from turning a lodging into a home.

Wondering idly what manner of woman she was, he had turned to go, when the whim seized him to glance at the name of the paper-covered volume she had been reading. *Franklyn Leyden* looked boldly up at him from the title-page. It was one of his own books.

Does one require to be abnormally vain to glean pleasure from so slight a matter? Leyden, at all events, being by temperament depressed or elated by trifles too insignificant to weigh with other men, was vastly pleased with his little discovery; and when, farthermore, he noticed that some of his especially pet passages has been singled out for marginal marking, the thin lips, which the annoyances of the afternoon had drawn into a straight line, relaxed into their ordinary curves of weak good-nature. He felt that something pleasant was about to happen, when he caught the soft rustle of a woman's gown in the adjoining room, and when the folding-doors opened, and Maxwell's successor came suddenly upon her unexpected guest, he feigned a momentary unconsciousness of her presence.

She, for her part, gave a gasp of surprise, possibly of fright, and Leyden turned round instantly, hat in one hand, book in the other.

---

1. An excuse used by people who wanted to evade visitors.

"Pray forgive my intrusion," he began, in his most dulcet tones, though the situation lost most of its charm so soon as he faced her. She was old enough to have mothered the girl he had unwittingly pictured. "I came up unannounced to call on my friend Maxwell, who used to lodge here until quite recently. Can you tell me what has happened to him? I had no idea he had moved."

She only stared at him instead of replying. Into her cheeks there came the slow-growing, lovely flush of a woman who has retained the pure colouring of her otherwise lost youth.

"You are . . . You must be . . . Forgive me, but surely you are Mr. Leyden?" she said, at last.

The tone hurried, then lagged, as the words stumbled over each other in her eagerness.

"I have seen pictures of you . . . every one has seen them . . . and I love . . . I reverence your work. Won't you . . . Won't you stop a little while? It is not my fault I am not Mr. Maxwell."

The glorious colour still flooding her face, and the ill-chosen, stammering words, were more than incense to Franklyn Leyden. It was for this he worked, and wrote, and had his somewhat indiscriminating being; it was for the attempt to baulk him of what he had grown to consider his due, that he could have strangled the paragraphist of that afternoon; and it was for the sake of her genuine hero-worship that he now forgave this woman her forty years and the lines on her careworn face, and cheerfully consented to do her bidding.

"Not Maxwell? No; that is my good fortune," he assured her. "You will think me very impertinent if I tell you the truth, but I was so charmed with the peaceful little home into which I had wandered, that I was quite longing to see its owner. You are," he turned to the fly-leaf of the novel, "you are Miss Suttaby?"

"Yes, I am Janet Suttaby." She still stood by the inner room where she had paused on first seeing him. "I will make enquiries about your friend. I know some gentleman left here on Saturday, and I think that was the name."

"We will find out presently," Leyden returned. He put down what he was holding, and pulled forward a chair. "Can't we have our talk first? It was curious, wasn't it, that you should recognise me? The pictures must be very like."

She surveyed him gravely as he leaned back in his seat, a fair-haired giant with china-blue eyes, and large hands which were extraordinarily white and mobile. When they had nothing else to work upon, the left was habitually fingering the lappet of his coat.

"You are younger than I thought," she told him.

She still looked at him as if he were some god who had dropped from another planet, but her nervousness was decreasing.

"What drew me first to your book was its deep knowledge of suffering. I thought you much older, to have lived through so much."

"Perhaps I am, actually, if with Bailey you 'count time by hearthrobs,'"[2] he said gently, while inwardly he was cogitating as to "what the deuce she meant."

Nothing amazed him so much about "Wrecked" as the number of times he had been told how he had suffered. He could only explain it as a fresh witness to the

---

2. Poet Philip James Bailey (1816–1905).

extreme faithfulness with which he had reproduced that poor chap in Algiers of whom he had made copy.

"Tell me the especial points. Ah, yes, do tell me. Has sorrow visited you too?"

From the exceeding diffidence with which she answered him, he gathered that she had seldom been asked so directly personal a question. This was quite easy to understand, he acknowledged, for, now that the flush had gone, it was undeniable that Miss Suttaby was really a plain person. She was also uninteresting, which was worse, or at least he knew she would be found uninteresting by most people; and he recalled Kingsley's contention that it takes a noble soul to see beauty in an ordinary careworn face.[3] For his own part, Miss Suttaby did interest him, and he found the pale face attractive.

She told him a little of her life,—the barest outlines merely, and even these were dragged from her, not indeed unwillingly, but as from one who was unaccustomed to talk of herself at all. Possibly she had never had time for our modern employment of thinking herself out, and appraising and cataloguing herself; possibly no one had ever cared to listen.

She was the daughter of a well-to-do farmer, who dying had left a second family to her charge, young, and cursed with the seeds of the lung trouble their mother had bequeathed them. Her life had been spent on these youngsters, whom she had tended, and watched, and slaved for, only to lose them one after another as they grew out of their teens. Bertie had lingered the longest, and Bertie had died last year.

Undoubtedly Franklyn Leyden made an admirable audience. Your good things might bore him, but your sad ones never, averred his friends, and in their whole-hearted enthusiasm they rarely noticed that all his kindnesses and all his considera-tion were called forth by what he saw, by what affected him personally. His best friend might be dying, and he would give him a wide berth for fear of a heart-ache; but if he came upon a little child who had tripped in the street, it would be impos-sible for him to pass it without attempted consolation. The child's wailing would have worried him else.

So betrayed by his curiosity in connection with the book into hearing something of the troubles of this stranger, he was speedily and very genuinely concerned about them.

"I am so sorry! So very heartily sorry!" was his comment, and Janet Suttaby found herself murmuring grateful thanks.

She had recognised the sincerity of the tone, and few of us, thank God! question that deeper sincerity, or the lack of it, which the tone may hide.

By the time he went away they both felt that they knew more about each other than a dozen mere ordinary meetings could have told them; and if on her side at least this impression was quite wrong, that did not detract at all from its pleasure.

"I shall come and see you again quite soon," he said, as they shook hands.

If he had been parting from Miss Elliott he knew he should have added, "if I may", but one soon catches the trick of how to bow from a pedestal, and with many men it is learned in an hour.

"Thursday or Friday. H'm. Yes. I will come in on Thursday."

It chanced, however, that Thursday, when it came, brought a pleasanter engage-ment, and it was not until a day or two later that he went to Museum Street. The

---

3. Charles Kingsley (1819–75), Victorian clergyman, author, and poet.

result of which alteration in dates was to teach him the means by which Miss Suttaby earned her livelihood. She wrote.

"But not what *you* would understand by writing. There is no art about it," she said ingenuously, when he accused her of keeping the fact a secret. "I just string things together for bread and butter, and they take them in little cheap-looking papers of which you have probably never heard. Here is the latest."

She pulled a weekly paper from under the pile of manuscript. It was one of the many serious-minded publications where religion, as understood by the particular sect the proprietor favours, is made palatable to every one but his staff.

"They give me seven-and-six a thousand, and I generally have to alter one-third, while they cut out another." Miss Suttaby explained. "But I know it is foolish to mind, for if I were fit for the magazines I should be paid more of course."

"Meanwhile, you should not buy daffodils."

"I don't in meat weeks. Daffodils mean bread and coffee; but I would rather. I am very strong."

Leyden picked up the paper.

"Do you mind if I have a cigarette? I will smoke and read this, and you shall get on with your work. You can't before me? Oh, nonsense! I am going to make myself quite comfortable and at home, and you'll get quite used to me in a minute or two."

The story proved far better than he had expected. The plot was hardly worth the very inferior type in which it was printed; but there were delicate little touches here and there in the working out, and a fair amount of originality was shown in the depicting of an old farmer who was represented in the rather blurred woodcut as a London dandy in the prime of life. It was difficult to make the right amount of allowance for editorial restrictions, but if she were given a free hand she would do well, he decided. Possibly she might achieve something really fine.

Then, because the easy-chair was comfortable, and to turn to his companion would have necessitated shifting his position, he left her to her writing for a bit longer, and began to think about his own affairs.

The book,—that confounded book!—how on earth was he to get it written? Two years ago he had been one of that band of young men whose names and productions are apt to become indistinctly glorious under the generic title of that of "our younger writers". He had tried his 'prentice hand at some small plays preparatory to taking the dramatic world by storm when he should be in the vein; and he had turned out two books of verse which not only sold as poems, but sold well. His publisher, who had seen too many versifiers perhaps to be especially impressed by this one, always declared that the soft voice and the white gesticulating hands were more responsible for the success than were the lines themselves; but as he only aired these opinions in private no harm was done, and certainly it was no fault of Leyden's that his personality was a good advertisement. Added to these slender pillars was the solid background of press work.

This had been his modest position when he had written "Wrecked", but the book had dragged him several rungs up the literary ladder, and he was now a person whom a certain set of aspiring nobodies used to point out to each other at first-nights and other society functions, and whom the real somebodies tolerated in a good-humoured fashion as a hanger-on who might speedily become one of themselves.

In other words, his first novel had contained such real promise that the majority were enthusiastic: the minority awaited fruition. They wanted to see what his second story would be like, said divers of the critics. If Mr. Franklyn Leyden were wise he would comprehend that "Wrecked" could only make an ephemeral reputation. If he wanted it sustained he must follow it up with something more equally written, and of more strength.

With this verdict Franklyn Leyden perfectly agreed. Indeed, he went farther, and told himself precisely wherein lay his weakness. He could not create. No one seemed to have discovered this as yet, for his critical powers were good, and his receptivity enormous; but unless some such chance came to him as that which had come during his fortnight's stay in Algiers, he knew that the book the reviewers wanted would never get written. Of course, to use Miss Suttaby's phrase, he could "string things together" to a required length, but he knew perfectly that if he could not improve upon "Wrecked", it would be far better for him to leave well severely alone.

Recalling it all as he sat quietly smoking, and watching the opposite houses through half-closed lids, he felt as if he almost owed Ned Jermyn a grudge for having decoyed him into his present position. The poor fellow had been dying at the hotel, when a chance had brought the two together, and possibly because he was weak and companionless, but more probably because of the other's intense sympathy of manner, he had told Leyden his life.

"It is a bit tragic, isn't it?" he had asked, with the indifference which besets a man who knows he will soon have ended his difficulties. "I started with the ten talents of the parable, but I've made an even bigger wreck of my life than the chap who had only one. You might do worse than tip me into one of your books some day, eh, Leyden?"

And Leyden, considering the wisdom of the self-mocking suggestion, had taken him at his word, and immediately upon his return to England, he had "tipped" poor Ned Jermyn, with all his sins and sorrows, into manuscript, and from manuscript they had emerged into print as soon after Jermyn's death as could be conveniently arranged. He had written it at a white heat, and the follies and the repentances . . . "People always talk as if repentance implied remorse," said the sick man querulously. "I don't regret what I've gone through. I am only sorry I did not pull it off better"; . . . the darkened room, with the glaring sunlight outside glinting through a broken bit in the wooden shutters; the weary voice, and the inert hands, lying open on the coverlet, had all found faithful reproduction. Jermyn had been a lonely man, and reticent, so he said; and it was extremely unlikely that anyone who knew one side of his character, or one part of his life, would know anything of any other. An alteration of names and places afforded an extra safety, though after all, if the truth were discovered, it could not possibly matter to him, Leyden told himself. He had the man's permission, and everything depended on the fashion of narration. He did not think one iota the less highly of himself that purely original work was beyond him. It did not happen to be his especial forte, that was all. Only, of course, the lack of it was awkward, when it came to the question of a second novel.

"Deucedly awkward!" he repeated, mentally, and turned round at last to survey Miss Suttaby.

"I am afraid you have finished some time ago. I seem to have missed the sound of your pen."

"Yes; some little time. I did not want to disturb you."

He looked at her gratefully. He had always understood that women of the class from which she sprang put on their best clothes in which to receive guests, and that being taken by surprise rendered them miserable. Yet here was Miss Suttaby in the painfully shabby serge she had worn when he had first seen her; and it did not appear to occur to her to deplore the fact, or to conceal the ink-stain on her finger. Unwilling to relinquish his pre-conceived theories, he settled in his own mind that her mother must have come of gentle blood, and have married beneath her; while aloud he thanked her warmly for allowing him to be happy in his own way.

". . . This is quite a little haven of refuge. The restfulness of it makes me terribly selfish," he added, and watched to see if such obvious underrating of himself would bring a show of that lovely colour which had gratified him the time before. That she uttered no verbal disclaimer to vulgarise it, added to his pleasure. "You look tired," he said, solicitously, wondering the while what other chord he could touch upon to obtain so instantaneous a response.

Every man knows the satisfaction of telling a good story when he can confidently count upon an appreciative laugh; and this feeling, which is perhaps mentally akin to the physical experience of a successful hunter, had been abnormally developed by Franklyn Leyden. It interested him if he were shut into a railway carriage with a complete stranger, to imagine of what mirth, for instance, or of what anger the man were capable; and then he would back himself within a given time to test the aptness of his theorising. The result of which apparently harmless piece of vanity was that he had grown to look upon his fellow-beings as so many pegs on which to hang his own emotions through the skilful drawing out of theirs; and it was largely owing to the fact that Winifred Elliott had declined to be viewed in this light, that their friendship had recently betrayed a tendency towards friction. At one time he had had an idea of marrying her, since she was quite the nicest girl . . . as a rule that was, of course, not when she contradicted . . . whom he knew; and in his heart he was attracted as strongly towards the class of ritual and ease and plenty, as are many of that class to the denizens of Bohemia. That idea had not died, though it was not prominently to the fore just at present, but meanwhile Miss Suttaby's "reverence" made a pleasing change, and it fortified him in his resolution to give his girl-friend time to miss him, and then to write and tell him of the miss.

When Miss Suttaby owned that he was right, and that she was very tired, he proposed they should go for a drive, and, growing keener as she demurred, finally gained his way, and went out to fetch a hansom.

"You are good enough to think highly of me, so you must let me do some little thing to live up to the position," he said, gaily.

His spirits had risen. He threw off all thought of his own worries, and of the unwritten book, and devoted himself to his companion.

"Can we go straight along Oxford Street? Why, of course we can! I feel that, too, that there is no point in driving towards Hampstead,[4] because one never walks there. In Oxford Street you can feel every inch of the way, 'Ah, how often I have trudged you!' and your cab becomes a coach and four by comparison . . . If you don't like the sunset glinting straight into your eyes, you must screw yourself into a sheltered angle . . . You do like it? I am so glad, for, do you know, so do I! It seems to me

---

4. Suburb that still retained a comparatively rural feeling—especially when compared to the major London thoroughfare, Oxford Street.

as wicked to shut out the sunshine as the sound of a little child's laughter. The day is sure to come when you will pine for them both."

Miss Suttaby drew a long breath. She seemed literally to be drinking in the soft spring breezes.

"I—I think this is *lovely*," she said. "I had never seen a famous writer until I saw you, and—please don't laugh!—I have never been in a cab until this afternoon."

"Never been in a cab?"

"Not a hansom. When Bertie and I first came to London we took a four-wheeler to our lodgings, because of the luggage, and since then it has always been omnibuses or walking."

"Nor seen a writer?"

She shook her head.

"Except in the Reading-Room[5] perhaps, but then I did not know who they were."

"Well, I never!" Leyden's astonishment vented itself in a prolonged stare. "Miss Suttaby, we must positively shake hands at once. You are more refreshing than April itself. I am glad that the cab, at all events, is a good specimen of its kind."

She hardly heard him as she leaned forward in undisguised enjoyment.

"How mauve the pavements look against the road. I never noticed that before. And aren't there quantities of flower-sellers? I wish I could give them, or someone, a happy hour in return for the one you are giving me."

"You shouldn't wish that. You should just enjoy it."

She looked round at him with a little laugh. It was the first he had heard from her, and it was musical.

"You are joking. The cream of the pleasure is the passing it on. Tonight I shall go upstairs to a sick girl on the top storey, and tell her of the colouring, and the wind which blows to-day as it used to blow over our fields. And of how it feels to be in the streets, and yet not to be tired, and not to be intent on getting somewhere else."

"And of me?" asked Franklyn Leyden. "See! We are nearing the park. Shall you tell her of me?"

It seemed a trick of Miss Suttaby's that she seldom answered questions which patently answered themselves. Her candid eyes spoke instead.

Later on, by way of amusing her, he began to talk of his fellow-workers, but this was hardly a success, and Leyden instantly felt that it was so, and desisted. He did not want to set them also on little pinnacles in her estimation, or his own height might thereby be lessened, and he could not tell her anecdotes, which, though possibly true, hardly tended to present them in a heroic light, when she met the attempt with such hurt wonderment.

"But *you* could not think that. You must be quoting. You always see the best in everybody."

He was nettled, albeit flattered.

"We may raise an altar to Art, Miss Suttaby, but neither you nor I can insist that only the worthiest shall be altar-servers. Many of them have shirked their apprenticeship, and the consequences are as disastrous as I tell you."

---

5. Main room of the British Library, where many writers worked.

He was not quite sure what he meant, though he thought it sounded well. But he had often found that women made a beautiful translation from a very imperfect original, and he waited for her answer, knowing it would furnish the keynote to what she believed she had discovered in him.

"Yes, I see," she said thoughtfully. They were on their return journey by now; the sunlight had faded and the wind was growing chill. "You mean that unless Life has taught you servitude at her other altars,—at those of duty and self-sacrifice, and conquered longings, perhaps especially,—one should not dare approach to the high altar of Art. Of necessity one would have no fruits to lay upon it. Yes, it is a beautiful idea, and I quite see what you mean."

"Exactly," said Franklyn Leyden.

After that he saw her continually, since one must have somewhere to spend odd hours, and the friendship grew apace. From the first she had interested him, and the interest deepened as he formed whimsical theories concerning her.

Physically, he knew she was ageing long before her time. For her there would be no Saint Martin's summer[6] to her days, when the audacities of youth should mellow into a middle age, which to many is as captivating, and to all far more gracious. Here there would be no tender dalliance with Time, for pressing anxiety and sharp actual need were already drawing upon her those gifts of furrowed cheeks and full-veined hands which he usually holds in patient reserve.

Yet this was merely physical; while in startling contrast to it, there looked out at him through the steadfast eyes, with their environing network of wrinkles, the girlish soul which circumstance had never allowed to grow.

The fancy proved arrestive. She had never had a lover in her life,—she told him so simply when the subject in its generalities came up between them one day in talk,—and the amazing candour of her gaze confirmed this statement. No woman's eyes, or so Leyden complacently told himself, as one who was a past master on such matters, no woman's eyes could have retained such absolute simplicity if they had ever dealt in the coquettish glances of youth, or had ever tried, and failed, to meet their lover in the first shy stages of her wooing. Something of the old sweetness and the old pain would always linger, ran his silent communings, and memories would make them their abiding place.

Despite the stretch of years between them, the temptation assailed him to flash into those eyes the love-light their serenity had never known, but strong though it was, he resisted it, applauding himself immensely for his self-denial, and offering a pious thanksgiving that he "was not blackguard enough" to initiate so absorbing a study. After all, his judgment may not have been so wrong, for when all is said and done, such a matter is probably one of degree, and being the man he was, that he still contrived to leave her peace undisturbed, may doubtless be counted unto him for righteousness.

On other points he held there was no need for scruple. There must be a multitude of tones in her voice which had never been brought out, and which corresponded to the capacities in her which lay dormant. There must be a whole gamut of delicious laughter which with her lay dumb, but which with other women

---

6. A period of mild late autumn weather.

stretches from the soft cooing of babyhood to the suppressed chuckle of quite old age. Had she ever laughed from a gleeful sense of pulsing blood? or because skies were blue and grass was green? She never seemed to have had any individual existence at all, since with her it had always been bound up with and dominated by "the others".

Leyden set himself to liberate the imprisoned powers, and was rewarded in a fashion which was quaintly refreshing. It was as if one should rescue withered roses of a bygone summer from between the pages of an old book, and placing them in water, should find them suddenly a-bloom with fragrance and beauty.

It was about this time that he asked her if she would care to show him any of her manuscripts. He might possibly be able to procure her better payment than she usually received. At all events he could try. He made the offer in pure good nature, but was secretly dismayed and inclined to back out of it, when she handed him a tattered pile of foolscap with the remark that she had submitted it to all the papers for which she worked, but that they would not even accept it on the ordinary terms of cutting and scoring what they pleased, and merely paying for the mutilated remainder.

"I am afraid it is very long; but if they took it as it is, it would mean ten pounds, and . . ."

"I understand," said Leyden, kindly. "I'll try to read it to-night; and you must not feel depressed about it. You are so absurdly humble-minded that it is quite possible you have not soared high enough in your efforts to place it, and that that is the reason it always comes back. Good-bye, Miss Suttaby. I will let you know very soon."

That he did not redeem his promise, or indeed go near her for the next week, was due in both cases to not knowing what to say. He had begun the reading with scant interest, and with his mind reverting to the old farmer whom the woodcut had transmogrified, but speedily his attention was enchained, and, though her hand was not easy to read, he did not put down the manuscript until he had arrived at the last page.

"There is no art about it," Miss Suttaby had said long ago when describing her writing, and he recalled her words now as a peculiarly apt criticism.

There was no art about it at all. She had produced no book before, and probably, if he could judge aright, and he thought he could, she would never produce one again. She had simply obeyed a forgotten mandate, and with perfect literalness. She had looked into her own heart, and written of what she found there, and what she wrote of was a great loneliness.

Her heroine was a deserted wife whose baby had died,—a woman who had revelled in intense happiness, who had passed through the first anguish of its loss, and who then had gone on enduring a twilight sort of existence, in which neither the one nor the other could ever touch her poignantly again. Her warmest greeting was at arm's-length now, being just a friendly hand-clasp instead of the old wealth of kisses, and this was typical of the changed attitude of her world. Everything was at arm's-length and never came right up to her, not even Death.

It was a miserable book, and in the latter part of it there was no relief, except that which was afforded by delicate little descriptions of country, where the wind seemed to blow as invigoratingly as she had said it blew over certain fields near the old home. But in spite of this monotony, and of the poverty of its construction, sometimes even of its language, it was a powerful book, because it bore so plainly the impress of truth.

Leyden returned to it again and again.

At first he refused to own to himself that his long doubt as to where his second novel was to come from, was now practically solved. He locked the thing away from him, and spent a day in strenuous efforts to forget it. With the evening he had an idea which he dignified to the height of an aspiration, since it allowed him to run riot on a line of thought which otherwise must have stayed debarred. He would have another look at the story, he decided, and amuse himself by arranging in his own mind what he would have done with it if Miss Suttaby had died and bequeathed it to him for his personal property. He would alter the position of the chapters for one thing, and work up two or three of the minor characters to something more imposing than their present shadowy condition. Towards the middle he might possibly interpolate that odd experience of his last year at the Hague; though he was not quite sure of this, since, though the book wanted lengthening, it must be done with the utmost delicacy. And certainly he would cut out one or two of the passages where the pathos of the loneliness of the woman was, to his thinking, much overstrained. For example, one could hardly ask one's readers to accept the notion of a woman who was otherwise sane taking a roll of baby clothes to bed with her in lieu of the dead child for whom she roused herself by feeling in her sleep; and though she might conceivably prefer to starve herself rather than omit the buying of certain flowers at certain given seasons in memory of birthdays and the like, did it not border upon the ridiculous to imagine she would always soil two cups in the solitary tea-drinking, rather than see only the one upon the board, and wash up only the one when the meal was over?

For the rest there was but little to suggest; and again reminding himself that the whole thing was farcical in the extreme, and a whimsical impossibility which he was concocting for his private amusement, he finally put down the manuscript and began devising imaginary reviews.

Naturally, what would strike the critics most would be his extraordinary versatility. Between "Wrecked" and this story, which was as yet unnamed, but which he should entitle "The Loneliness of a Woman", the difference of their style and treatment would be amazing. That had been largely incident,—Ned Jermyn's voice recurred to him, and the weak chuckle with which he had congratulated himself on the fullness with which he had packed his life: this was almost wholly introspective, for even the sins of the husband, of which much more might have been made, were touched upon very lightly, since to the woman's purity they were unknown, save for results.

There was only one quality which, the reviewers would point out, largely dominated both books; and that . . . a smile stole over Franklyn Leyden's lips, and his hand hugged the lappet of his opened coat . . . that was his enormous sympathy with suffering.

Heigh—o! He stretched out his arms, and rose with a sigh. What was the use of such roseate dreams? The manuscript which had so enthralled him was not his, but hers. She should . . . He hesitated a moment, disputing the word his imagination had supplied. Enthralled? Had it enthralled him? Was he not really enthralled of the book as he would have made it, rather than of the book as it actually was? Now he came to think of it, she would probably have great difficulty in getting it published. She was unknown, for one thing: those who had already seen it had rejected it: it was crude and unusual. It was highly probable no one would take it, and it was more than probable that if they did, she would never make a penny by the transaction. Whatever its merits, it was undeniably a book to enhance a reputation rather than make one.

He felt that the ground was a good deal cleared by the time he arrived at this conclusion. Naturally, he must think only of what was best for her; and it was very evident that to drop himself out of the matter would be very far from best for her. Yet, how to work it? He spent more than a week in indecision; but his thoughts were not occupied with how he was to make the story his own, and yet be enabled to repeat his thanksgiving anent blackguardism. They were solely concerned, he told himself daily, with the consideration of Miss Suttaby's interests.

"We must collaborate," he told her, when at length he betook himself to the dingy rooms in Museum Street. "Your story is much too good to be lost; and I should think . . ."

Miss Suttaby did not wait for him to finish his sentence.

"Collaborate?" She uttered a joyful, quivering cry. "You and I! Oh, Mr. Leyden, you must be joking! Why, it is like . . . like . . ."

All kinds of impossible similies presented themselves. It was like the sun-god asking a buttercup to ally its yellow gleams to his own. It was like . . . Oh! she did not know. She threw up her hands helplessly. Her eyes lost their gravity, and shone in bewildered excitement.

"Why not?" said Leyden quietly.

It was a pity her voice should have failed her just then, since she had seemed on the brink of a gratifying compliment. How extraordinary it was with this woman that her emotions seemed constantly getting in her way.

She had not even an elementary idea of using them gracefully, and if she ever cried, he felt convinced that instead of tears "like summer showers", she would blot and blur her face in a manner which would be quite sufficient to alienate sympathy.

"You don't think it would be to our mutual advantage?"

Miss Suttaby laughed.

"No, I don't," she said bluntly. "If you really think there is any good in it . . ."

"I really do."

". . . it must either go back to the drawer until I have time to polish it, or . . ."

"You musn't do that," Leyden cried sharply. "You would spoil it. It is perfect as it is."

Then he remembered that this was not what he had intended to say, because, of course, he did not think it.

"I mean, it is its unconsciousness which is its charm. You would only bungle it if you attempted improvement. But what is the alternative? 'Or,' you said."

"Or you must take it," said Miss Suttaby, quietly.

Leyden brought both his hands sharply down upon the table.

"Take it? What do you mean?"

"I mean, if there is anything worthy of your acceptance, please accept it."

Leyden's charm of manner was somewhat apt to evaporate when one came to know him well. When he had taken a friend's soundings, or believed he had taken them, and when in consequence his interest was upon the wane, quite unwittingly he saved himself for newer work. But those demurely spoken words brought it back with redoubled intensity.

"Miss Suttaby!" He leaned across the narrow table, and took one of the fast-ageing hands in both his own smooth ones. "This is one of the most beautiful gifts I ever had in my life. The thought, I mean, not the story itself, for of course I would never take that. How good of you! How infinitely gracious! I—I really don't know what to say to you, you kindest of friends. You have robbed me of words."

His warmth made her uncomfortable. She tried to withdraw her hand, and uneasily shifted her chair an inch or two.

"Robbed me of words!" murmured Leyden.

He wished she had not robbed herself of words as well. He would have liked her to look up at him with eyes becomingly humid, and tell him—what was indeed the truth—that he had done more for her, both in his book and in his friendship, than she could ever hope to repay. But as she said nothing of this, he was again obliged to break into ecstasy, grateful that he, at least, formed an appreciative audience to himself.

"Your generosity will make one of the red-letter days of my life. Your sweet sympathy . . ."

He paused. One cannot talk of sympathy to a woman who apparently does not want to listen. He released her hand.

"Miss Suttaby, let us strike a bargain. You say you are averse from collaboration. Probably you feel as I do, that it is not quite honest work. But let me strike a bargain with you. Let me buy this story from you out and out, and put it to what use I like. I think you said you might get ten pounds for it. I will give you thirty."

"That would buy a head-stone," Miss Suttaby said irrelevantly. She was oblivious of the fact that it would also buy bread and butter. "I promised Bertie. He thought that just a grass mound looked like a labourer's at our home. Mr. Leyden, I know it is too much, but since you will not take it as a gift, why . . . Bertie . . ."

Leyden was as kindly as ever. He talked away her scruples, and shared her tremulous delight, and it was only when he was upon his feet, and saying good-bye, that he referred to the tale.

"I must cut a good deal, I am afraid. Now Huldah cuddling those baby-clothes in bed, weren't you drawing a *little* too much on your imagination, eh, Miss Suttaby?"

She did not answer him at once, and accustomed as he had grown to her unaccountable fits of confusion, he could not but be struck by the paling cheeks and downcast eyes.

"One gets worked-up, and forgets probabilities, I find. But frankly it did not strike me as reading quite sanely, you know."

"I . . . I think a woman might, if her arms felt *very* empty," said Miss Suttaby.

Her voice sounded oddly muffled.

"Good-bye," said Leyden suddenly. "Write to me if I can ever be of the slightest use to you, won't you? You promise? That's right! Good-bye."

So it was she who had done that thing which he had branded in his own mind as preposterous! To women of her temperament, at least, it would read as supremely natural, and he was bound to confess that she had so amazed him that for aught he knew to the contrary they might form the generality. From that choked tone he had gathered much. Undoubtedly it was she, too, who had resorted to the ghastly fashion of preparing the solitary meal as if it were for two. He had been stupid, indeed, to think she could have evolved these and similar passages, when he knew her imagination to be so strictly limited. He would not cut a single line.

Next day he sent her ten pounds, with a promise of the remainder when the book should be out. He told her candidly he could not afford the whole of the amount at one fell swoop; and since he was invariably thoughtful in such matters, he tore up the cheque which she might have had some difficulty in cashing, and sent her notes instead.

Then he set to work in good earnest. Huldah should be no mere book-heroine, she should live. So far as he knew, the portrayal of a woman had never been done before in the only way in which fidelity is likely to be secured. She had never been drawn first by one who has suffered the actual suffering, and enjoyed the actual joys, and then by a second who has noted the visible results. She had never been the joint work of a woman dealing with the subtleties a man could not divine, and of a man writing of what a woman never notices.

He built upon Miss Suttaby's foundations, and for the purpose of keeping the work all of a piece and devoid of scrappiness, his material was Miss Suttaby herself. The narrowness and the pathos of the narrowness, the arrested growth of the gentle soul, her simplicities of movement and talk,—nothing of what he had observed escaped transmittal. He told himself she would never recognise her own portrait, and probably in this he was right, since people are mostly "unexplored Africas" to themselves. Ask any ordinary person how he cuts the loaf at breakfast, and he will gape in speechless ignorance. He has not the faintest idea if he jumps to his feet and saws away energetically, if he produces dainty symmetrical slices, or attacks the first corner that presents itself. All that makes the homely act individual to the onlooker, has never struck the actor at all.

No, no, he would be quite safe, or he would not risk wounding her for the world. And with all the reverence of which he was capable he went steadily on his way, until "her book" grew into "the book", and then to "mine". The last stage naturally saw its completion.

The following autumn and early winter found one man, at all events, blissfully content. Franklyn Leyden's new book had scored an immediate success, and the incense of adulation enveloped him in its clouds. It included, amongst other items, better business terms that he had expected, and a widely-advertised engagement to Lady Elliott's daughter, with whom he had long ago smoothed over old differences.

Once only had he heard from Miss Suttaby. She then wrote to tell him she had been ill, and unable to work. Would it be inconvenient to him to let her have at least a little of the money he had so generously promised? She gave a fresh address; two rooms were beyond her means.

Leyden was touched, and wrote back effusively, enclosing a couple of sovereigns. These were nothing to do with the sum she mentioned, he explained, but just a token of sincere friendship, which he begged her to accept in the spirit in which it was offered. In regard to what she asked, most certainly. He was only waiting until his royalties should have accumulated to allow of sending her a good round sum. It was all nonsense to refer to the paltry amount they had arranged: fifty pounds[7] would be far nearer the mark. He could never forget the gift she had wished to make him, and was exactly as grateful as if he had thought it right to accept it—Remaining, "ever faithfully", hers.

He found it such an expensive matter to be even contemplating marriage, that the carrying out of these benevolent intentions was unavoidably delayed; and when one day the post brought him a second appeal, he felt deservedly provoked. To worry him at such a time after all he had done, and was still doing, for her, surely showed a lamentable lack of consideration.

So he left the pencil-written note severely unanswered, fixing in his own mind the publication of the fifth edition of the book as a suitable time for writing again to his whilom acquaintance, and for settling the matter once and for all. It would be out in a week or two.

He kept his word on the very day of its appearance, and went to call on her personally, remembering what pleasure it would give her to see him again, and wondering if she would greet him with that lovely slow-growing flush.

The month was April, and the sight of the flower-sellers in Oxford Street reminded him of how she had once longed to share with them her own exceeding happiness, and what an important event she had made of a cab drive. He must see how the time went, but if he could possibly manage it, he would ask her to come out with him for another drive today. Such trifles pleased her.

He had so vividly pictured the delighted surprise with which she would recognise her visitor, that on reaching his destination he was considerably taken aback at being informed she had "gone away".

Yes, she had gone away from London altogether. And, no, she had left no address. On these two points the grim-visaged woman was certain, and as she was the "missus" of the house, as she carefully stated several times, who should be certain if not she herself? She "ud like ter know". She eyed him suspiciously the while, wondering what on earth he wanted with "that Miss Suttaby"; wondering, too, if he took her to be "flat enough" to admit to her lodger having died, especially when the alleged cause of "practical starvation" was so humiliating for any respectable landlady.

"I wish I could 'elp you, sir, but I can't."

Leyden thanked her courteously, and went away much crestfallen. The saving to his pocket he did not weigh for one moment against the hurt to his feelings. That she should have gone and not told him! He could not understand it.

Presently his mortification faded into a kindly pity. She was piqued, he supposed, that he had not instantly replied, and had therefore adopted this extraordinary method of punishing him, heedless of the fact that she was also punishing herself. Well! well! How like a woman!

---

7. A substantial sum, perhaps enough to sustain her for the better part of a year.

Here a passing carriage distracted his attention. By the time he reached home he was full of other thoughts. The whole episode had been too insignificant, and the heroine of it too homely to cut an enduring niche in his memory. Clearly it was no fault of his that she had chosen to drift out of his life.

So he simply forgot her.

It is probable that this is exactly what Miss Suttaby would have wished.

—1896

Fleet Street, London, c. 1894.

PART III

Mind and Body

Mind and Body: Introduction

In the 1890s, British cities were in crisis. Immigrants, agricultural migrants, and underpaid laborers crowded into festering slums—and when overworked, diseased, underfed people were crammed together without a reliable water supply or sewage system, conditions quickly became foul. Reformist investigators publicized the situation through the "New Journalism." W. T. Stead dressed as a homeless man to investigate the city's shelters and publicized youthful prostitution by "buying" an underage virgin. Novelists, too, took to the streets. Inspired by Émile Zola's naturalist philosophy, such writers as George Gissing, Israel Zangwill, and Arthur Morrison documented actual conditions, regardless of the moral effect on the reader. Their fiction treats lower-class subjects seriously, not just making them comic or pathetic foils for middle-class protagonists.

Other writers preferred to focus on the remnants of British rural life. Thomas Hardy appealed to readers' nostalgia by depicting the older world of agricultural labor, folk festivals, and rural villages. A. E. Housman set his spare, direct poems in a changeless natural world. In an era of rapid urbanization—of department stores, bicycles, typewriters, electric lights, and mass transit—it was sometimes restful to focus on the cherry tree's blossoms or the harvest supper.

Some *fin-de-siècle* writers, however, sought medical explanations for the condition of the urban poor. Today we can diagnose stunted and malformed bodies as the result of malnutrition, squalor, and medical neglect, but Victorians feared that fundamental biological differences were warping the British body. Could the poor be returning to a more primitive stage of human development, degenerating instead of evolving? Francis Galton, Darwin's cousin, thought that the risk justified "eugenics" (selective breeding).

Minds were also at risk. The new psychologists suggested that neurosis and hysteria constituted a kind of grey area between madness and sanity in which many people hovered. Max Nordau diagnosed a mental disorder in certain influential artists—Richard Wagner, Oscar Wilde, Sarah Grand—seeing culture as diseased. Nordau's theory impressed journalists like Hugh E. M. Stutfield and Janet E. Hogarth, but George Bernard Shaw objected: "I could prove Nordau to be an elephant on more evidence than he has brought to prove that our greatest men are degenerate lunatics." Sigmund Freud pioneered serious psychology; his early case study, "Dora," shows some of the ways he struggled to construct a workable model of the mind. Meanwhile, the new "sexologists" created medical categories for sexual behavior. Havelock Ellis's case studies and Edward Carpenter's defenses of male love helped define the new identity of "the homosexual." The novelist Henry James took readers deep inside characters' consciousnesses in his subtle, complex, turn-of-the-century psychological novels.

Whether suffering could be traced to medical, psychological, atavistic, or economic causes, the burning issue was how to alleviate it. Beatrice and Sidney Webb founded the Fabian party on idealistic socialist principles, and early socialist writing by John Ruskin and William Morris laid the foundations for George Bernard Shaw's critiques. Other 1890s writers preferred a spiritual solution. People during the *fin de siècle* were fascinated by séances, mediums, hypnosis, theories of other worlds, and life after death. Frederic W. H. Myers, cofounder of the Society for Psychical Research, aimed to map the unseen realm just as precisely as his fellow investigators categorized the city and the body.

At the *fin de siècle* it seemed possible to understand the body and the mind; to trace the medical, hereditary, sex-related, and psychological factors shaping them; to ameliorate suffering in a new society; and to imagine the possibilities beyond.

Body Fears: Degeneracy and Sexology

Francis Galton
1822–1911

How fitting that Francis Galton was a cousin of Charles Darwin. This multitalented African explorer, scientific writer (nine books and two hundred papers), meteorologist, psychologist, and statistician invented the term *eugenics* ("good birth") and launched eugenic study. An early subscriber to Darwinian evolution, Galton wanted to ensure racial improvement by guaranteeing that the most intelligent and talented people reproduced. Today, eugenic theory is discredited by both scientific and political results: genetics reveals that inheritance is highly complex and mediated by cultural factors, and the Nazis infamously used eugenic ideas to justify mass extermination. Yet, at the *fin de siècle*, eugenics was an exciting new idea for improving the world and was championed by the same radicals who supported the New Women movement, sexology, and Fabian socialism. In *Inquiries into Human Faculty and Its Development* (1883), Galton summed up his hopes for the capability and perfectability of the human race.

from Inquiries into Human Faculty and Its Development

Selection and Race.[1]

The fact of an individual being naturally gifted with high qualities, may be due either to his being an exceptionally good specimen of a poor race, or an average specimen of a high one. The difference of origin would betray itself in his descendants; they would revert towards the typical centre of their race, deteriorating in the first case but not in the second. The two cases, though theoretically distinct, are confused in reality, owing to the frequency with which exceptional personal qualities connote the departure of the entire nature of the individual from his ancestral type, and the formation of a new strain having its own typical centre. It is hardly necessary to add that it is in this indirect way that natural selection improves a race. The two events of selection and difference of race ought, however, to be carefully distinguished in broad practical considerations, while the frequency of their concurrence is borne in mind and allowed for.

So long as the race remains radically the same, the stringent selection of the best specimens to rear and breed from, can never lead to any permanent result. The attempt to raise the standard of such a race is like the labour of Sisyphus[2] in rolling his stone uphill; let the effort be relaxed for a moment, and the stone will roll back. Whenever a new typical centre appears, it is as though there was a facet upon the lower surface of the stone, on which it is capable of resting without rolling back. It affords a temporary sticking point in the forward progress of evolution.

The causes that check the unlimited improvement of highly-bred animals, so long as the race remains unchanged, are many and absolute.

In the first place there is an increasing delicacy of constitution;[3] the growing fineness of limb and structure end, after a few generations, in fragility. Overbred animals have little stamina, they resemble in this respect the "weedy" colts so often reared from first-class racers. One can perhaps see in a general way why this should be so. Each individual is the outcome of a vast number of organic elements of the most various species, just as some nation might be the outcome of a vast number of castes of individuals, each caste monopolising a special pursuit. Banish a number of the humbler castes—the bakers, the bricklayers, and the smiths, and the nation would soon come to grief. This is what is done in high breeding; certain qualities are bred for, and the rest are diminished as far as possible, but they cannot be dispensed with entirely.

The next difficulty lies in the diminished fertility of highly-bred animals. It is not improbable that its cause is of the same character as that of the delicacy of their constitution. Together with infertility is combined some degree of sexual indifference, or when passion is shown, it is not infrequently for some specimen of a coarser type. This is certainly the case with horses and with dogs.

It will be easily understood that these difficulties, which are so formidable in the case of plants and animals, which we can mate as we please and destroy when we please, would make the maintenance of a highly-selected breed of men an impossibility.

---

1. By "race" Galton means families; they may produce "high" (successful) or "poor" (underachieving) descendants.
2. In the Greek myth, Sisyphus's futile labor was to roll a stone uphill.
3. Bodily frame, general health.

Whenever a low race is preserved under conditions of life that exact a high level of efficiency, it must be subjected to rigorous selection. The few best specimens of that race can alone be allowed to become parents, and not many of their descendants can be allowed to live. On the other hand, if a higher race be substituted for the low one, all this terrible misery disappears. The most merciful form of what I ventured to call "eugenics" would consist in watching for the indications of superior strains or races, and in so favouring them that their progeny shall outnumber and gradually replace that of the old one. Such strains are of no infrequent occurrence. It is easy to specify families who are characterised by strong resemblances, and whose features and character are usually prepotent[4] over those of their wives or husbands in their joint offspring, and who are at the same time as prolific as the average of their class. These strains can be conveniently studied in the families of exiles, which, for obvious reasons, are easy to trace in their various branches.

The debt that most countries owe to the race of men whom they received from one another as immigrants, whether leaving their native country of their own free will, or as exiles on political or religious grounds, has been often pointed out, and may, I think, be accounted for as follows:—The fact of a man leaving his compatriots, or so irritating them that they compel him to go, is fair evidence that either he or they, or both, feel that his character is alien to theirs. Exiles are also on the whole men of considerable force of character; a quiet man would endure and succumb, he would not have energy to transplant himself or to become so conspicuous as to be an object of general attack. We may justly infer from this, that exiles are on the whole men of exceptional and energetic natures, and it is especially from such men as these that new strains of race are likely to proceed.

Influence of Man upon Race.

The influence of man upon the nature of his own race has already been very large, but it has not been intelligently directed, and has in many instances done great harm. Its action has been by invasions and migration of races, by war and massacre, by wholesale deportation of population, by emigration, and by many social customs which have a silent but widespread effect.

There exists a sentiment, for the most part quite unreasonable, against the gradual extinction of an inferior race. It rests on some confusion between the race and the individual, as if the destruction of a race was equivalent to the destruction of a large number of men. It is nothing of the kind when the process of extinction works silently and slowly through the earlier marriage of members of the superior race, through their greater vitality under equal stress, through their better chances of getting a livelihood, or through their prepotency in mixed marriages. That the members of an inferior class should dislike being elbowed out of the way is another matter; but it may be somewhat brutally argued that whenever two individuals struggle for a single place, one must yield, and that there will be no more unhappiness on the whole, if the inferior yield to the superior than conversely, whereas the world will be permanently enriched by the success of the superior. The conditions of happiness are, however, too complex to be disposed of by à priori[5]

---

4. Most powerful.
5. Prior ("from the first").

argument, it is safest to appeal to observation. I think it could be easily shown that when the differences between the races is not so great as to divide them into obviously different classes, and where their language, education, and general interests are the same, the substitution may take place gradually without any unhappiness. Thus the movements of commerce have introduced fresh and vigorous blood into various parts of England, the new-comers have intermarried with the residents, and their characteristics have been prepotent in the descendants of the mixed marriages. I have referred in the earlier part of the book to the changes of type in the English nature that have occurred during the last few hundred years. These have been effected so silently that we only know of them by the results. * * *

It is clear from what has been said, that men of former generations have exercised enormous influence over the human stock of the present day, and that the average humanity of the world now and in future years is and will be very different to what it would have been if the action of our forefathers had been different. The power in man of varying the future human stock vests a great responsibility in the hands of each fresh generation, which has not yet been recognised at its just importance, nor deliberately employed. It is foolish to fold the hands and to say that nothing can be done, inasmuch as social forces and self-interests are too strong to be resisted. They need not be resisted; they can be guided. It is one thing to check the course of a huge steam vessel by the shock of a sudden encounter when she is going at full speed in the wrong direction, and another to cause her to change her course slowly and gently by a slight turn of the helm. Nay, a ship may be made to describe a half circle, and to end by following a course exactly opposite to the first, without attracting the notice of the passengers. * * *

It will suffice to faintly sketch out some sort of basis for eugenics, it being now an understanding that we are provisionally agreed, for the sake of argument, that the improvement of race is an object of first-class importance, and that the popular feeling has been educated to regard it in that light.

The final object would be to devise means for favouring individuals who bore the signs of membership of a superior race, the proximate[6] aim would be to ascertain what those signs were, and these we will consider first.

The indications of superior breed are partly personal, partly ancestral. We need not trouble ourselves about the personal part, because full weight is already given to it in the competitive careers; energy, brain, morale, and health being recognised factors of success, while there can hardly be a better evidence of a person being adapted to his circumstances than that afforded by success. It is the ancestral part that is neglected, and which we have yet to recognise at its just value. A question that now continually arises is this; a youth is a candidate for permanent employment, his present personal qualifications are known, but how will he turn out in later years? The objections to competitive examinations[7] are notorious, in that they give undue prominence to youths whose receptive faculties are quick, and whose intellects are precocious. They give no indication of the direction in which the health, character,

---

6. Next.
7. Hiring candidates based on their test scores rather than their family connections.

and intellect of the youth will change through the development in their due course, of ancestral tendencies that are latent in youth, but will manifest themselves in after life. Examinations deal with the present, not with the future, although it is in the future of the youth that we are especially interested. Much of the needed guidance may be derived from his family history. I cannot doubt, if two youths were of equal personal merit, of whom one belonged to a thriving and long-lived family, and the other to a decaying and short-lived family, that there could be any hesitation in saying that the chances were greater of the first-mentioned youth becoming the more valuable public servant of the two.

A thriving family may be sufficiently defined or inferred by the successive occupations of its several male members in the previous generation, and of the two grandfathers. These are patent[8] facts attainable by almost every youth, which admit of being verified in his neighbourhood and attested in a satisfactory manner.

A healthy and long-lived family may be defined by the patent facts of ages at death, and number and ages of living relatives, within the degrees mentioned above, all of which can be verified and attested. A knowledge of the existence of longevity in the family would testify to the stamina of the candidate, and be an important addition to the knowledge of his present health in forecasting the probability of his performing a large measure of experienced work.

Owing to absence of data and the want of inquiry of the family antecedents of those who fail and of those who succeed in life, we are much more ignorant than we ought to be of their relative importance. In connection with this, I may mention some curious results published by Mr. F. M. Hollond[9] of Boston, U.S., as to the antecedent family history of persons who were reputed to be more moral than the average, and of those who were the reverse. He has been good enough to reply to questions that I sent to him concerning his criterion of morality, and other points connected with the statistics, in a way that seems satisfactory, and he has very obligingly furnished me with additional MS.[10] materials. One of his conclusions was that morality is more often found among members of large families than among those of small ones. It is reasonable to expect this would be the case owing to the internal discipline among members of large families, and to the wholesome sustaining and restraining effects of family pride and family criticism. Members of small families are apt to be selfish, and when the smallness of the family is due to the deaths of many of its members at early ages, it is some evidence either of weakness of the family constitution, or of deficiency of common sense or of affection on the part of the parents in not taking better care of them. Mr. Hollond quotes in his letter to me a piece of advice by Franklin to a young man in search of a wife, "to take one out of a bunch of sisters," and a popular saying that kittens brought up with others make the best pets, because they have learned to play without scratching. Sir William Gull[11] has remarked that those candidates for the Indian Civil Service who are members of large families are on the whole the strongest.

---

8. Obvious.

9. *Index Newspaper*, Boston, U.S. July 17, 1882 [Galton's note].

10. Manuscript.

11. *Blue Book*, C–1446, 1876. On the Selection and Training of Candidates for the Indian Civil Service [Galton's note].

Far be it from me to say that any scheme of marks for family merit would not require a great deal of preparatory consideration. Careful statistical inquiries have yet to be made into the family antecedents of public servants of mature age in connection with their place in examination lists at the earlier age when they first gained their appointments. This would be necessary in order to learn the amount of marks that should be assigned to various degrees of family merit. I foresee no peculiar difficulty in conducting such an inquiry; indeed, now that competitive examinations have been in general use for many years, the time seems ripe for it, but of course its conduct would require much confidential inquiry and a great deal of trouble in verifying returns. Still, it admits of being done, and if the results, derived from different sources, should confirm one another, they could be depended on.

Let us now suppose that a way was seen for carrying some such idea as this into practice, and that family merit, however defined, was allowed to count, for however little, in competitive examinations. The effect would be very great: it would show that ancestral qualities are of present current value; it would give an impetus to collecting family histories; it would open the eyes of every family and of society at large to the importance of marriage alliance with a good stock; it would introduce the subject of race into a permanent topic of consideration, which (on the supposition of its *bonâ fide* importance that has been assumed for the sake of argument) experience would show to be amply justified. Any act that first gives a guinea stamp to the sterling guinea's worth[12] of natural nobility might set a great social avalanche in motion.

—1883

Max Nordau
1849–1923

Hungarian doctor and journalist Max Nordau galvanized readers with *Degeneration* (English edition, 1895). The following excerpt shows how Nordau launched a medical critique of *fin-de-siècle* art. Artistic sensitivity, religious or philosophical inquiry, a longing for fame, the desire to buy things, insistence on a particular idea, and participation in an artistic school: all are symptoms of "semi-insanity," degeneration. Nordau attacked Oscar Wilde with particular venom, and when Wilde was convicted of sodomy a few months after *Degeneration* appeared, it seemed to confirm Nordau's diagnosis. Nordau's theory emboldened anti-aesthetic critics by giving them a "scientific" vocabulary. Although degeneration theory did not last long, Nordau went on to have an equally famous second career when he covered the scandalous trial of Alfred Dreyfus, falsely accused of espionage due to French anti-semitism, and became an influential early Zionist.

---

12. A guinea coin has value only after its face is stamped. Similarly, "natural nobility" needs an "act" to bring out its real value.

from Degeneration

from Ch. 3, "Diagnosis"

The manifestations described in the preceding chapter must be patent enough to everyone, be he never so narrow a Philistine.[1] The Philistine, however, regards them as a passing fashion and nothing more; for him the current terms, caprice, eccentricity, affectation of novelty, imitation, instinct, afford a sufficient explanation. The purely literary mind, whose merely æsthetic culture does not enable him to understand the connections of things, and to seize their real meaning, deceives himself and others as to his ignorance by means of sounding phrases, and loftily talks of a "restless quest of a new ideal by the modern spirit," "the richer vibrations of the refined nervous system of the present day," "the unknown sensations of an elect mind." But the physician, especially if he have devoted himself to the special study of nervous and mental maladies, recognises at a glance, in the *fin-de-siècle* disposition, in the tendencies of contemporary art and poetry, in the life and conduct of the men who write mystic, symbolic and "decadent" works, and the attitude taken by their admirers in the tastes and æsthetic instincts of fashionable society, the confluence of two well-defined conditions of disease, with which he is quite familiar, viz. degeneration (degeneracy) and hysteria, of which the minor stages are designated as neurasthenia.[2] These two conditions of the organism differ from each other, yet have many features in common, and frequently occur together; so that it is easier to observe them in their composite forms, than each in isolation. * * *

"The clearest notion we can form of degeneracy is to regard it as a *morbid deviation from an original type*. This deviation, even if, at the outset, it was ever so slight, contained transmissible elements of such a nature that anyone bearing in him the germs becomes more and more incapable of fulfilling his functions in the world; and mental progress, already checked in his own person, finds itself menaced also in his descendants."[3]

When under any kind of noxious influences an organism becomes debilitated, its successors will not resemble the healthy, normal type of the species, with capacities for development, but will form a new sub-species, which, like all others, possesses the capacity of transmitting to its offspring, in a continuously increasing degree, its peculiarities, these being morbid deviations from the normal form—gaps in development, malformations and infirmities. That which distinguishes degeneracy from the formation of new species (phylogeny) is, that the morbid variation does not continuously subsist and propagate itself, like one that is healthy, but, fortunately, is soon rendered sterile, and after a few generations often dies out before it reaches the lowest grade of organic degradation.

Degeneracy betrays itself among men in certain physical characteristics, which are denominated "stigmata," or brand-marks—an unfortunate term derived from a

---

1. Person with conventional middle-class tastes.
2. Degeneracy: each generation progressively deteriorates. Hysteria: excessive, uncontrollable emotional or sensory reaction (originally thought to be caused by the womb). Neurasthenia: weakness, depression, physical debility.
3. B.A. Morel's 1857 book, *Traité des dégénerescences physiques, intellectuals et morales de l'Espèce humaine et des causes qui produisent ces Variétés maladive* [Treatise on Physical, Intellectual, and Moral Degeneration in the Human Species and the Causes That Produce These Varieties of Illness]. Par le Dr. B. A. Morel. Paris 1857, p. 5 [Nordau's note].

false idea, as if degeneracy were necessarily the consequence of a fault, and the indication of it a punishment. Such stigmata consist of deformities, multiple and stunted growths in the first line of asymmetry, the unequal development of the two halves of the face and cranium; then imperfection in the development of the external ear, which is conspicuous for its enormous size, or protrudes from the head, like a handle, and the lobe of which is either lacking or adhering to the head, and the helix of which is not involuted; further, squint-eyes, hare-lips, irregularities in the form and position of the teeth; pointed or flat palates, webbed or supernumerary fingers (syn- and poly-dactylia), etc. * * *

Science, however, has found, together with these physical stigmata, others of a mental order, which betoken degeneracy quite as clearly as the former; and they allow of an easy demonstration from all the vital manifestations, and, in particular, from all the works of degenerates, so that it is not necessary to measure the cranium of an author, or to see the lobe of a painter's ear, in order to recognise the fact that he belongs to the class of degenerates. * * *

In the mental development of degenerates, we meet with the same irregularity that we have observed in their physical growth. The asymmetry of face and cranium finds, as it were, its counterpart in their mental faculties. Some of the latter are completely stunted, others morbidly exaggerated. That which nearly all degenerates lack is the sense of morality and of right and wrong. For them there exists no law, no decency, no modesty. In order to satisfy any momentary impulse, or inclination, or caprice, they commit crimes and trespasses with the greatest calmness and self-complacency, and do not comprehend that other persons take offence thereat. When this phenomenon is present in a high degree, we speak of "moral insanity" with Maudsley;[4] there are, nevertheless, low stages in which the degenerate does not, perhaps, himself commit any act which will bring him into conflict with the criminal code, but at least asserts the theoretical legitimacy of crime; seeks, with philosophically sounding fustian,[5] to prove that "good" and "evil," virtue and vice, are arbitrary distinctions; goes into raptures over evildoers and their deeds; professes to discover beauties in the lowest and most repulsive things; and tries to awaken interest in, and so-called "comprehension" of, every bestiality. The two psychological roots of moral insanity, in all its degrees of development, are, firstly, unbounded egoism, and, secondly, impulsiveness—i.e., inability to resist a sudden impulse to any deed; and these characteristics also constitute the chief intellectual stigmata of degenerates. * * *

Another mental stigma of degenerates is their emotionalism. Morel has even wished to make this peculiarity their chief characteristic—erroneously, it seems to me, for it is present in the same degree among hysterics, and, indeed, is to be found in perfectly healthy persons, who, from any transient cause, such as illness, exhaustion, or any mental shock, have been temporarily weakened. Nevertheless it is a phenomenon rarely absent in a degenerate. He laughs until he sheds tears, or weeps copiously without adequate occasion; a commonplace line of poetry or of prose sends a shudder down his back; he falls into raptures before indifferent pictures or statues; and music especially, even the most insipid and least commendable, arouses in him the most vehement

---

4. A pioneering British psychologist and fervent believer in degeneration (1835–1918).
5. Bombastic nonsense.

emotions. He is quite proud of being so vibrant a musical instrument, and boasts that where the Philistine remains completely cold, he feels his inner self confounded, the depths of his being broken up, and the bliss of the Beautiful possessing him to the tips of his fingers. His excitability appears to him a mark of superiority; he believes himself to be possessed by a peculiar insight lacking in other mortals, and he is fain to despise the vulgar herd for the dulness and narrowness of their minds. The unhappy creature does not suspect that he is conceited about a disease and boasting of a derangement of the mind; and certain silly critics, when, through fear of being pronounced deficient in comprehension, they make desperate efforts to share the emotions of a degenerate in regard to some insipid or ridiculous production, or when they praise in exaggerated expressions the beauties which the degenerate asserts he finds therein, are unconsciously simulating one of the stigmata of semi-insanity.

Besides moral insanity and emotionalism, there is to be observed in the degenerate a condition of mental weakness and despondency, which, according to the circumstances of his life, assumes the form of pessimism, a vague fear of all men, and of the entire phenomenon of the universe, or self-abhorrence. "These patients," says Morel, "feel perpetually compelled . . . to commiserate themselves, to sob, to repeat with the most desperate monotony the same questions and words. They have delirious presentations of ruin and damnation, and all sorts of imaginary fears." "Ennui never quits me," said a patient of this kind, whose case Roubinovitch[6] describes, "ennui of myself." "Among moral stigmata," says the same author, "there are also to be specified those undefinable apprehensions manifested by degenerates when they see, smell, or touch any object." And he further calls to notice "their unconscious fear of everything and everyone." In this picture of the sufferer from melancholia; downcast, sombre, despairing of himself and the world, tortured by fear of the Unknown, menaced by undefined but dreadful dangers, we recognise in every detail the man of the Dusk of the Nations and the *fin-de-siècle* frame of mind, described in the first chapter.

With this characteristic dejectedness of the degenerate, there is combined, as a rule, a disinclination to action of any kind, attaining possibly to abhorrence of activity and powerlessness to will (*aboulia*). * * * The degenerate who shuns action, and is without will-power, has no suspicion that his incapacity for action is a consequence of his inherited deficiency of brain. He deceives himself into believing that he despises action from free determination, and takes pleasure in inactivity; and, in order to justify himself in his own eyes, he constructs a philosophy of renunciation and of contempt for the world and men, asserts that he has convinced himself of the excellence of Quietism,[7] calls himself with consummate self-consciousness a Buddhist, and praises Nirvana in poetically eloquent phrases as the highest and worthiest ideal of the human mind. The degenerate and insane are the predestined disciples of Schopenhauer and Hartmann,[8] and need only to acquire a knowledge of Buddhism to become converts to it.

With the incapacity for action there is connected the predilection for inane reverie. The degenerate is not in a condition to fix his attention long, or indeed at all, on any subject, and is equally incapable of correctly grasping, ordering, or elabo-

---

6. J. Roubinovitch, *Hystérie mâle et Dégénérescence* (Male Hysteria and Degeneration; Paris, 1890).
7. 17th-c. mystical movement preaching self-surrender and passivity before God.
8. 19th-c. German philosophers of pessimism.

rating into ideas and judgments the impressions of the external world conveyed to his distracted consciousness by his defectively operating senses. It is easier and more convenient for him to allow his brain-centres to produce semi-lucid, nebulously blurred ideas and inchoate embryonic thoughts, and to surrender himself to the perpetual obfuscation of a boundless, aimless, and shoreless stream of fugitive ideas; and he rarely rouses himself to the painful attempt to check or counteract the capricious, and, as a rule, purely mechanical associations of ideas and succession of images, and bring under discipline the disorderly tumult of his fluid presentations. On the contrary, he rejoices in his faculty of imagination, which he contrasts with the insipidity of the Philistine, and devotes himself with predilection to all sorts of unlicensed pursuits permitted by the unshackled vagabondage of his mind; while he cannot endure well-ordered civil occupations, requiring attention and constant heed to reality. He calls this "having an idealist temperament," ascribes to himself irresistible æsthetic propinquities, and proudly styles himself an artist.

We will briefly mention some peculiarities frequently manifested by a degenerate. He is tormented by doubts, seeks for the basis of all phenomena, especially those whose first causes are completely inaccessible to us, and is unhappy when his inquiries and ruminations lead, as is natural, to no result. He is ever supplying new recruits to the army of system-inventing metaphysicians, profound expositors of the riddle of the universe, seekers for the philosopher's stone, the squaring of the circle and perpetual motion.[9] These last three subjects have such a special attraction for him, that the Patent Office at Washington is forced to keep on hand printed replies to the numberless memorials in which patents are constantly demanded for the solution of these chimerical problems. In view of Lombroso's researches,[10] it can scarcely be doubted that the writings and acts of revolutionists and anarchists are also attributable to degeneracy. The degenerate is incapable of adapting himself to existing circumstances. This incapacity, indeed, is an indication of morbid variation in every species, and probably a primary cause of their sudden extinction. He therefore rebels against conditions and views of things which he necessarily feels to be painful, chiefly because they impose upon him the duty of self-control, of which he is incapable on account of his organic weakness of will. Thus he becomes an improver of the world, and devises plans for making mankind happy, which, without exception, are conspicuous quite as much by their fervent philanthropy, and often pathetic sincerity, as by their absurdity and monstrous ignorance of all real relations.

Finally, a cardinal mark of degeneration which I have reserved to the last, is mysticism. * * *

I have enumerated the most important features characterizing the mental condition of the degenerate. The reader can now judge for himself whether or not the diagnosis "degeneration" is applicable to the originators of the new æsthetic tendencies. It must not for that matter be supposed that degeneration is synonymous with absence of talent. Nearly all the inquirers who have had degenerates under their observation expressly establish the contrary. "The degenerate," says Legrain,[11] "may

---

9. Famously impossible ideas. In alchemy, the "philosopher's stone" could supposedly transmute lead into gold and grant immortality.
10. This 19th-c. Italian criminologist theorized that criminals carried "stigmata."
11. Author of *Du Délire chez les Dégénérés* (Of the Delirium of Degenerates; Paris, 1886).

be a genius. A badly balanced mind is susceptible of the highest conceptions, while, on the other hand, one meets in the same mind with traits of meanness and pettiness all the more striking from the fact that they co-exist with the most brilliant qualities." We shall find this reservation in all authors who have contributed to the natural history of the degenerate. "As regards their intellect, they can," says Roubinovitch, "attain to a high degree of development, but from a moral point of view their existence is completely deranged. . . . A degenerate will employ his brilliant faculties quite as well in the service of some grand object as in the satisfaction of the basest propensities." Lombroso has cited a large number of undoubted geniuses who were equally undoubted mattoids,[12] graphomaniacs,[13] or pronounced lunatics; and the utterance of a French savant, Guérinsen, "Genius is a disease of the nerves," has become a "winged word."[14] This expression was imprudent, for it gave ignorant babblers a pretext, and apparently a right, to talk of exaggeration, and to condemn experts in nervous and mental diseases, because they professedly saw a lunatic in everyone who ventured to be something more than the most ordinary, characterless, average being. Science does not assert that every genius is a lunatic; there are some geniuses of superabundant power whose high privilege consists in the possession of one or other extraordinarily developed faculty, without the rest of their faculties falling short of the average standard. Just as little, naturally, is every lunatic a genius; most of them, even if we disregard idiots of different degrees, are much rather pitiably stupid and incapable; but in many, nay, in abundant cases, the "higher degenerate" of Magnan, just as he occasionally exhibits gigantic bodily stature or the disproportionate growth of particular parts, has some mental gift exceptionally developed at the cost, it is true, of the remaining faculties, which are wholly or partially atrophied. It is this which enables the well-informed to distinguish at the first glance between the sane genius, and the highly, or even the most highly, gifted degenerate. Take from the former the special capacity through which he becomes a genius, and there still remains a capable, often conspicuously intelligent, clever, moral, and judicious man, who will hold his ground with propriety in our social mechanism. Let the same be tried in the case of a degenerate, and there remains only a criminal or madman, for whom healthy humanity can find no use. If Goethe[15] had never written a line of verse, he would, all the same, have still remained a man of the world, of good principles, a fine art connoisseur, a judicious collector, a keen observer of nature. Let us, on the contrary, imagine a Schopenhauer who had written no astounding books, and we should have before us only a repulsive lusus naturæ,[16] whose morals would necesssarily exclude him from all respectable society, and whose fixed idea that he was a victim of persecution would point him out as a subject for a madhouse. The lack of harmony, the absence of balance, the singular incapacity of usefully applying, or deriving satisfaction from, their own special faculty among highly-gifted degenerates, strikes every healthy censor who does not allow himself to be prejudiced by the noisy admiration of critics, themselves degenerates: and will always prevent his

---

12. Semi-insane people.
13. Compulsive writers.
14. Widespread poeticism.
15. Johann Wolfgang von Goethe (1749–1832), German Romantic poet, novelist, and playwright, whose *Sorrows of Young Werther* (1774), about a suicidal lover, became an international bestseller.
16. Latin: freak of nature.

mistaking the mattoid for the same exceptional man who opens out new paths for humanity and leads it to higher developments. * * *

Added to this emotionalism and susceptibility to suggestion is a love of self never met with in a sane person in anything like the same degree. The hysterical person's own "I" towers up before his inner vision, and so completely fills his mental horizon that it conceals the whole of the remaining universe. He cannot endure that others should ignore him. He desires to be as important to his fellow-men as he is to himself. * * *

It is certainly unnecessary to draw the reader's attention in a special manner to the complete coincidence of this clinical picture of hysteria with the description of the peculiarities of the *fin-de-siècle* public, and to the fact that in the former we meet with all the features made familiar to us by the consideration of contemporary phenomena; in particular with the passion for imitating in externals—in dress, attitude, fashion of the hair and beard—the figures in old and modern pictures, and the feverish effort, through any sort of singularity, to make themselves talked about. The observation of pronounced cases of degeneration and hysteria, whose condition makes them necessary subjects for medical treatment, gives us also the key to the comprehension of subordinate details in the fashions of the day. The present rage for collecting, the piling up, in dwellings, of aimless bric-à-brac, which does not become any more useful or beautiful by being fondly called *bibelots*, appear to us in a completely new light when we know that Magnan has established the existence of an irresistible desire among the degenerate to accumulate useless trifles. It is so firmly imprinted and so peculiar that Magnan declares it to be a stigma of degeneration, and has invented for it the name "oniomania," or "buying craze." This is not to be confounded with the desire for buying, which possesses those who are in the first stage of general paralysis. The purchases of these persons are due to their delusion as to their own greatness. They lay in great supplies because they fancy themselves millionaires. The oniomaniac, on the contrary, neither buys enormous quantities of one and the same thing, nor is the price a matter of indifference to him as with the paralytic. He is simply unable to pass by any lumber without feeling an impulse to acquire it.

The curious style of certain recent painters—"impressionists," "stipplers," or "mosaists," "papilloteurs" or "quiverers," "roaring" colourists, dyers in gray and faded tints—becomes at once intelligible to us if we keep in view the researches of the Charcot[17] school into the visual derangements in degeneration and hysteria. The painters who assure us that they are sincere, and reproduce nature as they see it, speak the truth. The degenerate artist who suffers from *nystagmus*, or trembling of the eyeball, will, in fact, perceive the phenomena of nature trembling, restless, devoid of firm outline, and, if he is a conscientious painter, will give us pictures reminding us of the mode practised by the draughtsmen of the *Fliegende Blätter*[18] when they represent a wet dog shaking himself vigorously. If his pictures fail to produce a comic effect, it is only because the attentive beholder reads in them the desperate effort to reproduce fully an impression incapable of reproduction by the expedients of the painter's art as devised by men of normal vision.

17. Leading French neurologist of the 19th c. and Freud's teacher, famous for using hypnosis on hysterical patients.
18. German magazine founded in 1844.

There is hardly a hysterical subject whose retina is not partly insensitive. As a rule the insensitive parts are connected, and include the outer half of the retina. In these cases the field of vision is more or less contracted, and appears to him not as it does to the normal man—as a circle—but as a picture bordered by whimsically zigzag lines. Often, however, the insensitive parts are not connected, but are scattered in isolated spots over the entire retina. Then the sufferer will have all sorts of gaps in his field of vision, producing strange effects, and if he paints what he sees, he will be inclined to place in juxtaposition larger or smaller points or spots which are completely or partially dissociated. * * *

There is yet another phenomenon highly characteristic in some cases of degeneracy, in others of hysteria. This is the formation of close groups or schools uncompromisingly exclusive to outsiders, observable to-day in literature and art. Healthy artists or authors, in possession of minds in a condition of well-regulated equilibrium, will never think of grouping themselves into an association, which may at pleasure be termed a sect or band; of devising a catechism, of binding themselves to definite æsthetic dogmas, and of entering the lists for these with the fanatical intolerance of Spanish inquisitors. If any human activity is individualistic, it is that of the artist. True talent is always personal. In its creations it reproduces itself, its own views and feelings, and not the articles of faith learnt from any æsthetic apostle; it follows its creative impulses, not a theoretical formula preached by the founder of a new artistic or literary church; it constructs its work in the form organically necessary to it, not in that proclaimed by a leader as demanded by the fashion of the day. The mere fact that an artist or author allows himself to be sworn in to the party cry of any "ism," that he perambulates with jubilations behind a banner and Turkish music, is complete evidence of his lack of individuality—that is, of talent. If the mental movements of a period—even those which are healthy and prolific—range themselves, as a rule, under certain main tendencies, which receive each its distinguishing name, this is the work of historians of civilization or literature, who subsequently survey the combined picture of an epoch, and for their own convenience undertake divisions and classifications, in order that they may more correctly find their way among the multifariousness of the phenomena. These are, however, almost always arbitrary and artificial. Independent minds (we are not here speaking of mere imitators), united by a good critic into a group, may, it is true, have a certain resemblance to each other, but, as a rule, this resemblance will be the consequence, not of actual internal affinity, but of external influences. No one is able completely to withdraw himself from the influences of his time, and under the impression of events which affect all contemporaries alike, as well as of the scientific views prevailing at a given time, certain features develop themselves in all the works of an epoch, which stamp them as of the same date. But the same men who subsequently appear so naturally in each other's company, in historical works, that they seem to form a family, went when they lived their separate ways far asunder, little suspecting that at one time they would be united under one common designation. Quite otherwise it is when authors or artists consciously and intentionally meet together and found an æsthetic school, as a joint-stock bank[19] is founded, with a title for which, if possible, the protection of the law

---

19. Funded by shares rather than private capital.

is claimed, with by-laws, joint capital, etc. This may be ordinary speculation, but as a rule it is disease. * * *

This is the natural history of the æsthetic schools. Under the influence of an obsession, a degenerate mind promulgates some doctrine or other—realism, pornography, mysticism, symbolism, diabolism. He does this with vehement penetrating eloquence, with eagerness and fiery heedlessness. Other degenerate, hysterical, neurasthenical minds flock around him, receive from his lips the new doctrine, and live thenceforth only to propagate it.

In this case all the participants are sincere—the founder as well as the disciples. They act as, in consequence of the diseased constitution of their brain and nervous system, they are compelled to act. The picture, however, which from a clinical standpoint is perfectly clear, gets dimmed if the apostle of a craze and his followers succeed in attracting to themselves the attention of wider circles. He then receives a concourse of unbelievers, who are very well able to recognise the insanity of the new doctrine, but who nevertheless accept it, because they hope, as associates of the new sect, to acquire fame and money. In every civilized nation which has a developed art and literature there are numerous intellectual eunuchs, incapable of producing with their own powers a living mental work, but quite able to imitate the process of production. These cripples form, unfortunately, the majority of professional authors and artists, and their many noxious followers often enough stifle true and original talent. Now it is these who hasten to act as camp-followers[20] for every new tendency which seems to come into fashion. They are naturally the most modern of moderns, for no precept of individuality, no artistic knowledge, hinders them from bunglingly imitating the newest model with all the assiduity of an artisan. Clever in discerning externals, unscrupulous copyists and plagiarists, they crowd round every original phenomenon, be it healthy or unhealthy, and without loss of time set about disseminating counterfeit copies of it. To-day they are symbolists, as yesterday they were realists or pornographists. If they can promise themselves fame and a good sale, they write of mysteries with the same fluency as if they were spinning romances of knights and robbers, tales of adventure, Roman tragedies, and village stories at a time when newspaper critics and the public seemed to demand these things in preference to others. Now these practitioners, who, let it be again asserted, constitute the great majority of the mental workers of the fashionable sects in art and literature, and therefore of the associates of these sects also, are intellectually quite sane, even if they stand at a very low level of development, and were anyone to examine them, he might easily doubt the accuracy of the diagnosis "Degeneration" as regards the confessors of the new doctrines. Hence some caution must be exercised in the inquiry, and the sincere originators be always distinguished from the aping intriguers,—the founder of the religion and his apostles from the rabble to whom the Sermon on the Mount is of less concern than the miraculous draught of fishes and the multiplication of loaves.[21]

It has now been shown how schools originate. They arise from the degeneration of their founders and of the imitators they have convinced. That they come into fashion, and for a short time attain a noisy success, is due to the peculiarities of the recipient public, namely, to hysteria. * * * Thus the hysterical allow themselves without

---

20. Those who follow an army (servants, tradesmen, prostitutes).
21. Jesus's audience, overlooking his words because they can focus only on his miraculous provision of food.

more ado to be convinced of the magnificence of a work, and even find in it beauties of the highest kind, unthought of by the authors themselves and the appointed trumpeters of their fame. * * *

Thus a regular concourse is established about a victim of degeneration. The fashionable coxcomb, the æsthetic "gigerl,"[22] peeps over the shoulder of the hysterical whose admiration has been suggested to him; the intriguer marches at the heel of the dotard, simulating youth; and between all these comes pushing the inquisitive young street-loafer, who must always be in every place where "something is going on." And this crowd, because it is driven by disease, self-interest and vanity, makes very much more noise and bustle than a far larger number of sane men, who, without self-seeking after-thought, take quiet enjoyment in works of sane talent, and do not feel obliged to shout out their appreciation in the streets, and to threaten with death harmless passers-by who do not join in their jubilations. * * *

Decadentism has not been confined to France alone; it has also established a school in England. We have already mentioned, in the preceding book, one of the earliest and most servile imitators of Baudelaire—Swinburne.[23] I had to class him among the mystics, for the degenerative stigma of mysticism predominates in all his works. He has, it is true, been train-bearer to so many models that he may be ranked among the domestic servants of a great number of masters; but, finally, he will be assigned a place where he has served longest, and that is among the pre-Raphaelites.[24] From Baudelaire he has borrowed principally diabolism and Sadism, unnatural depravity, and a predilection for suffering, disease and crime. The ego-mania of decadentism, its love of the artificial, its aversion to nature, and to all forms of activity and movement, its megalomaniacal contempt for men and its exaggeration of the importance of art, have found their English representative among the "Æsthetes," the chief of whom is Oscar Wilde. * * *

When, therefore, an Oscar Wilde goes about in "æsthetic costume" among gazing Philistines, exciting either their ridicule or their wrath, it is no indication of independence of character, but rather from a purely anti-socialistic, ego-maniacal recklessness and hysterical longing to make a sensation, justified by no exalted aim; nor is it from a strong desire for beauty, but from a malevolent mania for contradiction.

Be that as it may, Wilde obtained, by his buffoon mummery, a notoriety in the whole Anglo-Saxon world that his poems and dramas would never have acquired for him. I have no reason to trouble myself about these, since they are feeble imitations of Rossetti[25] and Swinburne, and of dreary inanity. His prose essays, on the contrary, deserve attention, because they exhibit all the features which enable us to recognise in the "Æsthete" the comrade in art of the Decadent.

Like his French masters, Oscar Wilde despises Nature. "Whatever actually occurs is spoiled for art. All bad poetry springs from genuine feeling. To be natural is to be obvious, and to be obvious is to be inartistic."[26]

---

22. Fop.

23. 19th-c. poets celebrating sin and sexuality. Charles Baudelaire's *Les Fleurs du Mal* (Flowers of Evil; 1857), influenced Algernon Charles Swinburne, famous for his lyrical celebrations of necrophilia and masochism.

24. This controversial mid-Victorian artistic movement featured mystical symbols, medieval styles, and lush natural images.

25. Dante Gabriel Rossetti (1828–82), leading Pre-Raphaelite painter and poet.

26. In the following paragraphs, Nordau quotes from Wilde's essays "The Critic as Artist" and "Pen, Pencil and Poison," both published in *Intentions* (1891).

He is a "cultivator of the Ego," and feels deliciously indignant at the fact that Nature dares to be indifferent to his important person. "Nature is so indifferent, so unappreciative. Whenever I am walking in the park here, I always feel that I am no more to her than the cattle that browse on the slope."

With regard to himself and the human species, he shares the opinion of Des Esseintes.[27] "Ah! don't say that you agree with me. When people agree with me I always feel that I must be wrong."

His ideal of life is inactivity. "It is only the Philistine who seeks to estimate a personality by the vulgar test of production. This young dandy sought to be some-body rather than to do something." "Society often forgives the criminal; it never for-gives the dreamer. The beautiful sterile emotions that art excites in us are hateful in its eyes. . . . People . . . are always coming shamelessly up to one . . . and saying in a loud, stentorian voice, "What are you doing?" whereas, "What are you thinking?" is the only question that any civilized being should ever be allowed to whisper to another. . . . Contemplation . . . in the opinion of the highest culture, is the proper occupation of man. . . . It is to do nothing that the elect exist. Action is limited and relative. Unlimited and absolute is the vision of him who sits at ease and watches, who walks in loneliness and dreams." "The sure way of knowing nothing about life is to try to make one's self useful." "From time to time the world cries out against some charming artistic poet, because, to use its hackneyed and silly phrase, he has "nothing to say." But if he had something to say, he would probably say it, and the result would be tedious. It is just because he has no new message that he can do beautiful work."

Oscar Wilde apparently admires immorality, sin and crime. In a very affectionate biographical treatise on Thomas Griffith Wainwright, designer, painter, and author, and the murderer of several people, he says: "He was a forger of no mean or ordinary capabilities, and as a subtle and secret poisoner almost without rival in this or any age. This remarkable man, so powerful with 'pen, pencil, and poison,'" etc. "He sought to find expression by pen or poison." "When a friend reproached him with the murder of Helen Abercrombie, he shrugged his shoulders and said, 'Yes; it was a dreadful thing to do, but she had very thick ankles.'" "His crimes seem to have had an important effect upon his art. They gave a strong personality to his style, a qual-ity that his early work certainly lacked." "There is no sin except stupidity." "An idea that is not dangerous is unworthy of being called an idea at all."

He cultivates incidentally a slight mysticism in colours. "He," Wainwright, "had that curious love of green which in individuals is always the sign of a subtle, artistic temperament, and in nations is said to denote a laxity, if not a decadence of morals."

But the central idea of his tortuously disdainful prattling, pursuing as its chief aim the heckling of the Philistine, and laboriously seeking the opposite pole to sound com-mon-sense, is the glorification of art. Wilde sets forth in the following manner the sys-tem of the "Æsthetes": "Briefly, then, their doctrines are these: Art never expresses anything but itself. It has an independent life, just as Thought has, and develops purely on its own lines. . . . The second doctrine is this: All bad art comes from returning to Life and Nature, and elevating them into ideals. Life and Nature may sometimes be

---

27. Diseased, misanthropic main character of J. K. Huysmans's 1884 decadent novel À *Rebours* (Against the Grain).

used as part of Art's rough material, but before they are of any real service to Art they must be translated into artistic conventions. The moment Art surrenders its imaginative medium [?] it surrenders everything. As a method Realism is a complete failure, and the two things that every artist should avoid are modernity of form and modernity of subject matter. To us who live in the nineteenth century, any century is a suitable subject for art except our own. The only beautiful things are the things that do not concern us. . . . It is exactly because Hecuba is nothing to us that her sorrows are so suitable a motive for a tragedy. . . ." "The third doctrine is that Life imitates Art far more than Art imitates Life. This results not merely from Life's imitative instinct, but from the fact that the self-conscious aim of Life is to find expression, and that Art offers it certain beautiful forms through which it may realize that energy."

On this third point—the influence of art on life—Wilde does not refer to the fact, long ago established by me,[28] that the reciprocal relation between the work of art and the public consists in this, that the former exercises suggestion and the latter submits to it. What he actually wished to say was that nature—not civilized men—develops itself in the direction of forms given it by the artist. "Where, if not from the Impressionists, do we get those wonderful brown fogs that come creeping down our streets, blurring the gas-lamps and changing the houses into monstrous shadows? To whom, if not to them and their master, do we owe the lovely silver mists that brood over our river, and turn to faint forms of fading grace curved bridge and swaying barge? The extraordinary change that has taken place in the climate of London during the last ten years is entirely due to this particular school of Art." If he simply wished to affirm that formerly fog and mist were not felt to be beautiful, and that the artistic rendering of them first drew to them the attention of the multitude, nothing could be said in contradiction; he would have propounded just a hackneyed commonplace with misplaced sententiousness. He asserts, however, that painters have changed the climate, that for the last ten years there have been fogs in London, because the Impressionists have painted fogs—a statement so silly as to require no refutation. It is sufficient to characterize it as artistic mysticism. Lastly, Wilde teaches the following: "Æsthetics are higher than ethics. They belong to a more spiritual sphere. To discern the beauty of a thing is the finest point to which we can arrive. Even a colour-sense is more important in the development of the individual than a sense of right and wrong."

Thus the doctrine of the "Æsthetes" affirms, with the Parnassians, that the work of art is its own aim; with the Diabolists, that it need not be moral—nay, were better to be immoral; with the Decadents, that it is to avoid, and be diametrically opposed to, the natural and the true; and with all these schools of the ego-mania of degeneration, that art is the highest of all human functions. * * *

This rabble, which claims for itself a top place in the scale of intellectual rank, and freedom from the constraint of all moral laws as its most noble privilege, is certainly baser than the lowest scavenger. These creatures are of absolutely no use to the commonwealth, and injure true art by their productions, whose multitude and importunateness shut out from most men the sight of the genuine works of art—never very numerous—of the epoch. They are weaklings in will, unfitted for any activity requiring regular uniform efforts, or else victims to vanity, wishing to be more famous than

---

28. In Nordau's earlier study of the pathology of modern civilization, *Paradoxe* (1885).

is possible to a stone-breaker or a tailor. The uncertainty of comprehension and taste among the majority of mankind, and the incompetency of most professional critics, allow these intruders to make their nest among the arts, and to dwell there as parasites their life long. The buyer soon distinguishes a good boot from a bad one, and the journeyman cobbler who cannot properly sew on a sole finds no employment. But that a book or painting void of all originality is indifferent in quality, and for that reason superfluous, is by no means so easily recognised by the Philistine, or even by the man armed with the critical pen, and the producer of such chaff can apply himself undisturbed to his assiduous waste of time. These bunglers with pen, brush and modelling spattle,[29] strutting about in cap and doublet, naturally swear by the doctrine of the Æsthetes, carry themselves as if they were the salt of humanity, and make a parade of their contempt for the Philistine. They belong, however, to the elements of the race which are most inimical to society. Insensible to its tasks and interests, without the capacity to comprehend a serious thought or a fruitful deed, they dream only of the satisfaction of their basest instincts, and are pernicious—through the example they set as drones, as well as through the confusion they cause in minds insufficiently forewarned, by their abuse of the word "art" to mean demoralization and childishness. Ego-maniacs, Decadents and Æsthetes have completely gathered under their banner this refuse of civilized peoples, and march at its head.

—1895

Janet E. Hogarth
1865–1954

Pioneering New Woman Janet E. Hogarth had a prominent public career and a remarkable education, attending Oxford in 1884 and then Cheltenham Ladies' College, Dorothea Beale's famous institution for educating women. Hogarth became the first superintendent of the Bank of England's female clerks, helped start the *Times* book club, worked on the *Encyclopaedia Britannica*, and was acting editor of the *Fortnightly Review*. In her spare time, Hogarth did occasional journalism, and when she retired she wrote several books, including memoirs, a biography of her husband (the literary critic W. L. Courtney), and a history of the woman's movement in the 1930s. In spite of her interest in women's politics, Hogarth opposed suffrage; in spite of her own career, Hogarth felt ambivalent about women's participation in public life. In "Literary Degenerates" (1895), Hogarth applies Nordau's theory to women's writing.

Literary Degenerates

Have we emerged from the Dark Ages only to pass into the dusk of the nations? "Over the earth the shadows creep with deepening gloom, forms lose their outlines, there is a sound of rending in every tradition;" the high hopes of science have appar-

---

29. A spatula-shaped tool for working clay.

ently come to this, a despairing century tottering to its close. The end of an established order, a contempt for inherited views of custom and morality—that is what Dr. Max Nordau finds to be the essence of the much-abused phrase *fin-de-siècle*. But it is a matter rather for the physician than for the moralist. He may not, indeed, be able to minister to a mind diseased,[1] but it is he and none other than can say to a degenerate age, "Thou ailest here and here." He "recognises at a glance in the *fin-de-siècle* disposition, in the tendencies of contemporary art and poetry, in the life and conduct of the men who write mystic, symbolic, and decadent works, and in the attitude taken by their admirers, the confluence of two well-defined conditions of disease with which he is quite familiar, degeneration and hysteria." What is the cause of this strange disease of modern life? Chiefly a development of mechanical inventions and contrivances of civilisation, which has far outstripped even Nature's immense capacity for adapting organ to function. The growth of large towns is in itself an important factor in nerve wear and tear, not to mention the weariness of perpetual travelling, hourly posts, innumerable newspapers, and a veritable plague of modern novels. Our fathers had no time to adjust their nervous system to this vastly increased demand upon its resources. "Fatigue and exhaustion showed themselves in the first generation under the form of acquired hysteria, in the second as hereditary hysteria." The twilight mood thus produced is a sign of atavism, not progress; in one word it is literary degeneracy.

Degeneracy, then, or a morbid deviation from an original type, shows itself as clearly in certain mental characteristics as it does in certain physical traits, such as malformation of ears, asymmetry, inequalities in the two sides of the head, and other "stigmata." The minds of degenerates are as irregular as their bodies. Some faculties are completely stunted, others morbidly exaggerated. Nearly all lack the sense of right and wrong, and are indeed morally insane. Now the two psychological roots of moral insanity are, according to Max Nordau, unbounded egoism and impulsiveness. The degenerate is emotional, he is a pessimist, a prey to vague and causeless fears, of wavering will and disinclined to action, but with a strong predilection for inane reverie. He is tormented by doubts, he invents metaphysical systems, and he besieges the Patent Office with ingenious devices for squaring the circle. He rebels both in word and deed against the existing order of society, and he takes refuge in various forms of mysticism. On the other hand, he may often be a genius. Himself, in that case, a higher degenerate, his public consists chiefly of a vast number of "lower degenerates," reinforced by a crowd of foolish and imitative people, themselves affected by hysteria and neurasthenia. These hysterical subjects, whether higher or lower degenerates, are emotional and peculiarly susceptible to the influence of suggestion. They exhibit a love of self never met with in a sane person in anything like the same degree, and at the same time are often completely impervious to various forms of external excitation. Of such are the egomaniacs and the megalomaniacs, always supposing that the latter would not be better described as victims of excessive vanity. Then there are the Realists or Naturalists, like M. Zola,[2] though here, again, it seems a little difficult to distinguish between mental and moral weakness.

---

1. Macbeth's query about how to treat insanity (*Macbeth* 5.3).
2. French novelist Émile Zola (1840–1902) famously depicted unsavory scenes.

But to Dr. Nordau the moral is the mental, at least every form of vice may apparently be ascribed to nerve degeneracy, which is a form of insanity. He has chosen his examples so largely from France, that it has probably not occurred to him to vary their sex. Feminine talent plays but a small part in contemporary French literature, but if he had turned his eyes oftener to England, surely he would have found a promising field for speculation in our rising school of women writers. At least they would have served to swell the list of illustrations which he marshals under the three groups of Mystics, Egomaniacs, and Realists. So aptly have they caught his ideas, even before he had borrowed them from Dr. Lombroso, that it is difficult not to credit them with powers of clairvoyance.

If, as some critics uphold, æstheticism and Mr. Whistler have succeeded in modifying the London climate,[3] it is, perhaps, scarcely incredible that an advance in mental therapeutics should have exercised a powerful effect upon the literary atmosphere. Now that we know genius to be a disease of the nerves, what more natural than that women should use their favourite fallacy of simple conversion? It has yet to be proved that advanced views involve increasing logical accuracy, and if abnormal nerve excitement can be made to spell genius, what is to hinder every woman from obtaining the coveted distinction? The only question is whether it is a distinction, or, at any rate, whether it will remain so. The plain man might be forgiven even now, if he declared himself to be the real deviation from a commonplace type; there is some consolation in the thought that before the beginning of the twentieth century probably it will be a proud distinction to be sane. In the meantime, however, we have to face a flood of feminine literature, more or less admirable in manner, certainly more rather than less objectionable in matter. Even if we see in it an illustration of Max Nordau's canons of mental degeneracy, it is a little depressing that the ravings of lunacy should on the surface bear such a strong family likeness to what has hitherto been accepted as literature. True, the highest genius, as he reminds us, is sane, but why should a host of minor talents combine degenerate minds with such an undoubted ear for style? Perfection of literary manner, or even an approach to it, used to be thought the monopoly of classical scholarship. Can this be a mere academic prejudice, or is it just the substitution of something else for a classical training which explains at once the excellence of much modern writing and les défauts de ses qualités?[4] Most of the stories written by women, which deserve the epithet fin-de-siècle, are characterized by smartness of phrase, a happy choice of epithets, a certain capacity for presenting a scene with a few clear, bold strokes, and a marked predilection for sensual accessories of colour and perfume. They are impressionist, they are suggestive, in both senses of the word, and they often prove the existence of a nice discrimination for the finer shades of emotion, less frequently any firm grasp of character. They almost always raise a doubt as to the writer's capacity for sustained effort, and their promise appears likely for ever to lack fulfilment. External evidence would hardly justify us in assigning either their merits or demerits to a study of the classics. As a matter of fact, even in these days of the higher education, very few women have read their Homer or their Plato, and still fewer are as ready with their Horace as Mr. Gladstone.[5] Certainly the late Master of

---

3. Wilde's "The Decay of Lying" (see p. 19).
4. French: the defects of its qualities.
5. Prime Minister W. E. Gladstone (1809–98).

Balliol[6] has tempted a fair number to give an opinion upon the Platonic philosophy, but even those who have got beyond the community of wives are seldom sound upon anything except the myth of the Final Judgment.[7] Add to these philosophic studies a translation of Sophocles and perhaps a doubtful struggle with a play or two in the original; you will then have summed up pretty completely the Greek reading of any woman, even a woman who writes. Latin disturbs her even less; it is thought to be less closely associated with culture, and it can obviously have no connection with the "new Hellenism" for which she sighs.[8]

This she gets chiefly from a mis-reading of Mr. Pater, together with a closer study of poets like Mr. Swinburne and Mr. William Morris, or prose esssayists of the school of Mr. J. A. Symonds.[9] A faithful literary census, based perhaps on returns got from hypnotised subjects, would, I suspect, result in a list of authors strangely like Max Nordau's collection of literary degenerates. For the first places, probably Ibsen and Tolstoi[10] would be the chief competitors, though it is hinted that the second is already a little out of date. A classification by languages would put French first, and all the rest in comparison nowhere, so that Decadents, Diabolists, Parnassians, Symbolists, *et hoc genus omne*,[11] tread close upon the heels of the Scandinavian and Russian degenerates. But the internal evidence afforded by *fin de siècle* literature itself is even stronger than the presumption against a classical education, which can be based upon experience. A want of balance, a deficient sense of proportion with a resulting lack of humour, and a total absence of any sort of reticence in the expression of emotion, are its most characteristic notes. Nothing could be farther from the well-balanced serenity of the classical spirit, with its instinct for proportion and its love of restraint. What would become of the misnamed Independent Theatre[12] if it were forced to conform to the Greek canons of dramatic art? and where would the new Hellenists be if they realised that there were other schools of philosophy in Greece besides the Cyrenaics and Epicureans?[13] Truly, Mr. Pater has been evil-entreated by his disciples. Then, was it not the breeze which sets from Norway that wafted to us the last two stories of *Key Notes*, to take only one out of innumerable instances? Where but in Ibsen's *Ghosts* shall we find a parallel for the symptoms of the dying drunkard?[14] And is not the creator of Nora responsible for "the little woman with the great soul," who glides out of her garments in our presence, and invites us to share so many of the mysteries of the toilet? Perhaps there is a Parisian echo in the scented grey gloves, size five and three-quarters, which strew the paths of her romance; but surely the frames of white Aspinall, mounted in blue plush, which encase the portraits of the men who dared her to defy the world, can belong only to the taste of the barbaric North. But there are other than Northern influences at work. Even in its deepest depths of degradation, French art generally contrives to shroud the corpse

---

6. Renowned classical scholar Benjamin Jowett at Balliol College, Oxford.
7. Plato's *Republic* argues that male guardians should share women; his *Gorgias* takes up Zeus's rules for judging the dead.
8. Hope for a rebirth of Greek culture.
9. Writers accused of celebrating sensual pleasure.
10. Norwegian dramatist Henrik Ibsen and Russian novelist Leo Tolstoy were famous social radicals.
11. Latin: and all that type.
12. Founded in 1891 as a venue for realist drama, it sponsored plays by Ibsen and George Bernard Shaw.
13. The Cyrenaics valued feeling over virtue, while the Epicureans sought moderate indulgences. Hogarth is alluding to Pater's novel *Marius the Epicurean* (1885).
14. Hogarth is speculating about Ibsen's influence on the short stories of George Egerton.

of sensuality in the fair, white linen garment of a beautiful style. Most of the women who dissect their souls in the pages of the Yellow Book,[15] or in the novel with or without a purpose, have caught more than a passing echo of the saving grace of words. Like the impressionist school of artists,[16] they can seize the pictorial moment, and record a fleeting phase with a technical skill that often disarms the hostile critic.

Probably there are about as many definitions of impressionism as there are art critics. For the moment, however, let it stand for the portrayal, and hence the culture, of the emotions; or, if you prefer the phrase, for "living one's own life." The two definitions are more nearly related than appears at first sight. To represent emotion, say the modern sensualists, you must experience it; the literary artist or, indeed, any artist, must multiply his sensations as far as possible, regardless of whether they bring him pleasure or pain, and leaving their moral bearing wholly out of account. It is a new rendering of *tout savoir, c'est tout pardonner*, or, perhaps, the phrase should be *tout savoir, c'est tout pouvoir*.[17] Probably a woman will not have to make great efforts. Emotion fills so large a place already in the life, even of the normal woman, that it is scarcely surprising if its empire is soon supreme over the abnormal. If to be a creature of impulse is to be a mental degenerate, what woman can hope to be saved? Certainly no one who reads "Degeneration" and yields to the fascinating pastime of classifying her acquaintances under their appropriate forms of mania; for her own turn must come, and then she is bound to become an egomaniac, if to be an egomaniac is to dwell upon your internal experiences. And there are so many women of leisure with a taste for general reading. Why should France find its literary degenerates almost entirely amongst men? Probably the population statistics could solve the problem. Frenchwomen either have something better to do than to analyse their own emotions and to indulge in erotic hallucinations, or at least if they choose that form of indulgence they do not confide it to the world. In England we are less happy. There are no *mariages de convenance*,[18] or, at least, if there are, we do not admit it. Even if the system were introduced, where should we find the necessary partners, if one little literary year can bring us "A Superfluous Woman," a "One too Many," and a host of "Odd Women"?[19] With remarkable inconsistency the "odd" women invariably propose to interpret "living their own life" as living a life *à deux*.[20] If they are really "odd," it is a little difficult to know how they are all going to manage it; but it is at least consoling to learn that for the literary imagination there is no such thing as a "superfluous woman," she is merely a sacrifice to the exigencies of finding a new and striking title.

Seriously, however, a woman must have something upon which to expend her emotions. The source of the evil is to be sought in her detachment from family life, rather than in her excess of feeling. Can anything be more ludicrous or more pitiable than her attempt to inaugurate her own life by abandoning at the outset the very conditions of living it? Having shaken off the claims upon her affection with which she

---

15. The definitive aesthetic journal.
16. Controversial late-19th-c. French painters, including Cézanne, Monet, and Renoir, who depicted contemporary scenes with sketchy brushwork, bright color, and light.
17. French: to know all is to pardon all. Hogarth's revision: to know all is to be capable of all.
18. French: arranged marriages.
19. Recent New Women novels: Emma Brooke, *A Superfluous Woman* (1894); Eliza Lynn Linton, *One Too Many* (1894); George Gissing, *The Odd Women* (1893).
20. French: in a twosome, a couple. "Odd women" are spinsters.

was first surrounded, she has to set about creating fresh ones, or to revert to the original state of nature. Only to become a pure individualist of the school of Hobbes is certainly to mistake atavism for progress, and consequently to qualify as a degenerate.[21] Moreover, the capacity for indignation, which makes so many women perpetual protestants, is bound to find some object for attack. "The degenerate subject," says Max Nordau, "selects among the arrangements of civilisation such as are either immaterial or distinctly suitable in order to rebel against them." If marriage hardly falls under the first category, the advancing wisdom of mankind through centuries of evolution has generally included it under the second. To the *fin-de-siècle* authoress, however, this "distinctly suitable" arrangement is the head and front of society's offending. With the instinct of a true degenerate, and with wearisome iteration, she rings the changes on this single theme. The slavery of the marriage yoke, the mutual rights of men and women, and their growing mutual disgust, the degradation of the wife who is made her husband's plaything, her undue exaltation at the expense of her bolder sisters, who are prepared to follow nature and defy convention, and finally the delirious fancies of the victims of sex mania; we know the weary round, and would fain leave it behind us for ever. Gladly would we replace the divine right of instinct as an article of faith by a wholesome revival of the obsolete and unscientific doctrine of original sin. These literary phenomena may be pure madness, but for all Max Nordau's theories there is something to be said just now for a re-introduction of the devil. Mephistopheles has been too much forgotten of late to the great detriment of the Fausts who, in olden days, supposed themselves responsible for having entered upon his service.[22]

Still, no doubt, Max Nordau is within his rights if he chooses to call heartless selfishness egomania, and unbounded conceit megalomania. At any rate it would be a little hard to deny the prophet of degeneracy his own obsessions. If, as he says, "A sane man perceives little and rarely his internal excitations, but always and clearly his external impressions," most of the newer school of women writers are undoubtedly insane. Nor is the experience of experts in insanity without significance in this connection. Mr. Havelock Ellis has collected a large amount of testimony as to the peculiar forms which madness takes amongst women; it goes to prove that "in all forms of acute insanity the sexual element is more prominently shown in women than in men." Mr. Ellis adds, however, that the liability has its compensations. Though "the affectability of women exposes them to very diabolical manifestations, it is also the source of what is most angelic in woman. Poets have racked their brains to express and to account for this mixture of heaven and hell. We see that the key is really a very simple one; both the heaven and hell of women are but aspects of the same physiological affectability. Seeing this, we may see too that those worthy persons who are anxious to cut off the devil's tail might find, if they succeeded, that they had also shorn the angel of her wings." Was Shakespeare anticipating this pronouncement of modern science when he put those piteous songs into poor Ophelia's mouth, or was it a mere accident which added this faithful companion picture to his tragic study of "a noble mind o'erthrown" in its struggle with a time out of joint?[23]

---

21. 17th-c. political philosopher Thomas Hobbes imagined a pure state of nature, without government. Atavism is reversion to barbarism.
22. Legend of Dr. Faust selling his soul to the devil in exchange for fame and knowledge.
23. Discussions of Hamlet's apparent derangement and unsettled times (*Hamlet* 1.5 and 3.1).

May the angel soon find her wings again, or may she, at least, keep her diabolical manifestations out of print. Tolstoi, at his worst, is almost preferable to the flood of literature professing to lay bare the mysteries of sex with a daring only possible to a shameless depth of ignorance. Few people are without the germs of possible disease; but are the confused and morbid imaginings, which the sane hide deep within their breast, to be offered to the world at large as the discovery of a privileged few? To be silly and sinful is not necessarily to be singular. We commend this consideration to the authoress of *Theodora*.[24]

But, perhaps, women ought to be forgiven much of their want of balance for the sake of what they have suffered from over rapid emancipation. If the century as a whole has progressed by leaps and bounds, women have advanced at an almost immeasurable speed. Small wonder, therefore, that their self-control has not kept pace with the demands upon their nervous energy. When half-education has given way to a completer training, and when the independent woman attains the years which bring the philosophic mind, perhaps she may discover new objects upon which to expend her emotions, and may be content, therefore, to forego the psychological analysis of passion. After all, sex mania in art and literature can be but a passing phase, and possibly the modern heroine's admirable manner of expressing herself may outlast her repulsive qualities, to the exceeding great benefit of literature and of society. In a generation more the degenerate may be a mere sporadic survival, little likely to persist amid a race endowed with sound minds and healthy nerves. By that time probably even theatrical managers will recognise that of all things there cometh satiety, and that the woman with a past is no exception to this golden rule.

Meanwhile let us be grateful to Dr. Nordau for his display of graphomania.[25] It is not every higher degenerate whose passion for writing has made him so entertaining a critic. Or if there is really more method in his madness let moralists be left to find it out. In literature, as in bonnets, fashion is for ever turning the old into the new, and who knows whether the wheel may not come again full circle with a Shakespeare at the top and a Maeterlinckian[26] echo far beneath his feet?

—1895

George Bernard Shaw
1856–1950

With his fierce red beard, uncouth woolen outfits, and venomous language, George Bernard Shaw made an unforgettable impression. Shaw's plays are notable for their brilliant dialogue, mutable ideas, and comic contradictions; they include *Mrs. Warren's Profession* (1893), *Arms and the Man* (1894), *Candida* (1897), *Man and Superman* (1905), *Major Barbara* (1905),

---

24. "Victoria Crosse" (Vivian Cory), "Theodora: A Fragment," appeared in *The Yellow Book* in 1895.
25. Compulsive writing.
26. In spite of Hogarth's prediction, Belgian poet, dramatist, and philosopher Maurice Maeterlinck would win the Nobel Prize in 1911.

Pygmalion (1913), and *Heartbreak House* (1920). He won the Nobel Prize in 1925. At the *fin de siècle*, he was an influential critic and socialist essayist. Shaw also befriended (and had affairs with) several leading actresses and served as drama and music critic for several papers, including *The Pall Mall Gazette* (1885–88) and *Saturday Review* (1895–98). Shaw was born in Ireland to an unconventional family (his mother's lover lived in the household). He became a Fabian socialist in 1884. His writing is shaped by his fiery assertion of the absolute equality of every person and his remorselessly clever excoriation of accepted norms. No aesthete, Shaw wrote art for the sake of reform: "why would art if it was just for art's sake interest me at all?" His riposte to Nordau, originally commissioned by the anarchist paper *Liberty* in 1895, was revised and extended into the following pamphlet in 1908. For more information about Shaw, see p. 369.

from The Sanity of Art

Nordau's trick of calling rhyme echolalia[1] is reapplied in the case of authorship, which he calls graphomania[2] when he happens not to like the author. He insists that Wagner,[3] who was a voluminous author as well as a composer, was a graphomaniac; and his proof is that in his books we find "the restless repetition of one and the same strain of thought . . . Opera and Drama, Judaism in Music, Religion and the State, Art and Religion, and the Vocation of Opera are nothing more than the amplification of single passages in The Art-Work of the Future." This is a capital example of Nordau's limited power of attention. The moment that limited power is concentrated on his theory of degeneration, he loses sight of everything else, and drives his one borrowed horse into every obstacle on the road. To those of us who can attend to more than one thing at a time, there is no observation more familiar, and more frequently confirmed, than that this growth of pregnant single sentences into whole books which Nordau discovers in Wagner, balanced as it always is by the contraction of whole boyish chapters into single epigrams, is the process by which all great writers, speakers, artists, and thinkers elaborate their life-work. Let me take a writer after Nordau's own heart, a shrewd Yorkshireman, one whom he quotes as a trustworthy example of what he calls "the clear, mentally sane author, who, feeling himself impelled to say something, once for all expresses himself as distinctly and impressively as it is possible for him to do, and has done with it": namely, Dr. Henry Maudsley.[4] Dr. Maudsley is a clever and cultivated specialist in insanity, who has written several interesting books, consisting of repetitions, amplifications, and historical illustrations of the same idea, which is, if I may put it rather more bluntly than the urbane author, nothing less than the identification of religious with sexual ecstasy. And the upshot of it is the conventional scientific pessimism, from which Dr. Maudsley never gets away; so that his last book repeats his first book, instead of leaving it far behind, as Wagner's State and Religion leaves his Art and Revolution behind. But now that I have prepared the way by quoting Dr. Maudsley, why should I not ask Max Nordau himself to step before the looking-glass and tell us frankly whether, even in the ranks of his "psychiatrists" and lunacy doctors, he can pick out

---

1. Compulsive rhyming.
2. Compulsive writing.
3. German composer Richard Wagner (1813–83), famous for innovative operas based on German myths.
4. A pioneering British psychologist and a fervent believer in degeneration.

Max Beerbohm, [George Bernard Shaw] "Magnetic, he has the power to infect almost everyone with the delight he takes in himself" (1905).

a crank more hopelessly obsessed with one idea than himself? If you want an example of echolalia, can you find a more shocking one than this gentleman who, when
you say "mania," immediately begins to gabble Egomania, Graphomania,
Megalomania, Onomatomania, Pyromania, Kleptomania, Dipsomania, Erotomania,
Arithmomania, Oniomania, and is started off by the termination "phobia" with a
string of Agoraphobia, Claustrophobia, Rupophobia, Iophobia, Nosophobia,
Aichmophobia, Belenophobia, Cremnophobia, and Trichophobia?[5] After which he
suddenly observes: "This is simply philologico-medical trifling," a remark which looks
like returning sanity until he follows it up by clasping his temples in the true bed-
lamite manner, and complaining that "psychiatry is being stuffed with useless and disturbing designations," whereas, if the psychiatrists would only listen to him, they
would see that there is only one phobia and one mania: namely, degeneracy. That is,
the philologico-medical triflers are not crazy enough for him. He is so utterly mad on
the subject of degeneration that he finds the symptoms of it in the loftiest geniuses as
plainly as in the lowest jailbirds, the exceptions being himself, Lombroso, Krafft-
Ebing,[6] Dr. Maudsley, Goethe, Shakespear, and Beethoven. Perhaps he would have
dwelt on a case so convenient in many ways for his theory as Coleridge but that it
would spoil the connection between degeneration and "railway spine."[7] If a man's
senses are acute, he is degenerate, hyperæsthesia[8] having been observed in asylums.
If they are dull, he is degenerate, anæsthesia being the stigma of the craziness which
made old women confess to witchcraft. If he is particular as to what he wears, he is
degenerate: silk dressing-gowns and knee-breeches are grave symptoms, and woollen
shirts conclusive. If he is negligent in these matters, clearly he is inattentive, and
therefore degenerate. If he drinks, he is neurotic: if he is a vegetarian and teetotaller,
let him be locked up at once. If he lives an evil life, that fact condemns him without
further words: if on the other hand his conduct is irreproachable, he is a wretched
"mattoid,"[9] incapable of the will and courage to realize his vicious propensities in
action. If he writes verse, he is afflicted with echolalia; if he writes prose, he is a
graphomaniac; if in his books he is tenacious of his ideas, he is obsessed; if not, he is
"amorphous" and "inattentive." Wagner, as we have seen, contrived to be both
obsessed and inattentive, as might be expected from one who was "himself alone
charged with a greater abundance of degeneration than all the other degenerates put
together." And so on and so forth.

     There is, however, one sort of mental weakness, common among men who take
to science, as so many people take to art, without the necessary brain power, which
Nordau, with amusing unconsciousness of himself, has omitted. I mean the weakness
of the man who, when his theory works out into a flagrant contradiction of the facts,
concludes "So much the worse for the facts: let them be altered," instead of "So much
the worse for my theory." What in the name of common-sense is the value of a theory which identifies Ibsen, Wagner, Tolstoy, Ruskin, and Victor Hugo with the refuse

---

5. Nordau's terms for various types of neurotic obsession.
6. Italian criminologist Cesare Lombroso (1835–1909) strongly influenced Nordau; German psychologist and sexologist Richard von Krafft-Ebing (1840–1902) was interested in deviance.
7. Drug-addicted Romantic poet Samuel Taylor Coleridge (1772–1834) would fit Nordau's theory perfectly,
except that he would disprove Nordau's diagnosis since he predates the railway.
8. Extreme nervous sensitivity.
9. Degenerate.

of our prisons and lunatic asylums? What is to be said of the state of mind of an inveterate pamphleteer and journalist who, instead of accepting that identification as a *reductio ad absurdum*[10] of the theory, desperately sets to work to prove it by pointing out that there are numerous resemblances; that they all have heads and bodies, appetites, aberrations, whims, weaknesses, asymmetrical features, erotic impulses, fallible judgments, and the like common properties, not merely of all human beings, but all vertebrate organisms. Take Nordau's own list: "vague and incoherent thought, the tyranny of the association of ideas, the presence of obsessions, erotic excitability, religious enthusiasm, feebleness of perception, will, memory, and judgment, as well as inattention and instability." Is there a single man capable of understanding these terms who will not plead guilty to some experience of all of them, especially when he is accused vaguely and unscientifically, without any statement of the subject, or the moment, or the circumstances to which the accusation refers, or any attempt to fix a standard of sanity? I could prove Nordau to be an elephant on more evidence than he has brought to prove that our greatest men are degenerate lunatics. The papers in which Swift, having predicted the death of the sham prophet Bickerstaff on a certain date, did, after that date, immediately prove that he was dead,[11] are much more closely and fairly reasoned than any of Nordau's chapters. And Swift, though he afterwards died in a madhouse, was too sane to be the dupe of his own logic. At that rate, where will Nordau die? Probably in a highly respectable suburban villa.

—1895, 1908

Havelock Ellis
1859–1939

By documenting and categorizing sexual proclivities, leading British sexologist Havelock Ellis made desire into a medical condition. Although Ellis trained as a doctor, he left medicine when he became involved in radical groups in London and fell in love with South African novelist Olive Schreiner, with whom he wrote intimate letters for decades. Ellis later married Edith Lees, whose lesbian history he recorded in a case study. What is remarkable about Ellis is his sympathy for his subjects' different sexual interests. He not only refrains from the moral judgments his readers would have expected but actually proposes more liberal social accommodation for diverse desires. This was risky, and Ellis was traumatized when the study of same-sex love he coedited with John Addington Symonds, *Sexual Inversion*, was suppressed and nearly destroyed by Symonds's family, then used to prosecute a bookseller for distributing "indecent materials." The following excerpt from Ellis's major work, *Studies in the Psychology of Sex* (1901), reveals how sympathetically he regarded this most controversial of sexual behaviors.

---

10. Latin: reduction to absurdity.
11. 18th-c. satirist Jonathan Swift, writing as "Isaac Bickerstaff," published an elegy on the death of astrologer John Partridge and overruled Partridge's objection that he was still alive.

from Studies in the Psychology of Sex

The sexual invert[1] is specially liable to suffer from a high degree of neurasthenia,[2] often involving much nervous weakness and irritability, loss of self-control, and genital hyperæsthesia.[3] This is a condition which may be ameliorated, and it may be treated in much the same way as if no inversion existed, by physical and mental tonics, or, if necessary, sedatives; by regulated gymnastics and out-of-door exercises; and by occupations which employ, without overexerting, the mind. Very great and permanent benefit may be obtained by a prolonged course of such mental and physical hygiene; the associated neurasthenic conditions may be largely removed, with the morbid fears, suspicions, and irritabilities that are usually part of neurasthenia, and the invert may be brought into a fairly wholesome and tonic condition of self-control.

The inversion is not thus removed. Before deciding whether it is desirable to attempt so radical a change in the sexual impulse, it is necessary to have full knowledge of the patient and his history. If he is still young, and if the perversion does not appear to be deeply rooted in the organism, it is probable that—provided his own good-will is aiding—general hygienic measures, together with removal to a favorable environment, may gradually lead to the development of the normal sexual impulse. If it fails to do so, it becomes necessary to exercise great caution in recommending stronger methods. A brothel, on which Schrenck-Notzing[4] largely relies, is scarcely a desirable method of treatment from any point of view; to say no more, it is not calculated to attract an individual who is already inspired with disgust of women regarded as objects of desire. The assistance of an honest woman would be much better therapeutically, but it can very seldom be right and feasible to obtain the help of one who is likely to be successful. Purely "Platonic associations with the other sex," Moll[5] points out, "leads to better results than any prescribed attempt at coitus."

While there is, no doubt, a temptation to aid those who are anxious for aid to get rid of their abnormality, it is not possible to look upon the results of such aid, even if successful, with much satisfaction. Not only is the acquisition of the normal instinct by an invert very much on a level with the acquisition of a vice, but probably it seldom succeeds in eradicating the original inverted instinct. What usually happens is that the person becomes capable of experiencing both impulses, not a specially satisfactory state of things.

Moreover, it is often difficult prematurely to persuade an invert that his condition is changed; his health is perhaps improving, and if he experiences some slight attraction to a person of the opposite sex he hastily assumes that a deep and permanent change has occurred. This may be disastrous, especially if it leads to marriage, as it may do in an inverted man or still more easily in an inverted woman. The appar-

---

1. Theory that someone with same-sex desires has the body of one sex but the soul of the other.
2. Weakness, depression, physical debility.
3. Krafft-Ebing considers that the temporary or lasting association of homosexuality with neurasthenia having its root in congenital conditions is "almost invariable" [Ellis's note]. 19th-c. German physician Richard von Krafft-Ebing specialized in sexual deviance.
4. Baron Albert von Schrenck-Notzing, 19th-c. German medical psychologist and parapsychologist.
5. Albert Moll, 19th-c. German sexologist.

ent change does not turn out to be deep, and the invert's position is more unfortunate than his original position, both for himself and for his wife.[6]

Nor is it possible to view with satisfaction the prospects of inverts begetting or bearing children. Often, no doubt, the children turn out fairly well, but, for the most part, they bear witness that they belong to a neurotic and failing stock. Sometimes, indeed, the tendency to sexual inversion in eccentric and neurotic families seems merely to be Nature's merciful method of winding up a concern which, from her point of view, has ceased to be profitable.

No doubt the physician is often strongly tempted to advise marriage and to promise that the normal heterosexual impulse will appear. There is but too much evidence demonstrating the rashness and folly of those who give such advice, and hold forth such promises, without duly guarded qualification and with no proper examination of the individual case. Certainly, provided that the woman is in full possession of all the facts, and provided also that she has sufficient experience of life to realize what she is undertaking to do, marriage may not be unhappy. Similarly in the case of an inverted woman. But the inadvisability of parenthood still remains, and such marriages can never be absolutely satisfactory.

As a rule, inverts have no desire to be different from what they are, and, if they have any desire for marriage, it is usually only momentary. Very pathetic appeals for help are, however, sometimes made. I may quote from a letter addressed to me by a gentleman who desired advice on this matter: "In part, I write to you as a moralist and, in part, as to a physician. Dr. Q. has published a book in which, without discussion, hypnotic treatment of such cases was reported as successful. I am eager to know if your opinion remains what it was. This new assurance comes from a man whose moral firmness and delicacy are unquestionable, but you will easily imagine how one might shrink from the implantation of new impulses in the unconscious self, since newly created inclinations might disturb the conditions of life. At any rate, in my ignorance of hypnotism I fear that the effort to give the normal instinct might lead to marriage without the assurance that the normal instinct would be stable. I write, therefore, to explain my present condition and crave your counsel. It is with the greatest reluctance that I reveal the closely guarded secret of my life. I have no other abnormality and have not hitherto betrayed my abnormal instinct. I have never made any person the victim of passion: moral and religious feelings were too powerful. I have found my reverence for other souls a perfect safeguard against any approach to impurity. I have never had sexual interest in women. Once I had a great friendship with a beautiful and noble woman, without any mixture of sexual feeling on my part.

---

6. I have recently been told by a distinguished physician, who was consulted in the case, of a congenital invert highly placed in the English government service, who lately married in the hope of escaping his perversion, and was not even able to consummate the marriage. It is needless to insist on the misery which is created in such cases. It is not, of course, denied that such marriages may not sometimes become eventually happy. Thus Kiernan [. . .] reports the case of a thoroughly inverted girl who married the brother of the friend to whom she was previously attached merely in order to secure his sister's companionship. She was able to endure and even enjoy intercourse by imagining that her husband, who resembled his sister, was another sister. Liking and esteem for the husband gradually increased and after the sister died a child was born who much resembled her; "the wife's esteem passed through love of the sister to intense natural love of the daughter, as resembling the sister; through this to normal love of the husband as the father and brother." The final result may have been satisfactory, but this train of circumstances could not have been calculated beforehand [Ellis's note, quoting Kiernan, "Psychical Treatment of Congenital Sexual Inversion," *Review of Insanity and Nervous Diseases*, June 1894].

I was ignorant of my condition, and I have the bitter regret of having caused in her a hopeless love—proudly and tragically concealed to her death. My friendships with men, younger men, have been colored by passion, against which I have fought continually. The shame of this has made life a hell, and the horror of this abnormality, since I came to know it as such, has been an enemy to my religious faith. Here there could be no case of a divinely given instinct which I was to learn to use in a rational and chaste fashion, under the control of spiritual loyalty. The power which gave me life seemed to insist on my doing that for which the same power would sting me with remorse. If there is no remedy I must either cry out against the injustice of this life of torment between nature and conscience, or submit to the blind trust of baffled ignorance. If there is a remedy life will not seem to be such an intolerable ordeal. I am not pleading that I must succumb to impulse, I do not doubt that a pure celibate life is possible so far as action is concerned. But I cannot discover that friendship with younger men can go on uncolored by a sensuous admixture which fills me with shame and loathing. The gratification of passion—normal or abnormal—is repulsive to esthetic feeling. I am nearly 42 and I have always diverted myself from personal interests that threatened to become dangerous to me. More than a year ago, however, a new fate seemed to open to my unhappy and lonely life. I became intimate with a young man of twenty, of the rarest beauty of form and character. I am confident that he is and always has been pure. He lives an exalted moral and religious life dominated by the idea that he and all men are partners of the divine nature, and able in the strength of that nature to be free from evil. I believe him to be normal. He shows pleasure in the society of attractive young women and in an innocent light-hearted way refers to the time when he may be able to marry. He is a general favorite, but turned to me as to a friend and teacher. He is poor, and it was possible for me to guarantee him a good education. I began to help him from the longings of a lonely life. I wanted a son and a friend in my inward desolation. I craved the companionship of this pure and happy nature. I felt such a reverence for him that I hoped to find the sensuous element in me purged away by his purity. I am, indeed, utterly incapable of doing him harm; I am not morally weak; nevertheless the sensuous element is there, and it poisons my happiness. He is ardently affectionate and demonstrative. He spends the summers with me in Europe, and the tenderness he feels for me has prompted him at times to embrace and kiss me as he always has done to his father. Of late I have begun to fear that without will or desire I may injure the springs of feeling in him, especially if it is true that the homosexual tendency is latent in most men. The love he shows me is my joy, but a poisoned joy. It is the bread and wine of life to me; but I dare not think what his ardent affection might ripen into. I can go on fighting the battle of good and evil in my attachment to him, but I cannot define my duty to him. To shun him would be cruelty and would belie his trust in human fidelity. Without my friendship he will not take my money—the condition of a large career. I might, indeed, explain to him what I explain to you, but the ordeal and shame are too great, and I cannot see what good it would do. If he has the capacity of homosexual feeling he might be violently stimulated; if he is incapable of it, he would feel repulsion.

Suppose, then, that I should seek hypnotic treatment, I still do not know what tricks an abnormal nature might play me when diverted by suggestion. I might lose the joy of this friendship without any compensation. I am afraid; I am afraid! Might I not be influenced to shun the only persons who inspire unselfish feeling?

Bear with this account of my story. Many virtues are easy for me, and my life is spent in pursuits of culture. Alas, that all the culture with which I am credited, all the prayers and aspirations, all the strong will and heroic resolves have not rid my nature of this evil bent. What I long for is the right to love, not for the mere physical gratification, for the right to take another into the arms of my heart and profess all the tenderness I feel, to find my joy in planning his career with him, as one who is rightfully and naturally entitled to do so. I crave this since I cannot have a son. I leave the matter here.

When I read what I have written I see how pointless it is. It is possible, indeed, that brooding over my personal calamity magnifies in my mind the sense of danger to this friend through me, and that I only need to find the right relation of friendliness coupled with aloofness which will secure him against any too ardent attachment. Certainly I have no fear that I shall forget myself. Yet two things array themselves on the other side: I rebel inwardly against the necessity of isolating myself as if I were a pestilence, and I rebel against the taint of sensuous feeling. The normal man can feel that his instinct is no shame when the spirit is in control. I know that to the consciousness of others my instinct itself would be a shame and a baseness, and I have no tendency to construct a moral system for myself. I have, to be sure, moments when I declare to myself that I will have my sensuous gratification as well as other men, but, the moment I think of the wickedness of it, the rebellion is soon over. The disesteem of self, the sense of taint, the necessity of withdrawing from happiness lest I communicate my taint, that is a spiritual malady which makes the ground-tone of my existence one of pain and melancholy. Should you have only some moral consolation without the promise of medical assistance I should feel grateful."

In such a case as this one can do little more than advise the sufferer that, however painful his lot may be, it is not without its consolations, and that he would be best advised to pursue, as cheerfully as may be, the path that he has already long since marked out for himself. The invert sometimes fails to realize that for no man with high moral ideals, however normal he may be, is the conduct of life easy, and that if the invert has to be satisfied with affection without passion, and to live a life of chastity, he is doing no more than thousands of normal men have done, voluntarily and contentedly. As to hypnotism in such a case as this, it is altogether unreasonable to expect that suggestion will supplant the deeply-rooted organic impulses that have grown up during a life-time. * * *

We can seldom, therefore, safely congratulate ourselves on the success of any "cure" of inversion. The success is unlikely to be either permanent or complete, in the case of a decided invert; and in the most successful cases we have simply put into the invert's hands a power of reproduction which it is undesirable he should possess. The most satisfactory result is probably obtained if it is possible by direct and indirect methods to reduce the sexual hyperesthesia which usually exists when the medical treatment of inversion comes into question, and by psychic methods to refine and spiritualize the inverted impulse, so that the invert's natural perversion may not become a cause of acquired perversity in others. The invert is not only the victim of his own abnormal obsession, he is the victim of social hostility. We must seek to distinguish the part in his sufferings due to these two causes. When I review the cases I have brought forward and the mental history of inverts I have known, I am inclined to say that if we can enable an invert to be healthy, self-restrained, and self-respecting, we have often done better than to convert him into the mere feeble simulacrum[7] of a normal man. An appeal to the *paiderastia*[8] of the best Greek days, and the dignity, temperance, even chastity, which it involved, will sometimes find a ready response in the emotional, enthusiastic nature of the congenital invert. The "manly love" celebrated by Walt Whitman in *Leaves of Grass*, although it may be of more doubtful value for general use, furnishes a wholesome and robust ideal to the invert who is insensitive to normal ideals.[9] It is by some such method of self-treatment as this that most of the more highly intelligent men and women whose histories I have already briefly recorded have at last slowly and instinctively reached a condition of relative health and peace, both physical and moral. The method of self-restraint and self-culture, without self-repression, seems to be the most rational method of dealing with sexual inversion when that condition is really organic and deeply rooted. It is better that a man should be enabled to make the best of his own strong natural instincts, with all their disadvantages, than that he should be unsexed and perverted, crushed into a position which he has no natural aptitude to occupy. * * *

We have always to remember, and there is, indeed, no possibility of forgetting, that the question of homosexuality is a social question. Within certain limits, the gratification of the normal sexual impulse, even outside marriage, arouses no general or profound indignation; and is regarded as a private matter; rightly or wrongly, the gratification of the homosexual impulse is regarded as a public matter. This attitude is more or less exactly reflected in the law. Thus it happens that whenever a man is openly detected in a homosexual act, however exemplary his life may previously have been, however admirable it may still be in all other relations, every ordinary normal citizen, however licentious and pleasure-loving his own life may be, feels it a moral duty to regard the offender as hopelessly damned and to help in hounding him out of society. At very brief intervals cases occur, and without reaching the newspapers are more or less widely known, in which distinguished men in various fields, not seldom clergymen, suddenly disappear from the country or commit suicide in consequence of some such exposure or the threat of it. It is probable that many obscure tragedies could find their explanation in a homosexual cause. * * *

We regard all homosexuality with absolute and unmitigated disgust. We have been taught to venerate Alexander the Great, Epaminondas, Socrates,[10] and other antique heroes; but they are safely buried in the remote past, and do not affect our scorn of homosexuality in the present. There is undoubtedly a deeply founded reason for this horror and disgust, although in England it has only appeared during the last few centuries. Our modern attitude is sometimes traced back to the Jewish law and

---

7. Simulation, copy.

8. Classical Greek practice whereby an older man "mentored" a youth (hence the term "Greek love").

9. In this connection I may mention a forthcoming book entitled *Ioläus: an Anthology of Friendship*, edited by Edward Carpenter, not touching directly on sex matters, but dealing with the romance of friendship [Ellis's note]. 19th-c. American poet Walt Whitman's ideal of male comradeship offered an alternative to Greek love.

10. The conqueror Alexander the Great (356–323 B.C.E.) was devoted to his male lover, Hephaestion; Greek statesman and military leader Epaminondas (d. 326 B.C.E.) never married; the philosopher Socrates had romances with several young men.

its survival in St. Paul's opinion on this matter.[11] But the Jewish law itself had a foundation. Wherever the enlargement of the population becomes a strongly felt social need,—as it was among the Jews in their exaltation of family-life, and as it was when the European nations were constituted,—there homosexuality has been regarded as a crime, even punishable with death. The Incas of ancient Peru, in the fury of their devastation, even destroyed a whole town where sodomy had once been detected. I do not know if it has been pointed out before that there seems to be a certain relationship between the social reaction against homosexuality and against infanticide. Where the one is regarded leniently and favorably, there generally the other is also; where the one is stamped out, the other is usually stamped out. Even the forceful Normans could not go against the stream and obtain recognition for their strong homosexual instincts anywhere in Europe, except apparently in England, where legislation against sodomy, beginning under Henry VIII, has a somewhat special and recent origin.[12] * * *

The existing law in England is severe, but simple. Carnal knowledge *per anum* of either a man or a woman or an animal is a felony (under 24 or 25 Vict., c. 100, sec. 61) punishable by penal servitude for life as a maximum and ten years as a minimum; the attempt at such carnal knowledge is punishable by ten years' penal servitude. The Criminal Law Amendment Act of 1885 goes beyond this, and makes even "gross indecency" between males, however privately committed, a penal offense.[13] The Criminal Law Amendment Act is in many respects an admirable enactment: to it we owe the raising of the age at which it becomes lawful for a woman to consent to sexual intercourse from over twelve to over sixteen. But this Act appears to have been somewhat hastily carried through, and many of its provisions, as well as its omissions, have been justly subjected to severe criticism. The clause from which I have quoted is specially open to criticism. With the omission of the words "or private," the clause would be sound and in harmony with the most enlightened European legislation; but it must be pointed out that an act only becomes indecent when those who perform it or witness it regard it as indecent. The act which brought each of us into the world is not indecent; it would become so if carried on in public. If two male persons, who have reached years of discretion, consent together to perform some act of sexual intimacy in private, no indecency has been committed. If one of the consenting parties subsequently proclaims the act, indecency may doubtless be created, as may happen also in the case of normal sexual intercourse, but it seems contrary to good policy that such proclamation should convert the act itself into a penal offense. * * *

It may further be pointed out that legislation against homosexuality has no clear effect either in diminishing or increasing its prevalence. * * *

---

11. See Romans 1.26–27 and 1 Corinthians 6.9–10 for Paul's sexual condemnation.

12. In 1533 Henry VIII instituted a statute against sodomy, the penetration of men, women, or animals *per anum* (through the anus).

13. "Any male person who in public or private commits, or is a party to the commission of, any act of gross indecency with another male person, shall be guilty of a misdemeanor, and being convicted thereof, shall be liable at the discretion of the court to be imprisoned for any term not exceeding two years, with or without hard labor" [Ellis's note]. Wilde was convicted under this dangerously inclusive law. Radical Member of Parliament Henry Labouchère supposedly introduced this amendment to sabotage the Bill, never imagining it would pass.

In England the law is exceptionally severe; yet, according to the evidence of those who have an international acquaintance with these matters, homosexuality is fully as prevalent as on the Continent; some would say that it is more so. It cannot, therefore, be said that legislative enactments have very much influence on the prevalence of homosexuality. The chief effect seems to be that the attempt at suppression arouses the finer minds among sexual inverts to undertake the enthusiastic defense of homosexuality, while coarser minds are stimulated to cynical bravado.[14] * * *

The Oscar Wilde trial, with its wide publicity, and the fundamental nature of the questions it suggested, appears to have generally contributed to give definiteness and self-consciousness to the manifestations of homosexuality, and to have aroused inverts to take up a definite attitude. * * * One correspondent writes:—

"Up to the time of the Oscar Wilde trial I had not known what the condition of the law was. The moral question in itself—its relation to my own life and that of my friends—I reckoned I had solved; but I now had to ask myself how far I was justified in not only breaking the law, but in being the cause of a like breech in others, and others younger than myself. I have never allowed the *dictum* of the law to interfere with what I deemed to be a moral development in any youth for whom I am responsible. I cannot say that the trial made me alter my course of life, of the rightness of which I was too convincingly persuaded, but it made me much more careful, and it probably sharpened my sense of responsibility for the young. Reviewing the results of the trial as a whole, it doubtless did incalculable harm, and it intensified our national vice of hypocrisy. But I think it also may have done some good in that it made those who, like myself, have thought and experienced deeply in the matter—and there must be no small few—ready to strike a blow, when the time comes, for what we deem to be right, honorable, and clean."

From America a lady writes with reference to the moral position of inverts, though without allusion to the Wilde trial:—

"Inverts should have the courage and independence to be themselves, and to demand an investigation. If one strives to live honorably, and considers the greatest good to the greatest number, it is not a crime nor a disgrace to be an invert. I do not need the law to defend me, neither do I desire to have any concessions made for me, nor do I ask my friends to sacrifice their ideals for me. I too have ideals which I shall always hold. All that I desire—and I claim it as my right—is the freedom to exercise this divine gift of loving, which is not a menace to society nor a disgrace to me. Let it once be understood that the average invert is not a moral degenerate nor a mental degenerate, but simply a man or a woman who is less highly specialized, less completely differentiated, than other men and women, and I believe the prejudice against them will disappear, and if they live uprightly they will surely win the esteem and consideration of all thoughtful people. I know what it means to an invert—who feels himself set apart from the rest of mankind—to find one human heart who trusts him and understands him, and I know how almost impossible this is, and will be, until the world is made aware of these facts."

---

14. A man with homosexual habits, I have been told, declared he would be sorry to see the English law changed, as then he would find no pleasure in his practices [Ellis's note].

But, while the law has had no more influence in repressing abnormal sexuality than, wherever it has tried to do so, it has had in repressing the normal sexual instinct, it has served to foster another offense. What is called blackmailing in England, *chantage* in France, and *Erpressung* in Germany—in other words, the extortion of money by threats of exposing some real or fictitious offense—finds its chief field of activity in connection with homosexuality.[15] No doubt the removal of the penalty against simple homosexuality does not abolish blackmailing, as the existence of this kind of *chantage* in France shows, but it renders its success less probable.

On all these grounds, and taking into consideration the fact that the tendency of modern legislation generally, and the consensus of authoritative opinion in all countries, are in this direction, I am of opinion that neither "sodomy" (*i.e., immissio membri in anum hominis vel mulieris*)[16] nor "gross indecency" ought to be penal offenses, except under certain special circumstances. That is to say, that if two persons of either or both sexes, having reached years of discretion,[17] privately consent to practice some perverted mode of sexual relationship, the law cannot be called upon to interfere. It should be the function of the law in this matter to prevent violence, to protect the young, and to preserve public order and decency. Whatever laws are laid down beyond this must be left to the individuals themselves, to the moralist, and to social opinion. * * *

It is for us primarily a disgusting abomination, *i.e.*, a matter of taste, of esthetics; and, while unspeakably ugly to the majority, it is proclaimed as beautiful by a small minority. I do not know that we need find fault with this esthetic method of judging homosexuality. But it scarcely lends itself to legal purposes. To indulge in violent denunciation of the disgusting nature of homosexuality, and to measure the sentence by the disgust aroused, or to regret, as one English judge is reported to have regretted when giving sentence, that "gross indecency" is not punishable by death, is to import utterly foreign considerations into the matter. The judges who yield to this temptation would certainly never allow themselves to be consciously influenced on the bench by their political opinions. Yet esthetic opinions are quite as foreign to law as political opinions. * * *

It is clear that this public opinion, molded chiefly or entirely with reference to gross vice, tends to be unduly violent in its reaction. What, then, is the reasonable attitude of society toward the congenital sexual invert? It seems to lie in the avoidance of two extremes. On the one hand, it cannot be expected to tolerate the invert who flouts his perversion in its face and assumes that, because he would rather take his pleasure with a soldier or a policeman than with their sisters, he is of finer clay than the vulgar herd. On the other, it might well refrain from crushing with undiscerning ignorance beneath a burden of shame the subject of an abnormality which, as we have seen, has not been found incapable of fine uses. Inversion is an aberration from the usual course of nature. But the clash of contending elements which must often mark the history of such a deviation results now and again—by no means infrequently—in nobler activities than those yielded by the vast majority who are born to consume the fruits of the earth. It

---

15. The Criminal Law Amendment Act was nicknamed "the blackmailer's charter."

16. Latin: admitting the member into the anus of a man or woman.

17. Krafft-Ebing would place this age not under 16, the age at which in England girls may legally consent to normal sexual intercourse (*Psychopathia Sexualis*, 1893, p. 419). It certainly should not be lower [Ellis's note].

bears, for the most part, its penalty in the structure of its own organism. We are bound to protect the helpless members of society against the invert. If we go further, and seek to destroy the invert himself before he has sinned against society, we exceed the warrant of reason, and in so doing we may, perhaps, destroy also those children of the spirit which possess sometimes a greater worth than the children of the flesh.

—1901

Edward Carpenter
1844–1929

Edward Carpenter, a courageous advocate for decriminalizing male homosexuality, lived openly with his partner, George Merrill, from 1898 to 1929. Initially a clergyman, Carpenter left the church after two years to become a traveling lecturer. An inheritance from his father made him financially independent. He became a radical democrat and socialist, and his cottage, near Sheffield, became the center of socialist activity in the region. Of Carpenter's pamphlets on sexual liberty, the most famous is *The Intermediate Sex: A Study of Some Transitional Types of Men and Women* (1908). In it, he explained "Uranian" (same-sex) love by arguing that bodily sex need not match internal gender traits (individually proportioned mixtures of masculine and feminine) and that people were attracted to others whose gender mixtures corresponded to, and balanced, their own. Where Havelock Ellis's work was rigorous, scientific, and organized, Carpenter's writing was lyrical, persuasive, and emotive. The following essay, *Homogenic Love* (Greek for "same kind") was privately printed as a booklet in 1894. Because of the scandal of Oscar Wilde's trial, it could not be published until 1902 and was then revised and expanded in 1906 (the text here).

from Homogenic Love

Summarizing then some of our conclusions on this rather difficult question we may say that the homogenic love, as a distinct variety of the sex-passion, is in the main subject to the same laws as the ordinary love; that it probably demands and requires some amount of physical intimacy; that a wise humanity will quite recognise this; but that the degree of intimacy, in default of more certain physiological knowledge than we have, is a matter which can only be left to the good sense and feeling of those concerned; and that while we do not deny for a moment that excesses of physical appetite exist, these form no more reason for tabooing all expression of the sentiment than they do in the case of the more normal love. We may also say that if on the side of science much is obscure, there is no obscurity in the principles of healthy morality involved; that there is no exception here to the law that sensuality apart from love is degrading and something less than human; or to the law that love—true love—seeks nothing which is not consistent with the welfare of the loved one; and that here too the principle of Transmutation applies—the principle that Desire in man has its physical emotional and spiritual sides, and that when its outlet is checked along one channel, it will, within limits, tend to flow with more vehemence along the other channels—and that reasonable beings, perceiving this, will (again within limits) check the sensual and tend to throw the centre of their love-attraction upwards.

Probably in this, as in all love, it will be felt in the end by those who devote themselves to each other and to the truth, to be wisest to concentrate on the *real thing*, on the enduring deep affection which is the real satisfaction and outcome of the relation, and which like a young sapling they would tend with loving care till it grows into a mighty tree which the storms of a thousand years cannot shake; and those who do so heartily and truly can leave the physical to take care of itself. This indeed is per-haps the only satisfactory touchstone of the rightness and fitness of human relations generally, in sexual matters. People, not unnaturally, seek for an absolute rule in such matters, and a *fixed* line between the right and the wrong; but may we not say that there is no rule except that of Love—Love making use, of course, of whatever certain knowledge Science may from time to time be able to provide?

And speaking of the law of Transmutation and its importance, it is clear, I think, that in the homosexual love—whether between man and man or between woman and woman—the physical side, from the very nature of the case, can never find expression quite so freely and perfectly as in the ordinary heterosexual love; and therefore that there is a "natural" tendency for the former love to run rather more along emotional channels. And this no doubt throws light on the fact that love of the homogenic type has inspired such a vast amount of heroism and romance—and is indeed only paral-leled in this respect (as J. Addington Symonds has pointed out in his paper on Dantesque and Platonic ideals of Love)[1] by the loves of Chivalry, which of course owing to their special character, were subject to a similar transmutation. * * *

I have now said enough I think to show that though Science has not as yet been able to give any decisive utterance on the import of the physical and physiological side of the homogenic passion (and it must be remembered that its real understand-ing of this side of the ordinary sex-love is very limited), yet on its ethical and social sides—which cannot of course, in the last resort, be separated from the physiologi-cal—the passion is pregnant with meaning, and has received at various times in his-tory abundant justification. And in truth it seems the most natural thing in the world that just as the ordinary sex-love has a special function in the propagation of the race, so the other love should have its special function in social and heroic work, and in the generation—not of bodily children—but of those children of the mind, the philo-sophical conceptions and ideals which transform our lives and those of society. This without limiting too closely. In each case the main object may be said to be union. But as all love is also essentially creative, we naturally look for the creative activities of different kinds of love in different directions—and seem to find them so.

If there is any truth—even only a grain or two—in these speculations, it is easy to see that the love with which we are specially dealing is a very important factor in society, and that its neglect, or its repression, or its vulgar misapprehension, may be matters of considerable danger or damage to the common-weal. It is easy to see that while on the one hand the ordinary marriage is of indispensable importance to the

---

1. *In the Key of Blue* (1893).

State as providing the workshop as it were for the breeding and rearing of children, another form of union is almost equally indispensable to supply the basis for social activities of other kinds. Every one is conscious that without a close affectional tie of some kind his life is not complete, his powers are crippled, and his energies are inadequately spent. Yet it is not to be expected (though it may of course happen) that the man or woman who have dedicated themselves to each other and to family life should leave the care of their children and the work they have to do at home in order to perform social duties of a remote and less obvious, though may-be more arduous, character. Nor is it to be expected that a man or woman single-handed, without the counsel of a helpmate in the hour of difficulty, or his or her love in the hour of need, should feel equal to these wider activities. If—to refer once more to classic story—the love of Harmodius[2] had been for a wife and children at home, he would probably not have cared, and it would hardly have been his business, to slay the tyrant. And unless on the other hand each of the friends had had the love of his comrade to support him, the two could hardly have nerved themselves to this audacious and ever-memorable exploit. So it is difficult to believe that anything except that kind of comrade-union which satisfies and invigorates the two lovers and yet leaves them free from the responsibilities and *impedimenta* of family life can supply the force and liberate the energies required for social and mental activities of the most necessary kind.

For if the slaughter of tyrants is not the chief social duty now-a-days, we have with us hydra-headed monsters at least as numerous as the tyrants of old, and more difficult to deal with, and requiring no little courage to encounter. And beyond the extirpation of evils we have solid work waiting to be done in the patient and life-long building up of new forms of society, new orders of thought, and new institutions of human solidarity—all of which in their genesis will meet with opposition, ridicule, hatred, and even violence. Such campaigns as these—though different in kind from those of the Dorian mountaineers[3] described above—will call for equal hardihood and courage and will stand in need of a comradeship as true and valiant. It may indeed be doubted whether the higher heroic and spiritual life of a nation is ever quite possible without the sanction of this attachment in its institutions; and it is not unlikely that the markedly materialistic and commercial character of the last age of European civilised life is largely to be connected with the fact that the *only* form of love and love-union that it has recognised has been one founded on the quite necessary but comparatively materialistic basis of matrimonial sex-intercourse and child-breeding.[4]

Walt Whitman, the inaugurator, it may almost be said, of a new world of democratic ideals and literature, and—as one of the best of our critics[5] has remarked—the

---

2. Harmodius and his lover Aristogeiton, popular heroes for trying to assassinate Athenian tyrants in 514 B.C.E.

3. In his anonymous pamphlet *A Problem in Greek Ethics* (1901), John Addington Symonds argued that the Dorian warriors' comradely fidelity spurred their success.

4. It is interesting in this connection to notice the extreme fervor, almost of romance, of the bond which often unites lovers of like sex over a long period of years, in an unfailing tenderness of treatment and consideration towards each other, equal to that shown in the most successful marriages. The love of many such men, says Moll [. . .] "developed in youth lasts at times the whole life through. I know of such men, who had not seen their first love for years, even decades, and who yet on meeting showed the old fire of their first passion. In other cases a close love-intimacy will last unbroken for many years" [Carpenter's note]. Albert Moll was a German sexologist.

5. Symonds.

most Greek in spirit and in performance of modern writers, insists continually on this social function of "intense and loving comradeship, the personal and passionate attachment of man to man." "I will make," he says, "the most splendid race the sun ever shone upon, I will make divine magnetic lands. . . . I will make inseparable cities with their arms about each others necks, by the love of comrades." And again, in *Democratic Vistas*, "It is to the development, identification, and general prevalence of that fervid comradeship (the adhesive love at least rivaling the amative love hitherto possessing imaginative literature, if not going beyond it), that I look for the counter-balance and offset of materialistic and vulgar American Democracy, and for the spiritualisation thereof. . . . I say Democracy infers such loving comradeship, as its most inevitable twin or counterpart, without which it will be incomplete, in vain, and incapable of perpetuating itself."

Yet Whitman could not have spoken, as he did, with a kind of authority on this subject, if he had not been fully aware that through the masses of the people this attachment was already alive and working—though doubtless in a somewhat suppressed and unself-conscious form—and if he had not had ample knowledge of its effects and influence in himself and others around him. Like all great artists he could but give form and light to that which already existed dim and inchoate in the heart of the people. To those who have dived at all below the surface in this direction it will be familiar enough that the homogenic passion ramifies widely through all modern society, and that among the masses of the people as among the classes, below the stolid surface and reserve of British manners, letters pass and enduring attachments are formed, differing in no very obvious respect from those correspondences which persons of opposite sexes knit with each other under similar circumstances; but that hitherto while this passion has occasionally come into public notice through the police reports, etc., in its grosser and cruder forms, its more sane and spiritual manifestations—though really a moving force in the body politic—have remained unrecognised.

It is hardly needful in these days when social questions loom so large upon us to emphasise the importance of a bond which by the most passionate and lasting compulsion may draw members of the different classes together, and (as it often seems to do) none the less strongly because they are members of different classes. A moment's consideration must convince us that such a comradeship may, as Whitman says, have "deepest relations to general politics." It is noticeable, too, in this deepest relation to politics that the movement among women towards their own liberation and emancipation which is taking place all over the civilised world has been accompanied by a marked development of the homogenic passion among the female sex. It may be said that a certain strain in the relations between the opposite sexes which has come about owing to a growing consciousness among women that they have been oppressed and unfairly treated by men, and a growing unwillingness to ally themselves unequally in marriage—that this strain has caused the womankind to draw more closely together and to cement alliances of their own. But whatever the cause may be it is pretty certain that such comrade-alliances—and of a quite passionate kind—are becoming increasingly common, and especially perhaps among the more cultured classes of women, who are working out the great cause of their sex's liberation; nor is it difficult to see the importance of such alliances in such a campaign. In the United States where the battle of women's independence has been fought more vehemently perhaps than here, the tendency mentioned is even more strongly marked.

In conclusion there are a few words to be said about the legal aspect of this important question. It has to be remarked that the present state of the Law—arising as it does partly out of some of the misapprehensions above alluded to, and partly out of the sheer unwillingness of legislators to discuss the question—is really quite impracticable and unjustifiable, and will no doubt have to be altered.

The Law, of course, can only deal, and can only be expected to deal, with the outward and visible. It cannot control feeling; but it tries—in those cases where it is concerned—to control the expression of feeling. It has been insisted on in this essay that the Homogenic Love is a valuable social force, and, in cases, an indispensable factor of the noblest human character; also that it has a necessary root in the physical and sexual organism. This last is the point where the Law steps in. "We know nothing"—it says—"of what may be valuable social forces or factors of character, or of what may be the relation of physical things to things spiritual; but when you speak of a sexual element being present in this kind of love, we can quite understand that; and that is just what we mean to suppress. That sexual element is nothing but gross indecency, *any form of which by our Act of 1885 we make criminal.*"[6]

Whatever substantial ground the Law may have had for previous statutes on this subject—dealing with a specific act (sodomy)—it has surely quite lost it in passing so wide-sweeping a condemnation on all relations between male persons.[7] It has undertaken a censorship over private morals (entirely apart from social results) which is beyond its province, and which—even if it were its province—it could not possibly fulfil; it has opened wider than ever before the door to a real social evil and crime—that of blackmailing; and it has thrown a shadow over even the simplest and most natural expressions of an attachment which may, as we have seen, be of the greatest value in national life.[8]

That the homosexual passion may be improperly indulged in, that it may lead, like the heterosexual, to public abuses of liberty and decency we of course do not deny; but as, in the case of persons of opposite sex, the law limits itself on the whole to the maintenance of public order, the protection of the weak from violence and insult,[9] and of the young from their inexperience: so it should be here. Whatever teaching may be thought desirable on the general principles of morality concerned must be given—as it can only be given—by the spread of proper education and ideas, and not by the clumsy bludgeon of the statute-book.[10]

---

6. The Criminal Law Amendment Act, also called the Labouchère Amendment, which criminalized all forms of homosexual love.
7. Though, inconsistently enough, making no mention of females [Carpenter's note].
8. Dr. Moll maintains [. . .] that if familiarities between those of the same sex are made illegal, as immoral, self-abuse ought much more to be so made [Carpenter's note].
9. Though it is doubtful whether the marriage-laws even do this! [Carpenter's note].
10. In France, since the adoption of the Code Napoleon, sexual inversion is tolerated under the same restrictions as normal sexuality; and according to Carlier, formerly Chief of the French Police, Paris is not more depraved in this matter than London. Italy in 1889 also adopted the principles of the Code Napoleon on this point [Carpenter's note].

We have shown the special functions and really indispensable import of the homogenic or comrade love, in some form, in national life, and it is high time now that the modern States should recognise this in their institutions—instead of (as is also done in schools and places of education) by repression and disallowance perverting the passion into its least satisfactory channels. If the dedication of love were a matter of mere choice or whim, it still would not be the business of the State to compel that choice; but since no amount of compulsion can ever change the homogenic instinct in a person, where it is innate, the State in trying to effect such a change is only kicking vainly against the pricks of its own advantage—and trying, in view perhaps of the conduct of a licentious few, to cripple and damage a respectable and valuable class of its own citizens.

—1894

Political Solutions:
Philanthropy, Sociology, Socialism

William Morris
1834–1896

"Have nothing in your houses that you do not know to be useful, or believe to be beautiful," warned William Morris. This advice became the slogan for a generation of decorative reformers. The extraordinarily multitalented Morris was a socialist reformer, poet, utopian novelist, decorative artist, and Pre-Raphaelite painter, not to mention a translator of Icelandic sagas, a passionate preservationist, an all-around craftsman, and an innovative book designer. *The Defence of Guenevere and Other Poems* (1858) and *The Earthly Paradise* (1868) made him a contender for Poet Laureate, and he authored the novel *News from Nowhere* (1890). Morris & Co. ("The Firm") created a look that is still popular today, with hand-carved furniture and richly intricate wallpapers and tapestries featuring complex motifs of birds, fruits, and leaves, while his Kelmscott Press's lovingly handmade volumes led a revolution in book design. In all his work—literary, artistic, and political—Morris tried to recreate the sort of egalitarian, craftsman-oriented community in harmony with the natural world that he associated with an idealized Middle Ages. This ideal shaped his politics. Morris became an ardent socialist in 1883, delivering lectures to (and about) workers in which he argued passionately for a just society in which class distinctions would disappear and everyone would enjoy satisfyingly simple, unpretentious, well-designed lives. Morris married Jane Burden, one of the Pre-Raphaelites' favorite models. The marriage was unhappy, partly because of Jane's longstanding relationship with artist Dante Gabriel Rossetti, but it produced two daughters who became famous icons of Pre-Raphaelite style, including the noted craftswoman May Morris. Throughout his long life, Morris never faltered in his passion for justice, his adherence to principles of high craft, and his love of medievalism. No wonder that when he died, the doctor claimed the cause of death was "simply being William Morris, and having done more work than most ten men."

Useful Work versus Useless Toil

The above title may strike some of my readers as strange. It is assumed by most people nowadays that all work is useful, and by most *well-to-do* people that all work is desirable.[1] Most people, well-to-do or not, believe that, even when a man is doing work which appears to be useless, he is earning his livelihood by it—he is "employed," as the phrase goes; and most of those who are well-to-do cheer on the happy worker with congratulations and praises, if he is only "industrious" enough and deprives himself of all pleasure and holidays in the sacred cause of labour. In short, it has become an article of the creed of modern morality that all labour is good in itself—a convenient belief to those who live on the labour of others. But as to those on whom they live, I recommend them not to take it on trust, but to look into the matter a little deeper.

Let us grant, first, that the race of man must either labour or perish. Nature does not give us our livelihood gratis; we must win it by toil of some sort or degree. Let us see, then, if she does not give us some compensation for this compulsion to labour, since certainly in other matters she takes care to make the acts necessary to the continuance of life in the individual and the race not only endurable, but even pleasurable.

You may be sure that she does so, that it is of the nature of man, when he is not diseased, to take pleasure in his work under certain conditions. And, yet, we must say in the teeth of the hypocritical praise of all labour, whatsoever it may be, of which I have made mention, that there is some labour which is so far from being a blessing that it is a curse; that it would be better for the community and for the worker if the latter were to fold his hands and refuse to work, and either die or let us pack him off to the workhouse or prison—which you will.

Here, you see, are two kinds of work—one good, the other bad; one not far removed from a blessing, a lightening of life; the other a mere curse, a burden to life.

What is the difference between them, then? This: one has hope in it, the other has not. It is manly to do the one kind of work, and manly also to refuse to do the other.

What is the nature of the hope which, when it is present in work, makes it worth doing?

It is threefold, I think—hope of rest, hope of product, hope of pleasure in the work itself; and hope of these also in some abundance and of good quality; rest enough and good enough to be worth having; product worth having by one who is neither a fool nor an ascetic; pleasure enough for all for us to be conscious of it while we are at work; not a mere habit, the loss of which we shall feel as a fidgety man feels the loss of the bit of string he fidgets with.

I have put the hope of rest first because it is the simplest and most natural part of our hope. Whatever pleasure there is in some work, there is certainly some pain in all

---

1. Social reformer Thomas Carlyle popularized this position in *Past and Present* (1843): "there is a perennial nobleness, and even sacredness, in Work," for "destiny, on the whole, has no other way of cultivating us."

work, the beast-like pain of stirring up our slumbering energies to action, the beast-like dread of change when things are pretty well with us; and the compensation for this animal pain is animal rest. We must feel while we are working that the time will come when we shall not have to work. Also the rest, when it comes, must be long enough to allow us to enjoy it; it must be longer than is merely necessary for us to recover the strength we have expended in working, and it must be animal rest also in this, that it must not be disturbed by anxiety, else we shall not be able to enjoy it. If we have this amount and kind of rest we shall, so far, be no worse off than the beasts.

As to the hope of product, I have said that Nature compels us to work for that. It remains for *us* to look to it that we *do* really produce something, and not nothing, or at least nothing that we want or are allowed to use. If we look to this and use our wills we shall, so far, be better than machines.

The hope of pleasure in the work itself: how strange that hope must seem to some of my readers—to most of them! Yet I think that to all living things there is a pleasure in the exercise of their energies, and that even beasts rejoice in being lithe and swift and strong. But a man at work, making something which he feels will exist because he is working at it and wills it, is exercising the energies of his mind and soul as well as of his body. Memory and imagination help him as he works. Not only his own thoughts, but the thoughts of the men of past ages guide his hands; and, as a part of the human race, he creates. If we work thus we shall be men, and our days will be happy and eventful.

Thus worthy work carries with it the hope of pleasure in rest, the hope of pleasure in our using what it makes, and the hope of pleasure in our daily creative skill.

All other work but this is worthless; it is slaves' work—mere toiling to live, that we may live to toil.

Therefore, since we have, as it were, a pair of scales in which to weigh the work now done in the world, let us use them. Let us estimate the worthiness of the work we do, after so many thousand years of toil, so many promises of hope deferred, such boundless exultation over the progress of civilization and the gain of liberty.

Now, the first thing as to the work done in civilization and the easiest to notice is that it is portioned out very unequally amongst the different classes of society. First, there are people—not a few—who do no work, and make no pretence of doing any. Next, there are people, and very many of them, who work fairly hard, though with abundant easements and holidays, claimed and allowed; and lastly, there are people who work so hard that they may be said to do nothing else than work, and are accordingly called "the working classes," as distinguished from the middle classes and the rich, or aristocracy, whom I have mentioned above.

It is clear that this inequality presses heavily upon the "working" class, and must visibly tend to destroy their hope of rest at least, and so, in that particular, make them worse off than mere beasts of the field; but that is not the sum and end of our folly of turning useful work into useless toil, but only the beginning of it.

For first, as to the class of rich people doing no work, we all know that they consume a great deal while they produce nothing. Therefore, clearly, they have to be kept at the expense of those who do work, just as paupers have, and are a mere burden on the community. In these days there are many who have learned to see this, though they can see no further into the evils of our present system, and have formed no idea of any scheme for getting rid of this burden; though perhaps they have a vague hope that changes in the system of voting for members of the House of Commons[2] may, as if by magic, tend in that direction. With such hopes or superstitions we need not trouble ourselves. Moreover, this class, the aristocracy, once thought most necessary to the State, is scant of numbers, and has now no power of its own, but depends on the support of the class next below it—the middle class. In fact, it is really composed either of the most successful men of that class, or of their immediate descendants.

As to the middle class, including the trading, manufacturing, and professional people of our society, they do, as a rule, seem to work quite hard enough, and so at first sight might be thought to help the community, and not burden it. But by far the greater part of them, though they work, do not produce, and even when they do produce, as in the case of those engaged (wastefully indeed) in the distribution of goods, or doctors, or (genuine) artists and literary men, they consume out of all proportion to their due share. The commercial and manufacturing part of them, the most powerful part, spend their lives and energies in fighting amongst themselves for their respective shares of the wealth which they *force* the genuine workers to provide for them; the others are almost wholly the hangers-on of these; they do not work for the public, but a privileged class: they are the parasites of property, sometimes, as in the case of lawyers, undisguisedly so; sometimes, as the doctors and others above mentioned, professing to be useful, but too often of no use save as supporters of the system of folly, fraud, and tyranny of which they form a part. And all these we must remember have, as a rule, one aim in view; not the production of utilities, but the gaining of a position either for themselves or their children in which they will not have to work at all. It is their ambition and the end of their whole lives to gain, if not for themselves yet at least for their children, the proud position of being obvious burdens on the community. For their work itself, in spite of the sham dignity with which they surround it, they care nothing: save a few enthusiasts, men of science, art, or letters, who, if they are not the salt of the earth, are at least (and oh, the pity of it!) the salt of the miserable system of which they are the slaves, which hinders and thwarts them at every turn, and even sometimes corrupts them.

Here then is another class, this time very numerous and all-powerful, which produces very little and consumes enormously, and is therefore in the main supported, as paupers are, by the real producers. The class that remains to be considered produces all that is produced, and supports both itself and the other classes, though it is placed in a position of inferiority to them; real inferiority, mind you, involving a degradation both of mind and body. But it is a necessary consequence of this tyranny and folly that again many of these workers are not producers. A vast number of them once more are merely parasites of property, some of them openly so, as the soldiers by land and sea who are kept on foot for the perpetuating of national rivalries and enmities, and for the purposes of the national struggle for the share of the product of unpaid labour. But besides this obvious burden on the producers and the scarcely less obvious one of domestic servants, there is first the army of clerks, shop-assistants, and so forth, who are engaged in the service of the private war for wealth, which, as above said, is the real occupation of the well-to-do middle class. This is a larger body of workers than

---

2. The Reform Acts of 1867 and 1884 extended the vote.

might be supposed, for it includes amongst others all those engaged in what I should call competitive salesmanship, or, to use a less dignified word, the puffery[3] of wares, which has now got to such a pitch that there are many things which cost far more to sell than they do to make.

Next there is the mass of people employed in making all those articles of folly and luxury, the demand for which is the outcome of the existence of the rich non-producing classes; things which people leading a manly and uncorrupted life would not ask for or dream of. These things, whoever may gainsay me, I will for ever refuse to call wealth: they are not wealth, but waste. Wealth is what Nature gives us and what a reasonable man can make out of the gifts of Nature for his reasonable use. The sunlight, the fresh air, the unspoiled face of the earth, food, raiment and housing necessary and decent; the storing up of knowledge of all kinds, and the power of disseminating it; means of free communication between man and man; works of art, the beauty which man creates when he is most a man, most aspiring and thoughtful—all things which serve the pleasure of people, free, manly, and uncorrupted. This is wealth. Nor can I think of anything worth having which does not come under one or other of these heads. But think, I beseech you, of the product of England, the workshop of the world, and will you not be bewildered, as I am, at the thought of the mass of things which no sane man could desire, but which our useless toil makes—and sells?

Now, further, there is even a sadder industry yet, which is forced on many, very many, of our workers—the making of wares which are necessary to them and their brethren, *because they are an inferior class.* For if many men live without producing, nay, must live lives so empty and foolish that they *force* a great part of the workers to produce wares which no one needs, not even the rich, it follows that most men must be poor; and, living as they do on wages from those whom they support, cannot get for their use the *goods* which men naturally desire, but must put up with miserable makeshifts for them, with coarse food that does not nourish, with rotten raiment which does not shelter, with wretched houses which may well make a town-dweller in civilization look back with regret to the tent of the nomad tribe, or the cave of the prehistoric savage. Nay, the workers must even lend a hand to the great industrial invention of the age—adulteration, and by its help produce for their own use shams and mockeries of the luxury of the rich; for the wage-earners must always live as the wage-payers bid them, and their very habits of life are *forced* on them by their masters.

But it is waste of time to try to express in words due contempt of the productions of the much-praised cheapness of our epoch. It must be enough to say that this cheapness is necessary to the system of exploiting on which modern manufacture rests. In other words, our society includes a great mass of slaves, who must be fed, clothed, housed and amused as slaves, and that their daily necessity compels them to make the slave-wares whose use is the perpetuation of their slavery.

To sum up, then, concerning the manner of work in civilized States, these States are composed of three classes—a class which does not even pretend to work, a class which pretends to works but which produces nothing, and a class which works, but is compelled by the other two classes to do work which is often unproductive.

---

3. Sham praise.

Civilization therefore wastes its own resources, and will do so as long as the present system lasts. These are cold words with which to describe the tyranny under which we suffer; try then to consider what they mean.

There is a certain amount of natural material and of natural forces in the world, and a certain amount of labour-power inherent in the persons of the men that inhabit it. Men urged by their necessities and desires have laboured for many thousands of years at the task of subjugating the forces of Nature and of making the natural material useful to them. To our eyes, since we cannot see into the future, that struggle with Nature seems nearly over, and the victory of the human race over her nearly complete. And, looking backwards to the time when history first began, we note that the progress of that victory has been far swifter and more startling within the last two hundred years than ever before. Surely, therefore, we moderns ought to be in all ways vastly better off than any who have gone before us. Surely we ought, one and all of us, to be wealthy, to be well furnished with the good things which our victory over Nature has won for us.

But what is the real fact? Who will dare to deny that the great mass of civilized men are poor? So poor are they that it is mere childishness troubling ourselves to discuss whether perhaps they are in some ways a little better off than their forefathers. They are poor; nor can their poverty be measured by the poverty of a resourceless savage, for he knows of nothing else than his poverty; that he should be cold, hungry, houseless, dirty, ignorant, all that is to him as natural as that he should have a skin. But for us, for the most of us, civilization has bred desires which she forbids us to satisfy, and so is not merely a niggard but a torturer also.

Thus then have the fruits of our victory over Nature been stolen from us, thus has compulsion by Nature to labour in hope of rest, gain, and pleasure been turned into compulsion by man to labour in hope—of living to labour!

What shall we do then, can we mend it?

Well, remember once more that it is not our remote ancestors who achieved the victory over Nature, but our fathers, nay, our very selves. For us to sit hopeless and helpless then would be a strange folly indeed: be sure that we can amend it. What, then, is the first thing to be done?

We have seen that modern society is divided into two classes, one of which is *privileged* to be kept by the labour of the other—that is, it forces the other to work for it and takes from this inferior class everything that it *can* take from it, and uses the wealth so taken to keep its own members in a superior position, to make them beings of a higher order than the others: longer lived, more beautiful, more honourable, more refined than those of the other class. I do not say that it troubles itself about its members being *positively* long lived, beautiful or refined, but merely insists that they shall be so *relatively* to the inferior class. As also it cannot use the labour-power of the inferior class fairly in producing real wealth, it wastes it wholesale in the production of rubbish.

It is this robbery and waste on the part of the minority which keeps the majority poor; if it could be shown that it is necessary for the preservation of society that this should be submitted to, little more could be said on the matter, save that the despair of the oppressed majority would probably at some time or other destroy Society. But it has been shown, on the contrary, even by such incomplete experiments, for instance, as Co-operation (so-called), that the existence of a privileged class is by no means necessary for the production of wealth, but rather for the "government" of the producers of wealth, or, in other words, for the upholding of privilege.

The first step to be taken then is to abolish a class of men privileged to shirk their duties as men, thus forcing others to do the work which they refuse to do. All must work according to their ability, and so produce what they consume—that is, each man should work as well as he can for his own livelihood, and his livelihood should be assured to him; that is to say, all the advantages which society would provide for each and all of its members.

Thus, at last, would true Society be founded. It would rest on equality of condition. No man would be tormented for the benefit of another—nay, no one man would be tormented for the benefit of Society. Nor, indeed, can that order be called Society which is not upheld for the benefit of every one of its members.

But since men live now, badly as they live, when so many people do not produce at all, and when so much work is wasted, it is clear that, under conditions where all produced and no work was wasted, not only would every one work with the certain hope of gaining a due share of wealth by his work, but also he could not miss his due share of rest. Here, then, are two out of the three kinds of hope mentioned above as an essential part of worthy work assured to the worker. When class-robbery is abolished, every man will reap the fruits of his labour, every man will have due rest—leisure, that is. Some Socialists might say we need not go any further than this; it is enough that the worker should get the full produce of his work, and that his rest should be abundant. But though the compulsion of man's tyranny is thus abolished, I yet demand compensation for the compulsion of Nature's necessity. As long as the work is repulsive it will still be a burden which must be taken up daily, and even so would mar our life, even though the hours of labour were short. What we want to do is to add to our wealth without diminishing our pleasure. Nature will not be finally conquered till our work becomes a part of the pleasure of our lives.

That first step of freeing people from the compulsion to labour needlessly will at least put us on the way towards this happy end; for we shall then have time and opportunities for bringing it about. As things are now, between the waste of labour-power in mere idleness and its waste in unproductive work, it is clear that the world of civilization is supported by a small part of its people; when *all* were working *usefully* for its support, the share of work which each would have to do would be but small, if our standard of life were about on the footing of what well-to-do and refined people now think desirable. We shall have labour-power to spare, and shall, in short, be as wealthy as we please. It will be easy to live. If we were to wake up some morning now, under our present system, and find it "easy to live," that system would force us to set to work at once and make it hard to live; we should call that "developing our resources," or some such fine name. The multiplication of labour has become a necessity for us, and as long as that goes on no ingenuity in the invention of machines will be of any real use to us. Each new machine will cause a certain amount of misery among the workers whose special industry it may disturb; so many of them will be reduced from skilled to unskilled workmen, and then gradually matters will slip into their due grooves, and all will work apparently smoothly again; and if it were not that all this is preparing revolution, things would be, for the greater part of men, just as they were before the new wonderful invention.

But when revolution has made it "easy to live," when all are working harmoniously together and there is no one to rob the worker of his time, that is to say, his life; in those coming days there will be no compulsion on us to go on producing things we do not want, no compulsion on us to labour for nothing; we shall be able calmly and thoughtfully to consider what we shall do with our wealth of labour-power. Now, for my part, I think the first use we ought to make of that wealth, of that freedom, should be to make all our labour, even the commonest and most necessary, pleasant to everybody; for thinking over the matter carefully I can see that the one course which will certainly make life happy in the face of all accidents and troubles is to take a pleasurable interest in all the details of life. And lest perchance you think that an assertion too universally accepted to be worth making, let me remind you how entirely modern civilization forbids it; with what sordid, and even terrible, details it surrounds the life of the poor, what a mechanical and empty life she forces on the rich; and how rare a holiday it is for any of us to feel ourselves a part of Nature, and unhurriedly, thoughtfully, and happily to note the course of our lives amidst all the little links of events which connect them with the lives of others, and build up the great whole of humanity.

But such a holiday our whole lives might be, if we were resolute to make all our labour reasonable and pleasant. But we must be resolute indeed; for no half measures will help us here. It has been said already that our present joyless labour, and our lives scared and anxious as the life of a hunted beast, are forced upon us by the present system of producing for the profit of the privileged classes. It is necessary to state what this means. Under the present system of wages and capital the "manufacturer" (most absurdly so called, since a manufacturer means a person who makes with his hands) having a monopoly of the means whereby the power to labour inherent in every man's body can be used for production, is the master of those who are not so privileged; he, and he alone, is able to make use of this labour-power, which, on the other hand, is the only commodity by means of which his "capital," that is to say, the accumulated product of past labour, can be made productive to him. He therefore buys the labour-power of those who are bare of capital and can only live by selling it to him; his purpose in this transaction is to increase his capital, to make it breed. It is clear that if he paid those with whom he makes his bargain the full value of their labour, that is to say, all that they produced, he would fail in his purpose. But since he is the monopolist of the means of productive labour, he can *compel* them to make a bargain better for him and worse for them than that; which bargain is that after they have earned their livelihood, estimated according to a standard high enough to ensure their peaceable submission to his mastership, the rest (and by far the larger part as a matter of fact) of what they produce shall belong to him, shall be his *property* to do as he likes with, to use or abuse at his pleasure; which property is, as we all know, jealously guarded by army and navy, police and prison; in short, by that huge mass of physical force which superstition, habit, fear of death by starvation—IGNORANCE, in one word, among the propertyless masses, enables the propertied classes to use for the subjection of—their slaves.

Now, at other times, other evils resulting from this system may be put forward. What I want to point out now is the impossibility of our attaining to attractive labour under this system, and to repeat that it is this robbery (there is no other word for it) which wastes the available labour-power of the civilized world, forcing many men to do nothing, and many, very many more to do nothing useful; and forcing those who carry on really useful labour to most burdensome over-work. For understand once for all that the "manufacturer" aims primarily at producing, by means of the labour he has stolen from others, not goods but profits, that is, the "wealth" that is produced over and above the livelihood of his workmen, and the wear and tear of his machinery. Whether that "wealth" is real or sham matters nothing to him. If it sells and yields him a "profit" it is all right. I have said that, owing to there being rich people who have more money than they can spend reasonably, and who therefore buy sham wealth, there is waste on that side; and also that, owing to there being poor people who cannot afford to buy things which are worth making, there is waste on that side. So that the "demand" which the capitalist "supplies" is a false demand. The market in which he sells is "rigged" by the miserable inequalities produced by the robbery of the system of Capital and Wages.

It is this system, therefore, which we must be resolute in getting rid of, if we are to attain to happy and useful work for all. The first step towards making labour attractive is to get the means of making labour fruitful, the Capital, including the land, machinery, factories, &c., into the hands of the community, to be used for the good of all alike, so that we might all work at "supplying" the real "demands" of each and all—that is to say, work for livelihood, instead of working to supply the demand of the profit market—instead of working for profit—i.e., the power of compelling other men to work against their will.

When this first step has been taken and men begin to understand that Nature wills all men either to work or starve, and when they are no longer such fools as to allow some the alternative of stealing, when this happy day is come, we shall then be relieved from the tax of waste, and consequently shall find that we have, as aforesaid, a mass of labour-power available, which will enable us to live as we please within reasonable limits. We shall no longer be hurried and driven by the fear of starvation, which at present presses no less on the greater part of men in civilized communities than it does on mere savages. The first and most obvious necessities will be so easily provided for in a community in which there is no waste of labour, that we shall have time to look round and consider what we really do want, that can be obtained without over-taxing our energies; for the often-expressed fear of mere idleness falling upon us when the force supplied by the present hierarchy of compulsion is withdrawn, is a fear which is but generated by the burden of excessive and repulsive labour, which we most of us have to bear at present.

I say once more that, in my belief, the first thing which we shall think so necessary as to be worth sacrificing some idle time for, will be the attractiveness of labour. No very heavy sacrifice will be required for attaining this object, but some *will* be required. For we may hope that men who have just waded through a period of strife and revolution will be the last to put up long with a life of mere utilitarianism,[4] though Socialists are sometimes accused by ignorant persons of aiming at such a life. On the other hand, the ornamental part of modern life is already rotten to the core,

---

4. Practical use without beauty. The term also refers to a philosophy of practical value (the greatest good to the greatest number) developed by Jeremy Bentham in the 1820s.

and must be utterly swept away before the new order of things is realized. There is nothing of it—there is nothing which could come of it that could satisfy the aspirations of men set free from the tyranny of commercialism.

We must begin to build up the ornamental part of life—its pleasure, bodily and mental, scientific and artistic, social and individual—on the basis of work undertaken willingly and cheerfully, with the consciousness of benefiting ourselves and our neighbours by it. Such absolutely necessary work as we should have to do would in the first place take up but a small part of each day, and so far would not be burdensome; but it would be a task of daily recurrence, and therefore would spoil our day's pleasure unless it were made at least endurable while it lasted. In other words, all labour, even the commonest, must be made attractive.

How can this be done?—is the question the answer to which will take up the rest of this paper. In giving some hints on this question, I know that, while all Socialists will agree with many of the suggestions made, some of them may seem to some strange and venturesome. These must be considered as being given without any intention of dogmatizing, and as merely expressing my own personal opinion.

From all that has been said already it follows that labour, to be attractive, must be directed towards some obviously useful end, unless in cases where it is undertaken voluntarily by each individual as a pastime. This element of obvious usefulness is all the more to be counted on in sweetening tasks otherwise irksome, since social morality, the responsibility of man towards the life of man, will, in the new order of things, take the place of theological morality, or the responsibility of man to some abstract idea. Next, the day's work will be short. This need not be insisted on. It is clear that with work unwasted it *can* be short. It is clear also that much work which is now a torment, would be easily endurable if it were much shortened.

Variety of work is the next point, and a most important one. To compel a man to do day after day the same task, without any hope of escape or change, means nothing short of turning his life into a prison-torment. Nothing but the tyranny of profit-grinding makes this necessary. A man might easily learn and practise at least three crafts, varying sedentary occupation with outdoor—occupation calling for the exercise of strong bodily energy for work in which the mind had more to do. There are few men, for instance, who would not wish to spend part of their lives in the most necessary and pleasantest of all work—cultivating the earth. One thing which will make this variety of employment possible will be the form that education will take in a socially ordered community. At present all education is directed towards the end of fitting people to take their places in the hierarchy of commerce—these as masters, those as workmen. The education of the masters is more ornamental than that of the workmen, but it is commercial still; and even at the ancient universities learning is but little regarded, unless it can in the long run be made *to pay*. Due education is a totally different thing from this, and concerns itself in finding out what different people are fit for, and helping them along the road which they are inclined to take. In a duly ordered society, therefore, young people would be taught such handicrafts as they had a turn for as a part of their education, the discipline of their minds and bodies; and adults would also have opportunities of learning in the same schools, for the development of individual capacities would be of all things chiefly aimed at by education, instead, as now, the subordination of all capacities to the great end of "money-making" for oneself—or one's master. The amount of talent, and even genius, which the present system crushes, and which would be drawn out by such a system, would make our daily work easy and interesting.

Under this head of variety I will note one product of industry which has suffered so much from commercialism that it can scarcely be said to exist, and is, indeed, so foreign from our epoch that I fear there are some who will find it difficult to understand what I have to say on the subject, which I nevertheless must say, since it is really a most important one. I mean that side of art which is, or ought to be, done by the ordinary workman while he is about his ordinary work, and which has got to be called, very properly, Popular Art. This art, I repeat, no longer exists now, having been killed by commercialism. But from the beginning of man's contest with Nature till the rise of the present capitalistic system, it was alive, and generally flourished. While it lasted, everything that was made by man was adorned by man, just as everything made by Nature is adorned by her. The craftsman, as he fashioned the thing he had under his hand, ornamented it so naturally and so entirely without conscious effort, that it is often difficult to distinguish where the mere utilitarian part of his work ended and the ornamental began. Now the origin of this art was the necessity that the workman felt for variety in his work, and though the beauty produced by this desire was a great gift to the world, yet the obtaining variety and pleasure in the work by the workman was a matter of more importance still, for it stamped all labour with the impress of pleasure. All this has now quite disappeared from the work of civilization. If you wish to have ornament, you must pay specially for it, and the workman is compelled to produce ornament, as he is to produce other wares. He is compelled to pretend happiness in his work, so that the beauty produced by man's hand, which was once a solace to his labour, has now become an extra burden to him, and ornament is now but one of the follies of useless toil, and perhaps not the least irksome of its fetters.

Besides the short duration of labour, its conscious usefulness, and the variety which should go with it, there is another thing needed to make it attractive, and that is pleasant surroundings. The misery and squalor which we people of civilization bear with so much complacency as a necessary part of the manufacturing system, is just as necessary to the community at large as a proportionate amount of filth would be in the house of a private rich man. If such a man were to allow the cinders to be raked all over his drawing-room, and a privy[5] to be established in each corner of his dining-room, if he habitually made a dust and refuse heap of his once beautiful garden, never washed his sheets or changed his tablecloth, and made his family sleep five in a bed, he would surely find himself in the claws of a commission *de lunatico*.[6] But such acts of miserly folly are just what our present society is doing daily under the compulsion of a supposed necessity, which is nothing short of madness. I beg you to bring your commission of lunacy against civilization without more delay.

For all our crowded towns and bewildering factories are simply the outcome of the profit system. Capitalistic manufacture, capitalistic land-owning, and capitalistic exchange force men into big cities in order to manipulate them in the interests of

5. Toilet.
6. A commission of lunacy.

capital; the same tyranny contracts the due space of the factory so much that (for instance) the interior of a great weaving-shed is almost as ridiculous a spectacle as it is a horrible one. There is no other necessity for all this, save the necessity for grinding profits out of men's lives, and of producing cheap goods for the use (and subjection) of the slaves who grind. All labour is not yet driven into factories; often where it is there is no necessity for it, save again the profit-tyranny. People engaged in all such labour need by no means be compelled to pig together in close city quarters. There is no reason why they should not follow their occupations in quiet country homes, in industrial colleges, in small towns, or, in short, where they find it happiest for them to live.

As to that part of labour which must be associated on a large scale, this very factory system, under a reasonable order of things (though to my mind there might still be drawbacks to it), would at least offer opportunities for a full and eager social life surrounded by many pleasures. The factories might be centres of intellectual activity also, and work in them might well be varied very much: the tending of the necessary machinery might to each individual be but a short part of the day's work. The other work might vary from raising food from the surrounding country to the study and practice of art and science. It is a matter of course that people engaged in such work, and being the masters of their own lives, would not allow any hurry or want of foresight to force them into enduring dirt, disorder, or want of room. Science duly applied would enable them to get rid of refuse, to minimize, if not wholly to destroy, all the inconveniences which at present attend the use of elaborate machinery, such as smoke, stench, and noise; nor would they endure that the buildings in which they worked or lived should be ugly blots on the fair face of the earth. Beginning by making their factories, buildings, and sheds decent and convenient like their homes, they would infallibly go on to make them not merely negatively good, inoffensive merely, but even beautiful, so that the glorious art of architecture, now for some time slain by commercial greed, would be born again and flourish.

So, you see, I claim that work in a duly ordered community should be made attractive by the consciousness of usefulness, by its being carried on with intelligent interest, by variety, and by its being exercised amidst pleasurable surroundings. But I have also claimed, as we all do, that the day's work should not be wearisomely long. It may be said, "How can you make this last claim square with the others? If the work is to be so refined, will not the goods made by very expensive?"

I do admit, as I have said before, that some sacrifice will be necessary in order to make labour attractive. I mean that, if we *could* be contented in a free community to work in the same hurried, dirty, disorderly, heartless way as we do now, we might shorten our day's labour very much more than I suppose we shall do, taking all kinds of labour into account. But if we did, it would mean that our new-won freedom of condition would leave us listless and wretched, if not anxious, as we are now, which I hold is simply impossible. We should be contented to make the sacrifices necessary for raising our condition to the standard called out for as desirable by the whole community. Nor only so. We should, individually, be emulous to sacrifice quite freely still more of our time and our ease towards the raising of the standard of life. Persons, either by themselves or associated for such purposes, would freely, and for the love of the work and for its results—stimulated by the hope of the pleasure of creation—pro-

duce those ornaments of life for the service of all, which they are now bribed to produce (or pretend to produce) for the service of a few rich men. The experiment of a
civilized community living wholly without art or literature has not yet been tried.
The past degradation and corruption of civilization may force this denial of pleasure
upon the society which will arise from its ashes. If that must be, we will accept the
passing phase of utilitarianism as a foundation for the art which is to be. If the cripple and the starveling[7] disappear from our streets, if the earth nourish us all alike, if
the sun shine for all of us alike, if to one and all of us the glorious drama of the
earth—day and night, summer and winter—can be presented as a thing to understand and love, we can afford to wait awhile till we are purified from the shame of the
past corruption, and till art arises again amongst people freed from the terror of the
slave and the shame of the robber.

Meantime, in any case, the refinement, thoughtfulness, and deliberation of
labour must indeed be paid for, but not by compulsion to labour long hours. Our
epoch has invented machines which would have appeared wild dreams to the men of
past ages, and of those machines we have as yet *made no use.*

They are called "labour-saving" machines—a commonly used phrase which
implies what we expect of them; but we do not get what we expect. What they really
do is to reduce the skilled labourer to the ranks of the unskilled, to increase the number of the "reserve army of labour"—that is, to increase the precariousness of life
among the workers and to intensify the labour of those who serve the machines (as
slaves their masters). All this they do by the way, while they pile up the profits of the
employers of labour, or force them to expend those profits in bitter commercial war
with each other. In a true society these miracles of ingenuity would be for the first
time used for minimizing the amount of time spent in unattractive labour, which by
their means might be so reduced as to be but a very light burden on each individual.
All the more as these machines would most certainly be very much improved when
it was no longer a question as to whether their improvement would "pay" the individual, but rather whether it would benefit the community.

So much for the ordinary use of machinery, which would probably, after a time,
be somewhat restricted when men found out that there was no need for anxiety as
to mere subsistence, and learned to take an interest and pleasure in handiwork
which, done deliberately and thoughtfully, could be made more attractive than
machine work.

Again, as people freed from the daily terror of starvation find out what they
really wanted, being no longer compelled by anything but their own needs, they
would refuse to produce the mere inanities which are now called luxuries, or the poison and trash now called cheap wares. No one would make plush breeches when
there were no flunkies[8] to wear them, nor would anybody waste his time over making oleo-margarine[9] when no one was *compelled* to abstain from real butter.
Adulteration laws are only needed in a society of thieves—and in such a society they
are a dead letter.

---

7. Someone visibly malnourished.
8. Gaudily uniformed male servants.
9. Recently developed butter substitute.

Socialists are often asked how work of the rougher and more repulsive kind could be carried out in the new condition of things. To attempt to answer such questions fully or authoritatively would be attempting the impossibility of constructing a scheme of a new society out of the materials of the old, before we knew which of those materials would disappear and which endure through the evolution which is leading us to the great change. Yet it is not difficult to conceive of some arrangement whereby those who did the roughest work should work for the shortest spells. And again, what is said above of the variety of work applies specially here. Once more I say, that for a man to be the whole of his life hopelessly engaged in performing one repulsive and never-ending task, is an arrangement fit enough for the hell imagined by theologians, but scarcely fit for any other form of society. Lastly, if this rougher work were of any special kind, we may suppose that special volunteers would be called on to perform it, who would surely be forthcoming, unless men in a state of freedom should lose the sparks of manliness which they possessed as slaves.

And yet if there be any work which cannot be made other than repulsive, either by the shortness of its duration or the intermittency of its recurrence, or by the sense of special and peculiar usefulness (and therefore honour) in the mind of the man who performs it freely—if there be any work which cannot be but a torment to the worker, what then? Well, then, let us see if the heavens will fall on us if we leave it undone, for it were better that they should. The produce of such work cannot be worth the price of it.

Now we have seen that the semi-theological dogma that all labour, under any circumstances, is a blessing to the labourer, is hypocritical and false; that, on the other hand, labour is good when due hope of rest and pleasure accompanies it. We have weighed the work of civilization in the balance and found it wanting, since hope is mostly lacking to it, and therefore we see that civilization has bred a dire curse for men. But we have seen also that the work of the world might be carried on in hope and with pleasure if it were not wasted by folly and tyranny, by the perpetual strife of opposing classes.

It is Peace, therefore, which we need in order that we may live and work in hope and with pleasure. Peace so much desired, if we may trust men's words, but which has been so continually and steadily rejected by them in deeds. But for us, let us set our hearts on it and win it at whatever cost.

What the cost may be, who can tell? Will it be possible to win peace peaceably? Alas, how can it be? We are so hemmed in by wrong and folly, that in one way or other we must always be fighting against them: our own lives may see no end to the struggle, perhaps no obvious hope of the end. It may be that the best we can hope to see is that struggle getting sharper and bitterer day by day, until it breaks out openly at last into the slaughter of men by actual warfare instead of by the slower and crueller methods of "peaceful" commerce. If we live to see that, we shall live to see much; for it will mean the rich classes grown conscious of their own wrong and robbery, and consciously defending them by open violence; and then the end will be drawing near.

But in any case, and whatever the nature of our strife for peace may be, if we only aim at it steadily and with singleness of heart, and ever keep it in view, a reflection from that peace of the future will illumine the turmoil and trouble of our lives, whether the trouble be seemingly petty, or obviously tragic; and we shall, in our hopes at least, live the lives of men: nor can the present times give us any reward greater than that.

—1884

Oscar Wilde
1854–1900

Oscar Wilde's political conscience developed early. The son of two ardent Irish nationalists, he watched his mother publish patriotic verse and risk imprisonment in 1848 for her inflammatory editorials in the *Nation* advocating war with England. When he moved to England in 1874, Wilde dropped his Irish accent. Under the influence of socialist John Ruskin he helped build a road through the Oxford marshes (an experiment to teach students the value of labor). Throughout his life, Wilde retained his liking for working-class people, especially the men; he enjoyed meeting the Colorado miners on his American tour and befriended members of the urban underclass in London. An outsider by virtue of both national origin and sexual preference, Wilde had great fellow-feeling for others marginalized by Victorian society. In "The Soul of Man Under Socialism" he transforms the socialist lessons of Morris and Ruskin into a characteristically Wildean performance of bravura wit, scintillating paradoxes, and exciting redefinitions of art in its relation to life. For more information about Wilde, see pp. 19, 83, and 148.

from The Soul of Man Under Socialism

The chief advantage that would result from the establishment of Socialism is, undoubtedly, the fact that Socialism would relieve us from that sordid necessity of living for others which, in the present condition of things, presses so hardly upon almost everybody. In fact, scarcely any one at all escapes.

Now and then, in the course of the century, a great man of science, like Darwin; a great poet, like Keats; a fine critical spirit, like M. Renan; a supreme artist, like Flaubert,[1] has been able to isolate himself, to keep himself out of reach of the clamorous claims of others, to stand "under the shelter of the wall", as Plato puts it,[2] and so to realize the perfection of what was in him, to his own incomparable gain, and to the incomparable and lasting gain of the whole world. These, however, are exceptions. The majority of people spoil their lives by an unhealthy and exaggerated altruism—are forced, indeed, so to spoil them. They find themselves surrounded by hideous poverty, by hideous ugliness, by hideous starvation. It is inevitable that they should be strongly moved by all this. The emotions of man are stirred more quickly than man's intelligence; and, as I pointed out some time ago in an article on the func-

---

1. 19th-c. thinkers: evolutionary theorist Charles Darwin; Romantic poet John Keats; French historian and religious skeptic Ernest Renan; French novelist and uncompromising literary stylist Gustave Flaubert.
2. *The Republic*, Book VI.

tion of criticism,[3] it is much more easy to have sympathy with suffering than it is to have sympathy with thought. Accordingly, with admirable though misdirected intentions, they very seriously and very sentimentally set themselves to the task of remedying the evils that they see. But their remedies do not cure the disease: they merely prolong it. Indeed, their remedies are part of the disease.

They try to solve the problem of poverty, for instance, by keeping the poor alive; or, in the case of a very advanced school, by amusing the poor.[4]

But this is not a solution: it is an aggravation of the difficulty. The proper aim is to try and reconstruct society on such a basis that poverty will be impossible. And the altruistic virtues have really prevented the carrying out of this aim. Just as the worst slave-owners were those who were kind to their slaves, and so prevented the horror of the system being realized by those who suffered from it, and understood by those who contemplated it, so, in the present state of things in England, the people who do most harm are the people who try to do most good; and at last we have had the spectacle of men who have really studied the problem and know the life—educated men who live in the East-End[5]—coming forward and imploring the community to restrain its altruistic impulses of charity, benevolence and the like. They do so on the ground that such charity degrades and demoralizes. They are perfectly right. Charity creates a multitude of sins.

There is also this to be said. It is immoral to use private property in order to alleviate the horrible evils that result from the institution of private property. It is both immoral and unfair.

Under Socialism all this will, of course, be altered. There will be no people living in fetid dens and fetid rags, and bringing up unhealthy, hunger-pinched children in the midst of impossible and absolutely repulsive surroundings. The security of society will not depend, as it does now, on the state of the weather. If a frost comes we shall not have a hundred thousand men out of work, tramping about the streets in a state of disgusting misery, or whining to their neighbours for alms, or crowding round the doors of loathsome shelters to try and secure a hunch of bread and a night's unclean lodging. Each member of the society will share in the general prosperity and happiness of the society, and if a frost comes no one will practically be anything the worse.

Upon the other hand, Socialism itself will be of value simply because it will lead to Individualism.

Socialism, Communism, or whatever one chooses to call it, by converting private property into public wealth, and substituting cooperation for competition, will restore society to its proper condition of a thoroughly healthy organism, and ensure the material well-being of each member of the community. It will, in fact, give Life its proper basis and its proper environment. But for the full development of Life to its highest mode of perfection something more is needed. What is needed is Individualism. If the Socialism is Authoritarian; if there are Governments armed with economic power as they are now with political power; if, in a word, we are to

---

3. "The True Function and Value of Criticism: with some Remarks on the Importance of Doing Nothing" (*The Nineteenth Century*, 1890), substantially revised as "The Critic as Artist" in *Intentions* (1891).
4. "Missionary aestheticism," the movement to bring artistic enrichment to the urban slums.
5. Poorest area of London.

have Industrial Tyrannies, then the last state of man will be worse than the first. At present, in consequence of the existence of private property, a great many people are enabled to develop a certain very limited amount of Individualism. They are either under no necessity to work for their living, or are enabled to choose the sphere of activity that is really congenial to them and gives them pleasure. These are the poets, the philosophers, the men of science, the men of culture—in a word, the real men, the men who have realized themselves, and in whom all Humanity gains a partial realization. Upon the other hand, there are a great many people who, having no private property of their own, and being always on the brink of sheer starvation, are compelled to do the work of beasts of burden, to do work that is quite uncongenial to them, and to which they are forced by the peremptory, unreasonable, degrading Tyranny of want. These are the poor, and amongst them there is no grace of manner, or charm of speech, or civilization, or culture, or refinement in pleasures, or joy of life. From their collective force Humanity gains much in material prosperity. But it is only the material result that it gains, and the man who is poor is in himself absolutely of no importance. He is merely the infinitesimal atom of a force that, so far from regarding him, crushes him: indeed, prefers him crushed, as in that case he is far more obedient.

Of course, it might be said that the Individualism generated under conditions of private property is not always, or even as a rule, of a fine or wonderful type, and that the poor, if they have not culture and charm, have still many virtues. Both these statements would be quite true. The possession of private property is very often extremely demoralizing, and that is, of course, one of the reasons why Socialism wants to get rid of the institution. In fact, property is really a nuisance. Some years ago people went about the country saying that property has duties. They said it so often and so tediously that, at last, the Church has begun to say it. One hears it now from every pulpit. It is perfectly true. Property not merely has duties, but has so many duties that its possession to any large extent is a bore. It involves endless claims upon one, endless attention to business, endless bother. If property had simply pleasures we could stand it; but its duties make it unbearable. In the interest of the rich we must get rid of it. The virtues of the poor may be readily admitted, and are much to be regretted. We are often told that the poor are grateful for charity. Some of them are, no doubt, but the best amongst the poor are never grateful. They are ungrateful, discontented, disobedient and rebellious. They are quite right to be so. Charity they feel to be a ridiculously inadequate mode of partial restitution, or a sentimental dole, usually accompanied by some impertinent attempt on the part of the sentimentalist to tyrannize over their private lives. Why should they be grateful for the crumbs that fall from the rich man's table? They should be seated at the board, and are beginning to know it. As for being discontented, a man who would not be discontented with such surroundings and such a low mode of life would be a perfect brute. Disobedience, in the eyes of any one who has read history, is man's original virtue.[6] It is through disobedience that progress has been made, through disobedience and through rebellion. Sometimes the poor are praised for being thrifty. But to recommend thrift to the poor is both grotesque and insulting. It is like advising a man who is starving to eat less.

6. A reversal of "original sin," Eve's disobedience in the Garden of Eden.

For a town or country labourer to practise thrift would be absolutely immoral. Man should not be ready to show that he can live like a badly fed animal. He should decline to live like that, and should either steal or go on the rates,[7] which is considered by many to be a form of stealing. As for begging, it is safer to beg than to take, but it is finer to take than to beg. No: a poor man who is ungrateful, unthrifty, discontented and rebellious is probably a real personality, and has much in him. He is at any rate a healthy protest. As for the virtuous poor, one can pity them, of course, but one cannot possibly admire them. They have made private terms with the enemy, and sold their birthright for very bad pottage.[8] They must also be extraordinarily stupid. I can quite understand a man accepting laws that protect private property, and admit of its accumulation, as long as he himself is able under those conditions to realize some form of beautiful and intellectual life. But it is almost incredible to me how a man whose life is marred and made hideous by such laws can possibly acquiesce in their continuance.

However, the explanation is not really difficult to find. It is simply this. Misery and poverty are so absolutely degrading, and exercise such a paralysing effect over the nature of men, that no class is ever really conscious of its own suffering. They have to be told of it by other people, and they often entirely disbelieve them. What is said by great employers of labour against agitators is unquestionably true. Agitators are a set of interfering, meddling people, who come down to some perfectly contented class of the community and sow the seeds of discontent amongst them. That is the reason why agitators are so absolutely necessary. Without them, in our incomplete state, there would be no advance towards civilization. Slavery was put down in America, not in consequence of any action on the part of the slaves, or even any express desire on their part that they should be free. It was put down entirely through the grossly illegal conduct of certain agitators in Boston and elsewhere, who were not slaves themselves, nor owners of slaves, nor had anything to do with the question really. It was, undoubtedly, the Abolitionists who set the torch alight, who began the whole thing. And it is curious to note that from the slaves themselves they received, not merely very little assistance, but hardly any sympathy even; and when at the close of the war the slaves found themselves free, found themselves indeed so absolutely free that they were free to starve, many of them bitterly regretted the new state of things. To the thinker, the most tragic fact in the whole of the French Revolution is not that Marie Antoinette was killed for being a queen, but that the starved peasant of the Vendée voluntarily went out to die for the hideous cause of feudalism.[9]

It is clear, then, that no Authoritarian Socialism will do. For, while under the present system a very large number of people can lead lives of a certain amount of freedom and expression and happiness, under an industrial–barrack system,[10] or a system of economic tyranny, nobody would be able to have any such freedom at all. It is to be regretted that a portion of our community should be practically in slavery, but to propose to solve the problem by enslaving the entire community is childish.

---

7. The "poor rates," a fund amassed from property taxes to maintain the poor.
8. Elder brother Esau sells Jacob his inheritance in exchange for food, Genesis 25.29–34.
9. The queen was among thousands executed in the Reign of Terror. Peasants were horribly oppressed under the old feudal regime, yet peasants in the Vendée region (in western France) fought against the Revolution and suffered enormous loss of life.
10. A centralized, military-style governmental plan for the future.

Every man must be left quite free to choose his own work. No form of compulsion must be exercised over him. If there is, his work will not be good for him, will not be good in itself, and will not be good for others. And by work I simply mean activity of any kind.

I hardly think that any Socialist, nowadays, would seriously propose that an inspector should call every morning at each house to see that each citizen rose up and did manual labour for eight hours. Humanity has got beyond that stage, and reserves such a form of life for the people whom, in a very arbitrary manner, it chooses to call criminals. But I confess that many of the socialistic views that I have come across seem to me to be tainted with ideas of authority, if not of actual compulsion. Of course authority and compulsion are out of the question. All association must be quite voluntary. It is only in voluntary association that man is fine.

But it may be asked how Individualism, which is now more or less dependent on the existence of private property for its development, will benefit by the abolition of such private property. The answer is very simple. It is true that, under existing conditions, a few men who have had private means of their own, such as Byron, Shelley, Browning, Victor Hugo, Baudelaire,[11] and others, have been able to realize their personality more or less completely. Not one of these men ever did a single day's work for hire. They were relieved from poverty. They had an immense advantage. The question is whether it would be for the good of Individualism that such an advantage should be taken away. Let us suppose that it is taken away. What happens then to Individualism? How will it benefit?

It will benefit in this way. Under the new conditions Individualism will be far freer, far finer and far more intensified than it is now. I am not talking of the great imaginatively-realized Individualism of such poets as I have mentioned, but of the great actual Individualism latent and potential in mankind generally. For the recognition of private property has really harmed Individualism, and obscured it, by confusing a man with what he possesses. It has led Individualism entirely astray. It has made gain not growth its aim. So that man thought that the important thing was to have, and did not know that the important thing is to be. The true perfection of man lies, not in what man has, but in what man is. Private property has crushed true Individualism, and set up an Individualism that is false. It has debarred one part of the community from being individual by starving them. It has debarred the other part of the community from being individual, by putting them on the wrong road and encumbering them. Indeed, so completely has man's personality been absorbed by his possessions that the English law has always treated offences against a man's property with far more severity than offences against his person, and property is still the test of complete citizenship.[12] The industry necessary for the making of money is also very demoralizing. In a community like ours, where property confers immense distinction, social position, honour, respect, titles, and other pleasant things of the kind, man, being naturally ambitious, makes it his aim to accumulate this property, and goes on wearily and tediously accumulating it long after he has got far more than he wants, or can use, or enjoy, or perhaps even know of. Man will kill himself by overwork in

---

11. Famous 19th-c. authors: Romantic poets George Gordon, Lord Byron and Percy Bysshe Shelley; mid-Victorian poet Robert Browning; French realist novelist Victor Hugo; French decadent poet Charles Baudelaire.
12. The vote was limited to males who owned property worth at least £10.

order to secure property, and really, considering the enormous advantages that property brings, one is hardly surprised. One's regret is that society should be constructed on such a basis that man has been forced into a groove in which he cannot freely develop what is wonderful, and fascinating, and delightful in him—in which, in fact, he misses the true pleasure and joy of living. He is also, under existing conditions, very insecure. An enormously wealthy merchant may be—often is—at every moment of his life at the mercy of things that are not under his control. If the wind blows an extra point or so, or the weather suddenly changes, or some trivial thing happens, his ship may go down, his speculations may go wrong, and he finds himself a poor man, with his social position quite gone. Now, nothing should be able to harm a man except himself. Nothing should be able to rob a man at all. What a man really has, is what is in him. What is outside of him should be a matter of no importance.

With the abolition of private property, then, we shall have true, beautiful, healthy Individualism. Nobody will waste his life in accumulating things and the symbols for things. One will live. To live is the rarest thing in the world. Most people exist, that is all.

It is a question whether we have ever seen the full expression of a personality, except on the imaginative plane of art. In action, we never have. Caesar, says Mommsen,[13] was the complete and perfect man. But how tragically insecure was Caesar! Wherever there is a man who exercises authority, there is a man who resists authority. Caesar was very perfect, but his perfection travelled by too dangerous a road. Marcus Aurelius was the perfect man, says Renan. Yes; the great emperor was a perfect man. But how intolerable were the endless claims upon him! He staggered under the burden of the empire. He was conscious how inadequate one man was to bear the weight of that Titan and too vast orb.[14] What I mean by a perfect man is one who develops under perfect conditions; one who is not wounded, or worried, or maimed, or in danger. Most personalities have been obliged to be rebels. Half their strength has been wasted in friction. Byron's personality, for instance, was terribly wasted in its battle with the stupidity, and hypocrisy, and Philistinism of the English. Such battles do not always intensify strength: they often exaggerate weakness. Byron was never able to give us what he might have given us. Shelley escaped better.[15] Like Byron, he got out of England as soon as possible. But he was not so well known. If the English had had any idea of what a great poet he really was, they would have fallen on him with tooth and nail, and made his life as unbearable to him as they possibly could. But he was not a remarkable figure in society, and consequently he escaped, to a certain degree. Still, even in Shelley the note of rebellion is sometimes too strong. The note of the perfect personality is not rebellion but peace.

It will be a marvellous thing—the true personality of man—when we see it. It will grow naturally and simply, flower-like, or as a tree grows. It will not be at discord. It will never argue or dispute. It will not prove things. It will know everything. And yet it will not busy itself about knowledge. It will have wisdom. Its value will not be

---

13. 19th-c. German historian Theodor Mommsen.
14. Roman Emperor and Stoic philosopher Marcus Aurelius, who ruled during a turbulent period (161–80). The Titan god Atlas bore the weight of the world on his shoulders.
15. Shelley's atheism and radical politics angered the mainstream press, but because his poetry scarcely sold, he was less of a target than Byron, whose sex scandals garnered international publicity.

measured by material things. It will have nothing. And yet it will have everything, and whatever one takes from it, it will still have, so rich will it be. It will not be always meddling with others, or asking them to be like itself. It will love them because they will be different. And yet while it will not meddle with others it will help all, as a beautiful thing helps us, by being what it is. The personality of man will be very wonderful. It will be as wonderful as the personality of a child.

In its development it will be assisted by Christianity, if men desire that; but if men do not desire that, it will develop none the less surely. For it will not worry itself about the past, nor care whether things happened or did not happen. Nor will it admit any laws but its own laws; nor any authority but its own authority. Yet it will love those who sought to intensify it, and speak often of them. And of these Christ was one.

"Know Thyself"[16] was written over the portal of the antique world. Over the portal of the new world, "Be Thyself" shall be written. And the message of Christ to man was simply "Be thyself". That is the secret of Christ.

When Jesus talks about the poor he simply means personalities, just as when he talks about the rich he simply means people who have not developed their personalities. Jesus moved in a community that allowed the accumulation of private property just as ours does, and the gospel that he preached was not that in such a community it is an advantage for a man to live on scanty, unwholesome food, to wear ragged, unwholesome clothes, to sleep in horrid, unwholesome dwellings, and a disadvantage for a man to live under healthy, pleasant and decent conditions. Such a view would have been wrong there and then, and would of course be still more wrong now and in England; for as man moves northwards the material necessities of life become of more vital importance, and our society is infinitely more complex, and displays far greater extremes of luxury and pauperism than any society of the antique world. What Jesus meant was this. He said to man, "You have a wonderful personality. Develop it. Be your self. Don't imagine that your perfection lies in accumulating or possessing external things. Your perfection is inside of you. If only you could realize that, you would not want to be rich. Ordinary riches can be stolen from a man. Real riches cannot. In the treasury-house of your soul, there are infinitely precious things, that may not be taken from you. And so, try so to shape your life that external things will not harm you. And try also to get rid of personal property. It involves sordid preoccupation, endless industry, continual wrong. Personal property hinders Individualism at every step." It is to be noted that Jesus never says that impoverished people are necessarily good, or wealthy people necessarily bad. That would not have been true. Wealthy people are, as a class, better than impoverished people, more moral, more intellectual, more well-behaved. There is only one class in the community that thinks more about money than the rich, and that is the poor. The poor can think of nothing else. That is the misery of being poor. What Jesus does say is that man reaches his perfection, not through what he has, not even through what he does, but entirely through what he is. And so the wealthy young man who comes to Jesus is represented as a thoroughly good citizen, who has broken none of the laws of his state, none of the commandments of his religion. He is quite respectable, in the ordi-

---

16. The motto written over the doorway at the temple of Apollo at Delphi, and the central message of Socratic philosophy.

nary sense of that extraordinary word. Jesus says to him, "You should give up private property. It hinders you from realizing your perfection. It is a drag upon you. It is a burden. Your personality does not need it. It is within you, and not outside of you, that you will find what you really are, and what you really want." To his own friends he says the same thing. He tells them to be themselves, and not to be always worrying about other things. What do other things matter? Man is complete in himself. When they go into the world, the world will disagree with them. That is inevitable. The world hates Individualism. But that is not to trouble them. They are to be calm and self-centred. If a man takes their cloak, they are to give him their coat, just to show that material things are of no importance. If people abuse them, they are not to answer back. What does it signify? The things people say of a man do not alter a man. He is what he is. Public opinion is of no value whatsoever. Even if people employ actual violence, they are not to be violent in turn. That would be to fall to the same low level. After all, even in prison, a man can be quite free. His soul can be free. His personality can be untroubled. He can be at peace. And, above all things, they are not to interfere with other people or judge them in any way. Personality is a very mysterious thing. A man cannot always be estimated by what he does. He may keep the law, and yet be worthless. He may break the law, and yet be fine. He may be bad, without ever doing anything bad. He may commit a sin against society, and yet realize through that sin his true perfection.

There was a woman who was taken in adultery.[17] We are not told the history of her love, but that love must have been very great; for Jesus said that her sins were forgiven her, not because she repented, but because her love was so intense and wonderful. Later on, a short time before his death, as he sat at a feast, the woman came in and poured costly perfumes on his hair. His friends tried to interfere with her, and said that it was an extravagance, and that the money that the perfume cost should have been expended on charitable relief of people in want, or something of that kind. Jesus did not accept that view. He pointed out that the material needs of Man were great and very permanent, but that the spiritual needs of Man were greater still, and that in one divine moment, and by selecting its own mode of expression, a personality might make itself perfect. The world worships the woman, even now, as a saint.

Yes; there are suggestive things in Individualism. Socialism annihilates family life, for instance. With the abolition of private property, marriage in its present form must disappear. This is part of the programme. Individualism accepts this and makes it fine. It converts the abolition of legal restraint into a form of freedom that will help the full development of personality, and make the love of man and woman more wonderful, more beautiful, and more ennobling. Jesus knew this. He rejected the claims of family life, although they existed in his day and community in a very marked form. "Who is my mother? Who are my brothers?" he said, when he was told that they wished to speak to him. When one of his followers asked leave to go and bury his father, "Let the dead bury the dead," was his terrible answer.[18] He would allow no claim whatsoever to be made on personality.

And so he who would lead a Christlike life is he who is perfectly and absolutely himself. He may be a great poet, or a great man of science; or a young student at a

17. Mary Magdalen (John 8.4–8).
18. See Matthew 12.48 and 8.22.

University, or one who watches sheep upon a moor; or a maker of dramas, like Shakespeare, or a thinker about God, like Spinoza;[19] or a child who plays in a garden, or a fisherman who throws his nets into the sea. It does not matter what he is, as long as he realizes the perfection of the soul that is within him. All imitation in morals and in life is wrong. Through the streets of Jerusalem at the present day crawls one who is mad and carries a wooden cross on his shoulders. He is a symbol of the lives that are marred by imitation. Father Damien[20] was Christlike when he went out to live with the lepers, because in such service he realized fully what was best in him. But he was not more Christlike than Wagner,[21] when he realized his soul in music; or than Shelley, when he realized his soul in song. There is no one type for man. There are as many perfections as there are imperfect men. And while to the claims of charity a man may yield and yet be free, to the claims of conformity no man may yield and remain free at all.

Individualism, then, is what through Socialism we are to attain to. As a natural result the State must give up all idea of government. It must give it up because, as a wise man[22] once said many centuries before Christ, there is such a thing as leaving mankind alone; there is no such thing as governing mankind. All modes of government are failures. Despotism is unjust to everybody, including the despot, who was probably made for better things. Oligarchies are unjust to the many, and ochlocracies[23] are unjust to the few. High hopes were once formed of democracy; but democracy means simply the bludgeoning of the people by the people for the people.[24] It has been found out. I must say that it was high time, for all authority is quite degrading. It degrades those who exercise it, and degrades those over whom it is exercised. When it is violently, grossly and cruelly used, it produces a good effect, by creating, or at any rate bringing out, the spirit of revolt and Individualism that is to kill it. When it is used with a certain amount of kindness, and accompanied by prizes and rewards, it is dreadfully demoralizing. People, in that case, are less conscious of the horrible pressure that is being put on them, and so go through their lives in a sort of coarse comfort, like petted animals, without ever realizing that they are probably thinking other people's thoughts, living by other people's standards, wearing practically what one may call other people's second-hand clothes, and never being themselves for a single moment. "He who would be free," says a fine thinker,[25] "must not conform." And authority, by bribing people to conform, produces a very gross kind of over-fed barbarism amongst us.

With authority, punishment will pass away. This will be a great gain—a gain, in fact, of incalculable value. As one reads history, not in the expurgated editions written for schoolboys and passmen,[26] but in the original authorities of each time, one is absolutely sickened, not by the crimes that the wicked have committed, but by the

---

19. 17th-c. Dutch philosopher Baruch Spinoza proposed that all creation consists of different manifestations of God, the only substance.
20. 19th-c. Belgian Catholic missionary.
21. German composer Richard Wagner (1813–83).
22. Chuang Tsû, leader of Taoism (born 330 B.C.E.).
23. Oligarchies are governments led by small groups; ochlocracies are governments led by mobs.
24. Wilde applies Lincoln's famous phrase to the Chicago police killing demonstrators in the Haymarket riots (1886).
25. 19th-c. American philosopher Ralph Waldo Emerson.
26. University students content merely to pass their courses.

punishments that the good have inflicted; and a community is infinitely more brutalized by the habitual employment of punishment, than it is by the occasional occurrence of crime. It obviously follows that the more punishment is inflicted the more crime is produced, and most modern legislation has clearly recognized this, and has made it its task to diminish punishment as far as it thinks it can. Wherever it has really diminished it, the results have always been extremely good. The less punishment, the less crime. When there is no punishment at all, crime will either cease to exist, or if it occurs, will be treated by physicians as a very distressing form of dementia, to be cured by care and kindness. For what are called criminals nowadays are not criminals at all. Starvation, and not sin, is the parent of modern crime. That indeed is the reason why our criminals are, as a class, so absolutely uninteresting from any psychological point of view. They are not marvellous Macbeths and terrible Vautrins.[27] They are merely what ordinary, respectable, commonplace people would be if they had not got enough to eat. When private property is abolished there will be no necessity for crime, no demand for it; it will cease to exist. Of course all crimes are not crimes against property, though such are the crimes that the English law, valuing what a man has more than what a man is, punishes with the harshest and most horrible severity, if we except the crime of murder, and regard death as worse than penal servitude, a point on which our criminals, I believe, disagree. But though a crime may not be against property, it may spring from the misery and rage and depression produced by our wrong system of property-holding, and so, when that system is abolished, will disappear. When each member of the community has sufficient for his wants, and is not interfered with by his neighbour, it will not be an object of any interest to him to interfere with any one else. Jealousy, which is an extraordinary source of crime in modern life, is an emotion closely bound up with our conceptions of property, and under Socialism and Individualism will die out. It is remarkable that in communistic tribes jealousy is entirely unknown.

Now as the State is not to govern, it may be asked what the State is to do. The State is to be a voluntary association that will organize labour, and be the manufacturer and distributor of necessary commodities. The State is to make what is useful. The individual is to make what is beautiful. And as I have mentioned the word labour, I cannot help saying that a great deal of nonsense is being written and talked nowadays about the dignity of manual labour. There is nothing necessarily dignified about manual labour at all, and most of it is absolutely degrading. It is mentally and morally injurious to man to do anything in which he does not find pleasure, and many forms of labour are quite pleasureless activities, and should be regarded as such. To sweep a slushy crossing for eight hours on a day when the east wind is blowing is a disgusting occupation. To sweep it with mental, moral or physical dignity seems to me to be impossible. To sweep it with joy would be appalling. Man is made for something better than disturbing dirt. All work of that kind should be done by a machine.

And I have no doubt that it will be so. Up to the present, man has been, to a certain extent, the slave of machinery, and there is something tragic in the fact that as soon as man had invented a machine to do his work he began to starve. This, however, is, of course, the result of our property system and our system of competition.

---

27. Shakespeare's guilt-haunted murderer and Balzac's arch-villain.

One man owns a machine which does the work of five hundred men. Five hundred men are, in consequence, thrown out of employment, and having no work to do, become hungry and take to thieving. The one man secures the produce of the machine and keeps it, and has five hundred times as much as he should have, and probably, which is of much more importance, a great deal more than he really wants. Were that machine the property of all, every one would benefit by it. It would be an immense advantage to the community. All unintellectual labour, all monotonous, dull labour, all labour that deals with dreadful things, and involves unpleasant conditions, must be done by machinery. Machinery must work for us in coal mines, and do all sanitary services, and be the stoker[28] of steamers, and clean the streets, and run messages on wet days, and do anything that is tedious or distressing. At present machinery competes against man. Under proper conditions machinery will serve man. There is no doubt at all that this is the future of machinery, and just as trees grow while the country gentleman is asleep, so while Humanity will be amusing itself, or enjoying cultivated leisure—which, and not labour, is the aim of man—or making beautiful things, or reading beautiful things, or simply contemplating the world with admiration and delight, machinery will be doing all the necessary and unpleasant work. The fact is, that civilization requires slaves. The Greeks were quite right there. Unless there are slaves to do the ugly, horrible, uninteresting work, culture and contemplation become almost impossible. Human slavery is wrong, insecure and demoralizing. On mechanical slavery, on the slavery of the machine, the future of the world depends. And when scientific men are no longer called upon to go down to a depressing East-End and distribute bad cocoa and worse blankets to starving people, they will have delightful leisure in which to devise wonderful and marvellous things for their own joy and the joy of everyone else. There will be great storages of force for every city, and for every house if required, and this force man will convert into heat, light or motion, according to his needs. Is this Utopian? A map of the world that does not include Utopia is not worth even glancing at, for it leaves out the one country at which Humanity is always landing. And when Humanity lands there, it looks out, and, seeing a better country, sets sail. Progress is the realization of Utopias.

Now, I have said that the community by means of organization of machinery will supply the useful things, and that the beautiful things will be made by the individual. This is not merely necessary, but it is the only possible way by which we can get either the one or the other. An individual who has to make things for the use of others, and with reference to their wants and their wishes, does not work with interest, and consequently cannot put into his work what is best in him. Upon the other hand, whenever a community or a powerful section of a community, or a government of any kind, attempts to dictate to the artist what he is to do, Art either entirely vanishes, or becomes stereotyped, or degenerates into a low and ignoble form of craft. A work of art is the unique result of a unique temperament. Its beauty comes from the fact that the author is what he is. It has nothing to do with the fact that other people want what they want. Indeed, the moment that an artist takes notice of what other people want, and tries to supply the demand, he ceases to be an artist, and becomes a dull or an amusing craftsman, an honest or a dishonest tradesman. He has no further claim

---

28. Coal-shoveller.

to be considered as an artist. Art is the most intense mode of Individualism that the world has known. I am inclined to say that it is the only real mode of Individualism that the world has known. Crime, which, under certain conditions, may seem to have created Individualism, must take cognizance of other people and interfere with them. It belongs to the sphere of action. But alone, without any reference to his neighbours, without any interference, the artist can fashion a beautiful thing; and if he does not do it solely for his own pleasure, he is not an artist at all. * * *

It will, of course, be said that such a scheme as is set forth here is quite unpractical, and goes against human nature. This is perfectly true. It is unpractical, and it goes against human nature. This is why it is worth carrying out, and that is why one proposes it. For what is a practical scheme? A practical scheme is either a scheme that is already in existence, or a scheme that could be carried out under existing conditions. But it is exactly the existing conditions that one objects to; and any scheme that could accept these conditions is wrong and foolish. The conditions will be done away with, and human nature will change. The only thing that one really knows about human nature is that it changes. Change is the one quality we can predicate of it. The systems that fail are those that rely on the permanency of human nature, and not on its growth and development. The error of Louis XIV was that he thought human nature would always be the same. The result of his error was the French Revolution.[29] It was an admirable result. All the results of the mistakes of governments are quite admirable.

It is to be noted also that Individualism does not come to man with any sickly cant about duty, which merely means doing what other people want because they want it; or any hideous cant about self-sacrifice, which is merely a survival of savage mutilation. In fact, it does not come to man with any claims upon him at all. It comes naturally and inevitably out of man. It is the point to which all development tends. It is the differentiation[30] to which all organisms grow. It is the perfection that is inherent in every mode of life, and towards which every mode of life quickens. And so Individualism exercises no compulsion over man. On the contrary, it says to man that he should suffer no compulsion to be exercised over him. It does not try to force people to be good. It knows that people are good when they are let alone. Man will develop Individualism out of himself. Man is now so developing Individualism. To ask whether Individualism is practical is like asking whether Evolution is practical. Evolution is the law of life, and there is no evolution except towards Individualism. Where this tendency is not expressed, it is a case of artificially arrested growth, or of disease, or of death.

Individualism will also be unselfish and unaffected. It has been pointed out that one of the results of the extraordinary tyranny of authority is that words are absolutely distorted from their proper and simple meaning, and are used to express the obverse of their right signification. What is true about Art is true about Life. A man is called affected, nowadays, if he dresses as he likes to dress. But in doing that he is acting in a perfectly natural manner. Affectation, in such matters, consists in dressing according to the views of one's neighbour, whose views, as they are the views of the major-

---

29. The dazzling court of the "Sun King" Louis XIV (1638–1715) at Versailles led to the revolution against his descendant Louis XVI and Marie Antoinette.
30. Evolutionary specialization.

ity, will probably be extremely stupid. Or a man is called selfish if he lives in a manner that seems to him most suitable for the full realization of his own personality; if, in fact, the primary aim of his life is self-development. But this is the way in which every one should live. Selfishness is not living as one wishes to live, it is asking others to live as one wishes to live. And unselfishness is letting other people's lives alone, not interfering with them. Selfishness always aims at creating around it an absolute uniformity of type. Unselfishness recognizes infinite variety of type as a delightful thing, accepts it, acquiesces in it, enjoys it. It is not selfish to think for oneself. A man who does not think for himself does not think at all. It is grossly selfish to require of one's neighbour that he should think in the same way, and hold the same opinions. Why should he? If he can think, he will probably think differently. If he cannot think, it is monstrous to require thought of any kind from him. A red rose is not selfish because it wants to be a red rose. It would be horribly selfish if it wanted all the other flowers in the garden to be both red and roses. Under Individualism people will be quite natural and absolutely unselfish, and will know the meanings of the words, and realize them in their free, beautiful lives. Nor will men be egotistic as they are now. For the egotist is he who makes claims upon others, and the Individualist will not desire to do that. It will not give him pleasure. When man has realized Individualism, he will also realize sympathy and exercise it freely and spontaneously. Up to the present man has hardly cultivated sympathy at all. He has merely sympathy with pain, and sympathy with pain is not the highest form of sympathy. All sympathy is fine, but sympathy with suffering is the least fine mode. It is tainted with egotism. It is apt to become morbid. There is in it a certain element of terror for our own safety. We become afraid that we ourselves might be as the leper or as the blind, and that no man would have care of us. It is curiously limiting, too. One should sympathize with the entirety of life, not with life's sores and maladies merely, but with life's joy and beauty and energy and health and freedom. The wider sympathy is, of course, the more difficult. It requires more unselfishness. Anybody can sympathize with the sufferings of a friend, but it requires a very fine nature—it requires, in fact, the nature of a true Individualist—to sympathize with a friend's success. In the modern stress of competition and struggle for place, such sympathy is naturally rare, and is also very much stifled by the immoral ideal of uniformity of type and conformity to rule which is so prevalent everywhere, and is perhaps most obnoxious in England.

Sympathy with pain there will, of course, always be. It is one of the first instincts of man. The animals which are individual, the higher animals that is to say, share it with us. But it must be remembered that while sympathy with joy intensifies the sum of joy in the world, sympathy with pain does not really diminish the amount of pain. It may make man better able to endure evil, but the evil remains. Sympathy with consumption[31] does not cure consumption; that is what Science does. And when Socialism has solved the problem of disease, the area of the sentimentalists will be lessened, and the sympathy of man will be large, healthy, and spontaneous. Man will have joy in the contemplation of the joyous lives of others.

For it is through joy that the Individualism of the future will develop itself. Christ made no attempt to reconstruct society, and consequently the Individualism

31. Tuberculosis.

that he preached to man could be realized only through pain or in solitude. The ideals that we owe to Christ are the ideals of the man who abandons society entirely, or of the man who resists society absolutely. But man is naturally social. Even the Thebaid[32] became peopled at last. And though the cenobite[33] realizes his personality, it is often an impoverished personality that he so realizes. Upon the other hand, the terrible truth that pain is a mode through which man may realize himself exercised a wonderful fascination over the world. Shallow speakers and shallow thinkers in pulpits and on platforms often talk about the world's worship of pleasure, and whine against it. But it is rarely in the world's history that its ideal has been one of joy and beauty. The worship of pain has far more often dominated the world. Medievalism, with its saints and martyrs, its love of self-torture, its wild passion for wounding itself, its gashing with knives and its whipping with rods— Medievalism is real Christianity, and the medieval Christ is the real Christ. When the Renaissance dawned upon the world, and brought with it the new ideals of beauty of life and the joy of living, men could not understand Christ. Even Art shows us that. The painters of the Renaissance drew Christ as a little boy playing with another boy in a palace or a garden, or lying back in his mother's arms, smiling at her, or at a flower, or at a bright bird; or as a noble stately figure moving nobly through the world; or as a wonderful figure rising in a sort of ecstasy from death to life. Even when they drew him crucified they drew him as a beautiful God on whom evil men had inflicted suffering. But he did not preoccupy them much. What delighted them was to paint the men and women whom they admired, and to show the loveliness of this lovely earth. They painted many religious pictures—in fact, they painted far too many, and the monotony of type and motive is wearisome, and was bad for art. It was the result of the authority of the public in art-matters, and is to be deplored. But their soul was not in the subject. Raphael was a great artist when he painted his portrait of the Pope. When he painted his Madonnas and infant Christs, he is not a great artist at all. Christ had no message for the Renaissance, which was wonderful because it brought an ideal at variance with his, and to find the presentation of the real Christ we must go to medieval art. There, he is one maimed and marred; one who is not comely to look on, because Beauty is a joy; one who is not in fair raiment, because that may be a joy also: he is a beggar who has a marvellous soul; he is a leper whose soul is divine; he needs neither property nor health; he is a God realizing his perfection through pain.

The evolution of man is slow. The injustice of men is great. It was necessary that pain should be put forward as a mode of self-realization. Even now, in some places in the world, the message of Christ is necessary. No one who lived in modern Russia could possibly realize his perfection except by pain. A few Russian artists have realized themselves in Art, in a fiction that is medieval in character, because its dominant note is the realization of men through suffering. But for those who are not artists, and to whom there is no mode of life but the actual life of fact, pain is the only door to perfection. A Russian who lives happily under the present system of government in Russia must either believe that man has no soul, or that, if he has, it is not worth developing. A Nihilist who rejects all authority, because he knows authority to

---

32. Desert region of ancient Egypt.
33. Member of religious community.

be evil, and who welcomes all pain, because through that he realizes his personality, is a real Christian.[34] To him the Christian ideal is a true thing.

And yet, Christ did not revolt against authority. He accepted the imperial authority of the Roman Empire and paid tribute.[35] He endured the ecclesiastical authority of the Jewish Church, and would not repel its violence by any violence of his own. He had, as I said before, no scheme for the reconstruction of society. But the modern world has schemes. It proposes to do away with poverty and the suffering that it entails. It desires to get rid of pain and the suffering that pain entails. It trusts to Socialism and to Science as its methods. What it aims at is an Individualism expressing itself through joy. This Individualism will be larger, fuller, lovelier than any Individualism has ever been. Pain is not the ultimate mode of perfection. It is merely provisional and a protest. It has reference to wrong, unhealthy, unjust surroundings. When the wrong, and the disease and the injustice are removed, it will have no further place. It will have done its work. It was a great work, but it is almost over. Its sphere lessens every day.

Nor will man miss it. For what man has sought for is, indeed, neither pain nor pleasure, but simply Life. Man has sought to live intensely, fully, perfectly. When he can do so without exercising restraint on others, or suffering it ever, and his activities are all pleasurable to him, he will be saner, healthier, more civilized, more himself. Pleasure is Nature's test, her sign of approval. When man is happy, he is in harmony with himself and his environment. The new Individualism, for whose service Socialism, whether it wills it or not, is working, will be perfect harmony. It will be what the Greeks sought for, but could not, except in Thought, realize completely, because they had slaves, and fed them; it will be what the Renaissance sought for, but could not realize completely, except in Art, because they had slaves, and starved them. It will be complete, and through it each man will attain to his perfection. The new Individualism is the new Hellenism.[36]

—1891

George Bernard Shaw
1856–1950

As a friend told George Bernard Shaw, "what [you] call drama is nothing but explanation." During the *fin de siècle*, Shaw's already discursive plays began to feature additional prefaces and annotations, becoming political manifestos. This prodigious energy also found an outlet in political oratory and polemical essays. Growing up in an impoverished family in Dublin, Shaw already had a strong partisanship with the oppressed, and reading Marx's *Das Kapital* converted him to socialism. Convinced that everyone, regardless of gender, class, or race, needed access to art, education, and cultural benefits, Shaw became a major force in the Fabian Society (founded 1884), a moderate socialist group advocating gradual reform through parliamentary

---

34. Wilde's first play, *Vera, or, the Nihilists* (privately printed 1880, produced 1883) shows his interest in this Russian movement that aimed to overthrow oppression through indiscriminate destruction.
35. Taxes.
36. Popular *fin-de-siècle* notion of restoring the culture associated with ancient Greece.

legislation and eventually state ownership of property. Its *Fabian Essays in Socialism* (1889) sold 25,500 copies by 1893. Shaw's essay on the value of labor shows his best qualities as a political writer: his anti-sentimental pragmatism, his forceful outrage at social conditions, his direct and witty prose. For more information about Shaw, see p. 323.

from The Basis of Socialism

Wages.

I now ask you to pick up the dropped subject of the spread of cultivation. We had got as far as the appearance in the market of a new commodity—of the proletarian man compelled to live by the sale of himself! In order to realize at once the latent horror of this, you have only to apply our investigation of value, with its inevitable law that only by restricting the supply of a commodity can its value be kept from descending finally to zero. The commodity which the proletarian sells is one over the production of which he has practically no control. He is himself driven to produce it by an irresistible impulse. It was the increase of population that spread cultivation and civilization from the centre to the snowline, and at last forced men to sell themselves to the lords of the soil: it is the same force that continues to multiply men so that their exchange value[1] falls slowly and surely until it disappears altogether—until even black chattel slaves are released as not worth keeping in a land where men of all colors are to be had for nothing. This is the condition of our English laborers to-day: they are no longer even dirt cheap: they are valueless, and can be had for nothing. The proof is the existence of the unemployed, who can find no purchasers. By the law of indifference, nobody will buy men at a price when he can obtain equally serviceable men for nothing. What then is the explanation of the wages given to those who are in employment, and who certainly do not work for nothing? The matter is deplorably simple. Suppose that horses multiplied in England in such quantities that they were to be had for the asking, like kittens condemned to the bucket. You would still have to feed your horse—feed him and lodge him well if you used him as a smart hunter—feed him and lodge him wretchedly if you used him only as a drudge. But the cost of keeping would not mean that the horse had an exchange value. If you got him for nothing in the first instance—if no one would give you anything for him when you were done with him, he would be worth nothing, in spite of the cost of his keep. That is just the case of every member of the proletariat who could be replaced by one of the unemployed to-day. Their wage is not the price of themselves; for they are worth nothing: it is only their keep. For bare subsistence wages you can get as much common labor as you want, and do what you please with it within the limits of a criminal code which is sure to be interpreted by a proprietary-class[2] judge in your favor. If you have to give your footman a better allowance than your wretched hewer of match-wood, it is for the same reason that you have to give your hunter beans and a clean stall instead of chopped straw and a sty.[3] * * *

---

1. Market value.

2. Member of the class that owns everything.

3. When one of the conditions of earning a wage is the keeping up of a certain state, subsistence wages may reach a figure to which the term seems ludicrously inappropriate. For example, a fashionable physician in London cannot save out of £1,000 a year; and the post of Lord Lieutenant of Ireland can only be filled by a man who brings considerable private means to the aid of his official salary of £20,000 [Shaw's note].

"Overpopulation".

The introduction of the capitalistic system is a sign that the exploitation of the laborer toiling for a bare subsistence wage has become one of the chief arts of life among the holders of tenant rights.[4] It also produces a delusive promise of endless employment which blinds the proletariat to those disastrous consequences of rapid multiplication which are obvious to the small cultivator and peasant proprietor. But indeed the more you degrade the workers, robbing them of all artistic enjoyment, and all chance of respect and admiration from their fellows, the more you throw them back, reckless, on the one pleasure and the one human tie left to them—the gratification of their instinct for producing fresh supplies of men. You will applaud this instinct as divine until at last the excessive supply becomes a nuisance: there comes a plague of men; and you suddenly discover that the instinct is diabolic, and set up a cry of "over population". But your slaves are beyond caring for your cries: they breed like rabbits; and their poverty breeds filth, ugliness, dishonesty, disease, obscenity, drunkenness, and murder. In the midst of the riches which their labor piles up for you, their misery rises up too and stifles you. You withdraw in disgust to the other end of the town from them; you appoint special carriages on your railways and special seats in your churches and theatres for them; you set your life apart from theirs by every class barrier you can devise; and yet they swarm about you still: your face gets stamped with your habitual loathing and suspicion of them: your ears get so filled with the language of the vilest of them that you break into it when you lose your self-control: they poison your life as remorselessly as you have sacrificed theirs heartlessly. You begin to believe intensely in the devil. Then comes the terror of their revolting; the drilling and arming of bodies of them to keep down the rest; the prison, the hospital, paroxysms of frantic coercion, followed by paroxysms of frantic charity. And in the meantime, the population continues to increase!

"Illth."

It is sometimes said that during this grotesquely hideous march of civilization from bad to worse, wealth is increasing side by side with misery. Such a thing is eternally impossible: wealth is steadily decreasing with the spread of poverty. But riches are increasing, which is quite another thing. The total of the exchange values produced in the country annually is mounting perhaps by leaps and bounds. But the accumulation of riches, and consequently of an excessive purchasing power, in the hands of a class, soon satiates that class with socially useful wealth, and sets them offering a price for luxuries. The moment a price is to be had for a luxury, it acquires exchange value, and labor is employed to produce it. A New York lady, for instance, having a nature of exquisite sensibility, orders an elegant rosewood and silver coffin, upholstered in pink satin, for her dead dog. It is made; and meanwhile a live child is prowling barefooted and hunger-stunted in the frozen gutter outside. The exchange-value of the coffin is counted as part of the national wealth; but a nation which cannot afford food and clothing for its children cannot be allowed to pass as wealthy because it has provided a pretty coffin for a dead dog. Exchange value itself, in fact, has become bedev-

---

4. Property owners.

illed like everything else, and represents, no longer utility, but the cravings of lust, folly, vanity, gluttony, and madness, technically described by genteel economists as "effective demand". Luxuries are not social wealth: the machinery for producing them is not social wealth: labor skilled only to manufacture them is not socially useful labor: the men, women, and children who make a living by producing them are no more self-supporting than the idle rich for whose amusement they are kept at work. It is the habit of counting as wealth the exchange values involved in these transactions that makes us fancy that the poor are starving in the midst of plenty. They are starving in the midst of plenty of jewels, velvets, laces, equipages,[5] and racehorses; but not in the midst of plenty of food. In the things that are wanted for the welfare of the people we are abjectly poor; and England's social policy to-day may be likened to the domestic policy of those adventuresses who leave their children half-clothed and half-fed in order to keep a carriage and deal with a fashionable dressmaker. But it is quite true that whilst wealth and welfare are decreasing, productive power is increasing; and nothing but the perversion of this power to the production of socially useless commodities prevents the apparent wealth from becoming real. The purchasing power that commands luxuries in the hands of the rich, would command true wealth in the hands of all. Yet private property must still heap the purchasing power upon the few rich and withdraw it from the many poor. So that, in the end, the subject of the one boast that private property can make— the great accumulation of so-called "wealth" which it points so proudly to as the result of its power to scourge men and women daily to prolonged and intense toil, turns out to be a simulacrum. With all its energy, its Smilesian "self-help",[6] its merchant-princely enterprise, its ferocious sweating and slave-driving, its prodigality of blood, sweat and tears, what has it heaped up, over and above the pittance of its slaves? Only a monstrous pile of frippery, some tainted class literature and class art, and not a little poison and mischief.

This, then, is the economic analysis which convicts Private Property of being unjust even from the beginning, and utterly impossible as a final solution of even the individualist aspect of the problem of adjusting the share of the worker in the distribution of wealth to the labor incurred by him in its production. All attempts yet made to construct true societies upon it have failed: the nearest things to societies so achieved have been civilizations, which have rotted into centres of vice and luxury, and eventually been swept away by uncivilized races. That our own civilization is already in an advanced stage of rottenness may be taken as statistically proved. That further decay instead of improvement must ensue if the institution of private property be maintained, is economically certain. Fortunately, private property in its integrity is not now practicable. Although the safety valve of emigration has been furiously at work during this century, yet the pressure of population has forced us to begin the restitution to the people of the sums taken from them for the ground landlords, holders of tenant right, and capitalists, by the imposition of an income tax, and by compelling them to establish out of their revenues a national system of education, besides imposing restrictions—as yet only of the forcible-feeble sort—on

---

5. Elegant carriages.
6. Samuel Smiles's bestselling *Self-Help* (1859).

their terrible power of abusing the wage contract. These, however, are dealt with by Mr. Sidney Webb[7] in the historic essay which follows. I should not touch upon them at all, were it not that experience has lately convinced all economists that no exercise in abstract economics, however closely deduced, is to be trusted unless it can be experimentally verified by tracing its expression in history. It is true that the process which I have presented as a direct development of private property between free exchangers had to work itself out in the Old World indirectly and tortuously through a struggle with political and religious institutions and survivals quite antagonistic to it. It is true that cultivation did not begin in Western Europe with the solitary emigrant pre-empting his private property, but with the tribal communes in which arose subsequently the assertion of the right of the individual to private judgment and private action against the tyranny of primitive society. It is true that cultivation has not proceeded by logical steps from good land to less good; from less good to bad; and from bad to worse: the exploration of new countries and new regions, and the discovery of new uses for old products, has often made the margin of cultivation more fruitful than the centre, and, for the moment (whilst the centre was shifting to the margin), turned the whole movement of rent and wages directly counter to the economic theory. Nor is it true that, taking the world as one country, cultivation has yet spread from the snowline to the water's edge. There is free land still for the poorest East End match-box maker if she could get there, reclaim the wilderness there, speak the language there, stand the climate there, and be fed, clothed, and housed there whilst she cleared her farm; learned how to cultivate it; and waited for the harvest. Economists have been ingenious enough to prove that this alternative really secures her independence; but I shall not waste time in dealing with that. Practically, if there is no free land in England, the economic analysis holds good of England, in spite of Siberia, Central Africa, and the Wild West. Again, it is not immediately true that men are governed in production solely by a determination to realize the maximum of exchange value. The impulse to production often takes specific direction in the first instance; and a man will insist on producing pictures or plays although he might gain more money by producing boots or bonnets. But, his specific impulse once gratified, he will make as much money as he can. He will sell his picture or play for a hundred pounds rather than for fifty. In short, though there is no such person as the celebrated "economic man", man being wilful rather than rational, yet when the wilful man has had his way he will take what else he can get; and so he always does appear, finally if not primarily, as the economic man. On the whole, history, even in the Old World, goes the way traced by the economist. In the New World the correspondence is exact. The United States and the Colonies have been peopled by fugitives from the full-blown individualism of Western Europe, pre-empting private property precisely as assumed in this investigation of the conditions of cultivation. The economic relations of these cultivators have not since put on any of the old political disguises. Yet among them, in confirmation of the validity of our analysis, we see all the evils of our old civilizations growing up; and though with them the end is not yet, still it is from them to us that the great recent revival of the cry for nationalization of the land has come,

---

7. Sidney Webb and his wife Beatrice Potter Webb co-founded the Fabian Society.

articulated by a man[8] who had seen the whole tragedy of private property hurried through its acts with unprecedented speed in the mushroom cities of America.

On Socialism the analysis of the economic action of Individualism bears as a discovery, in the private appropriation of land, of the source of those unjust privileges against which Socialism is aimed. It is practically a demonstration that public property in land is the basic economic condition of Socialism. But this does not involve at present a literal restoration of the land to the people. The land is at present in the hands of the people: its proprietors are for the most part absentees. The modern form of private property is simply a legal claim to take a share of the produce of the national industry year by year without working for it. It refers to no special part or form of that produce; and in process of consumption its revenue cannot be distinguished from earnings, so that the majority of persons, accustomed to call the commodities which form the income of the proprietor his private property, and seeing no difference between them and the commodities which form the income of a worker, extend the term private property to the worker's subsistence also, and can only conceive an attack on private property as an attempt to empower everybody to rob everybody else all round. But the income of a private proprietor can be distinguished by the fact that he obtains it unconditionally and gratuitously by private right against the public weal,[9] which is incompatible with the existence of consumers who do not produce. Socialism involves discontinuance of the payment of these incomes, and addition of the wealth so saved to incomes derived from labor. As we have seen, incomes derived from private property consist partly of economic rent;[10] partly of pensions, also called rent, obtained by the subletting of tenant rights; and partly of a form of rent called interest, obtained by special adaptations of land to production by the application of capital: all these being finally paid out of the difference between the produce of the worker's labor and the price of that labor sold in the open market for wages, salary, fees, or profits.[11] The whole, except economic rent, can be added directly to the incomes of the workers by simply discontinuing its exaction from them. Economic rent, arising as it does from variations of fertility or advantages of situation, must always be held as common or social wealth, and used, as the revenues raised by taxation are now used, for public purposes, among which Socialism would make national insurance and the provision of capital matters of the first importance.

The economic problem of Socialism is thus solved; and the political question of how the economic solution is to be practically applied does not come within the scope of this essay. But if we have got as far as an intellectual conviction that the source of our social misery is no eternal well-spring of confusion and evil, but only an artificial system susceptible of almost infinite modification and readjustment—nay, of practical demolition and substitution at the will of Man, then a terrible weight will be lifted from the minds of all except those who are, whether avowedly to themselves or not, clinging to the present state of things from base motives. We have had in this century a stern series of lessons on the folly of believing anything for no better rea-

---

8. Naturalist Alfred Russel Wallace, who founded the Land Nationalization Society in 1881.
9. Benefit.
10. The value of fertile land.
11. This excess of the product of labor over its price is treated as a single category with impressive effect by Karl Marx, who called it "surplus value" (*mehrwerth*) [Shaw's note].

son than that it is pleasant to believe it. It was pleasant to look round with a con-sciousness of possessing a thousand a year, and say, with Browning's David, "All's love; and all's law."[12] It was pleasant to believe that the chance we were too lazy to take in this world would come back to us in another. It was pleasant to believe that a benev-olent hand was guiding the steps of society; overruling all evil appearances for good; and making poverty here the earnest of a great blessedness and reward hereafter. It was pleasant to lose the sense of worldly inequality in the contemplation of our equal-ity before God. But utilitarian[13] questioning and scientific answering turned all this tranquil optimism into the blackest pessimism. Nature was shewn to us as "red in tooth and claw":[14] if the guiding hand were indeed benevolent, then it could not be omnipotent; so that our trust in it was broken: if it were omnipotent, it could not be benevolent; so that our love of it turned to fear and hatred. We had never admitted that the other world, which was to compensate for the sorrows of this, was open to horses and apes (though we had not on that account been any the more merciful to our horses); and now came Science to shew us the corner of the pointed ear of the horse on our own heads, and present the ape to us as our blood relation. No proof came of the existence of that other world and that benevolent power to which we had left the remedy of the atrocious wrongs of the poor: proof after proof came that what we called Nature knew and cared no more about our pains and pleasures than we know or care about the tiny creatures we crush underfoot as we walk through the fields. Instead of at once perceiving that this meant no more than that Nature was unmoral and indifferent, we relapsed into a gross form of devil worship, and con-ceived Nature as a remorselessly malignant power. This was no better than the old optimism, and infinitely gloomier. It kept our eyes still shut to the truth that there is no cruelty and selfishness outside Man himself; and that his own active benevolence can combat and vanquish both. When the Socialist came forward as a meliorist[15] on these lines, the old school of political economists, who could see no alternative to pri-vate property, put forward in proof of the powerlessness of benevolent action to arrest the deadly automatic production of poverty by the increase of population, the very analysis I have just presented. Their conclusions exactly fitted in with the new ideas. It was Nature at it again—the struggle for existence—the remorseless extirpation of the weak—the survival of the fittest—in short, natural selection at work. Socialism seemed too good to be true: it was passed by as merely the old optimism foolishly run-ning its head against the stone wall of modern science. But Socialism now challenges individualism, scepticism, pessimism, worship of Nature personified as a devil, on their own ground of science. The science of the production and distribution of wealth is Political Economy. Socialism appeals to that science, and, turning on Individualism its own guns, routs it in incurable disaster. Henceforth the bitter cynic who still finds the world an eternal and unimprovable doghole, with the placid person of means who repeats the familiar misquotation, "the poor ye shall have always with you",[16] lose their usurped place among the cultured, and pass over to the ranks of the ignorant,

---

12. Robert Browning's "Saul" (1855): "all's love; yet all's law" (line 248).
13. Philosophy of practical value (the greatest good to the greatest number) developed by Jeremy Bentham in the 1820s.
14. Alfred, Lord Tennyson's "In Memoriam A.H.H.," section 56.
15. Improver.
16. Christ says, "For ye have the poor always with you; but me ye have not always" (Matthew 26.11).

the shallow, and the superstitious. As for the rest of us, since we were taught to revere proprietary respectability in our unfortunate childhood, and since we found our child-ish hearts so hard and unregenerate that they secretly hated and rebelled against respectability in spite of that teaching, it is impossible to express the relief with which we discover that our hearts were all along right, and that the current respectability of to-day is nothing but a huge inversion of righteous and scientific social order welter-ing in dishonesty, uselessness, selfishness, wanton misery, and idiotic waste of magnif-icent opportunities for noble and happy living. It was terrible to feel this, and yet to fear that it could not be helped—that the poor must starve and make you ashamed of your dinner—that they must shiver and make you ashamed of your warm overcoat. It is to economic science—once the Dismal, now the Hopeful—that we are indebted for the discovery that though the evil is enormously worse than we knew, yet it is not eternal—not even very long lived, if we only bestir ourselves to make an end of it.

—1889

Charles Booth
1840–1916

Charles Booth, a successful business manager of his family's steamship company, was annoyed when a socialist politician declared that 25 percent of Londoners lived in abject poverty. Determined to disprove him, Booth gathered a team of researchers who visited every street in London at least twice, and he spent his nights and weekends writing up the findings. The sev-enteen-volume *Life and Labour of the People in London* (1889–1903) charted populations, wages, and employment in different regions and classes with extraordinary thoroughness. (It turned out that 35 percent of Londoners were paupers.) Booth's pioneering sociological study spurred much late-Victorian philanthropic and social reform. His interest in poverty may stem from his upbringing in the Unitarian faith, which valued social conscience and broad-mindedness. Although Booth never became a full-fledged socialist, he argued for limited socialist reforms such as old-age pensions. The following excerpt from the first volume, describing the different neighborhoods of the poverty-stricken East End, shows both Booth's meticulous data and his vivid interest in the lives of his subjects.

from Life and Labour of the People in London
Ch. 3: "Concerning the Separate Districts"

For those who find an interest in such methods, I give on the next page a table [omit-ted here] showing for each district the percentage which each kind of occupation bears to the whole population. I can hardly hope to make the rows of figures in this table as luminous and picturesque to any other eye as they are to mine, and yet I am constrained to try to do so. I will take Whitechapel as a centre, and trace the figures east and west.

Of the population of Whitechapel 18¼ per cent. appear as employed in making clothes, 6½ per cent. in cigar making and food preparation, 8 per cent. are street sellers and general dealers, and 5¼ per cent. are small employers, mostly of the poor "sweater" type. All these are employments of the Jews.

Stepney, on the other hand, has few, if any, of these—only 7¼ per cent. all told against 38 per cent. in Whitechapel. Stepney is essentially the abode of labour: here the casual labourers reach their maximum of nearly 11 per cent. of the population, and have their homes in a mass of grimy streets and courts; and here are to be found also the largest proportion of regularly paid labour, viz., 24 per cent. of the population. In all, nearly 39 per cent. of the population of Stepney are counted in the five sections of labour against only about 18 per cent. so counted in Whitechapel.

Midway between Whitechapel and Stepney, in character as well as geographically, comes St. George's-in-the-East. Doubtless a line might be drawn which would fairly divide the population of St. George's into two portions, the one side falling naturally with Stepney and the Docks, the other side with Whitechapel and the Jewish quarters. The makers of clothes, 18 per cent. in Whitechapel, become 9½ per cent. in St. George's, and fall away to 1 per cent. in Stepney. The preparers of food and tobacco, 6½ per cent. in Whitechapel, become 4½ per cent. in St. George's, and drop to about 2 per cent. in Stepney. On the other hand, the casual labourers, who are 11 per cent. in Stepney, stand at 9 per cent. in St. George's, and fall away to 4 per cent. in Whitechapel; and so also with the other classes of labour, except those with irregular pay, who seem to bear a larger proportion to the population in St. George's than anywhere else. On the whole, it may be said that St. George's shares in the poor characteristics of both her neighbours, and is more entirely poverty stricken than either.

Passing from Whitechapel to Mile End Old Town, we more quickly get rid of the foreign element, but it is to be found in the westernmost angle or tongue; while in Poplar, where dress and food preparation and general dealers added together are only 4 per cent. as compared to 29 per cent. in Whitechapel, there is hardly any trace of it.

Passing north and west we see the same thing—food and dress fall to 12 per cent. in Bethnal Green—half of what they are in Whitechapel, to 9 per cent. in Shoreditch, and to 6 per cent. in Hackney.

In Bethnal Green and Shoreditch the four sections of artisans take the leading place, and amongst furniture and wood-work find here their home, accounting for 14 per cent. of the population.

Thus it will be seen that Whitechapel is the dwelling-place of the Jews—tailors, bootmakers, and tobacco-workers—and the centre of trading both small and large; Stepney and St. George's the district of ordinary labour; Shoreditch and Bethnal Green of the artisan; in Poplar sub-officials reach their maximum proportion, while Mile End, with a little of everything, very closely represents the average of the whole district; and finally Hackney stands apart with its well-to-do suburban population.

Each district has its character—its peculiar flavour. One seems to be conscious of it in the streets. It may be in the faces of the people, or in what they carry—perhaps a reflection is thrown in this way from the prevailing trades—or it may lie in the sounds one hears, or in the character of the buildings.

Of all the districts of that "inner ring" which surrounds the City,[1] St. George's-in-the-East is the most desolate. The other districts have each some charm or other—

---

1. Central business district of London.

a brightness not extinguished by, and even appertaining to, poverty and toil, to vice, and even to crime—a clash of contest, man against man, and men against fate—the absorbing interest of a battle-field—a rush of human life as fascinating to watch as the current of a river to which life is so often likened. But there is nothing of this in St. George's, which appears to stagnate with a squalor peculiar to itself.

The feeling that I have just described—this excitement of life which can accept murder as a dramatic incident, and drunkenness as the buffoonery of the stage—is especially characteristic of Whitechapel. And looked at in this way, what a drama it is! Whitechapel is a veritable Tom Tiddler's ground, the Eldorado of the East,[2] a gathering together of poor fortune seekers; its streets are full of buying and selling, the poor living on the poor. Here, just outside the old City walls, have always lived the Jews, and here they are now in thousands, both old established and new comers, seeking their livelihood under conditions which seem to suit them on the middle ground between civilization and barbarism.

The neighbourhood of old Petticoat Lane on Sunday is one of the wonders of London, a medley of strange sights, strange sounds, and strange smells. Streets crowded so as to be thoroughfares no longer, and lined with a double or treble row of hand-barrows, set fast with empty cases, so as to assume the guise of market stalls. Here and there a cart may have been drawn in, but the horse has gone and the tilt is used as a rostrum[3] whence the salemen with stentorian voices cry their wares, vying with each other in introducing to the surrounding crowd their cheap garments, smart braces, sham jewellery, or patent medicines.[4] Those who have something showy, noisily push their trade, while the modest merit of the utterly cheap makes its silent appeal from the lower stalls, on which are to be found a heterogeneous collection of such things as cotton sheeting, American cloth for furniture covers, old clothes, worn-out boots, damaged lamps, chipped china shepherdesses, rusty locks, and rubbish indescribable. Many, perhaps most, things of the "silent cheap" sort are bought in the way of business; old clothes to renovate, old boots to translate, hinges and door-handles to be furbished up again. Such things cannot *look* too bad, for the buyer may then persuade himself that he has a bargain unsuspected by the seller. Other stalls supply daily wants—fish is sold in large quantities—vegetables and fruit—queer cakes and outlandish bread. Except as regards these daily wants, the Jew is the seller, and the Gentile the buyer; Petticoat Lane is the exchange of the Jew, but the lounge of the Christian.

Nor is this great market the only scene of the sort in the neighbourhood on Sunday morning. Where Sclater Street crosses Brick Lane, near the Great Eastern Station,[5] is the market of the "fancy." Here the streets are blocked with those coming to buy, or sell, pigeons, canaries, rabbits, fowls, parrots, or guinea pigs, and with them or separately all the appurtenances of bird or pet keeping. Through this crowd the seller of shell-fish pushes his barrow; on the outskirts of it are moveable shooting galleries, and patent Aunt Sallies,[6] while some man standing up in a dog-cart[7] will dispose of racing tips in sealed envelopes to the East End sportsman.

---

2. Fabled places to pick up a fortune.
3. The slanted floor of the cart is used as a platform.
4. Fancy suspenders; fake jewelry; dubious medicinal compounds.
5. Today called Liverpool Street Station. The Brick Lane and Petticoat Lane outdoor markets still operate.
6. Carnival game where patrons shoot at a row of tin soldiers.
7. Modest two-wheeled cart.

Brick Lane should rightly be seen on Saturday night, though it is in almost all its length a gay and crowded scene every evening of the week, unless persistent rain drives both buyers and sellers to seek shelter. But this sight—the "market street"—is not confined to Brick Lane, nor peculiar to Whitechapel, nor even to the East End. In every poor quarter of London it is to be met with—the flaring lights, the piles of cheap comestibles,[8] and the urgent cries of the sellers. Everywhere, too, there is the same absolute indifference on the part of the buyer to these cries. They seem to be accepted on both sides as necessary, though entirely useless. Not infrequently the goods are sold by a sort of Dutch auction—then the prices named are usually double what the seller, and every bystander, knows to be the market price of the street and day, "Eightpence?" "Sevenpence?" "Sixpence?" "Fivepence?"——Say "Fourpence?"—well, then, "Threepence halfpenny?" A bystander, probably a woman, nods imperceptibly; the fish or whatever it is passes from the right hand of the seller on which it has been raised to view, on to the square of newspaper, resting on his left hand, is bundled up and quick as thought takes its place in the buyer's basket in exchange for the 3½d, which finds its place in the seller's apron or on the board beside the fish—and then begins again the same routine, "Eightpence?" "Sevenpence?" "Sixpence?" &c.

Lying between Middlesex Street and Brick Lane are to be found most of the common lodging houses, and in the immediate neighbourhood, lower still in reputation, there are streets of "furnished" houses, and houses where stairways and corners are occupied nightly by those without any other shelter. So lurid and intense is the light which murderous outrage[9] has lately thrown on these quarters, that the grey tones of the ordinary picture become invisible.

As to the registered Lodging Houses, it must be said and remembered that they did, and do, mark a great improvement. However bad their inmates may be, these houses undoubtedly represent the principles of order, cleanliness, and decency. It is useless to demand impossibilities from them. Those who frequent them come under some sort of regulation, and are under the eye of the deputy, who in his turn is under the eye of the police. Even in the worst of these houses there is a great mixture—strange bedfellows whom misfortune has brought together—and amongst the houses there are many grades. The worst are horrible dens, but the horror lies really in their inmates, who are incapable of any better way of living.

The plan of all alike is to have a common kitchen, with large hospitable fire, and dormitories above. The quarters for single men consist of large rooms packed close with dark-brown truckle beds[10]—room to move between bed and bed, and that is all—the women's rooms are, I believe, the same, while the quarters for the "married" are boxed off by partitions. There are some who are really married, many whose relations though illegal are of long standing, and others again who use the accommodation as a convenience in their way of life.

The registered Lodging Houses are, as I have said, better than the unregistered "furnished apartments," and so long as the low class exists at all, it must evidently lodge somewhere. This class tends (very naturally) to herd together; it is this tendency which must be combated, for by herding together, they—both the quarters

---

8. Foods.
9. Jack the Ripper murdered five prostitutes in the East End in 1888.
10. Trundle-beds, low beds that can be rolled under regular beds.

they occupy, and their denizens—tend to get worse. When this comes about destruction is the only cure, and in this neighbourhood there has been of late years a great change brought about by the demolition of bad property. If much remains to do, still much has been done in the clearing away of vile spots, which contained dwellings unfit for human use, and matched only by the people who inhabited them. The railways have cleared some parts, the Board of Works other parts. The transformation goes slowly on, business premises or great blocks of model dwellings covering the old sites. Meanwhile the inhabitants of the slums have been scattered, and though they must carry contamination with them wherever they go, it seems certain that such hotbeds of vice, misery, and disease as those from which they have been ousted are not again created. Many people must have altogether left the district, as the population showed a decrease of 5000 between 1871 and 1881; but with the completion of the new buildings the numbers have again reached the level of 1871. Probably few of those who leave return; but it may be doubted whether those whose houses are pulled down are the ones to leave the neighbourhood. It is not easy to say exactly how an ebb and flow of population works. It may be the expression in large of much individual hardship: but I am more inclined to suppose that pulling down Smith's house drives him into Brown's quarters, and that Brown goes elsewhere, to his great benefit; when the new buildings are ready they do not attract Brown back again, but draw their occupants from the surrounding streets—men of the stamp of Smith or Brown, according to the accommodation they offer; the vacant places are then taken by quite new-comers (in Whitechapel mostly poor foreigners) or by the natural increase in the population. The clearances have been principally confined to Whitechapel and St. George's, the rebuilding almost entirely to Whitechapel.

Stepney is rendered interesting by its long length of river frontage (about 2 miles, including all Wapping), and it is besides intersected by the Regent's Canal. It, like Whitechapel, has its foreign element, its haunts of crime, and strange picturesqueness. It, too, has been greatly changed in recent years. Ratcliff Highway hardly knows itself as St. George's Street; the policeman and the School Board visitor have "put a light in the darkness," and have begun to "make straight the way" here, as well as elsewhere in East London.[11]

Mile End Old Town—commonly denoted by the seeming strange letters M. E. O. T.—lies between the inner and outer ring, and looks very clean and new in spite of its name. Its streets, even the narrowest, look comparatively wide; the air is fresh and the squares and other small open spaces are frequent.[12]

Poplar, a huge district, consists of the subdivisions of Bow and Bromley as well as Poplar proper. Bow includes Old Ford, and Poplar itself includes the Isle of Dogs—transformed now into an Isle of Docks. In all it is a vast township, built, much of it, on low marshy land, bounded on the east by the river Lea, and on the south by a great bend in the Thames. In North Bow and other outlying parts there is a great deal of jerry building: desolate looking streets spring into existence, and fall into decay with startling rapidity, and are only made habitable by successive waves of occupation; anything will do so that the house be run up; any tenant will do, who will give the house

---

11. Quoting Psalms 112, John 1.23.
12. Mile End is, however, remarkable for the number of brothels to be found amongst its otherwise respectable streets [Booth's note].

a start by burning a little coal in it; the first tenants come and go, till one by one the houses find permanent occupants, the streets settle down to respectability and rents rise: or a street may go wrong and get into such a position that no course short of entire destruction seems possible. Among the early troubles of these streets are fevers, resulting it is said from the foul rubbish with which the hollow land has become levelled. This district has had many such troubles, and is steadily living them down.

In Bethnal Green are found the old weavers' houses, with large upper room, now usually partitioned off to make two ro three rooms or accommodate two families. In some cases the houses had originally only one room on each floor; and each floor, partitioned, now accommodates its family. In several cases a family (not weavers) have taken such a room, and while living in it themselves, let a weaver stand his loom or looms in it, getting rent for each loom. Weaving still lingers, but other trades have for the most part taken its place.

Of Shoreditch, or rather Hoxton, which is the most characteristic part of Shoreditch, I am tempted to recall a description by Mr. Besant, which will be remembered by all who have read "The Children of Gibeon."[13] There is, he says, nothing beautiful, or picturesque, or romantic in the place, there is only the romance of life in it, sixty thousand lives in Hoxton, everyone with its own story to tell. Its people quiet and industrious, folk who ask for nothing but steady work and fair wages. Everybody quite poor; yet, he says, and says truly, the place has a cheerful look. There may be misery, but it is not apparent; the people in the streets seem well fed, and are as rosy as London smoke and fog will allow.

On the other hand the northern and western part of Hackney, divided from Hoxton only by the canal, is almost entirely a middle class district. The old streets of De Beauvoir Town, or the new ones of Dalston and Upper Clapton, are alike of this kind, and in the old roads running through the new districts large and small houses are pulled down, and those of medium size erected.

—1889–1903

W. T. Stead
1849–1912

The most colorful, powerful, and controversial newspaper reporter of the *fin de siècle*, W. T. Stead helped invent modern investigative journalism. From editing the *Northern Echo*, Stead went on to work at and eventually edit the *Pall Mall Gazette* from 1880 to 1889, when he developed the sensationalistic, campaigning style of reportage that Matthew Arnold dubbed "New Journalism." When traditional papers such as the *Times* were still filling columns with verbatim transcriptions of parliamentary speeches, Stead's investigative zeal brought urban squalor to life. Stead's most famous stunt was to "buy" a young girl in order to expose underage prostitution in London. The popular, shocking articles he wrote as a result, "The Maiden

---

13. An 1886 novel by prolific popular novelist and social reformer Walter Besant.

Tribute of Modern Babylon" (1885), led to the sexual regulations of the Criminal Law Amendment Act of 1885. Stead was arrested for hiring a girl, but, in another publicity triumph, he happily edited the *Pall Mall Gazette* from prison for three months. Even Stead's death was spectacular: he went down on the Titanic in 1912. The following excerpt from the first installment of "The Maiden Tribute" shocked the newspaper-reading public on the morning of July 6, 1885.

from The Maiden Tribute of Modern Babylon

The Violation of Virgins

This branch of the subject is one upon which even the coolest and most scientific observer may well find it difficult to speak dispassionately in a spirit of calm and philosophic investigation. The facts, however, as they have been elucidated in the course of a careful and painstaking inquiry are so startling, and the horror which they excite so overwhelming, that it is doubly necessary to approach the subject with a scepticism proof against all but the most overwhelming demonstration. It is, however, a fact that there is in full operation among us a system of which the violation of virgins is one of the ordinary incidents; that these virgins are mostly of tender age, being too young in fact to understand the nature of the crime of which they are the unwilling victims; that these outrages are constantly perpetrated with almost absolute impunity; and that the arrangements for procuring, certifying, violating, repairing, and disposing of these ruined victims of the lust of London are made with a simplicity and efficiency incredible to all who have not made actual demonstration of the facility with which the crime can be accomplished.

To avoid misapprehension, I admit that the vast majority of those who are on the streets in London have not come there by the road of organized rape. Most women fall either by the seduction of individuals or by the temptation which well-dressed vice can offer to the poor. But there is a minority which has been as much the victim of violence as were the Bulgarian maidens with whose wrongs Mr. Gladstone made the world ring some eight years ago.[1] Some are simply snared, trapped and outraged either when under the influence of drugs or after a prolonged struggle in a locked room, in which the weaker succumbs to sheer downright force. Others are regularly procured; bought at so much per head in some cases, or enticed under various promises into the fatal chamber from which they are never allowed to emerge until they have lost what woman ought to value more than life. It is to this department of the subject that I now address myself.

Before beginning this inquiry I had a confidential interview with one of the most experienced officers who for many years was in a position to possess an intimate acquaintance with all phases of London crime. I asked him, "Is it or is it not a fact that, at this moment, if I were to go to the proper houses, well introduced, the keeper would, in return for money down, supply me in due time with a maid—a genuine article, I mean, not a mere prostitute tricked out as a virgin, but a girl who had never been seduced?" "Certainly," he replied without a moment's hesitation. "At what price?" I continued. "That is a difficult question," he said. "I remember one case

---

1. Gladstone's outrage about the Turks' brutality in the Balkans—and his denunciation of Prime Minister Disraeli's indifference—helped restore Gladstone to power in 1880.

which came under my official cognizance in Scotland-yard[2] in which the price agreed upon was stated to be £20. Some parties in Lambeth[3] undertook to deliver a maid for that sum—to a house of ill fame, and I have no doubt it is frequently done all over London." "But," I continued, "are these maids willing or unwilling parties to the transaction—that is, are they really maiden, not merely in being each a *virgo intacta* in the physical sense, but as being chaste girls who are not consenting parties to their seduction?" He looked surprised at my question, and then replied emphatically: "Of course they are rarely willing, and as a rule they do not know what they are coming for." "But," I said in amazement, "then do you mean to tell me that in very truth actual rapes, in the legal sense of the word, are constantly being perpetrated in London on unwilling virgins, purveyed and procured to rich men at so much a head by keepers of brothels?" "Certainly," said he, "there is not a doubt of it." "Why," I exclaimed, "the very thought is enough to raise hell." "It is true," he said; "and although it ought to raise hell, it does not even raise the neighbours." "But do the girls cry out?" "Of course they do. But what avails screaming in a quiet bedroom? Remember, the utmost limit of howling or excessively violent screaming, such as a man or woman would make if actual murder was being attempted, is only two minutes, and the limit of screaming of any kind is only five. Suppose a girl is being outraged in a room next to your house. You hear her screaming, just as you are dozing to sleep. Do you get up, dress, rush downstairs, and insist on admittance? Hardly. But suppose the screams continue and you get uneasy, you begin to think whether you should not do something? Before you have made up your mind and got dressed the screams cease, and you think you were a fool for your pains." "But the policeman on the beat?" "He has no right to interfere, even if he heard anything. Suppose that a constable had a right to force his way into any house where a woman screamed fearfully, policemen would be almost as regular attendants at childbed as doctors. Once a girl gets into such a house she is almost helpless, and may be ravished with comparative safety." "But surely rape is a felony punishable with penal servitude. Can she not prosecute?" "Whom is she to prosecute? She does not know her assailant's name. She might not even be able to recognize him if she met him outside. Even if she did, who would believe her? A woman who has lost her chastity is always a discredited witness. The fact of her being in a house of ill fame would possibly be held to be evidence of her consent. The keeper of the house and all the servants would swear she was a consenting party; they would swear that she had never screamed, and the woman would be condemned as an adventuress who wished to levy black mail." "And this is going on to-day?" "Certainly it is, and it will go on, and you cannot help it, as long as men have money, procuresses are skillful, and women are weak and inexperienced."

Virgins Willing and Unwilling.

So startling a declaration by so eminent an authority led me to turn my investigations in this direction. On discussing the matter with a well-known member of Parliament, he laughed and said: "I doubt the unwillingness of these virgins. That you can contract for maids at so much a head is true enough. I myself am quite ready to supply

---

2. Central police agency.
3. A poor district of London.

you with 100 maids at £25 each, but they will all know very well what they are about. There are plenty of people among us entirely devoid of moral scruples on the score of chastity, whose daughters are kept straight until they are sixteen or seventeen, not because they love virtue, but solely because their virginity is a realizable asset, with which they are taught they should never part except for value received. These are the girls who can be had at so much a head; but it is nonsense to say it is rape; it is merely the delivery as per contract of the asset virginity in return for cash down. Of course there may be some cases in which the girl is really unwilling, but the regular supply comes from those who take a strictly businesslike view of the saleable value of their maidenhead." My interlocutor referred me to a friend whom he described as the first expert on the subject, an evergreen[4] old gentleman to whom the brothels of Europe were as familiar as Notre Dame and St. Paul's.[5] This specialist, however, entirely denied that there was such a thing as the procuring of virgins, willing or unwilling, either here or on the Continent. Maidenheads, he maintained, were not assets that could be realized in the market, but he admitted that there were some few men whose taste led them to buy little girls from their mothers in order to abuse them. My respect for this "eminent authority" diminished, however, on receiving his assurance that all Parisian and Belgian brothels were managed so admirably that no minors could be harboured, and that no English girls were ever sent to the Continent for immoral purposes. Still even he admitted that little girls were bought and sold for vicious purposes, and this unnatural combination of slave trade, rape, and unnatural crime seemed to justify further inquiry.

I then put myself into direct and confidential communication with brothel-keepers in the West and East of London and in the provinces. Some of these were still carring on their business, others had abandoned their profession in disgust, and were now living a better life. The information which I received from them was, of course, confidential. I am not a detective, and much of the information which I received was given only after the most solemn pledge that I would not violate their confidence, so as to involve them in a criminal prosecution. It was somewhat unfortunate that this inquiry was only set on foot after the prosecution of Mrs. Jefferies.[6] The fine inflicted on her has struck momentary awe into the heart of the thriving community of "introducers." They could accommodate no one but their old customers. A new face suggested Mr. Minahan, and an inquiry for virgins or little girls by one who had not given his proofs, excited suspicion and alarm. But, aided by some trustworthy and experienced friends, I succeeded after a time in overcoming the preliminary obstacle so as to obtain sufficient evidence as to the reality of the crime.

The Confessions of a Brothel-Keeper.

Here, for instance, is a statement made to me by a brothel keeper, who formerly kept a noted house in the Mile-end road,[7] but who is now endeavouring to start

---

4. Perpetually young.
5. The landmark churches of Paris and London, respectively.
6. A Chelsea madam who boasted that she sold a hundred virgins to the King of Belgium each year and catered to the sexual needs of other wealthy men. She was arrested, pleaded guilty, and fined. Mr. Minahan was the detective who worked with reformer Josephine Butler to expose her.
7. Very poor area of London's East End.

life afresh as an honest man. I saw both him and his wife, herself a notorious prostitute whom he had married off the streets, where she had earned her living since she was fourteen:—

"Maids, as you call them—fresh girls as we know them in the trade—are constantly in request, and a keeper who knows his business has his eyes open in all directions, his stock of girls is constantly getting used up, and needs replenishing, and he has to be on the alert for likely 'marks' to keep up the reputation of his house. I have been in my time a good deal about the country on these errands. The getting of fresh girls takes time, but it is simple and easy enough when once you are in it. I have gone and courted girls in the country under all kinds of disguises, occasionally assuming the dress of a parson, and made them believe that I intended to marry them, and so got them in my power to please a good customer. How is it done? Why, after courting my girl for a time, I propose to bring her to London to see the sights. I bring her up, take her here and there, giving her plenty to eat and drink—especially drink. I take her to the theatre, and then I contrive it so that she loses her last train. By this time she is very tired, a little dazed with the drink and excitement, and very frightened at being left in town with no friends. I offer her nice lodgings for the night; she goes to bed in my house, and then the affair is managed. My client gets his maid, I get my £10 or £20 commission, and in the morning the girl, who has lost her character, and dare not go home, in all probability will do as the others do, and become one of my 'marks'—that is, she will make her living in the streets, to the advantage of my house. The brothel keeper's profit is, first, the commission down for the price of a maid, and secondly, the continuous profit of the addition of a newly seduced, attractive girl to his establishment. That is a fair sample case of the way in which we recruit. Another very simple mode of supplying maids is by breeding them. Many women who are on the streets have female children. They are worth keeping. When they get to be twelve or thirteen they become merchantable. For a very likely 'mark' of this kind you may get as much as £20 or £40. I sent my own daughter out on the streets from my own brothel. I know a couple of very fine little girls now who will be sold before very long. They are bred and trained for the life. They must take the first step some time, and it is bad business not to make as much out of that as possible. Drunken parents often sell their children to brothel keepers. In the East-end, you can always pick up as many fresh girls as you want. In one street in Dalston[8] you might buy a dozen. Sometimes the supply is in excess of the demand, and you have to seduce your maid yourself, or to employ some one else to do it, which is bad business in a double sense. There is a man called S—— whom a famous house used to employ to seduce young girls and make them fit for service when there was no demand for maids and there was a demand for girls who had been seduced. But as a rule the number seduced ready to hand is ample, especially among very young children. Did I ever do anything else in the way of recruiting? Yes. I remember one case very well. The girl, a likely 'mark,' was a simple country lass living in Horsham.[9] I had heard of her, and I went down to Horsham to see what I could do. Her parents believed that I was in regular business in London, and they were very glad when I proposed to engage their daughter. I

8. A run-down area on the edge of the East End.
9. Suburban town south of London.

brought her to town and made her a servant in our house. We petted her and made a good deal of her, gradually initiated her into the kind of life it was; and then I sold her to a young gentleman for £15. When I say that I sold her, I mean that he gave me the gold and I gave him the girl, to do what he liked with. He took her away and seduced her. I believe he treated her rather well afterwards, but that was not my affair. She was his after he paid for her and took her away. If her parents had inquired, I would have said that she had been a bad girl and run away with a young man. How could I help that? I once sold a girl twelve years old for £20 to a clergyman, who used to come to my house professedly to distribute tracts. The East is the great market for the children who are imported into West-end houses,[10] or taken abroad wholesale when trade is brisk. I know of no West-end houses, having always lived in Dalston or thereabouts, but agents pass to and fro in the course of business. They receive the goods, depart, and no questions are asked. Mrs. S., a famous procuress, has a mansion at ———, which is one of the worst centres of the trade, with four other houses in other districts, one at St. John's-wood.[11] This lady, when she discovers ability, cultivates it—that is, if a comely young girl of fifteen falls into her net, with some intelligence, she is taught to read and write, and to play the piano."

The London Slave Market.

This brothel-keeper was a smart fellow, and had been a commercial traveller once, but drink had brought him down. Anxious to test the truth of his statement, I asked him, through a trusty agent, if he would undertake to supply me in three days with a couple of fresh girls, maids, whose virginity would be attested by a doctor's certificate. At first he said that it would require a longer time. But on being pressed, and assured that money was no object, he said that he would make inquiries, and see what could be done. In two days I received from the same confidential source an intimation that for £10 commission he would undertake to deliver to my chambers, or to any other spot which I might choose to select, two young girls, each with a doctor's certificate of the fact that she was a *virgo intacta*. Hesitating to close with this offer, my agent received the following telegram:—"I think all right. I am with parties. Will tell you all to-morrow about twelve o'clock." On calling H—— said:—

"I will undertake to deliver at your rooms within two days two children at your chambers. Both are the daughters of brothel keepers whom I have known and dealt with, and the parents are willing to sell in both cases. I represented that they were intended for a rich old gentleman who has led a life of debauchery for years. I was suspected of baby-farming—that is, peaching,[12] at first, and it required all my knowledge of the tricks of the trade to effect my purpose. However, after champagne and liquors, my old friend G——, M—— lane, Hackney,[13] agreed to hand over her own child, a pretty girl of eleven, for £5, if she could get no more. The child was *virgo intacta*, so far as her mother knew. I then went to Mrs. N——, of B—— street, Dalston, (B—— street is a street of brothels from end to end). Mrs. N—— required little persuasion,

---

10. Wealthy district of London.
11. London district known for its "kept women" (their patrons liked the district's obscure, affordable houses).
12. Taking the children for himself.
13. A fairly prosperous London neighborhood.

but her price was higher. She would not part with her daughter under £5 or £10, as she was pretty and attractive, and a virgin, aged thirteen, who would probably fetch more in the open market. These two children I could deliver up within two days if the money was right. I would, on the same conditions, undertake to deliver half a dozen girls, ages varying from ten to thirteen, within a week or ten days."

I did not deem it wise to carry the negotiations any further. The purchase price was to be paid on delivery, but it was to be returned if the girls were found to have been tampered with.

That was fairly confirmatory evidence of the existence of the traffic to which official authority has pointed; but I was not content. Making inquiries at the other end of the town, by good fortune I was brought into intimate and confidential communication with an ex-brothel keeper. When a mere girl she had been seduced by Colonel S——, when a maidservant at Petersfield,[14] and had been thrown upon the streets by that officer at Manchester. She had subsequently kept a house of ill fame at a seaport town, and from thence had gravitated to the congenial neighbourhood of Regent's Park.[15] There she had kept a brothel for several years. About a year ago, however, she was picked up, when in a drunken fit, by some earnest workers, and after a hard struggle was brought back to a decent and moral life. She was a woman who bore traces of the rigorous mill through which she had passed. Her health was impaired; she looked ten years older than her actual age, and it was with the greatest reluctance she could be prevailed upon to speak of the incidents of her previous life, the horror of which seemed to cling to her like a nightmare. By dint of patient questioning, however, and the assurance that I would not criminate either herself or any of her old companions, she became more communicative, and answered my inquiries. Her narrative was straightforward; and I am fully convinced it was entirely genuine. I have since made strict inquiries among those who see her daily and know her most intimately, and I am satisfied that the woman was speaking the truth. She had no motive to deceive, and she felt very deeply the shame of her awful confession, which was only wrung from her by the conviction that it might help to secure the prevention of similar crimes in the future.

How Girls are Bought and Ruined.

Her story, or rather so much of it as is germane to the present inquiry, was somewhat as follows:—

"As a regular thing, the landlady of a bad house lets her rooms to gay women[16] and lives on their rent and the profits on the drink which they compel their customers to buy for the good of the house. She may go out herself or she may not. If business is very heavy, she will have to do her own share, but as a rule she contents herself with keeping her girls up to the mark, and seeing that they at least earn enough to pay their rent, and bring home sufficient customers to consume liquor enough to make it pay. Girls often shrink from going out, and need almost to be driven into the streets.

14. Town near the northern industrial city of Manchester.
15. Upscale London neighborhood.
16. Prostitutes.

If it was not for gin and the landlady they could never carry it on. Some girls I used to have would come and sit and cry in my kitchen and declare that they could not go out, they could not stand the life. I had to give them a dram and take them out myself, and set them agoing again, for if they did not seek gentlemen where was I to get my rent? Did they begin willingly? Some; others had no choice. How had they no choice? Because they never knew anything about it till the gentleman was in their bedroom, and it was too late. I or my girls would entice fresh girls in, and persuade them to stay out too late till they were locked out, and then a pinch of snuff in their beer would keep them snug until the gentleman had his way. Has that happened often? Lots of times. It is one of the ways by which you keep your house up. Every woman who has an eye to business is constantly on the lookout for likely girls. Pretty girls who are poor, and who have either no parents or are away from home, are easiest picked up. How is it done? You or your decoy find a likely girl, and then you track her down. I remember I once went a hundred miles and more to pick up a girl. I took a lodging close to the board school, where I could see the girls go backwards and forwards every day. I soon saw one that suited my fancy. She was a girl of about thirteen, tall and forward for her age, pretty, and likely to bring business. I found out she lived with her mother. I engaged her to be my little maid at the lodgings where I was staying. The very next day I took her off with me to London and her mother never saw her again. What became of her? A gentleman paid me £13 for the first of her, soon after she came to town. She was asleep when he did it—sound asleep. To tell the truth, she was drugged. It is often done. I gave her a drowse. It is a mixture of laudanum[17] and something else. Sometimes chloroform is used, but I always used either snuff or laudanum. We call it drowse or black draught, and they lie almost as if dead, and the girl never knows what has happened till morning. And then? Oh! then she cries a great deal from pain, but she is 'mazed, and hardly knows what has happened except that she can hardly move from pain. Of course we tell her it is all right; all girls have to go through it some time, that she is through it now without knowing it, and that it is no use crying. It will never be undone for all the crying in the world. She must now do as the others do. She can live like a lady, do as she pleases, have the best of all that is going, and enjoy herself all day. If she objects, I scold her and tell her she has lost her character, no one will take her in; I will have to turn her out on the streets as a bad and ungrateful girl. The result is that in nine cases out of ten, or ninety-nine out of a hundred, the child, who is usually under fifteen, frightened and friendless, her head aching with the effect of the drowse and full of pain and horror, gives up all hope, and in a week she is one of the attractions of the house. You say that some men say this is never done. Don't believe them; if these people spoke the truth, it might be found that they had done it themselves. Landladies who wish to thrive must humour their customers. If they want a maid we must get them one, or they will go elsewhere. We cannot afford to lose their custom; besides, after the maid is seduced, she fills up vacancies caused by disease or drink. There are very few brothels which are not occasionally recruited in that way. That case which I mentioned was by no means exceptional; in about seven years I remember selling two maids for £20 each, one at £16, one at £15, one at £13 and others for less. Of course, where I

---

17. Tincture of opium dissolved in alcohol.

bought I paid less than that. The difference represented my profit, commission, and payment for risk in procuring, drugging, &c."

Buying Girls at the East-end.

This experienced ex-procuress assured me that if she were to return to her old trade she would have no difficulty in laying her hands, through the agency of friends and relatives still in the trade, upon as many young girls as she needed. No house begins altogether with maids, but steps are at once taken to supply one or two young girls to train in. She did not think the alarm of the Jefferies trial had penetrated into the strata where she used to work. But said I, "Will these children be really maids, or will it merely be a plant to get off damaged articles under that guise?" Her reply was significant. "You do not know how it is done. Do you think I would buy a maid on her word? You can soon find out, if you are in the business, whether a child is really fresh or not. You have to trust the person who sells, no doubt, to some extent, but if you are in the trade they would not deceive you in a matter in which fraud can be so easily detected. If one house supplied another with girls who had been seduced, at the price of maids, it would get out, and their reputation would suffer. Besides you do not trust them very far. Half the commission is paid down on delivery, the other half is held over until the truth is proved." "How is that done?" "By a doctor or an experienced midwife. If you are dealing with a house you trust, you take their doctor's certificate. If they trust you they will accept the verdict of your doctor." "Does the girl know why you are taking her away?" "Very seldom. She thinks she is going to a situation.[18] When she finds out, it is too late. If she knew what it meant she either would not come or her readiness would give rise to a suspicion that she was not the article you wanted—that, in fact, she was no better than she should be." "Who are these girls?" "Orphans, daughters of drunken parents, children of prostitutes, girls whose friends are far away." "And their price?" "In the trade from £3 to £5 is, I should think, a fair thing. But if you doubt it I will make inquiries, if you like, in my old haunts and tell you what can be done next week."

As there is nothing like inquiry on the spot, I commissioned her to inquire as to the maids then in stock or procurable at short notice by a single bad house in the East of London, whose keeper she knew. The reply was businesslike and direct. If she wanted a couple of maids for a house in the country three would be brought to Waterloo railway station next Saturday at three, from whom two could be selected at £5 per head. One girl, not very pretty, about thirteen, could be had at once at £3. Offer to be accepted or confirmed by letter—which of course never arrived.

A Girl Escapes after being Sold.

Being anxious to satisfy myself as to the reality of these transactions, I instructed a thoroughly trustworthy woman to proceed with this ex-keeper to the house in question, and see if she could see any of the children whose price was quoted like that of lambs at so much a head. The woman of the house was somewhat suspicious, owing to the presence of a stranger, but after some conversation she said that she had one

---

18. Servant's job.

fresh girl within reach, whom she would make over at once if they could come to terms. The girl was sent for, and duly appeared. She was told that she was to have a good situation in the country within a few miles of London. She said that she had been brought up at a home at Streatham,[19] had been in service, but had been out of a place for three weeks. She was a pleasant, bright-looking girl, who seemed somewhat nervous when she heard so many inquiries and the talk about taking her into the country. The bargain, however, was struck. The keeper had to receive £2 down, and another sovereign when the girl was proved a maid. The money was paid, the girl handed over, but something said had alarmed her, and she solved the difficulty of disposing of her by making her escape. My friend who witnessed the whole transaction, and whose presence probably contributed something to the difficulty of the bargain, assures me that there was no doubt as to the sale and transfer of the girl. "Her escape," said the ex-keeper, "is one of the risks of the trade. If I had been really in for square business, I should never have agreed to take the girl from the house, partly in order to avoid such escape and partly for safety. It is almost invariably the rule that the seller must deliver the girl at some railway station. She is brought to you, placed in your cab or your railway carriage, and it is then your business, and an easy one, to see that she does not escape you. But the risks of delivery at a safe place are always taken by the seller."

A Dreadful Profession.

When I was prosecuting these inquiries at the East-end, I was startled by a discovery made by a confidential agent at the other end of the town. This was nothing less than the unearthing of a house, kept apparently by a highly respectable midwife, where children were taken by procurers to be certified as virgins before violation, and where, after violation, they were taken to be "patched up," and where, if necessary, abortion could be procured. The existence of the house was no secret. It was well known in the trade, and my agent was directed thither without much ado by a gay woman with whom he had made a casual acquaintance. No doubt the respectable old lady has other business of a less doubtful character, but in the trade her repute is unrivalled, first as a certificator of virginity, and secondly for the adroitness and skill with which she can repair the laceration caused by the subsequent outrage.

That surely was sufficiently horrible. Yet there stood the house, imperturbably respectable in its outward appearance, apparently an indispensable adjunct of modern civilization, its experienced proprietress maintaining confidential relations with the "best houses" in the West-end. This repairer of damaged virgins is not a procuress. Her mission is remedial. Her premises are not used for purposes of violation. She knows where it is done, but she cannot prevent that. What she does is to minimize pain and repair as effectively as possible the ravages of the lust which she did not create, and which she cannot control. But she is a wise woman, whom great experience has taught many secrets, and if she would but speak! Not that she is above giving a hint to those who seek her advice as to where little children can best be procured. A short time ago, she says, there was no difficulty. "Any of these houses," mentioning several of the best known foreign and English houses in the West and North-west,

---

19. Busy suburb of London.

"would supply children, but at present they are timid. You need to be an old customer to be served. But, after all, it is expensive getting young girls for them. If you really have a fancy that way, why do you not do as Mr. —— does? It is cheaper, simpler, and safer." "And how does Mr. —— do, and who is Mr. —— ?" "Oh, Mr. —— is a gentleman who has a great penchant for little girls. I do not know how many I have had to repair after him. He goes down to the East-end and the City, and watches when the girls come out of shops and factories for lunch or at the end of the day. He sees his fancy and marks her down. It takes a little time, but he wins the child's confidence. One day he proposes a little excursion to the West. She consents. Next day I have another subject, and Mr. —— is off with another girl." "And what becomes of the subjects on which you display your skill?" "Some go home, others go back to their situations, others again are passed on to those who have a taste for second-hand articles," and the good lady intimated that if my agent had such a taste, she was not without hopes that she might be able to do a little trade.

Why the Cries of the Victims are not Heard.

At this point in the inquiry, the difficulty again occurred to me how was it possible for these outrages to take place without detection. The midwife, when questioned, said there was no danger. Some of the houses had an underground room, from which no sound could be heard, and that, as a matter of fact, no one ever had been detected. The truth about the underground chambers is difficult to ascertain. Padded rooms for the purpose of stifling the cries of tortured victims of lust and brutality are familiar enough on the Continent. "In my house," said a most respectable lady, who keeps a villa in the west of London, "you can enjoy the screams of the girl with the certainty that no one else hears them but yourself." But to enjoy to the full the exclusive luxury of revelling in the cries of the immature child, it is not necessary to have a padded room, a double chamber, or an underground room. "Here," said the keeper of a fashionable villa, where in days bygone a prince of the blood is said to have kept for some months one of his innumerable sultanas,[20] as she showed her visitor over the well-appointed rooms, "Here is a room where you can be perfectly secure. The house stands in its own grounds. The walls are thick, there is a double carpet on the floor. The only window which fronts upon the back garden is double secured, first with shutters and then with heavy curtains. You lock the door and then you can do as you please. The girl may scream blue murder, but not a sound will be heard. The servants will be far away in the other end of the house. I only will be about seeing that all is snug." "But," remarked her visitor, "if you hear the cries of the child, you may yourself interfere, especially if, as may easily happen, I badly hurt and in fact all but kill the girl." "You will not kill her," she answered, "you have too much sense to kill the girl. Anything short of that, you can do as you please. As for me interfering, do you think I do not know my business?"

Flogging, both of men and women, goes on regularly in ordinary rooms, but the cry of the bleeding subject never attracts attention from the outside world. What chance is there, then, of the feeble, timid cry of the betrayed child penetrating the shuttered and curtained windows, or of moving the heart of the wily watcher—the woman whose

---

20. A sultan's concubine, here denoting a rich man's mistress.

business it is to secure absolute safety for her client. When means of stifling a cry—a pillow, a sheet, or even a pocket handerchief—lie all around, there is practically no danger. To some men, however, the shriek of torture is the essence of their delight, and they would not silence by a single note the cry of agony over which they gloat.

No Room for Repentance.

Whether the maids thus violated in the secret chambers of accommodation houses are willing or unwilling is a question on which a keeper shed a flood of light by a very pertinent and obvious remark: "I have never had a maid seduced in my house," he said, "unless she was willing. They are willing enough to come to my house to be seduced, but when the man comes they are never willing." And she proceeded to illustrate what she meant by descriptions of scenes which had taken place in her house when girls, who according to her story had implored her to allow them to be seduced in her rooms, had when the supreme moment arrived repented their willingness, and fought tooth and nail, when too late, for the protection of their chastity. To use her familiar phrase, they made "the devil's own row," and on at least one occasion it was evident that the girl's resistance had only been overcome after a prolonged and desperate fight, in which, what with screaming and violence, she was too exhausted to continue the struggle.

That was in the case of a full-grown woman. Children of twelve and thirteen cannot offer any serious resistance. They only dimly comprehend what it all means. Their mothers sometimes consent to their seduction for the sake of the price paid by their seducer. The child goes to the introducing house as a sheep to the shambles.[21] Once there, she is compelled to go through with it. No matter how brutal the man may be, she cannot escape. "If she wanted to be seduced, and came here to be seduced," says the keeper, "I shall see that she does not play the fool. The gentleman has paid for her, and he can do with her what he likes." Neither Rhadamanthus nor Lord Bramwell[22] could more sternly exact the rigorous fulfilment of the stipulations of the contract. "Once she is in my house," said a worthy landlady, "she does not go out till the job is done. She comes in willingly, but no matter how willing she may be to go out, she stays here till my gentleman has done with her. She repents too late when she repents after crossing my threshold."

Strapping Girls Down.

In the course of my investigations I heard some strange tales concerning the precautions taken to render escape impossible for the girl whose ruin, with or without her consent, has been resolved upon. One fact, which is of quite recent occurrence in a fashionable London suburb, the accuracy of which I was able to verify, is an illustration of the extent to which those engaged in this traffic are willing to go to supply the caprices of their customers. To oblige a wealthy customer who by riot and excess had impaired his vitality to such an extent that nothing could minister to his jaded senses but very young maidens, an eminently respectable lady undertook that whenever the girl was fourteen or fifteen years of age she should be strapped down hand and foot to

---

21. Slaughterhouse.
22. Stern judge of the underworld in Greek mythology and 19th-c. judge George William Wilshere Bramwell.

the four posts of the bedstead, so that all resistance save that of unavailing screaming would be impossible. Before the strapping down was finally agreed upon the lady of the house, a stalwart woman and experienced in the trade, had volunteered her services to hold the virgin down by force while her wealthy patron effected his purpose. That was too much even for him, and the alternative of fastening with straps padded on the under side was then agreed upon. Strapping down for violation used to be a common occurrence in Half-moon-street[23] and in Anna Rosenberg's brothel at Liverpool. Anything can be done for money, if you only know where to take it.

How the Law abets the Criminal.

The system of procuration, as I have already explained, is reduced to a science. The poorer brothel-keeper hunts up recruits herself, while the richer are supported by their agents. No prudent keeper of an introducing house will receive girls brought by other than her accredited and trusted agents. The devices of these agents are innumerable. They have been known to profess penitence in order to gain access to a home for fallen women, where they thought some Magdalens[24] repenting of their penitence might be secured for their house. They go into workhouses,[25] to see what likely girls are to be had. They use servants' registries.[26] They haunt the doors of gaols when girls in for their first offence are turned adrift on the expiry of their sentences. There are no subterfuges too cunning or too daring for them to resort to in the pursuit of their game. Against their wiles the law offers the girl over thirteen next to no protection. If a child of fourteen is cajoled or frightened, or overborne by anything short of direct force or the threat of immediate bodily harm, into however an unwilling acquiescence in an act the nature of which she most imperfectly apprehends, the law steps in to shield her violator. If permission is given, says "Stephen's Digest of the Criminal Law," "the fact that it was obtained by fraud, or that the woman did not understand the nature of the act is immaterial."

A Child of Thirteen Bought for £5.

Let me conclude the chapter of horrors by one incident, and only one of those which are constantly occurring in those dread regions of subterranean vice in which sexual crime flourishes almost unchecked. I can personally vouch for the absolute accuracy of every fact in the narrative.

At the beginning of this Derby week, a woman, an old hand in the work of procuration, entered a brothel in ——— st. M———, kept by an old acquaintance, and opened negotiations for the purchase of a maid.[27] One of the women who lodged in the house had a sister as yet untouched. Her mother was far away, her father was dead. The child was living in the house, and in all probability would be seduced and follow the profession of her elder sister. The child was between thirteen and fourteen,

---

23. In London's fashionable Mayfair district.
24. Fallen women, so called after Mary Magdalen in the New Testament.
25. Places to house the homeless poor.
26. Employment offices.
27. The Derby horse race is run on the first Wednesday in June. Stead employed Rebecca Jarret, a reformed prostitute who worked as a servant for the famous social reformer Josephine Butler, as his agent and had General Bramwell Booth of the Salvation Army witness the transaction.

and after some bargaining it was agreed that she should be handed over to the procuress for the sum of £5. The maid was wanted, it was said, to start a house with, and there was no disguise on either side that the sale was to be effected for immoral purposes. While the negotiations were going on, a drunken neighbour came into the house, and so little concealment was then used, that she speedily became aware of the nature of the transaction. So far from being horrified at the proposed sale of the girl, she whispered eagerly to the seller, "Don't you think she would take our Lily? I think she would suit." Lily was her own daughter, a bright, fresh-looking little girl, who was thirteen years old last Christmas. The bargain, however, was made for the other child, and Lily's mother felt she had lost her market.

The next day, Derby Day as it happened, was fixed for the delivery of this human chattel. But as luck would have it, another sister of the child who was to be made over to the procuress heard of the proposed sale. She was living respectably in a situation, and on hearing of the fate reserved for the little one she lost no time in persuading her dissolute sister to break off the bargain. When the woman came for her prey the bird had flown. Then came the chance of Lily's mother. The brothel-keeper sent for her, and offered her a sovereign for her daughter. The woman was poor, dissolute, and indifferent to everything but drink. The father, who was also a drunken man, was told his daughter was going to a situation. He received the news with indifference, without even inquiring where she was going to. The brothel-keeper having thus secured possession of the child, then sold her to the procuress in place of the child whose sister had rescued her from her destined doom for £5—£3 paid down and the remaining £2 after her virginity had been professionally certified. The little girl, all unsuspecting the purpose for which she was destined, was told that she must go with this strange woman to a situation. The procuress, who was well up to her work, took her away, washed her, dressed her up neatly, and sent her to bid her parents good-bye. The mother was so drunk she hardly recognized her daughter. The father was hardly less indifferent. The child left her home, and was taken to the woman's lodging in A—— street.

The first step had thus been taken. But it was necessary to procure the certification of her virginity—a somewhat difficult task, as the child was absolutely ignorant of the nature of the transaction which had transferred her from home to the keeping of this strange, but apparently kind-hearted woman. Lily[28] was a little cockney child, one of those who by the thousand annually develop into the servants of the poorer middle-class. She had been at school, could read and write, and although her spelling was extraordinary, she was able to express herself with much force and decision. Her experience of the world was limited to the London quarter in which she had been born. With the exception of two school trips to Richmond and one to Epping Forest,[29] she had never been in the country in her life, nor had she ever even seen the Thames excepting at Richmond. She was an industrious, warm-hearted little thing, a hardy English child, slightly coarse in texture, with dark black eyes, and short, sturdy figure. Her education was slight. She spelled write "right," for instance, and her grammar was very shaky. But she was a loving, affectionate child, whose kindly feeling for the drunken mother who sold her into nameless infamy was very

---

28. The child's real name was Liza Armstrong. Stead risked criminal charges for proceeding without the father's permission (he was told Liza would become a servant).

29. Popular recreation sites just outside London.

touching to behold. In a little letter of hers which I once saw, plentifully garlanded with kisses, there was the following ill-spelled childish verse:—

As I was in bed
Some little forths (thoughts) gave (came) in my head.
I forth (thought) of one, I forth (thought) of two;
But first of all I forth (thought) of you.[30]

The poor child was full of delight at going to her new situation, and clung affectionately to the keeper who was taking her away—where, she knew not.

The first thing to be done after the child was fairly severed from home was to secure the certificate of virginity without which the rest of the purchase-money would not be forthcoming. In order to avoid trouble she was taken in a cab to the house of a midwife, whose skill in pronouncing upon the physical evidences of virginity is generally recognized in the profession. The examination was very brief and completely satisfactory. But the youth, the complete innocence of the girl, extorted pity even from the hardened heart of the old abortionist. "The poor little thing," she exclaimed. "She is so small, her pain will be extreme. I hope you will not be too cruel with her"—as if to lust when fully roused the very acme of agony on the part of the victim has not a fierce delight. To quiet the old lady the agent of the purchaser asked if she could supply anything to dull the pain. She produced a small phial of chloroform. "This," she said, "is the best. My clients find this much the most effective." The keeper took the bottle, but unaccustomed to anything but drugging by the administration of sleeping potions, she would infallibly have poisoned the child had she not discovered by experiment that the liquid burned the mouth when an attempt was made to swallow it. £1 1s. was paid for the certificate of virginity—which was verbal and not written— while £1 10s. more was charged for the chloroform, the net value of which was probably less than a shilling. An arrangement was made that if the child was badly injured Madame would patch it up to the best of her ability, and then the party left the house.

From the midwife's the innocent girl was taken to a house of ill fame, No.—, P—— street, Regent-street, where, notwithstanding her extreme youth, she was admitted without question. She was taken up stairs, undressed, and put to bed, the woman who bought her putting her to sleep. She was rather restless, but under the influence of chloroform she soon went over. Then the woman withdrew. All was quiet and still. A few moments later the door opened, and the purchaser entered the bedroom.[31] He closed and locked the door. There was a brief silence. And then there rose a wild and piteous cry—not a loud shriek, but a helpless, startled scream like the bleat of a frightened lamb. And the child's voice was heard crying, in accents of terror, "There's a man in the room! Take me home; oh, take me home!"

And then all once more was still.

That was but one case among many, and by no means the worst. It only differs from the rest because I have been able to verify the facts. Many a similar cry will be raised this very night in the brothels of London, unheeded by man, but not unheard by the pitying ear of Heaven—

---

30. From a letter Liza wrote during the 12 weeks Stead kept her in France to ensure her safety.
31. Stead himself. He crept out quietly after hearing the cry.

For the child's sob in the darkness curseth deeper
Than the strong man in his wrath.[32]

—1885

Writing the City, Writing the Country

John Davidson
1857–1909

The Scots poet John Davidson became famous for his eloquent lines about the shabby, needy lives of underpaid urban clerks and newspapermen. Although he was a member of the male aesthetes' group, the Rhymer's Club, Davidson prided himself on his bluff masculinity and derided his fellow poets' affectations. Like his characters, Davidson earned a living from journalism while dreaming of literary success (in his case, as a playwright). Davidson wrote two blank-verse dramas celebrating self-expression, but when they failed, he committed suicide at the age of 52. Davidson's celebrated *Fleet Street Eclogues* (1893) are just as paradoxical as their name implies; they consist of eclogues, poems in praise of the countryside, yet they are written from the grimy newspaper district of London. Each eclogue celebrates a different season. In "Good-Friday," hard-bitten urban journalists surrender to dreams of spring, all the more poignant because they know they seek an impossible, lost Eden.

Good-Friday

BASIL   SANDY   BRIAN   MENZIES

SANDY
Pfff! journalists; the wind blows snell![1]

BRIAN
To-day we freeze, to-morrow fry.

BASIL
And yesterday the black rain fell
  In sheets from London's smoky sky,

Like water through a dirty sieve.   5

---

32. From Elizabeth Barrett Browning, "The Cry of the Children" (1843).

---

1. Bitter, severe.

MENZIES
March many-weathers, as they say,
In country nooks where proverbs live,
    And folk distinguish night from day.

SANDY
Well, we shall make a day of night;
    Behold with *gules* and *or*[2] a fire   10
Emblazoned, and a mellow light;
    And things that journalists require.

So let us open out our lore,
    And chat as snugly as the dead;
And damned be those who came before,   15
    And all our brilliant sayings said.

BRIAN
I love not brilliance; give me words
    Of meadow-growth and garden plot,
Of larks and blackcaps; gaudy birds,
    Gay flowers and jewels like me not.   20

BASIL
The age-end journalist it seems
    Can change his spots and turn his dress,
For you are he whose copy teems
    With paradox and preciousness.

BRIAN
Last night I watched the evening star   25
    Outshine the moon it so excelled;
And since my thought has been afar
    With deep and simple things of eld.

I heard in Fleet Street[3] all the day,
    While traffic rolled and bells were rung,   30
The sombre, wailing Tenebrae,
    The Sistine Miserere sung.[4]

---

2. Heraldic terms: "*gules*" is red; "*or*" is gold.
3. Site of London's newspaper business.
4. Catholic prayers during the last three days of Holy Week (leading up to Easter), called Tenebrae because the lights are gradually extinguished during the service. During this week the Sistine Chapel choirs sing the "Miserere" (a setting of Psalm 51).

I saw great people make their Maunds;[5]
   The prelate leave his lofty seat;
A kaiser break imperial bonds   35
   To serve the poor and wash their feet.

I saw where countless hearts besought
   Pardon, for heaven's sweet peace athirst;
And through my soul the tender thought
   Of Mary, Virgin-mother, pierced.   40

I saw a city kneeling down,
   I saw the gonfanon[6] unfurled,
I saw the Pope in triple crown
   Stand up for God and bless the world.

Templars[7] I saw, and monks and nuns,   45
   I saw frail priests strong kings command;
I thought how great the world was once
   When Heaven and Hell were close at hand.

The gloaming[8] came; I ceased to ache,
   For in my veins the springtime welled,   50
And soothed my fancy to forsake
   The deep and simple things of eld,

And fly away where blackbirds sing,
   To wander free in dale and down.

BASIL
I would that I could see the spring!   55

SANDY
Has any one been out of town?

MENZIES
I have for weeks.

BASIL
          For weeks? By heaven!
What deeds heroic have you wrought
That such a foretaste should be given   60
   Of Paradise?

---

5. Ritual abasement on Maundy Thursday (the day before Good Friday).
6. Small flag on a knight's lance.
7. The great medieval order of the Knights Templars became a powerful military unit in the Crusades.
8. Dusk.

MENZIES
   I earned it not.

'Twas accident: nor did I know
 Till now, that when they come to die
Good press-men to the country go.   65

   BRIAN
I think it's true.

   SANDY
   And so do I.

Heaven is to tread unpaven ground,
 And care no more for prose or rhyme.
Dear Menzies, talk of sight and sound,   70
 And make us feel the blossom-time.

   MENZIES
Then let my fancy dive and hale
 Pearls from my wandering memory,
Unstrung, unsorted, else I fail
 To see the spring and make you see.   75

Already round the oak at eve
 Good people prate of gain and loss;
With folded hands some sit and grieve—
 New mounds the green churchyard emboss.

The osier-peelers—ragged bands—   80
 In osier-holts[9] their business ply;
Like strokes of silver willow-wands
 On river banks a-bleaching lie.

The patchwork sunshine nets the lea;[10]
 The flitting shadows halt and pass;   85
Forlorn, the mossy humble-bee
 Lounges along the flowerless grass.

With unseen smoke as pure as dew,
 Sweeter than love or lovers are,
Wood-violets of watchet hue[11]   90
 Their secret hearths betray afar.

---

9. Willow groves; osiers are flexible willow shoots used in basket making.
10. Meadow.
11. Sky blue.

The vanguards of the daisies come,
   Summer's crusaders sanguine-stained,[12]
The only flowers that left their home
   When happiness in Eden reigned.   95

They strayed abroad, old writers tell,
   Hardy and bold, east, west, south, north:
Our guilty parents, when they fell,
   And flaming vengeance drove them forth,

Their haggard eyes in vain to God,   100
   To all the stars of heaven turned;
But when they saw where in the sod,
   The golden-hearted daisies burned,

Sweet thoughts that still within them dwelt
   Awoke, and tears embalmed their smart;   105
On Eden's daisies couched they felt
   They carried Eden in their heart.

BASIL
Oh, little flower so sweet and dear!

SANDY
   Oh, humanest of flowers that grow!

BRIAN
Oh, little brave adventurer!   110
   We human beings love you so!

MENZIES
We human beings love it so!
   And when a maiden's dainty shoe
Can cover nine, the gossips know
   The fulness of the Spring is due.   115

BRIAN
The gallant flower!

SANDY
   Its health! Come, drink!

MENZIES
Its health! By heaven, in Highland style![13]

---

12. Blood-colored.
13. Scottish style (the Scots were famed for being hard drinkers).

BASIL
The daisy's health! And now, we'll think
   Of Eden silently a while.   120

—1893

Arthur Symons
1865–1945

The decadent poet Arthur Symons celebrated the night world of London, the seamy, disreputable delights of drink and sex. Bohemian life at the *fin de siècle* attracted impecunious male artists who enjoyed the freedom to paint, dress, live, sleep, and love just as they pleased, freed from conventional moral rules. Symons was particularly enamored of the music-halls, popular entertainments for lower-class audiences where women performers belted out bawdy songs, often cross-dressing or barely dressing at all. In these poems Symons treats performance as a metaphor for a life emptied of everything meaningful, nothing left but rote recitation and a desire to please an audience. For more information about Symons, see pp. 71 and 75.

In Bohemia.

Drawn blinds and flaring gas within,
   And wine, and women, and cigars;
Without, the city's heedless din;
   Above, the white unheeding stars.

And we, alike from each remote,   5
   The world that works, the heaven that waits,
Con our brief pleasures o'er by rote,
   The favourite pastime of the Fates.

We smoke, to fancy that we dream,
   And drink, a moment's joy to prove,   10
And fain would love, and only seem
   To love because we cannot love.

Draw back the blinds, put out the light:[1]
   'Tis morning, let the daylight come.
God! how the women's cheeks are white,   15
   And how the sunlight strikes us dumb!

—1896

---

1. Echoes Othello's cry, "put out the light," just before killing Desdemona (5.2).

Prologue: In the Stalls.

My life is like a music-hall,
Where, in the impotence of rage,
Chained by enchantment to my stall,
I see myself upon the stage
Dance to amuse a music-hall.   5

'Tis I that smoke this cigarette,
Lounge here, and laugh for vacancy,
And watch the dancers turn; and yet
It is my very self I see
Across the cloudy cigarette.   10

My very self that turns and trips,
Painted, pathetically gay,
An empty song upon the lips
In make-believe of holiday:
I, I, this thing that turns and trips!   15

The light flares in the music-hall,
The light, the sound, that weary us;
Hour follows hour, I count them all,
Lagging, and loud, and riotous:
My life is like a music-hall.   20

—1902

To a Dancer.

Intoxicatingly
Her eyes across the footlights gleam,
(The wine of love, the wine of dream)
Her eyes, that gleam for me!

The eyes of all that see   5
Draw to her glances, stealing fire
From her desire that leaps to my desire;
Her eyes that gleam for me!

Subtly, deliciously,
A quickening fire within me, beat   10
The rhythms of her poising feet;
Her feet that poise to me!

Her body's melody,
In silent waves of wandering sound,
Thrills to the sense of all around,   15
Yet thrills alone for me!

And O, intoxicatingly,
When, at the magic moment's close,
She dies into the rapture of repose,
Her eyes that gleam for me!   20

—1895

Prologue: Before the Curtain.

We are the puppets of a shadow-play,
We dream the plot is woven of our hearts,
Passionately we play the self-same parts
Our fathers have played passionately yesterday,
And our sons play to-morrow. There's no speech   5
In all desire, nor any idle word,
Men have not said and women have not heard;
And when we lean and whisper each to each
Until the silence quickens to a kiss,
Even so the actor and the actress played   10
The lovers yesterday; when the lights fade
Before our feet, and the obscure abyss
Opens, and darkness falls about our eyes,
'Tis only that some momentary rage
Or rapture blinds us to forget the stage,   15
Like the wise actor, most in this thing wise.
We pass, and have our gesture; love and pain
And hope and apprehension and regret
Weave ordered lines into a pattern set
Not for our pleasure, and for us in vain.   20
The gesture is eternal; we who pass
Pass on the gesture; we, who pass, pass on
One after one into oblivion,
As shadows dim and vanish from a glass.[1]

—1902

---

1. Mirror.

A. E. Housman
1859–1936

Although his poetry is limpid, Alfred Edward Housman's personality was notoriously difficult. His merciless, even vicious, dissection of fellow scholars intimidated classicists when Housman served as a professor of Latin at University College London and Cambridge University. Housman became famous for his dispassionate, meticulous brilliance at parsing Latin literature, a remarkable achievement since he had failed his Oxford exams due to his tumultuous passion for fellow schoolmate Moses Jackson. Housman's poetry shows his mastery of disciplined, elegantly simple, highly concentrated verse forms and his aversion to deep feeling, except for a kind of enforced stoicism in the face of impending doom. Housman's plain words and pastoral subjects in his first book, *A Shropshire Lad* (1896), contrast with Wilde's baroque descriptions, Symons's decadent sensuality, Kipling's sturdy jingoism, and Davidson's urban modernity, showing the remarkable range of poetic styles produced at the *fin de siècle*.

II. Loveliest of trees, the cherry now

Loveliest of trees, the cherry now
Is hung with bloom along the bough,
And stands about the woodland ride
Wearing white for Eastertide.

Now, of my threescore years and ten,   5
Twenty will not come again,
And take from seventy springs a score,
It only leaves me fifty more.

And since to look at things in bloom
Fifty springs are little room,   10
About the woodlands I will go
To see the cherry hung with snow.

—1896

XIII. When I was one-and-twenty

When I was one-and-twenty
   I heard a wise man say,
"Give crowns and pounds and guineas[1]
   But not your heart away;
Give pearls away and rubies   5

---

1. British coins.

But keep your fancy free."
But I was one-and-twenty,
    No use to talk to me.

When I was one-and-twenty
    I heard him say again,   10
"The heart out of the bosom
    Was never given in vain;
'Tis paid with sighs a plenty
    And sold for endless rue."[2]
And I am two-and-twenty,   15
    And oh, 'tis true, 'tis true.

—1896

To an Athlete Dying Young

The time you won your town the race
We chaired you through the market-place;
Man and boy stood cheering by,
And home we brought you shoulder-high.

To-day, the road all runners come,   5
Shoulder-high we bring you home,
And set you at your threshold down,
Townsman of a stiller town.

Smart lad, to slip betimes away
From fields where glory does not stay,   10
And early though the laurel grows
It withers quicker than the rose.[1]

Eyes the shady night has shut
Cannot see the record cut,
And silence sounds no worse than cheers   15
After earth has stopped the ears:

Now you will not swell the rout
Of lads that wore their honours out,
Runners whom renown outran
And the name died before the man.   20

2. Repentence.

1. The laurel wreath symbolizes victory; the rose represents love.

So set, before its echoes fade,
The fleet foot on the sill of shade,
And hold to the low lintel up
The still-defended challenge-cup.

And round that early-laurelled head   25
Will flock to gaze the strengthless dead,
And find unwithered on its curls
The garland briefer than a girl's.

                                                       —1896

XXXI. On Wenlock Edge the wood's in trouble

On Wenlock Edge the wood's in trouble;
His forest fleece the Wrekin heaves;
The gale, it plies the saplings double,
And thick on Severn snow the leaves.[1]

'Twould blow like this through holt and hanger[2]   5
When Uricon[3] the city stood:
'Tis the old wind in the old anger,
But then it threshed another wood.

Then, 'twas before my time, the Roman
At yonder heaving hill would stare: 10
The blood that warms an English yeoman,
The thoughts that hurt him, they were there.

There, like the wind through woods in riot,
Through him the gale of life blew high;
The tree of man was never quiet: 15
Then 'twas the Roman, now 'tis I.

The gale, it plies the saplings double,
It blows so hard, 'twill soon be gone:
To-day the Roman and his trouble
Are ashes under Uricon.   20

                                                       —1896

---

1. Ridge, hill, and river in Shropshire, the western region where Housman grew up.
2. A holt is a grove; a hanger is a wood on the side of a steep hill.
3. Ancient Roman city Uriconium.

Thomas Hardy
1840–1928

Born in the southwestern agricultural region of Dorset, the son of a mason and a maidservant, Thomas Hardy wrote about the inarticulate rural poor with a passionate sympathy that won readers' admiration. Yet by the turn of the century, those very readers turned against him. Hardy's last novel, *Jude the Obscure* (1895), was nicknamed "Jude the Obscene," and his account of the sexual exploitation of a rural farm laborer, *Tess of the D'Ubervilles* (1891), raised a storm of protest. Critics begged him to return to the subject readers loved, the slow agrarian rhythms of the rural folk, the customs, speech, manners, and dress of a peasantry already viewed with nostalgia as Great Britain's urbanized modernity propelled itself forward. In *Far from the Madding Crowd* (1874), *The Return of the Native* (1878), and *The Mayor of Casterbridge* (1886), Hardy skillfully developed an imaginary region called "Wessex," adopting the medieval name for his Dorsetshire home and offering lovingly imagined, detailed settings of towns, villages, footpaths, fields, and rivers. When Hardy turned to writing poetry full-time after *Jude's* hostile reception, his *Wessex Poems* (1898) continued to explore the power of belonging to an ancient rural space in an era of modern industrialism. In these modest cottage and field settings, however, his poetic speakers and his fictional characters alike have moments of scrutinizing their own development, asking significant questions about memory, time, and chance, for Hardy believed that the universe was ruled by a blindly indifferent force, cruelly uninterested in human suffering.

Wessex Heights[1]

There are some heights in Wessex, shaped as if by a kindly hand
For thinking, dreaming, dying on, and at crises when I stand,
Say, on Ingpen Beacon eastward, or on Wylls-Neck westwardly,
I seem where I was before my birth, and after death may be.

In the lowlands I have no comrade, not even the lone man's friend—   5
Her who suffereth long and is kind;[2] accepts what he is too weak to mend:
Down there they are dubious and askance; there nobody thinks as I,
But mind-chains do not clank where one's next neighbour is the sky.

In the towns I am tracked by phantoms having weird detective ways—
Shadows of beings who fellowed with myself of earlier days: 10
They hang about at places, and they say harsh heavy things—
Men with a wintry sneer, and women with tart disparagings.

Down there I seem to be false to myself, my simple self that was,
And is not now, and I see him watching, wondering what crass cause

1. Hardy's imaginary region based on Dorset, in southwestern England.
2. Charity. See Corinthians 13.4.

Can have merged him into such a strange continuator as this,   15
Who yet has something in common with himself, my chrysalis.

I cannot go to the great grey Plain; there's a figure against the moon,
Nobody sees it but I, and it makes my breast beat out of tune;
I cannot go to the tall-spired town, being barred by the forms now passed
For everybody but me, in whose long vision they stand there fast.   20

There's a ghost at Yell'ham Bottom chiding loud at the fall of the night,
There's a ghost in Froom-side Vale, thin-lipped and vague, in a shroud of white,
There is one in the railway train whenever I do not want it near,
I see its profile against the pane, saying what I would not hear.

As for one rare fair woman, I am now but a thought of hers,   25
I enter her mind and another thought succeeds me that she prefers,
Yet my love for her in its fulness she herself even did not know;
Well, time cures hearts of tenderness, and now I can let her go.

So I am found on Ingpen Beacon, or on Wylls-Neck to the west,
Or else on homely Bulbarrow, or little Pilsdon Crest,   30
Where men have never cared to haunt, nor women have walked with me,
And ghosts then keep their distance; and I know some liberty.

—1898

The Darkling Thrush[1]

I leant upon a coppice[2] gate
   When Frost was spectre-gray,
And Winter's dregs made desolate
   The weakening eye of day.
The tangled bine-stems[3] scored the sky   5
   Like strings of broken lyres,
And all mankind that haunted nigh
   Had sought their household fires.

The land's sharp features seemed to be
   The Century's corpse outleant,   10
His crypt the cloudy canopy,
   The wind his death-lament.
The ancient pulse of germ[4] and birth
   Was shrunken hard and dry,
And every spirit upon earth   15
   Seemed fervourless as I.

---

1. This poem was published December 31, 1900, the last day of the 19th c.
2. Wood.
3. Stems of bushes.
4. Seed.

At once a voice arose among
  The bleak twigs overhead
In a full-hearted evensong[5]
  Of joy illimited;   20
An aged thrush, frail, gaunt, and small,
  In blast-beruffled plume,
Had chosen thus to fling his soul
  Upon the growing gloom.

So little cause for carolings   25
  Of such ecstatic sound
Was written on terrestrial things
  Afar or nigh around,
That I could think there trembled through
  His happy good-night air   30
Some blessed Hope, whereof he knew
  And I was unaware.

—1900

The Music Halls

From the 1840s through the 1920s, British music halls were raucous, cheerful, drunken, vibrant resorts where raw wit and outrageous comedy flourished. Stars such as Dan Leno, Marie Lloyd, Albert Chevalier, and Vesta Victoria sung in outrageously exaggerated Cockney (London working-class) accents, cross-dressed, feigned drunken staggering, and winked and drawled their heavily salacious lyrics. The songs, recording and parodying working-class urban life, tended to focus on appetite—for food, money, drink, sex. Mrs. Ormiston Chant made a career of trying to clean up the music halls' lewdness, without much success. A classic music-hall song made famous by singer Gus Elen, "If it Wasn't for the 'Ouses in Between," is typical in its urban setting and dialect and its mockery of the subject's pretensions. It is interesting, however, in the way it acknowledges the Londoner's desire for pastoral bliss—creating a comic poignancy akin to Davidson's *Fleet Street Eclogues*.

If it Wasn't for the 'Ouses in Between[1]

If you saw my little backyard, "Wot a pretty spot!" you'd cry,
It's a picture on a sunny summer day;
Wiv the turnip tops and cabbages wot peoples doesn't buy
I makes it on a Sunday look all gay.

---

5. Prayer offered at evening.

---

1. Words by Edgar Bateman, music by George Le Brunn.

The neighbours finks I grow 'em and you'd fancy you're in Kent,[2]   5
Or at Epsom if you gaze into the mews.[3]
It's a wonder as the landlord doesn't want to raise the rent,
Because we've got such nobby distant views.

CHORUS:
Oh it really is a wery pretty garden
And Chingford to the eastward could be seen;   10
Wiv a ladder and some glasses,
You could see to 'Ackney Marshes,
If it wasn't for the 'ouses in between.

We're as countrified as can be wiv a clothes prop for a tree,
The tub-stool makes a rustic little stile;   15
Ev'ry time the bloomin' clock strikes there's a cuckoo sings to me,
And I've painted up "To Leather Lane[4] a mile."
Wiv tomatoes and wiv radishes wot 'adn't any sale,
The backyard looks a puffick mass o' bloom;
And I've made a little beehive wiv some beetles in a pail,   20
And a pitchfork wiv a handle of a broom.

CHORUS:
Oh it really is a wery pretty garden,
And Rye 'ouse[5] from the cock-loft could be seen:
Where the chickweed man undresses,
To bathe 'mong the watercresses,   25
If it wasn't for the 'ouses in between.

There's the bunny shares 'is egg box wiv the cross-eyed cock and hen
Though they 'as got the pip and him the morf;[6]
In a dog's 'ouse on the line-post there was pigeons nine or ten,
Till someone took a brick and knocked it orf.   30
The dustcart though it seldom comes, is just like 'arvest 'ome
And we mean to rig a dairy up some'ow;
Put the donkey in the washouse wiv some imitation 'orns,
For we're teaching 'im to moo just like a cah.

CHORUS:
Oh it really is a wery pretty garden,   35
And 'Endon to the Westward could be seen;
And by climbing to the chimbley,

---

2. Charming countryside south of London. Other prized rural sites are named in ensuing stanzas.
3. Site of horse race, south of London. Mews are alleys between stables.
4. Commercial district.
5. 15th-c. manor house north of London.
6. Animal diseases.

You could see a cross to Wembley,
If it wasn't for the 'ouses in between.

Though the gas works[7] isn't wilets, they improve the rural scene,   40
For mountains they would very nicely pass.
There's the mushrooms in the dust-hole with the cowcumbers so green,
It only wants a bit o' 'ot-'ouse glass.[8]
I wears this milkman's nightshirt, and I sits outside all day,
Like the ploughboy cove what's mizzled o'er the Lea;[9]   45
And when I goes indoors at night they dunno what I say,
'Cause my language gets as yokel[10] as can be.

CHORUS:
Oh it really is a wery pretty garden,
And soap works from the 'ouse tops could be seen;
If I got a rope and pulley,   50
I'd enjoy the breeze more fully,
If it wasn't for the 'ouses in between.

—1899

Mental Hopes:
Psychology, Parapsychology, Fantasy

William James
1842–1910

Victorian readers frequently remarked that Henry James wrote fiction as if it were psychology, while his elder brother William wrote psychology as if it were fiction. William James was one of the most important early psychologists and philosophers of the late nineteenth century. He went to Harvard Medical School in 1864, although his chronic bad health prevented him from completing his studies until 1869, followed by a three-year collapse. He became Professor of Philosophy at Harvard in 1885 and a pioneer of "pragmatism," testing an idea by its practical consequences and concrete applications. James's enormously popular *Principles of Psychology*

---

7. Factories or enormous canisters for storing natural gas.
8. Hothouse (greenhouse) panes.
9. Thomas Gray's "Elegy Written in a Country Churchyard" (1751): "The lowing herd wind slowly o'er the lea, / The ploughman homeward plods his weary way."
10. Rough and rural.

(1890) is still in print. What is remarkable about it is that James explores subjective mental states without recourse to biological or anatomical facts. In the following excerpt, James describes his famous theory of the "stream of consciousness," the idea that one's thoughts appear to flow onward regardless of actual breaks, a notion that shaped much of modernist literature. Although James was fascinated by the way thought worked, he was rather dubious about his brother's subtle depictions of shifting modes of consciousness, for, as this excerpt shows, his own style was far more direct, clear, and dashing.

from Principles of Psychology

3) *Within each personal consciousness, thought is sensibly continuous.*

I can only define "continuous" as that which is without breach, crack, or division. I have already said that the breach from one mind to another is perhaps the greatest breach in nature. The only breaches that can well be conceived to occur within the limits of a single mind would either be *interruptions, time-*gaps during which the consciousness went out altogether to come into existence again at a later moment; or they would be breaks in the *quality,* or content, of the thought, so abrupt that the segment that followed had no connection whatever with the one that went before. The proposition that within each personal consciousness thought feels continuous, means two things:

1. That even where there is a time-gap the consciousness after it feels as if it belonged together with the consciousness before it, as another part of the same self;

2. That the changes from one moment to another in the quality of the consciousness are never absolutely abrupt.

The case of the time-gaps, as the simplest, shall be taken first. And first of all a word about time-gaps of which the consciousness may not be itself aware.

On [James's] page 200 we saw that such time-gaps existed, and that they might be more numerous than is usually supposed. If the consciousness is not aware of them, it cannot feel them as interruptions. In the unconsciousness produced by nitrous oxide and other anæsthetics, in that of epilepsy and fainting, the broken edges of the sentient life may meet and merge over the gap, much as the feelings of space of the opposite margins of the "blind spot" meet and merge over that objective interruption to the sensitiveness of the eye. Such consciousness as this, whatever it be for the onlooking psychologist, is for itself unbroken. It *feels* unbroken; a waking day of it is sensibly a unit as long as that day lasts, in the sense in which the hours themselves are units, as having all their parts next each other, with no intrusive alien substance between. To expect the consciousness to feel the interruptions of its objective continuity as gaps, would be like expecting the eye to feel a gap of silence because it does not hear, or the ear to feel a gap of darkness because it does not see. So much for the gaps that are unfelt.

With the felt gaps the case is different. On waking from sleep, we usually know that we have been unconscious, and we often have an accurate judgment of how long. The judgment here is certainly an inference from sensible signs, and its ease is due to long practice in the particular field.[1] The result of it, however, is that the con-

---

1. The accurate registration of the "how long" is still a little mysterious [James's note].

sciousness is, *for itself*, not what it was in the former case, but interrupted and discontinuous, in the mere sense of the words. But in the other sense of continuity, the sense of the parts being inwardly connected and belonging together because they are parts of a common whole, the consciousness remains sensibly continuous and one. What now is the common whole? The natural name for it is *myself, I*, or *me*.

When Paul and Peter wake up in the same bed, and recognize that they have been asleep, each one of them mentally reaches back and makes connection with but *one* of the two streams of thought which were broken by the sleeping hours. As the current of an electrode buried in the ground unerringly finds its way to its own similarly buried mate, across no matter how much intervening earth; so Peter's present instantly finds out Peter's past, and never by mistake knits itself on to that of Paul. Paul's thought in turn is as little liable to go astray. The past thought of Peter is appropriated by the present Peter alone. He may have a *knowledge*, and a correct one too, of what Paul's last drowsy states of mind were as he sank into sleep, but it is an entirely different sort of knowledge from that which he has of his own last states. He *remembers* his own states, whilst he only *conceives* Paul's. Remembrance is like direct feeling; its object is suffused with a warmth and intimacy to which no object of mere conception ever attains. This quality of warmth and intimacy and immediacy is what Peter's *present* thought also possesses for itself. So sure as this present is me, is mine, it says, so sure is anything else that comes with the same warmth and intimacy and immediacy, me and mine. What the qualities called warmth and intimacy may in themselves be will have to be matter for future consideration. But whatever past feelings appear with those qualities must be admitted to receive the greeting of the present mental state, to be owned by it, and accepted as belonging together with it in a common self. This community of self is what the time-gap cannot break in twain, and is why a present thought, although not ignorant of the time-gap, can still regard itself as continuous with certain chosen portions of the past.

Consciousness, then, does not appear to itself chopped up in bits. Such words as "chain" or "train" do not describe it fitly as it presents itself in the first instance. It is nothing jointed; it flows. A "river" or a "stream" are the metaphors by which it is most naturally described. *In talking of it hereafter, let us call it the stream of thought, of consciousness, or of subjective life*.

But now there appears, even within the limits of the same self, and between thoughts all of which alike have this same sense of belonging together, a kind of jointing and separateness among the parts, of which this statement seems to take no account. I refer to the breaks that are produced by sudden *contrasts in the quality* of the successive segments of the stream of thought. If the words "chain" and "train" had no natural fitness in them, how came such words to be used at all? Does not a loud explosion rend the consciousness upon which it abruptly breaks, in twain? Does not every sudden shock, appearance of a new object, or change in a sensation, create a real interruption, sensibly felt as such, which cuts the conscious stream across at the moment at which it appears? Do not such interruptions smite us every hour of our lives, and have we the right, in their presence, still to call our consciousness a continuous stream?

This objection is based partly on a confusion and partly on a superficial introspective view.

The confusion is between the thoughts themselves, taken as subjective facts, and the things of which they are aware. It is natural to make this confusion, but easy to avoid it when once put on one's guard. The things are discrete and discontinuous; they do pass before us in a train or chain, making often explosive appearances and rending each other in twain. But their comings and goings and contrasts no more break the flow of the thought that thinks them than they break the time and the space in which they lie. A silence may be broken by a thunder-clap, and we may be so stunned and confused for a moment by the shock as to give no instant account to ourselves of what has happened. But that very confusion is a mental state, and a state that passes us straight over from the silence to the sound. The transition between the thought of one object and the thought of another is no more a break in the *thought* than a joint in a bamboo is a break in the wood. It is a part of the *consciousness* as much as the joint is a part of the *bamboo*.

The superficial introspective view is the overlooking, even when the things are contrasted with each other most violently, of the large amount of affinity that may still remain between the thoughts by whose means they are cognized. Into the awareness of the thunder itself the awareness of the previous silence creeps and continues; for what we hear when the thunder crashes is not thunder *pure*, but thunder-breaking-upon-silence-and-contrasting-with-it. Our feeling of the same objective thunder, coming in this way, is quite different from what it would be were the thunder a continuation of previous thunder. The thunder itself we believe to abolish and exclude the silence; but the *feeling* of the thunder is also a feeling of the silence as just gone; and it would be difficult to find in the actual concrete consciousness of man a feeling so limited to the present as not to have an inkling of anything that went before. Here, again, language works against our perception of the truth. We name our thoughts simply, each after its thing, as if each knew its own thing and nothing else. What each really knows is clearly the thing it is named for, with dimly perhaps a thousand other things. It ought to be named after all of them, but it never is. Some of them are always things known a moment ago more clearly; others are things to be known more clearly a moment hence.[2] Our own bodily position, attitude, condition, is one of the things of which *some* awareness, however inattentive, invariably accompanies the knowledge of whatever else we know. We think; and as we think we feel our bodily selves as the seat of the thinking. If the thinking be *our* thinking, it must be suffused through all its parts with that peculiar warmth and intimacy that make it come as ours. Whether the warmth and intimacy be anything more than the feeling of the same old body always there, is a matter for the next chapter to decide. *Whatever* the content of the ego may be, it is habitually felt *with* everything else by us humans, and must form a *liaison* between all the things of which we become successively aware. * * *

---

2. James credits this idea to Rev. Jas. Wills in 1846, citing Wills at length, including: "the most dim shade of perception enters into, and in some infinitesimal degree modifies, the whole existing state" and "our mental states have always an *essential unity*, such that each state of apprehension, however variously compounded, is a single whole, of which every component is, therefore, strictly apprehended (so far as it is apprehended) as a part" ("Accidental Association," *The Transactions of the Royal Irish Academy* XXI:I [1846]).

The rhythm of a lost word may be there without a sound to clothe it; or the evanescent sense of something which is the initial vowel or consonant may mock us fitfully, without growing more distinct. Every one must know the tantalizing effect of the blank rhythm of some forgotten verse, restlessly dancing in one's mind, striving to be filled out with words.

Again, what is the strange difference between an experience tasted for the first time and the same experience recognized as familiar, as having been enjoyed before, though we cannot name it or say where or when? A tune, an odor, a flavor sometimes carry this inarticulate feeling of their familiarity so deep into our consciousness that we are fairly shaken by its mysterious emotional power. But strong and characteristic as this psychosis is—it probably is due to the submaximal excitement of wide-spreading associational brain-tracts[3]—the only name we have for all its shadings is "sense of familiarity."

When we read such phrases as "naught but," "either one or the other," "*a* is *b*, but," "although it is, nevertheless," "it is an excluded middle, there is no *tertium quid*,"[4] and a host of other verbal skeletons of logical relation, is it true that there is nothing more in our minds than the words themselves as they pass? What then is the meaning of the words which we think we understand as we read? What makes that meaning different in one phrase from what it is in the other? "Who?" "When?" "Where?" Is the difference of felt meaning in these interrogatives nothing more than their difference of sound? And is it not (just like the difference of sound itself) known and understood in an affection of consciousness correlative to it, though so impalpable to direct examination? Is not the same true of such negatives as "no," "never," "not yet"?

The truth is that large tracts of human speech are nothing but *signs of direction* in thought, of which direction we nevertheless have an acutely discriminative sense, though no definite sensorial image plays any part in it whatsoever. Sensorial images are stable psychic facts; we can hold them still and look at them as long as we like. These bare images of logical movement, on the contrary, are psychic transitions, always on the wing, so to speak, and not to be glimpsed except in flight. Their function is to lead from one set of images to another. As they pass, we feel both the waxing and the waning images in a way altogether peculiar and a way quite different from the way of their full presence. If we try to hold fast the feeling of direction, the full presence comes and the feeling of direction is lost. The blank verbal scheme of the logical movement gives us the fleeting sense of the movement as we read it, quite as well as does a rational sentence awakening definite imaginations by its words.

What is that first instantaneous glimpse of some one's meaning which we have, when in vulgar phrase we say we "twig" it?[5] Surely an altogether specific affection of our mind. And has the reader never asked himself what kind of a mental fact is his *intention of saying a thing* before he has said it? It is an entirely definite intention, distinct from all other intentions, an absolutely distinct state of consciousness, therefore; and yet how much of it consists of definite sensorial images, either of words or of things? Hardly anything! Linger, and the words and things come into the mind; the

---

3. Here "psychosis" means thought process; James refers to his theory of brain stimulation.
4. Latin: intermediate thing.
5. Understand it.

anticipatory intention, the divination is there no more. But as the words that replace it arrive, it welcomes them successively and calls them right if they agree with it, it rejects them and calls them wrong if they do not. It has therefore a nature of its own of the most positive sort, and yet what can we say about it without using words that belong to the later mental facts that replace it? The intention *to-say-so-and-so* is the only name it can receive. One may admit that a good third of our psychic life consists in these rapid premonitory perspective views of schemes of thought not yet articulate. How comes it about that a man reading something aloud for the first time is able immediately to emphasize all his words aright, unlesss from the very first he have a sense of at least the form of the sentence yet to come, which sense is fused with his consciousness of the present word, and modifies its emphasis in his mind so as to make him give it the proper accent as he utters it? Emphasis of this kind is almost altogether a matter of grammatical construction. If we read "no more" we expect presently to come upon a "than"; if we read "however" at the outset of a sentence it is a "yet," a "still," or a "nevertheless," that we expect. A noun in a certain position demands a verb in a certain mood and number, in another position it expects a relative pronoun. Adjectives call for nouns, verbs for adverbs, etc., etc. And this foreboding of the coming grammatical scheme combined with each successive uttered word is so practically accurate that a reader incapable of understanding four ideas of the book he is reading aloud, can nevertheless read it with the most delicately modulated expression of intelligence.

Some will interpret these facts by calling them all cases in which certain images, by laws of association, awaken others so very rapidly that we think afterwards we felt the very *tendencies* of the nascent images to arise, before they were actually there. For this school the only possible materials of consciousness are images of a perfectly definite nature. Tendencies exist, but they are facts for the outside psychologist rather than for the subject of the observation. The tendency is thus a *psychical* zero; only its *results* are felt.

Now what I contend for, and accumulate examples to show, is that "tendencies" are not only descriptions from without, but that they are among the *objects* of the stream, which is thus aware of them from within, and must be described as in very large measure constituted of *feelings* of *tendency*, often so vague that we are unable to name them at all. It is, in short, the re-instatement of the vague to its proper place in our mental life which I am so anxious to press on the attention. Mr. Galton and Prof. Huxley[6] have, as we shall see in Chapter XVIII, made one step in advance in exploding the ridiculous theory of Hume and Berkeley[7] that we can have no images but of perfectly definite things. Another is made in the overthrow of the equally ridiculous notion that, whilst simple objective qualities are revealed to our knowledge in subjective feelings, relations are not. But these reforms are not half sweeping and radical enough. What must be admitted is that the definite images of traditional psychology form but the very smallest part of our minds as they actually live. The traditional psychology talks like one who should say a river consists of nothing but pailsful, spoonsful, quartpotsful, barrelsful, and other moulded forms of water. Even were the pails and the pots all actually standing in the stream, still between them the free water

---

6. Prominent 19th-c. thinker Thomas Henry Huxley. For Galton, see p. 300.
7. 18th-c. philosophers David Hume and Bishop George Berkeley.

would continue to flow. It is just this free water of consciousness that psychologists resolutely overlook. Every definite image in the mind is steeped and dyed in the free water that flows round it. With it goes the sense of its relations, near and remote, the dying echo of whence it came to us, the dawning sense of whither it is to lead. The significance, the value, of the image is all in this halo or penumbra that surrounds and escorts it,—or rather that is fused into one with it and has become bone of its bone and flesh of its flesh; leaving it, it is true, an image of the same *thing* it was before, but making it an image of that thing newly taken and freshly understood.

What is that shadowy scheme of the "form" of an opera, play, or book, which remains in our mind and on which we pass judgment when the actual thing is done? What is our notion of a scientific or philosophical system? Great thinkers have vast premonitory glimpses of schemes of relation between terms, which hardly even as verbal images enter the mind, so rapid is the whole process.[8] We all of us have this permanent consciousness of whither our thought is going. It is a feeling like any other, a feeling of what thoughts are next to arise, before they have arisen. This field of view of consciousness varies very much in extent, depending largely on the degree of mental freshness or fatigue. When very fresh, our minds carry an immense horizon with them. The present image shoots its perspective far before it, irradiating in advance the regions in which lie the thoughts as yet unborn. Under ordinary conditions the halo of felt relations is much more circumscribed. And in states of extreme brain-fag[9] the horizon is narrowed almost to the passing word,—the associative machinery, however, providing for the next word turning up in orderly sequence, until at last the tired thinker is led to some kind of a conclusion. At certain moments he may find himself doubting whether his thoughts have not come to a full stop; but the vague sense of a *plus ultra*[10] makes him ever struggle on towards a more definite expression of what it may be; whilst the slowness of his utterance shows how difficult, under such conditions, the labor of thinking must be.

The awareness that our *definite* thought has come to a stop is an entirely different thing from the awareness that our thought is definitively completed. The expression of the latter state of mind is the falling inflection which betokens that the sentence is ended, and silence. The expression of the former state is "hemming and hawing," or else such phrases as "*et cetera*," or "and so forth." But notice that every part of the sentence to be left incomplete feels differently as it passes, by reason of the premonition we have that we shall be unable to end it. The "and so forth" casts its shadow back, and is as integral a part of the object of the thought as the distinctest of images would be.

—1890

---

8. Mozart describes thus his manner of composing: First bits and crumbs of the piece come and gradually join together in his mind; then the soul getting warmed to the work, the thing grows more and more, "and I spread it out broader and clearer, and at last it gets almost finished in my head, even when it is a long piece, so that I can see the whole of it at a single glance in my mind, as if it were a beautiful painting or a handsome human being; in which way I do not hear it in my imagination at all as a succession—the way it must come later—but all at once, as it were. It is a rare feast! All the inventing and making goes on in me as in a beautiful strong dream. But the best of all is the *hearing of it all at once*" [James's note].
9. Mental exhaustion.
10. Latin: better.

Sigmund Freud
1856–1939

What would modernity be like without Sigmund Freud? Concepts he pioneered—repression, the unconscious, neurosis, Oedipal syndrome—have become the fundamental categories by which we understand our own mental states in the Western world, even as their validity continues to be debated. As W. H. Auden wrote in his poem "In Memory of Sigmund Freud," "to us he is no more a person / now but a whole climate of opinion / under which we conduct our different lives." Freud grew up in a Jewish middle-class family in Vienna and received extensive medical training. Treating "hysterical" (emotionally uncontrolled) patients, Freud gradually developed his famous theory that repressed material needs to emerge into consciousness. Although this material can manage to surface through dreams, jokes, slips, and neurotic symptoms, Freud's theory of "psychoanalysis" or the "talking cure" held that an analyst could guide a patient into articulating his or her suppressed feelings. In dozens of books, Freud refined his model of the mind and dissociated it from neurology. He developed theories of sexuality, including infantile sexuality, the erotics of family life, homosexuality and narcissism; explored the "pleasure principle" and its counteracting force, the "death drive"; and speculated about the unconscious drives in civilizations and religions. By the time he died in 1939, in London, fleeing the Nazis, he was regarded as the master.

"Hysterics suffer mainly from reminiscences," wrote Freud—but so do psychoanalysts, especially when they fear they've done it wrong. Freud remained perennially dissatisfied with the early case study "Fragment of an Analysis of a Case of Hysteria" (generally known as "Dora"). Written in 1901 and published in 1905 (translated into English in 1925), "Dora" demonstrates Freud's literary gifts: he is both a writer piecing together a plot (like many of his case studies, "Dora" is a fascinating story) and a reader detecting hidden information in texts. "Dora" is as problematic as it is famous. To modern feminist theorists, Freud became the latest in a series of predatory adult men surveying Dora sexually. Traumatized by her parents' tawdry sexual bargains, Dora's plight is worsened by the psychoanalyst who brutally asserts that she really wanted it all along. Is Dora's decision to withdraw from treatment after only three months, then, a sign that Freud was getting uncomfortably close to the truth—or a strong woman's protest against her analyst's betrayal?

from Fragment of an Analysis of a Case of Hysteria (Dora)

The family circle of the eighteen-year-old girl who is the subject of this paper[1] included, besides herself, her two parents and a brother who was one and a half years her senior. Her father was the dominating figure in this circle, owing to his intelligence and his character as much as to the circumstances of his life. It was those circumstances which provided the framework for the history of the patient's childhood and illness. At the time at which I began the girl's treatment her father was in his late forties, a man of rather unusual activity and talents, a large manufacturer in very comfortable circumstances. His daughter was most tenderly attached to him, and for that

---

1. Ida Bauer.

reason her critical powers, which developed early, took all the more offence at many of his actions and peculiarities.

Her affection for him was still further increased by the many severe illnesses which he had been through since her sixth year. At that time he had fallen ill with tuberculosis and the family had consequently moved to a small town in a good climate, situated in one of our southern provinces. There his lung trouble rapidly improved; but, on account of the precautions which were still considered necessary, both parents and children continued for the next ten years or so to reside chiefly in this spot, which I shall call B——. When her father's health was good, he used at times to be away, on visits to his factories. During the hottest part of the summer the family used to move to a health-resort in the hills.

When the girl was about ten years old, her father had to go through a course of treatment in a darkened room on account of a detached retina. As a result of this misfortune his vision was permanently impaired. His gravest illness occurred some two years later. It took the form of a confusional attack, followed by symptoms of paralysis and slight mental disturbances.[2] * * * It is no doubt owing to this fortunate intervention of mine that four years later he brought his daughter, who had meanwhile grown unmistakably neurotic, and introduced her to me, and that after another two years he handed her over to me for psychotherapeutic treatment. * * *

The sympathies of the girl herself, who, as I have said, became my patient at the age of eighteen, had always been with the father's side of the family, and ever since she had fallen ill she had taken as her model the aunt who has just been mentioned.[3] There could be no doubt, too, that it was from her father's family that she had derived not only her natural gifts and her intellectual precocity but also the predisposition to her illness. I never made her mother's acquaintance. From the accounts given me by the girl and her father I was led to imagine her as an uncultivated woman and above all as a foolish one, who had concentrated all her interests upon domestic affairs, especially since her husband's illness and the estrangement to which it led. She presented the picture, in fact, of what might be called the "housewife's psychosis". She had no understanding of her children's more active interests, and was occupied all day long in cleaning the house with its furniture and utensils and in keeping them clean—to such an extent as to make it almost impossible to use or enjoy them. This condition, traces of which are to be found often enough in normal housewives, inevitably reminds one of forms of obsessional washing and other kinds of obsessional cleanliness. But such women (and this applied to the patient's mother) are entirely without insight into their illness, so that one essential characteristic of an "obsessional neurosis" is lacking. The relations between the girl and her mother had been unfriendly for years. The daughter looked down on her mother and used to criticize her mercilessly, and she had withdrawn completely from her influence.

During the girl's earlier years, her only brother (her elder by a year and a half) had been the model which her ambitions had striven to follow. But in the last few years the relations between the brother and sister had grown more distant. The young man used to try so far as he could to keep out of the family disputes; but when he was

---

2. Freud diagnosed syphilis and treated it successfully.
3. In whom Freud diagnosed "a severe form of psychoneurosis."

obliged to take sides he would support his mother. So that the usual sexual attraction had drawn together the father and daughter on the one side and the mother and son on the other.

The patient, to whom I shall in future give the name of "Dora", had even at the age of eight begun to develop neurotic symptoms. She became subject at that time to chronic dyspnoea with occasional accesses[4] in which the symptom was very much aggravated. The first onset occurred after a short expedition in the mountains and was accordingly put down to over-exertion. In the course of six months, during which she was made to rest and was carefully looked after, this condition gradually passed off. The family doctor seems to have had not a moment's hesitation in diagnosing the disorder as purely nervous and in excluding any organic cause for the dyspnoea; but he evidently considered this diagnosis compatible with the aetiology[5] of over-exertion.

The little girl went through the usual infectious diseases of childhood without suffering any lasting damage. As she herself told me—and her words were intended to convey a deeper meaning—her brother was as a rule the first to start the illness and used to have it very slightly, and she would then follow suit with a severe form of it. When she was about twelve she began to suffer from unilateral headaches in the nature of a migraine, and from attacks of nervous coughing. At first these two symptoms always appeared together, but they became separated later on and ran different courses. The migraine grew rarer, and by the time she was sixteen she had quite got over it. But attacks of *tussis nervosa*,[6] which had no doubt been started by a common catarrh,[7] continued to occur over the whole period. When, at the age of eighteen, she came to me for treatment, she was again coughing in a characteristic manner. The number of these attacks could not be determined; but they lasted from three to five weeks, and on one occasion for several months. The most troublesome symptom during the first half of an attack of this kind, at all events in the last few years, used to be a complete loss of voice. The diagnosis that this was once more a nervous complaint had been established long since; but the various methods of treatment which are usual, including hydrotherapy[8] and the local application of electricity, had produced no result. It was in such circumstances as these that the child had developed into a mature young woman of very independent judgement, who had grown accustomed to laugh at the efforts of doctors, and in the end to renounce their help entirely. Moreover, she had always been against calling in medical advice, though she had no personal objection to her family doctor. Every proposal to consult a new physician aroused her resistance, and it was only her father's authority which induced her to come to me at all.

I first saw her when she was sixteen, in the early summer. She was suffering from a cough and from hoarseness, and even at that time I proposed giving her psychological treatment. My proposal was not adopted, since the attack in question, like the others, passed off spontaneously, though it had lasted unusually long. During the next winter she came and stayed in Vienna with her uncle and his daughters after the

---

4. Difficulty breathing, with occasional fits.
5. Diagnosis.
6. Psychosomatic coughing.
7. A cold.
8. Water treatment.

death of the aunt of whom she had been so fond. There she fell ill of a feverish disorder which was diagnosed at the time as appendicitis. In the following autumn, since
her father's health seemed to justify the step, the family left the health-resort of
B—— for good and all. They first moved to the town where her father's factory was
situated, and then, scarcely a year later, settled permanently in Vienna.

Dora was by that time in the first bloom of youth—a girl of intelligent and engaging looks. But she was a source of heavy trials for her parents. Low spirits and an alteration in her character had now become the main features of her illness. She was
clearly satisfied neither with herself nor with her family; her attitude towards her
father was unfriendly, and she was on very bad terms with her mother, who was bent
upon drawing her into taking a share in the work of the house. She tried to avoid
social intercourse, and employed herself—so far as she was allowed to by the fatigue
and lack of concentration of which she complained—with attending lectures for
women and with carrying on more or less serious studies. One day her parents were
thrown into a state of great alarm by finding on the girl's writing-desk, or inside it, a
letter in which she took leave of them because, as she said, she could no longer
endure her life.[9] Her father, indeed, being a man of some perspicacity, guessed that
the girl had no serious suicidal intentions. But he was none the less very much
shaken; and when one day, after a slight passage of words between him and his daughter, she had a first attack of loss of consciousness—an event which was subsequently
covered by an amnesia—it was determined, in spite of her reluctance, that she should
come to me for treatment.

No doubt this case history, as I have so far outlined it, does not upon the whole
seem worth recording. It is merely a case of "*petite hystérie*"[10] with the commonest of
all somatic and mental symptoms: dyspnoea, *tussis nervosa*, aphonia, and possibly
migraines, together with depression, hysterical unsociability, and a *taedium vitae*[11]
which was probably not entirely genuine. More interesting cases of hysteria have no
doubt been published, and they have very often been more carefully described; for
nothing will be found in the following pages on the subject of stigmata of cutaneous
sensibility,[12] limitation of the visual field, or similar matters. I may venture to remark,
however, that all such collections of the strange and wonderful phenomena of hysteria have but slightly advanced our knowledge of a disease which still remains as great
a puzzle as ever. What is wanted is precisely an elucidation of the *commonest* cases and
of their most frequent and typical symptoms. I should have been very well satisfied if
the circumstances had allowed me to give a complete elucidation of this case of *petite
hystérie*. And my experiences with other patients leave me in no doubt that my ana-
lytic method would have enabled me to do so.

---

9. As I have already explained, the treatment of the case, and consequently my insight into the complex of events
composing it, remained fragmentary. There are therefore many questions to which I have no solution to offer, or
in which I can only rely upon hints and conjectures. This affair of the letter came up in the course of one of our
sessions and the girl showed signs of astonishment. "How on earth," she asked, "did they find the letter? It was
shut up in my desk." But since she knew that her parents had read this draft of a farewell letter, I conclude that
she had herself arranged for it to fall into their hands [Freud's note].

10. French: minor hysteria.

11. Aphonia is loss of the voice; *taedium vitae* means weariness of life.

12. Wounds testifying to skin sensitivity.

In 1896, shortly after the appearance of my *Studies on Hysteria* (written in conjunction with Dr. J. Breuer,[13] 1895), I asked an eminent fellow-specialist for his opinion on the psychological theory of hysteria put forward in that work. He bluntly replied that he considered it an unjustifiable generalization of conclusions which might hold good for a few cases. Since then I have seen an abundance of cases of hysteria, and I have been occupied with each case for a number of days, weeks, or years. In not a single one of them have I failed to discover the psychological determinants which were postulated in the *Studies*, namely, a psychical trauma, a conflict of affects,[14] and—an additional factor which I brought forward in later publications—a disturbance in the sphere of sexuality. It is of course not to be expected that the patient will come to meet the physician half-way with material which has become pathogenic for the very reason of its efforts to lie concealed; nor must the enquirer rest content with the first "No" that crosses his path.[15]

In Dora's case, thanks to her father's shrewdness which I have remarked upon more than once already, there was no need for me to look about for the points of contact between the circumstances of the patient's life and her illness, at all events in its most recent form. Her father told me that he and his family while they were at B—— had formed an intimate friendship with a married couple who had been settled there for several years. Frau K. had nursed him during his long illness, and had in that way, he said, earned a title to his undying gratitude. Herr K. had always been most kind to Dora. He had gone walks with her when he was there, and had made her small presents; but no one had thought any harm of that. Dora had taken the greatest care of the K.'s two little children, and been almost a mother to them. When Dora and her father had come to see me two years before in the summer, they had been just on their way to stop with Herr and Frau K., who were spending the summer on one of our lakes in the Alps. Dora was to have spent several weeks at the K.'s, while her father had intended to return home after a few days. During that time Herr K. had been staying there as well. As her father was preparing for his departure the girl had suddenly declared with the greatest determination that she was going with him, and she had in fact put her decision into effect. It was not until some days later that she had thrown any light upon her strange behaviour. She had then told her mother—intending that what she said should be passed on to her father—that Herr K. had had the audacity to make her a proposal[16] while they were on a walk after a trip upon the lake. Herr K. had been called to account by her father and uncle on the next occasion of their meeting, but he had denied in the most emphatic terms having on his side made any advances which could have been open to such a construction. He had then proceeded to throw suspicion upon the girl, saying that he had

---

13. Another Viennese Jew, Josef Breuer (1842–1925) was the first to treat a "hysteric" with hypnosis to recall buried memories. Breuer co-researched hysteria with Freud but broke with him in 1896.
14. Feelings.
15. In a lengthy footnote Freud cites a case treated by "another physician in Vienna." A 14-year-old girl "suffered from dangerous hysterical vomiting" but indignantly denied it when her physician asked if she had ever had a love affair with a man. When Freud took over the case he diagnosed the hysteria as the eruption of guilt over masturbation and her knowledge of an aunt's secret pregnancy. "The girl was looked upon as a 'mere child,'" writes Freud, "but she turned out to be initiated into all the essentials of sexual relations."
16. A sexual proposition.

heard from Frau K. that she took no interest in anything but sexual matters, and that she used to read Mantegazza's *Physiology of Love*[17] and books of that sort in their house on the lake. It was most likely, he had added, that she had been over-excited by such reading and had merely "fancied" the whole scene she had described.

"I have no doubt", continued her father, "that this incident is responsible for Dora's depression and irritability and suicidal ideas. She keeps pressing me to break off relations with Herr K. and more particularly with Frau K., whom she used positively to worship formerly. But that I cannot do. For, to begin with, I myself believe that Dora's tale of the man's immoral suggestions is a phantasy that has forced its way into her mind; and besides, I am bound to Frau K. by ties of honourable friendship and I do not wish to cause her pain. The poor woman is most unhappy with her husband, of whom, by the by, I have no very high opinion. She herself has suffered a great deal with her nerves, and I am her only support. With my state of health I need scarcely assure you that there is nothing wrong in our relations. We are just two poor wretches who give one another what comfort we can by an exchange of friendly sympathy. You know already that I get nothing out of my own wife. But Dora, who inherits my obstinacy, cannot be moved from her hatred of the K.'s. She had her last attack after a conversation in which she had again pressed me to break with them. Please try and bring her to reason."

Her father's words did not always quite tally with this pronouncement; for on other occasions he tried to put the chief blame for Dora's impossible behaviour on her mother—whose peculiarities made the house unbearable for every one. But I had resolved from the first to suspend my judgement of the true state of affairs till I had heard the other side as well.

The experience with Herr K.—his making love to her and the insult to her honour which was involved—seems to provide in Dora's case the psychical trauma which Breuer and I declared long ago to be the indispensable prerequisite for the production of a hysterical disorder. But this new case also presents all the difficulties which have since led me to go beyond that theory,[18] besides an additional difficulty of a special kind. For, as so often happens in histories of cases of hysteria, the trauma that we know of as having occurred in the patient's past life is insufficient to explain or to determine the *particular character* of the symptoms; we should understand just as much or just as little of the whole business if the result of the trauma had been symptoms quite other than *tussis nervosa*, aphonia, depression, and *taedium vitae*. But there is the further consideration that some of these symptoms (the cough and the loss of voice) had been produced by the patient years before the time of the trauma, and that their earliest appearances belong to her childhood, since they occurred in her eighth year. If, therefore, the trauma theory is not to be abandoned, we must go back to her childhood and look about there for any influences or impressions which might have had an effect analogous to that of a trauma. Moreover, it deserves to be remarked that in the inves-

---

17. By Italian sexologist Paolo Mantegazza, in the early 1870s.
18. I have gone beyond that theory, but I have not abandoned it; that is to say, I do not to-day consider the theory incorrect, but incomplete. All that I have abandoned is the emphasis laid upon the so-called "hypnoid state," which was supposed to be occasioned in the patient by the trauma, and to be the foundation for all the psychologically abnormal events which followed ∗ ∗ ∗ [Freud's note].

tigation even of cases in which the first symptoms had not already set in in childhood I have been driven to trace back the patients' life history to their earliest years.

When the first difficulties of the treatment had been overcome, Dora told me of an earlier episode with Herr K., which was even better calculated to act as a sexual trauma. She was fourteen years old at the time. Herr K. had made an arrangement with her and his wife that they should meet him one afternoon at his place of business in the principal square of B—— so as to have a view of a church festival. He persuaded his wife, however, to stay at home, and sent away his clerks, so that he was alone when the girl arrived. When the time for the procession approached, he asked the girl to wait for him at the door which opened on to the staircase leading to the upper story, while he pulled down the outside shutters. He then came back, and, instead of going out by the open door, suddenly clasped the girl to him and pressed a kiss upon her lips. This was surely just the situation to call up a distinct feeling of sexual excitement in a girl of fourteen who had never before been approached. But Dora had at that moment a violent feeling of disgust, tore herself free from the man, and hurried past him to the staircase and from there to the street door. She nevertheless continued to meet Herr K. Neither of them ever mentioned the little scene; and according to her account Dora kept it a secret till her confession during the treatment. For some time afterwards, however, she avoided being alone with Herr K. The K.'s had just made plans for an expedition which was to last for some days and on which Dora was to have accompanied them. After the scene of the kiss she refused to join the party, without giving any reason.

In this scene—second in order of mention, but first in order of time—the behaviour of this child of fourteen was already entirely and completely hysterical. I should without question consider a person hysterical in whom an occasion for sexual excitement elicited feelings that were preponderantly or exclusively unpleasurable; and I should do so whether or no the person were capable of producing somatic symptoms. The elucidation of the mechanism of this *reversal of affect* is one of the most important and at the same time one of the most difficult problems in the psychology of the neuroses. In my own judgement I am still some way from having achieved this end; and I may add that within the limits of the present paper I shall be able to bring forward only a part of such knowledge on the subject as I do possess.

In order to particularize Dora's case it is not enough merely to draw attention to the reversal of affect; there has also been a *displacement* of sensation. Instead of the genital sensation which would certainly have been felt by a healthy girl in such circumstances, Dora was overcome by the unpleasurable feeling which is proper to the tract of mucous membrane at the entrance to the alimentary canal—that is by disgust. The stimulation of her lips by the kiss was no doubt of importance in localizing the feeling at that particular place; but I think I can also recognize another factor in operation.[19]

The disgust which Dora felt on that occasion did not become a permanent symptom, and even at the time of the treatment it was only, as it were, potentially present. She was a poor eater and confessed to some disinclination for food. On the other

---

19. The causes of Dora's disgust at the kiss were certainly not adventitious, for in that case she could not have failed to remember and mention them. I happen to know Herr K., for he was the same person who had visited me with the patient's father, and he was still quite young and of prepossessing appearance [Freud's note].

hand, the scene had left another consequence behind it in the shape of a sensory hallucination which occurred from time to time and even made its appearance while she was telling me her story. She declared that she could still feel upon the upper part of her body the pressure of Herr K.'s embrace. In accordance with certain rules of symptom-formation which I have come to know, and at the same time taking into account certain other of the patient's peculiarities, which were otherwise inexplicable,—such as her unwillingness to walk past any man whom she saw engaged in eager or affectionate conversation with a lady,—I have formed in my own mind the following reconstruction of the scene. I believe that during the man's passionate embrace she felt not merely his kiss upon her lips but also the pressure of his erect member against her body. This perception was revolting to her; it was dismissed from her memory, repressed, and replaced by the innocent sensation of pressure upon her thorax, which in turn derived an excessive intensity from its repressed source. Once more, therefore, we find a displacement from the lower part of the body to the upper.[20] On the other hand, the compulsive piece of behaviour which I have mentioned was formed as though it were derived from the undistorted recollection of the scene: she did not like walking past any man who she thought was in a state of sexual excitement, because she wanted to avoid seeing for a second time the somatic sign which accompanies it.

It is worth remarking that we have here three symptoms—the disgust, the sensation of pressure on the upper part of the body, and the avoidance of men engaged in affectionate conversation—all of them derived from a single experience, and that it is only by taking into account the interrelation of these three phenomena that we can understand the way in which the formation of the symptoms came about. The disgust is the symptom of repression in the erotogenic oral zone,[21] which, as we shall hear, had been over-indulged in Dora's infancy by the habit of sensual sucking. The pressure of the erect member probably led to an analogous change in the corresponding female organ, the clitoris; and the excitation of this second erotogenic zone was referred by a process of displacement to the simultaneous pressure against the thorax and became fixed there. Her avoidance of men who might possibly be in a state of sexual excitement follows the mechanism of a phobia, its purpose being to safeguard her against any revival of the repressed perception.

In order to show that such a supplement to the story was possible, I questioned the patient very cautiously as to whether she knew anything of the physical signs of excitement in a man's body. Her answer, as touching the present, was "Yes", but, as touching the time of the episode, "I think not". From the very beginning I took the greatest pains with this patient not to introduce her to any fresh facts in the region of sexual knowledge; and I did this, not from any conscientious motives, but because I was anxious to subject my assumptions to a rigorous test in this case. Accordingly, I did not call a thing by its name until her allusions to it had become so unambiguous that there seemed very slight risk in translating them into direct speech. Her answer was always prompt and frank: she knew about it already. But the question of *where* her

---

20. The occurrence of displacements of this kind has not been assumed for the purpose of this single explanation; the assumption has proved indispensable for the explanation of a large class of symptoms. Since treating Dora I have come across another instance of an embrace (this time without a kiss) causing a fright. [* * *] There was no difficulty in tracing the fright back to an erection on the man's part, which she had perceived but had dismissed from her consciousness [Freud's note].

21. The erotic feelings associated with the mouth area.

knowledge came from was a riddle which her memories were unable to solve. She had forgotten the source of all her information on this subject.

If I may suppose that the scene of the kiss took place in this way, I can arrive at the following derivation for the feelings of disgust.[22] Such feelings seem originally to be a reaction to the smell (and afterwards also to the sight) of excrement. But the genitals can act as a reminder of the excretory functions; and this applies especially to the male member, for that organ performs the function of micturition[23] as well as the sexual function. Indeed, the function of micturition is the earlier known of the two, and the *only* one known during the pre-sexual period. Thus it happens that disgust becomes one of the means of affective expression in the sphere of sexual life. The Early Christian Father's "*inter urinas et faeces nascimur*"[24] clings to sexual life and cannot be detached from it in spite of every effort at idealization. I should like, however, expressly to emphasize my opinion that the problem is not solved by the mere pointing out of this path of association. The fact that this association *can* be called up does not show that it actually *will* be called up. And indeed in normal circumstances it will not be. A knowledge of the paths does not render less necessary a knowledge of the forces which travel along them.[25]

I did not find it easy, however, to direct the patient's attention to her relations with Herr K. She declared that she had done with him. The uppermost layer of all her associations during the sessions, and everything of which she was easily conscious and of which she remembered having been conscious the day before, was always connected with her father. It was quite true that she could not forgive her father for continuing his relations with Herr K. and more particularly with Frau K. But she viewed those relations in a very different light from that in which her father wished them to appear. In her mind there was no doubt that what bound her father to this young and beautiful woman was a common love-affair. Nothing that could help to confirm this view had escaped her perception, which in this connection was pitilessly sharp; *here there were no gaps to be found in her memory.* Their acquaintance with the K.'s had begun before her father's serious illness; but it had not become intimate until the young woman had officially taken on the position of nurse during that illness, while Dora's mother had kept away from the sick-room. During the first summer holidays after his recovery things had happened which must have opened every one's eyes to the true character of this "friendship". The two families had taken a suite of rooms in common at the hotel. One day Frau K. had announced that she could not keep the bedroom which she had up till then shared with one of her children. A few days later Dora's father had given up his bedroom, and they had both moved into new rooms— the end rooms, which were only separated by the passage, while the rooms they had

---

22. Here, as in all similar cases, the reader must be prepared to be met not by one but by several causes—by *overdetermination* [Freud's note].

23. Urination.

24. Latin: We are born between urine and feces.

25. All these discussions contain much that is typical and valid for hysteria in general. The subject of erection solves some of the most interesting hysterical symptoms. The attention that women pay to the outlines of men's genitals as seen through their clothing becomes, when it has been repressed, a source of the very frequent cases of avoiding company and of dreading society.—It is scarcely possible to exaggerate the pathogenic significance of the comprehensive tie uniting the sexual and the excremental, a tie which is at the basis of a very large number of hysterical phobias [Freud's note].

given up had not offered any such security against interruption. Later on, whenever she had reproached her father about Frau K., he had been in the habit of saying that he could not understand her hostility and that, on the contrary, his children had every reason for being grateful to Frau K. Her mother, whom she had asked for an explanation of this mysterious remark, had told her that her father had been so unhappy at that time that he had made up his mind to go into the wood and kill himself, and that Frau K., suspecting as much, had gone after him and had persuaded him by her entreaties to preserve his life for the sake of his family. Of course, Dora went on, she herself did not believe this story; no doubt the two of them had been seen together in the wood, and her father had thereupon invented this fairy tale of his suicide so as to account for their rendezvous.[26]

When they had returned to B——, her father had visited Frau K. every day at definite hours, while her husband was at his business. Everybody had talked about it and had questioned her about it pointedly. Herr K. himself had often complained bitterly to her mother, though he had spared her herself any allusions to the subject— which she seemed to attribute to delicacy of feeling on his part. When they had all gone for walks together, her father and Frau K. had always known how to manage things so as to be alone with each other. There could be no doubt that she had taken money from him, for she spent more than she could possibly have afforded out of her own purse or her husband's. Dora added that her father had begun to make handsome presents to Frau K., and in order to make these less conspicuous had at the same time become especially liberal towards her mother and herself. And, while previously Frau K. had been an invalid and had even been obliged to spend months in a sanatorium for nervous disorders because she had been unable to walk, she had now become a healthy and lively woman.

Even after they had left B—— for the manufacturing town, these relations, already of many years' standing, had been continued. From time to time her father used to declare that he could not endure the rawness of the climate, and that he must do something for himself; he would begin to cough and complain, until suddenly he would start off to B——, and from there write the most cheerful letters home. All these illnesses had only been pretexts for seeing his friend again. Then one day it had been decided that they were to move to Vienna and Dora began to suspect a hidden connection. And sure enough, they had scarcely been three weeks in Vienna when she heard that the K.'s had moved there as well. They were in Vienna, so she told me, at that very moment, and she frequently met her father with Frau K. in the street. She also met Herr K. very often, and he always used to turn round and look after her; and once when he had met her out by herself he had followed her for a long way, so as to make sure where she was going and whether she might not have a rendezvous.

On one occasion during the course of the treatment her father again felt worse, and went off to B—— for several weeks; and the sharp-sighted Dora had soon unearthed the fact that Frau K. had started off to the same place on a visit to her relatives there. It was at this time that Dora's criticisms of her father were the most frequent: he was insincere, he had a strain of falseness in his character, he only thought of his own enjoyment, and he had a gift for seeing things in the light which suited him best.

---

26. This is the point of connection with her own pretence at suicide, which may thus be regarded as the expression of a longing for a love of the same kind [Freud's note].

I could not in general dispute Dora's characterization of her father; and there was one particular respect in which it was easy to see that her reproaches were justified. When she was feeling embittered she used to be overcome by the idea that she had been handed over to Herr K. as the price of his tolerating the relations between her father and his wife; and her rage at her father's making such a use of her was visible behind her affection for him. At other times she was quite well aware that she had been guilty of exaggeration in talking like this. The two men had of course never made a formal agreement in which she was treated as an object for barter; her father in particular would have been horrified at any such suggestion. But he was one of those men who know how to evade a dilemma by falsifying their judgement upon one of the conflicting alternatives. If it had been pointed out to him that there might be danger for a growing girl in the constant and unsupervised companionship of a man who had no satisfaction from his own wife, he would have been certain to answer that he could rely upon his daughter, that a man like K. could never be dangerous to her, and that his friend was himself incapable of such intentions, or that Dora was still a child and was treated as a child by K. But as a matter of fact things were in a position in which each of the two men avoided drawing any conclusions from the other's behaviour which would have been awkward for his own plans. It was possible for Herr K. to send Dora flowers every day for a whole year while he was in the neighbourhood, to take every opportunity of giving her valuable presents, and to spend all his spare time in her company, without her parents noticing anything in his behaviour that was characteristic of love-making.[27] * * *

What the governess[28] had from time to time been to Dora, Dora had been to Herr K.'s children. She had been a mother to them, she had taught them, she had gone for walks with them, she had offered them a complete substitute for the slight interest which their own mother showed in them. Herr K. and his wife had often talked of getting a divorce; but it never took place, because Herr K., who was an affectionate father, would not give up either of the two children. A common interest in the children had from the first been a bond between Herr K. and Dora. Her preoccupation with his children was evidently a cloak for something else that Dora was anxious to hide from herself and from other people.

The same inference was to be drawn both from her behaviour towards the children, regarded in the light of the governess's behaviour towards herself, and from her silent acquiescence in her father's relations with Frau K.—namely, that she had all these years been in love with Herr K. When I informed her of this conclusion she did not assent to it. It is true that she at once told me that other people besides (one of her cousins, for instance—a girl who had stopped with them for some time at B——) had said to her: "Why you're simply wild about that man!" But she herself could not be got to recollect any feelings of the kind. Later on, when the quantity of material that had come up had made it difficult for her to persist in her denial, she admitted that she might have been in love with Herr K. at B——, but she declared that since the scene by the lake it had all been over. In any case it was

---

27. Wooing.

28. This "unmarried woman, no longer young, who was well-read and of advanced views" befriended Dora, told her about her father's affair with Frau K., and discussed "every sort of book on sexual life" with her. Dora soon realized that the governess's "pretended affection for her was really meant for her father."

quite certain that the reproaches which she made against her father of having been deaf to the most imperative calls of duty and of having seen things in the light which was most convenient from the point of view of his own passions—these reproaches recoiled on her own head.[29]

Her other reproach against her father was that his ill-health was only a pretext and that he exploited it for his own purposes. This reproach, too, concealed a whole section of her own secret history. One day she complained of a professedly new symptom, which consisted of piercing gastric pains. "Whom are you copying now?" I asked her, and found I had hit the mark. The day before she had visited her cousins, the daughters of the aunt who had died. The younger one had become engaged, and this had given occasion to the elder one for falling ill with gastric pains, and she was to be sent off to Semmering.[30] Dora thought it was all just envy on the part of the elder sister; she always got ill when she wanted something, and what she wanted now was to be away from home so as not to have to look on at her sister's happiness.[31] But Dora's own gastric pains proclaimed the fact that she identified herself with her cousin, who, according to her, was a malingerer. Her grounds for this identification were either that she too envied the luckier girl her love, or that she saw her own story reflected in that of the elder sister, who had recently had a love-affair which had ended unhappily. But she had also learned from observing Frau K. what useful things illnesses could become. Herr K. spent part of the year in travelling. Whenever he came back, he used to find his wife in bad health, although, as Dora knew, she had been quite well only the day before. Dora realized that the presence of the husband had the effect of making his wife ill, and that she was glad to be ill so as to be able to escape the conjugal duties which she so much detested. At this point in the discussion Dora suddenly brought in an allusion to her own alternations between good and bad health during the first years of her girlhood at B——; and I was thus driven to suspect that her states of health were to be regarded as depending upon something else, in the same way as Frau K.'s. (It is a rule of psycho-analytic technique that an internal connection which is still undisclosed will announce its presence by means of a contiguity—a temporal proximity—of associations; just as in writing, if "a" and "b" are put side by side, it means that the syllable "ab" is to be formed out of them.) Dora had had a very large number of attacks of coughing accompanied by loss of voice. Could it be that the presence or absence of the man she loved had had an influence upon the appearance and disappearance of the symptoms of her illness? If this were so, it must be possible to discover some coincidence or other which would betray the fact. I asked her what the average length of these attacks had been. "From three to six weeks, perhaps." How long had Herr K.'s absences lasted? "Three to six weeks, too", she was obliged to admit. Her illness was therefore a demonstration of her love for K., just as his wife's was a demonstration of her *dislike*. It was only necessary to suppose that her behaviour had been the opposite of Frau K.'s and that she had been ill when he was absent and well when he had come back. And this really seemed to have

---

29. The question then arises: If Dora loved Herr K., what was the reason for her refusing him in the scene by the lake? Or at any rate, why did her refusal take such a brutal form, as though she were embittered against him? And how could a girl who was in love feel insulted by a proposal which was made in a manner neither tactless nor offensive? [Freud's note].

30. A health resort fifty miles south of Vienna.

31. An event of everyday occurrence between sisters [Freud's note].

been so, at least during the first period of the attacks. Later on it no doubt became necessary to obscure the coincidence between her attacks of illness and the absence of the man she secretly loved, lest its regularity should betray her secret. The length of the attacks would then remain as a trace of their original significance.

I remembered that long before, while I was working at Charcot's clinic,[32] I had seen and heard how in cases of hysterical mutism[33] writing operated vicariously in the place of speech. Such patients were able to write more fluently, quicker, and better than others did or than they themselves had done previously. The same thing had happened with Dora. In the first days of her attacks of aphonia "writing had always come specially easy to her". No psychological elucidation was really required for this peculiarity, which was the expression of a physiological substitutive function enforced by necessity; it was noticeable, however, that such an elucidation was easily to be found. Herr K. used to write to her at length while he was travelling and to send her picture post-cards. It used to happen that she alone was informed as to the date of his return, and that his arrival took his wife by surprise. Moreover, that a person will correspond with an absent friend whom he cannot talk to is scarcely less obvious than that if he has lost his voice he will try to make himself understood in writing. Dora's aphonia, then, allowed of the following symbolic interpretation. When the man she loved was away she gave up speaking; speech had lost its value since she could not speak to *him*. On the other hand, writing gained in importance, as being the only means of communication with him in his absence. * * *

I now return to the reproach of malingering which Dora brought against her father. It soon became evident that this reproach corresponded to self-reproaches not only concerning her earlier states of ill-health but also concerning the present time. At such points the physician is usually faced by the task of guessing and filling in what the analysis offers him in the shape only of hints and allusions. I was obliged to point out to the patient that her present ill-health was just as much actuated by motives and was just as tendentious as had been Frau K.'s illness, which she had understood so well. There could be no doubt, I said, that she had an aim in view which she hoped to gain by her illness. That aim could be none other than to detach her father from Frau K. She had been unable to achieve this by prayers or arguments; perhaps she hoped to succeed by frightening her father (there was her farewell letter), or by awakening his pity (there were her fainting-fits), or if all this was in vain, at least she would be taking her revenge on him. She knew very well, I went on, how much he was attached to her, and that tears used to come into his eyes whenever he was asked after his daughter's health. I felt quite convinced that she would recover at once if only her father were to tell her that he had sacrificed Frau K. for the sake of her health. But, I added, I hoped he would not let himself be persuaded to do this, for then she would have learned what a powerful weapon she had in her hands, and she would certainly not fail on every future occasion to make use once more of her liability to ill-health. Yet if her father refused to give way to her, I was quite sure she would not let herself be deprived of her illness so easily. * * *

---

32. Freud studied with leading French neurologist and hysteria expert Jean Martin Charcot in 1885–86.
33. Inability to speak.

None of her father's actions seemed to have embittered her so much as his readiness to consider the scene by the lake as a product of her imagination. She was almost beside herself at the idea of its being supposed that she had merely fancied something on that occasion. For a long time I was in perplexity as to what the self-reproach could be which lay behind her passionate repudiation of this explanation of the episode. It was justifiable to suspect that there was something concealed, for a reproach which misses the mark gives no lasting offence. On the other hand, I came to the conclusion that Dora's story must correspond to the facts in every respect. No sooner had she grasped Herr K.'s intention than, without letting him finish what he had to say, she had given him a slap in the face and hurried away. Her behaviour must have seemed as incomprehensible to the man after she had left him as to us, for he must long before have gathered from innumerable small signs that he was secure of the girl's affections. In our discussion of Dora's second dream we shall come upon the solution of this riddle as well as upon the self-reproach which we have hitherto failed to discover.[34]

As she kept on repeating her complaints against her father with a wearisome monotony, and as at the same time her cough continued, I was led to think that this symptom might have some meaning in connection with her father. And apart from this, the explanation of the symptom which I had hitherto obtained was far from fulfilling the requirements which I am accustomed to make of such explanations. According to a rule which I had found confirmed over and over again by experience, though I had not yet ventured to erect it into a general principle, a symptom signifies the representation—the realization—of a phantasy with a sexual content, that is to say, it signifies a sexual situation. It would be better to say that at least *one* of the meanings of a symptom is the representation of a sexual phantasy, but that no such limitation is imposed upon the content of its other meanings. Any one who takes up psycho-analytic work will quickly discover that a symptom has more than one meaning and serves to represent several unconscious mental processes simultaneously. And I should like to add that in my estimation a single unconscious mental process or phantasy will scarcely ever suffice for the production of a symptom.

An opportunity very soon occurred for interpreting Dora's nervous cough in this way by means of an imagined sexual situation. She had once again been insisting that Frau K. only loved her father because he was "*ein vermögender Mann*".[35] Certain details of the way in which she expressed herself (which I pass over here, like most other purely technical parts of the analysis) led me to see that behind this phrase its opposite lay concealed, namely, that her father was "*ein unvermögender Mann*".[36] This could only be meant in a sexual sense—that her father, as a man, was without means, was impotent. Dora confirmed this interpretation from her conscious knowledge; whereupon I pointed out the contradiction she was involved in if on the one hand she continued to insist that her father's relation with Frau K. was a common love-affair, and on the other hand maintained that her father was impotent, or in other words incapable of carrying on an affair of such a kind. Her answer showed that she had no need to admit the contradiction. She knew very

---

34. Freud interpreted Dora's dream of a jewel-case as proof of her secret desire for Herr K.
35. German: a man of means (wealth).
36. German: a man without means. "Unvermögend" (unable) means both not rich and impotent.

well, she said, that there was more than one way of obtaining sexual gratification. (The source of this piece of knowledge, however, was once more untraceable.) I questioned her further, whether she referred to the use of organs other than the genitals for the purpose of sexual intercourse, and she replied in the affirmative. I could then go on to say that in that case she must be thinking of precisely those parts of the body which in her case were in a state of irritation,—the throat and the oral cavity. To be sure, she would not hear of going so far as this in recognizing her own thoughts; and indeed, if the occurrence of the symptom was to be made possible at all, it was essential that she should not be completely clear on the subject. But the conclusion was inevitable that with her spasmodic cough, which, as is usual, was referred for its exciting stimulus to a tickling in her throat, she pictured to herself a scene of sexual gratification *per os*[37] between the two people whose love-affair occupied her mind so incessantly. A very short time after she had tacitly accepted this explanation her cough vanished—which fitted in very well with my view; but I do not wish to lay too much stress upon this development, since her cough had so often before disappeared spontaneously.

This short piece of the analysis may perhaps have excited in the medical reader—apart from the scepticism to which he is entitled—feelings of astonishment and horror; and I am prepared at this point to look into these two reactions so as to discover whether they are justifiable. The astonishment is probably caused by my daring to talk about such delicate and unpleasant subjects to a young girl—or, for that matter, to any woman who is sexually active. The horror is aroused, no doubt, by the possibility that an inexperienced girl could know about practices of such a kind and could occupy her imagination with them. I would advise recourse to moderation and reasonableness upon both points. There is no cause for indignation either in the one case or in the other. It is possible for a man to talk to girls and women upon sexual matters of every kind without doing them harm and without bringing suspicion upon himself, so long as, in the first place, he adopts a particular way of doing it, and, in the second place, can make them feel convinced that it is unavoidable. A gynaecologist, after all, under the same conditions, does not hesitate to make them submit to uncovering every possible part of their body. The best way of speaking about such things is to be dry and direct; and that is at the same time the method furthest removed from the prurience with which the same subjects are handled in "society", and to which girls and women alike are so thoroughly accustomed. I call bodily organs and processes by their technical names, and I tell these to the patient if they—the names, I mean—happen to be unknown to her. *J'appelle un chat un chat.*[38] I have certainly heard of some people—doctors and laymen—who are scandalized by a therapeutic method in which conversations of this sort occur, and who appear to envy either me or my patients the titillation which, according to their notions, such a method must afford. But I am too well acquainted with the respectability of these gentry to excite myself over them. I shall avoid the temptation of writing a satire upon them. But there is one thing that I will mention: often, after I have for some time treated a patient who had not at first found it easy to be open about sexual mat-

---

37. Latin: by the mouth.
38. French: I call a cat a cat.

ters, I have had the satisfaction of hearing her exclaim: "Why, after all, your treatment is far more respectable than Mr. X.'s conversation!"

No one can undertake the treatment of a case of hysteria until he is convinced of the impossibility of avoiding the mention of sexual subjects, or unless he is prepared to allow himself to be convinced by experience. The right attitude is: "*pour faire une omelette il faut casser des œufs.*"[39] The patients themselves are easy to convince; and there are only too many opportunities of doing so in the course of the treatment. There is no necessity for feeling any compunction at discussing the facts of normal or abnormal sexual life with them. With the exercise of a little caution all that is done is to translate into conscious ideas what was already known in the unconscious; and, after all, the whole effectiveness of the treatment is based upon our knowledge that the affect attached to an unconscious idea operates more strongly and, since it cannot be inhibited, more injuriously than the affect attached to a conscious one. There is never any danger of corrupting an inexperienced girl. For where there is no knowledge of sexual processes even in the unconscious, no hysterical symptom will arise; and where hysteria is found there can no longer be any question of "innocence of mind" in the sense in which parents and educators use the phrase. With children of ten, of twelve, or of fourteen, with boys and girls alike, I have satisfied myself that the truth of this statement can invariably be relied upon.

As regards the second kind of emotional reaction, which is not directed against me this time, but against my patient—supposing that my view of her is correct—and which regards the perverse nature of her phantasies as horrible, I should like to say emphatically that a medical man has no business to indulge in such passionate condemnation. I may also remark in passing that it seems to me superfluous for a physician who is writing upon the aberrations of the sexual instincts to seize every opportunity of inserting into the text expressions of his personal repugnance at such revolting things. We are faced by a fact; and it is to be hoped that we shall grow accustomed to it, when we have put our own tastes on one side. We must learn to speak without indignation of what we call the sexual perversions—instances in which the sexual function has extended its limits in respect either to the part of the body concerned or to the sexual object chosen. The uncertainty in regard to the boundaries of what is to be called normal sexual life, when we take different races and different epochs into account, should in itself be enough to cool the zealot's ardour. We surely ought not to forget that the perversion which is the most repellent to us, the sensual love of a man for a man, was not only tolerated by a people so far our superiors in cultivation as were the Greeks, but was actually entrusted by them with important social functions. The sexual life of each one of us extends to a slight degree—now in this direction, now in that—beyond the narrow lines imposed as the standard of normality. The perversions are neither bestial nor degenerate in the emotional sense of the word. They are a development of germs all of which are contained in the undifferentiated sexual disposition of the child, and which, by being suppressed or by being diverted to higher, asexual aims—by being "sublimated"—are destined to provide the energy for a great number of our cultural achievements. When, therefore, any one has *become* a gross and manifest pervert, it would be more correct to say that he has

---

39. French: To make an omelette, one must break some eggs.

remained one, for he exhibits a certain stage of *inhibited development*. All psycho-
neurotics are persons with strongly marked perverse tendencies, which have been
repressed in the course of their development and have become unconscious.
Consequently their unconscious *phantasies* show precisely the same content as the
documentarily recorded *actions* of perverts—even though they have not read Krafft-
Ebing's *Psychopathia Sexualis*,[40] to which simple-minded people attribute such a large
share of the responsibility for the production of perverse tendencies. Psychoneuroses
are, so to speak, the *negative* of perversions. In neurotics their sexual constitution,
under which the effects of heredity are included, operates in combination with any
accidental influences in their life which may disturb the development of normal sexuality. A stream of water which meets with an obstacle in the river-bed is dammed up
and flows back into old channels which had formerly seemed fated to run dry. The
motive forces leading to the formation of hysterical symptoms draw their strength not
only from repressed *normal* sexuality but also from unconscious perverse activities.

The less repellent of the so-called sexual perversions are very widely diffused
among the whole population, as every one knows except medical writers upon the
subject. Or, I should rather say, they know it too; only they take care to forget it at
the moment when they take up their pens to write about it. So it is not to be wondered at that this hysterical girl of nearly nineteen, who had heard of the occurrence
of such a method of sexual intercourse (sucking at the male organ), should have
developed an unconscious phantasy of this sort and should have given it expression
by an irritation in her throat and by coughing. Nor would it have been very extraordinary if she had arrived at such a phantasy even without having had any enlightenment from external sources—an occurrence which I have quite certainly observed in
other patients. For in her case a noteworthy fact afforded the necessary somatic prerequisite for this independent creation of a phantasy which would coincide with the
practices of perverts. She remembered very well that in her childhood she had been
a thumb-sucker. Her father, too, recollected breaking her of the habit after it had persisted into her fourth or fifth year. Dora herself had a clear picture of a scene from her
early childhood in which she was sitting on the floor in a corner sucking her left
thumb and at the same time tugging with her right hand at the lobe of her brother's
ear as he sat quietly beside her. Here we have an instance of the complete form of self-
gratification by sucking, as it has also been described to me by other patients, who
had subsequently become anaesthetic and hysterical. * * *

Dora's incessant repetition of the same thoughts about her father's relations with
Frau K. made it possible to derive still further important material from the analysis.

A train of thought such as this * * * shows its pathological character in spite of its
apparently reasonable content, by the single peculiarity that no amount of conscious and
voluntary effort of thought on the patient's part is able to dissipate or remove it. A normal train of thought, however intense it may be, can eventually be disposed of. Dora felt
quite rightly that her thoughts about her father required to be judged in a special way. "I
can think of nothing else," she complained again and again. "I know my brother says we
children have no right to criticize this behaviour of Father's. He declares that we ought

---

40. Influential 1886 study by 19th-c. German psychologist and sexologist Richard von Krafft-Ebing.

not to trouble ourselves about it, and ought even to be glad, perhaps, that he has found a woman he can love, since Mother understands him so little. I can quite see that, and I should like to think the same as my brother, but I can't. I can't forgive him for it."[41]

Now what is one to do in the face of a supervalent thought like this, after one has heard what its conscious grounds are and listened to the ineffectual protests made against it? Reflection will suggest that *this excessively intense train of thought must owe its reinforcement to the unconscious*. It cannot be resolved by any effort of thought, either because it itself reaches with its root down into unconscious, repressed material, or because another unconscious thought lies concealed behind it. In the latter case, the concealed thought is usually the direct contrary of the supervalent one. Contrary thoughts are always closely connected with each other and are often paired off in such a way that *the one thought is excessively intensely conscious while its counterpart is repressed and unconscious*. This relation between the two thoughts is an effect of the process of repression. For repression is often achieved by means of an excessive reinforcement of the thought contrary to the one which is to be repressed. * * *

Let us now apply our theory to the instance provided by Dora's case. We will begin with the first hypothesis, namely, that her preoccupation with her father's relations to Frau K. owed its obsessive character to the fact that its root was unknown to her and lay in the unconscious. It is not difficult to divine the nature of that root from her circumstances and her conduct. Her behaviour obviously went far beyond what would have been appropriate to filial concern. She felt and acted more like a jealous wife—in a way which would have been comprehensible in her mother. By her ultimatum to her father ("either her or me"), by the scenes she used to make, by the suicidal intentions she allowed to transpire,—by all this she was clearly putting herself in her mother's place. If we have rightly guessed the nature of the imaginary sexual situation which underlay her cough, in that phantasy she must have been putting herself in Frau K.'s place. She was therefore identifying herself both with the woman her father had once loved and with the woman he loved now. The inference is obvious that her affection for her father was a much stronger one than she knew or than she would have cared to admit: in fact, that she was in love with him.

I have learnt to look upon unconscious love relations like this (which are marked by their abnormal consequences)—between a father and a daughter, or between a mother and a son—as a revival of germs of feeling in infancy. I have shown at length elsewhere[42] at what an early age sexual attraction makes itself felt between parents and children, and I have explained that the legend of Oedipus[43] is probably to be regarded as a poetical rendering of what is typical in these relations. Distinct traces are probably to be found in most people of an early partiality of this kind—on the part of a daughter for her father, or on the part of a son for his mother; but it must be assumed to be more intense from the very first in the case of those children whose constitution marks them down for a neurosis, who develop prematurely and have a

---

41. A supervalent thought of this kind is often the only symptom, beyond deep depression, of a pathological condition which is usually described as "melancholia," but which can be cleared up by psychoanalysis like a hysteria [Freud's note].

42. *Interpretation of Dreams* (1900) and *Three Essays on Sexuality* (1905).

43. Freud named the "Oedipus Complex" for the Greek tragedy of the son, thought dead in infancy, who unwittingly kills his father and marries his mother.

craving for love. At this point certain other influences, which need not be discussed here, come into play, and lead to a fixation of this rudimentary feeling of love or to a reinforcement of it; so that it turns into something (either while the child is still young or not until it has reached the age of puberty) which must be put on a par with a sexual inclination and which, like the latter, has the forces of the libido at its command.[44] The external circumstances of our patient were by no means unfavourable to such an assumption. The nature of her disposition had always drawn her towards her father, and his numerous illnesses were bound to have increased her affection for him. In some of these illnesses he would allow no one but her to discharge the lighter duties of nursing. He had been so proud of the early growth of her intelligence that he had made her his confidante while she was still a child. It was really she and not her mother whom Frau K.'s appearance had driven out of more than one position.

When I told Dora that I could not avoid supposing that her affection for her father must at a very early moment have amounted to her being completely in love with him, she of course gave me her usual reply: "I don't remember that." But she immediately went on to tell me something analogous about a seven-year-old girl who was her cousin (on her mother's side) and in whom she often thought she saw a kind of reflection of her own childhood. This little girl had (not for the first time) been the witness of a heated dispute between her parents, and, when Dora happened to come in on a visit soon afterwards, whispered in her ear: "You can't think how I hate that person!" (pointing to her mother), "and when she's dead I shall marry Daddy." I am in the habit of regarding associations such as this, which bring forward something that agrees with the content of an assertion of mine, as a confirmation from the unconscious of what I have said. No other kind of "Yes" can be extracted from the unconscious; there is no such thing at all as an unconscious "No".[45]

For years on end she had given no expression to this passion for her father. On the contrary, she had for a long time been on the closest terms with the woman who had supplanted her with her father, and she had actually, as we know from her self-reproaches, facilitated this woman's relations with her father. Her own love for her father had therefore been recently revived; and, if so, the question arises to what end this had happened. Clearly as a reactive symptom, so as to suppress something else—something, that is, that still exercised power in the unconscious. Considering how things stood, I could not help supposing in the first instance that what was suppressed was her love of Herr K. I could not avoid the assumption that she was still in love with him, but that, for unknown reasons, since the scene by the lake her love had aroused in her violent feelings of opposition, and that the girl had brought forward and reinforced her old affection for her father in order to avoid any further necessity for paying conscious attention to the love which she had felt in the first years of her girlhood and which had now become distressing to her. In this way I gained an insight

---

44. The decisive factor in this connection is no doubt the early appearance of true genital sensations, either spontaneously or as a result of seduction or masturbation [Freud's note].

45. There is another very remarkable and entirely trustworthy form of confirmation from the unconscious, which I had not recognized at the time this was written: namely, an exclamation on the part of the patient of "I didn't think that" or "I didn't think of that." This can be translated point-blank into: "Yes, I was unconscious of that" [Freud's note].

into a conflict which was well calculated to unhinge the girl's mind. On the one hand she was filled with regret at having rejected the man's proposal, and with longing for his company and all the little signs of his affection; while on the other hand these feelings of tenderness and longing were combated by powerful forces, amongst which her pride was one of the most obvious. Thus she had succeeded in persuading herself that she had done with Herr K.—that was the advantage she derived from this typical process of repression; and yet she was obliged to summon up her infantile affection for her father and to exaggerate it, in order to protect herself against the feelings of love which were constantly pressing forward into consciousness. The further fact that she was almost incessantly a prey to the most embittered jealousy seemed to admit of still another determination.

My expectations were by no means disappointed when this explanation of mine was met by Dora with a most emphatic negative. The "No" uttered by a patient after a repressed thought has been presented to his conscious perception for the first time does no more than register the existence of a repression and its severity; it acts, as it were, as a gauge of the repression's strength. If this "No", instead of being regarded as the expression of an impartial judgement (of which, indeed, the patient is incapable), is ignored, and if work is continued, the first evidence soon begins to appear that in such a case "No" signifies the desired "Yes". Dora admitted that she found it impossible to be as angry with Herr K. as he had deserved. She told me that one day she had met Herr K. in the street while she was walking with a cousin of hers who did not know him. The other girl had exclaimed all at once: "Why, Dora, what's wrong with you? You've gone as white as a sheet!" She herself had felt nothing of this change of colour; but I explained to her that the expression of emotion and the play of features obey the unconscious rather than the conscious, and are a means of betraying the former. Another time Dora came to me in the worst of tempers after having been uniformly cheerful for several days. She could give no explanation of this. She felt so contrary to-day, she said; it was her uncle's birthday, and she could not bring herself to congratulate him, she did not know why. My powers of interpretation were at a low ebb that day; I let her go on talking, and she suddenly recollected that it was Herr K.'s birthday too—a fact which I did not fail to use against her. And it was then no longer hard to explain why the handsome presents she had had on her own birthday a few days before had given her no pleasure. One gift was missing, and that was Herr K.'s, the gift which had plainly once been the most prized of all.

Nevertheless Dora persisted in denying my contention for some time longer, until, towards the end of the analysis, the conclusive proof of its correctness came to light.

I must now turn to consider a further complication to which I should certainly give no space if I were a man of letters engaged upon the creation of a mental state like this for a short story, instead of being a medical man engaged upon its dissection. The element to which I must now allude can only serve to obscure and efface the outlines of the fine poetic conflict which we have been able to ascribe to Dora. This element would rightly fall a sacrifice to the censorship of a writer, for he, after all, simplifies and abstracts when he appears in the character of a psychologist. But in the world of reality, which I am trying to depict here, a complication of motives, an accumulation and conjunction of mental activities—in a word, overdetermination—is the rule. For behind Dora's supervalent train of thought which was concerned with her father's relations with Frau K. there lay concealed a feeling of jealousy which had that lady as its *object*—a feeling, that is, which could only be based upon an affection on Dora's part for one of her own sex. It has long been known and often been pointed out that at the age of puberty boys and girls show clear signs, even in normal cases, of the existence of an affection for people of their own sex. A romantic and sentimental friendship with one of her school-friends, accompanied by vows, kisses, promises of eternal correspondence, and all the sensibility of jealousy, is the common precursor of a girl's first serious passion for a man. Thenceforward, in favourable circumstances, the homosexual current of feeling often runs completely dry. But if a girl is not happy in her love for a man, the current is often set flowing again by the libido in later years and is increased up to a greater or lesser degree of intensity. If this much can be established without difficulty of healthy persons, and if we take into account what has already been said about the fuller development in neurotics of the normal germs of perversion, we shall expect to find in these latter too a fairly strong homosexual predisposition. It must, indeed, be so; for I have never yet come through a single psycho-analysis of a man or a woman without having to take into account a very considerable current of homosexuality. When, in a hysterical woman or girl, the sexual libido which is directed towards men has been energetically suppressed, it will regularly be found that the libido which is directed towards women has become vicariously reinforced and even to some extent conscious.

I shall not in this place go any further into this important subject, which is especially indispensable to an understanding of hysteria in men, because Dora's analysis came to an end before it could throw any light on this side of her mental life. But I should like to recall the governess, whom I have already mentioned, and with whom Dora had at first enjoyed the closest interchange of thought, until she discovered that she was being admired and fondly treated not for her own sake but for her father's; whereupon she had obliged the governess to leave. She used also to dwell with noticeable frequency and a peculiar emphasis on the story of another estrangement which appeared inexplicable even to herself. She had always been on particularly good terms with the younger of her two cousins—the girl who had later on become engaged—and had shared all sorts of secrets with her. When, for the first time after Dora had broken off her stay by the lake, her father was going back to B——, she had naturally refused to go with him. This cousin had then been asked to travel with him instead, and she had accepted the invitation. From that time forward Dora had felt a coldness towards her, and she herself was surprised to find how indifferent she had become, although, as she admitted, she had very little ground for complaint against her. These instances of sensitiveness led me to inquire what her relations with Frau K. had been up till the time of the breach. I then found that the young woman and the scarcely grown girl had lived for years on a footing of the closest intimacy. When Dora stayed with the K.'s she used to share a bedroom with Frau K., and the husband used to be quartered elsewhere. She had been the wife's confidante and adviser in all the difficulties of her married life. There was nothing they had not talked about. Medea had been quite content that Creusa[46] should make friends with her two children; and she certainly did

---

46. In Greek myth, Medea fell in love with Jason; when he planned to marry Creusa, the Princess of Corinth, Medea sent her sons to Creusa with the gift of a murderous robe.

nothing to interfere with the relations between the girl and the children's father. How Dora managed to fall in love with the man about whom her beloved friend had so many bad things to say is an interesting psychological problem. We shall not be far from solving it when we realize that thoughts in the unconscious live very comfortably side by side, and even contraries get on together without disputes—a state of things which persists often enough even in the conscious.

When Dora talked about Frau K., she used to praise her "adorable white body" in accents more appropriate to a lover than to a defeated rival. Another time she told me, more in sorrow than in anger, that she was convinced the presents her father had brought her had been chosen by Frau K., for she recognized her taste. Another time, again, she pointed out that, evidently through the agency of Frau K., she had been given a present of some jewellery which was exactly like some that she had seen in Frau K.'s possession and had wished for aloud at the time. Indeed, I can say in general that I never heard her speak a harsh or angry word against the lady, although from the point of view of her supervalent thought she should have regarded her as the prime author of her misfortunes. She seemed to behave inconsequently; but her apparent inconsequence was precisely the manifestation of a complicating current of feeling. For how had this woman to whom Dora was so enthusiastically devoted behaved to her? After Dora had brought forward her accusation against Herr K., and her father had written to him and had asked for an explanation, Herr K. had replied in the first instance by protesting sentiments of the highest esteem for her and by proposing that he should come to the manufacturing town to clear up every misunderstanding. A few weeks later, when her father spoke to him at B——, there was no longer any question of esteem. On the contrary, Herr K. spoke of her with disparagement, and produced as his trump card the reflection that no girl who read such books and was interested in such things could have any title to a man's respect. Frau K., therefore, had betrayed her and had calumniated her; for it had only been with her that she had read Mantegazza and discussed forbidden topics. It was a repetition of what had happened with the governess: Frau K. had not loved her for her own sake but on account of her father. Frau K. had sacrificed her without a moment's hesitation so that her relations with her father might not be disturbed. This mortification touched her, perhaps, more nearly and had a greater pathogenic effect than the other one, which she tried to use as a screen for it,—the fact that she had been sacrificed by her father. Did not the obstinacy with which she retained the particular amnesia concerning the sources of her forbidden knowledge point directly to the great emotional importance for her of the accusation against her upon that score, and consequently to her betrayal by her friend?

I believe, therefore, that I am not mistaken in supposing that Dora's supervalent train of thought, which was concerned with her father's relations with Frau K., was designed not only for the purpose of suppressing her love for Herr K., which had once been conscious, but also to conceal her love for Frau K., which was in a deeper sense unconscious. The supervalent train of thought was directly contrary to the latter current of feeling. She told herself incessantly that her father had sacrificed her to this woman, and made noisy demonstrations to show that she grudged her the possession of her father; and in this way she concealed from herself the contrary fact, which was that she grudged her father Frau K.'s love, and had not forgiven the woman she loved for the disillusionment she had been caused by her betrayal. The jealous emotions of a woman were linked in the unconscious with a jealousy such as might have been felt by a man. These masculine or, more properly speaking, *gynaecophilic*[47] currents of feeling are to be regarded as typical of the unconscious erotic life of hysterical girls.

—1905

Frederic W. H. Myers
1843–1901

If science could chart the unconscious mind, why couldn't it map the equally intangible world of the spirits? So wondered Frederic William Henry Myers, the son of a clergyman, who studied classics and became a school inspector in the 1870s. Myers saw spiritualism as a way of reconciling religion with skeptical materialism—the two positions he himself oscillated between—and worked hard to apply the techniques of experimental psychology to the investigation of paranormal phenomena. He threw himself into the study of the mind, meeting the most prominent psychiatrists in France, Germany, and the United States (including William James, who became a close friend), and was one of the first to introduce Freud's theories to British readers. Myers's major contribution to psychology was his argument that the psyche was composed not only of the ordinary conscious mind ("supraliminal self") but also a submerged or subconscious mind ("subliminal self"). Myers helped found the Society for Psychical Research in 1882 with his mentor Henry Sidgwick and wrote many of the case studies published in its *Proceedings*. Although today the paranormal is regarded as a dubious pursuit, in the 1890s this field felt like the newest frontier for science. *Human Personality and Its Survival of Bodily Death* (1903) is a compendium of Myers's lifetime work of trying to prove "the survival of bodily death."

from Human Personality and Its Survival of Bodily Death

And thus we come face to face with the supreme problem;—if not all theoretical knowledge, at least of all knowledge as bearing upon the fate and the duty of man. The theoretical question of primary importance may be simply that of the existence or non-existence of a spiritual world. The human or practical question of supreme importance is that of man's presence or portion in that world, if it does exist. To prove that telepathy[1] implies a spiritual environment would be at once to lift our knowledge of the Cosmos to a higher level. To prove that man survives death would also be to transform and transfigure his whole life here and now. Before us, as of old, is that all-embracing problem; but before us also, for the first time, is some hint and indication as to the track which may be pursued towards its solution.

The old conception of the *ghost*—a conception which seemed to belong only to primitive animism and to modern folk-lore—has received a new meaning from observations of phenomena occurring between living men. We realise that a phantasmal

47. Woman-loving.

---

1. Myers coined this word.

figure may bear a true relation to some distant person whose semblance is thus shown; we learn by instances of directly provable coincidence that wraiths of this kind correspond with death too often to leave the correspondence attributable to chance alone. The vague question of former times narrows down, then, to the more precise question: Are there still coincidences, is there still evidence of some such definite type as this, showing that a phantasm can appear not only at but *after* a man's bodily death, and can still indicate connection with a persistent and individual life?

To this distinct question there can now be given, as I believe, a distinct and affirmative answer. When evidence has been duly analysed, when alternative hypotheses have been duly weighed, it seems to me that there is no real break in the appearance of veridical[2] phantasms, or in their causation at the moment of bodily death; but rather that (after setting aside all merely subjective post-mortem apparitions) there is evidence that the self-same living spirit is still operating, and it may be in the self-same way. And thus my general dogma will have received its specific confirmation. Telepathy, I have said, looks like a law prevailing in the spiritual as well as in the material world. And that it does so prevail, I now add, is proved by the fact that those who communicated with us telepathically in this world communicate with us telepathically from the other. Man, therefore, is not a planetary or a transitory being; he persists as very man among cosmic and eternal things.

If this bare fact be gained, we have a basis for such an edifice of knowledge as will take many generations to uprear. At first, indeed, the mere observation of these phantasms does not seem as though it could lead us far. It is like the observation of shooting stars—of meteors which appear without warning and vanish in a flash of fire. Yet systematic observation has learnt much as to these meteors; has learnt, for instance, the point in heaven from which they issue; their orbital relation to earth and sun. Somewhat similarly, continuous observation of these brief phantasmal appearances may tell us much of them at last; much, for instance, as to their relative frequency at different epochs after death; something as to their apparent knowledge of what has happened on earth since they left it. From the study of meteorites, again, a further unexpected discovery has been made. "The stone that fell down from Jupiter"[3] is nowhere alone in its glory. The solid earth, the ocean's floor, are covered with meteoric dust;—the dust of the cosmic wayside, which we have gathered in our rush through the constellations. Even thus we come to find that there are traces over all the earth of indeterminate and unrecognised communication from a world of unembodied intelligences;—*hauntings* of unknown purport, and bearing no perceptible relation to the thoughts or deeds of living men.

Much more, indeed, than would at first seem likely can be learnt by mere prolonged observation of spontaneous phantasms of the dead. Yet here as everywhere,— here more than anywhere,—the need of actual experiment is felt. For experiment here would mean the conversion of the scarce decipherable flash which flits before our spectroscope[4] into a steady glow; it would mean the enlistment of the departed in conscious and willing co-operation,—the long-desired opportunity to hear and to

---

2. Verifiable.

3. Anaxagoras mentions a stone that fell from Jupiter to Thrace (described by Roman writer Pliny, c. 24 C.E.).

4. Instrument for analyzing the spectrum.

answer;—*veras audire et reddere voces.*[5] And in fact such experiment turns out to be actually feasible. It is feasible in connection with each of the four forms of communication, of verbalisation, with which human life is familiar. There is a possibility of inducing a spiritual hearing and a spiritual picture-seeing or reading; and also a spiritually-guided writing and speech. Both our sensory automatism and our motor automatism may be initiated and directed by intelligence outside our own.

In Chapter VI., on Sensory Automatism, we shall already have discussed the passive methods in which communications of this kind may be awaited. We have now to consider in what ways Motor Automatism,—the unwilled activity of hand or voice,—may be used to convey messages which come to the automatist as though from without himself.

As though from without himself, I say; but of course their apparent externality does not prove that they have not originated in submerged strata of his own mind. In most cases, indeed, with motor as with sensory automatism, this is probably what really occurs. We find that a tendency to automatic writing is by no means uncommon among sane and healthy persons. But we also find that the messages thus given do not generally rise above the level of an incoherent dream. They seem to emerge from a region where scraps of thought and feeling exist confusedly, with no adequate central control. Yet sometimes the vague scrawling changes its character. It becomes veridical; it begins to convey a knowledge of actual facts of which the automatist has no previous information; it indicates some subliminal activity of his own, or some telepathic access to an external mind. Apparitions may flash their signals; the automatic script will lay the wire. For however inchoate and ill-controlled these written messages may be, if once they have been received at all we can assign no limit to their development as the expression of thought that passes incorporeally from mind to mind.

From mind to mind, as we have already seen ground to hope, independently of the question whether both minds, or one only, be still clad in flesh. There will often be great difficulty of interpretation; great perplexity as to the true relation between a message and its alleged source. But every year of late has added,—every year ought to add,—both to the mass of matter and to the feasibility of interpretation. These are not the hieroglyphs of the dead, but the hieroglyphs of the living.

Side by side with the automatism of arm and hand we must place the automatism of throat and tongue. Automatic utterance parallels automatic script throughout the scale of degrees by this time familiar. It begins, that is to say, with mere incoherence; but it assumes in some cases a veridical character; with knowledge delivered from some subliminal stratum or some external mind. And in some cases the special knowledge displayed in the utterances lends probability to their claim to proceed from a departed spirit.

When this occurs, when the utterance reaches this point of veracity and intensity, it is sometimes accompanied by certain other phenomena which for those who have witnessed them carry a sense of reality which description can hardly reproduce. The ordinary consciousness of the automatist appears to be suspended; he passes into a state of trance,—which in its turn seems but the preparation for an occupation by an invading intelligence,—by the surviving spirit, let us boldly say, of some recognisable departed friend. This friend then disposes of voice and hand almost as freely as

---

5. Latin: "to hear, to answer you with honest words" (Virgil's Aeneid 1.410, trans. Alan Mandelbaum).

though he were their legitimate owner. Nay, more than one intelligence may thus operate simultaneously, and the organism may thus appear as indeed no more than the organ of spiritual influences which make and break connection with it at will.

And here we reach a point which has become,—without my anticipation, and—as a matter (so to say) of mere scientific policy—even against my will,—the principal *nodus*[6] of the present work. This book, designed originally to carry on, as continuously and coherently as possible, the argument and exposition of facts which in *Phantasms of the Living* I had aided in setting before serious readers, has been forced unexpectedly forward by the sheer force of evidence, until it must now dwell largely on the extreme branch of the subject, far beyond the reserves and cautious approaches of the earlier work.

For in truth during the last ten years the centre of gravity of our evidence has shifted so profoundly that it can no longer be said that the relative masses of evidence for each class of phenomenon correspond roughly to the degree of strangeness—of apparent difficulty—which the phenomena themselves exhibit. Ten years ago there was *most* evidence for telepathy between the living; *next most* for phantasms of the dead; *least*, perhaps, for that actual possession and control of human organisms by departed spirits, which of all our phenomena is likely to be the hardest for the scientific mind to accept,—since it carries us back to the most outrageously savage group among the superstitions of the early world. With the recent development of trance-phenomena, however, this semblance of logical proportion has been quickly altered. We seem suddenly to have arrived, by a kind of short cut, at a direct solution of problems which we had till then been approaching by difficult inference or laborious calculation of chances. What need of computing coincidental death-wraiths,—of analysing the evidential details of post-mortem apparitions,—if here we have the departed ready to hear and answer questions, and to tell us frankly of the fate of souls? Might not these earlier lines of inquiry be now abandoned altogether?—nay, must not our former results seem useless now, in view of this overwhelming proof?

I reply to this, that it was soon evident, in the first place, that our previous disciplined search had been by no means wasted. There was need of our canons of evidence, our analysis of the sources of subliminal messages, in order to satisfy ourselves that these trance-utterances could in part, but in part only, be explained by telæsthesia[7] and telepathy,—operating among actual scenes and the minds of living men. Nay, further, that old evidence of ours at once explained and was explained by the new. Fresh light was thrown on many previous groups of phenomena, and they in their turn were seen to have preluded to the new phenomena in such fashion that the continuity of the whole series—albeit a series advancing by leaps and bounds—was intelligibly maintained for us.

Following on the first revelation of Mrs. Piper's[8] trance-phenomena came the permission accorded to me by the executors of Mr. Stainton Moses[9] to read and analyse his private records after his death. The strong impression which his phenomena had made upon me during his life was increased,—as the reader will after-

---

6. Latin: node.
7. Another Myers coinage: perception at a distance, without using sight or hearing.
8. Leonora Piper, famous 19th-c. American medium.
9. Prominent Anglican clergyman and spiritualist/medium, involved in Society for Psychical Research.

wards see,—by this posthumous and intimate study; and his history was seen to be in many respects analogous to Mrs. Piper's. A further parallel was afforded in 1898 by Mrs. Thompson;[10]—and it seems to me now that the evidence for communication with the spirits of identified deceased persons through the trance utterances and writings of sensitives[11] apparently controlled by those spirits is established beyond serious attack.

In saying this, however, I desire to explain,—in anticipation of obvious and legitimate criticism,—that throughout all this discussion of "spirit-possession" I use purposely the simplest and most popular terms, without by any means denying that terms more accurate and philosophical may be ultimately attainable. What I feel sure of is that such more accurate terms have not yet been attained;—that we are not yet justified in using any nomenclature which assumes that we possess a deeper knowledge of what is going on than the messages themselves have given us. I do not of course mean that we ought to accept the messages unquestioningly as being in all cases literally what they claim to be. We know of various *veræ causæ*,[12]—conscious or unconscious fraud, self-suggestion, telepathy between the living, and the like, which we are bound to regard as possibly operative, and which enable us to resolve many automatic messages into mere illustrations of agencies previously known. But I mean that where we get beyond these simpler causes,—where we are forced to accept the messages as representing in some way the continued identity of a former denizen of earth,—I do not think that either tradition or philosophy affords us any solid stand-point from which to criticise those messages;—any such knowledge of the nature or destiny of the human soul as can at present justify us in *translating* them, so to say, into any would-be interpretative terminology of our own. Such critical power we may perhaps achieve in the future; but we shall have to achieve it, I think, by careful collation of many more such messages than we as yet possess.

The reader who may feel disposed to give his adhesion to this culminating group of the long series of evidences which have pointed with more and more clearness to the survival of human personality, and to the possibility for men on earth of actual commerce with a world beyond, may feel perhaps that the *desiderium orbis catholici*,[13] the intimate and universal hope of every generation of men, has never till this day approached so near to fulfilment. There has never been so fair a prospect, for Life and Love. But the goal to which we tend is not an ideal of personal happiness alone. The anticipation of our own future is but one element in the prospect which opens to us now. Our inquiry has broadened into a wider scope. The point from which we started was an analysis of the latent faculties of man. The point towards which our argument has carried us is the existence of a spiritual environment in which those faculties operate, and of unseen neighbours who speak to us thence with slowly gathering power. Deep in this spiritual environment the cosmic secret lies. It is our business to collect the smallest indications; to carry out from this treasury of Rhampsinitus[14] so much as our bare hands can steal away. We have won our scraps of spiritual experi-

---

10. Mrs. Thompson's trances were reviewed in the *Proceedings of the Society for Psychical Research*.
11. People sensitive to supernatural influences who have entered a trance state.
12. Latin: true causes.
13. Latin: an ardent longing for all the world.
14. Roman historian Herodotus tells a story about wealthy King Rhampsinitus, who is so impressed by the clever thief who steals into his treasury that he marries his daughter to the man.

ance, our messages from behind the veil; we can try them in their connection with certain enigmas which philosophy hardly hoped to be able to put to proof. Can we, for instance, learn anything,—to begin with fundamental problems,—of the relation of spiritual phenomena to Space, to Time, to the material world?

As to the idea of Space, the evidence which will have been presented will enable us to speak with perhaps more clearness than could have been hoped for in such a matter. Spiritual life, we infer, is not bound and confined by space-considerations in the same way as the life of earth. But in what way is that greater freedom attained? It appears to be attained by the mere extension of certain licenses (so to call them) permitted to ourselves. We on earth submit to two familiar laws of the physical universe. A body can only act where it is. Only one body can occupy the same part of space at the same moment. Applied to common affairs these rules are of plain construction. But once get beyond ponderable matter,—once bring life and ether[15] into play, and definitions become difficult indeed. The orator, the poet, we say, can only act where he is;—but where is he? He has transformed the sheet of paper into a spiritual agency;—nay, the mere memory of him persists as a source of energy in other minds. Again, we may say that no other body can be in the same place as this writing-table; but what of the ether? What we have thus far learnt of spiritual operation seems merely to extend these two possibilities. Telepathy indefinitely extends the range of an unembodied spirit's potential presence. The interpenetration of the spiritual with the material environment leaves this ponderable planet unable to check or to hamper spiritual presence or operation. Strange and new though our evidence may be, it needs at present in its relation to space nothing more than an immense extension of conceptions which the disappearance of earthly limitations was certain immensely to extend.

How, then, does the matter stand with regard to our relation to Time? Do we find that our new phenomena point to any mode of understanding, or of transcending Time fundamentally different from those modes which we have at our command?

In dealing with Time Past we have memory and written record; in dealing with Time Future we have forethought, drawing inferences from the past.

Can, then, the spiritual knowledge of Past and Future which our evidence shows be explained by assuming that these existing means of knowledge are raised to a higher power? Or are we driven to postulate something in the nature of Time which is to us inconceivable;—some co-existence of Past and Future in an eternal Now? It is plainly with Time Past that we must begin the inquiry.

The knowledge of the past which automatic communications manifest is in most cases apparently referable to the actual memory of persons still existing beyond the tomb. It reaches us telepathically, as from a mind in which remote scenes are still imprinted. But there are certain scenes which are not easily assigned to the individual memory of any given spirit. And if it be possible for us to learn of present facts by telæsthesia as well as by telepathy;—by some direct supernormal percipience[16] without the intervention of any other mind to which the facts are already known,—may there not be also a retrocognitive[17] telæsthesia by which we may attain a direct knowledge of facts in the past?

---

15. The subtle intangible element believed to permeate the universe.
16. Perception, cognizance.
17. Knowledge of what has already occurred.

Some conception of this kind may possibly come nearest to the truth. It may even be that some World-Soul is perennially conscious of all its past; and that individual souls, as they enter into deeper consciousness, enter into something which is at once reminiscence and actuality. But nevertheless a narrower hypothesis will cover the actual cases with which we have to deal. Past facts are known to men on earth not from memory only, but by written record; and there may be records, of what kind we know not, which persist in the spiritual world. Our retrocognitions seem often a recovery of isolated fragments of thought and feeling, pebbles still hard and rounded amid the indecipherable sands over which the mighty waters are "rolling evermore."

When we look from Time Past to Time Future we are confronted with essentially the same problems, though in a still more perplexing form, and with the world-old mystery of Free Will *versus* Necessity looming in the background. Again we find that, just as individual memory would serve to explain a large proportion of Retrocognition, so individual forethought—a subliminal forethought, based often on profound organic facts not normally known to us—will explain a large proportion of Precognition.[18] But here again we find also precognitions which transcend what seems explicable by the foresight of any mind such as we know; and we are tempted to dream of a World-Soul whose Future is as present to it as its Past. But in this speculation also, so vast and vague an explanation seems for the present beyond our needs; and it is safer—if aught be safe in this region which only actual evidence could have emboldened us to approach—to take refuge in the conception of intelligences not infinite, yet gifted with a foresight which strangely transcends our own.

Closely allied to speculations such as these is another speculation, more capable of being subjected to experimental test, yet which remains still inconclusively tested, and which has become for many reasons a stumbling-block rather than a corroboration in the spiritual inquiry. I refer to the question whether any influence is exercised by spirits upon the gross material world otherwise than through ordinary organic structures. We know that the spirit of a living man controls his own organism, and we shall see reason to think that discarnate[19] spirits may also control, by some form of "possession," the organisms of living persons,—may affect directly, that is to say, some portions of matter which we call living, namely, the brain of the entranced sensitive. There seems to me, then, no paradox in the supposition that some effect should be produced by spiritual agency—possibly through the mediation of some kind of energy derived from living human beings—upon inanimate matter as well. And I believe that as a fact such effects have been observed and recorded in a trustworthy manner by Sir W. Crookes, the late Dr. Speer, and others, in the cases especially of D. D. Home and of W. Stainton Moses.[20] If, indeed, I call these and certain other records still inconclusive, it is mainly on account of the mass of worthless narratives with which they have been in some sense smothered; the long history of so-called investigations which have consisted merely in an interchange of credulity and fraud. For the present the evidence of this kind which has real value is better presented, I think, in separate records than collected or discussed in any generalised form. All that I propose in this work, therefore, is briefly to indicate the relation which these "physical

---

18. Knowledge of what has not yet occurred.
19. Disembodied.
20. Crookes and Speer were spiritualist researchers; Home was a prominent medium; for Moses, see n. 9.

phenomena" hold to the psychical phenomena with which my book is concerned. Alongside of the faculty or achievement of man's ordinary or supraliminal self I shall demarcate the faculty or achievement which I ascribe to his subliminal self;[21] and alongside of this again I shall arrange such few well-attested phenomena as seem *primâ facie*[22] to demand the physical intervention of discarnate intelligencies.

I have traced the utmost limits to which any claim to a scientific basis for these inquiries can at present be pushed. Yet the subject-matter has not yet been exhausted of half its significance. The conclusions to which our evidence points are not such as can be discussed or dismissed as a mere matter of speculative curiosity. They affect every belief, every faculty, every hope and aim of man; and they affect him the more intimately as his interests grow more profound. Whatever meaning be applied to ethics, to philosophy, to religion, the concern of all these is here.

It would have been inconsistent with my main purpose had I interpolated considerations of this kind into the body of this work. For that purpose was above all to show that realms left thus far to philosophy or to religion,—too often to mere superstition and idle dream,—might in the end be brought under steady scientific rule. I contend that Religion and Science are no separable or independent provinces of thought or action; but rather that each name implies a different aspect of the same ideal;—that ideal being the completely normal reaction of the individual spirit to the whole of cosmic law.

Assuredly this deepening response of man's spirit to the Cosmos deepening round him must be affected by all the signals which now are glimmering out of night to tell him of his inmost nature and his endless fate. Who can think that either Science or Revelation has spoken as yet more than a first half-comprehended word? But if in truth souls departed call to us, it is to them that we shall listen most of all. We shall weigh their undesigned concordances,[23] we shall analyse the congruity of their message with the facts which such a message should explain. To some thoughts which may thus be generated I shall try to give expression in an Epilogue to the present work.

—1903

Henry James
1843–1916

A ponderous elephant picking up pins with his extra-sensitive trunk was fellow-novelist Marie Corelli's memorable description of Henry James's prose. H. G. Wells agreed, commenting that a James novel "is like a church lit but without a congregation to distract you, with every light and line focused on the high altar. And on the altar, very reverently placed, intensely there, is a dead kitten, an egg-shell, and a bit of string." Indeed, reading James must have been a bewildering experience for *fin-de-siècle* readers. All that carefully described material, for nothing but

---

21. Myers held that the subconscious mind ("subliminal self") can receive and exercise paranormal force.
22. Latin: from the first.
23. Their unintentional agreements.

a momentary perception? For in a mature James novel, all the action—the complications, the suspense, the resolution—occur in the depths of a character's consciousness. James requires his reader to trace the most minute psychological tremors, register the subtlest shifts in awareness, feel breathless from the suspense of knowledge. James's psychological novels pioneered a new way of depicting the mind—and made it clear that the mind was the new realm for the novelist to explore.

Born into a wealthy, cosmopolitan family (led by his socially prominent father), Henry James spent his youth in constant travel across France, Switzerland, England, Albany, and New York, meeting the intellectual, artistic, critical, and religious leaders of the period. He shared his rich impressions with brilliant siblings: his psychologist brother William James and his sister, diarist Alice James. As an adult, James decided to live in England, where he developed such an extensive social life that, famously, in the winter of 1878–79, he accepted 107 dinner invitations. However, James never formed closer ties. Although attracted to men, it is unclear whether he ever acted on those urgings, and he remained a lifelong bachelor, his sexuality sublimated, redirected, and mystified in his writing. He was prolific, turning out hundreds of pieces of journalism, incisive literary essays, volumes of travel writing and autobiography, plays, dozens of short stories, and twenty novels. Although his earlier work achieved popularity, especially the delightful *Daisy Miller* (1879), James was traumatized by the humiliating failure of his play *Guy Domville* (1895) and began producing increasingly difficult fiction for a highly elite audience with the leisure and training to enjoy his densely written language. From *Daisy Miller* through *Portrait of a Lady* (1881) to *The Ambassadors* (1903), James explored the "international theme": a naïvely cheerful American is enticed and eventually destroyed by a European culture encrusted with layers of complex, cruel, unspoken traditions. Other work of his middle period includes *The Bostonians* (1886), *The Princess Casamassima* (1886), and the chillingly indeterminate ghost story, "The Turn of the Screw," (1898); the three great novels of the late period are *The Ambassadors*, *The Wings of the Dove* (1902), and *The Golden Bowl* (1904). "The Beast in the Jungle" (1903) renders the intensely shifting, subtle flow of its character's consciousness and finds its climax in the reader's recognition of the unbearably bitter irony of that character's fate.

The Beast in the Jungle

I

What determined the speech that startled him in the course of their encounter scarcely matters, being probably but some words spoken by himself quite without intention—spoken as they lingered and slowly moved together after their renewal of acquaintance. He had been conveyed by friends an hour or two before to the house at which she was staying; the party of visitors at the other house, of whom he was one, and thanks to whom it was his theory, as always, that he was lost in the crowd, had been invited over to luncheon. There had been after luncheon much dispersal, all in the interest of the original motive, a view of Weatherend itself and the fine things, intrinsic features, pictures, heirlooms, treasures of all the arts, that made the place almost famous; and the great rooms were so numerous that guests could wander at their will, hang back from the principal group and in cases where they took such matters with the last seriousness give themselves up to mysterious appreciations and measurements. There were persons to be observed, singly or in couples, bending toward objects in out-of-the-way corners with their hands on their knees and their heads nodding quite as with the emphasis of an excited sense of smell. When they were two they either mingled their sounds of ecstasy or melted into silences of even

Max Beerbohm, Mr. *Henry James* (c. 1904).

deeper import, so that there were aspects of the occasion that gave it for Marcher much the air of the "look round," previous to a sale highly advertised, that excites or quenches, as may be, the dream of acquisition. The dream of acquisition at Weatherend would have had to be wild indeed, and John Marcher found himself, among such suggestions, disconcerted almost equally by the presence of those who knew too much and by that of those who knew nothing. The great rooms caused so much poetry and history to press upon him that he needed some straying apart to feel in a proper relation with them, though this impulse was not, as happened, like the gloating of some of his companions, to be compared to the movements of a dog sniffing a cupboard. It had an issue promptly enough in a direction that was not to have been calculated.

It led, briefly, in the course of the October afternoon, to his closer meeting with May Bartram, whose face, a reminder, yet not quite a remembrance, as they sat much separated at a very long table, had begun merely by troubling him rather pleasantly. It affected him as the sequel of something of which he had lost the beginning. He knew it, and for the time quite welcomed it, as a continuation, but didn't know what it continued, which was an interest or an amusement the greater as he was also somehow aware—yet without a direct sign from her—that the young woman herself hadn't lost the thread. She hadn't lost it, but she wouldn't give it back to him, he saw, without some putting forth of his hand for it; and he not only saw that, but saw several things more, things odd enough in the light of the fact that at the moment some accident of grouping brought them face to face he was still merely fumbling with the idea that any contact between them in the past would have had no importance. If it had had no importance he scarcely knew why his actual impression of her should so seem to have so much; the answer to which, however, was that in such a life as they all appeared to be leading for the moment one could but take things as they came. He was satisfied, without in the least being able to say why, that this young lady might roughly have ranked in the house as a poor relation; satisfied also that she was not there on a brief visit, but was more or less a part of the establishment—almost a working, a remunerated part. Didn't she enjoy at periods a protection that she paid for by helping, among other services, to show the place and explain it, deal with the tiresome people, answer questions about the dates of the building, the styles of the furniture, the authorship of the pictures, the favourite haunts of the ghost? It wasn't that she looked as if you could have given her shillings—it was impossible to look less so. Yet when she finally drifted toward him, distinctly handsome, though ever so much older—older than when he had seen her before—it might have been as an effect of her guessing that he had, within the couple of hours, devoted more imagination to her than to all the others put together, and had thereby penetrated to a kind of truth that the others were too stupid for. She *was* there on harder terms than any one; she was there as a consequence of things suffered, one way and another, in the interval of years; and she remembered him very much as she was remembered—only a good deal better.

By the time they at last thus came to speech they were alone in one of the rooms—remarkable for a fine portrait over the chimney-place—out of which their friends had passed, and the charm of it was that even before they had spoken they had practically arranged with each other to stay behind for talk. The charm, happily, was in other things too—partly in there being scarce a spot at Weatherend without something to stay behind for. It was in the way the autumn day looked into the high windows as it waned; the way the red light, breaking at the close from under a low sombre sky, reached out in a long shaft and played over old wainscots, old tapestry, old gold, old colour. It was most of all perhaps in the way she came to him as if, since she had been turned on to deal with the simpler sort, he might, should he choose to keep the whole thing down, just take her mild attention for a part of her general business. As soon as he heard her voice, however, the gap was filled up and the missing link supplied; the slight irony he divined in her attitude lost its advantage. He almost jumped at it to get there before her. "I met you years and years ago in Rome. I remember all about it." She confessed to disappointment—she had been so sure he didn't; and to prove how well he did he began to pour forth the particular recollections that popped up as he called for them. Her face and her voice, all at his service now, worked the miracle—the impression operating like the torch of a lamp-lighter who touches into flame, one by one, a long row of gas-jets. Marcher flattered himself the illumination was brilliant, yet he was really still more pleased on her showing him, with amusement, that in his haste to make everything right he had got most things rather wrong. It hadn't been at Rome—it had been at Naples; and it hadn't been eight years before—it had been more nearly ten. She hadn't been, either, with her uncle and aunt, but with her mother and brother; in addition to which it was not with the Pembles *he* had been, but with the Boyers, coming down in their company from Rome—a point on which she insisted, a little to his confusion, and as to which she had her evidence in hand. The Boyers she had known, but didn't know the Pembles, though she had heard of them, and it was the people he was with who had made them acquainted. The incident of the thunderstorm that had raged round them with such violence as to drive them for refuge into an excavation—this incident had not occurred at the Palace of the Cæsars, but at Pompeii,[1] on an occasion when they had been present there at an important find.

He accepted her amendments, he enjoyed her corrections, though the moral of them was, she pointed out, that he *really* didn't remember the least thing about her; and he only felt it as a drawback that when all was made strictly historic there didn't appear much of anything left. They lingered together still, she neglecting her office—for from the moment he was so clever she had no proper right to him—and both neglecting the house, just waiting as to see if a memory or two more wouldn't again breathe on them. It hadn't taken them many minutes, after all, to put down on the table, like the cards of a pack, those that constituted their respective hands; only what came out was that the pack was unfortunately not perfect—that the past, invoked, invited, encouraged, could give them, naturally, no more than it had. It had made them anciently meet—her at twenty, him at twenty-five; but nothing was so strange, they seemed to say to each other, as that, while so occupied, it hadn't done a little more for them. They looked at each other as with the feeling of an occasion missed; the present would have been so much better if the other, in the far distance, in the foreign land, hadn't been so stupidly meagre. There weren't apparently, all

---

1. Major archaeological sites and 19th-c. tourist attractions, both fairly recently excavated.

counted, more than a dozen little old things that had succeeded in coming to pass between them; trivialities of youth, simplicities of freshness, stupidities of ignorance, small possible germs, but too deeply buried—too deeply (didn't it seem?) to sprout after so many years. Marcher could only feel he ought to have rendered her some service—saved her from a capsized boat in the bay or at least recovered her dressing-bag, filched from her cab in the streets of Naples by a lazzarone with a stiletto.[2] Or it would have been nice if he could have been taken with fever all alone at his hotel, and she could have come to look after him, to write to his people, to drive him out in convalesence. *Then* they would be in possession of the something or other that their actual show seemed to lack. It yet somehow presented itself, this show, as too good to be spoiled; so that they were reduced for a few minutes more to wondering a little helplessly why—since they seemed to know a certain number of the same people—their reunion had been so long averted. They didn't use that name for it, but their delay from minute to minute to join the others was a kind of confession that they didn't quite want it to be a failure. Their attempted supposition of reasons for their not having met but showed how little they knew of each other. There came in fact a moment when Marcher felt a positive pang. It was vain to pretend she was an old friend, for all the communities were wanting, in spite of which it was as an old friend that he saw she would have suited him. He had new ones enough—was surrounded with them for instance on the stage of the other house; as a new one he probably wouldn't have so much as noticed her. He would have liked to invent something, get her to make-believe with him that some passage of a romantic or critical kind *had* originally occurred. He was really almost reaching out in imagination—as against time—for something that would do, and saying to himself that if it didn't come this sketch of a fresh start would show for quite awkwardly bungled. They would separate, and now for no second or no third chance. They would have tried and not succeeded. Then it was, just at the turn, as he afterwards made it out to himself, that, everything else failing, she herself decided to take up the case and, as it were, save the situation. He felt as soon as she spoke that she had been consciously keeping back what she said and hoping to get on without it; a scruple in her that immensely touched him when, by the end of three or four minutes more, he was able to measure it. What she brought out, at any rate, quite cleared the air and supplied the link—the link it was so odd he should frivolously have managed to lose.

"You know you told me something I've never forgotten and that again and again has made me think of you since; it was that tremendously hot day when we went to Sorrento,[3] across the bay, for the breeze. What I allude to was what you said to me, on the way back, as we sat under the awning of the boat enjoying the cool. Have you forgotten?"

He had forgotten, and was even more surprised than ashamed. But the great thing was that he saw in this no vulgar reminder of any "sweet" speech. The vanity of women had long memories, but she was making no claim on him of a compliment or a mistake. With another woman, a totally different one, he might have feared the recall possibly even of some imbecile "offer." So, in having to say that he had indeed forgotten, he was conscious rather of a loss than of a gain; he already saw an interest

---

2. Beggar with a knife.
3. Town near Naples.

in the matter of her mention. "I try to think—but I give it up. Yet I remember the Sorrento day."

"I'm not very sure you do," May Bartram after a moment said; "and I'm not very sure I ought to want you to. It's dreadful to bring a person back at any time to what he was ten years before. If you've lived away from it," she smiled, "so much the better."

"Ah if *you* haven't why should I?" he asked.

"Lived away, you mean, from what I myself was?"

"From what *I* was. I was of course an ass," Marcher went on; "but I would rather know from you just the sort of ass I was than—from the moment you have something in your mind—not know anything."

Still, however, she hesitated. "But if you've completely ceased to be that sort——?"

"Why I can then all the more bear to know. Besides, perhaps I haven't."

"Perhaps. Yet if you haven't," she added, "I should suppose you'd remember. Not indeed that *I* in the least connect with my impression the invidious name you use. If I had only thought you foolish," she explained, "the thing I speak of wouldn't so have remained with me. It was about yourself." She waited as if it might come to him; but as, only meeting her eyes in wonder, he gave no sign, she burnt her ships. "Has it ever happened?"

Then it was that, while he continued to stare, a light broke for him and the blood slowly came to his face, which began to burn with recognition. "Do you mean I told you——?" But he faltered, lest what came to him shouldn't be right, lest he should only give himself away.

"It was something about yourself that it was natural one shouldn't forget—that is if one remembered you at all. That's why I ask you," she smiled, "if the thing you then spoke of has ever come to pass?"

Oh then he saw, but he was lost in wonder and found himself embarrassed. This, he also saw, made her sorry for him, as if her allusion had been a mistake. It took him but a moment, however, to feel it hadn't been, much as it had been a surprise. After the first little shock of it her knowledge on the contrary began, even if rather strangely, to taste sweet to him. She was the only other person in the world then who would have it, and she had had it all these years, while the fact of his having so breathed his secret had unaccountably faded from him. No wonder they couldn't have met as if nothing had happened. "I judge," he finally said, "that I know what you mean. Only I had strangely enough lost any sense of having taken you so far into my confidence."

"Is it because you've taken so many others as well?"

"I've taken nobody. Not a creature since then."

"So that I'm the only person who knows?"

"The only person in the world."

"Well," she quickly replied, "I myself have never spoken. I've never, never repeated of you what you told me." She looked at him so that he perfectly believed her. Their eyes met over it in such a way that he was without a doubt. "And I never will."

She spoke with an earnestness that, as if almost excessive, put him at ease about her possible derision. Somehow the whole question was a new luxury to him—that is from the moment she was in possession. If she didn't take the sarcastic view she clearly took the sympathetic, and that was what he had had, in all the long time, from no one whomsoever. What he felt was that he couldn't at present have begun to tell her, and yet could profit perhaps exquisitely by the accident of having done so of old. "Please don't then. We're just right as it is."

"Oh I am," she laughed, "if you are!" To which she added: "Then you do still feel in the same way?"

It was impossible he shouldn't take to himself that she was really interested, though it all kept coming as a perfect surprise. He had thought of himself so long as abominably alone, and lo he wasn't alone a bit. He hadn't been, it appeared, for an hour—since those moments on the Sorrento boat. It was *she* who had been, he seemed to see as he looked at her—she who had been made so by the graceless fact of his lapse of fidelity. To tell her what he had told her—what had it been but to ask something of her? something that she had given, in her charity, without his having, by a remembrance, by a return of the spirit, failing another encounter, so much as thanked her. What he had asked of her had been simply at first not to laugh at him. She had beautifully not done so for ten years, and she was not doing so now. So he had endless gratitude to make up. Only for that he must see just how he had figured to her. "What, exactly, was the account I gave——?"

"Of the way you did feel? Well, it was very simple. You said you had had from your earliest time, as the deepest thing within you, the sense of being kept for something rare and strange, possibly prodigious and terrible, that was sooner or later to happen to you, that you had in your bones the foreboding and the conviction of, and that would perhaps overwhelm you."

"Do you call that very simple?" John Marcher asked.

She thought a moment. "It was perhaps because I seemed, as you spoke, to understand it."

"You do understand it?" he eagerly asked.

Again she kept her kind eyes on him. "You still have the belief?"

"Oh!" he exclaimed helplessly. There was too much to say.

"Whatever it's to be," she clearly made out, "it hasn't yet come."

He shook his head in complete surrender now. "It hasn't yet come. Only, you know, it isn't anything I'm to *do*, to achieve in the world, to be distinguished or admired for. I'm not such an ass as *that*. It would be much better, no doubt, if I were."

"It's to be something you're merely to suffer?"

"Well, say to wait for—to have to meet, to face, to see suddenly break out in my life; possibly destroying all further consciousness, possibly annihilating me; possibly, on the other hand, only altering everything, striking at the root of all my world and leaving me to the consequences, however they shape themselves."

She took this in, but the light in her eyes continued for him not to be that of mockery. "Isn't what you describe perhaps but the expectation—or at any rate the sense of danger, familiar to so many people—of falling in love?"

John Marcher thought. "Did you ask me that before?"

"No—I wasn't so free-and-easy then. But it's what strikes me now."

"Of course," he said after a moment, "it strikes you. Of course it strikes *me*. Of course what's in store for me may be no more than that. The only thing is," he went on, "that I think if it had been that I should by this time know."

"Do you mean because you've *been* in love?" And then as he but looked at her in silence: "You've been in love, and it hasn't meant such a cataclysm, hasn't proved the great affair?"

"Here I am, you see. It hasn't been overwhelming."

"Then it hasn't been love," said May Bartram.

"Well, I at least thought it was. I took it for that—I've taken it till now. It was agreeable, it was delightful, it was miserable," he explained. "But it wasn't strange. It wasn't what *my* affair's to be."

"You want something all to yourself—something that nobody else knows or *has* known?"

"It isn't a question of what I 'want'—God knows I don't want anything. It's only a question of the apprehension that haunts me—that I live with day by day."

He said this so lucidly and consistently that he could see it further impose itself. If she hadn't been interested before she'd have been interested now.

"Is it a sense of coming violence?"

Evidently now too again he liked to talk of it. "I don't think of it as—when it does come—necessarily violent. I only think of it as natural and as of course above all unmistakeable. I think of it simply as *the* thing. *The* thing will of itself appear natural."

"Then how will it appear strange?"

Marcher bethought himself. "It won't—to *me*."

"To whom then?"

"Well," he replied, smiling at last, "say to you."

"Oh then I'm to be present?"

"Why you *are* present—since you know."

"I see." She turned it over. "But I mean at the catastrophe."

At this, for a minute, their lightness gave way to their gravity; it was as if the long look they exchanged held them together. "It will only depend on yourself—if you'll watch with me."

"Are you afraid?" she asked.

"Don't leave me *now*," he went on.

"Are you afraid?" she repeated.

"Do you think me simply out of my mind?" he pursued instead of answering. "Do I merely strike you as a harmless lunatic?"

"No," said May Bartram. "I understand you. I believe you."

"You mean you feel how my obsession—poor old thing—may correspond to some possible reality?"

"To some possible reality."

"Then you *will* watch with me?"

She hesitated, then for the third time put her question. "Are you afraid?"

"Did I tell you I was—at Naples?"

"No, you said nothing about it."

"Then I don't know. And I should *like* to know," said John Marcher. "You'll tell me yourself whether you think so. If you'll watch with me you'll see."

"Very good then." They had been moving by this time across the room, and at the door, before passing out, they paused as for the full wind-up of their understanding. "I'll watch with you," said May Bartram.

II

The fact that she "knew"—knew and yet neither chaffed him nor betrayed him—had in a short time begun to constitute between them a goodly bond, which became more marked when, within the year that followed their afternoon at Weatherend, the opportunities for meeting multiplied. The event that thus promoted these occasions was the death of the ancient lady her great-aunt, under whose wing, since losing her mother, she had to such an extent found shelter, and who, though but the widowed mother of the new successor to the property, had succeeded—thanks to a high tone and a high temper—in not forfeiting the supreme position at the great house. The deposition of this personage arrived but with her death, which, followed by many changes, made in particular a difference for the young woman in whom Marcher's expert attention had recognised from the first a dependent with a pride that might ache though it didn't bristle. Nothing for a long time had made him easier than the thought that the aching must have been much soothed by Miss Bartram's now finding herself able to set up a small home in London. She had acquired property, to an amount that made that luxury just possible, under her aunt's extremely complicated will, and when the whole matter began to be straightened out, which indeed took time, she let him know that the happy issue was at last in view. He had seen her again before that day, both because she had more than once accompanied the ancient lady to town and because he had paid another visit to the friends who so conveniently made of Weatherend one of the charms of their own hospitality. These friends had taken him back there; he had achieved there again with Miss Bartram some quiet detachment; and he had in London succeeded in persuading her to more than one brief absence from her aunt. They went together, on these latter occasions, to the National Gallery and the South Kensington Museum,[4] where, among vivid reminders, they talked of Italy at large—not now attempting to recover, as at first, the taste of their youth and their ignorance. That recovery, the first day at Weatherend, had served its purpose well, had given them quite enough; so that they were, to Marcher's sense, no longer hovering about the head-waters of their stream, but had felt their boat pushed sharply off and down the current.

They were literally afloat together; for our gentleman this was marked, quite as marked as that the fortunate cause of it was just the buried treasure of her knowledge. He had with his own hands dug up this little hoard, brought to light—that is to within reach of the dim day constituted by their discretions and privacies—the object of value the hiding-place of which he had, after putting it into the ground himself, so strangely, so long forgotten. The rare luck of his having again just stumbled on the spot made him indifferent to any other question; he would doubtless have devoted more time to the odd accident of his lapse of memory if he hadn't been moved to devote so much to the sweetness, the comfort, as he felt, for the future, that this accident itself had helped to keep fresh. It had never entered into his plan that any one should "know," and mainly for the reason that it wasn't in him to tell any one. That would have been impossible, for nothing but the amusement of a cold world would have waited on it. Since, however, a mysterious fate had opened his mouth betimes, in spite of him, he would count that a compensation and profit by it to the utmost.

---

4. Major art museums in London.

That the right person *should* know tempered the asperity of his secret more even than his shyness had permitted him to imagine; and May Bartram was clearly right, because—well, because there she was. Her knowledge simply settled it; he would have been sure enough by this time had she been wrong. There was that in his situation, no doubt, that disposed him too much to see her as a mere confidant, taking all her light for him from the fact—the fact only—of her interest in his predicament; from her mercy, sympathy, seriousness, her consent not to regard him as the funniest of the funny. Aware, in fine, that her price for him was just in her giving him this constant sense of his being admirably spared, he was careful to remember that she had also a life of her own, with things that might happen to *her*, things that in friendship one should likewise take account of. Something fairly remarkable came to pass with him, for that matter, in this connexion—something represented by a certain passage of his consciousness, in the suddenest way, from one extreme to the other.

He had thought himself, so long as nobody knew, the most disinterested person in the world, carrying his concentrated burden, his perpetual suspense, ever so quietly, holding his tongue about it, giving others no glimpse of it nor of its effect upon his life, asking of them no allowance and only making on his side all those that were asked. He hadn't disturbed people with the queerness of their having to know a haunted man, though he had had moments of rather special temptation on hearing them say they were forsooth "unsettled." If they were as unsettled as he was—he who had never been settled for an hour in his life—they would know what it meant. Yet it wasn't, all the same, for him to make them, and he listened to them civilly enough. This was why he had such good—though possibly such rather colourless—manners; this was why, above all, he could regard himself, in a greedy world, as decently—as in fact perhaps even a little sublimely—unselfish. Our point is accordingly that he valued this character quite sufficiently to measure his present danger of letting it lapse, against which he promised himself to be much on his guard. He was quite ready, none the less, to be selfish, just a little, since surely no more charming occasion for it had come to him. "Just a little," in a word, was just as much as Miss Bartram, taking one day with another, would let him. He never would be in the least coercive, and would keep well before him the lines on which consideration for her—the very highest—ought to proceed. He would thoroughly establish the heads under which her affairs, her requirements, her peculiarities—he went so far as to give them the latitude of that name—would come into their intercourse. All this naturally was a sign of how much he took the intercourse itself for granted. There was nothing more to be done about *that*. It simply existed; had sprung into being with her first penetrating question to him in the autumn light there at Weatherend. The real form it should have taken on the basis that stood out large was the form of their marrying. But the devil in this was that the very basis itself put marrying out of the question. His conviction, his apprehension, his obsession, in short, wasn't a privilege he could invite a woman to share; and that consequence of it was precisely what was the matter with him. Something or other lay in wait for him, amid the twists and the turns of the months and the years, like a crouching Beast in the Jungle. It signified little whether the crouching Beast were destined to slay him or to be slain. The definite point was the inevitable spring of the creature; and the definite lesson from that was that a man of feeling didn't cause himself to be accompanied by a lady on a tiger-hunt. Such was the image under which he had ended by figuring his life.

They had at first, none the less, in the scattered hours spent together, made no allusion to that view of it; which was a sign he was handsomely alert to give that he didn't expect, that he in fact didn't care, always to be talking about it. Such a feature in one's outlook was really like a hump on one's back. The difference it made every minute of the day existed quite independently of discussion. One discussed of course *like* a hunchback, for there was always, if nothing else, the hunchback face. That remained, and she was watching him; but people watched best, as a general thing, in silence, so that such would be predominantly the manner of their vigil. Yet he didn't want, at the same time, to be tense and solemn; tense and solemn was what he imagined he too much showed for with other people. The thing to be, with the one person who knew, was easy and natural—to make the reference rather than be seeming to avoid it, to avoid it rather than be seeming to make it, and to keep it, in any case, familiar, facetious even, rather than pedantic and portentous. Some such consideration as the latter was doubtless in his mind for instance when he wrote pleasantly to Miss Bartram that perhaps the great thing he had so long felt as in the lap of the gods was no more than this circumstance, which touched him so nearly, of her acquiring a house in London. It was the first allusion they had yet again made, needing any other hitherto so little; but when she replied, after having given him the news, that she was by no means satisfied with such a trifle as the climax to so special a suspense, she almost set him wondering if she hadn't even a larger conception of singularity for him than he had for himself. He was at all events destined to become aware little by little, as time went by, that she was all the while looking at his life, judging it, measuring it, in the light of the thing she knew, which grew to be at last, with the consecration of the years, never mentioned between them save as "the real truth" about him. That had always been his own form of reference to it, but she adopted the form so quietly that, looking back at the end of a period, he knew there was no moment at which it was traceable that she had, as he might say, got inside his idea, or exchanged the attitude of beautifully indulging for that of still more beautifully believing him.

It was always open to him to accuse her of seeing him but as the most harmless of maniacs, and this, in the long run—since it covered so much ground—was his easiest description of their friendship. He had a screw loose for her but she liked him in spite of it and was practically, against the rest of the world, his kind wise keeper, unremunerated but fairly amused and, in the absence of other near ties, not disreputably occupied. The rest of the world of course thought him queer, but she, she only, knew how, and above all why, queer; which was precisely what enabled her to dispose the concealing veil in the right folds. She took his gaiety from him—since it had to pass with them for gaiety—as she took everything else; but she certainly so far justified by her unerring touch his finer sense of the degree to which he had ended by convincing her. *She* at least never spoke of the secret of his life except as "the real truth about you," and she had in fact a wonderful way of making it seem, as such, the secret of her own life too. That was in fine how he so constantly felt her as allowing for him; he couldn't on the whole call it anything else. He allowed for himself, but she, exactly, allowed still more; partly because, better placed for a sight of the matter, she traced his unhappy perversion through reaches of its course into which he could scarce follow it. He knew how he felt, but, besides knowing that, she knew how he *looked* as well; he knew each of the things of importance he was insidiously kept from doing, but she could add up the amount they made, understand how much, with a lighter weight on his spirit, he might have done, and thereby establish how, clever as he was, he fell short. Above all she was in the secret of the difference between the forms he went through—those of his little office under Government, those of caring for his modest patrimony, for his library, for his garden in the country, for the people in London whose invitations he accepted and repaid—and the detachment that reigned beneath them and that made of all behaviour, all that could in the least be called behaviour, a long act of dissimulation. What it had come to was that he wore a mask painted with the social simper, out of the eye-holes of which there looked eyes of an expression not in the least matching the other features. This the stupid world, even after years, had never more than half discovered. It was only May Bartram who had, and she achieved, by an art indescribable, the feat of at once—or perhaps it was only alternately—meeting the eyes from in front and mingling her own vision, as from over his shoulder, with their peep through the apertures.

So while they grew older together she did watch with him, and so she let this association give shape and colour to her own existence. Beneath *her* forms as well detachment had learned to sit, and behaviour had become for her, in the social sense, a false account of herself. There was but one account of her that would have been true all the while and that she could give straight to nobody, least of all to John Marcher. Her whole attitude was a virtual statement, but the perception of that only seemed called to take its place for him as one of the many things necessarily crowded out of his consciousness. If she had moreover, like himself, to make sacrifices to their real truth, it was to be granted that her compensation might have affected her as more prompt and more natural. They had long periods, in this London time, during which, when they were together, a stranger might have listened to them without in the least pricking up his ears; on the other hand the real truth was equally liable at any moment to rise to the surface, and the auditor would then have wondered indeed what they were talking about. They had from an early hour made up their mind that society was, luckily, unintelligent, and the margin allowed them by this had fairly become one of their commonplaces. Yet there were still moments when the situation turned almost fresh—usually under the effect of some expression drawn from herself. Her expressions doubtless repeated themselves, but her intervals were generous. "What saves us, you know, is that we answer so completely to so usual an appearance: that of the man and woman whose friendship has become such a daily habit—or almost—as to be at last indispensable." That for instance was a remark she had frequently enough had occasion to make, though she had given it at different times different developments. What we are especially concerned with is the turn it happened to take from her one afternoon when he had come to see her in honour of her birthday. This anniversary had fallen on a Sunday, at a season of thick fog and general outward gloom; but he had brought her his customary offering, having known her now long enough to have established a hundred small traditions. It was one of his proofs to himself, the present he made her on her birthday, that he hadn't sunk into real selfishness. It was mostly nothing more than a small trinket, but it was always fine of its kind, and he was regularly careful to pay for it more than he thought he could afford. "Our habit saves you, at least, don't you see? because it makes you, after all, for the vulgar, indistinguishable from other men. What's the most inveterate mark of men in general? Why the capacity to spend endless time with dull women—to spend it I won't say without being bored, but without minding that they are, without being driven off at a tangent by it; which comes to the same thing. I'm your dull woman, a part of the daily bread for which you pray at church. That covers your tracks more than anything."

"And what covers yours?" asked Marcher, whom his dull woman could mostly to this extent amuse. "I see of course what you mean by your saving me, in this way and that, so far as other people are concerned—I've seen it all along. Only what is it that saves *you*? I often think, you know, of that."

She looked as if she sometimes thought of that too, but rather in a different way. "Where other people, you mean, are concerned?"

"Well, you're really so in with me, you know—as a sort of result of my being so in with yourself. I mean of my having such an immense regard for you, being so tremendously mindful of all you've done for me. I sometimes ask myself if it's quite fair. Fair I mean to have so involved and—since one may say it—interested you. I almost feel as if you hadn't really had time to do anything else."

"Anything else but be interested?" she asked. "Ah what else does one ever want to be? If I've been 'watching' with you, as we long ago agreed I was to do, watching's always in itself an absorption."

"Oh certainly," John Marcher said, "if you hadn't had your curiosity——! Only doesn't it sometimes come to you as time goes on that your curiosity isn't being particularly repaid?"

May Bartram had a pause. "Do you ask that, by any chance, because you feel at all that yours isn't? I mean because you have to wait so long."

Oh he understood what she meant! "For the thing to happen that never does happen? For the Beast to jump out? No, I'm just where I was about it. It isn't a matter as to which I can *choose*, I can decide for a change. It isn't one as to which there *can* be a change. It's in the lap of the gods. One's in the hands of one's law—there one is. As to the form the law will take, the way it will operate, that's its own affair."

"Yes," Miss Bartram replied; "of course one's fate's coming, of course it *has* come in its own form and its own way, all the while. Only, you know, the form and the way in your case were to have been—well, something so exceptional and, as one may say, so particularly *your* own."

Something in this made him look at her with suspicion. "You say 'were to *have* been,' as if in your heart you had begun to doubt."

"Oh!" she vaguely protested.

"As if you believed," he went on, "that nothing will now take place."

She shook her head slowly but rather inscrutably. "You're far from my thought."

He continued to look at her. "What then is the matter with you?"

"Well," she said after another wait, "the matter with me is simply that I'm more sure than ever my curiosity, as you call it, will be but too well repaid."

They were frankly grave now; he had got up from his seat, had turned once more about the little drawing-room to which, year after year, he brought his inevitable topic; in which he had, as he might have said, tasted their intimate community with every sauce, where every object was as familiar to him as the things of his own house and the very carpets were worn with his fitful walk very much as the desks in old counting-houses are worn by the elbows of generations of clerks. The generations of his nervous moods had been at work there, and the place was the written history of his whole middle life. Under the impression of what his friend had just said he knew himself, for some reason, more aware of these things; which made him, after a moment, stop again before her. "Is it possibly that you've grown afraid?"

"Afraid?" He thought, as she repeated the word, that his question had made her, a little, change colour; so that, lest he should have touched on a truth, he explained very kindly: "You remember that that was what you asked *me* long ago—that first day at Weatherend."

"Oh yes, and you told me you didn't know—that I was to see for myself. We've said little about it since, even in so long a time."

"Precisely," Marcher interposed—"quite as if it were too delicate a matter for us to make free with. Quite as if we might find, on pressure, that I *am* afraid. For then," he said, "we shouldn't, should we? quite know what to do."

She had for the time no answer to this question. "There have been days when I thought you were. Only, of course," she added, "there have been days when we have thought almost anything."

"Everything. Oh!" Marcher softly groaned, as with a gasp, half spent, at the face, more uncovered just then than it had been for a long while, of the imagination always with them. It had always had its incalculable moments of glaring out, quite as with the very eyes of the very Beast, and, used as he was to them, they could still draw from him the tribute of a sigh that rose from the depths of his being. All they had thought, first and last, rolled over him; the past seemed to have been reduced to mere barren speculation. This in fact was what the place had just struck him as so full of—the simplification of everything but the state of suspense. That remained only by seeming to hang in the void surrounding it. Even his original fear, if fear it had been, had lost itself in the desert. "I judge, however," he continued, "that you see I'm not afraid now."

"What I see, as I make it out, is that you've achieved something almost unprecedented in the way of getting used to danger. Living with it so long and so closely you've lost your sense of it; you know it's there, but you're indifferent, and you cease even, as of old, to have to whistle in the dark. Considering what the danger is," May Bartram wound up, "I'm bound to say I don't think your attitude could well be surpassed."

John Marcher faintly smiled. "It's heroic?"

"Certainly—call it that."

It was what he would have liked indeed to call it. "I *am* then a man of courage?"

"That's what you were to show me."

He still, however, wondered. "But doesn't the man of courage know what he's afraid of—or *not* afraid of? I don't know *that*, you see. I don't focus it. I can't name it. I only know I'm exposed."

"Yes, but exposed—how shall I say?—so directly. So intimately. That's surely enough."

"Enough to make you feel then—as what we may call the end and the upshot of our watch—that I'm not afraid?"

"You're not afraid. But it isn't," she said, "the end, of our watch. That is it isn't the end of yours. You've everything still to see."

"Then why haven't *you*?" he asked. He had had, all along, to-day, the sense of her keeping something back, and he still had it. As this was his first impression of that it quite made a date. The case was the more marked as she didn't at first answer; which in turn made him go on. "You know something I don't." Then his voice, for that of a man of courage, trembled a little. "You know what's to happen." Her silence, with the face she showed, was almost a confession—it made him sure. "You know, and you're afraid to tell me. It's so bad that you're afraid I'll find out."

All this might be true, for she did look as if, unexpectedly to her, he had crossed some mystic line that she had secretly drawn round her. Yet she might, after all, not have worried; and the real climax was that he himself, at all events, needn't. "You'll never find out."

III

It was all to have made, none the less, as I have said, a date; which came out in the fact that again and again, even after long intervals, other things that passed between them wore in relation to this hour but the character of recalls and results. Its immediate effect had been indeed rather to lighten insistence—almost to provoke a reaction; as if their topic had dropped by its own weight and as if moreover, for that matter, Marcher had been visited by one of his occasional warnings against egotism. He had kept up, he felt, and very decently on the whole, his consciousness of the importance of not being selfish, and it was true that he had never sinned in that direction without promptly enough trying to press the scales the other way. He often repaired his fault, the season permitting, by inviting his friend to accompany him to the opera; and it not infrequently thus happened that, to show he didn't wish her to have but one sort of food for her mind, he was the cause of her appearing there with him a dozen nights in the month. It even happened that, seeing her home at such times, he occasionally went in with her to finish, as he called it, the evening, and, the better to make his point, sat down to the frugal but always careful little supper that awaited his pleasure. His point was made, he thought, by his not eternally insisting with her on himself; made for instance, at such hours, when it befell that, her piano at hand and each of them familiar with it, they went over passages of the opera together. It chanced to be on one of these occasions, however, that he reminded her of her not having answered a certain question he had put to her during the talk that had taken place between them on her last birthday. "What is it that saves *you*?"—saved her, he meant, from that appearance of variation from the usual human type. If he had practically escaped remark, as she pretended, by doing, in the most important particular, what most men do—find the answer to life in patching up an alliance of a sort with a woman no better than himself—how had she escaped it, and how could the alliance, such as it was, since they must suppose it had been more or less noticed, have failed to make her rather positively talked about?

"I never said," May Bartram replied, "that it hadn't made me a good deal talked about."

"Ah well then you're not 'saved.'"

"It hasn't been a question for me. If you've had your woman I've had," she said, "my man."

"And you mean that makes you all right?"

Oh it was always as if there were so much to say! "I don't know why it shouldn't make me—humanly, which is what we're speaking of—as right as it makes you."

"I see," Marcher returned. "'Humanly,' no doubt, as showing that you're living for something. Not, that is, just for me and my secret."

May Bartram smiled. "I don't pretend it exactly shows that I'm not living for you. It's my intimacy with you that's in question."

He laughed as he saw what she meant. "Yes, but since, as you say, I'm only, so far as people make out, ordinary, you're—aren't you? no more than ordinary either. You help me to pass for a man like another. So if I *am*, as I understand you, you're not compromised. Is that it?"

She had another of her waits, but she spoke clearly enough. "That's it. It's all that concerns me—to help you to pass for a man like another."

He was careful to acknowledge the remark handsomely. "How kind, how beautiful, you are to me! How shall I ever repay you?"

She had her last grave pause, as if there might be a choice of ways. But she chose. "By going on as you are."

It was into this going on as he was that they relapsed, and really for so long a time that the day inevitably came for a further sounding of their depths. These depths, constantly bridged over by a structure firm enough in spite of its lightness and of its occasional oscillation in the somewhat vertiginous air, invited on occasion, in the interest of their nerves, a dropping of the plummet and a measurement of the abyss. A difference had been made moreover, once for all, by the fact that she had all the while not appeared to feel the need of rebutting his charge of an idea within her that she didn't dare to express—a charge uttered just before one of the fullest of their later discussions ended. It had come up for him then that she "knew" something and that what she knew was bad—too bad to tell him. When he had spoken of it as visibly so bad that she was afraid he might find it out, her reply had left the matter too equivocal to be let alone and yet, for Marcher's special sensibility, almost too formidable again to touch. He circled about it at a distance that alternately narrowed and widened and that still wasn't much affected by the consciousness in him that there was nothing she could "know," after all, any better than he did. She had no source of knowledge he hadn't equally—except of course that she might have finer nerves. That was what women had where they were interested; they made out things, where people were concerned, that the people often couldn't have made out for themselves. Their nerves, their sensibility, their imagination, were conductors and revealers, and the beauty of May Bartram was in particular that she had given herself so to his case. He felt in these days what, oddly enough, he had never felt before, the growth of a dread of losing her by some catastrophe—some catastrophe that yet wouldn't at all be *the* catastrophe: partly because she had almost of a sudden begun to strike him as more useful to him than ever yet, and partly by reason of an appearance of uncertainty in her health, coincident and equally new. It was characteristic of the inner detachment he had hitherto so successfully cultivated and to which our whole account of him is a reference, it was characteristic that his complications, such as they were, had never yet seemed so as at this crisis to thicken about him, even to the point of making him ask himself if he were, by any chance, of a truth, within sight or sound, within touch or reach, within the immediate jurisdiction, of the thing that waited.

When the day came, as come it had to, that his friend confessed to him her fear of a deep disorder in her blood, he felt somehow the shadow of a change and the chill of a shock. He immediately began to imagine aggravations and disasters, and above all to think of her peril as the direct menace for himself of personal privation. This indeed gave him one of those partial recoveries of equanimity that were agreeable to him—it showed him that what was still first in his mind was the loss she herself might suffer. "What if she should have to die before knowing, before seeing——?" It would have been brutal, in the early stages of her trouble, to put that question to her; but it had immediately sounded for him to his own concern, and the possibility was what most made him sorry for her. If she did "know," moreover, in the sense of her having had some—what should he think?—mystical irresistible light, this would make the matter not better, but worse, inasmuch as her original adoption of his own curiosity had quite become the basis of her life. She had been living to see what would *be* to be seen, and it would quite lacerate her to have to give up before the accomplishment of the vision. These reflexions, as I say, quickened his generosity; yet, make them as he might, he saw himself, with the lapse of the period, more and more disconcerted. It lapsed for him with a strange steady sweep, and the oddest oddity was that it gave him, independently of the threat of much inconvenience, almost the only positive surprise his career, if career it could be called, had yet offered him. She kept the house as she had never done; he had to go to her to see her—she could meet him nowhere now, though there was scarce a corner of their loved old London in which she hadn't in the past, at one time or another, done so; and he found her always seated by her fire in the deep old-fashioned chair she was less and less able to leave. He had been struck one day, after an absence exceeding his usual measure, with her suddenly looking much older to him than he had ever thought of her being; then he recognised that the suddenness was all on his side—he had just simply and suddenly noticed. She looked older because inevitably, after so many years, she *was* old, or almost; which was of course true in still greater measure of her companion. If she was old, or almost, John Marcher assuredly was, and yet it was her showing of the lesson, not his own, that brought the truth home to him. His surprises began here; when once they had begun they multiplied; they came rather with a rush: it was as if, in the oddest way in the world, they had all been kept back, sown in a thick cluster, for the late afternoon of life, the time at which for people in general the unexpected has died out.

One of them was that he should have caught himself—for he *had* so done—*really* wondering if the great accident would take form now as nothing more than his being condemned to see this charming woman, this admirable friend, pass away from him. He had never so unreservedly qualified her as while confronted in thought with such a possibility; in spite of which there was small doubt for him that as an answer to his long riddle the mere effacement of even so fine a feature of his situation would be an abject anticlimax. It would represent, as connected with his past attitude, a drop of dignity under the shadow of which his existence could only become the most grotesque of failures. He had been far from holding it a failure—long as he had waited for the appearance that was to make it a success. He had waited for quite another thing, not for such a thing as that. The breath of his good faith came short, however, as he recognised how long he had waited, or how long at least his companion had. That she, at all events, might be recorded as having waited in vain—this affected him sharply, and all the more because of his at first having done little more than amuse himself with the idea. It grew more grave as the gravity of her condition grew, and the state of mind it produced in him, which he himself ended by watching as if it had been some definite disfigurement of his outer person, may pass for another of his surprises. This conjoined itself still with another, the really stupefying consciousness of a question that he would have allowed to shape itself had he dared. What did everything mean—what, that is, did *she* mean, she and her vain waiting and her probable death and the soundless admonition of it all—unless, that, at this time of day, it was simply, it was overwhelmingly too late? He had never at any stage of his queer consciousness admitted the whisper of such a correction; he had never till within these last few months been so false to his conviction as not to hold that what was to come to him had time, whether *he* struck himself as having it or not. That at last, at last, he certainly hadn't it, to speak of, or had it but in the scantiest measure—such, soon enough, as things went with him, became the inference with which his old obsession had to reckon: and this it was not helped to do by the more and more confirmed appearance that the great vagueness casting the long shadow in which he had lived had, to attest itself, almost no margin left. Since it was in Time that he was to have met his fate, so it was in Time that his fate was to have acted; and as he waked up to the sense of no longer being young, which was exactly the sense of being stale, just as that, in turn, was the sense of being weak, he waked up to another matter beside. It all hung together; they were subject, he and the great vagueness, to an equal and indivisible law. When the possibilities themselves had accordingly turned stale, when the secret of the gods had grown faint, had perhaps even quite evaporated, that, and that only, was failure. It wouldn't have been failure to be bankrupt, dishonoured, pilloried, hanged; it was failure not to be anything. And so, in the dark valley into which his path had taken its unlooked-for twist, he wondered not a little as he groped. He didn't care what awful crash might overtake him, with what ignominy or what monstrosity he might yet be associated—since he wasn't after all too utterly old to suffer—if it would only be decently proportionate to the posture he had kept, all his life, in the threatened presence of it. He had but one desire left—that he shouldn't have been "sold."

IV

Then it was that, one afternoon, while the spring of the year was young and new she met all in her own way his frankest betrayal of these alarms. He had gone in late to see her, but evening hadn't settled and she was presented to him in that long fresh light of waning April days which affects us often with a sadness sharper than the greyest hours of autumn. The week had been warm, the spring was supposed to have begun early, and May Bartram sat, for the first time in the year, without a fire; a fact that, to Marcher's sense, gave the scene of which she formed part a smooth and ultimate look, an air of knowing, in its immaculate order and cold meaningless cheer, that it would never see a fire again. Her own aspect—he could scarce have said why—intensified this note. Almost as white as wax, with the marks and signs in her face as numerous and as fine as if they had been etched by a needle, with soft white draperies relieved by a faded green scarf on the delicate tone of which the years had further refined, she was the picture of a serene and exquisite but impenetrable sphinx,[5] whose head, or indeed all whose person, might have been powdered with silver. She was a sphinx, yet with her white petals and green fronds she might have been a lily too—only an artificial lily, wonderfully imitated and constantly kept, without dust or stain, though not exempt from a slight droop and a complexity of faint creases, under some clear glass bell. The perfection of household care, of high polish and finish, always reigned in her rooms, but they now looked most as if every-thing had been wound up, tucked in, put away, so that she might sit with folded hands and with nothing more to do. She was "out of it," to Marcher's vision; her work was over; she communicated with him as across some gulf or from some island of rest that she had already reached, and it made him feel strangly abandoned. Was it—or rather wasn't it—that if for so long she had been watching with him the answer to their question must have swum into her ken and taken on its name, so that her occupation was verily gone? He had as much as charged her with this in say-ing to her, many months before, that she even then knew something she was keep-ing from him. It was a point he had never since ventured to press, vaguely fearing as he did that it might become a difference, perhaps a disagreement, between them. He had in this later time turned nervous, which was what he in all the other years had never been; and the oddity was that his nervousness should have waited till he had begun to doubt, should have held off so long as he was sure. There was something, it seemed to him, that the wrong word would bring down on his head, something that would so at least ease off his tension. But he wanted not to speak the wrong word; that would make everything ugly. He wanted the knowledge he lacked to drop on him, if drop it could, by its own august weight. If she was to forsake him it was surely for her to take leave. This was why he didn't directly ask her again what she knew; but it was also why, approaching the matter from another side, he said to her in the course of his visit: "What do you regard as the very worst that at this time of day *can* happen to me?"

He had asked her that in the past often enough; they had, with the odd irregu-lar rhythm of their intensities and avoidances, exchanged ideas about it and then had seen the ideas washed away by cool intervals, washed like figures traced in sea-sand. It had ever been the mark of their talk that the oldest allusions in it required but a little dismissal and reaction to come out again, sounding for the hour as new. She could thus at present meet his enquiry quite freshly and patiently. "Oh yes, I've repeatedly thought, only it always seemed to me of old that I couldn't quite make up my mind. I thought of dreadful things, between which it was difficult to choose; and so must you have done."

---

5. Greek mythological creature who speaks of human fate in riddles.

"Rather! I feel now as if I had scarce done anything else. I appear to myself to have spent my life in thinking of nothing *but* dreadful things. A great many of them I've at different times named to you, but there were others I couldn't name."

"They were too, too dreadful?"

"Too, too dreadful—some of them."

She looked at him a minute, and there came to him as he met it an inconsequent sense that her eyes, when one got their full clearness, were still as beautiful as they had been in youth, only beautiful with a strange cold light—a light that somehow was a part of the effect, if it wasn't rather a part of the cause, of the pale hard sweetness of the season and the hour. "And yet," she said at last, "there are horrors we've mentioned."

It deepened the strangeness to see her, as such a figure in such a picture, talk of "horrors," but she was to do in a few minutes something stranger yet—though even of this he was to take the full measure but afterwards—and the note of it already trembled. It was, for the matter of that, one of the signs that her eyes were having again the high flicker of their prime. He had to admit, however, what she said. "Oh yes, there were times when we did go far." He caught himself in the act of speaking as if it all were over. Well, he wished it were; and the consummation depended for him clearly more and more on his friend.

But she had now a soft smile. "Oh far——!"

It was oddly ironic. "So you mean you're prepared to go further?"

She was frail and ancient and charming as she continued to look at him, yet it was rather as if she had lost the thread. "Do you consider that we went far?"

"Why I thought it the point you were just making—that we *had* looked most things in the face."

"Including each other?" She still smiled. "But you're quite right. We've had together great imaginations, often great fears; but some of them have been unspoken."

"Then the worst—we haven't faced that. I *could* face it, I believe, if I knew what you think it. I feel," he explained, "as if I had lost my power to conceive such things." And he wondered if he looked as blank as he sounded. "It's spent."

"Then why do you assume," she asked, "that mine isn't?"

"Because you've given me signs to the contrary. It isn't a question for you of conceiving, imagining, comparing. It isn't a question now of choosing." At last he came out with it. "You know something I don't. You've shown me that before."

These last words had affected her, he made out in a moment, exceedingly, and she spoke with firmness. "I've shown you, my dear, nothing."

He shook his head. "You can't hide it."

"Oh, oh!" May Bartram sounded over what she couldn't hide. It was almost a smothered groan.

"You admitted it months ago, when I spoke of it to you as of something you were afraid I should find out. Your answer was that I couldn't, that I wouldn't, and I don't pretend I have. But you had something therefore in mind, and I see now how it must have been, how it still is, the possibility that, of all possibilities, has settled itself for you as the worst. This," he went on, "is why I appeal to you. I'm only afraid of ignorance to-day—I'm not afraid of knowledge." And then as for a while she said nothing: "What makes me sure is that I see in your face and feel here, in this air and amid these appearances, that you're out of it. You've done. You've had your experience. You leave me to my fate."

Well, she listened, motionless and white in her chair, as on a decision to be made, so that her manner was fairly an avowal, though still, with a small fine inner stiffness, an imperfect surrender. "It *would* be the worst," she finally let herself say. "I mean the thing I've never said."

It hushed him a moment. "More monstrous than all the monstrosities we've named?"

"More monstrous. Isn't that what you sufficiently express," she asked, "in calling it the worst?"

Marcher thought. "Assuredly—if you mean, as I do, something that includes all the loss and all the shame that are thinkable."

"It would if it *should* happen," said May Bartram. "What we're speaking of, remember, is only my idea."

"It's your belief," Marcher returned. "That's enough for me. I feel your beliefs are right. Therefore if, having this one, you give me no more light on it, you abandon me."

"No, no!" she repeated. "I'm with you—don't you see?—still." And as to make it more vivid to him she rose from her chair—a movement she seldom risked in these days—and showed herself, all draped and all soft, in her fairness and slimness. "I haven't forsaken you."

It was really, in its effort against weakness, a generous assurance, and had the success of the impulse not, happily, been great, it would have touched him to pain more than to pleasure. But the cold charm in her eyes had spread, as she hovered before him, to all the rest of her person, so that it was for the minute almost a recovery of youth. He couldn't pity her for that; he could only take her as she showed— as capable even yet of helping him. It was as if, at the same time, her light might at any instant go out; wherefore he must make the most of it. There passed before him with intensity the three or four things he wanted most to know; but the question that came of itself to his lips really covered the others. "Then tell me if I shall consciously suffer."

She promptly shook her head. "Never!"

It confirmed the authority he imputed to her, and it produced on him an extraordinary effect. "Well, what's better than that? Do you call that the worst?"

"You think nothing is better?" she asked.

She seemed to mean something so special that he again sharply wondered, though still with the dawn of a prospect of relief. "Why not, if one doesn't *know?*" After which, as their eyes, over his question, met in a silence, the dawn deepened, and something to his purpose came prodigiously out of her very face. His own, as he took it in, suddenly flushed to the forehead, and he gasped with the force of a perception to which, on the instant, everything fitted. The sound of his gasp filled the air; then he became articulate. "I see—if I don't suffer!"

In her own look, however, was doubt. "You see what?"

"Why what you mean—what you've always meant."

She again shook her head. "What I mean isn't what I've always meant. It's different."

"It's something new?"

She hung back from it a little. "Something new. It's not what you think. I see what you think."

His divination drew breath then; only her correction might be wrong. "It isn't that I *am* a blockhead?" he asked between faintness and grimness. "It isn't that it's all a mistake?"

"A mistake?" she pityingly echoed. *That* possibility, for her, he saw, would be monstrous; and if she guaranteed him the immunity from pain it would accordingly not be what she had in mind. "Oh no," she declared; "it's nothing of that sort. You've been right."

Yet he couldn't help asking himself if she weren't, thus pressed, speaking but to save him. It seemed to him he should be most in a hole if his history should prove all a platitude. "Are you telling me the truth, so that I shan't have been a bigger idiot than I can bear to know? I *haven't* lived with a vain imagination, in the most besotted illusion? I haven't waited but to see the door shut in my face?"

She shook her head again. "However the case stands *that* isn't the truth. Whatever the reality, it *is* a reality. The door isn't shut. The door's open," said May Bartram.

"Then something's to come?"

She waited once again, always with her cold sweet eyes on him. "It's never too late." She had, with her gliding step, diminished the distance between them, and she stood nearer to him, close to him, a minute, as if still charged with the unspoken. Her movement might have been for some finer emphasis of what she was at once hesitating and deciding to say. He had been standing by the chimney-piece, fireless and sparely adorned, a small perfect old French clock and two morsels of rosy Dresden[6] constituting all its furniture; and her hand grasped the shelf while she kept him waiting, grasped it a little as for support and encouragement. She only kept him waiting, however; that is he only waited. It had become suddenly, from her movement and attitude, beautiful and vivid to him that she had something more to give him; her wasted face delicately shone with it—it glittered almost as with the white luster of silver in her expression. She was right, incontestably, for what he saw in her face was the truth, and strangely, without consequence, while their talk of it as dreadful was still in the air, she appeared to present it as inordinately soft. This, prompting bewilderment, made him but gape the more gratefully for her revelation, so that they continued for some minutes silent, her face shining at him, her contact imponderably pressing, and his stare all kind but all expectant. The end, none the less, was that what he had expected failed to come to him. Something else took place instead, which seemed to consist at first in the mere closing of her eyes. She gave way at the same instant to a slow, fine shudder, and though he remained staring—though he stared in fact but the harder—turned off and regained her chair. It was the end of what she had been intending, but it left him thinking only of that.

"Well, you don't say——?"

---

6. Valuable china figurines.

She had touched in her passage a bell near the chimney and had sunk back strangely pale. "I'm afraid I'm too ill."

"Too ill to tell me?" It sprang up sharp to him, and almost to his lips, the fear she might die without giving him light. He checked himself in time from so expressing his question, but she answered as if she had heard the words.

"Don't you know—now?"

"'Now'——?" She had spoken as if some difference had been made within the moment. But her maid, quickly obedient to her bell, was already with them. "I know nothing." And he was afterwards to say to himself that he must have spoken with odious impatience, such an impatience as to show that, supremely disconcerted, he washed his hands of the whole question.

"Oh!" said May Bartram.

"Are you in pain?" he asked as the woman went to her.

"No," said May Bartram.

Her maid, who had put an arm round her as if to take her to her room, fixed on him eyes that appealingly contradicted her; in spite of which, however, he showed once more his mystification. "What then has happened?"

She was once more, with her companion's help, on her feet, and, feeling withdrawal imposed on him, he had blankly found his hat and gloves and had reached the door. Yet he waited for her answer. "What *was* to," she said.

V.

He came back the next day, but she was then unable to see him, and as it was literally the first time this had occurred in the long stretch of their acquaintance he turned away, defeated and sore, almost angry—or feeling at least that such a break in their custom was really the beginning of the end—and wandered alone with his thoughts, especially with the one he was least able to keep down. She was dying and he would lose her; she was dying and his life would end. He stopped in the Park, into which he had passed, and stared before him at his recurrent doubt. Away from her the doubt pressed again; in her presence he had believed her, but as he felt his forlornness he threw himself into the explanation that, nearest at hand, had most of a miserable warmth for him and least of a cold torment. She had deceived him to save him—to put him off with something in which he should be able to rest. What could the thing that was to happen to him be, after all, but just this thing that had begun to happen? Her dying, her death, his consequent solitude—*that* was what he had figured as the Beast in the Jungle, that was what had been in the lap of the gods. He had had her word for it as he left her—what else on earth could she have meant? It wasn't a thing of a monstrous order; not a fate rare and distinguished; not a stroke of fortune that overwhelmed and immortalised; it had only the stamp of the common doom. But poor Marcher at this hour judged the common doom sufficient. It would serve his turn, and even as the consummation of infinite waiting he would bend his pride to accept it. He sat down on a bench in the twilight. He hadn't been a fool. Something had *been*, as she had said, to come. Before he rose indeed it had quite struck him that the final fact really matched with the long avenue through which he had had to reach it. As sharing his suspense and as giving herself all, giving her life, to bring it to an end, she had come with him every step of the way. He had lived by her aid, and to leave her behind would be cruelly, damnably to miss her. What could be more overwhelming that that?

Well, he was to know within the week, for though she kept him a while at bay, left him restless and wretched during a series of days on each of which he asked about her only again to have to turn away, she ended his trial by receiving him where she had always received him. Yet she had been brought out at some hazard into the presence of so many of the things that were, consciously, vainly, half their past, and there was scant service left in the gentleness of her mere desire, all too visible, to check his obsession and wind up his long trouble. That was clearly what she wanted; the one thing more for her own peace while she could still put out her hand. He was so affected by her state that, once seated by her chair, he was moved to let everything go; it was she herself therefore who brought him back, took up again, before she dismissed him, her last word of the other time. She showed how she wished to leave their business in order. "I'm not sure you understood. You've nothing to wait for more. It *has* come."

Oh how he looked at her! "Really?"

"Really."

"The thing that, as you said, *was* to?"

"The thing that we began in our youth to watch for."

Face to face with her once more he believed her; it was a claim to which he had so abjectly little to oppose. "You mean that it has come as a positive definite occurrence, with a name and a date?"

"Positive. Definite. I don't know about the 'name,' but, oh with a date!"

He found himself again too helplessly at sea. "But come in the night—come and passed me by?"

May Bartram had her strange faint smile. "Oh no, it hasn't passed you by!"

"But if I haven't been aware of it and it hasn't touched me——?"

"Ah your not being aware of it"—and she seemed to hesitate an instant to deal with this—"your not being aware of it is the strangeness *in* the strangeness. It's the wonder *of* the wonder." She spoke as with the softness almost of a sick child, yet now at last, at the end of all, with the perfect straightness of a sibyl.[7] She visibly knew that she knew, and the effect on him was of something co-ordinate, in its high character, with the law that had ruled him. It was the true voice of the law; so on her lips would the law itself have sounded. "It *has* touched you," she went on. "It has done its office. It has made you all its own."

"So utterly without my knowing it?"

"So utterly without your knowing it." His hand, as he leaned to her, was on the arm of her chair, and, dimly smiling always now, she placed her own on it. "It's enough if *I* know it."

"Oh!" he confusedly breathed, as she herself of late so often had done.

"What I long ago said is true. You'll never know now, and I think you ought to be content. You've *had* it," said May Bartram.

"But had what?"

---

7. Female prophet, in classical mythology.

"Why what was to have marked you out. The proof of your law. It has acted. I'm too glad," she then bravely added, "to have been able to see what it's *not*."

He continued to attach his eyes to her, and with the sense that it was all beyond him, and that *she* was too, he would still have sharply challenged her hadn't he so felt it an abuse of her weakness to do more than take devoutly what she gave him, take it hushed as to a revelation. If he did speak, it was out of the foreknowledge of his loneliness to come. "If you're glad of what it's 'not' it might then have been worse?"

She turned her eyes away, she looked straight before her; with which after a moment: "Well, you know our fears."

He wondered. "It's something then we never feared?"

On this slowly she turned to him. "Did we ever dream, with all our dreams, that we should sit and talk of it thus?"

He tried for a little to make out that they had; but it was as if their dreams, numberless enough, were in solution in some thick cold mist through which thought lost itself. "It might have been that we couldn't talk."

"Well"—she did her best for him—"not from this side. This, you see," she said, "is the *other* side."

"I think," poor Marcher returned, "that all sides are the same to me." Then, however, as she gently shook her head in correction: "We mightn't, as it were, have got across——?"

"To where we are—no. We're *here*"—she made her weak emphasis.

"And much good does it do us!" was her friend's frank comment.

"It does us the good it can. It does us the good that *it* isn't here. It's past. It's behind," said May Bartram. "Before——" but her voice dropped.

He had got up, not to tire her, but it was hard to combat his yearning. She after all told him nothing but that his light had failed—which he knew well enough without her. "Before——?" he blankly echoed.

"Before you see, it was always to *come*. That kept it present."

"Oh I don't care what comes now! Besides," Marcher added, "it seems to me I liked it better present, as you say, than I can like it absent with *your* absence."

"Oh mine!"—and her pale hands made light of it.

"With the absence of everything." He had a dreadful sense of standing there before her for—so far as anything but this proved, this bottomless drop was concerned—the last time of their life. It rested on him with a weight he felt he could scarce bear, and this weight it apparently was that still pressed out what remained in him of speakable protest. "I believe you; but I can't begin to pretend I understand. *Nothing*, for me, is past; nothing *will* pass till I pass myself, which I pray my stars may be as soon as possible. Say, however," he added, "that I've eaten my cake, as you contend, to the last crumb—how can the thing I've never felt at all be the thing I was marked out to feel?"

She met him perhaps less directly, but she met him unperturbed. "You take your 'feelings' for granted. You were to suffer your fate. That was not necessarily to know it."

"How in the world—when what is such knowledge but suffering?"

She looked up at him a while in silence. "No—you don't understand."

"I suffer," said John Marcher.

"Don't, don't!"

"How can I help at least *that?*"

"*Don't!*" May Bartram repeated.

She spoke it in a tone so special, in spite of her weakness, that he stared an instant—stared as if some light, hitherto hidden, had shimmered across his vision. Darkness again closed over it, but the gleam had already become for him an idea. "Because I haven't the right——?"

"Don't *know*—when you needn't," she mercifully urged. "You needn't—for we shouldn't."

"Shouldn't?" If he could but know what she meant!

"No—it's too much."

"Too much?" he still asked but with a mystification that was the next moment of a sudden to give way. Her words, if they meant something, affected him in this light— the light also of her wasted face—as meaning *all*, and the sense of what knowledge had been for herself came over him with a rush which broke through into a question. "Is it of that then you've dying?"

She but watched him, gravely at first, as to see, with this, where he was, and she might have seen something or feared something that moved her sympathy. "I would live for you still—if I could." Her eyes closed for a little, as if, withdrawn into herself, she were for a last time trying. "But I can't!" she said as she raised them again to take leave of him.

She couldn't indeed, as but too promptly and sharply appeared, and he had no vision of her after this that was anything but darkness and doom. They had parted for ever in that strange talk; access to her chamber of pain, rigidly guarded, was almost wholly forbidden him; he was feeling now moreover, in the face of doctors, nurses, the two or three relatives attracted doubtless by the presumption of what she had to "leave," how few were the rights, as they were called in such cases, that he had to put forward, and how odd it might even seem that their intimacy shouldn't have given him more of them. The stupidest fourth cousin had more, even though she had been nothing in such a person's life. She had been a feature of features in *his*, for what else was it to have been so indispensable? Strange beyond saying were the ways of existence, baffling for him the anomaly of his lack, as he felt it to be, of producible claim. A woman might have been, as it were, everything to him, and it might yet present him in no connexion that any one seemed held to recognise. If this was the case in these closing weeks it was the case more sharply on the occasion of the last offices rendered, in the great grey London cemetery, to what had been mortal, to what had been precious, in his friend. The concourse at her grave was not numerous, but he saw himself treated as scarce more nearly concerned with it than if there had been a thousand others. He was in short from this moment face to face with the fact that he was to profit extraordinarily little by the interest May Bartram had taken in him. He couldn't quite have said what he expected, but he hadn't surely expected this approach to a double privation. Not only had her interest failed him, but he seemed to feel himself unattended—and for a reason he couldn't seize—by the distinction, the dignity, the propriety, if nothing else, of the man markedly bereaved. It was as if, in the view of society, he had not *been* markedly bereaved, as if there still failed some sign or proof of it, and as if none the less his character could never be affirmed nor the deficiency ever made up. There were moments as the weeks went by when he would have liked, by some almost aggressive act, to take his stand on the intimacy of his loss, in order that it *might* be questioned and his retort, to the relief of his spirit, so recorded; but the moments of an irritation more helpless followed fast on these, the moments during which, turning things over with a good conscience but with a bare horizon, he found himself wondering if he oughtn't to have begun, so to speak, further back.

He found himself wondering indeed at many things, and this last speculation had others to keep it company. What could he have done, after all, in her lifetime, without giving them both, as it were, away? He couldn't have made known she was watching him, for that would have published the superstition of the Beast. This was what closed his mouth now—now that the Jungle had been threshed to vacancy and that the Beast had stolen away. It sounded too foolish and too flat; the difference for him in this particular, the extinction in his life of the element of suspense, was such as in fact to surprise him. He could scarce have said what the effect resembled; the abrupt cessation, the positive prohibition, of music perhaps, more than anything else, in some place all adjusted and all accustomed to sonority and to attention. If he could at any rate have conceived lifting the veil from his image at some moment of the past (what had he done, after all, if not lift it to *her*?) so to do this to-day, to talk to people at large of the Jungle cleared and confide to them that he now felt it as safe, would have been not only to see them listen as to a goodwife's tale, but really to hear himself tell one. What it presently came to in truth was that poor Marcher waded through his beaten grass, where no life stirred, where no breath sounded, where no evil eye seemed to gleam from a possible lair, very much as if vaguely looking for the Beast, and still more as if acutely missing it. He walked about in an existence that had grown strangely more spacious, and, stopping fitfully in places where the undergrowth of life struck him as closer, asked himself yearningly, wondered secretly and sorely, if it would have lurked here or there. It would have at all events *sprung*; what was at least complete was his belief in the truth itself of the assurance given him. The change from his old sense to his new was absolute and final: what was to happen *had* so absolutely and finally happened that he was as little able to know a fear for his future as to know a hope; so absent in short was any question of anything still to come. He was to live entirely with the other question, that of his unidentified past, that of his having to see his fortune impenetrably muffled and masked.

The torment of this vision became then his occupation; he couldn't perhaps have consented to live but for the possibility of guessing. She had told him, his friend, not to guess; she had forbidden him, so far as he might, to know, and she had even in a sort denied the power in him to learn: which were so many things, precisely, to deprive him of rest. It wasn't that he wanted, he argued for fairness, that anything past and done should repeat itself; it was only that he shouldn't, as an anticlimax, have been taken sleeping so sound as not to be able to win back by an effort of thought the lost stuff of consciousness. He declared to himself at moments that he would either win it back or have done with consciousness for ever; he made this idea his one motive in fine, made it so much his passion that none other, to compare with it, seemed ever to have touched him. The lost stuff of consciousness became thus for him as a strayed or stolen child to an unappeasable father; he hunted it up and down very much as if he were knocking at doors and enquiring of the police. This was the spirit in which, inevitably, he set himself to travel; he started on a journey that was to be as long as he could make it; it danced before him that, as the other side of the globe couldn't possibly have less to say to him, it might, by a possibility of suggestion, have more. Before he quitted London, however, he made a pilgrimage to May Bartram's grave, took his way to it through the endless avenues of the grim suburban necropolis,[8] sought it out in the wilderness of tombs, and, though he had come but for the renewal of the act of farewell, found himself, when he had at last stood by it, beguiled into long intensities. He stood for an hour, powerless to turn away and yet powerless to penetrate the darkness of death; fixing with his eyes her inscribed name and date, beating his forehead against the fact of the secret they kept, drawing his breath, while he waited, as if some sense would in pity of him rise from the stones. He kneeled on the stones, however, in vain; they kept what they concealed; and if the face of the tomb did become a face for him it was because her two names became a pair of eyes that didn't know him. He gave them a last long look, but no palest light broke.

VI

He stayed away, after this, for a year; he visited the depths of Asia, spending himself on scenes of romantic interest, of superlative sanctity; but what was present to him everywhere was that for a man who had known what *he* had known the world was vulgar and vain. The state of mind in which he had lived for so many years shone out to him, in reflexion, as a light that coloured and refined, a light beside which the glow of the East was garish cheap and thin. The terrible truth was that he had lost—with everything else—a distinction as well; the things he saw couldn't help being common when he had become common to look at them. He was simply now one of them himself—he was in the dust, without a peg for the sense of difference; and there were hours when before the temples of gods and the sepulchres of kings, his spirit turned for nobleness of association to the barely discriminated slab in the London suburb. That had become for him, and more intensely with time and distance, his one witness of a past glory. It was all that was left to him for proof or pride, yet the past glories of Pharaohs were nothing to him as he thought of it. Small wonder then that he came back to it on the morrow of his return. He was drawn there this time as irresistibly as the other, yet with a confidence, almost, that was doubtless the effect of the many months that had elapsed. He had lived, in spite of himself, into his change of feeling, and in wandering over the earth had wandered, as might be said, from the circumference to the centre of his desert. He had settled to his safety and accepted perforce his extinction; figuring to himself, with some colour, in the likeness of certain little old men he remembered to have seen, of whom, all meagre and wizened as they might look, it was related that they had

---

8. City of the dead.

in their time fought twenty duels or been loved by ten princesses. They indeed had been wondrous for others while he was but wondrous for himself; which, however, was exactly the cause of his haste to renew the wonder by getting back, as he might put it, into his own presence. That had quickened his steps and checked his delay. If his visit was prompt it was because he had been separated so long from the part of himself that alone he now valued.

It's accordingly not false to say that he reached his goal with a certain elation and stood there again with a certain assurance. The creature beneath the sod *knew* of his rare experience, so that strangely now, the place had lost for him its mere blankness of expression. It met him in mildness—not, as before, in mockery; it wore for him the air of conscious greeting that we find, after absence, in things that have closely belonged to us and which seem to confess of themselves to the connexion. The plot of ground, the green tablet, the tended flowers affected him so as belonging to him that he resembled for the hour a contented landlord reviewing a piece of property. Whatever had happened—well, had happened. He had not come back this time with the vanity of that question, his former worrying "What, *what?*" now practically so spent. Yet he would none the less never again so cut himself off from the spot; he would come back to it every month, for if he did nothing else by its aid he at least held up his head. It thus grew for him, in the oddest way, a positive resource; he carried out his idea of periodical returns, which took their place at last among the most inveterate of his habits. What it all amounted to, oddly enough, was that in his finally so simplified world this garden of death gave him the few square feet of earth on which he could still most live. It was as if, being nothing anywhere else for any one, nothing even for himself, he were just everything here, and if not for a crowd of witnesses or indeed for any witness but John Marcher, then by clear right of the register that he could scan like an open page. The open page was the tomb of his friend, and *there* were the facts of the past, there the truth of his life, there the backward reaches in which he could lose himself. He did this from time to time with such effect that he seemed to wander through the old years with his hand in the arm of a companion who was, in the most extraordinary manner, his other, his younger self; and to wander, which was more extraordinary yet, round and round a third presence—not wandering she, but stationary, still, whose eyes, turning with his revolution, never ceased to follow him, and whose seat was his point, so to speak, of orientation. Thus in short he settled to live—feeding all on the sense that he once *had* lived, and dependent on it not alone for a support but for an identity.

It sufficed him in its way for months and the year elapsed; it would doubtless even have carried him further but for an accident, superficially slight, which moved him, quite in another direction, with a force beyond any of his impressions of Egypt or of India. It was a thing of the merest chance—the turn, as he afterwards felt, of a hair, though he was indeed to live to believe that if light hadn't come to him in this particular fashion it would still have come in another. He was to live to believe this, I say, though he was not to live, I may not less definitely mention, to do much else. We allow him at any rate the benefit of the conviction, struggling up for him at the end, that, whatever might have happened or not happened, he would have come round of himself to the light. The incident of an autumn day had put the match to the train laid from of old by his misery. With the light before him he knew that even of late his ache had only been smothered. It was strangely drugged, but it throbbed; at the touch it began to bleed. And the touch, in the event, was the face of a fellow-mortal. This face, one grey afternoon when the leaves were thick in the alleys, looked into Marcher's own, at the cemetery, with an expression like the cut of a blade. He felt it, that is, so deep down that he winced at the steady thrust. The person who so mutely assaulted him was a figure he had noticed, on reaching his own goal, absorbed by a grave a short distance away, a grave apparently fresh, so that the emotion of the visitor would probably match it for frankness. This fact alone forbade further attention, though during the time he stayed he remained vaguely conscious of his neighbour, a middle-aged man apparently, in mourning, whose bowed back, among the clustered monuments and mortuary yews, was constantly presented. Marcher's theory that these were elements in contact with which he himself revived, had suffered, on this occasion, it may be granted, a marked, an excessive check. The autumn day was dire for him as none had recently been, and he rested with a heaviness he had not yet known on the low stone table that bore May Bartram's name. He rested without power to move, as if some spring in him, some spell vouchsafed, had suddenly been broken for ever. If he could have done that moment as he wanted he would simply have stretched himself on the slab that was ready to take him, treating it as a place prepared to receive his last sleep. What in all the wide world had he now to keep awake for? He stared before him with the question, and it was then that, as one of the cemetery walks passed near him, he caught the shock of the face.

His neighbour at the other grave had withdrawn, as he himself, with force enough in him, would have done by now, and was advancing along the path on his way to one of the gates. This brought him close, and his pace was slow, so that—and all the more as there was a kind of hunger in his look—the two men were for a minute directly confronted. Marcher knew him at once for one of the deeply stricken—a perception so sharp that nothing else in the picture comparatively lived, neither his dress, his age, nor his presumable character and class; nothing lived but the deep ravage of the features that he showed. He *showed* them—that was the point; he was moved, as he passed, by some impulse that was either a signal for sympathy or, more possibly, a challenge to an opposed sorrow. He might already have been aware of our friend, might at some previous hour have noticed in him the smooth habit of the scene, with which the state of his own senses so scantly consorted, and might thereby have been stirred as by an overt discord. What Marcher was at all events conscious of was in the first place that the image of scarred passion presented to him was conscious too—of something that profaned the air; and in the second that, roused, startled, shocked, he was yet the next moment looking after it, as it went, with envy. The most extraordinary thing that had happened to him—though he had given that name to other matters as well—took place, after his immediate vague stare, as a consequence of this impression. The stranger passed, but the raw glare of his grief remained, making our friend wonder in pity what wrong, what wound it expressed, what injury not to be healed. What had the man *had*, to make him by the loss of it so bleed and yet live?

Something—and this reached him with a pang—that *he*, John Marcher, hadn't; the proof of which was precisely John Marcher's arid end. No passion had ever touched him, for this was what passion meant; he had survived and maundered and pined, but where had been *his* deep ravage? The extraordinary thing we speak of was the sudden rush of the result of this question. The sight that had just met his eyes named to him, as in letters of quick flame, something he had utterly, insanely missed, and what he had missed made these things a train of fire, made them mark themselves in an anguish of inward throbs. He had seen *outside* of his life, not learned it within, the way a woman was mourned when she had been loved for herself: such was the force of his conviction of the meaning of the stranger's face, which still flared for him as a smoky torch. It hadn't come to him, the knowledge, on the wings of experience; it had brushed him, jostled him, upset him, with the disrespect of chance, the insolence of accident. Now that the illumination had begun, however, it blazed to the zenith, and what he presently stood there gazing at was the sounded void of his life. He gazed, he drew breath, in pain; he turned in his dismay, and, turning, he had before him in sharper incision than ever the open page of his story. The name on the table smote him as the passage of his neighbour had done, and what it said to him, full in the face, was that *she* was what he had missed. This was the awful thought, the answer to all the past, the vision at the dread clearness of which he turned as cold as the stone beneath him. Everything fell together, confessed, explained, overwhelmed; leaving him most of all stupefied at the blindness he had cherished. The fate he had been marked for he had met with a vengeance—he had emptied the cup to the lees; he had been the man of his time, *the* man, to whom nothing on earth was to have happened. That was the rare stroke—that was his visitation. So he saw it, as we say, in pale horror, while the pieces fitted and fitted. So *she* had seen it while he didn't, and so she served at this hour to drive the truth home. It was the truth, vivid and monstrous, that all the while he had waited the wait was itself his portion. This the companion of his vigil had at a given moment made out, and she had then offered him the chance to baffle his doom. One's doom, however, was never baffled, and on the day she told him his own had come down she had seen him but stupidly stare at the escape she offered him.

The escape would have been to love her; then, *then* he would have lived. *She* had lived—who could say now with what passion?—since she had loved him for himself; whereas he had never thought of her (ah how it hugely glared at him!) but in the chill of his egotism and the light of her use. Her spoken words came back to him—the chain stretched and stretched. The Beast had lurked indeed, and the Beast, at its hour, had sprung; it had sprung in that twilight of the cold April when, pale, ill, wasted, but all beautiful, and perhaps even then recoverable, she had risen from her chair to stand before him and let him imaginably guess. It had sprung as he didn't guess; it had sprung as she hopelessly turned from him, and the mark, by the time he left her, had fallen where it *was* to fall. He had justified his fear and achieved his fate; he had failed, with the last exactitude, of all he was to fail of; and a moan now rose to his lips as he remembered she had prayed he mightn't know. This horror of waking—*this* was knowledge, knowledge under the breath of which the very tears in his eyes seemed to freeze. Through them, none the less, he tried to fix it and hold it; he kept it there before him so that he might feel the pain. That at least, belated and bitter, had something of the taste of life. But the bitterness suddenly sickened him, and it was as if, horribly, he saw, in the truth, in the cruelty of his image, what had been appointed and done. He saw the Jungle of his life and saw the lurking Beast; then, while he looked, perceived it, as by a stir of the air, rise, huge and hideous, for the leap that was to settle him. His eyes darkened—it was close; and, instinctively turning, in his hallucination, to avoid it, he flung himself, face down, on the tomb.

—1903

Max Beerbohm, Mr. *Rudyard Kipling takes a bloomin' day aht, on the Blasted 'Eath, along with Brittania, 'is gurl* (1904).

PART IV

England and Its Others

England and Its Others: Introduction

Between 1870 and 1900 the British Empire occupied four million square miles, administering territories in Southern and Central Africa, Australia and New Zealand, Canada, the West Indies (the Bahamas and Antilles islands), Burma, Hong Kong, Afghanistan, Egypt, Malaysia, and India. It is an almost unimaginably vast task: the British had to study local languages, customs, and religions; build entire infrastructures, from transit systems to hotels to universities; install and maintain legal systems; detect and defeat rebellions; define borders; support missionaries; arrange political alliances; administer every detail of a civil service bureaucracy; and govern nations far larger than Great Britain itself. They had to do this thousands of miles from home, in dozens of different regions, each with its own particular needs. The Empire gave the British national and religious pride, enormous wealth, and a claim to superiority over their colonial subjects. At the *fin de siècle*, imperialism was a popular ideology with widespread support. The word *jingoism*, aggressive patriotism, came from a music-hall song during this period: in 1878, G. W. Hunt sang, "We don't want to fight, yet by jingo! if we do, / We've got the ships, we've got the men, and got the money too."

Yet the British Empire did not always present a reassuring prospect for the colonial masters. Native people often resented their subjection, challenging the comforting myth that the British were bringing Christian civilization to the savages. Moreover, those native people often proved themselves capable of doing things as well as—or better than—the British themselves. In such cases, British observers had to wonder: What justified one group's control of the other? What, indeed, made British culture "British" if an Indian woman such as Toru Dutt or a West Indian man such as J. J. Thomas could use English literary techniques so beautifully? Another problem: although the British might have liked to imagine a powerful, centrally controlled global Empire, in reality it was much more like a ramshackle assemblage of differently governed, partially autonomous, mutinous colonies, creatively reworking

British culture. Instead of the British conquering and imposing themselves on natives, the cultures fused, permanently altering one another. Colonial subjects could use the English language and English verse forms to retell Celtic myths or Bengali tales. Nobody embodies these paradoxes more vividly than Rudyard Kipling, who urged fanatical imperialist expansionism while showing profound sympathy for the colonized. Kipling's writing is both fundamentally Indian and ardently British; no less than Toru Dutt's, it represents the new composite cultures springing from the imperial project.

"Writing Empire" offers a selection of texts from across the British Empire, while special sections on Africa, India, and Ireland focus on the areas of greatest ferment during the *fin de siècle*. In each case, these writers engage in a passionate conversation—fighting each other and themselves—to define the natives' capabilities, the local culture and geography, the Europeans' role in the region, the symbolic qualities projected onto the region, and the changing, emerging nature of colonial identity.

Writing Empire

This section begins with famous jingoistic poems by Sir Henry Newbolt and Rudyard Kipling (and Henry Labouchère's deft, devastating parody of Kipling), showing us the intense emotions undergirding the imperial project. We then turn to the West Indies, a region that had been central to the slave trade, which brought enslaved West Africans to labor on sugar plantations in the Caribbean islands. Britain abolished slavery in 1833, but it continued in all but name for several more years, and when it was finally eradicated, the economy was badly affected. Plantations collapsed, the ex-slaves were desperately impoverished, and there were few alternative economic structures in place. Governmental chaos and frequent uprisings further destabilized the region. Most infamous was the Morant Bay Rebellion in Jamaica in 1865, which Governor Edward Eyre suppressed with indiscriminate shootings, state executions, and floggings (many inflicted on people who had nothing to do with the riots). The storm of controversy back in Britain foregrounded the question of the West Indians' identity: Were they threatening beasts to be exterminated, or human beings with rights who had been brutally ill-treated? This is the debate undergirding the excerpts from the writings of James Anthony Froude and J. J. Thomas.

While the West Indies was associated with atrocious violence, an island archipelago on the other side of the world accrued a more mythic status. The Pacific islands, remote from Great Britain and without many exploitable natural resources, were claimed by France and England and visited mostly by missionaries in the nineteenth century. Writers depicted Polynesian islands like Tahiti as sensual paradises of naked women, endless fruit, perfect weather, and utter sexual license but condemned Melanesian islands like Fiji for cannibalism and savagery. Practices such as tattooing and tabooing worried the British, too. In the 1890s Robert Louis Stevenson traveled to the South Seas for his health, and his accounts provide some of the most sensitive and penetrating depictions of daily life in these islands.

Some of those Pacific islands shared in the growing prosperity of the region's two great countries, Australia and New Zealand. Australia had begun its colonial history as a penal colony, and Britain transported convicts there from 1788 to the 1860s. While New Zealand was seen as rural and remote, Australia was known as a rough place where unsuccessful men might find one last chance, farming sheep or digging gold (its gold rush began in the 1850s). The 1890s saw a new Australian literary movement, mostly associated with the *Bulletin* literary magazine, that celebrated life in the bush, a tough world of unrelenting weather, desperate loneliness, and male adventure. The rugged landscape and the vast distances inspired Australian writers, but Dorothea Mackellar's decision to depict the continent as attractive because of its emptiness may provoke the question of why (and whether) the aborigines had to be erased from this construction of Australia.

Like the Australian writers, Canadian writers of the *fin de siècle* praised vast unpopulated plains, brutally extreme weather, and unfamiliar flora—and, like the Australians, they had to figure out what space the indigenous inhabitants could occupy in that poetic landscape. In 1867 Canada became a self-governing colony under British rule. But this political affiliation was complicated by historical ties with France (which controlled much of Canada through the mid-eighteenth century), geographical proximity to the United States, and the presence of Native Americans. What, then, did it mean to be Canadian? "Said the Canoe" by Isabella Valancy Crawford offers a fascinating answer in using the conventions of European love lyrics to describe Native American culture and North American landscape.

All the readings in this section show colonial identities as spaces of contestation. British subjects in the West Indies, Pacific islands, Australia, and Canada encountered bodies, landscapes, and voices that spoke in other languages. These *fin-de-siècle* writings reveal the stress, the danger, and the excitement in this new, and mutual, scrutiny, both in what gets said and what (and whom) gets silenced.

Sir Henry Newbolt
1862–1938

Once widely admired for his vigorous patriotic and nautical verses, Sir Henry Newbolt has now been almost completely forgotten except for "Vitaï Lampada." Newbolt, who trained as a lawyer, also wrote novels, edited poetry anthologies, edited *The Monthly Review*, and produced the official naval history of World War I. A liberal and progressive thinker, his love of country infused his poems with deep fervor. For the late Victorians "Vitaï Lampada" was profoundly inspirational. It sums up the almost touchingly innocent pre-war British pride in the way public-school sports taught patriotism, manliness, honor, and teamwork. This kind of boys' bonding experience did make the work of Empire possible by facilitating troop loyalty, but it did not stand up against the guns of World War I.

Vitaï Lampada[1]

There's a breathless hush in the Close to-night—
   Ten to make and the match to win[2]—
A bumping pitch and a blinding light,
   An hour to play and the last man in.
And it's not for the sake of a ribboned coat,   5
   Or the selfish hope of a season's fame,
But his Captain's hand on his shoulder smote—
   "Play up! play up! and play the game!"

The sand of the desert is sodden red,—
   Red with the wreck of a square[3] that broke;—   10
The Gatling's[4] jammed and the Colonel dead,
   And the regiment blind with dust and smoke.
The river of death has brimmed his banks,
   And England's far, and Honour a name,
But the voice of a schoolboy rallies the ranks: 15
   "Play up! play up! and play the game!"

This is the word that year by year,
   While in her place the School is set,
Every one of her sons must hear,
   And none that hears it dare forget.   20
This they all with a joyful mind
   Bear through life like a torch in flame,
And falling fling to the host behind—
   "Play up! play up! and play the game!"

—1897

Rudyard Kipling
1865–1936

Henry James called him "the infant monster" and Max Beerbohm caricatured him as a stout, florid little man, blasting a horn on behalf of Britannia. But was Rudyard Kipling really such a blatantly masculinist imperialist? Born in India, he had an idyllic early childhood with Hindustani as his main language and was miserable when sent to England at age five. In 1882 he returned to his beloved India as a journalist and began to produce tales of Indian (especially

---

1. Latin: the torch of life (from Roman poet Lucretius, *De Rerum Natura* 2.79).
2. They're playing cricket on the school fields.
3. A protective troop formation. At the battle of Abu Klea (1885), the Sudanese broke the square.
4. First rapid-fire gun, used in British combat in Africa.

Anglo-Indian) life, characterized by startlingly realistic physical and linguistic details. The British public had never read such vivid evocations of Indian life, and Kipling became a celebrity when he was only in his twenties. His energetic, economical, vernacular prose style differed drastically from the aesthetes' languidly baroque archaisms. His poetry, too, moved with a vigorous rhythmic swing, as it worked to celebrate the "Tommies," the ordinary soldiers of Empire. Kipling also became famous for his children's tales, the "Just-So" stories, and he reported from South Africa during the Boer War. He was awarded the Nobel Prize in 1902. His best work memorializes the unromantic hard, everyday service that built the Empire, commemorating both the expatriates and the native people involved in British overseas administrations. But as Kipling aged, his imperialism hardened, opposing Home Rule in India and celebrating what he infamously dubbed "the white man's burden." As he got older, too, his writing became more somber, especially when he lost his only son in World War I and wrote, "If any question why we died / Tell them, because our fathers lied." This couplet, with its double, contradictory, tragic identification ("we" are soldiers, but it is written by a father) sums up the complexity of Kipling's work at its best. For more information about Kipling, see p. 527.

The White Man's Burden[1]

Take up the White Man's burden—
Send forth the best ye breed—
Go, bind your sons to exile
To serve your captives' need;
To wait, in heavy harness,   5
On fluttered folk and wild—
Your new-caught, sullen peoples,
Half devil and half child.

Take up the White Man's burden—
In patience to abide,   10
To veil the threat of terror
And check the show of pride;
By open speech and simple,
An hundred times made plain,
To seek another's profit   15
And work another's gain.

Take up the White Man's burden—
The savage wars of peace—
Fill full the mouth of Famine,
And bid the sickness cease;   20
And when your goal is nearest
(The end for others sought)
Watch sloth and heathen folly
Bring all your hope to nought.

---

1. Written to commemorate the U.S. acquisition of the Philippines in 1899.

Take up the White Man's burden—   25
No iron rule of kings,
But toil of serf and sweeper—
The tale of common things.
The ports ye shall not enter,
The roads ye shall not tread,   30
Go, mark them with your living
And mark them with your dead.

Take up the White Man's burden,
And reap his old reward—
The blame of those ye better   35
The hate of those ye guard—
The cry of hosts ye humour
(Ah, slowly!) toward the light:—
"Why brought ye us from bondage,
Our loved Egyptian night?"[2]   40

Take up the White Man's burden—
Ye dare not stoop to less—
Nor call too loud on Freedom
To cloak your weariness.
By all ye will or whisper,   45
By all ye leave or do,
The silent sullen peoples
Shall weigh your God and you.

Take up the White Man's burden!
Have done with childish days—   50
The lightly-proffered laurel,[3]
The easy ungrudged praise:
Comes now, to search your manhood
Through all the thankless years,
Cold, edged with dear-bought wisdom,   55
The judgment of your peers.

                                                                  —1899

---

2. The "white men" are like Moses leading the Israelites out of Egyptian bondage.
3. Symbol of victory and public honor.

Henry Labouchère
1831–1912

If you admire Oscar Wilde, you may know Henry Labouchère's name. He was the Member of Parliament responsible for the law under which Wilde was convicted, the Criminal Law Amendment Act of 1885 ("the Labouchère Amendment"). It is terribly ironic that this radical politician is now best known for his most reactionary legislation. In fact, Labouchère was a pioneering radical, agnostic, crusading journalist, an anti-imperialist and a staunch defender of feminist causes. Historians speculate that he sponsored the Criminal Law Amendment Act hoping that its cruelly punitive provisions would prevent it from passing and was appalled when it was voted in. Labouchère became famous for his *Daily News* dispatches from Paris under siege in the Franco-Prussian War (1870–71) and for exposing a forger responsible for a letter incriminating the leader of the Irish independence movement, Charles Parnell. As a Member of Parliament, Labouchère opposed the Boer War and demanded the abolition of the House of Lords. His newspaper, *Truth*, publicized radical causes and exposed frauds. "The Brown Man's Burden" (1899) shows his witty style and indignant politics.

The Brown Man's Burden

Pile on the brown man's burden
  To gratify your greed;
Go clear away the "niggers"
  Who progress would impede;
Be very stern, for truly   5
  'Tis useless to be mild
With new-caught, sullen peoples,
  Half devil and half child.

Pile on the brown man's burden;
  And if ye rouse his hate,   10
Meet his old-fashioned reasons
  With Maxims up to date.
With shells and dumdum bullets[1]
  A hundred times made plain
The brown man's loss must ever   15
  Imply the white man's gain.

Pile on the brown man's burden,
  Compel him to be free;
Let all your manifestoes
  Reek with philanthropy.   20

---

1. Initially introduced by the British in India, dumdum bullets expand upon impact to create maximum damage.

And if with heathen folly
  He dares your will dispute,
Then in the name of freedom
  Don't hesitate to shoot.

Pile on the brown man's burden,   25
  And if his cry be sore,
That surely need not irk you—
  Ye've driven slaves before.
Seize on his ports and pastures,
  The fields his people tread;   30
Go make from them your living,
  And mark them with his dead.

Pile on the brown man's burden,
  Nor do not deem it hard
If you should earn the rancor   35
  Of these ye yearn to guard,
The screaming of your eagle
  Will drown the victim's sob—
Go on through fire and slaughter.
  There's dollars in the job.   40

Pile on the brown man's burden,
  And through the world proclaim
That ye are freedom's agent—
  There's no more paying game!
And should your own past history   45
  Straight in your teeth be thrown,
Retort that independence
  Is good for whites alone.

Pile on the brown man's burden,
  With equity have done;   50
Weak, antiquated scruples
  Their squeamish course have run,
And though 'tis freedom's banner
  You're waving in the van,[2]
Reserve for home consumption   55
  The sacred "rights of man"![3]

And if by chance ye falter,
  Or lag along the course,

---

2. The foremost, advancing part of the army.
3. Famous slogan from the French Revolution, internationally popularized by Thomas Paine's *The Rights of Man* (1791).

If, as the blood flows freely,
    Ye feel some slight remorse,   60
Hie ye to Rudyard Kipling,
    Imperialism's prop,
And bid him, for your comfort,
    Turn on his jingo stop.[4]

—1899

James Anthony Froude
1818–1894

Author of a twelve-volume history of sixteenth-century England and a four-volume biography of the Victorian sage Thomas Carlyle, James Anthony Froude developed a new way to write history. Froude started as a clergyman with a fellowship at Exeter College, but his writing career began when he published a novel expressing religious doubt; he had to resign when the rector publicly burnt copies of the book. Although Froude's *The Science of History* made an important case for using original documents when writing history, his vivid style, his skepticism about historical truth, and his eagerness to engage in theological and racial debates of the period often made his work very controversial. His highly opinionated *History of England in the Sixteenth Century* alienated other historians, and his harsh biography of Carlyle shocked readers accustomed to reverential memoirs. For modern readers, however, Froude's colonialist writing is his most outrageous work. In *The English in Ireland in the Eighteenth Century* (1872–74), he argues that the Irish are incapable of governing themselves, and he makes the same claim about West Indians in *The English in the West Indies* (1888), where he constructs the colonial subjects as childlike: happy, innocent, ignorant, and eager for British rule.

from The English in the West Indies

West Indian civilisation is old-fashioned, and has none of the pushing manners which belong to younger and perhaps more thriving communities. The West Indians themselves, though they may be deficient in energy, are uniformly ladies and gentlemen, and all their arrangements take their complexion from the general tone of society. There is a refinement visible at once in the subsidiary vessels of the mail service which ply among the islands. They are almost as large as those which cross the Atlantic, and never on any line in the world have I met with officers so courteous and cultivated. The cabins were spacious and as cool as a temperature of 80°, gradually rising as we went south, would permit. Punkahs[1] waved over us at dinner. In our berths a single sheet was all that was provided for us, and this was one more than we needed. A sea was running when we cleared out from under the land. Among the

---

4. Kipling can mechanically turn on his jingoism, like a switch on a player piano.

---

1. Palm-frond fans.

cabin passengers was a coloured family in good circumstances moving about with nurses and children. The little things, who had never been at sea before, sat on the floor, staring out of their large helpless black eyes, not knowing what was the matter with them. Forward there were perhaps two or three hundred coloured people going from one island to another, singing, dancing, and chattering all night long, as radiant and happy as carelessness and content could make them. Sick or not sick made no difference. Nothing could disturb the imperturbable good humour and good spirits.

It was too hot to sleep; we sat several of us smoking on deck, and I learnt the first authentic particulars of the present manner of life of these much misunderstood people. Evidently they belonged to a race far inferior to the Zulus and Caffres,[2] whom I had known in South Africa. They were more coarsely formed in limb and feature. They would have been slaves in their own country if they had not been brought to ours, and at the worst had lost nothing by the change. They were good-natured, innocent, harmless, lazy perhaps, but not more lazy than is perfectly natural when even Europeans must be roused to activity by cocktail.

In the Antilles generally, Barbadoes being the only exception, negro families have each their cabin, their garden ground, their grazing for a cow. They live surrounded by most of the fruits which grew in Adam's paradise—oranges and plantains, bread-fruit, and cocoa-nuts, though not apples. Their yams and cassava grow without effort, for the soil is easily worked and inexhaustibly fertile. The curse is taken off from nature, and like Adam again they are under the covenant of innocence. Morals in the technical sense they have none, but they cannot be said to sin, because they have no knowledge of a law, and therefore they can commit no breach of the law. They are naked and not ashamed. They are *married* as they call it, but not *parsoned*. The woman prefers a looser tie that she may be able to leave a man if he treats her unkindly. Yet they are not licentious. I never saw an immodest look in one of their faces, and never heard of any venal profligacy. The system is strange, but it answers. A missionary told me that a connection rarely turns out well which begins with a legal marriage. The children scramble up anyhow, and shift for themselves like chickens as soon as they are able to peck. Many die in this way by eating unwholesome food, but also many live, and those who do live grow up exactly like their parents. It is a very peculiar state of things, not to be understood, as priest and missionary agree, without long acquaintance. There is evil, but there is not the demoralising effect of evil. They sin, but they sin only as animals, without shame, because there is no sense of doing wrong. They eat the forbidden fruit, but it brings with it no knowledge of the difference between good and evil. They steal, but if detected they fall back upon the Lord. It was de will of de Lord that they should do this or that. De Lord forbid that they should go against his holy pleasure. In fact these poor children of darkness have escaped the consequences of the Fall, and must come of another stock after all.

Meanwhile they are perfectly happy. In no part of the globe is there any peasantry whose every want is so completely satisfied as her Majesty's black subjects in these West Indian islands. They have no aspirations to make them restless. They have no guilt upon their consciences. They have food for the picking up. Clothes they need not, and lodging in such a climate need not be elaborate. They have perfect liberty,

---

2. Caffres (Kaffirs), an old derogatory term for black Africans at the Cape, including the Zulu tribe.

and are safe from dangers, to which if left to themselves they would be exposed, for the English rule prevents the strong from oppressing the weak. In their own country they would have remained slaves to more warlike races. In the West Indies their fathers underwent a bondage of a century or two, lighter at its worst than the easiest form of it in Africa; their descendants in return have nothing now to do save to laugh and sing and enjoy existence. Their quarrels, if they have any, begin and end in words. If happiness is the be all and end all of life, and those who have most of it have most completely attained the object of their being, the "nigger" who now basks among the ruins of the West Indian plantations is the supremest specimen of present humanity.

We retired to our berths at last. At waking we were at anchor off St. Vincent, an island of volcanic mountains robed in forest from shore to crest. Till late in the last century it was the headquarters of the Caribs, who kept up a savage independence there, recruited by runaway slaves from Barbadoes or elsewhere. Brandy and Sir Ralph Abercrombie reduced them to obedience in 1796,[3] and St. Vincent throve tolerably down to the days of free trade. Even now when I saw it, Kingston, the principal town, looked pretty and well to do, reminding me, strange to say, of towns in Norway, the houses stretching along the shore painted in the same tints of blue or yellow or pink, with the same red-tiled roofs, the trees coming down the hill sides to the water's edge, villas of modest pretensions shining through the foliage, with the patches of cane fields, the equivalent in the landscape of the brilliant Norwegian grass. The prosperity has for the last forty years waned and waned. There are now two thousand white people there, and forty thousand coloured people, and the proportion alters annually to our disadvantage. The usual remedies have been tried. The constitution has been altered a dozen times. Just now I believe the Crown is trying to do without one, having found the results of the elective principle not encouraging, but we shall perhaps revert to it before long; any way, the tables show that each year the trade of the island decreases, and will continue to decrease while the expenditure increases and will increase.

I did not land, for the time was short, and as a beautiful picture the island was best seen from the deck. The characteristics of the people are the same in all the Antilles, and could be studied elsewhere. * * *

In the West Indies there is indefinite wealth waiting to be developed by intelligence and capital; and men with such resources, both English and American, might be tempted still to settle there, and lead the blacks along with them into more settled manners and higher forms of civilisation. But the future of the blacks, and our own influence over them for good, depend on their being protected from themselves and from the schemers who would take advantage of them. However little may be the share to which the mass of a population be admitted in the government of their country, they are never found hard to manage where they prosper and are justly dealt with. The children of darkness are even easier of control than the children of light.[4] Under an administration formed on the model of that of our Eastern Empire[5] these islands would be peopled in a generation or two with dusky citizens, as proud as the rest of

---

3. The British took St. Vincent in 1783, but Carib resistance continued until Abercrombie, leading the British forces, crushed them in 1796.

4. Froude's racism also alludes to Jesus's teachings about how cheaters succeed more than the virtuous: "the children of this world are in their generation wiser than the children of light" (Luke 16.8).

5. India.

us of the flag under which they will have thriven, and as willing to defend it against any invading enemy as they are now unquestionably indifferent. Partially elected councils, local elected boards, &c., serve only as contrivances to foster discontent and encourage jobbery.[6] They open a rift which time will widen, and which will create for us, on a smaller scale, the conditions which have so troubled us in Ireland, where each concession of popular demands makes the maintenance of the connection more difficult. In the Pacific colonies self-government is a natural right; the colonists are part of ourselves, and have as complete a claim to the management of their own affairs as we have to the management of ours. The less we interfere with them the more heartily they identify themselves with us. But if we choose besides to indulge our ambition with an empire, if we determine to keep attached to our dominion countries which, like the East Indies, have been conquered by the sword, countries, like the West Indies, which, however acquired, are occupied by races enormously outnumbering us, many of whom do not speak our language, are not connected with us by sentiment, and not visibly connected by interest, with whom our own people will not intermarry or hold social intercourse, but keep aloof from, as superior from inferior—to impose on such countries forms of self-government at which we have ourselves but lately arrived, to put it in the power of these overwhelming numbers to shake us off if they please, and to assume that when our real motive has been only to save ourselves trouble they will be warmed into active loyalty by gratitude for the confidence which we pretend to place in them, is to try an experiment which we have not the slightest right to expect to be successful, and which if it fails is fatal.

Once more, if we mean to keep the blacks as British subjects, we are bound to govern them, and to govern them well. If we cannot do it, we had better let them go altogether.

—1888

J. J. Thomas
1840–1889

Born in Trinidad just a few years after the British ended slavery, and fascinated by the Creole dialect, John Jacob Thomas taught himself linguistics while teaching and working in the Civil Service. He wrote his pioneering *The Theory and Practice of Creole Grammar* in 1869. Outraged by Froude's *The English in the West Indies*, Thomas published critical articles in the Grenada newspaper, which he collected in *Froudacity*. In this book, a West Indian of African descent dared to critique one of the major British intellectual figures of his generation, a remarkably courageous act. The style of *Froudacity* also shows how hard Thomas had to work to gain his readers' respect. His frequent Latin tags and learned allusions, along with the rigorously close analyses of Froude's style, demonstrate that Thomas was a serious intellectual himself, a colonial subject better informed than his colonial master.

---

6. Using public service for personal gain.

from **Froudacity**

Barbados.

Our distinguished voyager visited many of the British West Indies, landing first at Barbados, his social experience whereof is set forth in a very agreeable account. Our immediate business, however, is not with what West Indian hospitality, especially among the well-to-do classes, can and does accomplish for the entertainment of visitors, and particularly visitors so eminent as Mr. Froude. We are concerned with what Mr. Froude has to say concerning our dusky brethren and sisters in those Colonies. We have, thus, much pleasure in being able at the outset to extract the following favourable verdict of his respecting them—premising, at the same time, that the balcony from which Mr. Froude surveyed the teeming multitude in Bridgetown[1] was that of a grand hotel at which he had, on invitation, partaken of the refreshing beverage mentioned in the citation:—

"Cocktail over, and walking in the heat of the sun being a thing not to be thought of, I sat for two hours in the balcony, watching the people, who were as thick as bees in swarming time. Nine-tenths of them were pure black. You rarely saw a white face, but still less would you see a discontented one, imperturbable good humour and self-satisfaction being written on the features of every one. The women struck me especially. They were smartly dressed in white calico, scrupulously clean, and tricked out with ribands and feathers; but their figures were so good, and they carried themselves so well and gracefully, that although they might make themselves absurd, they could not look vulgar. Like the Greek and Etruscan women, they are trained from childhood to carry weights on their heads. They are thus perfectly upright, and plant their feet firmly and naturally on the ground. They might serve for sculptors' models, and are well aware of it."

Regarding the other sex, Mr. Froude says:—

"The men were active enough, driving carts, wheeling barrows, and selling flying-fish," &c.

He also speaks with candour of the entire absence of drunkenness and quarrelling, and the agreeable prevalence of good humour and light-heartedness among them. Some critic might, on reading the above extract from our author's account of the men, be tempted to ask—"But what is the meaning of that little word 'enough' occurring therein?" We should be disposed to hazard a suggestion that Mr. Froude, being fair-minded and loyal to truth, as far as is compatible with his sympathy for his hapless "Anglo-West Indians,"[2] could not give an entirely ungrudging testimony in favour of the possible, nay probable, voters by whose suffrages the supremacy of the Dark Parliament[3] will be ensured, and the relapse into obeahism,[4] devil-worship, and children-eating be inaugurated. Nevertheless, *Si sic omnia dixisset*—if he had said all things thus! Yes, if Mr. Froude had, throughout his volume, spoken in this strain, his occasional want of patience and fairness with regard to our male kindred might have found condonation in his even more than chivalrous

---

1. Commercial port town.
2. The British ruling class.
3. West Indian self-governance; suffrages: votes.
4. Folk religion involving sorcery.

appreciation of our womankind. But it has been otherwise. So we are forced to try conclusions with him in the arena of his own selection—unreflecting spokesman that he is of British colonialism, which, we grieve to learn through Mr. Froude's pages, has, like the Bourbon family, not only forgotten nothing, but, unfortunately for its own peace, learnt nothing also.[5]

St. Vincent.

The following are the words in which our traveller embodies the main motive and purpose of his voyage:—

"My own chief desire was to see the human inhabitants, to learn what they were doing, how they were living, and what they were thinking about. . . . "

But, alas, with the mercurialism of temperament in which he has thought proper to indulge when only Negroes and Europeans not of "Anglo-West Indian" tendencies were concerned, he jauntily threw to the winds all the scruples and cautious minuteness which were essential to the proper execution of his project. At Barbados, as we have seen, he satisfies himself with sitting aloft, at a balcony-window, to contemplate the movements of the sable throng below, of whose character, moral and political, he nevertheless professes to have become a trustworthy delineator. From the above-quoted account of his impressions of the external traits and deportment of the Ethiopic folk thus superficially gazed at, our author passes on to an analysis of their mental and moral idiosyncrasies, and other intimate matters, which the very silence of the book as to his method of ascertaining them is a sufficient proof that his knowledge in their regard has not been acquired directly and at first hand. Nor need we say that the generally adverse cast of his verdicts on what he had been at no pains to study for himself points to the "hostileness" of the witnesses whose testimony alone has formed the basis of his conclusions. Throughout Mr. Froude's tour in the British Colonies his intercourse was exclusively with "Anglo-West Indians," whose aversion to the Blacks he has himself, perhaps they would think indiscreetly, placed on record. In no instance do we find that he condescended to visit the abode of any Negro, whether it was the mansion of a gentleman of the hut of a peasant of that race. The whole tenor of the book indicates his rigid adherence to this onesided course, and suggests also that, as a traveller, Mr. Froude considers maligning on hearsay to be just as convenient as reporting facts elicited by personal investigation. Proceed we, however, to strengthen our statement regarding his definitive abandonment, and that without any apparent reason, of the plan he had professedly laid down for himself at starting, and failing which no trustworthy data could have been obtained concerning the character and disposition of the people about whom he undertakes to thoroughly enlighten his readers. Speaking of St. Vincent, where he arrived immediately after leaving Barbados, our author says:—

"I did not land, for the time was short, and as a beautiful picture the island was best seen from the deck. The characteristics of the people are the same in all the Antilles, and could be studied elsewhere."

---

5. Politician Charles-Maurice de Talleyrand's (1754–1838) remark about the French ruling family after the French Revolution and Napoleonic wars.

Now, it is a fact, patent and notorious, that "the characteristics of the people are" *not* "the same in all the Antilles." A man of Mr. Froude's attainments, whose studies have made him familiar with ethnological facts, must be aware that difference of local surroundings and influences does, in the course of time, inevitably create difference of characteristic and deportment. Hence there is in nearly every Colony a marked dissimilarity of native qualities amongst the Negro inhabitants, arising not only from the causes above indicated, but largely also from the great diversity of their African ancestry. We might as well be told that because the nations of Europe are generally white and descended from Japhet,[6] they could be studied one by the light derived from acquaintance with another. We venture to declare that, unless a common education from youth has been shared by them, the Hamitic[7] inhabitants of one island have very little in common with those of another, beyond the dusky skin and woolly hair. In speech, character, and deportment, a coloured native of Trinidad differs as much from one of Barbados as a North American black does from either, in all the above respects.

Grenada.

In Grenada, the next island he arrived at, our traveller's procedure with regard to the inhabitants was very similar. There he landed in the afternoon, drove three or four miles inland to dine at the house of a "gentleman who was a passing resident," returned in the dark to his ship, and started for Trinidad. In the course of this journey back, however, as he sped along in the carriage, Mr. Froude found opportunity to look into the people's houses along the way, where, he tells us, he "could see and was astonished to observe signs of comfort, and even signs of taste—armchairs, sofas, side-boards with cut-glass upon them, engravings and coloured prints upon the walls." As a result of this nocturnal examination, *à vol d'oiseau*,[8] he has written paragraph upon paragraph about the people's character and prospects in the island of Grenada. To read the patronizing terms in which our historian-traveller has seen fit to comment on Grenada and its people, one would believe that his account is of some half-civilized, out-of-the-way region under British sway, and inhabited chiefly by a horde of semi-barbarian ignoramuses of African descent. If the world had not by this time thoroughly assessed the intrinsic value of Mr. Froude's utterances, one who knows Grenada might have felt inclined to resent his causeless depreciation of the intellectual capacity of its inhabitants; but considering the estimate which has been pretty generally formed of his historical judgment, Mr. Froude may be dismissed, as regards Grenada and its people, with a certain degree of scepticism. Such scepticism, though lost upon himself, is unquestionably needful to protect his readers from the hallucination which the author's singular contempt for accuracy is but too liable to induce.

—1889

---

6. Noah's son, the supposed ancestor of the Greeks and Northern Europeans.
7. Ham was another son of Noah, the supposed ancestor of the Egyptians and Africans.
8. French: bird's-eye view.

Robert Louis Stevenson
1850–1894

A haggard, skeletal, shadowy man strides out of his own picture in John Singer Sargent's famous portrait. The combination of vigorous motion and illness is exactly right for Robert Louis Stevenson, who was famous for popular tales of swashbuckling adventure (especially *Kidnapped* [1886] and *Treasure Island* [1883]) but had adventure enough just trying to stay alive. Born in Edinburgh, Stevenson trained as a lawyer and an engineer, and throughout his life he retained great affection for Scottish speech and customs, faithfully recorded in novels like *The Master of Ballantrae* (1889) and *Thrawn Janet* (1881). Because of his Calvinist upbringing, Stevenson was deeply concerned with evil and predestination, a preoccupation visible in his famous *Strange Case of Dr. Jekyll and Mr. Hyde* (1886), which also demonstrates the period's fascination with the unconscious mind. In his twenties, Stevenson's lungs became badly diseased, forcing him to avoid the harsh Scottish winters. Wandering through the United States, France, and the South of England with his American wife, Fanny, he finally ended up voyaging through the South Pacific and adopting Samoa as his home, where he died. *The Beach of Falesá* (1893) and *In the South Seas* (1896), written with a sympathetic interest in Pacific cultures, leave behind historical romance for a kind of realism that respected the daily difficulties of life in Polynesia.

The House of Temoana

The history of the Marquesas[1] is, of late years, much confused by the coming and going of the French. At least twice they have seized the archipelago, at least once deserted it; and in the meanwhile the natives pursued almost without interruption their desultory cannibal wars. Through these events and changing dynasties, a single considerable figure may be seen to move: that of the high chief, a king, Temoana. Odds and ends of his history came to my ears: how he was at first a convert of the Protestant mission; how he was kidnapped or exiled from his native land, served as cook aboard a whaler, and was shown, for small charge, in English seaports; how he returned at last to the Marquesas, fell under the strong and benign influence of the late bishop, extended his influence in the group, was for a while joint ruler with the prelate, and died at last the chief supporter of Catholicism and the French. His widow remains in receipt of two pounds a month from the French Government. Queen she is usually called, but in the official almanac she figures as "*Madame Vaekehu, Grande Chefesse.*" His son (natural or adoptive, I know not which), Stanislao Moanatini, chief of Akaui, serves in Tai-o-hae as a kind of Minister of Public Works, and the daughter of Stanislao is High Chiefess of the southern island of Tauata. These, then, are the greatest folk of the archipelago; we thought them also the most estimable. This is the rule in Polynesia, with few exceptions; the higher the family, the better the man—better in sense, better in manners, and usually taller and stronger in body. A stranger advances blindfold. He scrapes acquain-

---

1. These islands, part of French Polynesia since 1842, are about 1,000 miles northeast of Tahiti.

John Singer Sargent, detail from *Robert Louis Stevenson and His Wife* (1885).

tance as he can. Save the tattoo in the Marquesas, nothing indicates the difference of rank; and yet almost invariably we found, after we had made them, that our friends were persons of station. I have said "usually taller and stronger." I might have been more absolute,—over all Polynesia, and a part of Micronesia, the rule holds good; the great ones of the isle, and even of the village, are greater of bone and muscle, and often heavier of flesh, than any commoner. The usual explanation—that the high-born child is more industriously shampooed,[2] is probably the true one. In

2. Massaged.

New Caledonia, at least, where the difference does not exist or has never been remarked, the practice of shampooing seems to be itself unknown. Doctors would be well employed in a study of the point.

Vaekehu lives at the other end of the town from the Residency, beyond the buildings of the mission. Her house is on the European plan: a table in the midst of the chief room; photographs and religious pictures on the wall. It commands to either hand a charming vista: through the front door, a peep of green lawn, scurrying pigs, the pendent fans of the coco-palm and the splendor of the bursting surf: through the back, mounting forest glades and coronals of precipice. Here, in the strong thorough-draught, Her Majesty received us in a simple gown of print, and with no mark of royalty but the exquisite finish of her tattooed mittens, the elaboration of her manners, and the gentle falsetto in which all the highly refined among Marquesan ladies (and Vaekehu above all others) delight to sing their language. An adopted daughter interpreted, while we gave the news, and rehearsed by name our friends of Anaho. As we talked, we could see, through the landward door, another lady of the household at her toilet under the green trees; who presently, when her hair was arranged, and her hat wreathed with flowers, appeared upon the back verandah with gracious salutations.

Vaekehu is very deaf; "*merci*" is her only word of French; and I do not know that she seemed clever. An exquisite, kind refinement, with a shade of quietism, gathered perhaps from the nuns, was what chiefly struck us. Or rather, upon that first occasion, we were conscious of a sense as of district-visiting on our part, and reduced evangelical gentility on the part of our hostess. The other impression followed after she was more at ease, and came with Stanislao and his little girl to dine on board the *Casco*.[3] She had dressed for the occasion: wore white, which very well became her strong brown face; and sat among us, eating or smoking her cigarette, quite cut off from all society, or only now and then included through the intermediary of her son. It was a position that might have been ridiculous, and she made it ornamental; making believe to hear and to be entertained; her face, whenever she met our eyes, lighting with the smile of good society; her contributions to the talk, when she made any, and that was seldom, always complimentary and pleasing. No attention was paid to the child, for instance, but what she remarked and thanked us for. Her parting with each, when she came to leave, was gracious and pretty, as had been every step of her behaviour. When Mrs. Stevenson held out her hand to say good-bye, Vaekehu took it, held it, and a moment smiled upon her; dropped it, and then, as upon a kindly afterthought, and with a sort of warmth of condescension, held out both hands and kissed my wife upon both cheeks. Given the same relation of years and of rank, the thing would have been so done on the boards of the *Comédie Française*; just so might Madame Brohan have warmed and condescended to Madame Broisat in the *Marquis de Villemer*.[4] It was my part to accompany our guests ashore: when I kissed the little girl good-bye at the pier steps, Vaekehu gave a cry of gratification, reached down her hand into the

---

3. Stevenson's ship.
4. Ethelie Madeleine Brohan and Emilie Broisat, 19th-c. actresses in the troupe of the French national theater (Comédie Française), which performed George Sand's play *Marquis de Villemer* in 1867.

boat, took mine, and pressed it with that flattering softness which seems the coquetry of the old lady in every quarter of the earth. The next moment she had taken Stanislao's arm, and they moved off along the pier in the moonlight, leaving me bewildered. This was a queen of cannibals; she was tattooed from hand to foot, and perhaps the greatest masterpiece of that art now extant, so that a while ago, before she was grown prim, her leg was one of the sights of Tai-o-hae; she had been passed from chief to chief; she had been fought for and taken in war; perhaps, being so great a lady, she had sat on the high place, and throned it there, alone of her sex, while the drums were going twenty strong and the priests carried up the bloodstained baskets of long-pig.[5] And now behold her, out of that past of violence and sickening feasts, step forth, in her age, a quiet, smooth, elaborate old lady, such as you might find at home (mittened also, but not often so well mannered) in a score of country houses. Only Vaekehu's mittens were of dye, not of silk; and they had been paid for, not in money, but the cooked flesh of men. It came in my mind with a clap, what she could think of it herself, and whether at heart, perhaps, she might not regret and aspire after the barbarous and stirring past. But when I asked Stanislao—"Ah!" said he, "she is content; she is religious, she passes all her days with the sisters."

Stanislao (Stanislaos, with the final consonant evaded after the Polynesian habit) was sent by Bishop Dordillon[6] to South America, and there educated by the fathers. His French is fluent, his talk sensible and spirited, and in his capacity of ganger-in-chief, he is of excellent service to the French. With the prestige of his name and family, and with the stick when needful, he keeps the natives working and the roads passable. Without Stanislao and the convicts, I am in doubt what would become of the present regimen in Nuka-hiva; whether the highways might not be suffered to close up, the pier to wash away, and the Residency to fall piecemeal about the ears of impotent officials. And yet though the hereditary favourer, and one of the chief props of French authority, he has always an eye upon the past. He showed me where the old public place had stood, still to be traced by random piles of stone; told me how great and fine it was, and surrounded on all sides by populous houses, whence, at the beating of the drums, the folk crowded to make holiday. The drumbeat of the Polynesian has a strange and gloomy stimulation for the nerves of all. White persons feel it—at these precipitate sounds their hearts beat faster; and, according to old residents, its effect on the natives was extreme. Bishop Dordillon might entreat; Temoana himself command and threaten; at the note of the drum wild instincts triumphed. And now it might beat upon these ruins, and who should assemble? The houses are down, the people dead, their lineage extinct; and the sweepings and fugitives of distant bays and islands encamp upon their graves. The decline of the dance Stanislao especially laments. "*Chaque pays à ses coutumes,*"[7] said he; but in the report of any gendarme, perhaps corruptly eager to increase the number of *dèlits*[8] and the instruments of his own power, custom after custom is placed on the expurgatorial index. "*Tenez, une danse qui n'est pas permise,*" said Stanislao: "*je ne sais pas pourquoi,*

---

5. Human flesh.
6. René-Ildefonse Dordillon was bishop of the Marquesas, 1855–88.
7. French: Each country has its costumes.
8. French: criminal offenses.

elle est très jolie, elle va comme çà,"[9] and sticking his umbrella upright in the road, he sketched the steps and gestures. All his criticisms of the present, all his regrets for the past, struck me as temperate and sensible. The short term of office of the Resident he thought the chief defect of the administration; that officer having scarce begun to be efficient ere he was recalled. I thought I gathered, too, that he regarded with some fear the coming change from a naval to a civil governor. I am sure at least that I regard it so myself; for the civil servants of France have never appeared to any foreigner as at all the flower of their country, while her naval officers may challenge competition with the world. In all his talk, Stanislao was particular to speak of his own country as a land of savages; and when he stated an opinion of his own, it was with some apologetic preface, alleging that he was "a savage who had travelled." There was a deal, in this elaborate modesty, of honest pride. Yet there was something in the precaution that saddened me; and I could not but fear he was only forestalling a taunt that he had heard too often.

I recall with interest two interviews with Stanislao. The first was a certain afternoon of tropic rain, which we passed together in the verandah of the club; talking at times with heightened voices as the showers redoubled overhead, passing at times into the billiard-room, to consult, in the dim, cloudy daylight, that map of the world which forms its chief adornment. He was naturally ignorant of English history, so that I had much of news to communicate. The story of Gordon I told him in full, and many episodes of the Indian Mutiny, Lucknow, the second battle of Cawnpore, the relief of Arrah, the death of poor Spottiswoode, and Sir Hugh Rose's hotspur, midland campaign.[10] He was intent to hear; his brown face, strongly marked with small-pox, kindled and changed with each vicissitude. His eyes glowed with the reflected light of battle; his questions were many and intelligent, and it was chiefly these that sent us so often to the map. But it is of our parting that I keep the strongest sense. We were to sail on the morrow, and the night had fallen, dark, gusty, and rainy, when we stumbled up the hill to bid farewell to Stanislao. He had already loaded us with gifts; but more were waiting. We sat about the table over cigars and green cocoa-nuts; claps of wind blew through the house and extinguished the lamp, which was always instantly relighted with a single match; and these recurrent intervals of darkness were felt as a relief. For there was something painful and embarrassing in the kindness of that separation. "*Ah, vous devriez rester ici, mon cher ami!*" cried Stanislao. "*Vous êtes les gens qu'il faut pour les Kanaques; vous êtes doux, vous et votre famille; vous seriez obéis dans toutes les îles.*"[11] We had been civil; not always that, my conscience told me, and never anything beyond; and all this to-do is a measure, not of our considerateness, but of the want of it in others. The rest of the evening, on to Vaekehu's and back as far as to the pier, Stanislao walked with my arm and sheltered

---

9. French: "There's a dance that's not allowed, I don't know why not, it is very pretty, it goes like this."

10. General Charles Gordon (1833–85) became a hero for holding out against Sudanese rebels in the siege of Khartoum, only to be killed two days before the relief party arrived. The rest are episodes during the Indian Mutiny of 1857: at Lucknow, the British successfully withstood a siege; at Cawnpore, the British hung Indian prisoners to retaliate for murders of British women and children; at Arrah, a small force of British soldiers held out in a siege; Col. Henry Spottiswoode shot himself when learning of his troops' mutiny in 1857; Field Marshal Hugh Henry Rose routed rebel forces although his soldiers were vastly outnumbered and fought in searing heat.

11. French: "Ah, you should stay here, my dear friend! You are the people who are necessary for the Kanaks [native islanders]; you are kind, you and your family; you would be obeyed in all the islands."

me with his umbrella; and after the boat had put off, we could still distinguish, in the murky darkness, his gestures of farewell. His words, if there were any, were drowned by the rain and the loud surf.

I have mentioned presents, a vexed question in the South Seas; and one which well illustrates the common, ignorant habit of regarding races in a lump. In many quarters the Polynesian gives only to receive. I have visited islands where the population mobbed me for all the world like dogs after the waggon of cat's-meat; and where the frequent proposition, "You my pleni (friend)," or (with more of pathos) "You all 'e same my father," must be received with hearty laughter and a shout. And perhaps everywhere, among the greedy and rapacious, a gift is regarded as a sprat to catch a whale. It is the habit to give gifts and to receive returns, and such characters, complying with the custom, will look to it nearly that they do not lose. But for persons of a different stamp the statement must be reversed. The shabby Polynesian is anxious till he has received the return gift; the generous is uneasy until he has made it. The first is disappointed if you have not given more than he; the second is miserable if he thinks he has given less than you. This is my experience; if it clash with that of others, I pity their fortune, and praise mine: the circumstance cannot change what I have seen, nor lessen what I have received. And indeed I find that those who oppose me often argue from a ground of singular presumptions; comparing Polynesians with an ideal person, compact of generosity and gratitude, whom I never had the pleasure of encountering; and forgetting that what is almost poverty to us is wealth almost unthinkable to them. I will give one instance: I chanced to speak with consideration of these gifts of Stanislao's with a certain clever man, a great hater and contemner of Kanakas. "Well! what were they?" he cried. "A pack of old men's beards. Trash!" And the same gentleman, some half an hour later, being upon a different train of thought, dwelt at length on the esteem in which the Marquesans held that sort of property, how they preferred it to all others except land, and what fancy prices it would fetch. Using his own figures, I computed that, in this commodity alone, the gifts of Vaekehu and Stanislao represented between two and three hundred dollars; and the queen's official salary is of two hundred and forty in the year.

But generosity on the one hand, and conspicuous meanness on the other, are in the South Seas, as at home, the exception. It is neither with any hope of gain, nor with any lively wish to please, that the ordinary Polynesian chooses and presents his gifts. A plain social duty lies before him, which he performs correctly, but without the least enthusiasm. And we shall best understand his attitude of mind, if we examine our own to the cognate absurdity of marriage presents. There we give without any special thought of a return; yet if the circumstance arise, and the return be withheld, we shall judge ourselves insulted. We give them usually without affection, and almost never with a genuine desire to please; and our gift is rather a mark of our own status than a measure of our love to the recipients. So in a great measure and with the common run of the Polynesians: their gifts are formal; they imply no more than social recognition; and they are made and reciprocated, as we pay and return our morning visits. And the practice of marking and measuring events and sentiments by presents is universal in the island world. A gift plays with them the part of stamp and seal; and has entered profoundly into the mind of islanders. Peace and war, marriage, adoption and naturalisation, are celebrated or declared by the acceptance or the refusal of gifts; and it is as natural for the islander to bring a gift as for us to carry a card-case.[12]

—1896

Dorothea Mackellar
1885–1968

Isobel Marion Dorothea Mackellar wrote Australia's quintessential patriotic poem when she was nineteen, homesick, and living in England. "I love a sunburnt country" became an anthem for Australians, expressing a national pride in the distinctive aspects of Australia's landscape: its barren, rugged terrain and tropical climate. Mackellar seems an unlikely celebrant of the Australian bush, for she was raised in a prosperous urban family in Sydney, the daughter of prominent physician and member of parliament Charles Kinnaird Mackellar, and traveled internationally in her youth. However, her poems were inspired by her brothers' farms near Gunnedah in New South Wales. A third-generation Australian, she could trace her ancestry back to grandparents who arrived in 1839. Although she published several books of poetry and novels, none achieved the fame of "My Country." Just before she died, Mackellar received the Order of the British Empire to recognize her contributions to Australian poetry.

My Country

The love of field and coppice,[1]
   Of green and shaded lanes,
Of ordered woods and gardens
   Is running in your veins.
Strong love of grey-blue distance   5
   Brown streams and soft, dim skies—
I know but cannot share it,
   My love is otherwise.

I love a sunburnt country,
   A land of sweeping plains,   10
Of ragged mountain ranges,
   Of droughts and flooding rains.
I love her far horizons,
   I love her jewel-sea,

---

12. For calling-cards.

---

1. Thicket, small wood.

Her beauty and her terror—   15
    The wide brown land for me!

The stark white ring-barked forests,
    All tragic to the moon,
The sapphire-misted mountains,
    The hot gold hush of noon.   20
Green tangle of the brushes,
    Where lithe lianas[2] coil,
And orchids deck the tree tops
    And ferns the warm dark soil.

Core of my heart, my country!   25
    Her pitiless blue sky,
When sick at heart, around us,
    We see the cattle die—
But then the grey clouds gather,
    And we can bless again   30
The drumming of an army,
    The steady, soaking rain.

Core of my heart, my country!
    Land of the Rainbow Gold,
For flood and fire and famine,   35
    She pays us back three-fold.
Over the thirsty paddocks,
    Watch, after many days,
The filmy veil of greenness
    That thickens as we gaze . . .   40

An opal-hearted country,
    A wilful, lavish land—
All you who have not loved her,
    You will not understand—
Though earth holds many splendours,   45
    Wherever I may die,
I know to what brown country
    My homing thoughts will fly.

              —1908

---

2. Tropical vines.

Isabella Valancy Crawford
1850–1887

This obscure, impoverished young woman would have surely been gratified to learn that within a century she would become widely revered as a major Canadian writer, indeed, one of the first distinctly Canadian poets. Irish by birth, Isabella Valancy Crawford moved to Canada at age eight and experienced the hardships typical of the frontier. Crawford grew up in an isolated village where her parents taught her Latin and French and tutored her in classic literature, but the family fell into poverty and tragedy. Nine of the twelve children died within a few years, and the surviving family members relied on Crawford's journalism for support. Crawford therefore had to write prolifically and swiftly, until she died of heart failure at thirty-six. She had poems, short stories, and at least a dozen novels under way when she died, but the only book published in her lifetime was *Old Spookses' Pass* (1884). She had to pay the publication costs and sold very few copies. Today, however, her work is widely anthologized. She was influenced by Catherine Parr Traill, another early Canadian writer, and by local Ojibway legends (probably learned when the Ojibway came to her doctor father, Stephen Dennis Crawford, for treatment). "Said the Canoe" exemplifies her regional orientation, her interest in Native American culture, and her admiration of the Canadian landscape.

Said the Canoe

My masters twain made me a bed
Of pine-boughs resinous, and cedar;
Of moss, a soft and gentle breeder
Of dreams of rest; and me they spread
With furry skins and, laughing, said: 5
"Now she shall lay her polished sides
As queens do rest, or dainty brides,
Our slender lady of the tides!"

My masters twain their camp-soul lit;
Streamed incense from the hissing cones;   10
Large crimson flashes grew and whirled;
Thin golden nerves of sly light curled
Round the dun camp; and rose faint zones,
Half way about each grim bole knit,
Like a shy child that would bedeck   15
With its soft clasp a Brave's red neck,
Yet sees the rough shield on his breast,
The awful plumes shake on his crest,
And, fearful, drops his timid face,
Nor dares complete the sweet embrace.   20

Into the hollow hearts of brakes—
Yet warm from sides of does and stags
Passed to the crisp, dark river-flags—
Sinuous, red as copper-snakes,
Sharp-headed serpents, made of light,   25
Glided and hid themselves in night.

My masters twain the slaughtered deer
Hung on forked boughs with thongs of leather:
Bound were his stiff, slim feet together,
His eyes like dead stars cold and drear.   30
The wandering firelight drew near
And laid its wide palm, red and anxious,
On the sharp splendour of his branches,
On the white foam grown hard and sere
    On flank and shoulder.   35
Death—hard as breast of granite boulder—
    Under his lashes
Peered thro' his eyes at his life's grey ashes.

My masters twain sang songs that wove—
As they burnished hunting-blade and rifle—   40
A golden thread with a cobweb trifle,
Loud of the chase and low of love:

"O love! art thou a silver fish,
Shy of the line and shy of gaffing,[1]
Which we do follow, fierce, yet laughing,   45
Casting at thee the light-winged wish?
And at the last shall we bring thee up
From the crystal darkness, under the cup
    Of lily folden
    On broad leaves golden?   50

"O Love! art thou a silver deer
With feet as swift as wing of swallow,
While we with rushing arrows follow?
And at the last shall we draw near
And o'er thy velvet neck cast thongs   55
Woven of roses, stars and songs—
    New chains all moulden
    Of rare gems olden?"

---

1. Catching with an iron fishhook.

They hung the slaughtered fish like swords
  On saplings slender; like scimitars,   60
  Bright, and ruddied from new-dead wars,
Blazed in the light the scaly hordes.

They piled up boughs beneath the trees,
  Of cedar web and green fir tassel.
  Low did the pointed pine tops rustle,   65
The camp-fire blushed to the tender breeze.

The hounds laid dewlaps on the ground
  With needles of pine, sweet, soft and rusty,
  Dreamed of the dead stag stout and lusty;
A bat by the red flames wove its round.   70

The darkness built its wigwam walls
  Close round the camp, and at its curtain
  Pressed shapes, thin, woven and uncertain
As white locks of tall waterfalls.

—1905

The Scramble for Africa

In "the scramble for Africa," Britain battled with France and Belgium to control territory. Nowhere was the economic motive for Empire more obvious. Britain plundered much of Central Africa and occupied Egypt in order to protect the trade route of the Suez Canal. This view of Africa as a resource to be exploited, with the Africans themselves merely impediments, underlies H. M. Stanley's infamously ruthless voyages. Mary Kingsley, on the other hand, produced respectful, sympathetic accounts of African tribal groups and their customs and cultures.

In the 1890s, three events shaped British colonization in Africa. Gold was discovered in 1886, sparking a gold rush to the Cape Colony (now South Africa) and bringing thriving infrastructures and booming economies to the region. But then Britain's failures as a colonizing power became evident in the Boer War, 1899–1902. Meanwhile, publications climaxing in Joseph Conrad's *Heart of Darkness* (1899) exposed the atrocious cruelty of Belgian King Leopold II's exploitation of the Belgian Congo and caused British readers to ask how much their nation was complicit in these practices.

The Boer War was fought between the British and the Dutch settlers (Boers, or Afrikaners) for control of the Cape region and its gold. The Boers initially won most of the battles, but when Lord Kitchener and Lord Roberts conquered the capitals of the two Boer republics, the Boer army officially surrendered. However, guerrilla warfare persisted, and the British responded by burning Boer farms and imprisoning Boer families in detention centers or concentration camps. The ensuing scandal (discussed by David Lloyd George) and continued British losses led to negotiations, and the Boers finally surrendered in 1902, giving the Boer republics up to Britain.

It may seem that an inconclusive series of guerilla battles half the world away could not have affected the British very much, but in fact the Boer War proved deeply disturbing. That it took three years for the vaunted British Army to defeat small groups of Dutch farmers destroyed the myth of national invincibility and exposed serious structural weaknesses in the military. Although the Boer War became a flash-point for patriotism, it also revealed that the nation's major institutions were riddled with dangerous incompetence, disorganization, and cruelty. The casual murder and maltreatment of innocent human beings in Africa was not just Stanley's adventure tale, or something the Belgians did, but Britain's state policy.

Sir Henry Morton Stanley
1841–1904

The most famous of African explorers, Sir Henry Morton Stanley made his name as the intrepid reporter for the *New York Herald* who made it through Central Africa in 1871 to find the lost Scottish missionary David Livingstone. Fighting hostile Africans, diseases, and impen-etrable swamps, Stanley finally found Livingstone, asking, with famously deadpan courtesy, "Dr. Livingstone, I presume?" Stanley's life story was, in its way, just as adventurous. An ille-gitimate child growing up in poverty in a Welsh workhouse, originally named John Rowlands, he ran away to North America and fought on both sides in the Civil War. He took the name of his mentor (the owner of a New Orleans plantation) and became a reporter. In *How I Found Livingstone* (1872) and *Through the Dark Continent* (1878), Stanley popularized a vision of African exploration as a heroic, ruthless combat to open up the region to Christianizing influ-ences and trade opportunities. He became Belgian King Leopold II's agent and representative for Leopold's notoriously exploitative colony in the Congo, which enslaved Africans to get ivory (the basis of Conrad's *Heart of Darkness*). While Stanley had some important achieve-ments—he mapped the source of the Congo river and the lakes of Central Africa—he is mainly remembered today for his cruelty. In the expedition to map Central Africa recorded in *Through the Dark Continent*, all three of Stanley's English companions and half of his African crew died. More members of his Emin Pasha Relief Expedition of 1887 died than in any other recorded African expedition. The following excerpt from *Through the Dark Continent* shows Stanley's gleefully bellicose attitude to Africa and Africans.

from Through the Dark Continent

Dec. 29. [1876]— * * * Below Kaimba Island and its neighbour, the Livingstone[1] assumes a breadth of 1800 yards. The banks are very populous: the villages of the left bank comprise the district of Luavala. We thought for some time we should be per-

---

1. His name for the Congo river.

"H. M. Stanley's Expedition fighting the Bangala," Central Africa (*The Graphic*, 1877).

mitted to pass by quietly, but soon the great wooden drums, hollowed out of huge trees, thundered the signal along the river that there were strangers. In order to lessen all chances of a rupture between us, we sheered off to the middle of the river, and quietly lay on our paddles. But from both banks at once, in fierce concert, the natives, with their heads gaily feathered, and armed with broad black wooden shields and long spears, dashed out towards us.

Tippu-Tib[2] before our departure had hired to me two young men of Ukusu—cannibals—as interpreters. These were now instructed to cry out the word "Sennenneh!" ("Peace!"), and to say that we were friends.

---

2. Stanley's Arab-trader escort through hostile territory.

But they would not reply to our greeting, and in a bold peremptory manner told us to return.

"But we are doing no harm, friends. It is the river that takes us down, and the river will not stop, or go back."

"This is our river."

"Good. Tell it to take us back, and we will go."

"If you do not go back, we will fight you."

"No, don't; we are friends."

"We don't want you for our friends; we will eat you."

But we persisted in talking to them, and as their curiosity was so great they persisted in listening, and the consequence was that the current conveyed us near to the right bank; and in such near neighbourhood to another district, that our discourteous escort had to think of themselves, and began to skurry hastily up river, leaving us unattacked.

The villages on the right bank also maintained a tremendous drumming and blowing of war-horns, and their wild men hurried up with menace towards us, urging their sharp-prowed canoes so swiftly that they seemed to skim over the water like flying-fish. Unlike the Luavala villagers, they did not wait to be addressed, but as soon as they came within fifty or sixty yards they shot out their spears, crying out, "Meat! meat! Ah! ha! We shall have plenty of meat! Bo-bo-bo-bo, Bo-bo-bo-bo-o o!"

Undoubtedly these must be relatives of the terrible "Bo-bo-bo's" above, we thought, as with one mind we rose to respond to this rabid man-eating tribe. Anger we had none for them. It seemed to me so absurd to be angry with people who looked upon one only as an epicure would regard a fat capon. Sometimes also a faint suspicion came to my mind that this was all but a part of a hideous dream. Why was it that I should be haunted with the idea that there were human beings who regarded me and my friends only in the light of meat? Meat! We? Heavens! what an atrocious idea!

"Meat! Ah! we shall have meat to day. Meat! meat! meat!"

There was a fat-bodied wretch in a canoe, whom I allowed to crawl within spear-throw of me; who, while he swayed the spear with a vigour far from assuring to one who stood within reach of it, leered with such a clever hideousness of feature that I felt, if only within arm's length of him, I could have bestowed upon him a hearty thump on the back, and cried out applaudingly, "Bravo, old boy! You do it capitally!"

Yet not being able to reach him, I was rapidly being fascinated by him. The rapid movements of the swaying spear, the steady wide-mouthed grin, the big square teeth, the head poised on one side with the confident pose of a practised spear-thrower, the short brow and square face, hair short and thick. Shall I ever forget him? It appeared to me as if the spear partook of the same cruel inexorable look as the grinning savage. Finally, I saw him draw his right arm back, and his body incline backwards, with still that same grin on his face, and I felt myself begin to count, one, two, three, four—and *whizz*! The spear flew over my back, and hissed as it pierced the water. The spell was broken.

It was only five minutes' work clearing the river. * * *

Jan. 4. [1877]— * * * At 4 P.M. we came opposite a river about 200 yards wide, which I have called the Leopold River, in honour of his Majesty Leopold II., King of the Belgians, and which the natives called either the Kankora, Mikonju, or Munduku. Perhaps the natives were misleading me, or perhaps they really possessed a superfluity of names, but I think that whatever name they give it should be mentioned in connection with each stream.

Soon after passing by the confluence, the Livingstone, which above had been 2500 yards wide, perceptibly contracted, and turned sharply to the east-north-east, because of a hill which rose on the left bank about 300 feet above the river. Close to the elbow of the bend on the right bank we passed by some white granite rocks, from one to six feet above the water, and just below these we heard the roar of the First Cataract of the Stanley Falls series.

But louder than the noise of the falls rose the piercing yells of the savage Mwana Ntaba from both sides of the great river. We now found ourselves confronted by the inevitable necessity of putting into practice the resolution which we had formed before setting out on the wild voyage—to conquer or die. What should we do? Shall we turn and face the fierce cannibals, who with hideous noise drown the solemn roar of the cataract, or shall we cry out "Mambu Kwa Mungu"—"Our fate is in the hands of God"—and risk the cataract with its terrors!

Meanwhile, we are sliding smoothly to our destruction, and a decision must therefore be arrived at instantly. God knows, I and my fellows would rather have it not to do, because possibly it is only a choice of deaths, by cruel knives or drowning. If we do not choose the knives, which are already sharpened for our throats, death by drowning is certain. So finding ourselves face to face with the inevitable, we turn to the right bank upon the savages, who are in the woods and on the water. We drop our anchors and begin the fight, but after fifteen minutes of it find that we cannot force them away. We then pull up anchors and ascend stream again, until, arriving at the elbow above mentioned, we strike across the river and divide our forces. Manwa Sera[3] is to take four canoes and to continue up stream a little distance, and, while we occupy the attention of the savages in front, is to lead his men through the woods and set upon them in rear. At 5.30 P.M. we make the attempt, and keep them in play for a few minutes, and on hearing a shot in the woods dash at the shore, and under a shower of spears and arrows effect a landing. From tree to tree the fight is continued until sunset, when, having finally driven the enemy off, we have earned peace for the night.

Until about 10 P.M. we are busy constructing an impenetrable stockade or boma of brushwood, and then at length, we lay our sorely fatigued bodies down to rest, without comforts of any kind and without fires, but (I speak for myself only) with a feeling of gratitude to Him who had watched over us in our trouble, and a humble prayer that His protection may be extended to us, for the terrible days that may yet be to come. * * *

---

3. Stanley's second-in-command.

Feb. 1.— ＊ ＊ ＊ We emerge out of the shelter of the deeply wooded banks in presence of a vast affluent,[4] nearly 2000 yards across at the mouth. As soon as we have fairly entered its waters, we see a great concourse of canoes hovering about some islets, which stud the middle of the stream. The canoe-men, standing up, give a loud shout as they discern us, and blow their horns louder than ever. We pull briskly on to gain the right bank, and come in view of the right branch of the affluent, when, looking up stream, we see a sight that sends the blood tingling through every nerve and fibre of the body, arouses not only our most lively interest, but also our most lively apprehensions—a flotilla of gigantic canoes bearing down upon us, which both in size and numbers utterly eclipse anything encountered hitherto! Instead of aiming for the right bank, we form in line, and keep straight down river, the boat taking position behind. Yet after a moment's reflection, as I note the numbers of the savages, and the daring manner of the pursuit, and the desire of our canoes to abandon the steady compact line, I give the order to drop anchor. Four of our canoes affect not to listen, until I chase them, and threaten them with my guns. This compelled them to return to the line, which is formed of eleven double canoes, anchored 10 yards apart. The boat moves up to the front, and takes position 50 yards above them. The shields are next lifted by the non-combatants, men, women, and children, in the bows, and along the outer lines, as well as astern, and from behind these, the muskets and rifles are aimed.

We have sufficient time to take a view of the mighty force bearing down on us, and to count the number of the war-vessels which have been collected from the Livingstone and its great affluent. There are fifty-four of them! A monster canoe leads the way, with two rows of upstanding paddles, forty men on a side, their bodies bending and swaying in unison as with a swelling barbarous chorus they drive her down towards us. In the bow, standing on what appears to be a platform, are ten prime young warriors, their heads gay with feathers of the parrot, crimson and grey: at the stern, eight men, with long paddles, whose tops are decorated with ivory balls, guide the monster vessel; and dancing up and down from stem to stern are ten men, who appear to be chiefs. All the paddles are headed with ivory balls, every head bears a feather crown, every arm shows gleaming white ivory armlets. From the bow of the canoe streams a thick fringe of the long white fibre of the Hyphene palm. The crashing sound of large drums, a hundred blasts from ivory horns, and a thrilling chant from two thousand human throats, do not tend to soothe our nerves or to increase our confidence. However, it is "neck or nothing." We have no time to pray, or to take sentimental looks at the savage world, or even to breathe a sad farewell to it. So many other things have to be done speedily and well.

As the foremost canoe comes rushing down, and its consorts on either side beating the water into foam, and raising their jets of water with their sharp prows, I turn to take a last look at our people, and say to them:—

---

4. Tributary stream.

"Boys, be firm as iron; wait until you see the first spear, and then take good aim. Don't fire all at once. Keep aiming until you are sure of your man. Don't think of running away, for only your guns can save you."

Frank[5] is with the *Ocean* on the right flank, and has a choice crew, and a good bulwark of black wooden shields. Manwa Sera has the *London Town*—which he has taken in charge instead of the *Glasgow*[6]—on the left flank, the sides of the canoe bristling with guns, in the hands of tolerably steady men.

The monster canoe aims straight for my boat, as though it would run us down; but, when within fifty yards off, swerves aside, and, when nearly opposite, the warriors above the manned prow let fly their spears, and on either side there is a noise of rushing bodies. But every sound is soon lost in the ripping, crackling musketry. For five minutes we are so absorbed in firing that we take no note of anything else; but at the end of that time we are made aware that the enemy is reforming about 200 yards above us.

Our blood is up now. It is a murderous world, and we feel for the first time that we hate the filthy, vulturous ghouls who inhabit it. We therefore lift our anchors, and pursue them up-stream along the right bank, until rounding a point we see their villages. We make straight for the banks, and continue the fight in the village streets with those who have landed, hunt them out into the woods, and there only sound the retreat, having returned the daring cannibals the compliment of a visit.

While mustering my people for re-embarkation, one of the men came forward and said that in the principal village there was a "Meskiti," a "pembé"—a church, or temple, of ivory—and that ivory was "as abundant as fuel." In a few moments I stood before the ivory temple, which was merely a large circular roof supported by thirty-three tusks of ivory, erected over an idol 4 feet high, painted with camwood dye, a bright vermilion, with black eyes and beard and hair. The figure was very rude, still it was an unmistakable likeness of a man. The tusks being wanted by the Wangwana, they received permission to convey them into the canoes. One hundred other pieces of ivory were collected, in the shape of log wedges, long ivory war-horns, ivory pestles to pound cassava[7] into meal and herbs for spinach, ivory armlets and balls, and ivory mallets to beat the figbark into cloth.

—1878

---

5. Stanley's three white companions were Frederick Barker, Francis Pocock, and Francis's brother Edward. All died on the expedition.
6. The names of the expedition's canoes.
7. Edible starch.

Mary Kingsley
1862–1900

Imagine a Victorian spinster in a long black gown—wading through neck-deep mud, covered in leeches—and you will understand why Mary Kingsley amazed Victorian readers. In 1893 the quiet stay-at-home daughter of an invalid mother suddenly leapt into national prominence as a fearless explorer, naturalist, anthropologist, and advocate for West Africa. Kingsley would have only seven years to pursue this career, but those few years were packed with brilliant research. Kingsley was born into one of the most famous literary dynasties in England. Her uncle was the author Charles Kingsley, and her father George, uncle Henry, and cousin Mary were also respected novelists. Yet Kingsley had little access to intellectual life. Her father traveled constantly, leaving Kingsley at home with her isolated and invalid mother, an ex-servant who may have been illiterate and was never fully accepted by the Kingsley clan. As she noted, "being allowed to learn German was all the paid-for education I ever had. Two thousand pounds was spent on my brother's, I still hope not in vain." As soon as her parents died and her brother released her, Kingsley left. She went to West Africa to collect fish and study tribal religions, and soon she developed a passionate expertise in, and affinity for, West African cultures, landscapes, and people. Back in England she defended her adopted region against colonialist assumptions, and in her two books on West Africa she became the master of a prose style of limpid, self-deprecating, absurdist wit. She died at age 38 from enteric fever (typhoid), contracted from the Boer prisoners she was nursing in South Africa. These excerpts from *Travels in West Africa* show her strong admiration for African ways coexisting with earlier assumptions about African capabilities, and her objections to Stanley's dehumanizing brutality.

from Travels in West Africa

It was in 1893[1] that, for the first time in my life, I found myself in possession of five or six months which were not heavily forestalled, and feeling like a boy with a new half-crown, I lay about in my mind, as Mr. Bunyan[2] would say, as to what to do with them. "Go and learn your tropics," said Science. Where on earth am I to go, I wondered, for tropics are tropics wherever found, so I got down an atlas and saw that either South America or West Africa must be my destination, for the Malayan region was too far off and too expensive. Then I got Wallace's *Geographical Distribution*[3] and after reading that master's article on the Ethiopian region I hardened my heart and closed with West Africa. I did this the more readily because while I knew nothing of the practical condition of it, I knew a good deal both by tradition and report of South East America, and remembered that Yellow Jack[4] was endemic, and that a certain naturalist, my superior physically and mentally, had come very near getting starved to

---

1. Kingsley's parents died in 1892 and her brother departed for China in 1893.
2. John Bunyan, author of *The Pilgrim's Progress* (1678).
3. Alfred Russel Wallace (1823–1913) codeveloped the theory of natural selection with Charles Darwin (1809–82).
4. Yellow fever.

death in the depressing society of an expedition slowly perishing of want and miscellaneous fevers up the Parana.[5]

My ignorance regarding West Africa was soon removed. And although the vast cavity in my mind that it occupied is not even yet half filled up, there is a great deal of very curious information in its place. I use the word curious advisedly, for I think many seemed to translate my request for practical hints and advice into an advertisement that "Rubbish may be shot here." This same information is in a state of great confusion still, although I have made heroic efforts to codify it. I find, however, that it can almost all be got in under the following different headings, namely and to wit:—

The dangers of West Africa.
The disagreeables of West Africa.
The diseases of West Africa.
The things you must take to West Africa.
The things you find most handy in West Africa.
The worst possible things you can do in West Africa.

I inquired of all my friends as a beginning what they knew of West Africa. The majority knew nothing. A percentage said, "Oh, you can't possibly go there; that's where Sierra Leone is, the white man's grave,[6] you know." If these were pressed further, one occasionally found that they had had relations who had gone out there after having been "sad trials," but, on consideration of their having left not only West Africa, but this world, were now forgiven and forgotten. One lady however kindly remembered a case of a gentleman who had resided some few years at Fernando Po,[7] but when he returned an aged wreck of forty he shook so violently with ague as to dislodge a chandelier, thereby destroying a valuable tea-service and flattening the silver teapot in its midst.

No; there was no doubt about it, the place was not healthy, and although I had not been "a sad trial," yet neither had the chandelier-dislodging Fernando Po gentleman. So I next turned my attention to cross-examining the doctors. "Deadliest spot on earth," they said cheerfully, and showed me maps of the geographical distribution of disease. Now I do not say that a country looks inviting when it is coloured in Scheele's green[8] or a bilious yellow, but these colours may arise from lack of artistic gift in the cartographer. There is no mistaking what he means by black, however, and black you'll find they colour West Africa from above Sierra Leone to below the Congo. "I wouldn't go there if I were you," said my medical friends, "you'll catch something; but if you must go, and you're as obstinate as a mule, just bring me——" and then followed a list of commissions from here to New York, any one of which——but I only found that out afterwards. * * *

Fortunately I could number among my acquaintances one individual who had lived on the Coast for seven years. Not, it is true, on that part of it which I was

---

5. South American river.
6. Nickname for Sierra Leone, later applied to West Africa generally.
7. Island in Bight of Biafra in West Africa.
8. Bright green.

bound for. Still his advice was pre-eminently worth attention, because, in spite of his long residence in the deadliest spot of the region, he was still in fair going order. I told him I intended going to West Africa, and he said, "When you have made up your mind to go to West Africa the very best thing you can do is to get it unmade again and go to Scotland instead; but if your intelligence is not strong enough to do so, abstain from exposing yourself to the direct rays of the sun, take 4 grains of quinine[9] every day for a fortnight before you reach the Rivers, and get some introductions to the Wesleyans; they are the only people on the Coast who have got a hearse with feathers."

My attention was next turned to getting ready things to take with me. Having opened upon myself the sluice gates of advice, I rapidly became distracted. My friends and their friends alike seemed to labour under the delusion that I intended to charter a steamer and was a person of wealth beyond the dreams of avarice. The only thing to do in this state of affairs was to gratefully listen and let things drift. They showered on me various preparations of quinine and other so-called medical comforts, mustard leaves, a patent filter, a hot-water bottle, and last but not least a large square bottle purporting to be malt and cod-liver oil, which, rebelling against an African temperature, arose in its wrath, ejected its cork, and proclaimed itself an efficient but not too savoury glue.

Not only do the things you have got to take, but the things you have got to take them in, present a fine series of problems to the young traveller. Crowds of witnesses testified to the forms of baggage holders they had found invaluable, and these, it is unnecessary to say, were all different in form and material.

With all this *embarras de choix*[10] I was too distracted to buy anything new in the way of baggage except a long waterproof sack neatly closed at the top with a bar and handle. Into this I put blankets, boots, books, in fact anything that would not go into my portmanteau or black bag. From the first I was haunted by a conviction that its bottom would come out, but it never did, and in spite of the fact that it had ideas of its own about the arrangement of its contents, it served me well throughout my voyage.

It was the beginning of August '93 when I first left England for "the Coast." Preparations of quinine with postage partially paid arrived up to the last moment, and a friend hastily sent two newspaper clippings, one entitled "A Week in a Palm-oil Tub," which was supposed to describe the sort of accommodation, companions, and fauna likely to be met with on a steamer going to West Africa, and on which I was to spend seven to *The Graphic* contributor's one; the other from *The Daily Telegraph*, reviewing a French book of "Phrases in common use" in Dahomey.[11] The opening sentence in the latter was, "Help, I am drowning." Then came the inquiry, "If a man is not a thief?" and then another cry, "The boat is upset." "Get up, you lazy scamps," is the next exclamation, followed almost immediately by the question, "Why has not this man been buried?" "It is fetish that has killed him, and he must lie here exposed with nothing on him until only the bones remain," is the cheerful answer. This sounded discouraging to a person whose occupation would necessitate going about

---

9. Anti-malarial drug.
10. French: embarrassment of riches.
11. Part of French West Africa.

considerably in boats, and whose fixed desire was to study fetish. So with a feeling of foreboding gloom I left London for Liverpool—none the more cheerful for the matter-of-fact manner in which the steamboat agents had informed me that they did not issue return tickets by the West African lines of steamers.

I will not go into the details of that voyage here, much as I am given to discursiveness. They are more amusing than instructive, for on my first voyage out I did not know the Coast, and the Coast did not know me, and we mutually terrified each other. I fully expected to get killed by the local nobility and gentry; they thought I was connected with the World's Women's Temperance Association,[12] and collecting shocking details for subsequent magic-lantern[13] lectures on the liquor traffic; so fearful misunderstandings arose, but we gradually educated each other, and I had the best of the affair; for all I had got to teach them was that I was only a beetle and fetish hunter, and so forth, while they had to teach me a new world, and a very fascinating course of study I found it. And whatever the Coast may have to say against me—for my continual desire for hair-pins, and other pins, my intolerable habit of getting into water, the abominations full of ants, that I brought into their houses, or things emitting at unexpectedly short notice vivid and awful stenches—they cannot but say that I was a diligent pupil, who honestly tried to learn the lessons they taught me so kindly, though some of those lessons were hard to a person who had never previously been even in a tame bit of tropics, and whose life for many years had been an entirely domestic one in a University town.[14] * * *

There is an uniformity in the habits of West Coast rivers, from the Volta to the Coanza,[15] which is, when you get used to it, very taking. Excepting the Congo, the really great river comes out to sea with as much mystery as possible; lounging lazily along among its mangrove swamps in a what's-it-matter-when-one-comes-out and where's-the-hurry style, through quantities of channels inter-communicating with each other. Each channel, at first sight as like the other as peas in a pod, is bordered on either side by green-black walls of mangroves, which Captain Lugard[16] graphically described as seeming "as if they had lost all count of the vegetable proprieties, and were standing on stilts with their branches tucked up out of the wet, leaving their gaunt roots exposed in mid-air." High-tide or low-tide, there is little difference in the water; the river, be it broad or narrow, deep or shallow, looks like a pathway of polished metal; for it is as heavy weighted with sticking mud as water e'er can be, ebb or flow, year out and year in. But the difference in the banks, though an unending alternation between two appearances, is weird.

At high-water you do not see the mangroves displaying their ankles in the way that shocked Captain Lugard. They look most respectable, their foliage rising densely in a wall irregularly striped here and there by the white line of an aërial root, coming straight down into the water from some upper branch as straight as a plummet, in the strange, knowing way an aërial root of a mangrove does, keeping the hard straight line until it gets some two feet above water-level, and then spreading out into blunt

---

12. Organization trying to prohibit alcoholic drinks.
13. Precursor of slide show.
14. Cambridge.
15. The Volta flows through what is now Ghana; the Kwanza (Coanza) is in modern Angola.
16. Established British rule in Uganda in 1890.

fingers with which to dip into the water and grasp the mud. Banks indeed at high water can hardly be said to exist, the water stretching away into the mangrove swamps for miles and miles, and you can then go, in a suitable small canoe, away among these swamps as far as you please.

This is a fascinating pursuit. For people who like that sort of thing it is just the sort of thing they like, as the art critic of a provincial town wisely observed anent an impressionist picture recently acquired for the municipal gallery. But it is a pleasure to be indulged in with caution; for one thing, you are certain to come across crocodiles. Now a crocodile drifting down in deep water, or lying asleep with its jaws open on a sand-bank in the sun, is a picturesque adornment to the landscape when you are on the deck of a steamer, and you can write home about it and frighten your relations on your behalf; but when you are away among the swamps in a small dug-out canoe, and that crocodile and his relations are awake—a thing he makes a point of being at flood tide because of fish coming along—and when he has got his foot upon his native heath—that is to say, his tail within holding reach of his native mud—he is highly interesting, and you may not be able to write home about him—and you get frightened on your own behalf. For crocodiles can, and often do, in such places, grab at people in small canoes. I have known of several natives losing their lives in this way; some native villages are approachable from the main river by a short cut, as it were, through the mangrove swamps, and the inhabitants of such villages will now and then go across this way with small canoes instead of by the constant channel to the village, which is almost always winding. In addition to this unpleasantness you are liable—until you realise the danger from experience, or have native advice on the point—to get tide-trapped away in the swamps, the water falling round you when you are away in some deep pool or lagoon, and you find you cannot get back to the main river. For you cannot get out and drag your canoe across the stretches of mud that separate you from it, because the mud is of too unstable a nature and too deep, and sinking into it means staying in it, at any rate until some geologist of the remote future may come across you, in a fossilised state, when that mangrove swamp shall have become dry land. Of course if you really want a truly safe investment in Fame, and really care about Posterity, and Posterity's Science, you will jump over into the black batter-like, stinking slime, cheered by the thought of the terrific sensation you will produce 20,000 years hence, and the care you will be taken of then by your fellow-creatures, in a museum. But if you are a mere ordinary person of a retiring nature, like me, you stop in your lagoon until the tide rises again; most of your attention is directed to dealing with an "at home" to crocodiles and mangrove flies, and with the fearful stench of the slime round you. What little time you have over you will employ in wondering why you came to West Africa, and why, after having reached this point of absurdity, you need have gone and painted the lily and adorned the rose, by being such a colossal ass as to come fooling about in mangrove swamps. Twice this chatty little incident, as Lady MacDonald would call it,[17] has happened to me, but never again if I can help it. On one occasion, the last, a mighty Silurian,[18] as The Daily Telegraph would call him, chose to get his front paws over the stern of my canoe, and

---

17. Lady Ethel MacDonald, wife of the governor of the Niger Coast Protectorate, and Kingsley's traveling companion from Calabar to Fernando Po in 1895.
18. Crocodile.

endeavoured to improve our acquaintance. I had to retire to the bows, to keep the balance right,[19] and fetch him a clip on the snout with a paddle, when he withdrew, and I paddled into the very middle of the lagoon, hoping the water there was too deep for him or any of his friends to repeat the performance. Presumably it was, for no one did it again. I should think that crocodile was eight feet long; but don't go and say I measured him, or that this is my outside measurement for crocodiles. I have measured them when they have been killed by other people, fifteen, eighteen, and twenty-one feet odd. This was only a pushing young creature who had not learnt manners. * * *

So I went down to where the canoes were tied by their noses to the steep bank, and finding a paddle, a broken one, I unloosed the smallest canoe. Unfortunately this was fifteen feet or so long, but I did not know the disadvantage of having, as it were, a long-tailed canoe then—I did shortly afterwards.

The promontories running out into the river on each side of the mission beach give a little stretch of slack water between the bank and the mill-race-like current of the Ogowé,[20] and I wisely decided to keep in the slack water, until I had found out how to steer—most important thing steering. I got into the bow of the canoe, and shoved off from the bank all right; then I knelt down—learn how to paddle standing up by and by—good so far. I rapidly learnt how to steer from the bow, but I could not get up any pace. Intent on acquiring pace, I got to the edge of the slack water; and then displaying more wisdom, I turned round to avoid it, proud as a peacock, you understand, at having found out how to turn round. At this moment, the current of the greatest equatorial river in the world, grabbed my canoe by its tail. We spun round and round for a few seconds, like a teetotum,[21] I steering the whole time for all I was worth, and then the current dragged the canoe ignominiously down river, tail foremost.

Fortunately a big tree was at that time temporarily hanging against the rock in the river, just below the sawmill beach. Into that tree the canoe shot with a crash, and I hung on, and shipping my paddle, pulled the canoe into the slack water again, by the aid of the branches of the tree, which I was in mortal terror would come off the rock, and insist on accompanying me and the canoe, viâ Kama country,[22] to the Atlantic Ocean; but it held, and when I had got safe against the side of the pinnacle-rock I wiped a perspiring brow, and searched in my mind for a piece of information regarding navigation that would be applicable to the management of long-tailed Adooma canoes. I could not think of one for some minutes. Captain Murray[23] has imparted to me at one time and another an enormous mass of hints as to the management of vessels, but those vessels were all presupposed to have steam power. But he having been the first man to take an ocean-going steamer up to Matadi[24] on the Congo, through the terrific currents that whirl and fly in Hell's Cauldron,[25] knew about currents, and I remembered he had said regarding taking vessels through them, "Keep all the headway you can on her." Good! that hint inverted will fit this

---

19. It is no use saying because I was frightened, for this miserably understates the case [Kingsley's note].
20. River in the French Congo (now Gabon).
21. A top.
22. Region on the banks of the Ogowé river occupied by the Kama (now Kumu) tribe.
23. Captain of the steamer that took Kingsley to West Africa in 1893, who taught her African navigation.
24. Town in Congo.
25. Famous whirlpool.

situation like a glove, and I'll keep all the tailway I can off her. Feeling now as safe as only a human being can feel who is backed up by a sound principle, I was cautiously crawling to the tail-end of the canoe, intent on kneeling in it to look after it, when I heard a dreadful outcry on the bank. Looking there I saw Mme. Forget, Mme. Gacon, M. Gacon,[26] and their attributive crowd of mission children all in a state of frenzy. They said lots of things in chorus. "What?" said I. They said some more and added gesticulations. Seeing I was wasting their time as I could not hear, I drove the canoe from the rock and made my way, mostly by steering to the bank close by; and then tying the canoe firmly up I walked over the mill stream and divers other things towards my anxious friends. "You'll be drowned," they said. "Gracious goodness!" said I, "I thought that half an hour ago, but it's all right now; I can steer." After much conversation I lulled their fears regarding me, and having received strict orders to keep in the stern of the canoe, because that is the proper place when you are managing a canoe single-handed, I returned to my studies. I had not however lulled my friends' interest regarding me, and they stayed on the bank watching.

I found first, that my education in steering from the bow was of no avail; second, that it was all right if you reversed it. For instance, when you are in the bow, and make an inward stroke with the paddle on the right-hand side, the bow goes to the right; whereas, if you make an inward stroke on the right-hand side, when you are sitting in the stern, the bow then goes to the left. Understand? Having grasped this law, I crept along up river; and, by Allah! before I had gone twenty yards, if that wretch, the current of the greatest, &c., did not grab hold of the nose of my canoe, and we teetotummed round again as merrily as ever. My audience screamed. I knew what they were saying, "You'll be drowned! Come back! Come back!" but I heard them and I heeded not. If you attend to advice in a crisis you're lost; besides, I couldn't "Come back" just then. However, I got into the slack water again, by some very showy, high-class steering. Still steering, fine as it is, is not all you require and hanker after. You want pace as well, and pace, except when in the clutches of the current, I had not so far attained. Perchance, thought I, the pace region in a canoe may be in its centre; so I got along on my knees into the centre to experiment. Bitter failure; the canoe took to sidling down river broadside on, like Mr. Winkle's horse.[27] Shouts of laughter from the bank. Both bow and stern education utterly inapplicable to centre; and so, seeing I was utterly thrown away there, I crept into the bows, and in a few more minutes I steered my canoe, perfectly, in among its fellows by the bank and secured it there. Mme. Forget ran down to meet me and assured me she had not laughed so much since she had been in Africa, although she was frightened at the time lest I should get capsized and drowned. * * *

Well, when I got down to Lembarene[28] I naturally went on with my canoeing studies, in pursuit of the attainment of pace. Success crowned my efforts, and I can honestly and truly say that there are only two things I am proud of—one is that Doctor Günther[29] has approved of my fishes, and the other is that I can paddle an Ogowé canoe. Pace, style, steering and all, "All same for one" as if I were an Ogowé

26. Kingsley's hosts, French missionaries in Talagouga.
27. Comic scene from Charles Dickens's *The Pickwick Papers* (1836–37).
28. The head of the Ogowé river delta.
29. Kingsley collected fish for Albert Gunther, eminent ichthyologist at the British Museum.

African. A strange, incongruous pair of things: but I often wonder what are the things other people are really most proud of; it would be a quaint and repaying subject for investigation. * * *

My most favourite form of literature, I may remark, is accounts of mountaineering exploits, though I have never seen a glacier or a permanent snow mountain in my life. I do not care a row of pins how badly they may be written, and what form of bumble-puppy grammar and composition is employed, as long as the writer will walk along the edge of a precipice with a sheer fall of thousands of feet on one side and a sheer wall on the other; or better still crawl up an *arête*[30] with a precipice on either. Nothing on earth would persuade me to do either of these things myself, but they remind me of bits of country I have been through where you walk along a narrow line of security with gulfs of murder looming on each side, and where in exactly the same way you are as safe as if you were in your easy chair at home, as long as you get sufficient holding ground: not on rock in the bush village inhabited by murderous cannibals, but on ideas in those men's and women's minds; and these ideas, which I think I may say you will always find, give you safety. It is not advisable to play with them, or to attempt to eradicate them, because you regard them as superstitious; and never, never shoot too soon. I have never had to shoot, and hope never to have to; because in such a situation, one white alone with no troops to back him means a clean finish. But this would not discourage me if I had to start, only it makes me more inclined to walk round the obstacle, than to become a mere blood splotch against it, if this can be done without losing your self-respect, which is the mainspring of your power in West Africa.

As for flourishing about a revolver and threatening to fire, I hold it utter idiocy. I have never tried it, however, so I speak from prejudice which arises from the feeling that there is something cowardly in it. Always have your revolver ready loaded in good order, and have your hand on it when things are getting warm, and in addition have an exceedingly good bowie knife, not a hinge knife, because with a hinge knife you have got to get it open—hard work in a country where all things go rusty in the joints—and hinge knives are liable to close on your own fingers. The best form of knife is the bowie, with a shallow half moon cut out of the back at the point end, and this depression sharpened to a cutting edge. A knife is essential, because after wading neck deep in a swamp your revolver is neither use nor ornament until you have had time to clean it. But the chances are you may go across Africa, or live years in it, and require neither. It is just the case of the gentleman who asked if one required a revolver in Carolina? and was answered, "You may be here one year, and you may be here two and never want it; but when you do want it you'll want it very bad."

The cannibalism of the Fans, although a prevalent habit, is no danger, I think, to white people, except as regards the bother it gives one in preventing one's black companions from getting eaten. The Fan is not a cannibal from sacrificial motives like the negro. He does it in his common sense way. Man's flesh, he says, is good to eat, very good, and he wishes you would try it. Oh dear no, he never eats it himself, but the next door town does. He is always very much abused for eating his relations, but he really does not do this. He will eat his next door neighbour's relations

---

30. French: mountain ridge.

and sell his own deceased to his next door neighbour in return; but he does not buy slaves and fatten them up for his table as some of the Middle Congo tribes I know of do. He has no slaves, no prisoners of war, no cemeteries, so you must draw your own conclusions. * * *

One village in particular did we have a lively time at. Obanjo[31] had a wife and home there, likewise a large herd of goats, some of which he was desirous of taking down with us to sell at Gaboon. It was a pleasant-looking village, with a clean yellow beach which most of the houses faced. But it had ramifications in the interior. I being very lazy, did not go ashore, but watched the pantomime from the bamboo staging. The whole flock of goats enter at right end of stage, and tear violently across the scene, disappearing at left. Two minutes elapse. Obanjo and his gallant crew enter at right hand of stage, leg it like lamplighters across front, and disappear at left. Fearful pow-wow behind the scenes. Five minutes elapse. Enter goats at right as before, followed by Obanjo and company as before, and so on da capo.[32] It was more like a fight I once saw between the armies of Macbeth and Macduff[33] than anything I have seen before or since; only our Rembwé play was better put on, more supers, and noise, and all that sort of thing, you know. It was a spirited performance I assure you and I and the inhabitants of the village, not personally interested in goat-catching, assumed the rôle of audience and cheered it to the echo. While engaged in shouting "Encore" to the third round, I received a considerable shock by hearing a well-modulated evidently educated voice saying in most perfect English:

"Most diverting spectacle, madam, is it not?"

Now you do not expect to hear things called "diverting spectacles" on the Rembwé; so I turned round and saw standing on the bank against which our canoe was moored, what appeared to me to be an English gentleman who had from some misfortune gone black all over and lost his trousers and been compelled to replace them with a highly ornamental table-cloth. The rest of his wardrobe was in exquisite condition, with the usual white jean coat, white shirt and collar, very neat tie, and felt hat affected by white gentlemen out here. Taking a large and powerful cigar from his lips with one hand, he raised his hat gracefully with the other and said:

"Pray excuse me, madam."

I said, "Oh, please go on smoking."

"May I?" he said, offering me a cigar-case.

"Oh, no thank you," I replied.

"Many ladies do now," he said, and asked me whether I "preferred Liverpool, London, or Paris."

I said, "Paris; but there were nice things in both the other cities."

"Indeed that is so," he said; "they have got many very decent works of art in the St. George's Hall."[34]

I agreed, but said I thought the National Gallery[35] preferable because there you got such fine representative series of works of the early Italian schools. I felt I had got

31. Leader of Kingsley's African crew.
32. Italian musical phrase: from the top.
33. Climactic battle in Shakespeare's *Macbeth*.
34. Museum in Liverpool.
35. Famous London museum.

to rise to this man whoever he was, somehow, and having regained my nerve, I was coming up hand over hand to the level of his culture when Obanjo and the crew arrived, carrying goats. Obanjo dropped his goat summarily into the hold, and took off his hat with his very best bow to my new acquaintance, who acknowledged the salute with a delicious air of condescension.

"Introduce me," said the gentleman.

"I cannot," said Obanjo.

"I regret, madam," said the gentleman, "I have not brought my card-case with me. One little expects in such a remote region to require one; my name is Prince Makaga."[36]

I said I was similarly card-caseless for reasons identical with his own, but gave him my name and address, and Obanjo, having got all aboard, including a member of the crew, fetched by the leg, shoved off, and with many bows we and the black gentleman parted. As soon as we were out of earshot from shore "Who is he, Obanjo?" said I. Obanjo laughed, and said he was a M'pongwe gentleman who had at one time been agent for one of the big European firms at Gaboon, and had been several times to Europe. Thinking that he could make more money on his own account, he had left the firm and started trading all round this district. At first he made a great deal of money, but a lot of his trust had recently gone bad and he was doubtless up here now looking after some such matter. Obanjo evidently thought him too much of a lavender-kid-glove gentleman to deal with bush trade, and held it was the usual way; a man got spoilt by going to Europe. I quite agree with him on general lines, but Prince Makaga had a fine polish on him without the obvious conceit usually found in men who have been home.

—1897

David Lloyd George
1863–1945

An energetic, charismatic young orator and lawyer, David Lloyd George arrived in Parliament in 1890 as an ardent reformer, defending Welsh interests, opposing the Boer War, and supporting socialist-inspired reforms such as pensions and welfare. By the beginning of World War I, this radical's politics began to change, and Lloyd George, Prime Minister from 1916 to 1922, became a member of the Conservative Party. The following speech shows him in his youthful, fiery mode. One of the great scandals of the Boer War was the British use of a new technique, the concentration camp. Camp conditions were so appalling that the camps backfired by becoming a scandal and a shock to British self-esteem; the outrage is evident in Lloyd George's speech.

---

36. "Makaga, an honourable name, which only one man, and he the bravest and best hunter in the tribe, may bear. The office of the Makaga is to lead all desperate affairs . . ." [from Kingsley's note, quoting *Du Chaillu's Explorations and Adventures in Equatorial Africa* (1861)].

from South African War—Mortality in Camps of Detention

Mr. Lloyd-George: After the answer which the Secretary of State has given this afternoon, I do not think that any apology is necessary for this motion. About three weeks ago the hon. Member for East Mayo and myself called attention to this subject, but the facts which have been revealed since showed that we considerably understated the case at that time. On 2nd May the right hon. Gentleman said that in the Transvaal[1] there were 284 deaths from 1st January, and on 7th May he said that the deaths in the Orange River Colony camps since February had been 41 men, 80 women, and 261 children. The answer given to-day proves that, so far from this being the result of temporary conditions, it is growing worse. The deaths in these camps in the Transvaal in a single month were 336—that is a mortality rate, according to the rough computation I have made, of 120 per thousand. For the sake of the credit and good name of this country something should be done to put an end to this condition of things, which is going from bad to worse. A newspaper published last week the details of mortality in one camp. Full particulars were given, including the names of those who had died; a question was based on them, and the right hon. Gentleman consented to ask Lord Kitchener[2] as to the facts. We are constantly hearing of the calumnies of the pro-Boer press. But it is not for hon. Gentlemen opposite to talk about calumnies in view of those recently circulated by their own press. Lord Kitchener, it turns out, confirmed every figure of the Return which had been published in the newspaper, and admitted that the death-rate in this one camp had been 450 per thousand. A deputation went out to these camps from this country. One was a former Member of this House—Mr. Joshua Rowntree—and everyone who knows him will be convinced of the accuracy of every statement he makes. His word is as good as his oath. An English lady went out also.[3] She was permitted to go as far as Bloemfontein;[4] but Mr. Rowntree was not permitted to go beyond Cape Town, though a great deal of persuasion was brought to bear on Sir Alfred Milner,[5] as he then was. No doubt what has happened since in these camps and elsewhere has entitled him to his peerage. What has he done? He has allowed one lady to proceed as far as Bloemfontein, but no farther. We now know the reason why no one is permitted to proceed beyond Bloemfontein. The facts revealed by the right hon. Gentleman, which have come straight from Lord Kitchener, show that there was a state of things at Johannesburg which the Government were afraid to exhibit. This lady has made some reports as to what was taking place in the best of these camps—the best equipped and the longest established—and they are sufficiently deplorable. These were camps, not of fighting men, every one of whom would pass a physical test, but of women, many of whom were in a weak condition, and of children. Food, insufficient; such as was supplied, bad; the women herded together, sometimes twelve in a tent; tents leaking; clothes saturated; not much clothing allowed; little children half

---

1. One of the Boer republics.
2. Lord Kitchener and Lord Roberts led the British troops in the Boer War.
3. Emily Hobhouse's *A Letter to the Committee of the South African Women and Children's Distress Fund* (1901) revealed the terrible conditions in the camps.
4. Capital of one of the Boer republics; the British conquered it and established a concentration camp there in 1900.
5. Top British administrator in the region during the Boer War; later made a baron and a viscount.

starved; the food they had, bad; their clothes soaked through with rain and dew. What marvel is it that the right hon. Gentleman has to tell us this tale of hundreds of children dying? [A Nationalist Member: Another Weyler.][6] The quantity of the food is less—I carefully compared it—than the amount allowed in this country to criminals under hard labour. Here is the official Report of the medical officer in this very camp about which we are inquiring to-day—

> "Examined samples of the mealies,[7] and of the sugar used. Sample one: mouldy and contains mite; unfit for human consumption."

This is given to little children.

> "Sample 2: contains mite, but I could not discover any living mite; it is very dangerous as human food. Sample 3: a moist sample of brown sugar; smells somewhat sour, but with microscope could not find ferment or other foreign matter, except water; the sugar is unfit for the use of young children."

Until recently there were two scales in these camps. The full scale for children was—flour and meal, half a pound; meat, half a pound; milk, quarter of a tin; and so on. But this is for children under six years of age. If relatives on commando,[8] no flour; and only one-third of the quantity of meat given to other children. Little children under six years of age to have no flour, one-third the quantity of milk, and no meat at all on five days a week, because their relatives are on commando! [A Nationalist Member: Generous England!] When this statement was first made the right hon. Gentleman denied it very violently, and it is to his credit that he did so, for he did not believe it possible that such inhumanity could be committed by anybody in authority. The warmth of his indignation is creditable to the right hon. Gentleman, and it is still more creditable that when he discovered that it was a fact he stopped at any rate that part of the transaction. That the state of things with regard to the clothing is very bad is proved by the appeal which has been made to America by the wife of the Military Governor at Pretoria to raise funds—

> "for the purpose of providing warm clothing for the Boer women and children in the refugee camps in South Africa, many of whom are totally destitute, and unable to provide against the cold weather which is now setting in."

Then she goes on to say—

> "It is in the name of little children who are living in open tents, without fires, and possessing only the scantiest clothing, that I ask for help."

An appeal has to be sent by the wife of the Military Governor of Johannesburg to America to provide for the women and children we have taken under our protection.

---

6. Valeriano Weyler, the Spanish governor of Cuba who established "reconcentration camps" there in 1897.
7. Ground corn, a South African staple.
8. Participating in the Boer army's guerilla warfare.

This, Sir, is the idea of bringing a great war to a successful issue. We are told that war is war, and that, after all, these are the necessary consequences of a state of war. I do not think that is so. We know perfectly well that this is the result of a deliberate policy. I cannot challenge that policy at the present moment, and I do not propose to do so. I say that this is the result of a deliberate and settled policy. It is not a thing which has been done in twenty-four hours, for it has taken months and months to do it. The military authorities knew perfectly well it was to be done, and they had ample time to provide for it. They started clearing the country about six months ago, and it is disgraceful that five or six months after that children should be dying at the rate of hundreds per month in the different camps. But let me point this out to the House. The rate of mortality among children—and I think this is the most disgraceful fact in the whole situation—is higher than that amongst the soldiers who have braved all the risks of the field. The mortality amongst our own troops is something like thirty-six per thousand. When the epidemic was at its height in Bloemfontein the death rate was fifty-two per thousand. Even taking the argument that war is war, and that women and children should not be altogether exempt from its dangers, it is unfair to class the mortality of soldiers in the field with that of women and children. But while the rate of mortality amongst the soldiers in the field is fifty-two per thousand, the mortality amongst the women and children in these camps is 450 per thousand, and we have no right to put the women and children in this position. What is the assumption of the right hon. Gentleman? He says that it is by voluntary submission on the part of these women and children that they are refugees, and that they sought our protection. If they are seeking our protection, then we are ill requiting their confidence. They are British subjects, and they are voluntarily British subjects. They came voluntarily to seek the protection of the British flag, and how do we treat them? Why, we half starve them. We give them bad food, no shelter, we clothe them badly, their houses are burned, and their stock taken away. This is how you treat those who have voluntarily submitted to us. This is the first object lesson for them under British rule.

Mr. Nolan (Louth, S.): We know all about that in Ireland. [Ministerial laughter.]

Mr. Cullinan (Tipperary, S.): Yes, it is common in Ireland; laugh at it if you like.

Mr. Lloyd-George: The right hon. Gentleman says they sought our protection. Protection against whom? Is it against their own kith and kin? Is it against the natives? Is there a single case recorded where the natives have attacked these poor women and children out on the veldt?[9] No, but they have been driven and compelled to come in. I have got case after case which I might quote to the House where they were compelled to come in—cases where the husband never fought against us, and cases where the husbands are now on commando. There were no charges against the women, and there could be none against the poor little children, but they were compelled to come into these camps. The right hon. Gentleman says he is perfectly willing that they shall go elsewhere if they have anyone to protect them. They have sent petitions in to the military authorities begging to be allowed to leave these camps. [The hon. Member read one of the petitions referred to, and continued:] We are told that these people are voluntary refugees

---

9. Open grasslands.

who ask for our protection, but if this is so will the right hon. Gentleman explain why the terms of this petition at Kimberley were refused, and why there was a barbed wire fence surrounding the whole camp? If such a camp is not a prison, it is very like one. All round the camp there are sentries outside. These refugees have asked permission to be allowed to go away, and it has been refused. There are cases in which relatives in Cape Colony have offered to take these women and children under their protection and to pay the expense of conveying them and of keeping them, and even this offer has been refused.

The right hon. Gentleman cannot possibly state, in face of all these facts, that these are voluntary refugees. I say that it is the very worst policy in the world to keep these women and children there in these camps against their will, and under such conditions. It is perfectly impossible, owing to the circumstances, that these children should not suffer. You cannot have children of eighteen months and three or four years old under these tents, in all sorts of weather, without injury to their health. You cannot give them the class of food which you can give to a man in full health and strength, and there certainly ought to be some means of protecting them rather than herding them together in these refugee camps, and I appeal to the right hon. Gentleman to do something in this respect. He must know that it is quite impossible under the conditions existing in the Orange River Colony and the Transvaal to do anything to adequately provide for women and children in those parts. There are two camps which are fairly good, I am told, at Port Elizabeth and Norval's Point, in Cape Colony. There the refugees are within reach of a sympathetic population, and I put it to the Government that it is better to send these people to places where they will have the sympathy of their kinsmen, for it is too much to expect of flesh and blood that they will not sympathise with these refugees.

—1901

The Eastern Empire: India

For more than three hundred years, the British controlled India, fundamentally reshaping its language, literature, religion, and behavior. During the seventeenth and eighteenth centuries, the British East India Company established trade in India in order to export Indian cotton. Starting out with small trading posts, it eventually ended up managing cities and sponsoring armies, and by the nineteenth century, it had become the governmental authority, aiming to "civilize" India by providing it with European-style governments, legal systems, religious institutions, and schools.

In 1857, everything changed. Soldiers in the Bengal army mutinied and shot their British officers. A rash of brutal and indiscriminate murders erupted on both sides; civilians, women, and children were massacred. Popularly known as "the Mutiny" (although today it is sometimes considered the first Indian War of Independence), this year-long bloodshed shocked the British public, revealing the bitterness of Indians' resentment of their colonial masters.

Terrified of provoking another violent uprising, the British became much more careful to sustain Indian traditions. After the Mutiny, the Crown took over the control of India directly, with Queen Victoria pronouncing herself Empress of India in 1876. During this period, the British laid down a vast railway and canal system, fundamentally altering travel, trade, and communication within India. Indian universities started to produce a new educated coterie comfortable with both Indian beliefs and European culture. By the 1890s, India was a thriving nation with modern railways, publishers, universities, and roads, boasting its own composite "Anglo-Indian" culture merging the colonial masters' material with homegrown traditions.

The most famous chronicler of Anglo-Indian culture was undoubtedly Rudyard Kipling, whose "Gunga Din" and "Without Benefit of Clergy" express British visitors' complex mix of love, loyalty, disdain, and distaste for the native people who served them. But in "In the Next Room," Alice Perrin adds the ingredient of sexualized fear to show how quickly this relationship could turn toxic. It was easier to generalize about Indian exoticism at home, where Sherlock Holmes could symbolically exorcise the demonic cruelty of the East. Similarly, Laurence Hope relied heavily on the British association of breathless sensuality with India in her popular poems. The last word, however, belongs to Toru Dutt, who forged a remarkably rich synthesis of European poetic forms with Indian ideas. Kipling, an English man brought up in India, and Dutt, an Indian woman educated in Europe, bookend this section. They both managed—in their different ways and for their different purposes—to express their love for Indian culture in English literary style, thereby exemplifying the new possibilities for Anglo-Indian literature in the twentieth century and beyond.

Rudyard Kipling
1865–1936

This brash, brilliant young journalist brought a different kind of voice into English literature: the language of Anglo-Indian culture. British readers of Rudyard Kipling's early books, especially his wildly successful poems, *Barrack-Room Ballads* (1889), and short stories, *Life's Handicap* (1891), found themselves in the rough, dusty work of the British soldier or the lonely, yearning life of a British civil servant, in a place with unfamiliar and resonant words, glaring sunlight, spicy food, colorful silk, and jangling gold. Kipling rarely falls into the Victorian habit of describing India as an exotic paradise of sensual license, a savage heart of darkness, or a comic spectacle of native buffoonery. Instead, he makes the colony the central place, with Britain as the outpost and British readers as outsiders. Yet Kipling's politics are more ambivalent. Both "Gunga Din" and "Without Benefit of Clergy" tenderly depict an interracial alliance (either of friendship or of love), but only on the terms of the Indian partner's devoted service and early death and in emphatic preservation of imperial values. Kipling constructs an India of unprecedented realism—but it represents the reality he chooses to affirm. For more information about Kipling, see p. 484.

Gunga Din

You may talk o' gin an' beer
When you're quartered safe out 'ere,
An' you're sent to penny-fights an' Aldershot[1] it;
But if it comes to slaughter
You will do your work on water,   5
An' you'll lick the bloomin' boots of 'im that's got it.
Now in Injia's sunny clime,
Where I used to spend my time
A-servin' of 'Er Majesty the Queen,
Of all them black-faced crew   10
The finest man I knew
Was our regimental *bhisti*, Gunga Din.

    He was "Din! Din! Din!
    You limping lump o' brick-dust, Gunga Din!
    Hi! *slippy hitherao!*[2]   15
    Water, get it! *Panee lao!*[3]
    You squidgy-nosed old idol, Gunga Din!"

The uniform 'e wore
Was nothin' much before,
An' rather less than 'arf o' that be'ind,   20
For a twisty piece o' rag
An' a goatskin water-bag
Was all the field-equipment 'e could find.
When the sweatin' troop-train lay
In a sidin' through the day,   25
Where the 'eat would make your bloomin' eye-brows crawl,
We shouted "Harry By!"[4]
Till our throats were bricky-dry,
Then we wopped 'im 'cause 'e couldn't serve us all.

    It was "Din! Din! Din!   30
    You 'eathen, where the mischief 'ave you been?
    You put some *juldee*[5] in it,
    Or I'll *marrow*[6] you this minute
    If you don't fill up my helmet, Gunga Din!"

---

1. Penny-fights are skirmishes. Aldershot is a military camp in Hampshire.
2. Come here!
3. Bring water swiftly!
4. Hey, brother! (Hari bhai.)
5. Speed.
6. Hit.

'E would dot an' carry one   35
Till the longest day was done,
An' 'e didn't seem to know the use o' fear.
If we charged or broke or cut,
You could bet your bloomin' nut,
'E'd be waitin' fifty paces right flank rear.   40
With 'is *mussick*[7] on 'is back,
'E would skip with our attack,
An' watch us till the bugles made "Retire."
An' for all 'is dirty 'ide
'E was white, clear white, inside   45
When 'e went to tend the wounded under fire!

    It was "Din! Din! Din!"
    With the bullets kickin' dust-spots on the green.
    When the cartridges ran out,
    You could 'ear the front-files shout: 50
    "Hi! ammunition-mules an' Gunga Din!"

I sha'n't forgit the night
When I dropped be'ind the fight
With a bullet where my belt-plate should 'a' been.
I was chokin' mad with thirst,   55
An' the man that spied me first
Was our good old grinnin', gruntin' Gunga Din.
'E lifted up my 'ead,
An' 'e plugged me where I bled,
An' 'e guv me 'arf-a-pint o' water—green: 60
It was crawlin' and it stunk,
But of all the drinks I've drunk,
I'm gratefullest to one from Gunga Din.

    It was "Din! Din! Din!
    'Ere's a beggar with a bullet through 'is spleen;   65
    'E's chawin' up the ground an' 'e kickin' all around:
    For Gawd's sake git the water, Gunga Din!"

'E carried me away
To where a *dooli*[8] lay,
An' a bullet come an' drilled the beggar clean.   70
'E put me safe inside,
An' just before 'e died:
    "I 'ope you liked your drink," sez Gunga Din.
So I'll meet 'im later on

---

7. Water-bag.
8. Stretcher.

In the place where 'e is gone—   75
Where it's always double drill and no canteen;
'E'll be squattin' on the coals
Givin' drink to pore damned souls,
An' I'll get a swig in Hell from Gunga Din!

    Din! Din! Din!   80
    You Lazarushian-leather[9] Gunga Din!
    Tho' I've belted you an' flayed you,
    By the livin' Gawd that made you,
    You're a better man than I am, Gunga Din!

                                                            —1890

Without Benefit of Clergy[1]

Before my Spring I garnered Autumn's gain,
    Out of her time my field was white with grain,
The year gave up her secrets to my woe.
    Forced and deflowered each sick season lay,
In mystery of increase and decay;
    I saw the sunset ere men saw the day,
Who am too wise in that I should not know.
                                —Bitter Waters.[2]

1

"But if it be a girl?"

    "Lord of my life, it cannot be. I have prayed for so many nights, and sent gifts to Sheikh Badl's shrine so often, that I know God will give us a son—a man-child that shall grow into a man. Think of this and be glad. My mother shall be his mother till I can take him again, and the mullah[3] of the Pattan mosque shall cast his nativity[4]— God send he be born in an auspicious hour!—and then, and then thou wilt never weary of me, thy slave."

    "Since when hast thou been a slave, my queen?"

    "Since the beginning—till this mercy[5] came to me. How could I be sure of thy love when I knew that I had been bought with silver?"

    "Nay, that was the dowry. I paid it to thy mother."

    "And she has buried it, and sits upon it all day long like a hen. What talk is yours of dower! I was bought as though I had been a Lucknow dancing-girl[6] instead of a child."

---

9. Combines Russian leather (heavily tanned like Gunga Din's skin) with Lazarus, the beggar who goes to heaven while the rich man who scorned him begs for a drink of water in hell (Luke 16).

---

1. Not legally married.
2. Kipling's poem.
3. Muslim cleric.
4. Make his astrological chart.
5. Pregnancy.
6. A prostitute.

"Art thou sorry for the sale?"

"I have sorrowed; but to-day I am glad. Thou wilt never cease to love me now?—answer, my king."

"Never—never. No."

"Not even though the *mem-log*—the white women of thy own blood—love thee? And remember, I have watched them driving in the evening; they are very fair."

"I have seen fire-balloons[7] by the hundred. I have seen the moon, and—then I saw no more fire-balloons."

Ameera clapped her hands and laughed. "Very good talk," she said. Then with an assumption of great stateliness: "It is enough. Thou hast my permission to depart,—if thou wilt."

The man did not move. He was sitting on a low red-lacquered couch in a room furnished only with a blue and white floor-cloth, some rugs, and a very complete collection of native cushions. At his feet sat a woman of sixteen, and she was all but all the world in his eyes. By every rule and law she should have been otherwise, for he was an Englishman, and she a Mussulman's daughter bought two years before from her mother, who, being left without money, would have sold Ameera shrieking to the Prince of Darkness if the price had been sufficient.

It was a contract entered into with a light heart; but even before the girl had reached her bloom she came to fill the greater portion of John Holden's life. For her, and the withered hag her mother, he had taken a little house overlooking the great red-walled city, and found,—when the marigolds had sprung up by the well in the courtyard, and Ameera had established herself according to her own ideas of comfort, and her mother had ceased grumbling at the inadequacy of the cooking-places, the distance from the daily market, and at matters of house-keeping in general,—that the house was to him his home. Any one could enter his bachelor's bungalow by day or night, and the life that he led there was an unlovely one. In the house in the city his feet only could pass beyond the outer courtyard to the women's rooms; and when the big wooden gate was bolted behind him he was king in his own territory, with Ameera for queen. And there was going to be added to this kingdom a third person whose arrival Holden felt inclined to resent. It interfered with his perfect happiness. It disarranged the orderly peace of the house that was his own. But Ameera was wild with delight at the thought of it, and her mother not less so. The love of a man, and particularly a white man, was at the best an inconstant affair, but it might, both women argued, be held fast by a baby's hands. "And then," Ameera would always say, "then he will never care for the white *mem-log*. I hate them all—I hate them all."

"He will go back to his own people in time," said the mother; "but by the blessing of God that time is yet afar off."

Holden sat silent on the couch thinking of the future, and his thoughts were not pleasant. The drawbacks of a double life are manifold. The Government, with singular care, had ordered him out of the station for a fortnight on special duty in the place of a man who was watching by the bedside of a sick wife. The verbal notification of the transfer had been edged by a cheerful remark that Holden ought to think himself lucky in being a bachelor and a free man. He came to break the news to Ameera.

---

7. Hot-air balloons.

"It is not good," she said slowly, "but it is not all bad. There is my mother here, and no harm will come to me—unless indeed I die of pure joy. Go thou to thy work and think no troublesome thoughts. When the days are done I believe . . . nay, I am sure. And—and then I shall lay *him* in thy arms, and thou wilt love me for ever. The train goes tonight, at midnight is it not? Go now, and do not let thy heart be heavy by cause of me. But thou wilt not delay in returning? Thou wilt not stay on the road to talk to the bold white *mem-log*. Come back to me swiftly, my life."

As he left the courtyard to reach his horse that was tethered to the gatepost, Holden spoke to the white-haired old watchman who guarded the house, and bade him under certain contingencies despatch the filled-up telegraph-form that Holden gave him. It was all that could be done, and with the sensations of a man who has attended his own funeral Holden went away by the night-mail to his exile. Every hour of the day he dreaded the arrival of the telegram, and every hour of the night he pictured to himself the death of Ameera. In consequence his work for the State was not of first-rate quality, nor was his temper towards his colleagues of the most amiable. The fortnight ended without a sign from his home, and, torn to pieces by his anxieties, Holden returned to be swallowed up for two precious hours by a dinner at the club, wherein he heard, as a man hears in a swoon, voices telling him how execrably he had performed the other man's duties, and how he had endeared himself to all his associates. Then he fled on horseback through the night with his heart in his mouth. There was no answer at first to his blows on the gate, and he had just wheeled his horse round to kick it in when Pir Khan appeared with a lantern and held his stirrup.

"Has aught occurred?" said Holden.

"The news does not come from my mouth, Protector of the Poor, but—" He held out his shaking hand as befitted the bearer of good news who is entitled to a reward.

Holden hurried through the courtyard. A light burned in the upper room. His horse neighed in the gateway and he heard a shrill little wail that sent all the blood into the apple of his throat. It was a new voice, but it did not prove that Ameera was alive.

"Who is there?" he called up the narrow brick staircase.

There was a cry of delight from Ameera, and then the voice of the mother, tremulous with old age and pride—"We be two women and—the—man—thy—son."

On the threshold of the room Holden stepped on a naked dagger, that was laid there to avert ill-luck, and it broke at the hilt under his impatient heel.

"God is great!" cooed Ameera in the half-light. "Thou hast taken his misfortunes on thy head."

"Ay, but how is it with thee, life of my life? Old woman, how is it with her?"

"She has forgotten her sufferings for joy that the child is born. There is no harm; but speak softly," said the mother.

"It only needed thy presence to make me all well," said Ameera. "My king, thou hast been very long away. What gifts hast thou for me? Ah, ah! It is I that bring gifts this time. Look, my life, look. Was there ever such a babe? Nay, I am too weak even to clear my arm from him."

"Rest then, and do not talk. I am here, *bachari* (little woman)."

"Well said, for there is a bond and a heel-rope (*peecharee*) between us now that nothing can break. Look—canst thou see in this light? He is without spot or blemish.

Never was such a man-child. *Ya illah!* [My God] he shall be a pundit[8]—no, a trooper of the Queen. And, my life, dost thou love me as well as ever, though I am faint and sick and worn? Answer truly."

"Yea. I love as I have loved, with all my soul. Lie still, pearl, and rest."

"Then do not go. Sit by my side here—so. Mother, the lord of this house needs a cushion. Bring it." There was an almost imperceptible movement on the part of the new life that lay in the hollow of Ameera's arm. "Aho!" she said, her voice breaking with love. "The babe is a champion from his birth. He is kicking me in the side with mighty kicks. Was there ever such a babe! And he is ours to us—thine and mine. Put thy hand on his head, but carefully, for he is very young, and men are unskilled in such matters."

Very cautiously Holden touched with the tips of his fingers the downy head.

"He is of the Faith," said Ameera; "for lying here in the night-watches I whispered the call to prayer and the profession of faith into his ears. And it is most marvellous that he was born upon a Friday,[9] as I was born. Be careful of him, my life; but he can almost grip with his hands."

Holden found one helpless little hand that closed feebly on his finger. And the clutch ran through his limbs till it settled about his heart. Till then his sole thought had been for Ameera. He began to realize that there was some one else in the world, but he could not feel that it was a veritable son with a soul. He sat down to think, and Ameera dozed lightly.

"Get hence, *sahib*,"[10] said her mother under her breath. "It is not good that she should find you here on waking. She must be still."

"I go," said Holden submissively. "Here be rupees. See that my *baba* gets fat and finds all that he needs."

The chink of the silver roused Ameera. "I am his mother, and no hireling," she said weakly. "Shall I look to him more or less for the sake of money? Mother, give it back. I have born my lord a son."

The deep sleep of weakness came upon her almost before the sentence was completed. Holden went down to the courtyard very softly with his heart at ease. Pir Khan, the old watchman, was chuckling with delight. "This house is now complete," he said, and without further comment thrust into Holden's hands the hilt of a sabre worn many years ago when he, Pir Khan, served the Queen in the police. The bleat of a tethered goat came from the well-kerb.

"There be two," said Pir Khan, "two goats of the best. I bought them, and they cost much money; and since there is no birth-party assembled their flesh will be all mine. Strike craftily, *sahib*! 'Tis an ill-balanced sabre at the best. Wait till they raise their heads from cropping the marigolds."

"And why?" said Holden, bewildered.

"For the birth-sacrifice. What else? Otherwise the child being unguarded from fate may die. The Protector of the Poor knows the fitting words to be said."

Holden had learned them once with little thought that he would ever speak them in earnest. The touch of the cold sabre-hilt in his palm turned suddenly to the

---

8. Teacher.
9. Islamic holy day.
10. Master.

clinging grip of the child up stairs—the child that was his own son—and a dread of loss filled him.

"Strike!" said Pir Khan. "Never life came into the world but life was paid for it. See, the goats have raised their heads. Now! With a drawing cut!"

Hardly knowing what he did Holden cut twice as he muttered the Mohammedan prayer that runs:—"Almighty! In place of this my son I offer life for life, blood for blood, head for head, bone for bone, hair for hair, skin for skin." The waiting horse snorted and bounded in his pickets at the smell of the raw blood that spirted over Holden's riding-boots.

"Well smitten!" said Pir Khan wiping the sabre. "A swordsman was lost in thee. Go with a light heart, Heaven-born. I am thy servant, and the servant of thy son. May the Presence live a thousand years and. . . . the flesh of the goats is all mine?" Pir Khan drew back richer by a month's pay. Holden swung himself into the saddle and rode off through the low-hanging wood-smoke of the evening. He was full of riotous exultation, alternating with a vast vague tenderness directed towards no particular object, that made him choke as he bent over the neck of his uneasy horse. "I never felt like this in my life," he thought. "I'll go to the club and pull myself together."

A game of pool was beginning, and the room was full of men. Holden entered, eager to get to the light and the company of his fellows, singing at the top of his voice:

> In Baltimore a-walking, a lady I did meet!

"Did you?" said the club-secretary from his corner. "Did she happen to tell you that your boots were wringing wet? Great goodness, man, it's blood!"

"Bosh!" said Holden, picking his cue from the rack. "May I cut in? It's dew. I've been riding through high crops. My faith! my boots are in a mess though!

> And if it be a girl she shall wear a wedding ring,
> And if it be a boy he shall fight for his king,
> With his dirk, and his cap, and his little jacket blue,
> He shall walk the quarter-deck—"

"Yellow on blue—green next player," said the marker monotonously.

"*He shall walk the quarter-deck*,—am I green, marker? *He shall walk the quarter-deck*,—eh! that's a bad shot,—*as his daddy used to do!*"

"I don't see that you have anything to crow about," said a zealous junior civilian acidly. "The Government is not exactly pleased with your work when you relieved Sanders."

"Does that mean a wigging[11] from head-quarters?" said Holden with an abstracted smile. "I think I can stand it."

The talk beat up round the ever-fresh subject of each man's work, and steadied Holden till it was time to go to his dark empty bungalow, where his butler received

---

11. Scolding.

him as one who knew all his affairs. Holden remained awake for the greater part of the night, and his dreams were pleasant ones.

2

"How old is he now?"

"*Ya illah!* What a man's question! He is all but six weeks old; and on this night I go up to the house-top with thee, my life, to count the stars. For that is auspicious. And he was born on a Friday under the sign of the sun, and it has been told to me that he will outlive us both and get wealth. Can we wish for aught better, beloved?"

"There is nothing better. Let us go up to the roof, and thou shalt count the stars—but a few only, for the sky is heavy with cloud."

"The winter rains are late, and maybe they come out of season. Come, before all the stars are hid. I have put on my richest jewels."

"Thou hast forgotten the best of all."

"*Ai!* Ours. He comes also. He has never yet seen the skies."

Ameera climbed the narrow staircase that led to the flat roof. The child, placid and unwinking, lay in the hollow of her right arm, gorgeous in silver-fringed muslin with a small skull-cap on his head. Ameera wore all that she valued most. The diamond nose-stud that takes the place of the Western patch[12] in drawing attention to the curve of the nostril, the gold ornament in the centre of the forehead studded with tallow-drop emeralds and flawed rubies, the heavy circlet of beaten gold that was fastened round her neck by the softness of the pure metal, and the chinking curb-patterned silver anklets hanging low over the rosy ankle-bone. She was dressed in jade-green muslin as befitted a daughter of the Faith,[13] and from shoulder to elbow and elbow to wrist ran bracelets of silver tied with floss silk, frail glass bangles slipped over the wrist in proof of the slenderness of the hand, and certain heavy gold bracelets that had no part in her country's ornaments but, since they were Holden's gift and fastened with a cunning European snap, delighted her immensely.

They sat down by the low white parapet of the roof, overlooking the city and its lights.

"They are happy down there," said Ameera. "But I do not think that they are as happy as we. Nor do I think the white *mem-log* are as happy. And thou?"

"I know they are not."

"How dost thou know?"

"They give their children over to the nurses."

"I have never seen that," said Ameera with a sigh, "nor do I wish to see. *Ahi!*"—she dropped her head on Holden's shoulder,—"I have counted forty stars, and I am tired. Look at the child, love of my life, he is counting too."

The baby was staring with round eyes at the dark of the heavens. Ameera placed him in Holden's arms, and he lay there without a cry.

"What shall we call him among ourselves?" she said. "Look! Art thou ever tired of looking? He carries thy very eyes. But the mouth—"

"Is thine, most dear. Who should know better than I?"

---

12. 18th-c. women pasted "beauty marks" on their cheeks.
13. Green is associated with Islam; the dress also conceals her body according to Muslim codes of female modesty.

"'Tis such a feeble mouth. Oh, so small! And yet it holds my heart between its lips. Give him to me now. He has been too long away."

"Nay, let him lie; he has not yet begun to cry."

"When he cries thou wilt give him back—eh! What a man of mankind thou art! If he cried he were only the dearer to me. But, my life, what little name shall we give him?"

The small body lay close to Holden's heart. It was utterly helpless and very soft. He scarcely dared to breathe for fear of crushing it. The caged green parrot that is regarded as a sort of guardian spirit in most native households moved on its perch and fluttered a drowsy wing.

"There is the answer," said Holden. "Mian Mittu has spoken. He shall be the parrot. When he is ready he will talk mightily and run about. Mian Mittu is the parrot in thy—in the Mussulman tongue, is it not?"

"Why put me so far off?" said Ameera fretfully. "Let it be like unto some English name—but not wholly. For he is mine."

"Then call him Tota, for that is likest English."

"Ay, Tota, and that is still the parrot. Forgive me, my lord, for a minute ago, but in truth he is too little to wear all the weight of Mian Mittu for name. He shall be Tota—our Tota to us. Hearest thou, oh, small one? Littlest, thou art Tota." She touched the child's cheek, and he waking wailed, and it was necessary to return him to his mother, who soothed him with the wonderful rhyme of *Aré koko, Faré koko!* which says:

> Oh, crow! Go crow! Baby's sleeping sound,
> And the wild plums grow in the jungle, only a penny a pound.
> Only a penny a pound, *baba*, only a penny a pound.

Reassured many times as to the price of those plums, Tota cuddled himself down to sleep. The two sleek, white well-bullocks in the courtyard were steadily chewing the cud of their evening meal; old Pir Khan squatted at the head of Holden's horse, his police sabre across his knees, pulling drowsily at a big water-pipe that croaked like a bull-frog in a pond. Ameera's mother sat spinning in the lower verandah, and the wooden gate was shut and barred. The music of a marriage procession came to the roof above the gentle hum of the city, and a string of flying-foxes crossed the face of the low moon.

"I have prayed," said Ameera after a long pause, "I have prayed for two things. First, that I may die in thy stead if thy death is demanded, and in the second that I may die in the place of the child. I have prayed to the Prophet and to Beebee Miriam [the Virgin Mary]. Thinkest thou either will hear?"

"From thy lips who would not hear the lightest word?"

"I asked for straight talk, and thou hast given me sweet talk. Will my prayers be heard?"

"How can I say? God is very good."

"Of that I am not sure. Listen now. When I die, or the child dies, what is thy fate? Living, thou wilt return to the bold white *mem-log*, for kind calls to kind."

"Not always."

"With a woman, no; with a man it is otherwise. Thou wilt in this life, later on, go back to thine own folk. That I could almost endure, for I should be dead. But in thy very death thou wilt be taken away to a strange place and a paradise that I do not know."

"Will it be paradise?"

"Surely, for who would harm thee? But we two—I and the child—shall be elsewhere, and we cannot come to thee, nor canst thou come to us. In the old days, before the child was born, I did not think of these things; but now I think of them always. It is very hard talk."

"It will fall as it will fall. Tomorrow we do not know, but to-day and love we know well. Surely we are happy now."

"So happy that it were well to make our happiness assured. And thy Beebee Miriam should listen to me; for she is also a woman. But then she would envy me! It is not seemly for men to worship a woman."

Holden laughed aloud at Ameera's little spasm of jealousy.

"Is it not seemly? Why didst thou not turn me from worship of thee, then?"

"Thou a worshipper! And of me! My king, for all thy sweet words, well I know that I am thy servant and thy slave, and the dust under thy feet. And I would not have it otherwise. See!"

Before Holden could prevent her she stooped forward and touched his feet; recovering herself with a little laugh she hugged Tota closer to her bosom. Then, almost savagely—

"Is it true that the bold white *mem-log* live for three times the length of my life? Is it true that they make their marriages not before they are old women?"

"They marry as do others—when they are women."

"That I know, but they wed when they are twenty-five. Is that true?"

"That is true."

"*Ya illah!* At twenty-five! Who would of his own will take a wife even of eighteen? She is a woman—ageing every hour. Twenty-five! I shall be an old woman at that age, and—Those *mem-log* remain young for ever. How I hate them!"

"What have they to do with us?"

"I cannot tell. I know only that there may now be alive on this earth a woman ten years older than I who may come to thee and take thy love ten years after I am an old woman, grey headed, and the nurse of Tota's son. That is unjust and evil. They should die too."

"Now, for all thy years thou art a child, and shalt be picked up and carried down the staircase."

"Tota! Have a care for Tota, my lord! Thou at least art as foolish as any babe!" Ameera tucked Tota out of harm's way in the hollow of her neck, and was carried down stairs laughing in Holden's arms, while Tota opened his eyes and smiled after the manner of the lesser angels.

He was a silent infant, and, almost before Holden could realize that he was in the world, developed into a small gold-coloured little god and unquestioned despot of the house overlooking the city. Those were months of absolute happiness to Holden and Ameera—happiness withdrawn from the world, shut in behind the wooden gate that Pir Khan guarded. By day Holden did his work with an immense pity for such as were not so fortunate as himself, and a sympathy for small children that amazed and amused many mothers at the little station-gatherings. At nightfall he returned to Ameera,—Ameera full of the wondrous doings of Tota, how he had been seen to clap his hands together and move his fingers with intention and purpose—which was manifestly a miracle—how later, he had of his own initiative crawled out of his low bedstead on to the floor and swayed on both feet for the space of three breaths.

"And they were long breaths, for my heart stood still with delight," said Ameera.

Then he took the beasts into his councils—the well-bullocks, the little grey squirrels, the mongoose that lived in a hole near the well, and especially Mian Mittu, the parrot, whose tail he grievously pulled, and Mian Mittu screamed till Ameera and Holden arrived.

"Oh, villain! Child of strength! This to thy brother on the house-top! *Tobah, tobah!* Fie! Fie! But I know a charm to make him wise as Suleiman and Aflatoun [Solomon and Plato]. Now look," said Ameera. She drew from an embroidered bag a handful of almonds. "See! we count seven. In the name of God!"

She placed Mian Mittu, very angry and rumpled, on the top of his cage, and seating herself between the babe and the bird she cracked and peeled an almond less white than her teeth. "This is a true charm, my life, and do not laugh. See! I give the parrot one half and Tota the other." Mian Mittu with careful beak took his share from between Ameera's lips, and she kissed the other half into the mouth of the child, who ate it slowly with wondering eyes. "This I will do each day of seven, and without doubt he who is ours will be a bold speaker and wise. Eh, Tota, what wilt thou be when thou art a man and I am grey-headed?" Tota tucked his fat legs into adorable creases. He could crawl, but he was not going to waste the spring of his youth in idle speech. He wanted Mian Mittu's tail to tweak.

When he was advanced to the dignity of a silver belt—which, with a magic-square engraved on silver and hung round his neck, made up the greater part of his clothing—he staggered on a perilous journey down the garden to Pir Khan and proffered him all his jewels in exchange for one little ride on Holden's horse, having seen his mother's mother chaffering with pedlars in the verandah. Pir Khan wept and set the untried feet on his own grey head in sign of fealty, and brought the bold adventurer to his mother's arms, vowing that Tota would be a leader of men ere his beard was grown.

One hot evening while he sat on the roof between his father and mother watching the never-ending warfare of the kites, that the city boys flew, he demanded a kite of his own with Pir Khan to fly it, because he had a fear of dealing with anything larger than himself, and when Holden called him a "spark," he rose to his feet and answered slowly in defence of his newfound individuality: "*Hum 'park nahin hai. Hom admi hai.* (I am no spark, but a man.)"

The protest made Holden choke and devote himself very seriously to a consideration of Tota's future. He need hardly have taken the trouble. The delight of that life was too perfect to endure. Therefore it was taken away as many things are taken away in India—suddenly and without warning. The little lord of the house, as Pir Khan called him, grew sorrowful and complained of pains who had never known the meaning of pain. Ameera, wild with terror, watched him through the night, and in the dawning of the second day the life was shaken out of him by fever—the seasonal autumn fever. It seemed altogether impossible that he could die, and neither Ameera nor Holden at first believed the evidence of the little body on the bedstead. Then Ameera beat her head against the wall and would have flung herself down the well in the garden had Holden not restrained her by main force.

One mercy only was granted to Holden. He rode to his office in broad daylight and found waiting him an unusually heavy mail that demanded concentrated attention and hard work. He was not, however, alive to this kindness of the gods.

3

The first shock of a bullet is no more than a brisk pinch. The wrecked body does not send in its protest to the soul till ten or fifteen seconds later. Holden realized his pain slowly, exactly as he had realized his happiness, and with the same imperious necessity for hiding all trace of it. In the beginning he only felt that there had been a loss, and that Ameera needed comforting, where she sat with her head on her knees shivering as Mian Mittu from the house-top called, *Tota! Tota! Tota!* Later all his world and the daily life of it rose up to hurt him. It was an outrage that any one of the children at the band-stand in the evening should be alive and clamorous, when his own child lay dead. It was more than mere pain when one of them touched him, and stories told by over-fond fathers of their children's latest performances cut him to the quick. He could not declare his pain. He had neither help, comfort, nor sympathy; and Ameera at the end of each weary day would lead him through the hell of self-questioning reproach which is reserved for those who have lost a child, and believe that with a little—just a little more care—it might have been saved.

"Perhaps," Ameera would say, "I did not take sufficient heed. Did I, or did I not? The sun on the roof that day when he played so long alone and I was—*ahi!* braiding my hair—it may be that the sun then bred the fever. If I had warned him from the sun he might have lived. But, oh my life, say that I am guiltless! Thou knowest that I loved him as I love thee. Say that there is no blame on me, or I shall die—I shall die!"

"There is no blame,—before God, none. It was written and how could we do aught to save? What has been, has been. Let it go, beloved."

"He was all my heart to me. How can I let the thought go when my arm tells me every night that he is not here? *Ahi! Ahi!* Oh Tota come back to me—come back again, and let us be all together as it was before!"

"Peace, peace! For thine own sake, and for mine also, if thou lovest me—rest."

"By this I know thou dost not care; and how shouldst thou? The white men have hearts of stone and souls of iron. Oh that I had married a man of mine own people—though he beat me, and had never eaten the bread of an alien!"

"Am I an alien—mother of my son?"

"What else—*sahib?* . . . Oh forgive me—forgive! The death has driven me mad. Thou art the life of my heart, and the light of my eyes, and the breath of my life, and—and I have put thee from me though it was but for a moment. If thou goest away to whom shall I look for help? Do not be angry. Indeed, it was the pain that spoke and not thy slave."

"I know, I know. We be two who were three. The greater need therefore that we should be one."

They were sitting on the roof as of custom. The night was a warm one in early spring, and sheet-lightning was dancing on the horizon to a broken tune played by far-off thunder. Ameera settled herself in Holden's arms.

"The dry earth is lowing like a cow for the rain, and I—I am afraid. It was not like this when we counted the stars. But thou lovest me as much as before, though a bond is taken away? Answer!"

"I love more because a new bond has come out of the sorrow that we have eaten together, and that thou knowest."

"Yea, I knew," said Ameera in a very small whisper. "But it is good to hear thee say so, my life, who art so strong to help. I will be a child no more, but a woman and an aid to thee. Listen! Give me my *sitar*[14] and I will sing bravely."

She took the light silver-studded *sitar* and began a song of the great hero Rajah Rasalu. The hand failed on the strings, the tune halted, checked, and at a low note turned off to the poor little nursery-rhyme about the wicked crow:

> And the wild plums grow in the jungle, only a penny a pound.
> Only a penny a pound, *baba*—only . . .

Then came the tears, and the piteous rebellion against fate till she slept, moaning a little in her sleep, with the right arm thrown clear of the body as though it protected something that was not there. It was after this night that life became a little easier for Holden. The ever-present pain of loss drove him into his work, and the work repaid him by filling up his mind for eight or nine hours a day. Ameera sat alone in the house and brooded, but grew happier when she understood that Holden was more at ease, according to the custom of women. They touched happiness again, but this time with caution.

"It was because we loved Tota that he died. The jealousy of God was upon us," said Ameera. "I have hung up a large black jar before our window to turn the evil eye from us, and we must make no protestations of delight but go softly underneath the stars, lest God find us out. Is that not good talk, worthless one?"

She had shifted the accent on the word that means "beloved," in proof of the sincerity of her purpose. But the kiss that followed the new christening was a thing that any deity might have envied. They went about henceforward saying, "It is naught, it is naught;" and hoping that all the Powers heard.

The Powers were busy on other things. They had allowed thirty million people four years of plenty wherein men fed well and the crops were certain and the birthrate rose year by year: the districts reported a purely agricultural population varying from nine hundred to two thousand to the square mile of the overburdened earth; and the Member for Lower Tooting,[15] wandering about India in top-hat and frock-coat talked largely of the benefits of British rule, and suggested as the one thing needful the establishment of a duly qualified electoral system and a general bestowal of the franchise. His long-suffering hosts smiled and made him welcome, and when he paused to admire, with pretty picked words, the blossom of the blood-red *dhak* tree that had flowered untimely for a sign of what was coming, they smiled more than ever.

It was the Deputy Commissioner of Kot-Kumharsen, staying at the club for a day, who lightly told a tale that made Holden's blood run cold as he overheard the end.

---

14. Indian stringed instrument.
15. Caricature of an ignorant British Member of Parliament.

"He won't bother any one any more. Never saw a man so astonished in my life. By Jove, I thought he meant to ask a question in the House about it. Fellow-passenger in his ship—dined next him—bowled over by cholera[16] and died in eighteen hours. You needn't laugh, you fellows. The Member for Lower Tooting is awfully angry about it; but he's more scared. I think he's going to take his enlightened self out of India."

"I'd give a good deal if he were knocked over. It might keep a few vestrymen of his kidney to their own parish.[17] But what's this about cholera? It's full early for anything of that kind," said a warden of an unprofitable salt-lick.

"Don't know," said the Deputy Commissioner reflectively. "We've got locusts with us. There's sporadic cholera all along the north—at least we're calling it sporadic for decency's sake. The spring crops are short in five districts, and nobody seems to know where the rains are. It's nearly March now. I don't want to scare anybody, but it seems to me that Nature's going to audit her accounts with a big red pencil this summer."

"Just when I wanted to take leave, too!" said a voice across the room.

"There won't be much leave this year, but there ought to be a great deal of promotion. I've come in to persuade the Government to put my pet canal on the list of famine relief-works. It's an ill-wind that blows no good. I shall get that canal finished at last."

"Is it the old programme then," said Holden; "famine, fever, and cholera?"

"Oh no. Only local scarcity and an unusual prevalence of seasonal sickness. You'll find it all in the reports if you live till next year. You're a lucky chap. You haven't got a wife to put out of harm's way. The hill-stations ought to be full of women this year."

"I think you're inclined to exaggerate the talk in the *bazars*," said a young civilian in the Secretariat. "Now I have observed——"

"I dare say you have," said the Deputy Commissioner, "but you've a great deal more to observe, my son. In the meantime, I wish to observe to you—" and he drew him aside to discuss the construction of the canal that was so dear to his heart. Holden went to his bungalow and began to understand that he was not alone in the world, and also that he was afraid for the sake of another,—which is the most soul-satisfying fear known to man.

Two months later, as the Deputy had foretold, Nature began to audit her accounts with a red pencil. On the heels of the spring-reapings came a cry for bread, and the Government, which had decreed that no man should die of want, sent wheat. Then came the cholera from all four quarters of the compass. It struck a pilgrim-gathering of half a million at a sacred shrine. Many died at the feet of their god; the others broke and ran over the face of the land carrying the pestilence with them. It smote a walled city and killed two hundred a day. The people crowded the trains, hanging on to the foot-boards and squatting on the roofs of the carriages, and the cholera followed them, for at each station they dragged out the dead and the dying.

---

16. Disease spread by contaminated water, especially in regions with poor sanitary conditions; it kills people through rapid dehydration. Cholera epidemics in the 1830s and 1840s devastated England's industrial cities and parts of India.

17. Vestrymen are local church officials; this is a disrespectful way to wish officials like the Member of Parliament would stay home.

They died by the roadside, and the horses of the Englishmen shied at the corpses in the grass. The rains did not come, and the earth turned to iron lest man should escape death by hiding in her. The English sent their wives away to the hills and went about their work, coming forward as they were bidden to fill the gaps in the fighting-line. Holden, sick with fear of losing his chiefest treasure on earth, had done his best to persuade Ameera to go away with her mother to the Himalayas.

"Why should I go?" said she one evening on the roof.

"There is sickness, and people are dying, and all the white *mem-log* have gone."

"All of them?"

"All—unless perhaps there remain some old scald-head who vexes her husband's heart by running risk of death."

"Nay; who stays is my sister, and thou must not abuse her, for I will be a scald-head too. I am glad all the bold *mem-log* are gone."

"Do I speak to a woman or a babe? Go to the hills and I will see to it that thou goest like a queen's daughter. Think, child. In a red-lacquered bullock cart, veiled and curtained, with brass peacocks upon the pole and red cloth hangings. I will send two orderlies for guard and—"

"Peace! Thou art the babe in speaking thus. What use are those toys to me? He would have patted the bullocks and played with the housings. For his sake, perhaps,—thou hast made me very English—I might have gone. Now, I will not. Let the *mem-log* run."

"Their husbands are sending them, beloved."

"Very good talk. Since when hast thou been my husband to tell me what to do? I have but born thee a son. Thou art only all the desire of my soul to me. How shall I depart when I know that if evil befall thee by the breadth of so much as my littlest fingernail—is that not small?—I should be aware of it though I were in paradise. And here, this summer thou mayst die—*ai, janee*, die! and in dying they might call to tend thee a white woman, and she would rob me in the last of thy love!"

"But love is not born in a moment or on a death-bed!"

"What dost thou know of love, stone-heart? She would take thy thanks at least and, by God and the Prophet and Beebee Miriam the mother of thy Prophet, that I will never endure. My lord and my love, let there be no more foolish talk of going away. Where thou art, I am. It is enough." She put an arm round his neck and a hand on his mouth.

There are not many happinesses so complete as those that are snatched under the shadow of the sword. They sat together and laughed, calling each other openly by every pet name that could move the wrath of the gods. The city below them was locked up in its own torments. Sulphur fires blazed in the streets; the conches in the Hindu temples screamed and bellowed, for the gods were inattentive in those days. There was a service in the great Mahomedan shrine, and the call to prayer from the minarets was almost unceasing. They heard the wailing in the houses of the dead, and once the shriek of a mother who had lost a child and was calling for its return. In the grey dawn they saw the dead borne out through the city gates, each litter with its own little knot of mourners. Wherefore they kissed each other and shivered.

It was a red and heavy audit, for the land was very sick and needed a little breathing-space ere the torrent of cheap life should flood it anew. The children of immature fathers and undeveloped mothers made no resistance. They were cowed and sat still, waiting till the sword should be sheathed in November if it were so willed. There were gaps among the English, but the gaps were filled. The work of superintending famine-relief, cholera-sheds, medicine-distribution, and what little sanitation was possible, went forward because it was so ordered.

Holden had been told to keep himself in readiness to move to replace the next man who should fall. There were twelve hours in each day when he could not see Ameera, and she might die in three. He was considering what his pain would be if he could not see her for three months, or if she died out of his sight. He was absolutely certain that her death would be demanded—so certain that when he looked up from the telegram and saw Pir Khan breathless in the doorway, he laughed aloud, "And?" said he,——

"When there is a cry in the night and the spirit flutters into the throat, who has a charm that will restore? Come swiftly, Heaven-born! It is the black cholera."

Holden galloped to his home. The sky was heavy with clouds, for the long deferred rains were near and the heat was stifling. Ameera's mother met him in the courtyard, whimpering, "She is dying. She is nursing herself into death. She is all but dead. What shall I do, *sahib?*"

Ameera was lying in the room in which Tota had been born. She made no sign when Holden entered because the human soul is a very lonely thing and, when it is getting ready to go away, hides itself in a misty borderland where the living may not follow. The black cholera does its work quietly and without explanation. Ameera was being thrust out of life as though the Angel of Death had himself put his hand upon her. The quick breathing seemed to show that she was neither afraid nor in pain, but neither eyes nor mouth gave any answer to Holden's kisses. There was nothing to be said or done. Holden could only wait and suffer. The first drops of the rain began to fall on the roof and he could hear shouts of joy in the parched city.

The soul came back a little and the lips moved. Holden bent down to listen. "Keep nothing of mine," said Ameera. "Take no hair from my head. *She* would make thee burn it later on. That flame I should feel. Lower! Stoop lower! Remember only that I was thine and bore thee a son. Though thou wed a white woman to-morrow, the pleasure of receiving in thy arms thy first son is taken from thee for ever. Remember me when thy son is born—the one that shall carry thy name before all men. His misfortunes be on my head. I bear witness—I bear witness"—the lips were forming the words on his ear—"that there is no God but—thee, beloved!"

Then she died. Holden sat still, and all thought was taken from him,—till he heard Ameera's mother lift the curtain.

"Is she dead, *sahib?*"

"She is dead."

"Then I will mourn, and afterwards take an inventory of the furniture in this house. For that will be mine. The *sahib* does not mean to resume it? It is so little, so very little, *sahib,* and I am an old woman. I would like to lie softly."

"For the mercy of God be silent, a while. Go out and mourn where I cannot hear."

"*Sahib,* she will be buried in four hours."

"I know the custom. I shall go ere she is taken away. That matter is in thy hands. Look to it, that the bed on which—on which she lies—"

"Aha! That beautiful red-lacquered bed. I have long desired——"

"That the bed is left here untouched for my disposal. All else in the house is thine. Hire a cart, take everything, go hence, and before sunrise let there be nothing in this house but that which I have ordered thee to respect."

"I am an old woman. I would stay at least for the days of mourning, and the rains have just broken. Whither shall I go?"

"What is that to me? My order is that there is a going. The house-gear is worth a thousand rupees and my orderly shall bring thee a hundred rupees to-night."

"That is very little. Think of the cart-hire."

"It shall be nothing unless thou goest, and with speed. O woman, get hence and leave me to my dead!"

The mother shuffled down the staircase, and in her anxiety to take stock of the house-fittings forgot to mourn. Holden stayed by Ameera's side and the rain roared on the roof. He could not think connectedly by reason of the noise, though he made many attempts to do so. Then four sheeted ghosts glided dripping into the room and stared at him through their veils. They were the washers of the dead. Holden left the room and went out to his horse. He had come in a dead, stifling calm through ankle-deep dust. He found the court-yard a rain-lashed pond alive with frogs; a torrent of yellow water ran under the gate, and a roaring wind drove the bolts of the rain like buck-shot against the mud walls. Pir Khan was shivering in his little hut by the gate, and the horse was stamping uneasily in the water.

"I have been told the *sahib's* order," said Pir Khan. "It is well. This house is now desolate. I go also, for my monkey-face would be a reminder of that which has been. Concerning the bed, I will bring that to thy house yonder in the morning; but remember, *sahib*, it will be to thee a knife turned in a green wound. I go upon a pilgrimage, and I will take no money. I have grown fat in the protection of the Presence whose sorrow is my sorrow. For the last time I hold his stirrup."

He touched Holden's foot with both hands and the horse sprang out into the road, where the creaking bamboos were whipping the sky and all the frogs were chuckling. Holden could not see for the rain in his face. He put his hands before his eyes and muttered,

"Oh you brute! You utter brute!"

The news of his trouble was already in his bungalow. He read the knowledge in his butler's eyes when Ahmed Khan brought in food, and for the first and last time in his life laid a hand upon his master's shoulder, saying: "Eat, *sahib*, eat. Meat is good against sorrow. I also have known. Moreover the shadows come and go, *sahib*; the shadows come and go. These be curried eggs."

Holden could neither eat nor sleep. The heavens sent down eight inches of rain in that night and washed the earth clean. The waters tore down walls, broke roads, and scoured open the shallow graves on the Mahomedan burying-ground. All next day it rained, and Holden sat still in his house considering his sorrow. On the morning of the third day he received a telegram which said only: "Rickells, Myndonie. Dying. Holden relieve. Immediate." Then he thought that before he departed he would look at the house wherein he had been master and lord. There was a break in the weather, and the rank earth steamed with vapour.

He found that the rains had torn down the mud pillars of the gateway, and the heavy wooden gate that had guarded his life hung lazily from one hinge. There was grass three inches high in the courtyard; Pir Khan's lodge was empty, and the sodden thatch sagged between the beams. A gray squirrel was in possession of the verandah, as if the house had been untenanted for thirty years instead of three days. Ameera's mother had removed everything except some mildewed matting. The *tick-tick* of the little scorpions as they hurried across the floor was the only sound in the house. Ameera's room and the other one where Tota had lived were heavy with mildew; and the narrow staircase leading to the roof was streaked and stained with rain-borne mud. Holden saw all these things, and came out again to meet in the road Durga Dass, his landlord,—portly, affable, clothed in white muslin, and driving a C-spring buggy.[18] He was overlooking his property to see how the roofs stood the stress of the first rains.

"I have heard," said he, "you will not take this place any more, *sahib?*"

"What are you going to do with it?"

"Perhaps I shall let it again."

"Then I will keep it on while I am away."

Durga Dass was silent for some time. "You shall not take it on, *sahib*," he said. "When I was a young man I also——, but to-day I am a member of the Municipality. Ho! Ho! No. When the birds have gone what need to keep the nest? I will have it pulled down—the timber will sell for something always. It shall be pulled down, and the Municipality shall make a road across, as they desire, from the burning-*ghaut*[19] to the city wall, so that no man may say where this house stood."

—1890

Alice Perrin
1867–1934

Like Kipling, Alice Robinson Perrin was born in India but educated in England and returned to India as an adult. Like the other prewar Anglo-Indian romance writers (including Bithia Mary Croker and Maud Diver), Perrin stressed domestic, romantic, and emotional experience. She married Charles Perrin, an officer in the Indian Civil Service, and they traveled around the country before returning to England near the turn of the century. In several collections of short stories and novels, Perrin demonstrates familiarity with daily life in India. *Punch* remarked that her "cleverly-written stories . . . are second only to the 'Plain Tales' by Rudyard Kipling," while a reviewer in *The Standard* called her "one of the finest short-story writers we have." Perrin specialized in depicting newcomers to India, evoking the disorientation, fear, physical discomfort, and anxiety—as well as the arrogance—of the civil servants and young women in a very alien place. The uneasiness of these British subjects usually climaxes in a horrific supernatural event, a crisis that both represents and confirms their fears of India and the Indians.

---

18. Modern carriage with expensive springs.
19. Crematorium.

In the Next Room

Long years after I had shaken the sandy soil of Usapore[1] from my feet, I met a lady on board a P. and O. steamer[2] to whom I told the story of Arnold.

"I could tell you a story about Usapore, too," she said, "only nobody ever believes a word of it."

"I would believe anything you told me," I replied, "and anything about Usapore that was unpleasant. Tell me the story now, we have half an hour before dinner, and your husband is still playing whist."

So she allowed herself to be persuaded, and it appeared that only the previous year "George," her husband, who was a Bengal civilian, had been suddenly ordered to Usapore in the middle of the hot weather, and she, being a model wife, made prompt preparations to accompany him.

"And would you believe it," she said, still sore at the recollection, "my cook and butler refused to come with me! I had been so kind to them, given them good wages, and clothes, and medicine, and everything they wanted, and I imagined they would never leave us. However, they did, and we had to rely on picking up others at Usapore. We had an awful journey, the heat, flies and dust simply indescribable, and the dâk bungalow[3] to end with. You must know what a ghastly little building that is."

"Indeed, I do," I sighed in sympathy.

"Well, then we could not get a house, every bungalow was occupied, and our predecessor had been a bachelor and chummed[4] with some other men. So at last we had to take a ruin belonging to a native, that had been built in the old days long before the Mutiny. Perhaps you remember it? Down by the river."

"I think I do," I said, searching my memory; "but it was only occupied by natives then as far as I recollect."

"It is pulled down now, I believe, and a good thing too, for, in spite of what George or anyone else may say, that house was haunted!"

"Really!"

"Yes, and you shall hear all about it if you have the patience to listen. It was a rambling old stone building, with fairly good verandahs, but filthy dirty and very much out of repair. However, three of the rooms were quite habitable, which were really all we needed, as we only expected to remain in the place for about three months. We had brought our camp furniture[5] with us, and were soon able to leave the miseries of the dâk bungalow. I had got a cook, but no khansamah,[6] and had almost made up my mind to do without one, when a man suddenly presented himself and his written characters and requested to be taken into our service. The characters were good and the man's appearance respectable, so I engaged him.

"The first night in our new quarters passed quietly enough, but the next morning, just after George had started for office, my ayah[7] entered my room crying.

---

1. Perhaps Perrin's invention, as no such town appears on 19th-c. maps of India.
2. The Peninsula and Oriental Steam Navigation Company (P & O) ran ships between Britain and India.
3. House for travelers.
4. Lodged with.
5. Folding portable furniture.
6. Butler or household steward.
7. Nanny.

"'Mem-sahib,'[8] she whimpered, 'do not keep the new khansamah. The watchman's wife tells me—'

"I interrupted her and said I would not listen to tales of the other servants, so she said no more, but all the same I felt a little curious, and in consequence observed the new man closely when he came for orders. There certainly was something rather peculiar about him, though what I could not exactly say, and as I had no fault to find with him I dismissed him from my thoughts.

"A fortnight passed away, and then one night I awoke very suddenly with a conviction that something had roused me. I first thought that the punkah[9] had stopped, but found I was mistaken, and gradually I became aware of a sound in the drawing-room, out of which our bedroom opened, and I sat up to listen.

"An indistinct murmur of two voices was going on in the next room, with something in the sound that was oddly familiar to me, though at the moment I could not name what it recalled to my mind. Thinking that for some reason the servants must have come into the house, I called out, but received no answer, neither did the low murmur cease. I got out of bed, and, taking the hand lamp from the dressing-table, I peered with it into the drawing-room. All was dark, and the noise suddenly stopped. I called two or three times, and the watchman, hearing me, came into the verandah. He declared nobody had been about, that all the servants, with the exception of himself and the punkah-coolies,[10] were asleep in their quarters, and no one had entered the bungalow. I concluded I must have been dreaming, and went back to bed puzzled and restless.

"The incident worried me so that I told my husband about it in the morning, and as he only said that it must have been the punkah-coolies talking, I dropped the subject to avoid argument. I saw him drive off to the Courts, and then sent for the khansamah to bring me his daily accounts. He began reading them out in the usual nasal monotone, 'soup—eggs—fowls,' etc., when it flashed across me in a second that this was what the sounds had reminded me of the previous night—a servant and his mistress going through the daily accounts! The murmur of the voices came back to me with redoubled distinctness, and I could only imagine that I had dreamt I was listening to myself taking down the items.

"Two or three nights afterwards the same thing happened again. I woke up with a start, and instantly my thoughts reverted to my dream, but this time I was positive I was wide awake. Nevertheless, there was a low murmur of voices in the drawing-room. I could have sworn to its being a native giving in his accounts to his mistress, and I could even distinguish the woman's voice as she acknowledged each item. I woke George, then sprang out of bed, and rushed with the lamp to the drawing-room door, followed sleepily by my husband, but directly I entered the room not a sound was to be heard except the chirrup of a musk-rat as it scuttled round the walls.

"'Dreaming again,' said George.

"In spite of his unbelief I insisted on his going through all the rooms and verandahs with me, and even out into the garden, where we found the watchman asleep, and while the unlucky sleeper was being shaken and abused I went back to bed feeling

---

8. Title meaning mistress.
9. Large fan.
10. Derogatory term for the servants who operated the fan.

somewhat small, but at the same time determined to leave no stone unturned until the mystery was solved. With great difficulty I persuaded George to stay awake for an hour, but to my intense annoyance we heard nothing. I began to doubt my own senses, and George made idiotic jokes about my having eaten cheese toast at dinner.

"News came the next day of a disturbance in the district, and George was obliged to hurry off at a moment's notice, making the best arrangements he could, as he did not expect to get back for the night. The same evening I went for a long ride by myself, and returned rather late. I paused on my way through the drawing-room to turn up the shaded lamps, and as I did so I was surprised to see Eli Bux, the new khansamah, standing by my writing-table with a kitchen knife and an old account book in his hands. Then I saw him walk into my bedroom, and, calling his name, I followed him. But when I entered the room he was not there.

"I knew my eyes had not deceived me, for I particularly remarked that the man seemed to stoop a good deal, which I had never observed in him before. I called the ayah and asked if Eli Bux had passed through my room, but she declared he had not. I sent her into the kitchen to inquire what he had been doing in the drawing-room, but she returned with the startling announcement that the khansamah had gone to the city early in the afternoon and had not yet returned. The ayah naturally concluded that I should be vexed at the idea of his absenting himself just when dinner should have claimed his attention, and, seizing the opportunity, she once more burst forth into abuse of Eli Bux, but I snubbed her again, as, in any case, it was none of her business.

"I felt a little nervous when I went to bed that night, and lay sleepless for a long time, half expecting to hear the voices in the drawing-room, and hardly knowing whether I hoped or dreaded that I should do so. I wondered again if I had really heard them, or if they simply existed in my imagination. If the former, I felt that there must be something strange in connection with the house; if the latter, that I must be out of sorts and require a doctor's advice.

"I must at last have fallen into a doze, for I suddenly opened my eyes to see by the dim, lowered light of the lamp, the figure of a native man standing by my dressing-table with his back towards me. I caught sight of his face reflected in the glass. It was Eli Bux!

"I watched him for about a minute, and saw that he was ransacking my dressing-table drawers and opening the various little boxes in which I kept pins and scraps of jewellery. He put his hand under the looking-glass, and I knew he was feeling for the rings and brooch I wore every day. I was literally paralysed with fright, and felt as if I had been turned to stone, when the man looked into the mirror and caught sight of my reflection, open-mouthed and horror-struck, watching him from the bed. He turned slowly round, and in his hand was a long, sharp knife.

"I tried to scream, but my voice failed me, and we remained motionless staring at one another. The punkah was still, and the mosquitoes were buzzing savagely round my bed. The man took a step towards me. Then another. His eyes glittered, and his fingers felt along the edge of the knife—

"Suddenly a sound broke the stillness. The voices were in the drawing-room, and this time louder and clearer than they had ever been before. Eli Bux started and looked wildly round. So he, too, could hear the voices! He listened for a second.

Then an expression of abject terror crossed his face, and with a hoarse yell he rushed out into the verandah. I heard a muffled cry as of someone choking, followed by a heavy fall.

"I felt sure he was murdering the punkah-coolies, and then my presence of mind returned. I sprang out of bed and ran into the drawing-room; all was quiet there again, not a sound to be heard. I ran through the hall and into the front verandah, where I called and shouted at the top of my voice, and stepped down on to the gravel path meaning to make my way to the servants' quarters. But I had hardly gone two yards when my heart again stood still with fear. I saw something moving in the deep shadow of the trees, and a pariah dog flitted past me in the moonlight, uttering a long, dismal howl.

"It was more than my over-strung nerves could bear. Scarcely knowing what I was doing, I fled like a hunted creature back into the house, and had barely reached my room when I fell to the floor in a dead faint.

"When I recovered consciousness it was broad daylight, and George and the doctor were bending over my bed, while the ayah stood weeping copiously in the background expressing her firm conviction that I was quite dead. When I had swallowed some brandy, and been made to keep quiet for an hour, I was strong enough to tell George my story, not forgetting the part that 'the voices' had played. He heard me to the end with a grave face, and then told me that Eli Bux had been discovered dead in my verandah. The watchman and the two coolies had been drugged, and on the ayah coming to call me in the morning she had found the two coolies still in a heavy sleep, with the dead body of Eli Bux between them. My watch and rings were found in his pocket, and it was subsequently proved on examination that he had died from heart disease, from which he must have been suffering for years previously.

"When I was better I called the ayah and gave her leave to tell me all she knew about the khansamah, and, delighted at obtaining a hearing, she poured forth a voluble tale as to Eli Bux having been an accomplished scoundrel, and added that his father had been a great deal worse. Then she paused, and I impatiently told her to continue.

"'Surely the mem-sahib has heard what happened in this house?' she said, and when I shook my head she told me that the father of Eli Bux had been khansamah to a lady in that very bungalow when the Mutiny broke out, that her husband was shot while he was at office, and that the butler cut his mistress's throat in the drawing-room and ran off with all the jewellery and money he could find.

"'And the watchman's wife,' continued the ayah with relish, 'says that Eli Bux had lots of that poor mem-sahib's jewellery buried somewhere, given him by his old father when he lay dying.'

"After this I felt I could stay in that horrible bungalow no longer. George did not believe the ayah's story, and declared it was all a native yarn, but I know it was true, for I heard the spirit voices of that unfortunate woman and her murderer, and the man I saw in the drawing-room was the ghost of Eli Bux's father. Those voices saved my life, for if Eli Bux had not heard them and, knowing what they were, died of the fright, he would have cut my throat. What do *you* think about it?" she concluded abruptly.

"I entirely agree with you," I responded with fervour. "Did you ever hear the voices again?"

"No, George sent me off to the hills, and joined me there directly his three months at Usapore were over, but he lived on in that awful house till he left the place. He says he never saw or heard anything unnatural, and to this day he exasperates me beyond words if I mention the story before him, by making silly references to cheese toast and indigestion!"

—1901

Sir Arthur Conan Doyle
1859–1930

Sir Arthur Conan Doyle had the misfortune of creating a character he could not escape. Doyle wanted to be regarded as a serious author, but the public clamored for more Sherlock Holmes. Even the death of Holmes could not stop the demand, and Doyle reluctantly resurrected his hero a few years later. It was during medical training at the University of Edinburgh that he met Dr. Joseph Bell, whose apparently miraculous deductions about his patients' lives later inspired Doyle to invent Holmes. Doyle also became deeply involved in studies of psychic phenomena, becoming perhaps the most famous publicist of the spiritualist movement and devoting his final years to that cause. When the Boer War began, Doyle was one of the government's most prominent defenders. Knighted for his patriotism in 1902, Doyle also served in World War I and produced enormous amounts of wartime journalism, including a six-volume history, *The British Campaign in France and Flanders*. Moreover, Doyle defended people who had been imprisoned on spurious evidence. Although Doyle was an energetic activist, deeply involved in medicine, politics, sports, the judicial system, and spiritualism, he was proudest of his historical novels—and yet it is not surprising that his fame rests on the short stories and novels starring Sherlock Holmes, mostly published in *The Strand Magazine* between 1892 and 1927. In an era haunted by the Jack the Ripper murders in 1888, the messy war in South Africa, labor unrest, and urban squalor, Holmes offered a powerful counter-fantasy. He embodied the idea that pure intellect, rational deduction, careful organization, and close observation could resolve the dark problems of his society. In "The Adventure of the Speckled Band," we see how Holmes's cool ratiocination combats the menace associated with gypsies and India.

The Adventure of the Speckled Band

On glancing over my notes of the seventy odd cases in which I have during the last eight years studied the methods of my friend Sherlock Holmes, I find many tragic, some comic, a large number merely strange, but none commonplace; for, working as he did rather for the love of his art than for the acquirement of wealth, he refused to associate himself with any investigation which did not tend towards the unusual, and even the fantastic. Of all these varied cases, however, I cannot recall any which presented more singular features than that which was associated with the well-known Surrey[1] family of the Roylotts of Stoke Moran. The events in question occurred in

---

1. Southeastern region of England.

the early days of my association with Holmes, when we were sharing rooms as bachelors in Baker Street.[2] It is possible that I might have placed them upon record before, but a promise of secrecy was made at the time, from which I have only been freed during the last month by the untimely death of the lady to whom the pledge was given. It is perhaps as well that the facts should now come to light, for I have reasons to know that there are wide-spread rumors as to the death of Dr. Grimesby Roylott which tend to make the matter even more terrible than the truth.

It was early in April in the year '83 that I woke one morning to find Sherlock Holmes standing, fully dressed, by the side of my bed. He was a late riser as a rule, and as the clock on the mantel-piece showed me that it was only a quarter past seven, I blinked up at him in some surprise, and perhaps just a little resentment, for I was myself regular in my habits.

"Very sorry to knock you up,[3] Watson," said he, "but it's the common lot this morning. Mrs. Hudson has been knocked up, she retorted upon me, and I on you."

"What is it, then—a fire?"

"No; a client. It seems that a young lady has arrived in a considerable state of excitement, who insists upon seeing me. She is waiting now in the sitting-room. Now, when young ladies wander about the metropolis at this hour of the morning, and knock sleepy people up out of their beds, I presume that it is something very pressing which they have to communicate. Should it prove to be an interesting case, you would, I am sure, wish to follow it from the outset. I thought, at any rate, that I should call you and give you the chance."

"My dear fellow, I would not miss it for anything."

I had no keener pleasure than in following Holmes in his professional investigations, and in admiring the rapid deductions, as swift as intuitions, and yet always founded on a logical basis, with which he unravelled the problems which were submitted to him. I rapidly threw on my clothes, and was ready in a few minutes to accompany my friend down to the sitting-room. A lady dressed in black and heavily veiled, who had been sitting in the window, rose as we entered.

"Good-morning, madam," said Holmes, cheerily. "My name is Sherlock Holmes. This is my intimate friend and associate, Dr. Watson, before whom you can speak as freely as before myself. Ha! I am glad to see that Mrs. Hudson has had the good sense to light the fire. Pray draw up to it, and I shall order you a cup of hot coffee, for I observe that you are shivering."

"It is not cold which makes me shiver," said the woman, in a low voice, changing her seat as requested.

"What, then?"

"It is fear, Mr. Holmes. It is terror." She raised her veil as she spoke, and we could see that she was indeed in a pitiable state of agitation, her face all drawn and gray, with restless, frightened eyes, like those of some hunted animal. Her features and figure were those of a woman of thirty, but her hair was shot with premature gray, and her expression was weary and haggard. Sherlock Holmes ran her over with one of his quick, all-comprehensive glances.

---

2. In the early stories, before Watson marries, Holmes and Watson share quarters at 22B Baker Street.
3. Wake you up.

"You must not fear," said he, soothingly, bending forward and patting her forearm. "We shall soon set matters right, I have no doubt. You have come in by train this morning, I see."

"You know me, then?"

"No, but I observe the second half of a return ticket in the palm of your left glove. You must have started early, and yet you had a good drive in a dog-cart,[4] along heavy roads, before you reached the station."

The lady gave a violent start, and stared in bewilderment at my companion.

"There is no mystery, my dear madam," said he, smiling. "The left arm of your jacket is spattered with mud in no less than seven places. The marks are perfectly fresh. There is no vehicle save a dog-cart which throws up mud in that way, and then only when you sit on the left-hand side of the driver."

"Whatever your reasons may be, you are perfectly correct," said she. "I started from home before six, reached Leatherhead[5] at twenty past, and came in by the first train to Waterloo.[6] Sir, I can stand this strain no longer; I shall go mad if it continues. I have no one to turn to—none, save only one, who cares for me, and he, poor fellow, can be of little aid. I have heard of you, Mr. Holmes; I have heard of you from Mrs. Farintosh, whom you helped in the hour of her sore need. It was from her that I had your address. Oh, sir, do you not think that you could help me, too, and at least throw a little light through the dense darkness which surrounds me? At present it is out of my power to reward you for your services, but in a month or six weeks I shall be married, with the control of my own income, and then at least you shall not find me ungrateful."

Holmes turned to his desk, and unlocking it, drew out a small case-book, which he consulted.

"Farintosh," said he. "Ah yes, I recall the case; it was concerned with an opal tiara. I think it was before your time, Watson. I can only say, madam, that I shall be happy to devote the same care to your case as I did to that of your friend. As to reward, my profession is its own reward; but you are at liberty to defray whatever expenses I may be put to, at the time which suits you best. And now I beg that you will lay before us everything that may help us in forming an opinion upon the matter."

"Alas!" replied our visitor, "the very horror of my situation lies in the fact that my fears are so vague, and my suspicions depend so entirely upon small points, which might seem trivial to another, that even he to whom of all others I have a right to look for help and advice looks upon all that I tell him about it as the fancies of a nervous woman. He does not say so, but I can read it from his soothing answers and averted eyes. But I have heard, Mr. Holmes, that you can see deeply into the manifold wickedness of the human heart. You may advise me how to walk amid the dangers which encompass me."

"I am all attention, madam."

"My name is Helen Stoner, and I am living with my step-father, who is the last survivor of one of the oldest Saxon[7] families in England, the Roylotts of Stoke Moran, on the western border of Surrey."

---

4. Two-wheeled carriage with seats placed back to back.
5. Major town in Surrey.
6. Waterloo Station, the London terminus for southeastern rail lines.
7. The Angles and Saxons were early occupants of Britain, predating the Norman Conquest of 1066. At the *fin de siècle* there was a strong interest in returning to native Saxon roots.

Holmes nodded his head. "The name is familiar to me," said he.

"The family was at one time among the richest in England, and the estates extended over the borders into Berkshire in the north, and Hampshire in the west. In the last century, however, four successive heirs were of a dissolute and wasteful disposition, and the family ruin was eventually completed by a gambler in the days of the Regency.[8] Nothing was left save a few acres of ground, and the two-hundred-year-old house, which is itself crushed under a heavy mortgage. The last squire dragged out his existence there, living the horrible life of an aristocratic pauper; but his only son, my step-father, seeing that he must adapt himself to the new conditions, obtained an advance from a relative, which enabled him to take a medical degree, and went out to Calcutta, where, by his professional skill and his force of character, he established a large practice. In a fit of anger, however, caused by some robberies which had been perpetrated in the house, he beat his native butler to death, and narrowly escaped a capital sentence. As it was, he suffered a long term of imprisonment, and afterwards returned to England a morose and disappointed man.

"When Dr. Roylott was in India he married my mother, Mrs. Stoner, the young widow of Major-general Stoner, of the Bengal Artillery. My sister Julia and I were twins, and we were only two years old at the time of my mother's re-marriage. She had a considerable sum of money—not less than £1000 a year—and this she bequeathed to Dr. Roylott entirely while we resided with him, with a provision that a certain annual sum should be allowed to each of us in the event of our marriage. Shortly after our return to England my mother died—she was killed eight years ago in a railway accident near Crewe.[9] Dr. Roylott then abandoned his attempts to establish himself in practice in London, and took us to live with him in the old ancestral house at Stoke Moran. The money which my mother had left was enough for all our wants, and there seemed to be no obstacle to our happiness.

"But a terrible change came over our step-father about this time. Instead of making friends and exchanging visits with our neighbors, who had at first been overjoyed to see a Roylott of Stoke Moran back in the old family seat, he shut himself up in his house, and seldom came out save to indulge in ferocious quarrels with whoever might cross his path. Violence of temper approaching to mania has been hereditary in the men of the family, and in my step-father's case it had, I believe, been intensified by his long residence in the tropics.[10] A series of disgraceful brawls took place, two of which ended in the police-court, until at last he became the terror of the village, and the folks would fly at his approach, for he is a man of immense strength, and absolutely uncontrollable in his anger.

"Last week he hurled the local blacksmith over a parapet into a stream, and it was only by paying over all the money which I could gather together that I was able to avert another public exposure. He had no friends at all save the wandering gypsies, and he would give these vagabonds leave to encamp upon the few acres of bramble-covered land which represent the family estate, and would accept in return the hospitality of their tents, wandering away with them sometimes for weeks on end. He has

---

8. 1811–20, a period associated with upper-class license and pleasure, when the playboy Prince of Wales ruled in place of the mad George III.
9. Town in northwest England.
10. Victorians believed that the heat of the tropics exacerbated passion and sensuality.

a passion also for Indian animals, which are sent over to him by a correspondent, and he has at this moment a cheetah and a baboon, which wander freely over his grounds, and are feared by the villagers almost as much as their master.

"You can imagine from what I say that my poor sister Julia and I had no great pleasure in our lives. No servant would stay with us, and for a long time we did all the work of the house. She was but thirty at the time of her death, and yet her hair had already begun to whiten, even as mine has."

"Your sister is dead, then?"

"She died just two years ago, and it is of her death that I wish to speak to you. You can understand that, living the life which I have described, we were little likely to see any one of our own age and position. We had, however, an aunt, my mother's maiden sister, Miss Honoria Westphail, who lives near Harrow,[11] and we were occasionally allowed to pay short visits at this lady's house. Julia went there at Christmas two years ago, and met there a half-pay major of marines, to whom she became engaged. My step-father learned of the engagement when my sister returned, and offered no objection to the marriage; but within a fortnight of the day which had been fixed for the wedding, the terrible event occurred which has deprived me of my only companion."

Sherlock Holmes had been leaning back in his chair with his eyes closed and his head sunk in a cushion, but he half opened his lids now and glanced across at his visitor.

"Pray be precise as to details," said he.

"It is easy for me to be so, for every event of that dreadful time is seared into my memory. The manor-house is, as I have already said, very old, and only one wing is now inhabited. The bedrooms in this wing are on the ground floor, the sitting-rooms being in the central block of the buildings. Of these bedrooms the first is Dr. Roylott's, the second my sister's, and the third my own. There is no communication between them, but they all open out into the same corridor. Do I make myself plain?"

"Perfectly so."

"The windows of the three rooms open out upon the lawn. That fatal night Dr. Roylott had gone to his room early, though we knew that he had not retired to rest, for my sister was troubled by the smell of the strong Indian cigars which it was his custom to smoke. She left her room, therefore, and came into mine, where she sat for some time, chatting about her approaching wedding. At eleven o'clock she rose to leave me but she paused at the door and looked back.

"'Tell me, Helen,' said she, 'have you ever heard any one whistle in the dead of the night?'

"'Never,' said I.

"'I suppose that you could not possibly whistle, yourself, in your sleep?'

"'Certainly not. But why?'

"'Because during the last few nights I have always, about three in the morning, heard a low, clear whistle. I am a light sleeper, and it has awakened me. I cannot tell where it came from—perhaps from the next room, perhaps from the lawn. I thought that I would just ask you whether you had heard it.'

---

11. A town outside London, famous for its private school.

"'No, I have not. It must be those wretched gypsies in the plantation.'

"'Very likely. And yet if it were on the lawn, I wonder that you did not hear it also.'

"'Ah, but I sleep more heavily than you.'

"'Well, it is of no great consequence, at any rate.' She smiled back at me, closed my door, and a few moments later I heard her key turn in the lock."

"Indeed," said Holmes. "Was it your custom always to lock yourselves in at night?"

"Always."

"And why?"

"I think that I mentioned to you that the doctor kept a cheetah and a baboon. We had no feeling of security unless our doors were locked."

"Quite so. Pray proceed with your statement."

"I could not sleep that night. A vague feeling of impending misfortune impressed me. My sister and I, you will recollect, were twins, and you know how subtle are the links which bind two souls which are so closely allied. It was a wild night. The wind was howling outside, and the rain was beating and splashing against the windows. Suddenly, amid all the hubbub of the gale, there burst forth the wild scream of a terrified woman. I knew that it was my sister's voice. I sprang from my bed, wrapped a shawl round me, and rushed into the corridor. As I opened my door I seemed to hear a low whistle, such as my sister described, and a few moments later a clanging sound, as if a mass of metal had fallen. As I ran down the passage, my sister's door was unlocked, and revolved slowly upon its hinges. I stared at it horror-stricken, not knowing what was about to issue from it. By the light of the corridor-lamp I saw my sister appear at the opening, her face blanched with terror, her hands groping for help, her whole figure swaying to and fro like that of a drunkard. I ran to her and threw my arms round her, but at that moment her knees seemed to give way and she fell to the ground. She writhed as one who is in terrible pain, and her limbs were dreadfully convulsed. At first I thought that she had not recognized me, but as I bent over her she suddenly shrieked out in a voice which I shall never forget, 'Oh, my God, Helen! It was the band! The speckled band!' There was something else which she would fain have said, and she stabbed with her finger into the air in the direction of the doctor's room, but a fresh convulsion seized her and choked her words. I rushed out, calling loudly for my step-father, and I met him hastening from his room in his dressing-gown. When he reached my sister's side she was unconscious, and though he poured brandy down her throat and sent for medical aid from the village, all efforts were in vain, for she slowly sank and died without having recovered her consciousness. Such was the dreadful end of my beloved sister."

"One moment," said Holmes; "are you sure about this whistle and metallic sound? Could you swear to it?"

"That was what the county coroner asked me at the inquiry. It is my strong impression that I heard it, and yet, among the crash of the gale and the creaking of an old house, I may possibly have been deceived."

"Was your sister dressed?"

"No, she was in her night-dress. In her right hand was found the charred stump of a match, and in her left a match-box."

"Showing that she had struck a light and looked about her when the alarm took place. That is important. And what conclusions did the coroner come to?"

"He investigated the case with great care, for Dr. Roylott's conduct had long been notorious in the county, but he was unable to find any satisfactory cause of death. My evidence showed that the door had been fastened upon the inner side, and the windows were blocked by old-fashioned shutters with broad iron bars, which were secured every night. The walls were carefully sounded, and were shown to be quite solid all round, and the flooring was also thoroughly examined, with the same result. The chimney is wide, but is barred up by four large staples. It is certain, therefore, that my sister was quite alone when she met her end. Besides, there were no marks of any violence upon her."

"How about poison?"

"The doctors examined her for it, but without success."

"What do you think that this unfortunate lady died of, then?"

"It is my belief that she died of pure fear and nervous shock, though what it was that frightened her I cannot imagine."

"Were there gypsies in the plantation at the time?"

"Yes, there are nearly always some there."

"Ah, and what did you gather from this allusion to a band—a speckled band?"

"Sometimes I have thought that it was merely the wild talk of delirium, sometimes that it may have referred to some band of people, perhaps to these very gypsies in the plantation. I do not know whether the spotted handkerchiefs which so many of them wear over their heads might have suggested the strange adjective which she used."

Holmes shook his head like a man who is far from being satisfied.

"These are very deep waters," said he; "pray go on with your narrative."

"Two years have passed since then, and my life has been until lately lonelier than ever. A month ago, however, a dear friend, whom I have known for many years, has done me the honor to ask my hand in marriage. His name is Armitage—Percy Armitage—the second son of Mr. Armitage, of Crane Water, near Reading.[12] My step-father has offered no opposition to the match, and we are to be married in the course of the spring. Two days ago some repairs were started in the west wing of the building, and my bedroom wall has been pierced, so that I have had to move into the chamber in which my sister died, and to sleep in the very bed in which she slept. Imagine, then, my thrill of terror when last night, as I lay awake, thinking over her terrible fate, I suddenly heard in the silence of the night the low whistle which had been the herald of her own death. I sprang up and lit the lamp, but nothing was to be seen in the room. I was too shaken to go to bed again, however, so I dressed, and as soon as it was daylight I slipped down, got a dog-cart at the 'Crown Inn,' which is opposite, and drove to Leatherhead, from whence I have come on this morning with the one object of seeing you and asking your advice."

"You have done wisely," said my friend. "But have you told me all?"

"Yes, all."

"Miss Roylott, you have not. You are screening your step-father."

"Why, what do you mean?"

For answer Holmes pushed back the frill of black lace which fringed the hand that lay upon our visitor's knee. Five little livid spots, the marks of four fingers and a thumb, were printed upon the white wrist.

---

12. Bustling city west of London.

"You have been cruelly used," said Holmes.

The lady colored deeply and covered over her injured wrist. "He is a hard man," she said, "and perhaps he hardly knows his own strength."

There was a long silence, during which Holmes leaned his chin upon his hands and stared into the crackling fire.

"This is a very deep business," he said, at last. "There are a thousand details which I should desire to know before I decide upon our course of action. Yet we have not a moment to lose. If we were to come to Stoke Moran to-day, would it be possible for us to see over these rooms without the knowledge of your step-father?"

"As it happens, he spoke of coming into town to-day upon some most important business. It is probable that he will be away all day, and that there would be nothing to disturb you. We have a house-keeper now, but she is old and foolish, and I could easily get her out of the way."

"Excellent. You are not averse to this trip, Watson?"

"By no means."

"Then we shall both come. What are you going to do yourself?"

"I have one or two things which I would wish to do now that I am in town. But I shall return by the twelve o'clock train, so as to be there in time for your coming."

"And you may expect us early in the afternoon. I have myself some small business matters to attend to. Will you not wait and breakfast?"

"No, I must go. My heart is lightened already since I have confided my trouble to you. I shall look forward to seeing you again this afternoon." She dropped her thick black veil over her face and glided from the room.

"And what do you think of it all, Watson?" asked Sherlock Holmes, leaning back in his chair.

"It seems to me to be a most dark and sinister business."

"Dark enough and sinister enough."

"Yet if the lady is correct in saying that the flooring and walls are sound, and that the door, window, and chimney are impassable, then her sister must have been undoubtedly alone when she met her mysterious end."

"What becomes, then, of these nocturnal whistles, and what of the very peculiar words of the dying woman?"

"I cannot think."

"When you combine the ideas of whistles at night, the presence of a band of gypsies who are on intimate terms with this old doctor, the fact that we have every reason to believe that the doctor has an interest in preventing his step-daughter's marriage, the dying allusion to a band, and, finally, the fact that Miss Helen Stoner heard a metallic clang, which might have been caused by one of those metal bars which secured the shutters falling back into their place, I think that there is good ground to think that the mystery may be cleared along those lines."

"But what, then, did the gypsies do?"

"I cannot imagine."

"I see many objections to any such theory."

"And so do I. It is precisely for that reason that we are going to Stoke Moran this day. I want to see whether the objections are fatal, or if they may be explained away. But what in the name of the devil!"

The ejaculation had been drawn from my companion by the fact that our door had been suddenly dashed open, and that a huge man had framed himself in the aperture. His costume was a peculiar mixture of the professional and of the agricultural, having a black top-hat, a long frock-coat, and a pair of high gaiters, with a hunting-crop swinging in his hand. So tall was he that his hat actually brushed the cross bar of the doorway, and his breadth seemed to span it across from side to side. A large face, seared with a thousand wrinkles, burned yellow with the sun, and marked with every evil passion, was turned from one to the other of us, while his deep-set, bile-shot eyes, and his high, thin, fleshless nose, gave him somewhat the resemblance to a fierce old bird of prey.

"Which of you is Holmes?" asked this apparition.

"My name, sir; but you have the advantage of me," said my companion, quietly.

"I am Dr. Grimesby Roylott, of Stoke Moran."

"Indeed, doctor," said Holmes, blandly. "Pray take a seat."

"I will do nothing of the kind. My step-daughter has been here. I have traced her. What has she been saying to you?"

"It is a little cold for the time of the year," said Holmes.

"What has she been saying to you?" screamed the old man, furiously.

"But I have heard that the crocuses promise well," continued my companion, imperturbably.

"Ha! You put me off, do you?" said our new visitor, taking a step forward and shaking his hunting-crop. "I know you, you scoundrel! I have heard of you before. You are Holmes, the meddler."

My friend smiled.

"Holmes, the busybody!"

His smile broadened.

"Holmes, the Scotland-yard Jack-in-office!"[13]

Holmes chuckled heartily. "Your conversation is most entertaining," said he. "When you go out close the door, for there is a decided draught."

"I will go when I have said my say. Don't you dare to meddle with my affairs. I know that Miss Stoner has been here. I traced her! I am a dangerous man to fall foul of! See here." He stepped swiftly forward, seized the poker, and bent it into a curve with his huge brown hands.

"See that you keep yourself out of my grip," he snarled, and hurling the twisted poker into the fireplace, he strode out of the room.

"He seems a very amiable person," said Holmes, laughing. "I am not quite so bulky, but if he had remained I might have shown him that my grip was not much more feeble than his own." As he spoke he picked up the steel poker, and with a sudden effort straightened it out again.

"Fancy his having the insolence to confound me with the official detective force![14] This incident gives zest to our investigation, however, and I only trust that our little friend will not suffer from her imprudence in allowing this brute to trace her. And now,

---

13. Scotland Yard is the central detective agency in London. A Jack-in-office is an insolent official.
14. No paid police officer, Holmes is proud of his status as a gentleman amateur who detects crime for love of the sport. Britain's professional detective force dated back only to 1829, and its reputation suffered from its inability to solve the Jack the Ripper murders.

Watson, we shall order breakfast, and afterwards I shall walk down to Doctors' Commons,[15] where I hope to get some data which may help us in this matter."

It was nearly one o'clock when Sherlock Holmes returned from his excursion. He held in his hand a sheet of blue paper, scrawled over with notes and figures.

"I have seen the will of the deceased wife," said he. "To determine its exact meaning I have been obliged to work out the present prices of the investments with which it is concerned. The total income, which at the time of the wife's death was little short of £1100, is now, through the fall in agricultural prices, not more than £750. Each daughter can claim an income of £250, in case of marriage. It is evident, therefore, that if both girls had married, this beauty would have had a mere pittance, while even one of them would cripple him to a very serious extent. My morning's work has not been wasted, since it has proved that he has the very strongest motives for standing in the way of anything of the sort. And now, Watson, this is too serious for dawdling, especially as the old man is aware that we are interesting ourselves in his affairs; so if you are ready, we shall call a cab and drive to Waterloo. I should be very much obliged if you would slip your revolver into your pocket. An Eley's No. 2[16] is an excellent argument with gentlemen who can twist steel pokers into knots. That and a tooth-brush are, I think, all that we need."

At Waterloo we were fortunate in catching a train for Leatherhead, where we hired a trap[17] at the station inn, and drove for four or five miles through the lovely Surrey lanes. It was a perfect day, with a bright sun and a few fleecy clouds in the heavens. The trees and way-side hedges were just throwing out their first green shoots, and the air was full of the pleasant smell of the moist earth. To me at least there was a strange contrast between the sweet promise of the spring and this sinister quest upon which we were engaged. My companion sat in the front of the trap, his arms folded, his hat pulled down over his eyes, and his chin sunk upon his breast, buried in the deepest thought. Suddenly, however, he started, tapped me on the shoulder, and pointed over the meadows.

"Look there!" said he.

A heavily-timbered park stretched up in a gentle slope, thickening into a grove at the highest point. From amid the branches there jutted out the gray gables and high roof-tree of a very old mansion.

"Stoke Moran?" said he.

"Yes, sir, that be the house of Dr. Grimesby Roylott," remarked the driver.

"There is some building going on there," said Holmes; "that is where we are going."

"There's the village," said the driver, pointing to a cluster of roofs some distance to the left; "but if you want to get to the house, you'll find it shorter to get over this stile,[18] and so by the foot-path over the fields. There it is, where the lady is walking."

"And the lady, I fancy, is Miss Stoner," observed Holmes, shading his eyes. "Yes, I think we had better do as you suggest."

---

15. London civil-law establishment with jurisdiction over licenses, wills, and other legal documents.
16. A small heavy gun.
17. A small two-wheeled carriage.
18. Rough steps for surmounting a fence or wall.

We got off, paid our fare, and the trap rattled back on its way to Leatherhead.

"I thought it as well," said Holmes, as we climbed the stile, "that this fellow should think we had come here as architects, or on some definite business. It may stop his gossip. Good-afternoon, Miss Stoner. You see that we have been as good as our word."

Our client of the morning had hurried forward to meet us with a face which spoke her joy. "I have been waiting so eagerly for you," she cried, shaking hands with us warmly. "All has turned out splendidly. Dr. Roylott has gone to town, and it is unlikely that he will be back before evening."

"We have had the pleasure of making the doctor's acquaintance," said Holmes, and in a few words he sketched out what had occurred. Miss Stoner turned white to the lips as she listened.

"Good heavens!" she cried, "he has followed me, then."

"So it appears."

"He is so cunning that I never know when I am safe from him. What will he say when he returns?"

"He must guard himself, for he may find that there is some one more cunning than himself upon his track. You must lock yourself up from him to-night. If he is violent, we shall take you away to your aunt's at Harrow. Now, we must make the best use of our time, so kindly take us at once to the rooms which we are to examine."

The building was of gray, lichen-blotched stone, with a high central portion, and two curving wings, like the claws of a crab, thrown out on each side. In one of these wings the windows were broken, and blocked with wooden boards, while the roof was partly caved in, a picture of ruin. The central portion was in little better repair, but the right-hand block was comparatively modern, and the blinds in the windows, with the blue smoke curling up from the chimneys, showed that this was where the family resided. Some scaffolding had been erected against the end wall, and the stone-work had been broken into, but there were no signs of any workmen at the moment of our visit. Holmes walked slowly up and down the ill-trimmed lawn, and examined with deep attention the outsides of the windows.

"This, I take it, belongs to the room in which you used to sleep, the centre one to your sister's, and the one next to the main building to Dr. Roylott's chamber?"

"Exactly so. But I am now sleeping in the middle one."

"Pending the alterations, as I understand. By-the-way, there does not seem to be any very pressing need for repairs at that end wall."

"There were none. I believe that it was an excuse to move me from my room."

"Ah! that is suggestive. Now, on the other side of this narrow wing runs the corridor from which these three rooms open. There are windows in it, of course?"

"Yes, but very small ones. Too narrow for any one to pass through."

"As you both locked your doors at night, your rooms were unapproachable from that side. Now, would you have the kindness to go into your room and bar your shutters."

Miss Stoner did so, and Holmes, after a careful examination through the open window, endeavored in every way to force the shutter open, but without success. There was no slit through which a knife could be passed to raise the bar. Then with his lens he tested the hinges, but they were of solid iron, built firmly into the massive masonry. "Hum!" said he, scratching his chin in some perplexity; "my theory certainly presents some difficulties. No one could pass these shutters if they were bolted. Well, we shall see if the inside throws any light upon the matter."

A small side door led into the whitewashed corridor from which the three bed-rooms opened. Holmes refused to examine the third chamber, so we passed at once to the second, that in which Miss Stoner was now sleeping, and in which her sister had met with her fate. It was a homely little room, with a low ceiling and a gaping fireplace, after the fashion of old country-houses. A brown chest of drawers stood in one corner, a narrow white-counterpaned bed in another, and a dressing-table on the left-hand side of the window. These articles, with two small wicker-work chairs, made up all the furniture in the room, save for a square of Wilton carpet[19] in the centre. The boards round and the panelling of the walls were of brown, worm-eaten oak, so old and discolored that it may have dated from the original building of the house. Holmes drew one of the chairs into a corner and sat silent, while his eyes travelled round and round and up and down, taking in every detail of the apartment.

"Where does that bell communicate with?" he asked, at last, pointing to a thick bell-rope which hung down beside the bed, the tassel actually lying upon the pillow.

"It goes to the house-keeper's room."

"It looks newer than the other things?"

"Yes, it was only put there a couple of years ago."

"Your sister asked for it, I suppose?"

"No, I never heard of her using it. We used always to get what we wanted for ourselves."

"Indeed, it seemed unnecessary to put so nice a bell-pull there. You will excuse me for a few minutes while I satisfy myself as to this floor." He threw himself down upon his face with his lens in his hand, and crawled swiftly backward and forward, examining minutely the cracks between the boards. Then he did the same with the wood-work with which the chamber was panelled. Finally he walked over to the bed, and spent some time in staring at it, and in running his eye up and down the wall. Finally he took the bell-rope in his hand and gave it a brisk tug.

"Why, it's a dummy," said he.

"Won't it ring?"

"No, it is not even attached to a wire. This is very interesting. You can see now that it is fastened to a hook just above where the little opening for the ventilator is."

"How very absurd! I never noticed that before."

"Very strange!" muttered Holmes, pulling at the rope. "There are one or two very singular points about this room. For example, what a fool a builder must be to open a ventilator into another room, when, with the same trouble, he might have communicated with the outside air!"

"That is also quite modern," said the lady.

"Done about the same time as the bell-rope?" remarked Holmes.

"Yes, there were several little changes carried out about that time."

"They seem to have been of a most interesting character—dummy bell-ropes, and ventilators which do not ventilate. With your permission, Miss Stoner, we shall now carry our researches into the inner apartment."

---

19. Made of durable, plain wool.

Dr. Grimesby Roylott's chamber was larger than that of his step-daughter, but was as plainly furnished. A camp-bed,[20] a small wooden shelf full of books, mostly of a technical character, an arm-chair beside the bed, a plain wooden chair against the wall, a round table, and a large iron safe were the principal things which met the eye. Holmes walked slowly round and examined each and all of them with the keenest interest.

"What's in here?" he asked, tapping the safe.

"My step-father's business papers."

"Oh! you have seen inside, then?"

"Only once, some years ago. I remember that it was full of papers."

"There isn't a cat in it, for example?"

"No. What a strange idea!"

"Well, look at this!" He took up a small saucer of milk which stood on the top of it.

"No; we don't keep a cat. But there is a cheetah and a baboon."

"Ah, yes, of course! Well, a cheetah is just a big cat, and yet a saucer of milk does not go very far in satisfying its wants, I dare say. There is one point which I should wish to determine." He squatted down in front of the wooden chair, and examined the seat of it with the greatest attention.

"Thank you. That is quite settled," said he, rising and putting his lens in his pocket. "Hello! Here is something interesting!"

The object which had caught his eye was a small dog-lash hung on one corner of the bed. The lash, however, was curled upon itself, and tied so as to make a loop of whip-cord.

"What do you make of that, Watson?"

"It's a common enough lash. But I don't know why it should be tied."

"That is not quite so common, is it? Ah, me! it's a wicked world, and when a clever man turns his brains to crime it is the worst of all. I think that I have seen enough now, Miss Stoner, and with your permission we shall walk out upon the lawn."

I had never seen my friend's face so grim or his brow so dark as it was when we turned from the scene of this investigation. We had walked several times up and down the lawn, neither Miss Stoner nor myself liking to break in upon his thoughts before he roused himself from his reverie.

"It is very essential, Miss Stoner," said he, "that you should absolutely follow my advice in every respect."

"I shall most certainly do so."

"The matter is too serious for any hesitation. Your life may depend upon your compliance."

"I assure you that I am in your hands."

"In the first place, both my friend and I must spend the night in your room."

Both Miss Stoner and I gazed at him in astonishment.

"Yes, it must be so. Let me explain. I believe that that is the village inn over there?"

"Yes, that is the 'Crown.'"

"Very good. Your windows would be visible from there?"

"Certainly."

---

20. A small folding bed.

"You must confine yourself to your room, on pretence of a headache, when your step-father comes back. Then when you hear him retire for the night, you must open the shutters of your window, undo the hasp, put your lamp there as a signal to us, and then withdraw quietly with everything which you are likely to want into the room which you used to occupy. I have no doubt that, in spite of the repairs, you could manage there for one night."

"Oh yes, easily."

"The rest you will leave in our hands."

"But what will you do?"

"We shall spend the night in your room, and we shall investigate the cause of this noise which has disturbed you."

"I believe, Mr. Holmes, that you have already made up your mind," said Miss Stoner, laying her hand upon my companion's sleeve.

"Perhaps I have."

"Then for pity's sake tell me what was the cause of my sister's death."

"I should prefer to have clearer proofs before I speak."

"You can at least tell me whether my own thought is correct, and if she died from some sudden fright."

"No, I do not think so. I think that there was probably some more tangible cause. And now, Miss Stoner, we must leave you, for if Dr. Roylott returned and saw us, our journey would be in vain. Good-bye, and be brave, for if you will do what I have told you, you may rest assured that we shall soon drive away the dangers that threaten you."

Sherlock Holmes and I had no difficulty in engaging a bedroom and sitting-room at the "Crown Inn." They were on the upper floor, and from our window we could command a view of the avenue gate, and of the inhabited wing of Stoke Moran Manor House. At dusk we saw Dr. Grimesby Roylott drive past, his huge form looming up beside the little figure of the lad who drove him. The boy had some slight difficulty in undoing the heavy iron gates, and we heard the hoarse roar of the doctor's voice, and saw the fury with which he shook his clinched fists at him. The trap drove on, and a few minutes later we saw a sudden light spring up among the trees as the lamp was lit in one of the sitting-rooms.

"Do you know, Watson," said Holmes, as we sat together in the gathering darkness, "I have really some scruples as to taking you to-night. There is a distinct element of danger."

"Can I be of assistance?"

"Your presence might be invaluable."

"Then I shall certainly come."

"It is very kind of you."

"You speak of danger. You have evidently seen more in these rooms than was visible to me."

"No, but I fancy that I may have deduced a little more. I imagine that you saw all that I did."

"I saw nothing remarkable save the bell-rope, and what purpose that could answer I confess is more than I can imagine."

"You saw the ventilator, too?"

"Yes, but I do not think that it is such a very unusual thing to have a small opening between two rooms. It was so small that a rat could hardly pass through."

"I knew that we should find a ventilator before ever we came to Stoke Moran."

"My dear Holmes!"

"Oh yes, I did. You remember in her statement she said that her sister could smell Dr. Roylott's cigar. Now, of course that suggested at once that there must be a communication between the two rooms. It could only be a small one, or it would have been remarked upon at the coroner's inquiry. I deduced a ventilator."

"But what harm can there be in that?"

"Well, there is at least a curious coincidence of dates. A ventilator is made, a cord is hung, and a lady who sleeps in the bed dies. Does not that strike you?"

"I cannot as yet see any connection."

"Did you observe anything very peculiar about that bed?"

"No."

"It was clamped to the floor. Did you ever see a bed fastened like that before?"

"I cannot say that I have."

"The lady could not move her bed. It must always be in the same relative position to the ventilator and to the rope—for so we may call it, since it was clearly never meant for a bell-pull."

"Holmes," I cried, "I seem to see dimly what you are hinting at. We are only just in time to prevent some subtle and horrible crime."

"Subtle enough and horrible enough. When a doctor does go wrong, he is the first of criminals. He has nerve and he has knowledge. Palmer and Pritchard[21] were among the heads of their profession. This man strikes even deeper, but I think, Watson, that we shall be able to strike deeper still. But we shall have horrors enough before the night is over; for goodness' sake let us have a quiet pipe, and turn our minds for a few hours to something more cheerful."

About nine o'clock the light among the trees was extinguished, and all was dark in the direction of the Manor House. Two hours passed slowly away, and then, suddenly, just at the stroke of eleven, a single bright light shone out right in front of us.

"That is our signal," said Holmes, springing to his feet, "it comes from the middle window."

As we passed out he exchanged a few words with the landlord, explaining that we were going on a late visit to an acquaintance, and that it was possible that we might spend the night there. A moment later we were out on the dark road, a chill wind blowing in our faces, and one yellow light twinkling in front of us through the gloom to guide us on our sombre errand.

There was little difficulty in entering the grounds, for unrepaired breaches gaped in the old park wall. Making our way among the trees, we reached the lawn, crossed it, and were about to enter through the window, when out from a clump of laurel bushes there darted what seemed to be a hideous and distorted child, who threw itself upon the grass with writhing limbs, and then ran swiftly across the lawn into the darkness.

"My God!" I whispered; "did you see it?"

Holmes was for the moment as startled as I. His hand closed like a vice upon my wrist in his agitation. Then he broke into a low laugh, and put his lips to my ear.

---

21. Doctors who poisoned their own families: William Palmer in 1849, Edward William Pritchard in 1865.

"It is a nice household," he murmured. "That is the baboon."

I had forgotten the strange pets which the doctor affected. There was a cheetah, too; perhaps we might find it upon our shoulders at any moment. I confess that I felt easier in my mind when, after following Holmes's example and slipping off my shoes, I found myself inside the bedroom. My companion noiselessly closed the shutters, moved the lamp onto the table, and cast his eyes round the room. All was as we had seen it in the daytime. Then creeping up to me and making a trumpet of his hand, he whispered into my ear again so gently that it was all that I could do to distinguish the words:

"The least sound would be fatal to our plans."

I nodded to show that I had heard.

"We must sit without light. He would see it through the ventilator."

I nodded again.

"Do not go asleep; your very life may depend upon it. Have your pistol ready in case we should need it. I will sit on the side of the bed, and you in that chair."

I took out my revolver and laid it on the corner of the table.

Holmes had brought up a long thin cane, and this he placed upon the bed beside him. By it he laid the box of matches and the stump of a candle. Then he turned down the lamp, and we were left in darkness.

How shall I ever forget that dreadful vigil? I could not hear a sound, not even the drawing of a breath, and yet I knew that my companion sat open-eyed, within a few feet of me, in the same state of nervous tension in which I was myself. The shutters cut off the least ray of light, and we waited in absolute darkness. From outside came the occasional cry of a night-bird, and once at our very window a long drawn cat-like whine, which told us that the cheetah was indeed at liberty. Far away we could hear the deep tones of the parish clock, which boomed out every quarter of an hour. How long they seemed, those quarters! Twelve struck, and one and two and three, and still we sat waiting silently for whatever might befall.

Suddenly there was a momentary gleam of a light up in the direction of the ventilator, which vanished immediately, but was succeeded by a strong smell of burning oil and heated metal. Some one in the next room had lit a dark-lantern.[22] I heard a gentle sound of movement, and then all was silent once more, though the smell grew stronger. For half an hour I sat with straining ears. Then suddenly another sound became audible—a very gentle, soothing sound, like that of a small jet of steam escaping continually from a kettle. The instant that we heard it, Holmes sprang from the bed, struck a match, and lashed furiously with his cane at the bell-pull.

"You see it, Watson?" he yelled. "You see it?"

But I saw nothing. At the moment when Holmes struck the light I heard a low, clear whistle, but the sudden glare flashing into my weary eyes made it impossible for me to tell what it was at which my friend lashed so savagely. I could, however, see that his face was deadly pale, and filled with horror and loathing.

He had ceased to strike, and was gazing up at the ventilator, when suddenly there broke from the silence of the night the most horrible cry to which I have ever listened. It swelled up louder and louder, a hoarse yell of pain and fear and anger all

---

22. A lantern with sliding panels to conceal the light.

mingled in the one dreadful shriek. They say that away down in the village, and even in the distant parsonage, that cry raised the sleepers from their beds. It struck cold to our hearts, and I stood gazing at Holmes, and he at me, until the last echoes of it had died away into the silence from which it rose.

"What can it mean?" I gasped.

"It means that it is all over," Holmes answered. "And perhaps, after all, it is for the best. Take your pistol, and we will enter Dr. Roylott's room."

With a grave face he lit the lamp and led the way down the corridor. Twice he struck at the chamber door without any reply from within. Then he turned the handle and entered, I at his heels, with the cocked pistol in my hand.

It was a singular sight which met our eyes. On the table stood a dark-lantern with the shutter half open, throwing a brilliant beam of light upon the iron safe, the door of which was ajar. Beside this table, on the wooden chair, sat Dr. Grimesby Roylott, clad in a long gray dressing-gown, his bare ankles protruding beneath, and his feet thrust into red heelless Turkish slippers. Across his lap lay the short stock with the long lash which we had noticed during the day. His chin was cocked upward and his eyes were fixed in a dreadful, rigid stare at the corner of the ceiling. Round his brow he had a peculiar yellow band, with brownish speckles, which seemed to be bound tightly round his head. As we entered he made neither sound nor motion.

"The band! the speckled band!" whispered Holmes.

I took a step forward. In an instant his strange head-gear began to move, and there reared itself from among his hair the squat diamond-shaped head and puffed neck of a loathsome serpent.

"It is a swamp adder!" cried Holmes, "the deadliest snake in India. He has died within ten seconds of being bitten. Violence does, in truth, recoil upon the violent, and the schemer falls into the pit which he digs for another.[23] Let us thrust this creature back into its den, and we can then remove Miss Stoner to some place of shelter, and let the county police know what has happened."

As he spoke he drew the dog-whip swiftly from the dead man's lap, and throwing the noose round the reptile's neck, he drew it from its horrid perch, and carrying it at arm's length, threw it into the iron safe, which he closed upon it.

Such are the true facts of the death of Dr. Grimesby Roylott, of Stoke Moran. It is not necessary that I should prolong a narrative which has already run to too great a length, by telling how we broke the sad news to the terrified girl, how we conveyed her by the morning train to the care of her good aunt at Harrow, of how the slow process of official inquiry came to the conclusion that the doctor met his fate while indiscreetly playing with a dangerous pet. The little which I had yet to learn of the case was told me by Sherlock Holmes as we travelled back next day.

"I had," said he, "come to an entirely erroneous conclusion which shows, my dear Watson, how dangerous it always is to reason from insufficient data. The presence of the gypsies, and the use of the word 'band,' which was used by the poor girl, no doubt to explain the appearance which she had caught a hurried glimpse

---

23. Paraphrase of Psalms 7.15–16.

of by the light of her match, were sufficient to put me upon an entirely wrong scent. I can only claim the merit that I instantly reconsidered my position when, however, it became clear to me that whatever danger threatened an occupant of the room could not come either from the window or the door. My attention was speedily drawn, as I have already remarked to you, to this ventilator, and to the bell-rope which hung down to the bed. The discovery that this was a dummy, and that the bed was clamped to the floor, instantly gave rise to the suspicion that the rope was there as bridge for something passing through the hole, and coming to the bed. The idea of a snake instantly occurred to me, and when I coupled it with my knowledge that the doctor was furnished with a supply of creatures from India, I felt that I was probably on the right track. The idea of using a form of poison which could not possibly be discovered by any chemical test was just such a one as would occur to a clever and ruthless man who had had an Eastern training. The rapidity with which such a poison would take effect would also, from his point of view, be an advantage. It would be a sharp-eyed coroner, indeed, who could distinguish the two little dark punctures which would show where the poison fangs had done their work. Then I thought of the whistle. Of course he must recall the snake before the morning light revealed it to the victim. He had trained it, probably by the use of the milk which we saw, to return to him when summoned.[24] He would put it through this ventilator at the hour that he thought best, with the certainty that it would crawl down the rope and land on the bed. It might or might not bite the occupant, perhaps she might escape every night for a week, but sooner or later she must fall a victim.

"I had come to these conclusions before ever I had entered his room. An inspection of his chair showed me that he had been in the habit of standing on it, which of course would be necessary in order that he should reach the ventilator. The sight of the safe, the saucer of milk, and the loop of whip-cord were enough to finally dispel any doubts which may have remained. The metallic clang heard by Miss Stoner was obviously caused by her step-father hastily closing the door of his safe upon its terrible occupant. Having once made up my mind, you know the steps which I took in order to put the matter to the proof. I heard the creature hiss, as I have no doubt that you did also, and I instantly lit the light and attacked it."

"With the result of driving it through the ventilator."

"And also with the result of causing it to turn upon its master at the other side. Some of the blows of my cane came home, and roused its snakish temper, so that it flew upon the first person it saw. In this way I am no doubt indirectly responsible for Dr. Grimesby Roylott's death, and I cannot say that it is likely to weigh very heavily upon my conscience."

—1892

---

24. This solution is famously impossible, since snakes are deaf, can't climb, and do not drink milk. There is also no such animal as an "Indian swamp adder."

Laurence Hope
1865–1904

"Laurence Hope" (Adela Nicolson) might seem like a conventional Anglo-Indian: the wife of a colonel in the Indian army, stationed in remote military outposts throughout the 1890s. But Colonel Malcolm Nicolson was fluent in Indian languages and enamored of Indian culture, and his wife shared that passion. Hope came from an artistic and literary family. Her sister "Victoria Cross" wrote the daringly erotic "Theodora: A Fragment," published in the aesthetic magazine *The Yellow Book* in 1895. Hope was often depicted as Kipling's female counterpart. Like Kipling, she was born in India and returned there as a teenager after being brought up in England. It may even have been her father, editor of a Karachi newspaper, who gave Kipling his first job. Hope's poems express the British idea that the East, especially India, oozed with sensuality, fatalism, decadence, sexuality, and exotic beauty. Indeed, Hope represented the popular notion of India so perfectly that readers argued over whether the poems were authentic translations of Indian verses or original poems. "Kashmiri Song" and "Till I Wake" are two of the "Four Indian Love Lyrics," made famous when Amy Woodforde-Finden set them to music. After her husband died in surgery, Hope committed suicide at age thirty-nine.

Kashmiri Song

Pale hands I loved beside the Shalimar,[1]
   Where are you now? Who lies beneath your spell!
Whom do you lead on Rapture's roadway, far,
   Before you agonise them in farewell?

Oh, pale dispensers of my Joys and Pains,   5
   Holding the doors of Heaven and of Hell,
How the hot blood rushed wildly through the veins
   Beneath your touch, until you waved farewell.

Pale hands, pink tipped, like Lotus buds that float
   On those cool waters where we used to dwell,   10
I would have rather felt you round my throat
   Crushing out life; than waving me farewell!

                                      —1901

---

1. Famous gardens built by Shah Jahangir in Kashmir in the 17th c.

Till I Wake

When I am dying, lean over me tenderly, softly,
  Stoop, as the yellow roses droop in the wind
                    from the South.
So I may, when I wake, if there be an Awakening,
  Keep, what lulled me to sleep, the touch of your   5
                    lips on my mouth.

—1901

Toru Dutt
1856–1877

Toru Dutt was one of three brilliant and tragically short-lived children of a Hindu family that
converted to Christianity. She was educated in French and English schools, becoming fluent
in both languages, but also studied Indian culture (including Sanskrit) in depth. This unusual
background enabled Dutt to combine her familiarity with European literary form with a profound knowledge of Indian history, religious ideas, and folkloric traditions, lending her poetry
a double authority. Dutt wrote two novels and translated French poems, but it was *Ancient
Ballads and Legends of Hindustan* (published posthumously in 1882) that made her famous. The
first work of female-authored Indian poetry to be published in English, it consists mainly of traditional Bengali tales rendered into ballad form. Only twenty-one when she died, Dutt
nonetheless helped create a new style of Anglo-Indian poetry, celebrating ancient legends in
modern verse. Her youth, her deep knowledge of Romantic poetry, and her early death from
consumption earned her the nickname of "the Keats of Indo-English literature."

Jogadhya Uma[1]

"Shell-bracelets ho! Shell-bracelets ho!
  Fair maids and matrons come and buy!"
Along the road, in morning's glow,
  The pedlar raised his wonted cry.
The road ran straight, a red, red line,   5
  To Khirogram,[2] for cream renowned,
Through pasture-meadows where the kine,[3]
  In knee-deep grass, stood magic bound
And half awake, involved in mist,
  That floated in dun coils profound,   10

---

1. Based on an old folktale Dutt heard from the family nurse.
2. In West Bengal.
3. Cattle.

Till by the sudden sunbeams kist
   Rich rainbow hues broke all around.

"Shell-bracelets ho! Shell-bracelets ho!"
   The roadside trees still dripped with dew,
And hung their blossoms like a show.   15
   Who heard the cry? 'Twas but a few,
A ragged herd-boy, here and there,
   With his long stick and naked feet;
A ploughman wending to his care,
   The field from which he hopes the wheat;   20
An early traveller, hurrying fast
   To the next town; an urchin slow
Bound for the school; these heard and past,
   Unheeding all,—"Shell-bracelets ho!"

Pellucid spread a lake-like tank   25
   Beside the road now lonelier still,
High on three sides arose the bank
   Which fruit-trees shadowed at their will;
Upon the fourth side was the Ghat,[4]
   With its broad stairs of marble white,   30
And at the entrance-arch there sat,
   Full face against the morning light,
A fair young woman with large eyes,
   And dark hair falling to her zone,[5]
She heard the pedlar's cry arise,   35
   And eager seemed his ware to own.

"Shell-bracelets ho! See, maiden see!
   The rich enamel sunbeam-kist!
Happy, oh happy, shalt thou be,
   Let them but clasp that slender wrist;   40
These bracelets are a mighty charm,
   They keep a lover ever true,
And widowhood avert, and harm,
   Buy them, and thou shalt never rue.
Just try them on!"—She stretched her hand,   45
   "Oh what a nice and lovely fit!
No fairer hand, in all the land,
   And lo! the bracelet matches it."

---

4. A staircase down to the water.
5. Waist.

Dazzled the pedlar on her gazed
   Till came the shadow of a fear,   50
While she the bracelet arm upraised
   Against the sun to view more clear.
Oh she was lovely, but her look
   Had something of a high command
That filled with awe. Aside she shook   55
   Intruding curls by breezes fanned
And blown across her brows and face,
   And asked the price, which when she heard
She nodded, and with quiet grace
   For payment to her home referred.   60

"And where, O maiden, is thy house?
   But no, that wrist-ring has a tongue,
No maiden art thou, but a spouse,
   Happy, and rich, and fair, and young."
"Far otherwise, my lord is poor,   65
   And him at home thou shalt not find;
Ask for my father; at the door
   Knock loudly; he is deaf, but kind.
Seest thou that lofty gilded spire
   Above these tufts of foliage green?   70
That is our place; its point of fire
   Will guide thee o'er the tract between."

"That is the temple spire."—"Yes, there
   We live; my father is the priest,
The manse is near, a building fair   75
   But lowly, to the temple's east.
When thou hast knocked, and seen him, say
   His daughter, at Dhamaser Ghat,
Shell-bracelets bought from thee to-day,
   And he must pay so much for that.   80
Be sure, he will not let thee pass
   Without the value, and a meal,
If he demur, or cry alas!
   No money hath he,—then reveal,

Within the small box, marked with streaks   85
   Of bright vermilion, by the shrine,
The key whereof has lain for weeks
   Untouched, he'll find some coin,—'tis mine.
That will enable him to pay
   The bracelet's price, now fare thee well!"   90
She spoke, the pedlar went away,
   Charmed with her voice, as by some spell;

While she left lonely there, prepared
   To plunge into the water pure,
And like a rose her beauty bared,   95
   From all observance quite secure.

Not weak she seemed, nor delicate,
   Strong was each limb of flexile grace,
And full the bust; the mien elate,
   Like her's, the goddess of the chase   100
On Latmos hill,[6]—and oh, the face
   Framed in its cloud of floating hair,
No painter's hand might hope to trace
   The beauty and the glory there!
Well might the pedlar look with awe,   105
   For though her eyes were soft, a ray
Lit them at times, which kings who saw
   Would never dare to disobey.

Onwards through groves the pedlar sped
   Till full in front the sunlit spire   110
Arose before him. Paths which led
   To gardens trim in gay attire
Lay all around. And lo! the manse,
   Humble but neat with open door!
He paused, and blest the lucky chance   115
   That brought his bark to such a shore.
Huge straw ricks, log huts full of grain,
   Sleek cattle, flowers, a tinkling bell,
Spoke in a language sweet and plain,
   "Here smiling Peace and Plenty dwell."   120

Unconsciously he raised his cry,
   "Shell-bracelets ho!" And at his voice
Looked out the priest, with eager eye,
   And made his heart at once rejoice.
"Ho, *Sankha* pedlar![7] Pass not by,   125
   But step thou in, and share the food
Just offered on our altar high,
   If thou art in a hungry mood.
Welcome are all to this repast!
   The rich and poor, the high and low!   130
Come, wash thy feet, and break thy fast,
   Then on thy journey strengthened go."

---

6. Artemis. Dutt may be alluding to Keats's "Endymion," in which Cynthia (the moon) loves the beautiful
Ladmian shepherd-prince Endymion.
7. Sankha are bracelets made of conch shells.

"Oh thanks, good priest! Observance due
    And greetings! May thy name be blest!
I came on business, but I knew,   135
    Here might be had both food and rest
Without a charge; for all the poor
    Ten miles around thy sacred shrine
Know that thou keepest open door,
    And praise that generous hand of thine: 140
But let my errand first be told,
    For bracelets sold to thine this day,
So much thou owest me in gold,
    Hast thou the ready cash to pay?

The bracelets were enamelled,—so   145
    The price is high."—"How! Sold to mine?
Who bought them, I should like to know."
    "Thy daughter, with the large black eyne,[8]
Now bathing at the marble ghat."
    Loud laughed the priest at this reply,   150
"I shall not put up, friend, with that;
    No daughter in the world have I,
An only son is all my stay;
    Some minx has played a trick, no doubt,
But cheer up, let thy heart be gay.   155
    Be sure that I shall find her out."

"Nay, nay, good father, such a face
    Could not deceive, I must aver;
At all events, she knows thy place,
    'And if my father should demur   160
To pay thee,'—thus she said,—'or cry
    He has no money, tell him straight
The box vermilion-streaked to try,
    That's near the shrine.'" "Well, wait, friend, wait!"
The priest said thoughtful, and he ran   165
    And with the open box came back,
"Here is the price exact, my man,
    No surplus over, and no lack.

How strange! how strange! Oh blest art thou
    To have beheld her, touched her hand,   170
Before whom Vishnu's[9] self must bow,
    And Brahma[10] and his heavenly band!

---

8. Eyes.
9. Hindu god, the preserver.
10. Hindu god, the creator.

Here have I worshipped her for years
   And never seen the vision bright;
Vigils and fasts and secret tears   175
   Have almost quenched my outward sight;
And yet that dazzling form and face
   I have not seen, and thou, dear friend,
To thee, unsought for, comes the grace,
   What may its purport be, and end?   180

How strange! How strange! Oh happy thou!
   And couldst thou ask no other boon
Than thy poor bracelet's price? That brow
   Resplendent as the autumn moon
Must have bewildered thee, I trow,   185
   And made thee lose thy senses all."
A dim light on the pedlar now
   Began to dawn; and he let fall
His bracelet basket in his haste,
   And backward ran the way he came;   190
What meant the vision fair and chaste,
   Whose eyes were they,—those eyes of flame?

Swift ran the pedlar as a hind,[11]
   The old priest followed on his trace,
They reached the Ghat but could not find   195
   The lady of the noble face.
The birds were silent in the wood,
   The lotus flowers exhaled a smell
Faint, over all the solitude,
   A heron as a sentinel   200
Stood by the bank. They called,—in vain,
   No answer came from hill or fell,[12]
The landscape lay in slumber's chain,
   E'en Echo slept within her cell.

Broad sunshine, yet a hush profound!   205
   They turned with saddened hearts to go;
Then from afar there came a sound
   Of silver bells;—the priest said low.
"O Mother, Mother, deign to hear,
   The worship-hour has rung; we wait   210

---

11. Deer.
12. Uncultivated lands, wild pastures.

In meek humility and fear.
   Must we return home desolate?
Oh come, as late thou cam'st unsought,
   Or was it but an idle dream?
Give us some sign if it was not,   215
   A word, a breath, or passing gleam."

Sudden from out the water sprung
   A rounded arm, on which they saw
As high the lotus buds among
   It rose, the bracelet white, with awe.   220
Then a wide ripple tost and swung
   The blossoms on that liquid plain,
And lo! the arm so fair and young
   Sank in the waters down again.
They bowed before the mystic Power,   225
   And as they home returned in thought,
Each took from thence a lotus flower
   In memory of the day and spot.

Years, centuries, have passed away,
   And still before the temple shrine   230
Descendants of the pedlar pay
   Shell bracelets of the old design
As annual tribute. Much they own
   In lands and gold,—but they confess
From that eventful day alone   235
   Dawned on their industry,—success.
Absurd may be the tale I tell,
   Ill-suited to the marching times,
I loved the lips from which it fell,
   So let it stand among my rhymes.   240

—1882

Celts and Colonialism: Ireland

Unlike Britain's global colonies, Ireland was an integral part of the United Kingdom, with a European climate, landscape, and population. Yet its economic and emotional misery derived from a colonial situation. Irish resources were sent back to England, supporting absentee English landlords, while Irish infrastructure decayed, living conditions worsened, and the economy failed. During the catastrophic potato famine of 1845–50, 0.5 to 1.5 million Irish starved to death, and over 1 million emigrated. The English response was scandalously inadequate.

Like other colonized subjects, the Irish were regarded as savages and forced into a foreign language and culture, and like other "natives," they suffered, rebelled, and rewrote their occupiers' culture. Like their counterparts in India, the West Indies, the Pacific, and Africa, Irish writers sought to recover (or create) an indigenous literary tradition, even within the acquired language of English. If modern Irish history was a sobering litany of poverty, famine, disease, and distress, returning to misty Celtic origins promised a glamorous alternative, a national inheritance of romantic love, dashing glory, mythic grandeur, epic tragedy, and spiritual beauty. W. B. Yeats based early poems on Irish fairy tales, sagas, and Gaelic legends. He was soon joined by allies like J. M. Synge, Katharine Tynan, and Lady Augusta Gregory to form the "Celtic Revival," also called the "Irish Literary Renaissance." "I made my song a coat / Covered with embroideries / Out of old mythologies / From heel to throat," Yeats reminisced in 1914. These mythologies helped sustain the Irish people and create a nationalist consciousness. By the twentieth century, however, modernism had moved into starker styles, the Irish national struggle had turned violent, and, as Yeats himself soberly concluded, "there's more enterprise / In walking naked."

W. B. Yeats
1865–1939

The first Irish writer to win the Nobel Prize in Literature, William Butler Yeats created an enduring myth of Ireland as a romantic and doomed nation. He was born into a creative Anglo-Irish Protestant family. His father was the famous portraitist John Yeats, his sisters ran the Dun Emer Press, and his brother Jack became a celebrated artist. Although he grew up in Dublin, he spent summers in Sligo with his mother's family, the Pollexfens, and developed an enduring affection for that area, where he would be buried. Yeats's hopeless passion for Maud Gonne—he proposed to her four times—fundamentally shaped his work. After decades of unrequited love, including a desperate proposal to her daughter Iseult, he finally married his friend Georgie (Georgiana) Hyde-Lees, a successful union that produced a son and a daughter. When Yeats became a member of the Irish Senate in 1922, he described himself wryly as "a sixty-year-old smiling public man."

Yeats was, of course, more than that; as the Nobel Prize committee commented in 1923, "his always inspired poetry . . . in a highly artistic form gives expression to the spirit of a whole nation." Yeats's moving, powerful language forged a sense of national spirit for Ireland, express-ing enduring fascination with ancient mythology, mysticism, the craggy, misty landscape, and simple, kindly country folk. His early poems were deeply influenced by aestheticism (see pp. 80–82), and by co-founding the Rhymer's Club with Ernest Rhys he gave male aesthetic poets a cohesive identity. An early prose work, *The Celtic Twilight*, praises the lush, mysterious, sym-bolic mood of these poems. It is no surprise that during the 1890s Yeats also participated in the period's mystical and spiritual movements like the Order of the Golden Dawn. Yet this was also the decade in which Yeats provided practical support for an emerging Irish artistic movement. He founded the Abbey Theatre in 1904, which staged his own plays, as well as those by Lady Augusta Gregory, J. M. Synge, and others. In 1902, with his sisters Lily and Lolly, he founded the Dun Emer Press (later the Cuala Press) to publish Irish writers. After the turn of the century, Yeats began embracing a more direct style. Grappling with the increasing violence of the Irish independence movement, he had to rethink his vague idealism. "Romantic Ireland's dead and gone / It's with O'Leary in the grave," he wrote mournfully in 1913. The excerpt and poems here show how Yeats made Ireland romantic in the first place. For more information about Yeats, see p. 80.

from The Celtic Twilight

Suddenly it seemed to me that he was peering about him a little eagerly. "Do you see anything, X——?" I said. "A shining, winged woman, covered by her long hair, is standing near the doorway," he answered, or some such words. "Is it the influence of some living person who thinks of us, and whose thoughts appear to us in that symbolic form?" I said; for I am well instructed in the ways of the visionaries and in the fashion of their speech. "No," he replied; "for if it were the thoughts of a person who is alive I should feel the living influence in my living body, and my heart would beat and my breath would fail. It is a spirit. It is some one who is dead or who has never lived."

I asked what he was doing, and found he was clerk in a large shop. His pleasure, however, was to wander about upon the hills, talking to half-mad and visionary peasants, or to persuade queer and conscience-stricken persons to deliver up the keeping of their troubles into his care. Another night, when I was with him in his own lodging, more than one turned up to talk over their beliefs and disbeliefs, and sun them as it were in the subtle light of his mind. Sometimes visions come to him as he talks with them, and he is rumoured to have told divers people true matters of their past days and distant friends, and left them hushed with dread of their strange teacher, who seems scarce more than a boy, and is so much more subtle than the oldest among them.

The poetry he recited me was full of his nature and his visions. Sometimes it told of other lives he believes himself to have lived in other centuries, sometimes of people he had talked to, revealing them to their own minds. I told him I would write an article upon him and it, and was told in turn that I might do so if I did not mention his name, for he wished to be always "unknown, obscure, impersonal." Next day a bundle of his poems arrived, and with them a note in these words: "Here are copies of verses you said you liked. I do not think I could ever write or paint any more. I prepare myself for a cycle of other activities in some other life. I will make rigid my roots and branches. It is not now my turn to burst into leaves and flowers."

The poems are all endeavours to capture some high, impalpable mood in a net of obscure images. But something can be known of their charm from three verses which I rescue gladly from the caprice of the gods who rule over a mystic's manuscript. They are addressed to a girl, whom he knew, I understand, in another life, and tell how he died out of a dream of love centuries before his present body was born.

As from our dreams we died away
    Far off I felt the outer things,
Your wind-blown tresses round me play,
    Your bosom's gentle murmurings.

And far away our faces met   5
    As on the verge of the vast spheres;
And in the night our cheeks were wet,
    I could not say with dew or tears.

As one within the Mother's heart,
    In that hushed dream upon the hight,   10
We lived, and then rose up to part,
    Because her ways are infinite.

One or two other poems have a like perfection of feeling, but deal with more impalpable matters. There are fine passages in all, but these will often be imbedded in thoughts which have evidently a special value to the writer's mind, but are to other men merely the counters of an unknown coinage. To them they seem merely so much brass or copper or tarnished silver at the best. Sometimes he illustrates his verses with Blake-like drawings,[1] in which rather incomplete anatomy does not altogether hide extreme beauty of feeling. The faeries in whom he believes have given him many subjects, notably Thomas of Ercildoune[2] sitting motionless in the twilight while a young and beautiful creature leans softly out of the shadow and whispers in his ear. He delights above all in strong effects of colour: spirits who have upon their heads instead of hair the feathers of peacocks; a phantom reaching from a swirl of flame towards a star; a spirit passing with a globe of iridescent crystal—symbol of the soul—half shut within his hand. But always under this largess of colour lies some tender homily addressed to man's fragile hopes. This spiritual eagerness draws to him all those who, like himself, seek for illumination or else mourn for a joy that has gone. One of these especially comes to mind. A winter or two ago he spent much of the night walking up and down upon the mountain talking to an old peasant who, dumb to most men, poured out his cares for him. Both were unhappy: X—— because he had then first decided that art and poetry were not for him, and the old peasant because his life was ebbing out with no achievement remaining and no hope left him. Both how Celtic! how full of striving after a something never to be completely expressed in word or deed. The peasant was wandering in his mind with prolonged sorrow. Once he burst out with "God possesses the heavens—God possesses the heavens—but He covets the world"; and once he lamented that his old neighbours were gone, and that all had forgotten him: they used to draw a chair to the fire for him in every cabin, and now they said, "Who is that old fellow there?" "The fret" [Irish for doom] "is over me," he repeated, and then went on to talk once more of God and heaven. More than once also he said, waving his arm towards the mountain, "Only myself knows what happened under the thorn tree forty years ago;" and as he said it the tears upon his face glistened in the moonlight.

    This old man always rises before me when I think of X——. Both seek—one in wandering sentences, the other in symbolic pictures and subtle allegoric

---

1. Romantic poet William Blake was also admired for his visual representations of his private spiritual world.
2. 13th-c. Scottish wizard, also called Thomas the Rhymer, who supposedly fell in love with a fairy who gave him the gift of prophecy.

poetry—to express a something that lies beyond the range of expression; and both, if X—— will forgive me, have within them the vast and vague extravagance that lies at the bottom of the Celtic heart. The peasant visionaries that are, the land-lord duelists that were, and the whole hurly-burly of legends—Cuchulin fighting the sea for two days until the waves pass over him and he dies, Caolte storming the palace of the gods, Oisin seeking in vain for three hundred years to appease his insatiable heart with all the pleasures of faeryland,[3] these two mystics walking up and down upon the mountains uttering the central dreams of their souls in no less dream-laden sentences, and this mind that finds them so interesting—all are a por-tion of that great Celtic phantasmagoria whose meaning no man has discovered, nor any angel revealed.

—1893

To the Rose Upon the Rood of Time[1]

Red Rose, proud Rose, sad Rose of all my days!
Come near me, while I sing the ancient ways:
Cuchulain[2] battling with the bitter tide;
The Druid,[3] grey, wood-nurtured, quiet-eyed,
Who cast round Fergus[4] dreams, and ruin untold;   5
And thine own sadness, whereof stars, grown old
In dancing silver-sandalled on the sea,
Sing in their high and lonely melody.
Come near, that no more blinded by man's fate,
I find under the boughs of love and hate,   10
In all poor foolish things that live a day,
Eternal beauty wandering on her way.

Come near, come near, come near—Ah, leave me still
A little space for the rose-breath to fill!
Lest I no more hear common things that crave;   15
The weak worm hiding down in its small cave,
The field-mouse running by me in the grass,
And heavy mortal hopes that toil and pass;
But seek alone to hear the strange things said
By God to the bright hearts of those long dead,   20
And learn to chaunt a tongue men do not know.

---

3. Irish legends: Cuchulain and Caolte were heroic warriors; Oisin (or Ossian), another legendary hero, lived in fairyland with his bride Niamh for 300 years.

1. Yeats belonged to the mystic Order of the Golden Dawn; one of its symbols was the Rosy Cross, the Rose of Beauty suffering upon the Rood (or Cross) of Time.
2. Legendary Irish hero.
3. Ancient priest.
4. Visionary Fergus MacRoy, king of Ulster, commanded the Red Branch warriors.

Come near; I would, before my time to go,
Sing of old Eire[5] and the ancient ways:
Red Rose, proud Rose, sad Rose of all my days.

—1893

To Ireland in the Coming Times

Know, that I would accounted be
True brother of a company
That sang, to sweeten Ireland's wrong,
Ballad and story, rann[1] and song;
Nor be I any less of them,   5
Because the red-rose-bordered hem
Of her, whose history began
Before God made the angelic clan,
Trails all about the written page.
When Time began to rant and rage   10
The measure of her flying feet
Made Ireland's heart begin to beat;
And Time bade all his candles flare
To light a measure here and there;
And may the thoughts of Ireland brood   15
Upon a measured quietude.

Nor may I less be counted one
With Davis, Mangan, Ferguson,[2]
Because, to him who ponders well,
My rhymes more than their rhyming tell   20
Of things discovered in the deep,
Where only body's laid asleep.
For the elemental creatures go
About my table to and fro,
That hurry from unmeasured mind   25
To rant and rage in flood and wind,
Yet he who treads in measured ways
May surely barter gaze for gaze.
Man ever journeys on with them
After the red-rose-bordered hem.   30
Ah, faeries, dancing under the moon,
A Druid land, a Druid tune!

5. Gaelic: Ireland.

1. Gaelic: verse.
2. Thomas Davis, James Clarence Mangan, and Samuel Ferguson were patriotic poets whose work incorporated Irish myth and history.

While still I may, I write for you
The love I lived, the dream I knew.
From our birthday, until we die,   35
Is but the winking of an eye;
And we, our singing and our love,
What measurer Time has lit above,
And all benighted things that go
About my table to and fro,   40
Are passing on to where may be,
In truth's consuming ecstasy,
No place for love and dream at all;
For God goes by with white footfall.
I cast my heart into my rhymes,   45
That you, in the dim coming times,
May know how my heart went with them
After the red-rose-bordered hem.

—1893

The Hosting of the Sidhe[1]

The host is riding from Knocknarea[2]
And over the grave of Clooth-na-Bare;[3]
Caoilte[4] tossing his burning hair,
And Niamh[5] calling *Away, come away:*
Empty your heart of its mortal dream.   5
The winds awaken, the leaves whirl round,
Our cheeks are pale, our hair is unbound,
Our breasts are heaving, our eyes are agleam,
Our arms are waving, our lips are apart;
And if any gaze on our rushing band,   10
We come between him and the deed of his hand,
We come between him and the hope of his heart.
The host is rushing 'twixt night and day,
And where is there hope or deed as fair?
Caoilte tossing his burning hair,   15
And Niamh calling *Away, come away.*

—1899

---

1. The Sidhe were the gods of ancient Ireland.
2. Mountain in Sligo where mythic Queen Maeve is supposedly buried.
3. The half-human Old Woman of Beare, who tried to drown her fairy side in a Sligo lake.
4. Mythic poet and warrior, associated with the wind.
5. The fairy Niamh of the Golden Hair took her husband Oisin away to the Country of the Young.

Katharine Tynan
1861–1931

In her youth, Katharine Tynan was the ardent poet of the Celtic Revival; after her marriage to Henry Albert Hinkson in 1898, she became a prosperous churner-out of popular fiction, producing over a hundred novels, plus collections of short stories, autobiographies, and other prose. Born into a large family (twelve children) and convent-educated, Tynan came to poetry with a strong Irish Catholic identity. She counted among her closest friends Alice Meynell, Rosamund Marriott Watson, Oscar Wilde, and W. B. Yeats. She collaborated with Yeats on the first major anthology of the Irish Literary Revival, *Poems and Ballads of Young Ireland* (1888), and in 1907 Yeats edited and published a collection of Tynan's poems. Her poetry typifies the Irish Literary Renaissance, celebrating the legends of Catholic and pagan ancient Ireland in lilting balladic meter and evocative imagery. "The Children of Lir," which Yeats particularly admired, is Tynan's best-known poem. It is based on a famous Irish folktale, sometimes called "the second sorrowful tale," about a witch who has punished her stepchildren by transforming them into swans for nine hundred years.

The Children of Lir

"And their stepmother, being jealous of their father's great love for them, cast upon the King's children, by sorcery, the shape of swans, and bade them go roaming, even till Patrick's mass-bell should sound in Erin,—but no farther in time than that did her power extend."
—*The Fate of the Children of Lir.*[1]

Out upon the sand-dunes thrive the coarse long grasses,
    Herons standing knee-deep in the brackish pool,
Overhead the sunset fire and flame amasses,
    And the moon to eastward rises pale and cool:
Rose and green around her, silver-grey and pearly,   5
    Chequered with the black rooks[2] flying home to bed;
For, to wake at daybreak birds must couch them early,
    And the day's a long one since the dawn was red.

On the chilly lakelet, in that pleasant gloaming,
    See the sad swans sailing: they shall have no rest: 10
Never a voice to greet them save the bittern's booming
    Where the ghostly sallows sway against the West.
"Sister," saith the grey swan, "Sister, I am weary,"
    Turning to the white swan wet, despairing eyes;
"Oh," she saith, "my young one," "Oh," she saith, "my dearie,"   15
    Casts her wings about him with a storm of cries.

---

1. The swans can be restored to human shape only when St. Patrick comes to Ireland (Erin).
2. Crows.

Woe for Lir's sweet children whom their vile stepmother
    Glamoured with her witch-spells for a thousand years;[3]
Died their father raving—on his throne another—
    Blind before the end came from the burning tears.   20
She—the fiends possess her, torture her for ever.
    Gone is all the glory of the race of Lir;
Gone and long forgotten like a dream of fever:
    But the swans remember all the days that were.

Hugh, the black and white swan with the beauteous feathers,   25
    Fiachra, the black swan with the emerald breast,
Conn, the youngest, dearest, sheltered in all weathers,
    Him his snow-white sister loves the tenderest.
These her mother gave her as she lay a-dying,
    To her faithful keeping, faithful hath she been,   30
With her wings spread o'er them when the tempest's crying
    And her songs so hopeful when the sky's serene.

Other swans have nests made 'mid the reeds and rushes,
    Lined with downy feathers where the cygnets sleep
Dreaming, if a bird dreams, till the daylight blushes,   35
    Then they sail out swiftly on the current deep.
With the proud swan-father, tall, and strong, and stately,
    . And the mild swan-mother, grave with household cares,
All well-born and comely, all rejoicing greatly:
    Full of honest pleasure is a life like theirs.   40

But alas for my swans, with the human nature,
    Sick with human longings, starved for human ties,
With their hearts all human cramped in a bird's stature,
    And the human weeping in the bird's soft eyes,
Never shall my swans build nests in some green river,   45
    Never fly to Southward in the autumn grey,
Rear no tender children, love no mates for ever,
    Robbed alike of bird's joys and of man's are they.

Babbled Conn the youngest, "Sister, I remember
    At my father's palace how I went in silk,   50
Ate the juicy deer-flesh roasted from the ember,
    Drank from golden goblets my child's draught of milk.
Once I rode a-hunting, laughed to see the hurly,[4]
    Shouted at the ball-play, on the lake did row,

---

3. Lir married the princess Aobh and had four children; after Aobh's death he married her sister, who resented his love for his children and avenged herself on them.
4. A traditional Gaelic sport.

You had for your beauty gauds[5] that shone so rarely:"   55
  "Peace," saith Fionnuala, "that was long ago."

"Sister," saith Fiachra, "well do I remember
  How the flaming torches lit the banquet-hall,
And the fire leapt skyward in the mid-December,
  And amid the rushes slept our staghounds tall.   60
By our father's right hand you sat shyly gazing,
  Smiling half and sighing, with your eyes a-glow
As the bards sang loudly all your beauty praising:"
  "Peace," saith Fionnuala, "that was long ago."

"Sister," then saith Hugh, "most do I remember   65
  One I called my brother, you, earth's goodliest man,
Strong as forest oaks are where the wild vines clamber,
  First at feast or hunting, in the battle's van.[6]
Angus, you were handsome, wise and true and tender,
  Loved by every comrade, feared by every foe: 70
Low, low, lies your beauty, all forgot your splendour:"
  "Peace," saith Fionnuala, "that was long ago."

Dews are in the clear air, and the roselight paling,
  Over sands and sedges shines the evening star,
And the moon's disk lonely high in heaven is sailing,   75
  Silvered all the spear-heads of the rushes are,—
Housèd warm are all things as the night grows colder,
  Water-fowl and sky-fowl dreamless in the nest;
But the swans go drifting, drooping wing and shoulder
  Cleaving the still waters where the fishes rest.   80

—1891

J. M. Synge
1871–1909

When the aimless young playwright John Millington Synge visited the windswept, nearly desolate Aran Islands off the west coast of Ireland in 1898, he found his calling. On these remote
islands lived some of the last Gaelic-speaking communities, and Synge immersed himself in
their language, their myths, and their daily lives. The Aran Islands inspired his mature plays,
Riders to the Sea, *The Shadow of the Glen*, and *The Playboy of the Western World*. He joined Yeats

---

5. Jewels.
6. Front.

and Lady Gregory in developing the Abbey Theatre in Dublin to foster Irish nationalist drama, but Synge's plays offered a version of Ireland that scandalized the nation. Synge wrote Ireland as a contemporary realm of bleak poverty, amoral misery, and fundamental paganism. Yet this grim daily life gets recounted in mellifluous language that evokes a rich oral literary tradition. When *Playboy* opened at the Abbey Theatre in 1907, there were riots. Synge's sense of fellowship with the Irish peasantry is surprising given his upbringing in a traditional Protestant Anglo-Irish family, patriotic toward England and hostile to Irish independence. Synge grew up studying music and lived in Paris much of his adult life. He died of Hodgkin's disease at age thirty-eight, just as he was preparing to marry and in the full spate of his career. Astoundingly, he wrote all his plays within only six years. *Riders to the Sea*, an early one-act play, movingly depicts the inexorable destruction of an Irish fishing family—and the community they represent—because they are forced to depend on the sea that destroys them.

Riders to the Sea

A Play in One Act.

First performed at the Molesworth Hall, Dublin, February 25th, 1904.

PERSONS:—
    MAURYA (an old woman)
    BARTLEY (her son)
    CATHLEEN (her daughter)
    NORA (a younger daughter)
    MEN AND WOMEN

SCENE.—An Island off the West of Ireland.[1]

(*Cottage kitchen, with nets, oil-skins, spinning wheel, some new boards standing by the wall, etc. Cathleen, a girl of about twenty, finishes kneading cake, and puts it down in the pot-oven[2] by the fire; then wipes her hands, and begins to spin at the wheel. Nora, a young girl, puts her head in at the door.*)

NORA (*in a low voice*): Where is she?
CATHLEEN: She's lying down, God help her, and may be sleeping, if she's able.
    (*Nora comes in softly, and takes a bundle from under her shawl.*)
CATHLEEN (*spinning the wheel rapidly*): What is it you have?
NORA: The young priest is after bringing them. It's a shirt and a plain stocking were got off a drowned man in Donegal.
    (*Cathleen stops her wheel with a sudden movement, and leans out to listen.*)
NORA: We're to find out if it's Michael's they are, some time herself will be down looking by the sea.
CATHLEEN: How would they be Michael's, Nora. How would he go the length of that way to the far north?
NORA: The young priest says he's known the like of it. "If it's Michael's they are," says he, "you can tell herself he's got a clean burial by the grace of God, and if they're

---

1. Synge editor Ann Saddlemyer suggests Inishmaan, the Aran Island where Synge did most of his research.
2. An iron plate covered with a pot, with hot embers piled around it.

not his, let no one say a word about them, for she'll be getting her death," says he, "with crying and lamenting."

(*The door which Nora half closed is blown open by a gust of wind.*)

CATHLEEN (*looking out anxiously*): Did you ask him would he stop Bartley going this day with the horses to the Galway fair?

NORA: "I won't stop him," says he, "but let you not be afraid. Herself does be saying prayers half through the night, and the Almighty God won't leave her destitute," says he, "with no son living."

CATHLEEN: Is the sea bad by the white rocks, Nora?

NORA: Middling bad, God help us. There's a great roaring in the west, and it's worse it'll be getting when the tide's turned to the wind. (*She goes over to the table with the bundle.*) Shall I open it now?

CATHLEEN: Maybe she'd wake up on us, and come in before we'd done (*coming to the table*). It's a long time we'll be, and the two of us crying.

NORA (*Goes to the inner door and listens*): She's moving about on the bed. She'll be coming in a minute.

CATHLEEN: Give me the ladder, and I'll put them up in the turf-loft,[3] the way she won't know of them at all, and maybe when the tide turns she'll be going down to see would he be floating from the east.

(*They put the ladder against the gable of the chimney; Cathleen goes up a few steps and hides the bundle in the turf-loft. Maurya comes from the inner room.*)

MAURYA (*looking up at Cathleen and speaking querulously*): Isn't it turf enough you have for this day and evening?

CATHLEEN: There's a cake baking at the fire for a short space (*throwing down the turf*), and Bartley will want it when the tide turns if he goes to Connemara.[4]

(*Nora picks up the turf and puts it round the pot-oven.*)

MAURYA (*sitting down on a stool at the fire*): He won't go this day with the wind rising from the south and west. He won't go this day, for the young priest will stop him surely.

NORA: He'll not stop him, mother, and I heard Eamon Simon and Stephen Pheety and Colum Shawn saying he would go.

MAURYA: Where is he itself?

NORA: He went down to see would there be another boat sailing in the week, and I'm thinking it won't be long till he's here now, for the tide's turning at the green head,[5] and the hooker's[6] tacking from the east.

CATHLEEN: I hear some one passing the big stones.

NORA (*looking out*): He's coming now, and he in a hurry.

BARTLEY (*comes in and looks round the room. Speaking sadly and quietly*): Where is the bit of new rope, Cathleen, was bought in Connemara?

CATHLEEN (*coming down*): Give it to him, Nora; it's on a nail by the white boards. I hung it up this morning, for the pig with the black feet was eating it.

NORA (*giving him a rope*): Is that it, Bartley?

---

3. For storing peat, blocks of dried earth used for fuel.
4. Port nearest the Aran Islands, on the west coast of Ireland.
5. Grassy headland.
6. Small sailboat.

MAURYA: You'd do right to leave that rope, Bartley, hanging by the boards (*Bartley takes the rope*). It will be wanting in this place, I'm telling you, if Michael is washed up to-morrow morning, or the next morning, or any morning in the week, for it's a deep grave we'll make him by the grace of God.

BARTLEY (*beginning to work with the rope*): I've no halter the way I can ride down on the mare, and I must go now quickly. This is the one boat going for two weeks or beyond it, and the fair will be a good fair for horses I heard them saying below.

MAURYA: It's a hard thing they'll be saying below if the body is washed up and there's no man in it to make the coffin, and I after giving a big price for the finest white boards you'ld find in Connemara.

(*She looks round at the boards.*)

BARTLEY: How would it be washed up, and we after looking each day for nine days, and a strong wind flowing a while back from the west and south?

MAURYA: If it isn't found itself, that wind is raising the sea, and there was a star up against the moon, and it rising in the night. If it was a hundred horses, or a thousand horses you had itself, what is the price of a thousand horses against a son where there is one son only?

BARTLEY (*working at the halter, to Cathleen*): Let you go down each day, and see the sheep aren't jumping in on the rye, and if the jobber[7] comes you can sell the pig with the black feet if there is a good price going.

MAURYA: How would the like of her get a good price for a pig?

BARTLEY (*to Cathleen*): If the west wind holds with the last bit of the moon let you and Nora get up weed enough for another cock for the kelp.[8] It's hard set we'll be from this day with no one in it but one man to work.

MAURYA: It's hard set we'll be surely the day you're drown'd with the rest. What way will I live and the girls with me, and I an old woman looking for the grave?

(*Bartley lays down the halter, takes off his old coat, and puts on a newer one of the same flannel.*)

BARTLEY (*to Nora*): Is she coming to the pier?

NORA (*looking out*): She's passing the green head and letting fall her sails.

BARTLEY (*getting his purse and tobacco*): I'll have half an hour to go down, and you'll see me coming again in two days, or in three days, or maybe in four days if the wind is bad.

MAURYA (*turning round to the fire, and putting her shawl over her head*): Isn't it a hard and cruel man won't hear a word from an old woman, and she holding him from the sea?

CATHLEEN: It's the life of a young man to be going on the sea, and who would listen to an old woman with one thing and she saying it over?

BARTLEY (*taking the halter*): I must go now quickly. I'll ride down on the red mare, and the gray pony 'll run behind me. . . The blessing of God on you.

(*He goes out.*)

MAURYA (*crying out as he is in the door*): He's gone now, God spare us, and we'll not see him again. He's gone now, and when the black night is falling I'll have no son left me in the world.

---

7. Reseller, middleman.
8. Cocks were piles of dried seaweed (kelp), used for fertilizer.

CATHLEEN: Why wouldn't you give him your blessing and he looking round in the door? Isn't it sorrow enough is on every one in this house without your sending him out with an unlucky word behind him, and a hard word in his ear?

(*Maurya takes up the tongs and begins raking the fire aimlessly without looking round.*)

NORA (*turning towards her*): You're taking away the turf from the cake.

CATHLEEN (*crying out*): The Son of God forgive us, Nora, we're after forgetting his bit of bread.

(*She comes over to the fire.*)

NORA: And it's destroyed he'll be going till dark night, and he after eating nothing since the sun went up.

CATHLEEN (*turning the cake out of the oven*): It's destroyed he'll be, surely. There's no sense left on any person in a house where an old woman will be talking for ever.

(*Maurya sways herself on her stool.*)

CATHLEEN (*cutting off some of the bread and rolling it in a cloth; to Maurya*): Let you go down now to the spring well and give him this and he passing. You'll see him then and the dark word will be broken, and you can say "God speed you," the way he'll be easy in his mind.

MAURYA (*taking the bread*): Will I be in it as soon as himself?

CATHLEEN: If you go now quickly.

MAURYA (*standing up unsteadily*): It's hard set I am to walk.

CATHLEEN (*looking at her anxiously*): Give her the stick, Nora, or maybe she'll slip on the big stones.

NORA: What stick?

CATHLEEN: The stick Michael brought from Connemara.

MAURYA (*taking a stick Nora gives her*): In the big world the old people do be leaving things after them for their sons and children, but in this place it is the young men do be leaving things behind for them that do be old.

(*She goes out slowly. Nora goes over to the ladder.*)

CATHLEEN: Wait, Nora, maybe she'd turn back quickly. She's that sorry, God help her, you wouldn't know the thing she'd do.

NORA: Is she gone round by the bush?

CATHLEEN (*looking out*): She's gone now. Throw it down quickly, for the Lord knows when she'll be out of it again.

NORA (*getting the bundle from the loft*): The young priest said he'd be passing to-morrow, and we might go down and speak to him below if it's Michael's they are surely.

CATHLEEN (*taking the bundle*): Did he say what way they were found?

NORA (*coming down*): "There were two men," says he, "and they rowing round with poteen before the cocks crowed, and the oar of one of them caught the body, and they passing the black cliffs of the north."

CATHLEEN (*trying to open the bundle*): Give me a knife, Nora, the string's perished with the salt water, and there's a black knot on it you wouldn't loosen in a week.

NORA (*giving her a knife*): I've heard tell it was a long way to Donegal.[9]

---

9. Northern county.

CATHLEEN (*cutting the string*): It is surely. There was a man in here a while ago—the man sold us that knife—and he said if you set off walking from the rocks beyond, it would be seven days you'd be in Donegal.

NORA: And what time would a man take, and he floating?

(*Cathleen opens the bundle and takes out a bit of a stocking. They look at them eagerly.*)

CATHLEEN (*in a low voice*): The Lord spare us, Nora! isn't it a queer hard thing to say if it's his they are surely?

NORA: I'll get his shirt off the hook the way we can put the one flannel on the other. (*She looks through some clothes hanging in the corner.*) It's not with them, Cathleen, and where will it be?

CATHLEEN: I'm thinking Bartley put it on him in the morning, for his own shirt was heavy with the salt in it (*pointing to the corner*). There's a bit of a sleeve was of the same stuff. Give me that and it will do.

(*Nora brings it to her and they compare the flannel.*)

CATHLEEN: It's the same stuff, Nora; but if it is itself aren't there great rolls of it in the shops of Galway, and isn't it many another man may have a shirt of it as well as Michael himself?

NORA (*who has taken up the stocking and counted the stitches, crying out*): It's Michael, Cathleen, it's Michael; God spare his soul, and what will herself say when she hears this story, and Bartley on the sea?

CATHLEEN (*taking the stocking*): It's a plain stocking.

NORA: It's the second one of the third pair I knitted, and I put up three score stitches, and I dropped four of them.

CATHLEEN (*counts the stitches*): It's that number is in it (*crying out*). Ah, Nora, isn't it a bitter thing to think of him floating that way to the far north, and no one to keen[10] him but the black hags[11] that do be flying on the sea?

NORA (*swinging herself half round, and throwing out her arms on the clothes*): And isn't it a pitiful thing when there is nothing left of a man who was a great rower and fisher, but a bit of an old shirt and a plain stocking?

CATHLEEN (*after an instant*): Tell me is herself coming, Nora? I hear a little sound on the path.

NORA (*looking out*): She is, Cathleen. She's coming up to the door.

CATHLEEN: Put these things away before she'll come in. Maybe it's easier she'll be after giving her blessing to Bartley, and we won't let on we've heard anything the time he's on the sea.

NORA (*helping Cathleen to close the bundle*): We'll put them here in the corner. (*They put them into a hole in the chimney corner. Cathleen goes back to the spinning-wheel.*)

NORA: Will she see it was crying I was?

CATHLEEN: Keep your back to the door the way the light'll not be on you.

---

10. Mourn.
11. Literal translation of the Irish for cormorants.

(*Nora sits down at the chimney corner, with her back to the door. Maurya comes in very slowly, without looking at the girls, and goes over to her stool at the other side of the fire. The cloth with the bread is still in her hand. The girls look at each other, and Nora points to the bundle of bread.*)

CATHLEEN (*after spinning for a moment*): You didn't give him his bit of bread?

(*Maurya begins to keen softly, without turning round.*)

CATHLEEN: Did you see him riding down?

(*Maurya goes on keening.*)

CATHLEEN (*a little impatiently*): God forgive you; isn't it a better thing to raise your voice and tell what you seen, than to be making lamentation for a thing that's done? Did you see Bartley, I'm saying to you.

MAURYA (*with a weak voice*): My heart's broken from this day.

CATHLEEN (*as before*): Did you see Bartley?

MAURYA: I seen the fearfulest thing.

CATHLEEN (*leaves her wheel and looks out*): God forgive you; he's riding the mare now over the green head, and the gray pony behind him.

MAURYA (*starts, so that her shawl falls back from her head and shows her white tossed hair. With a frightened voice*): The gray pony behind him. . .

CATHLEEN (*coming to the fire*): What is it ails you, at all?

MAURYA (*speaking very slowly*): I've seen the fearfulest thing any person has seen, since the day Bride Dara seen the dead man with the child in his arms.[12]

CATHLEEN and NORA: Uah.

(*They crouch down in front of the old woman at the fire.*)

NORA: Tell us what it is you seen.

MAURYA: I went down to the spring well, and I stood there saying a prayer to myself. Then Bartley came along, and he riding on the red mare with the gray pony behind him (*she puts up her hands, as if to hide something from her eyes*). The Son of God spare us, Nora!

CATHLEEN: What is it you seen?

MAURYA: I seen Michael himself.

CATHLEEN (*speaking softly*): You did not, mother; It wasn't Michael you seen, for his body is after being found in the far north, and he's got a clean burial by the grace of God.

MAURYA (*a little defiantly*): I'm after seeing him this day, and he riding and galloping. Bartley came first on the red mare; and I tried to say "God speed you," but something choked the words in my throat. He went by quickly; and "the blessing of God on you," says he, and I could say nothing. I looked up then, and I crying, at the gray pony, and there was Michael upon it—with fine clothes on him, and new shoes on his feet.

CATHLEEN (*begins to keen*): It's destroyed we are from this day. It's destroyed, surely.

NORA: Didn't the young priest say the Almighty God won't leave her destitute with no son living?

MAURYA (*in a low voice, but clearly*): It's little the like of him knows of the sea. . . . Bartley will be lost now, and let you call in Eamon and make me a good coffin out

---

12. A supernatural portent. Bride is a nickname for Bridget.

of the white boards, for I won't live after them. I've had a husband, and a husband's father, and six sons in this house—six fine men, though it was a hard birth I had with every one of them and they coming to the world—and some of them were found and some of them were not found, but they're gone now the lot of them. . . There were Stephen, and Shawn, were lost in the great wind, and found after in the Bay of Gregory of the Golden Mouth,[13] and carried up the two of them on one plank, and in by that door.

(*She pauses for a moment, the girls start as if they heard something through the door that is half open behind them.*)

NORA (*in a whisper*): Did you hear that, Cathleen? Did you hear a noise in the north-east?

CATHLEEN (*in a whisper*): There's some one after crying out by the seashore.

MAURYA (*continues without hearing anything*): There was Sheamus and his father, and his own father again, were lost in a dark night, and not a stick or sign was seen of them when the sun went up. There was Patch after was drowned out of a curagh[14] that turned over. I was sitting here with Bartley, and he a baby, lying on my two knees, and I seen two women, and three women, and four women coming in, and they crossing themselves, and not saying a word. I looked out then, and there were men coming after them, and they holding a thing in the half of a red sail, and water dripping out of it—it was a dry day, Nora—and leaving a track to the door.

(*She pauses again with her hand stretched out towards the door. It opens softly and old women begin to come in, crossing themselves on the threshold, and kneeling down in front of the stage with red petticoats over their heads.*)

MAURYA (*half in a dream, to Cathleen*): Is it Patch, or Michael, or what is it at all?

CATHLEEN: Michael is after being found in the far north, and when he is found there how could he be here in this place?

MAURYA: There does be a power of young men floating round in the sea, and what way would they know if it was Michael they had, or another man like him, for when a man is nine days in the sea, and the wind blowing, it's hard set his own mother would be to say what man was in it.

CATHLEEN: It's Michael, God spare him, for they're after sending us a bit of his clothes from the far north.

(*She reaches out and hands Maurya the clothes that belonged to Michael. Maurya stands up slowly, and takes them in her hands. Nora looks out.*)

NORA: They're carrying a thing among them and there's water dripping out of it and leaving a track by the big stones.

CATHLEEN (*in a whisper to the women who have come in*): Is it Bartley it is?

ONE OF THE WOMEN: It is surely, God rest his soul.

(*Two younger women come in and pull out the table. Then men carry in the body of Bartley, laid on a plank, with a bit of a sail over it, and lay it on the table.*)

CATHLEEN (*to the women, as they are doing so*): What way was he drowned?

---

13. Gregory Sound separates two of the Aran Islands (Saddlemyer). Synge may be conflating two early Church fathers, St. John Chrysostom (Greek: the Golden Mouth) and St. Gregory I.
14. Fragile light rowing boat.

ONE OF THE WOMEN: The gray pony knocked him over into the sea, and he was washed out where there is a great surf on the white rocks.

(*Maurya has gone over and knelt down at the head of the table. The women are keening softly and swaying themselves with a slow movement. Cathleen and Nora kneel at the other end of the table. The men kneel near the door.*)

MAURYA (*raising her head and speaking as if she did not see the people around her*): They're all gone now, and there isn't anything more the sea can do to me.... I'll have no call now to be up crying and praying when the wind breaks from the south, and you can hear the surf is in the east, and the surf is in the west, making a great stir with the two noises, and they hitting one on the other. I'll have no call now to be going down and getting Holy Water in the dark nights after Samhain,[15] and I won't care what way the sea is when the other women will be keening. (*To Nora.*) Give me the Holy Water, Nora, there's a small sup[16] still on the dresser.

(*Nora gives it to her.*)

MAURYA (*drops Michael's clothes across Bartley's feet, and sprinkles the Holy Water over him*): It isn't that I haven't prayed for you, Bartley, to the Almighty God. It isn't that I haven't said prayers in the dark night till you wouldn't know what I'ld be saying; but it's a great rest I'll have now, and it's time surely. It's a great rest I'll have now, and great sleeping in the long nights after Samhain, if it's only a bit of wet flour we do have to eat, and maybe a fish that would be stinking.

(*She kneels down again, crossing herself, and saying prayers under her breath.*)

CATHLEEN (*to an old man*): Maybe yourself and Eamon would make a coffin when the sun rises. We have fine white boards herself bought, God help her, thinking Michael would be found, and I have a new cake you can eat while you'll be working.

THE OLD MAN (*looking at the boards*): Are there nails with them?

CATHLEEN: There are not, Colum; we didn't think of the nails.

ANOTHER MAN: It's a great wonder she wouldn't think of the nails, and all the coffins she's seen made already.

CATHLEEN: It's getting old she is, and broken.

(*Maurya stands up again very slowly and spreads out the pieces of Michael's clothes beside the body, sprinkling them with the last of the Holy Water.*)

NORA (*in a whisper to Cathleen*): She's quiet now and easy; but the day Michael was drowned you could hear her crying out from this to the spring well. It's fonder she was of Michael, and would any one have thought that?

CATHLEEN (*slowly and clearly*): An old woman will be soon tired with anything she will do, and isn't it nine days herself is after crying and keening, and making great sorrow in the house?

MAURYA (*puts the empty cup mouth downwards on the table, and lays her hands together on Bartley's feet*): They're all together this time, and the end is come. May the Almighty God have mercy on Bartley's soul, and on Michael's soul, and on the souls of Sheamus and Patch, and Stephen and Shawn (*bending her head*); and

---

15. Festival of the dead, celebrated November 1.
16. Bottle.

may He have mercy on my soul, Nora, and on the soul of every one is left living in the world.

(*She pauses, and the keen rises a little more loudly from the women, then sinks away.*)

MAURYA (*continuing*): Michael has a clean burial in the far north, by the grace of the Almighty God. Bartley will have a fine coffin out of the white boards, and a deep grave surely. What more can we want than that? No man at all can be living for ever, and we must be satisfied.

(*She kneels down again and the curtain falls slowly.*)

—1904

Credits

Part I: Aestheticism

Arguing for Art: Aesthetic Prose

1. Walter Pater, "Leonardo da Vinci," "Conclusion," *The Longman Anthology of British Literature*, vol. 2, ed. David Damrosch (New York: Addison-Wesley Longman, 1999), 1762–65.

2. James McNeill Whistler, *Mr. Whistler's Ten O'Clock* (Boston and New York: Houghton Mifflin and Co., 1888), 7–16.

3. Oscar Wilde, "The Decay of Lying," *The Complete Works of Oscar Wilde*, ed. Merlin Holland (New York: HarperCollins, 1966), 970–92.

4. Oscar Wilde, "Preface to *The Picture of Dorian Gray*," *The Longman Anthology of British Literature*, vol. 2, ed. David Damrosch (New York: Addison-Wesley Longman, 1999), 1881–82.

5. "Vernon Lee" (Violet Paget), *Baldwin: Being Dialogues on Views and Aspirations* (Boston: Roberts Brothers, 1886), 198–209, 210–13, 218–23, 270–74, 275–78.

6. Alice Meynell, "The Colour of Life," *Essays* (New York: Charles Scribner's Sons, 1914), 171–75.

7. Max Beerbohm, "A Defence of Cosmetics" and "A Letter to the Editor," *Aesthetes and Decadents of the 1890's*, ed. Karl Beckson (Chicago: Academy Chicago Publishers, 1981), 48–66.

8. Arthur Symons, "The Decadent Movement in Literature," *Harper's New Monthly Magazine* November 1893: 858–59.

Incantatory Art: Aesthetic Poems

1. Ernest Dowson, "Non Sum Qualis Eram Bonae Sub Regno Cynarae," *The Poems of Ernest Dowson*, ed. Mark Longaker (Philadelphia: University of Pennsylvania Press, 1962), 58.

2. Lionel Johnson, "The Destroyer of a Soul" and "A Decadent's Lyric," *The Longman Anthology of British Literature*, vol. 2, ed. David Damrosch (New York: Addison-Wesley Longman, 1999), 1958, 1960.

3. Arthur Symons, "Renée," *Poems by Arthur Symons* (New York: John Lane Company, 1916), 82.

4. Arthur Symons, "White Heliotrope," *The Longman Anthology of British Literature*, vol. 2, ed. David Damrosch (New York: Addison-Wesley Longman, 1999), 1953.

5. Arthur Symons, "Morbidezza" and "Maquillage," *Silhouettes* (London: Leonard Smithers, 1896, first ed. 1892), 13, 14.

6. Lord Alfred Douglas, "Two Loves," *The Longman Anthology of British Literature*, vol. 2, ed. David Damrosch (New York: Addison-Wesley Longman, 1999), 1961–63.

7. W. B. Yeats, "When You are Old," "The Lover Tells of the Rose in His Heart," "He Remembers Forgotten Beauty," "The Secret Rose," and "He Wishes for the Cloths of Heaven," *W. B. Yeats: Selected Poetry*, ed. A. Norman Jeffares (London: Macmillan & Co. Ltd., 1963), 17, 24–25, 29–30, 33–34, 35.

8. Oscar Wilde, "The Sphinx," "The Harlot's House," and "The Ballad of Reading Gaol," *Oscar Wilde: Plays, Prose Writings and Poems*, ed. Isobel Murray (London: J. M. Dent & Sons Ltd., 1975), 397–99, 399–401, 403–4, 395–96, 377–94.

9. Oscar Wilde, "Impression du Matin," *The Longman Anthology of British Literature*, vol. 2, ed. David Damrosch (New York: Addison-Wesley Longman, 1999), 1856–57.

10. "Michael Field" (Edith Cooper, Katharine Bradley), "Come, Gorgo, put the rug in place," "I Love You With My Life," "The Mummy Invokes his Soul," and "Unbosoming," *Victorian Women Poets*, eds. Angela Leighton and Margaret Reynolds (Oxford: Blackwell, 1995), 490–91, 496, 499–500, 500.

11. "Michael Field" (Edith Cooper, Katharine Bradley), "La Gioconda" and "A Pen-Drawing of Leda," *The Longman Anthology of British Literature*, vol. 2, ed. David Damrosch (New York: Addison-Wesley Longman, 1999), 1946.

12. Amy Levy, "To Vernon Lee" and "Xantippe," *Victorian Women Poets*, eds. Angela Leighton and Margaret Reynolds (Oxford: Blackwell, 1995), 609, 591–97.

13. Alice Meynell, "Renouncement," "Cradle-Song at Twilight," "Why Wilt Thou Chide?" and "Easter Night," *The Poems of Alice Meynell* (New York: Charles Scribner's Sons, 1923), 28, 32, 62, 94.

14. Alice Meynell, "Maternity," *Victorian Women Poets*, eds. Angela Leighton and Margaret Reynolds (Oxford: Blackwell, 1995), 522.

15. "Graham R. Tomson" (Rosamund Marriott Watson), "Aubade," *Victorian Women Poets*, ed. Virginia Blain (New York: Longman, 2001), 266–67.

16. "Graham R. Tomson" (Rosamund Marriott Watson), "Ballad of the Bird-Bride," *Victorian Women Poets*, eds. Angela Leighton and Margaret Reynolds (Oxford: Blackwell, 1995), 583–85.

17. Olive Custance, "Doubts," *Opals* (London: John Lane, 1897), 51–53.

18. Olive Custance, "The White Witch," *The Longman Anthology of British Literature*, vol. 2, ed. David Damrosch (New York: Addison-Wesley Longman, 1999), 1965–66.

The Art of Conversation: Aesthetic Fiction and Drama

1. W. S. Gilbert, "If You're Anxious for to Shine," *The Longman Anthology of British Literature*, vol. 2, ed. David Damrosch (New York: Addison-Wesley Longman, 1999), 1938–40.

2. Max Beerbohm, "Enoch Soames," *The Longman Anthology of British Literature*, vol. 2, ed. David Damrosch (New York: Addison-Wesley Longman, 1999), 2091–2109.

3. Oscar Wilde, *The Importance of Being Earnest*, from *The Longman Anthology of British Literature*, vol. 2, ed. David Damrosch (New York: Addison-Wesley Longman, 1999), 1883–1922.

4. Una Ashworth Taylor, "Seed of the Sun" and "The Truce of God," *Nets for the Wind* (London: John Lane, 1896), 122–34, 156–72.

Part II: New Women

New Women in the Popular Press

1. Sarah Grand, "The New Aspect of the Woman Question," *North American Review* 158 (March 1894): 270–76.

2. "Ouida" (Marie Louise de la Ramée), "The New Woman," *North American Review* 158 (May 1894): 610–19.

3. B. A. Crackanthorpe, "The Revolt of the Daughters," *The Nineteenth Century* 35 (1894): 23–31.

4. Kathleen Cuffe, "A Reply from the Daughters," *The Nineteenth Century* 35 (1894): 437–50.

5. A. G. P. Sykes, "The Evolution of the Sex," *The Westminster Review* 143 (1895): 396–400.

6. Mona Caird, "Does Marriage Hinder a Woman's Self-development?" *The Daughters of Danaus* (New York: The Feminist Press at CUNY, 1989, first pub. 1899), 535–39.

7. Alice Meynell, "A Woman in Grey," *Alice Meynell Prose and Poetry, Centenary Volume* (London: Jonathan Cape, 1947, first pub. in *The Colour of Life*, 1896), 208–12.

New Women Poetry

1. May Kendall, "Woman's Future," *Victorian Women Poets: A New Annotated Anthology*, ed. Virginia Blain (New York: Longman, 2001), 318–20.

2. Constance Naden, "The New Orthodoxy," *Victorian Women Poets: A New Annotated Anthology*, ed. Virginia Blain (New York: Longman, 2001), 249.

3. Dora Sigerson Shorter, "Cecilia's Way," *New Women Poets: An Anthology*, ed. Linda Hughes (London: The Eighteen Nineties Society, 2001), 19.

4. E. Nesbit, "Accession," *New Women Poets: An Anthology*, ed. Linda Hughes (London: The Eighteen Nineties Society, 2001), 31.

5. Dollie Radford, "From Our Emancipated Aunt in Town," *New Women Poets: An Anthology*, ed. Linda Hughes (London: The Eighteen Nineties Society, 2001), 44–47.

6. Amy Levy, "Captivity," *New Women Poets: An Anthology*, ed. Linda Hughes (London: The Eighteen Nineties Society, 2001), 47–48.

7. "Graham R. Tomson" (Rosamund Marriott Watson), "On the Road," *New Women Poets: An Anthology*, ed. Linda Hughes (London: The Eighteen Nineties Society, 2001), 54.

8. Mathilde Blind, "Prelude: Wings," *New Women Poets: An Anthology*, ed. Linda Hughes (London: The Eighteen Nineties Society, 2001), 67.

New Women Fiction

1. "George Egerton" (Mary Chavelita Dunne Clairmonte Bright), "A Cross Line," *Keynotes* (London: Elkin Matthews and John Lane, 1893), 9–44.

2. Ella D'Arcy, "The Pleasure-Pilgrim," *Monochromes* (Boston: Roberts Brothers, 1895), 165–218.

3. Mabel E. Wotton, "The Fifth Edition," *Daughters of Decadence: Women Writers of the Fin de Siècle*, ed. Elaine Showalter (New Brunswick: Rutgers University Press, 1993), 139–64. First published in *Day-Books* (London: John Lane, 1896).

Part III: Mind and Body

Body Fears: Degeneracy and Sexology

1. Francis Galton, *Inquiries into Human Faculty and Its Development* (London: Macmillan and Co., 1883), 305–9, 317, 323–28.

2. Max Nordau, *Degeneration* (London: William Heinemann, 1895), 15–24, 26–33, 317, 319–22, 337.

3. Janet E. Hogarth, "Literary Degenerates," *The Fortnightly Review* 63 (1895): 586–92.

4. George Bernard Shaw, *The Sanity of Art: An Exposure of the Current Nonsense About Artists Being Degenerate* (London: The New Age Press, 1908), 85–92; http://www.modjourn.brown.edu/MJP_Books.htm.

5. Havelock Ellis, *Studies in the Psychology of Sex*, vol. II (Philadelphia: F. A. Davis Company, 1908, first ed. 1901), 196–203, 206, 209–16.

6. Edward Carpenter, *Homogenic Love, and Its Place in a Free Society* (Manchester: The Labour Press Society Limited, 1894), 35–37, 42–51.

Political Solutions: Philanthropy, Sociology, Socialism

1. William Morris, "Useful Work versus Useless Toil," *William Morris on Art and Socialism*, ed. Norman Kelvin (New York: Dover, 1999, lecture delivered 1884), 128–43.

2. Oscar Wilde, "The Soul of Man Under Socialism," *The Soul of Man Under Socialism and Selected Critical Prose*, ed. Linda Dowling (London: Penguin, 2001, first written 1891), 127–42, 155–60.

3. George Bernard Shaw, "The Basis of Socialism," *Fabian Essays in Socialism* (London: Walter Scott Ltd, 1889), 18–19, 21–29.

4. Charles Booth, *Life and Labour of the People in London: First Series: Poverty* (New York: AMS Press, Inc., 1970, rpt. 1889 ed.), 63–72.

5. W. T. Stead, "The Maiden Tribute of Modern Babylon," *The Pall Mall Gazette* (July 6, 1885): 3–6; http://www.attackingthedevil.co.uk/pmg/tribute/mt1.php.

Writing the City, Writing the Country

1. John Davidson, "Good-Friday," *Fleet Street Eclogues* (London: Elkin Matthews and John Lane, 1893), 31–39.

2. Arthur Symons, "In Bohemia," *Silhouettes* (London: Leonard Smithers, 1896, 2nd ed.), 23.

3. Arthur Symons, "Prologue: In the Stalls," "To a Dancer," and "Prologue: Before the Curtain," *Poems by Arthur Symons*, vol. I (New York: John Lane Company, 1916), 80, 81, 79.

4. A. E. Housman, "II. Loveliest of trees, the cherry now," "XIII. When I was one-and-twenty," "To an Athlete Dying Young," and "XXXI. On Wenlock Edge the wood's in trouble," *A Shropshire Lad* (London: Grant Richards, 1906), 3–4, 20–21, 26–28, 45–46.

5. Thomas Hardy, "Wessex Heights" and "The Darkling Thrush," *The Longman Anthology of British Literature*, vol. 2, ed. David Damrosch (New York: Addison-Wesley Longman, 1999), 2082, 2083–84.

6. The Music Halls, "If it Wasn't for the 'Ouses in Between," *Songs of the British Music Hall*, ed. Peter Davison (New York: Oak Publications, 1971), 192–94.

Mental Hopes: Psychology, Parapsychology, Fantasy

1. William James, *Principles of Psychology* (New York: Henry Holt & Company, 1890), 237–39.

2. Sigmund Freud, "Fragment of an Analysis of a Case of Hysteria" ("Dora"), *The Standard Edition of the Complete Psychological Works of Sigmund Freud, Vol. VII (1901–1905)*, trans. and ed. James Strachey (London: The Hogarth Press, 1925), 18–35, 37–40, 42, 46–51, 54–55, 55–63.

3. Frederic W. H. Myers, *Human Personality and its Survival of Bodily Death*, vol. I (London: Longmans, Green, and Co., 1903), 25–33.

4. Henry James, "The Beast in the Jungle," *Selected Tales of Henry James* (London: The Richards Press, 1947), 219–67.

Part IV: England and Its Others

Writing Empire

1. Sir Henry Newbolt, "Vitaï Lampada," *Poems: New and Old* (London: John Murray, 1912), 78–79.

2. Rudyard Kipling, "The White Man's Burden," *The Literary Digest* (Feb. 25, 1899), 219.

3. Henry Labouchère, "The Brown Man's Burden," *The Literary Digest* (Feb. 25, 1899), 219.

4. James Anthony Froude, *The English in the West Indies* (London: Longmans, Green, and Co, 1888), 48–51, 90–91.

5. J. J. Thomas, *Froudacity: West Indian Fables by James Anthony Froude* (Philadelphia: Gebbie and Co., 1890), 41–49.

6. Robert Louis Stevenson, "The House of Temoana," *In the South Seas* (New York: C. Scribner's Sons, 1896), 76–85.

7. Dorothea Mackellar, "My Country," *The Oxford Anthology of Australian Literature*, eds. Leonie Kramer and Adrian Mitchell (Melbourne: Oxford University Press, 1985), 141–42.

8. Isabella Valancy Crawford, "Said the Canoe," *Empire Writing: An Anthology of Colonial Literature 1870–1918*, ed. Elleke Boehmer (Oxford: Oxford University Press, 1998), 164–67.

The Scramble for Africa

1. Sir Henry Morton Stanley, *Through the Dark Continent*, from *The Longman Anthology of British Literature*, vol. 2, ed. David Damrosch (New York: Addison-Wesley Longman, 1999), 1841–44.

2. Mary Kingsley, *Travels in West Africa* (London: Macmillan and Co., 1897), 1–6, 87–90, 197–200, 329–32, 339–41.

3. David Lloyd George, "South African War—Mortality in Camps of Detention," *Hansard's Parliamentary Debates* XCV (June 17, 1901), 573–78.

The Eastern Empire: India

1. Rudyard Kipling, "Gunga Din," *The Poems of Rudyard Kipling* (New York: A. L. Burt, 1900), 32–37.

2. Rudyard Kipling, "Without Benefit of Clergy," *The Longman Anthology of British Literature*, vol. 2, ed. David Damrosch (New York: Addison-Wesley Longman, 1999), 1790–1804.

3. Alice Perrin, "In the Next Room," *East of Suez* (London: Chatto & Windus, 1909, rpt. of 1901 edition), 155–68.

4. Sir Arthur Conan Doyle, "The Adventure of the Speckled Band," *The Adventures of Sherlock Holmes* (New York and London: Harper and Brothers, 1902), 176–204. (Orig. published as No. 8 of "The Adventures of Sherlock Holmes," *The Strand* 3 (Jan.–June 1892), [142]–157.)

5. Laurence Hope, "Kashmiri Song" and "Till I Wake," *India's Love Lyrics, Including The Garden of Kama* (New York: Dodd, Mead, 1906), 133.

6. Toru Dutt, "Jogadhya Uma," *Ancient Ballads and Legends of Hindustan* (Madras: Kalidas & Co., 1927), 54–64.

Celts and Colonialism: Ireland

1. W. B. Yeats, *The Celtic Twilight* (London: A. H. Bullen, 1902, rpt. of 1893 edition), 18–25.

2. W. B. Yeats, "To the Rose Upon the Rood of Time," "To Ireland in the Coming Times," and "The Hosting of the Sidhe," *W. B. Yeats: Selected Poetry*, ed. A. Norman Jeffares (London: Macmillan & Co. Ltd, 1963), 10, 22–23, 24.

3. Katharine Tynan, "The Children of Lir," *Ballads and Lyrics* (London: Kegan Paul, Trench, Trübner & Co., 1891), 1–5.

4. J. M. Synge, *Riders to the Sea*, from *The Shadow of the Glen and Riders to the Sea* (London: Elkin Matthews, 1910), 39–63.

Bibliography

Recommendations for additional reading:

Note: This list offers general studies. Single-author studies and additional recommendations can be found in: • *The Longman Anthology of British Literature* (3rd edition), vols. 2b and 2c • The Longman Cultural Edition of *Heart of Darkness, The Man Who Would Be King, and Other Works on Empire*, Joseph Conrad and Rudyard Kipling (ed. David Damrosch) • The Longman Cultural Edition of *The Picture of Dorian Gray*, Oscar Wilde (ed. Andrew Elfenbein)

Studies of the *fin de siècle*: • Osbert Burdett, *The Beardsley Period: An Essay in Perspective*, 1925 • G. A. Cevasco, *The 1890s: An Encyclopedia of British Literature, Art, and Culture*, 1993 • Bram Djikstra, *Idols of Perversity: Fantasies of Feminine Evil in Fin-de-Siècle Culture*, 1986 • Holbrook Jackson, *The Eighteen Nineties*, 1922 • Peter Keating, *The Haunted Study: A Social History of the English Novel 1875–1914*, 1991 • Richard Le Gallienne, *The Romantic '90s*, 1926 • Nikki Lee Manos and Meri-Jane Rochelson, *Transforming Genres: New Approaches to British Fiction of the 1890s*, 1994 • W. G. Blaikie Murdoch, *The Renaissance of the Nineties*, 1911 • Elizabeth Robins Pennell, *Nights: Rome and Venice in the Aesthetic Eighties, London and Paris in the Fighting Nineties*, 1916 • Elaine Showalter, *Sexual Anarchy: Gender and Culture at the Fin de Siècle*, 1990 • John Stokes, *Fin de Siècle/Fin du Globe: Fears and Fantasies of the Late Nineteenth Century*, 1992 • John Stokes, *In the Nineties*, 1989 • Gaye Tuchman and Nina E. Fortin, *Edging Women Out: Victorian Novelists, Publishers, and Social Change*, 1989 • W. B. Yeats, "The Tragic Generation," *The Trembling of the Veil*, 1922

Part I: Aestheticism

Recommended novels and plays: • Max Beerbohm, *The Happy Hypocrite*, 1897 • Max Beerbohm, *Zuleika Dobson*, 1911 • "Ouida" (Marie Louise de la Ramée), "Afternoon," 1883 • "Ouida" (Marie Louise de la Ramée), *Moths*, 1880 • "Ouida" (Marie Louise de la Ramée), *Princess Napraxine*, 1884 • John Meade Falkner, *The Lost Stradivarius*, 1895 • "Lucas Malet" (Mary St Leger Kingsley Harrison), *The Gateless Barrier*, 1900 • "Lucas Malet" (Mary St Leger Kingsley Harrison), *The History of Sir Richard Calmady*, 1901 • "Lucas Malet" (Mary St Leger Kingsley Harrison), *The Wages of Sin*, 1890 • J. K. Huysmans, *À Rebours*

(*Against the Grain*), 1884 • Henry James, *The Golden Bowl*, 1904 • Henry James, *Portrait of a Lady*, 1881 • Henry James, *The Spoils of Poynton*, 1897 • "Vernon Lee" (Violet Paget), *Miss Brown*, 1884 • Walter Pater, *Marius the Epicurean*, 1885 • Oscar Wilde, *De Profundis*, 1897 • Oscar Wilde, *An Ideal Husband*, 1895 • Oscar Wilde, *Lady Windermere's Fan*, 1892 • Oscar Wilde, *The Picture of Dorian Gray*, 1890–91 • Oscar Wilde, *Salome*, 1892 • Oscar Wilde, *A Woman of No Importance*, 1893

Recommended criticism: • James Eli Adams, *Dandies and Desert Saints: Styles of Victorian Masculinity*, 1995 • Joseph Bristow, ed., *The Fin de Siècle Poem: English Literary Culture and the 1890s*, 2005 • Liz Constable, Dennis Denisoff, and Matthew Potolsky, eds., *Perennial Decay: On the Aesthetics and Politics of Decadence*, 1998 • Richard Dellamora, *Masculine Desire: The Sexual Politics of Victorian Aestheticism*, 1990 • Dennis Denisoff, *Aestheticism and Sexual Parody, 1840–1940*, 2001 • Linda Dowling, *Language and Decadence in the Victorian Fin de Siècle*, 1985 • Linda Dowling, *The Vulgarization of Art: The Victorians and Aesthetic Democracy*, 1996 • Jessica Feldman, *Victorian Modernism: Pragmatism and the Varieties of Aesthetic Experience*, 2002 • Rita Felski, *The Gender of Modernity*, 1995 • Jonathan Freedman, *Professions of Taste: Henry James, British Aestheticism, and Commodity Culture*, 1993 • Graham Hough, *The Last Romantics*, 1976 • Diana Maltz, *British Aestheticism and the Urban Working Classes, 1870–1900: Beauty for the People*, 2005 • Katherine Lyons Mix, *A Study in Yellow: The Yellow Book and Its Contributors*, 1960 • Yopie Prins, *Victorian Sappho*, 1999 • Kathy Alexis Psomiades, *Beauty's Body: Femininity and Representation in British Aestheticism*, 1997 • Talia Schaffer, *The Forgotten Female Aesthetes: Literary Culture in Late-Victorian England*, 2000 • Talia Schaffer and Kathy Alexis Psomiades, eds., *The Women's World of British Aestheticism*, 1999 • Margaret Stetz and Mark Samuels Lasner, *England in the 1890s: Literary Publishing at the Bodley Head*, 1990 • Ana Parejo Vadillo, *Women Poets and Urban Aestheticism*, 2005 • David Weir, *Decadence and the Making of Modernism*, 1995

Part II: New Women

Recommended novels and plays: • Grant Allen, *The Woman Who Did*, 1895 • Mona Caird, *The Daughters of Danaus*, 1894 • Mary Cholmondeley, *Red Pottage*, 1899 • Kate Chopin, *The Awakening*, 1899 • Ella Hepworth Dixon, *The Story of a Modern Woman*, 1894 • Charlotte Perkins Gilman, *Herland*, 1912 • Charlotte Perkins Gilman, "The Yellow Wallpaper," 1892 • George Gissing, *The Odd Women*, 1893 • "Sarah Grand" (Frances Bellenden Clarke), *The Beth Book*, 1897 • "Sarah Grand" (Frances Bellenden Clarke), *The Heavenly Twins*, 1893 • Thomas Hardy, *Jude the Obscure*, 1895 • "Iota" (Kathleen Mannington Caffyn), *A Yellow Aster*, 1894 • "Lucas Malet" (Mary St Leger Kingsley Harrison), *The Wages of Sin*, 1890 • "George Paston" (Emily Morse Symonds), *A Writer of Books*, 1899 • Olive Schreiner, *The Story of an African Farm*, 1883 • Mary Ward, *Marcella*, 1894 • H. G. Wells, *Ann Veronica*, 1909

Recommended criticism: • Ann Ardis, *Modernism and Cultural Conflict, 1880–1922*, 2002 • Ann Ardis, *New Women, New Novels: Feminism and Early Modernism*, 1991 • Gail Cunningham, *The New Woman and the Victorian Novel*, 1978 • Ann Heilmann, *New Woman Fiction: Women Writing First-Wave Feminism*, 2000 • Ann Heilmann, *New Woman Strategies: Sarah Grand, Olive Schreiner, Mona Caird*, 2004 • Ann Heilmann, ed., *Feminist Forerunners: New Womanism and Feminism in the Early Twentieth Century*, 2001 • Sally Ledger, *The New Woman: Fiction and Feminism at the Fin de Siècle*, 1997 • Jane Eldridge Miller, *Rebel Women: Feminism, Modernism, and the Edwardian Novel*, 1997 • Sally Mitchell, *The New Girl: Girls' Culture in England, 1880–1915*, 1995 • Patricia Murphy, *Time Is of the Essence: Temporality, Gender, and the New Woman*, 2001 • Lyn Pykett, *The "Improper" Feminine: The Women's Sensation Novel and the New Woman Writing*, 1992 • Angelique Richardson, *Love and Eugenics in the Late Nineteenth Century: Rational Reproduction and the New Woman*, 2003 • Angelique Richardson and Chris Willis, eds., *The New Woman in Fiction and in Fact: Fin de Siècle Feminisms*, 2001 • LeeAnne M. Richardson, *New Woman and Colonial Adventure Fiction in Victorian Britain: Gender, Genre, and Empire*, 2006 • David Rubinstein, *Before the Suffragettes: Women's Emancipation in the 1890s*, 1986 • Beth Sutton-Ramspeck, *Raising the Dust: The Literary Housekeeping of Mary Ward, Sarah Grand, and Charlotte Perkins Gilman*, 2004

Part III: Mind and Body

Recommended novels and plays: • J. M. Barrie, *Peter Pan*, 1904 • Sir Arthur Conan Doyle, *The Adventures of Sherlock Holmes*, 1892 • Sir Arthur Conan Doyle, *The Hound of the Baskervilles*, 1902 • Sir Arthur Conan Doyle, *The Sign of Four*, 1890 • Sir Arthur Conan Doyle, *A Study in Scarlet*, 1887 • George du Maurier, *Trilby*, 1894 • George Gissing, *The Netherworld*, 1889 • George Gissing, *New Grub Street*, 1891 • George and Weedon Grossmith, *Diary of a Nobody*, 1892 • Thomas Hardy, *Jude the Obscure*, 1895 • Thomas Hardy, *The Mayor of Casterbridge*, 1886 • Thomas Hardy, *Tess of the d'Urbervilles*, 1891 • Thomas Hardy, *The Well-Beloved*, 1897 • Margaret Harkness, *In Darkest London*, 1891 • Margaret Harkness, *Out of Work*, 1888 • Annie E. Holdsworth, *The Years That the Locusts Hath Eaten*, 1897 • Henry James, *The Turn of the Screw*, 1898 • Jerome K. Jerome, *Three Men in a Boat, To Say Nothing of the Dog!* 1889 • George Moore, *Esther Waters*, 1894 • Arthur Morrison, *A Child of the Jago*, 1896 • George Bernard Shaw, *Major Barbara*, 1905 • Robert Louis Stevenson, *Strange Case of Dr. Jekyll and Mr. Hyde*, 1886 • Bram Stoker, *Dracula*, 1897 • Robert Tressell, *The Ragged-Trousered Philanthropists*, 1914 • Mary Ward, *Robert Elsmere*, 1888 • H. G. Wells, *The Island of Doctor Moreau*, 1896 • H. G. Wells, *Kipps*, 1905 • H. G. Wells, *Love and Mr. Lewisham*, 1900 • H. G. Wells, *The Time Machine*, 1895 • H. G. Wells, *The War of the Worlds*, 1898 • Oscar Wilde, *The Happy Prince and Other Tales*, 1888 • Israel Zangwill, *Children of the Ghetto*, 1892

Recommended criticism: • Ruth Brandon, *The Spiritualists: The Passion for the Occult in the Nineteenth and Twentieth Centuries*, 1983 • J. Edward Chamberlain and

Sander Gilman, eds., *Degeneration: The Dark Side of Progress*, 1985 • Nicholas Daly, *Literature, Technology, and Modernity 1860–2000*, 2004 • William Greenslade, *Degeneration, Culture and the Novel 1880–1940*, 1994 • Gareth Stedman Jones, *Outcast London*, 1971 • P. J. Keating, *The Working Classes in Victorian Fiction*, 1979 • Stephen Kern, *The Culture of Time and Space, 1880–1918*, 2003 • Seth Koven, *Slumming: Sexual and Social Politics in Victorian London*, 2004 • Keith Laybourn, *The Rise of Socialism in Britain*, 1997 • Diana Maltz, *British Aestheticism and the Urban Working Classes, 1870–1900: Beauty for the People*, 2005 • Lynda Nead, *Victorian Babylon: People, Streets, and Images in Nineteenth-Century London*, 2005 • Deborah Epstein Nord, *Walking the Victorian Streets: Women, Representation, and the City*, 1995 • Daniel Pick, *Faces of Degeneration: A European Disorder c. 1848–1918*, 1989 • Roy Porter, *London: A Social History*, 1984 • Angelique Richardson, *Love and Eugenics in the Late Nineteenth Century: Rational Reproduction and the New Woman*, 2003 • John Saville, *The Labour Movement in Britain*, 1988 • Andrew Scull, *Madhouses, Mad-Doctors, and Madmen: The Social History of Psychology in the Victorian Era*, 1981 • Pamela Thurschwell, *Literature, Technology, and Magical Thinking, 1880–1920*, 2001 • Pamela Thurschwell and Nicola Bown, eds., *The Victorian Supernatural*, 2004 • Ana Parejo Vadillo, *Women Poets and Urban Aestheticism*, 2005 • Judith Walkowitz, *City of Dreadful Delight: Narratives of Sexual Danger in Late-Victorian London*, 1992

Part IV: England and Its Others

Recommended novels and plays: • Joseph Conrad, *Heart of Darkness*, 1902 • Joseph Conrad, *Lord Jim*, 1900 • Bithia Mary Croker, *Diana Barrington. A Romance of Central India*, 1888 • Lady Augusta Gregory, *Cuchulain of Muirthemne*, 1902 • H. Rider Haggard, *King Solomon's Mines*, 1885 • H. Rider Haggard, *She*, 1886 • G. A. Henty, *With Clive in India: or, The Beginnings of an Empire*, 1884 • Anthony Hope (Anthony Hawkins), *The Prisoner of Zenda*, 1894 • Rudyard Kipling, *Kim*, 1901 • Rudyard Kipling, *Plain Tales from the Hills*, 1888 • Olive Schreiner, *Story of an African Farm*, 1883 • Olive Schreiner, *Trooper Halket of Mashonaland*, 1897 • George Bernard Shaw, *John Bull's Other Island*, 1904 • Edith Somerville and "Martin Ross" (Violet Martin), *The Real Charlotte*, 1894 • Flora Annie Steel, *On the Face of the Waters*, 1896 • Robert Louis Stevenson, *The Beach at Falesá*, 1893 • Robert Louis Stevenson, *The Ebb-Tide*, 1894 • Robert Louis Stevenson, *Kidnapped*, 1886 • Robert Louis Stevenson, *Treasure Island*, 1883 • Bram Stoker, *Dracula*, 1897 • J. M. Synge, *The Playboy of the Western World*, 1907

Recommended criticism: • Stephen Arata, *Fictions of Loss in the Victorian Fin de Siècle: Identity and Empire*, 1996 • Patrick Brantlinger, *Crusoe's Footprints: Cultural Studies in Britain and America*, 1990 • Patrick Brantlinger, *Rule of Darkness: British Literature and Imperialism, 1830–1914*, 1988 • Joseph Bristow, *Empire Boys: Adventures in a Man's World*, 1991 • Nicholas Daly, *Modernism, Romance, and the Fin de Siècle: Popular Fiction and British Culture, 1880–1914*, 2000 • Richard Fallis, *The Irish Renaissance*, 1995 • E. J. Hobsbawm, *The Age of*

Empire, 1875–1914, 1987 • Paula Krebs, *Gender, Race, and the Writing of Empire: Public Discourse and the Boer War*, 2004 • Anne McClintock, *Imperial Leather: Race, Gender, and Sexuality in the Imperial Contest*, 1995 • Thomas R. Metcalf, *Forging the Raj: Essays on British India in the Heyday of Empire*, 2005 • Thomas Pakenham, *The Scramble for Africa, 1876–1912*, 1991 • Thomas Richards, *The Imperial Archive: Knowledge and the Fantasy of Empire*, 1993 • LeeAnne M. Richardson, *New Woman and Colonial Adventure Fiction in Victorian Britain: Gender, Genre, and Empire*, 2006 • Jenny Sharpe, *Allegories of Empire: The Figure of Woman in the Colonial Text*, 1993 • George W. Stocking, *Victorian Anthropology*, 1987

For Index of Authors and Titles,
see pages xv-xix.